A
Century
of
Planting

A Century of Planting

A History of the American Friends Mission in India

by

E. ANNA NIXON
Missionary to India, 1940-1984

A CENTURY OF PLANTING

International Standard Book Number:
0-913342-54-8   Paper
0-913342-55-6   Cloth

Library of Congress Catalog Card Number: 85-72070

Other books by E. Anna Nixon:

More than Shadow, *a story of village life in India*
Christian Eduation in the Third World
"Delayed Manila," *autobiographical account of concentration camp
experience during World War II*
Dr. Grace of Bundelkhand, *biography of Bundelkhand's
first woman doctor*

Design, composition, and lithography by
The Barclay Press, Newberg, Oregon, United States of America

Dedicated
to the
women of the past century
in the
Evangelical Friends Church — Eastern Region
who first accepted the challenge
of a mission in India
and kept it going

Contents

Preface

THE MISSIONARIES IN INDIA and the members of the Church that sent them were ordinary people, subject to the limitations of their times. The quality that made them different, however, was their deep sense of the reality of a personal God. No mere pioneering spirit but the call of God sent Friends from America to India in 1892. Missionaries have continued to this day responding to the same call.

Crossing the water conferred no supernatural gifts or immunities on the missionaries. With the faith and knowledge they possessed they had to face the hard realities of diverse religions, cultural adjustments, illness, disappointment, hostility, and death. Their plans often went down in defeat; their problems baffled them; human relationships had to be worked through. This account deals with people more than plans, faith more than finance, service more than success, effort more than efficiency, and prayer more than power. Less emphasis is placed on policies and strategies than on people who made them and carried them out.

After traveling the rugged paths to backward areas, spending and being spent in telling villagers about Jesus, year after year the missionaries came home again empty-handed. "It would be an unspeakable joy were we able to tell you of marvelous conversions and great ingatherings of souls," said Delia Fistler after twelve years in India, "but we have no such record to present."[1] Yet a sense of the compassionate, longsuffering, and loving God, reaching out through these missionaries to a humble people in Bundelkhand, is constantly present. In an earlier report Delia wrote, "'The harvest is white, but the laborers are few.'[2] Oh, friends, pray on. These dying multitudes must be reached *soon*. God needs more spirit-filled messengers in this vast field. Friends! pray them out to the foreign field. Pray them out of your houses if need be, out of easy places, out of their indecision and shrinking, into the midst of the vast harvest field where the need is greater than pen can describe, where the number of Christ's ambassadors is so pitifully small that angels might well weep and wonder."[3]

For the first twenty years only women answered the call, sent by a board made up — until 1905 — entirely of women. They often failed in dark times, but rose in the triumph of the cross to serve again. They knew that the cross of Christ was central and that there was no other way of salvation. They knew it was the holiness of God and not compassion that redeems. People everywhere must repent. They did not lose the sense of God's holiness and therefore of human sin. And though they showed much compassion to famine sufferers and the poor in the villages and to the orphans they rescued from starvation, they never lost sight of the need of redemption of every one of them.[4]

With faith based firmly on the promises of God, the Friends Church in India — the *Bundelkhand Masihi Mitra Samaj* — continues reaching out, going again and again to the villages. Those promises of the past century still stand, "unchanged, undiminished, and undimmed."[5] This book has been written, therefore, to increase the awareness of the readers of their privilege in standing with the Christians in Bundelkhand in strong hope and earnest prayer for abundant harvest.

— E. Anna Nixon

Acknowledgments

WRITING THIS HISTORY has drawn help from many sympathetic and interested people who have encouraged, advised, and corrected. Credit should first of all be given to all the Friends India missionaries who are yet living, for their willingness to read and approve the scripts of the portions concerning their time in India. Recalling painful situations brought tears but also the desire that the telling of such would be a guide to others who seek to find a better way.

The Friends Foreign Missionary Society of Evangelical Friends Church — Eastern Region and Malone College furnished archival materials and allowed the use of their photocopiers. Malone College Library also gave space for the organization of files as the writing was in the beginning stages. The author expresses gratitude to them. The FFMS also appointed a committee to give support and advice to the author as the history was being written. Lucy Anderson, Margaret Mosher, and Esther Hess volunteered their time and gave invaluable support throughout the whole process of writing.

As long ago as 1972 the author began gathering materials for this project. At that time Vijay Prakash, the present representative consultant for the FFMS of EFC — ER in India, assisted the author with forty-six interviews of leading Indian Christians in Bundelkhand.

Stuti Prakash, Vishal Mangalwadi, Dr. D. W. Mategaonker, Victor Mangalwadi, Gabriel Massey, and Norma Freer all gave special help through answering questions and sending materials. Kamal B. Lall in India and Connie Bancroft in America gave invaluable assistance in typing. Catherine Cattell and Dr. Ezra and Frances DeVol assisted in the choice of pictures. Robert Hess kindly consented to write the introduction. The author's sister, Hazel Adams of Eckert, Colorado, provided a quiet office for nearly two months of crucial writing, and a dozen friends in Newberg volunteered their assistance in final preparation of the glossary, index, appendix, and bibliography; and two supplied typewriters.[6]

Last but not least, the author wishes to express gratitude to Arthur O. Roberts, Newberg, Oregon; June Preston, College Park, Georgia; and Blanche Pearson, Akron, Ohio, for voluntarily reading through the script and making excellent suggestions on organization, content, balance, and style. The author took the liberty of correcting a few spelling and grammatical errors in quotations from letters, carefully guarding against changing the intended meaning, emphasis, or style. Spelling of towns, cities, and people varied from letter to letter and from time to time. The author sought to use current spelling consistently.

The author is aware of the awesome responsibility of writing about a work in which she herself has been so deeply involved. Without the call of God she would never have attempted it, and without the constant presence and help of the Lord of History, she would never have finished it. Most of all, there is deep gratitude to God for His call to be a part of what He is doing in establishing a work for the glory of His name in Bundelkhand.

Introduction

HISTORIANS WRITE with a certain point of view. The quality of their writing is much improved if this particular viewpoint is wisely used to select historical events and to balance them together honestly. Should the point of view misrepresent facts and distort events, then the history must be dismissed. A completely neutral or objective approach to history is probably impossible and where attempted makes insipid reading.

Anna Nixon, who writes this particular history, is well qualified to comment on India. A Friends missionary for 44 years, she speaks the national language, Hindi, with fluency and has demonstrated much sympathy with the feelings and aspirations of the Indian people, particularly those of the Bundelkhand area, which is the focus of her survey.

Philosophically, she agrees with the missionaries and national leaders whom she describes. The dress styles, eating habits, and modes of transportation have changed considerably since the Friends Mission began in central India in 1896, but the content of faith has not. Belief that Jesus Christ was sent of God in fulfillment of Old Testament biblical prophecy, that He taught, healed, was executed, and rose from the dead for every person's spiritual redemption is basic. His life, His word, His commands are normative. Early Quakers in the 1650s called themselves Friends because Jesus had said, "You are my friends if you do whatever I command you." His last major command was to preach the Gospel to every creature. Delia Fistler, Esther Baird, Anna Nixon, and many other Friends went to Bundelkhand largely with this motivation.

Christian missionaries, like their contemporaries, are also influenced by compassion, by the desire to be recognized, by the love of adventure, and by other strong personalities. However, in the final analysis, the Christian missionary is constrained by the love of Christ.

So much, then, for motivation for writing this history. It deals far more with mission personalities and mission policy than with the social, cultural, and economic history of the period. The adopted mission policy, more by necessity than by choice, was an orphanage-centered approach for the first forty years. During the latter half of the period studied, the method was what is now called "peoples movement." Ably described by Bishop J. W. Pickett and Donald McGavran, this is the attempt to concentrate evangelism on one ethnic or caste group until the Church grows strong enough to survive. Everett Cattell capably developed this approach in Bundelkhand. In both methods preaching the Gospel of Christ was primary.

Mission policy in Bundelkhand complemented proclamation with education and medicine from the beginning. The first school for girls in Bundelkhand was the Mission one. The early dispensaries and later Christian hospital are equated in the minds of many with Mission. The discussion of whether policy or personality is more important is not just academic, for planning and setting goals assists every type person. These policies were implemented by dedicated personalities.

Traditional India is largely Hindu in cultural trappings, though Islam has made a heavy impact since A.D. 1200. Political and ethnic invasions have come, like ocean tides, through her northwestern and sometimes northeastern valleys, but most of them have been assimilated into the wide sea that is Hindu culture. Islamic invasions, through what are now Afghanistan and Pakistan, are notable exceptions. Even they did not entirely displace Hinduism but rather became cultural islands in various parts of India.

Describing Hinduism is like the proverbial story of the six blind men seeking to evaluate an elephant. This is the religion — or better, culture — of some 725 million people and has existed for at least twenty-five hundred years. During this time there have been additions and deletions, but Hindu leaders speak of four permissible goals or aims in life.

One of these is *Kama*, pleasure, realized mainly through love. This includes conjugal happiness in married and family life. Another is *Artha*, power or material possessions. One can seek wealth and power, like *Kama*, but both these are inferior to the last two goals. *Dharma* is religious and moral style of life. Here one seeks to do his duty to his family, caste, and community. Joy is found in moral development, but this leads to the fourth and highest goal, *Moksha*, or salvation. This means freedom or release from endless transmigration and absorption into fullness of being.

Modern secular India has often relegated *Moksha* to lesser importance, but its influence is pervasive. The teaching of salvation on the sophisticated as well as on the simple level springs from ancient convictions of *Karma* and transmigration. Because humans and the world in general are characteristically moral, then every act performed is evaluated on an ethical scale. Lives are many and repeat themselves in order to repair *Karma* deficiencies. The Indian villager in Bundelkhand has seen and heard the creaking waterwheel with its many clay pots. This age-old irrigation system is a persistent parable: as the vessel comes up on each circle full of water, then empties it out, so is our life. One learns to accept present status because it was determined by ethical behavior in a previous life. But all is not passive resignation, for if one lives well, performs the *Dharma* of the group — caste — in this life, then he shall be reborn higher in another life. One finally becomes free from the wheel of rebirths through salvation and is absorbed in the universal being.

Popular Hinduism in Bundelkhand, and other parts of India, has much in common with the development of gods and goddesses in other parts of the world. There are three major deities who with their consorts have special functions. Brahma, seldom worshiped, is the remote god who brings the world periodically back into a new cycle. Vishnu, called the preserver, is very popular, especially in the form of one or more of his nine incarnations. When evil grows preponderant he assumes an incarnation, most popular of which have been Rama and Krishna. Shiva, pictured with many arms dancing in a ring of fire, is the destroyer, both feared and worshiped. The adoration of these gods and their wives is related to the fertility cults characteristic of nature worship.

Since Hinduism is eclectic, combining easily — if slowly — other types of worship, it has become pervasive all over India and in many parts of southeast Asia. The stories of the major gods and goddesses have become the common, beloved literature of Hindus wherever they settle. Thus, one finds statues and stories of thousands of deities around India. A chief way of salvation (moksha) for the common Hindu is personal devotion to one of these gods or goddesses. The philosopher seeks salvation through introspective meditation. The ordinary villager defers to one or to several deities as life crises occur.

That this system of teaching has challenged thoughtful minds is understandable. It has given continuity to one of earth's oldest civilizations. Rigorous social groupings in India have been buttressed by this explanation. Almost every attempt at social, scientific religious reform in India has been impeded by caste. The origin and development of the caste system has received much comment. It has been influenced by color distinctions, by occupational groupings, and by ritual taboos on eating as well as the prevailing philosophy.

At the writing of this history, many of the caste strictures have weakened. The framers of the India Constitution have outlawed it as a system. The veteran missionary statesman, E. Stanley Jones, used to say that when caste weakens, India will become Christian. Certainly there is wide respect for the Christian message and especially the person of Christ. The people of Bundeklhand saw and heard the missionaries and the national Christians with eyes and ears conditioned by Hinduism. Many of them were the untouchables or outcastes. Their reluctance to accept could be based upon strong opposition to a "foreign" religion or to misunderstanding of the message. The survey described in this book reveals the sincere and dedicated attempt of a group of Christians to share their faith by both proclamation and deeds of mercy for many years. The author has given an accurate and readable account of the expatriates and national Christians who believed that the Gospel of Jesus Christ could flourish as a fruitful vine in India.

During the time covered in this book, India experienced a gradual political transformation. The British came to India to trade in the seventeenth and eighteenth centuries. By 1757 their traders assumed political authority. At first the area ruled was small, but by persuasion and force they had some sort of control over most of India in 1850. In certain areas their administration used the local ruler, or maharaja, to direct civil affairs. The area of Bundelkhand was one of these. These local rulers cooperated with the British who controlled their defense and external affairs. British officials who were Christian looked upon their work in India as a divinely bestowed trust; others felt responsibility to disseminate the English common law and enlightened education as ends in themselves. Still others saw India as a lucrative market for developing the factory system of England and Europe.

Toward the end of the last century, sensitive Indians began to protest the educational and economic disparity between conquerors and conquered. Nationalism in India had two major emphases as the twentieth century began. These emphases reflected the personality and methods of their proponents. One was a fiery revolutionary named Tilak. The other, Gokhale, sought change and self-government but through education and persuasion. He preferred evolution to revolution.

Neither of these leaders, nor their methods, brought India to independence. This came through Mahatma Gandhi. Trained in London, experienced in agitation against repression in South Africa, he returned home in 1915. He realized two basic truths about his country and people. The majority lived simply in the countryside and possessed great reserves of emotional strength. This was in decided contrast to the elite leaders of the independence movement. Gandhi wore a loincloth to identify with the poor. He merged the goals of independence and morality. His methods were fasting and nonviolence. Many of his emphases were in the stream of Hindu morality. But his nonviolence was one that the British could hardly oppose. Frequently quoting Christ's teachings, he put the rulers on the defensive. Gandhi's word became the command for millions of followers. "He . . . succeeded in tapping the great emotional reserves of the people and made them potent instruments of a massive political movement, impressive though non-violent." (Nihal Singh, *My India*, Vikas Publishing House, Delhi, 1982)

India gained independence in 1947. Deep feelings of animosity and widespread fears brought with independence a time of Hindu-Muslim tension that led to vicious slaughter. A great population shift occurred as Pakistan and (now) Bangladesh separated from India proper. Jawaharlal Nehru, Gandhi's disciple, developed a unified secular state that became a leader among developing countries. His successors and particularly Nehru's daughter, Indira, and grandson Rajiv Gandhi, have continued to this date policies of political nonalignment, socialism in politics, and a strong emphasis upon economic development. The railroads, post offices, insurance, and airlines are nationalized. Private industries in textiles, tea exports, and other forms of business exist side by side with the huge government projects. A modern Indian student quickly learns that western (British) imperialism curtailed India factory development in order to favor their own. Britain, after Independence, was the scapegoat to explain almost all backwardness.

Thirty-eight years after Independence there have been many signs of progress. Food grain production is now 142 million tons. Industrial growth is averaging 5 percent annually. Building of transport systems has been extended to many remote areas. Indian scholars have been in the vanguard in nuclear physics, in modern medicine, and in communications. But poverty is still very real. The annual per capita income is $71.21. Millions go to bed hungry. A contemporary Indian Christian writes, "There is a moral crisis everywhere. Corruption has become a way of life. The caste system is still formidable. The basic reasons are selfishness and superstition." (F. Sunderaraj, *AIM Magazine*, August 1984)

The efforts to establish a church in Bundelkhand are thoroughly and interestingly described here. Religious, economic, social, and many personal factors have influenced it. In reading the account, one at times wonders about the investment in lives, time, and finance. Some deep convictions, some criticisms, and a healthy respect for those described are the outcome of reading this. It helps to know that this is only one scene in a much wider mosaic.

—*W. Robert Hess*
General Superintendent of the
Evangelical Friends Church—Eastern Region

July 1985

PART I

DELIA FISTLER

1892-1916

Esther Baird and Delia Fistler. The first missionaries appointed to India by Friends of Ohio Yearly Meeting.

Sarah Jenkins, first FFMS
President 1884-1895

Elisabeth M. Jenkins, second
FFMS President 1895-1913

Nowgong, Bundelkhand, India — the first home of the American Friends Mission

Bazaar day in Nowgong

Blind Charlotte Bai with rescued
famine waifs of 1896

"What Can
Take Away
My Hunger?"
—A famine
victim

"What Can Wash Away
My Sin?"–Thakur P. Singh,
first village convert

Jagat Sagar (pond) where people go
to wash away their sins

Anna Edgerton   Charlotte Bai and Mary Bai

Eva Allen,
Carrie Wood,
Dr. Goddard

Louise Pierson Memorial Chapel, Nowgong

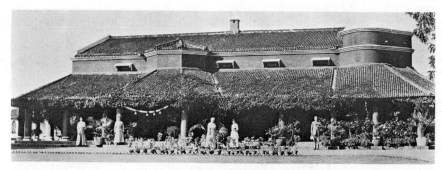

Nowgong Missionary Bungalow

The Orphanage and Matron's Quarters

Nowgong Missionary Cottage

Occupying a Field

"Behold, I have set before thee an open door, and no man can shut it." Revelation 3:8

Called to India

In the day of no airplanes, India, by way of slow boats, seemed an eternal distance from the U.S.A. But in Ohio through what seems to have been a remarkable visitation of the Spirit of God in 1892, India blazed into significance for a small group of people called Friends. On Sunday morning, August 21, in Cleveland, J. Walter and Emma B. Malone were as usual in the pulpit of First Friends Church. The congregation waited in their pews to hear God speak, for it was the unusual sense of His presence that drew people to the simple Quaker worship. Present that morning among others were two young women for whom India became extremely important. One was Delia Fistler, 25, a gifted preacher and evangelist who had led many to Christ. She emphasized the baptism of the Holy Spirit, which was at that time the Quaker terminology for defining the second work of grace, or sanctification, as taught by the Wesleyans. The other was Esther Baird, 33, a graduate nurse who attended some of the ministerial training classes the Malones conducted daily (the beginning of today's Malone College).

After the service, Delia Fistler went one way and Esther Baird another, each to her own home in distant parts of the city. That afternoon, the Malones, Esther Baird, and Delia Fistler, each without the knowledge of the other, knelt to pray about India.

Delia Fistler thought back over her life. As a child, she had sensed time and again that God was calling her to India.[1] At the age of nineteen she had been converted and had joined the Evangelical Church of her parents. Later she had come into contact with Friends and had been baptized with the Holy Spirit. She had since found her ministry in the fellowship of Friends. As she prayed that afternoon, God's clear call to India came into focus, and she determined to present herself as a candidate to India when the Friends Foreign Missionary Society Board met the next week at Yearly Meeting.

Esther Baird, on the other side of the city, was dealing with the same call. How could it be possible, she reasoned, to go so far? Considering her training and her age, she realized if she were ever to say "yes" to such a call it would have to be now. She opened her heart to the possibility and set about to follow through with the next step in working it out.

At the First Friends parsonage, J. Walter and Emma B. Malone had each gone to a separate place to pray. An hour later as they came out of their prayer closets they both started talking at once. They discovered, as they had prayed for India, each had felt without a doubt that God wanted Esther Baird and Delia Fistler in India.

A Courageous Women's Board

The following week at Yearly Meeting, Delia Fistler went straight to the Mission Board and told them of her call. Esther Baird was more timid; she approached Sarah Jenkins, the president of the board. Members of the board must have exclaimed as did Mary when Angel Gabriel appeared to her: "How can these things be!" This new Mission Board made up entirely of women had sent Esther Butler to China in 1887 and Amanda Kirkpatrick in 1888.[2] Having taken this one giant step of faith to China, was God indeed urging them to take another—this time to India? They called J. Walter Malone for confirmation. He immediately favored their proposition and suggested they send Delia Fistler and Esther Baird. Only then did he learn that both these young women had already offered themselves.[3] Along with them, also, was one other. Martha Barber (sometimes called Matti), a recorded minister of Adrian Quarterly Meeting, at that same Yearly Meeting offered herself as a candidate to India with full support already pledged.[4] So on August 30, 1892, just nine days after that unusual Sunday, the Friends Foreign Missionary Society announced:

> We united in the prayer that the coming year may be even more fruitful than the past. Our dear sisters, Delia Fistler, Matti Barber and Esther Baird, feeling called of God to go as missionaries to India, offered themselves to the Missionary Board for this work.[5]

The Methodist Umbrella

These three young women wanted to step from Damascus Yearly Meeting House directly onto a ship, but the Mission Board needed time to think through some of the implications of their decision. Financially, they were not ready to launch a full-blown mission in India, nor did they consider these three gifted young women as qualified to start such a mission. They were as yet totally ignorant of the language and inexperienced in foreign culture. Delia expressed her impatience at the unnecessary delays, and Sarah Jenkins chided her for being too anxious.[6] She pointed out that the Mission Board would send them out only under the care of another mission already working in India. Martha Barber knew Mr. Fuller of the Christian and Missionary Alliance in Akola. There was much correspondence and serious consideration of associating with them. But just before deciding finally, Bishop Thoburn, the first missionary bishop of the Methodist Church in Asia, came to Cleveland. J. Walter Malone and other board members met him. He opened his Methodist arms to them. "Come along and work with us while learning the language and customs of the people," he invited. "Then when you feel the time has come, you may be released and take up your own work."[7]

This arrangement pleased the Board, the missionary candidates, and the Bishop. As plans for sailing were made, Mrs. Loomis, who had agreed to support Martha, also added the support of Mary Thomas.[8] There was no time for the board to arrange an interview with Mary before the ship sailed, but Mrs. Loomis's recommendations were so good they accepted Mary both as a member of the Friends Church and as a missionary without ever having met her.[9] The contract was signed by mail and Mary met the other three in New York and sailed with them November 23, 1892, on the SS *City of Paris*.[10]

Adjustments and New Experiences

Once out on the high seas, the ship rolled and pitched. Mary Thomas wrote, "Our voyage to India was a most tempestuous one, and we were sometimes glad to think of the time when there will be 'no more sea.'"[11] On shipboard the four missionaries for the first time were thrown together—literally! They soon discovered in spite of consecration, Christian experience, and joyous adventure, they had not left behind their weaknesses, prejudices, or their own peculiar dispositions. Even before reaching the shores of India friction flared and misunderstandings had to be wrestled through. When seasickness abated enough, they read a steamer letter from Sarah Jenkins, the Board president:

> My dear girls one and all (read on shipboard)
>
> As the time has now arrived that you are to leave your native land and the fields of service you have been familiar with, and go to scenes so very different, I can but feel solicitous that nothing may in any wise mar the sweet unity and Christian fellowship which should ever be the

bond to bind together those that love the Lord, and are going out, to carry the precious Gospel message to those who are in darkness . . . . In *all* the *close* relationships of life there is abundant need for great condescension and charity, and coming together as you do in your new relationships each with your established views, and lines of thought, and which have no doubt been somewhat different, you will need to deal tenderly and patiently with each other.[12]

News of the friction never appeared in print, but Sarah Jenkins, on hearing about it, answered, "I do hope every shade of unpleasantness has disappeared and healing from the sun of righteousness has come and that you are all sweetly united."

On December 28, 1892, they arrived in Bombay. The weather was pleasantly cool and the atmosphere electric with promises of new adventures. They were soon swallowed up in a sea of humanity — coolies, beggars, British soldiers, curious crowds of people, and small vendors who came as close as possible to ply their trade with the newly arrived passengers. One trunk didn't get through, but the Methodists who met them at the ship knew just how to trace that trunk. They also knew the immediate plans for the new missionaries. They were all hustled off to attend the Methodist Decennial Conference, where they met many of their future co-workers. After that, Delia and Esther went to Muthura, North India. Delia was put in charge of a Training School for Christian Workers, and because of her preaching ability, she received many calls to speak in conferences and meetings. Esther, a trained nurse, fit immediately into the dispensary, where within a year she was in full charge. Mary and Martha were sent to Bareilley, in the North Western India Conference. From there they were assigned to Bijnor, a center of a large native district where four English families were stationed. Learning the Hindi language had top priority, but they both also started visiting women in their homes (*zenana* work). Sometimes they taught through interpreters and did many things — Mary Thomas reported —"with a good bit of wrestling with the elements."[13]

Four months after their arrival in India, the missionaries began to experience India's famous hot season. All things green disappeared and trees shed their leaves. Hot burning wind called the *loo* whistled through the land, and to escape, they shut their doors and windows from early morning until late evening. The streets were swept of life. Animals grazing in the open or walking on the roads sought shady nooks and waited silently for the cool of the evening. Darkness afforded scant relief. To get sleep the missionaries took refuge under mosquito nets beneath the stars. Energy drained from their fingertips, and progress halted. Accepting the advice of experienced foreigners in India, they packed their bags and went to the Himalayan foothills for the two hottest months of May and June. Esther and Delia went to Naini Tal and Mary and Martha to Mussoorie. There were many English people in both of these stations, and they were tempted to let their own cultural social life push aside their chief purpose for coming to India. But they disciplined themselves, and while enjoying some social life with those they readily understood, they gave the major part of their time to catching up on foreign correspondence and continuing with their language study.

Birth Pangs of a Friends Mission

All four missionaries' understanding and use of Hindi increased daily, and their confidence in being able to launch out on their own to open a Friends Mission grew apace. Letters home began to carry large requests for authorization to launch such a Mission. The Board, however, fended off such requests. "We have felt very sorry that we could not see the way to gratify your desire to have a Friends Mission in India," wrote Emelyn J. Cattell, secretary of the Mission Board. "We felt it was all we could do to pay the salaries of two missionaries in India."[14] Underlining the stringent times the Board was facing, they requested the India missionaries to consider taking a cut in salary from $600 to $550 a year. Evidently there was some effort to bring salaries in line with those paid to the missionaries in China.

The missionaries did not object to lower salaries, but they did continue their requests for a Friends Mission, and little by little they began to have their way. The first grant of money beyond salaries came from the Missionary Board for the purchase of a bullock cart. This was to help Delia and Esther reach the villages as yet untaught and thus "carry the tidings to those who have not heard. It will be new ground even in India."[15]

Another event pointed toward the future. Brought to Esther Baird in the dispensary was a little boy whose English father and Indian mother both died in an epidemic. She could not bear to turn him away. When no relatives could be found, Esther adopted him. The Mission Board, on hearing this, expressed alarm, wondering how many more helpless waifs would be adopted, involving them in an outlay of funds far beyond their means. They also foresaw problems arising between the Methodist and Friends boards if such a course were pursued. Surely, they considered, the care of a child would eat away Esther Baird's time for language study and deflect her from wider service. The objections, however, had been drowned by the tender cries of a little boy needing help, and Esther Baird kept him. She named him Eugene Franklin Baird.[16]

Suddenly illness stopped all activities including language study and requests to the Mission Board. First, Delia was stricken down with a fever so severe that no one thought she would recover. By the time news of her illness reached the Board, they felt they should bring her to America immediately. They wrote Bishop Thoburn for an assessment of the situation. Many weeks later, on receiving their letter, he replied that Delia's illness "was not of a climatic character," and assured them she was recovering in India.[17]

Soon after that, Bishop Thoburn came to America and met members of the Mission Board in Mt. Pleasant, Ohio. He praised the Friends missionaries, saying Esther Baird was able to prescribe for ordinary diseases as though she were a regular physician. He called her an all-around missionary because she was good wherever she was placed. Martha Barber and Mary Thomas had been transferred from Bijnor to Allahabad, and he felt they were well fitted for the work of evangelism among Eurasians in that city as well as visiting a native village once a week. He appreciated Delia Fistler's free witness for Christ and her ability to reach others spiritually.[18] Hearing such things pleased the Mission Board members very much. When the Board shared with Bishop Thoburn the many requests they had from the missionaries to start a work of their own, a ripple of uncertainty stirred the calm of the meeting. Indeed those young women in India were not just the ordinary type, and the Bishop realized they must have a challenge big enough to hold their interest, especially in a country like India where the need is so great. He promised to seek further opportunities for their ministry within the Methodist framework. He said frankly that he felt they would accomplish more for the Kingdom of the Lord working with the Methodists than in a separate work. He recommended that the Board leave the missionaries' salaries at $600 a year.[19] Though this was listened to carefully, even the $550 was later dropped to $500 because of financial stress.

Had the Bishop and the Board members known what was happening in India during this meeting in America, they would indeed have been alarmed. Esther had come down with a very severe case of typhoid fever.[20] Delia, still weak from her own illness, had to lay aside everything to care for Esther. Co-workers joined in the battle to save her life. When the Mission Board finally did receive word, they were again filled with anxiety until word eventually came through that she was going to recover. With this news came renewed and urgent requests for a Friends Mission in India.

Putting the young missionaries out on their own clearly took more courage than the Board had. They not only felt more comfortable with their missionaries working under the leadership of Bishop Thoburn, but they also sought to avoid the frightening financial responsibility in the course the missionaries proposed. All the "powers that be" converged to deflect the missionaries from that direction.

"Suppose we should have our treasury so enriched by a bequest and could enlarge our work, what kind of work would you want to open? Will you not do more good where you are than in separate work?"[21] asked Emelyn J. Cattell.

Delia found no time to reply, for Esther's illness persisted so stubbornly that even after four months she was still too weak to write a report. Delia wrote for them both:

> God's ways are often mysterious, but always good. His providences to us, too, have at times seemed strange. Sickness almost unto death has come to us; we have been led through severe trials; we have seen our plans thwarted again and again; yet we have ever felt assured that all which was of His wise permitting, even though contrary to our planning, must be for our good.[22]

Health returned slowly, and by November Esther had recovered her strength. She and Delia were then transferred from Muthura to Lucknow and were put in charge of a deaconess home, zenana work, and a home for homeless women.[23] The work taxed their strength and abilities while they learned empathy for the poor and homeless, but they were more confined than when in Muthura, where they sometimes went out preaching in their bullock cart. This led to increased pressure on the Board to establish a Friends Mission focused on evangelism among untaught villages. Emelyn C. Lupton answered for the Board:

> Letters have been received . . . asking what prospect there is for a Friends Mission in India and requesting that we again prayerfully consider whether it is not the Lord's will that we open denominational work there next year. We see no light on it whatever — other societies are having to cut down expenses . . . . But while this is true, if the Lord wants us to open a Friends Mission in India, we want to do just what will please Him . . . . We cannot give any pledges for placing you in a work of our own in India or even a word of encouragement in that line, but in order to intelligently consider it, will you give us your plans . . . . What kind of work would you want to do, and what is your estimate of the annual expense?[24]

By Yearly Meeting 1895, their propositions were before the Board: "We do not ask to start a large mission, but simply request permission to enter an unoccupied field and live simply among the people, doing evangelistic village work," wrote Delia. Their budget was modest indeed: $350 for the year, above their salaries.

The Christian Endeavor Society offered $400 annually on Delia Fistler's salary. The Board considered and prayed much about the request. Then they took the plunge of faith. "We feel we are able to go up and possess the land, trusting in Him who says, 'The silver and gold is mine, and all power is given me in heaven and earth,'" they recorded.[25] So on December 9, 1895, the missionaries were given permission to open the American Friends Mission in India, with Delia as superintendent, Esther as treasurer, and Martha as auditor.[26]

Choosing a Place

As the cool and pleasant months slipped away, they searched diligently for a place. They found need everywhere but no open doors. Guna was an untouched field but with no suitable housing. Gwalior presented a terrific challenge—and a closed door.[27] "Which way shall we turn? Guide Thou our feet," they prayed.[28] At the same time, Friends in America called a special day of prayer. Shortly after that, a Wesleyan chaplain visiting Lucknow, in casual conversation, mentioned Nowgong. This military outpost nineteen miles from the railway and sixty-five miles from Jhansi was headquarters for a British regiment, the political agent, and the superintendent of police. It was the central town for a group of native states in which more than a million people lived in villages that had never been evangelized. The area, called Bundelkhand, covered 9,852 square miles. The chaplain said, "I believe this is the very place for you. You have not only the untouched district to which your hearts call you, but in Nowgong you would also have the advantage of an organized community with the protection it would afford."[29]

Delia Fistler went to Nowgong, was convinced this was God's choice, and immediately rented an officer's bungalow.

Famine

On a sweltering night, April 1, 1896, Delia, Esther, and Martha arrived in Nowgong to open the Friends Mission.[30] The hot season had begun and would relentlessly hang on for at least three months, while fields lay parched and bare and hot winds swirled loose dust and sand through the alleyways. Thirst would seldom be quenched. Enervating temperatures hovering between 110° and 120° F would sap their energy and the will to work. Even so, the next morning the women rose early to set their house in order. Their first battle was with white ants invading their living room. This would be a recurring battle for the rest of their lives in India. Before everything was in place, gaunt, listless people—more than a hundred— appeared at their door.[31] They spoke to the people of Christ, but received scant response. Each day they went early to nearby villages before the sun became unbearable. They were appalled to see the mobs of emaciated men, women, and children who came to them, not primarily to hear their message, but to beg for food. This was the third year of a severe famine in the land. Some were starving, not having eaten for three days. Children grabbed up roots and leaves and stuffed them in their mouths to stop their gnawing hunger. Esther, Delia, and Martha were in no way prepared for ministry to these needs, but compassion led them to take along grain as they went out to preach. As they were running out of money, an Englishman, who knew the ravages of famine from former experience, gave them fifteen dollars toward grain for the famine victims, but it was not enough. The cost of moving, feeding the hungry, and taking in children quickly ate up all their resources and revealed to the missionaries how naive they had been in asking for only $350 a year. They hoped the pathetic situation would move people at home to send more. Babies and little children whose parents had died of hunger were brought to them. "We have already taken in and are caring for seven such little waifs," wrote Delia. "We could not do otherwise . . . and we believe that God will in some way send the means to support them."[32] They cleaned out a stable in which to put them and called it the "Children's Refuge." Martha Barber took charge. Esther, the nurse, was pulled into medical work by the stark needs of the children and the people. Delia, the superintendent, conducted regular church services on the veranda of their home every Sunday afternoon. As many as fifty people attended regularly, including prominent men in the town. During the week Delia and Martha frequently conducted services for British soldiers.[33] When the rains came, the famine did not end as they had hoped. Severe and widespread, it covered an area of 225,000 square miles and affected a population of 65,000,000 people. In Bundelkhand the death rate doubled and the population decreased by nearly 9 percent between 1891 and 1901.[34]

After reports were sent for Yearly Meeting, the missionaries expected letters and donations to flood the mails, but as time passed, nothing came. All supplies were exhausted. With faith that funds would surely come, the missionaries begged credit from the government bakery and dairy in Nowgong to feed the babies, at least, for ten weeks. Still no letters came. Delia Fistler, in desperation, wrote: "Are we to understand that the yearly meeting who sent us forth as its representatives with blessings and prayers and such hearty promise to support a work in India has paid no attention to the pressure upon us?"[35]

Shocked into action, the Board replied with a seven-page letter containing such assurance of love and concern that all doubt must have been wiped away. The word of the famine had indeed stirred the people at Yearly Meeting, and in less than thirty minutes a sum of $1,600 was subscribed without pressure.[36] Later, many local churches, Sunday school classes, and other small groups gave heartily. Other Friends groups and interested individuals also gave — a total of $4,210.56 by the end of the year, even though economic problems plagued the U.S.A. and the treasury had never been so low.[37]

For the next two years famine work demanded all the energy and resources of the missionaries. They distributed blankets, clothing, and bags of grain by the cartloads throughout the district. Delia and Esther followed the carts, traveling part way by oxcart and part way by elephant.

The Orphanage

As Esther and Delia found more destitute children, they took them to Martha.[38] Many parents left children with the promise of coming back for them when the famine became lighter. They never came. At first the thought of being tied to an orphanage took the heart out of the missionaries. Dedicated to village evangelism, they first considered the daily care of the children a hindrance to their main task. They had already nearly reached the end of their term and had not seen a single convert from Bundelkhand's villages. Gradually, however, they began to view the care of these children in an entirely different light. Nurtured and brought to Christ, these orphans could in turn become evangelists to their own people. With renewed dedication, they accepted all who came. The "Children's Refuge" eventually became temporary home for more than 500 children.[39] In no way were they equipped to care for so many, but as they prayed for help, God sent the great Indian saint, Pandita Ramabai.

After her conversion to Christianity, Pandita Ramabai dedicated her life to helping destitute widows and the outcaste of India. Three times she came from Kedgaon near Pune to Nowgong to take some of the orphans, widows, and cast-off child wives — many not yet twelve years old. But she could not take them all. The Friends Mission kept twenty-one boys and three girls as their permanent family.[40] Then they began to search for more skilled staff to relieve Martha Barber, whose furlough was due. The first permanent national employee of the Friends Mission was blind Charlotte Bai from Lucknow. In spite of her handicap, Charlotte impressed them with her ability and great capacity to love. A thoroughly dedicated Christian, she became a spiritual pillar in the newly established orphanage and was loved by the children she disciplined. They would never forget her or stop singing her praises as long as they lived.[41]

The care of children led to schools, and Eliza Frankland, a retired English Friends missionary in India, moved to Nowgong with the concern to teach the orphan children and also start a school for girls in the bazaar.[42] Girls had never before been taught in Bundelkhand. Eliza's presence filled a great need on the staff so that two missionaries would remain on the field as furloughs came due. Delia was scheduled to go first, then Martha, and finally Esther.[43]

CHAPTER
II | # Planting a Church

*"Upon this rock I will build my church; and the gates
of hell shall not prevail against it."* Matthew 16:18

A Time to Build

"Thus far our work has been seed sowing. Our faith is not failing," Delia
Fistler wrote as she prepared for furlough. With moving arguments and
strong logic she placed before the Board a request for $5,000 to build per-
manent headquarters at once. Already they had been forced to move
twice from rented houses and were facing a third move—a drain on both
funds and energy. The famine-stricken victims could do the building.
"Thus not only could hundreds of families be supported, but every stroke
of work would be an advantage to our mission."[1]

The Board's viewpoint was strikingly opposite. They could hardly
find passage money to bring the missionaries home for furlough over the
next two years. People were stretching to meet the budget, even doing
without life's necessities to fulfill their pledges. "Butter and meat are often
left from the table for Jesus' sake," Elizabeth Jenkins wrote, "and the early
subscriptions are unchanged."[2] The Loomis funds to support Martha Barber were depleted.[3] With finances so tight, they doubted seriously if they
could continue an India Mission. They objected to beginning the building
when no one would be on the field to supervise the work except Esther
Baird, who was already loaded with medical work. So they said a prayerfully kind but flat "No" to Delia's disturbing proposal.[4]

Delia arrived in the U.S.A. in early November 1897,[5] fully aware of
the building program in China, including a hospital. She pointedly
accused the Board of discrimination against India. Most members of the
Board hardly knew Delia Fistler, but at their first meeting they became

19

aware of the strength of her spirit, the determination of her faith, and her incisive way of dealing with problems. Delia's understanding of the Board's difficulties also deepened. Not only was the India Mission new, but the Board also was young and still learning by trial and error. As they met, unity, love, understanding, and willingness to venture resulted, and the Board's faith quickened.[6] The Board had received a legacy from Dr. A. H. Hussey to build the hospital in China. They prayed for another to cover the building needs in India, but none came. Instead, Delia took to the road and challenged the people of Ohio Yearly Meeting, and as they came in contact with her, they gave many small subscriptions — enough to cover the cost of building. The Board marveled at the capacity of self-denial of their people. To Delia they said, "If thee had not come, this would not have happened."[7]

Martha Barber returned to the U.S.A. in September 1898. Because Loomises could no longer support her, she never returned to the field.[8] In her place stepped Anna V. Edgerton, fully supported by North Carolina Yearly Meeting.[9] She and Delia sailed together with deep faith and great hope and arrived in India early in 1899.[10]

Delia was delighted to find nine new converts among the non-Christian workers and ten among the orphans. As the missionaries sat and sipped their tea, Eliza Frankland and Esther Baird talked of exhausting trips to distant villages to heal, teach, and preach. Eliza Frankland told them about the success of the girls' school in the bazaar. People no longer were saying, "You might as well teach a cow." British soldiers also were hearing the Gospel and being converted. Under the discipline and training of Charlotte Bai, the orphans were learning good manners and Christian principles. As Delia in turn added her story of money in America for permanent headquarters, Esther was so thrilled that she wanted to cancel her furlough. She probably would have done just that had severe, recurring headaches not forced her to go. Taking Eugene, her adopted son, she left Bombay for furlough on April 8, 1899.[11]

Throughout the rest of that year, securing a headquarters consumed most of Delia's time and energy. Just as she settled on what seemed financially feasible and all was ready except the signature on the deed, the Political Agent was transferred. The new P.A. looked at the proposition with a jaundiced eye and refused to sign the deed. The orphanage, he said, would be too close to the Agency. His alternative was an offer to lease ten or more acres, well situated, on which they could build. When Delia Fistler saw the property he had in mind, she realized it was exactly what they longed for but had never dared hope for. Delia accepted, realizing the new location, though much more costly, would in the end be far better.[12] She then wrote to the Board: "Let not a few hundred dollars infuence your decision, but join your faith with ours that God will provide all needed means.[13] And that is exactly what happened, for though there were no extra funds, there was faith, prayer, and openness to God. This led to careful estimating, frugal planning, and excellent communication between field and Board.[14]

On June 28, 1900, thirteen acres of choice land was leased to the Mission for $18 a year. Even as the papers were signed, the clouds gathered, lightning split the sky, and raindrops began turning into sheets of rain as the monsoon set in. Tree planting and laying out of roads and paths proceeded on bright days. Silk-cotton trees took root along the side of the road leading from the front gate to the site of the bungalow, flowering golden mohrs and large neems were planted to the right and left, and papaya trees in the garden. A pepul tree shaded a platform for plants, and there was plenty of room for vegetables and flowers. As rains washed over Bundelkhand, bringing coolness and fertility, showers of blessing poured over the homeland, too. Just as the lease was signed in India, a legacy was left to the FFMS to pay extra costs of building.[15]

Esther Baird, free from headaches, returned to India and plunged into building. She and Delia ordered second- and third-class bricks and laboriously counted them to be sure the quantity and quality were right. They watched wily workmen and measured every foot of lumber. No calculations were taken for granted; every bit was checked against scheduled rates.[16]

By June 1901 the orphans' home was completed. To the children given shelter in a stable, it seemed like a palace. It was made of sunbaked brick and plastered with mud. Mud floors stayed dry under a tile roof laid on a bamboo frame. Inside was no ceiling and no furniture, though platforms made of brick substituted for beds. Worship was conducted in the schoolroom, which, in addition to two storage rooms, divided the girls' side from the boys'. A cottage on one side where the missionaries would sleep by turns and two rooms on the other side for Bible women and Matron Charlotte Bai, provided quarters for supervisors.[17]

With the building of the orphanage, funds were exhausted; but by February 1902,[18] the foundation for the bungalow was laid and money came. Then other delays caused by unacceptable materials, unskilled and lethargic workers, long holidays, and the enervating hot season tried the patience of the missionaries. A year later, in January 1903, even though the building was not finished, the missionaries moved in. There were four bedrooms in the bungalow and three good wells with an adequate water supply.[19] By April the whole project — orphanage and bungalow — was finished and paid for at a cost of slightly more than $5,200.[20]

Eliza Frankland had not moved in with the others. After nearly six years of volunteer service in Nowgong, she left in Anna Edgerton's care the first girls' school ever to be established in Bundelkhand. She sailed home to England to retire in November 1902.[21]

A year later, Dr. Abigail G. Goddard, fully supported by New England Yearly Meeting, joined them in celebrating their first Christmas in the new bungalow.[22] Delia Fistler moved to the cottage at the corner of the orphanage to free one room in the bungalow for the doctor to use as a dispensary.[23]

A Friends Church in Bundelkhand

Delia Fistler held regular services in Hindi on the bungalow veranda and in English at the military barracks for soldiers and their children. There were many converts in the barracks — a great contrast to the village work, which took the heart out of the missionaries but produced no fruit.[24] Delia was overjoyed when two of the older boys, Dalsaiya and Bhagwana, begged to go to the villages with her. "We want to learn how to do the Lord's work," they said, "for that is what we intend to do when we get older." So they jostled along by oxcart and tonga as far as forty miles, visiting hundreds of villages and distributing tracts and Gospels at large melas.[25] They also rented a small building in the bazaar as a preaching point and used it for the girls' school and for Sunday school. "Great crowds listen," Delia wrote home wistfully. "Many show deep interest; some come to the bungalow for further instruction; there's every reason to believe that a few are fully convinced; but they have not yet found courage to openly confess Him."[26]

Little by little, however, a group of believers was being gathered, and a letter from America late in 1901 gave Delia Fistler authority to found a church as a part of Ohio Yearly Meeting:

> Delia A. Fistler who is now in Nowgong, India, a missionary from Ohio Yearly Meeting of the Friends Church, is fully authorized by that body and by the Lord Jesus Christ Whose servant and minister she is, to organize, institute and govern a church or churches in said mission field, as she and her co-workers, or their successors may judge wise and right, under the guidance of the Holy Spirit and the Word of God; and that said Churches shall constitute an integral part of Ohio Yearly Meeting.[27]

On April 11, 1902, the Friends Church in Bundelkhand was founded. Delia Fistler read and explained the declaration of faith and asked the people to stand who wanted to be members. Forty-nine responded. Thirty-one were received as full members, and the rest were enrolled as probationary.[28]

The newly organized church, challenged with a vision of their responsibility in evangelism, rented houses in some five villages and sent young men out to hold weekly evangelistic services in each one.[29] The second year they added three more villages. For transportation they sometimes used Eliza Frankland's parting gift of the little pony cart pulled by the horse that children in America paid for and prayed for. Zenana work was increased with the coming of Mary Bai of Lucknow,[30] to also be a companion for Charlotte Bai.

Education and Marriage for Adult Young People

The organized church and permanent home for work led to vigorous expansion of the work. Schools were emphasized, and the bazaar girls' school continued to thrive under Anna Edgerton. A library of more than 100 books was kept in the school and used even though the literacy rate was then only 2 percent.[31] Since no Christian teachers were yet available, the Mission hired a Hindu. She was cooperative and competent, but she worshiped idols and participated in Hindu festivals. Delia's conscience troubled her. At the next mission council meeting, she expressed her conviction that a Hindu teacher in a Christian school was not God's will. The missionaries wrestled with this policy, dreading the repercussions in the bazaar on dismissing the teacher and wondering how the school could function without her since Anna Edgerton was leaving for furlough. Spurning expediency and adopting a policy that held for eighty years, they agreed to have only Christian teachers. The school situation was cared for by shifting the small orphan boys who had been studying with the girls to the boys' school.[32] Then, as if the Lord wanted to give them a sign of His approval, the Board appointed Eva H. Allen of New England Yearly Meeting in Anna Edgerton's place. Eva had special kindergarten training. Under her, the attendance increased and the school prospered.[33]

As the years rolled by, more orphans were given a home and the earlier ones became adults. Most of the older boys were not scholars and quickly lost interest in books. Many, however, had aptitudes for various trades. The Mission opened an industrial school for fourteen of them and by 1904 built a new workshed. A man was needed for this work, but since there was none, Esther Baird was given the responsibility. Classes were opened in gardening, blacksmithing, and tailoring. Masonry, weaving, and shoe-making were added later as competent instructors were found.[34] It was a profitable enterprise, and Delia wrote the Board, "We wonder how we ever managed without it."[35]

Many of the young people were already past the usual marriage age in Bundelkhand, and since marriages are arranged in India, the missionaries had to function as parents. Knowing no other place to find Christian marriage partners for their children, they looked within the orphanage itself. The first marriage was celebrated when the two oldest orphans were joined in holy matrimony in September 1904.[36] Dalsaiya and Sundariya moved from the orphanage to a separate room on the same compound. Since Dalsaiya was an evangelist and Sundariya a worker, their support from the Mission neither increased nor decreased.

The earlier concept of training the orphans to live among their own people was temporarily set aside. After all, who were their own people? Famine had cut them off from all relatives. The orphans were not conscious of their caste and did not seem to know or care which village they had come from. The hostility of a Hindu society isolated them socially even as they isolated themselves. When the next couple were married, the groom had a call to preach and the bride was a tutor in the mission school. They were assigned to Harpalpur, where the husband served as an evangelist and the wife opened a girls' school.[37] Thus, a seemingly unavoidable precedent of continued dependence was set that would weigh on the Mission with each newly established family. It is not surprising that the next marriageable young man also got a call to preach.[38] During the next three years as five more weddings took place, there was great rejoicing about the new Christian homes as the mission budget continued increasing as babies were born.[39]

Caring for the Ill

Esther Baird expanded the medical work as more and more patients came for treatment. With Dr. Abigail Goddard on the field, even more patients came. The doctor treated 3,307 patients at the bungalow dispensary during her first year while studying Hindi.[40] Every week, in a horse-drawn, two-wheel cart, she and Esther Baird drove west for nineteen miles to Harpalpur in the state of Alipura. The trip took two days — one going and one treating the ill and returning home at night. They rented a small house in which they slept, preached, and cared for the ill. The first year, 434 patients received treatment there. The Raja of Alipura was so impressed that he offered the ladies a free grant of land on which to build a dispensary.[41] The building was soon put up, largely through the missionaries' tithes.[42]

At the same time they started praying for an outstation in the state capital, Chhatarpur, located fifteen miles east of Nowgong. The first evangelistic meetings were held in Chhatarpur for four days in late 1906, and the missionaries prepared to station a worker there.[43] The Board immediately saw the strategic significance of this step and supported it with their prayers and financial assistance.[44]

The Burden of the Board

In only eight years since taking the leap of faith to open the Mission in India, the Board, made up entirely of women, quickly moved from caution to courage. They kept information flowing to the whole Church. Pastors gathered in the tithes. Women's auxiliaries emphasized prayer and "proportionate and systematic giving."[45] Young people and children also learned about missions and supported projects. The superintendent for junior and juvenile work said, "The children now have six boys, two girls, two beds, and the horse to pray for."[46] Not on bequests or legacies, but on small, regular donations of many concerned Friends who channeled their donations through their local churches, the Mission survived.

Words of challenge rang through the halls of Ohio Yearly Meeting in 1905 as the corresponding secretary of the Women's Board, Emelyn J. Cattell Lupton, gave her twenty-first annual report:

"All power is given unto me in heaven and in earth . . . . Go ye therefore and teach all nations." There is no other way for His saving grace to reach the heathen but through His Church — and what need of any other since His command is upon His people and His power promised . . . . The first *great expense* of building has been met . . . . The *day* is *upon us* when we ought to *push* the work in all departments as never before.[47]

The Friends Foreign Missionary Society as this point changed its constitution to bring men onto the Board as well as women. Edward Mott (treasurer), John Benedict and Elbert Benedict (members at large) were elected.[48]

The Cost of Revival

The new Indian Church ached with its responsibility of disciplining and excommunicating two recalcitrant members. Being fewer than fifty, and wanting desperately not to subtract but to add more members, they suffered.[49]

They began to pray for a chapel in which to meet, but no one could have realized at what great cost that prayer would be answered. Louise B. Pierson of the Woman's Union Missionary Society in Calcutta came to Nowgong in October as a guest in the new bungalow. She was delighted to be shown every room. While there, she became ill with typhoid fever, and on November 2, 1903, she died and was buried in the Nowgong Christian cemetery.[50] On hearing of Louise's death, her grief-stricken father, Dr. Arthur T. Pierson, and other relatives sent money to build a chapel in Nowgong in her memory. The Louise B. Pierson Chapel, with a seating capacity of 300, was dedicated on January 25, 1906.[51] After dedication, the building was used during the week for the girls' school.[52]

In spite of the progress in buildings, schools, outstations, medical work, literature distribution, and evangelistic effort, the missionaries were distressed. The Church's preaching every week in eight centers around Nowgong and the Mission's visits to 175 or more villages each year had still not produced a single village convert. The missionaries had bought two strong tents in which to live as they preached for weeks at a time in distant villages, where frightened villagers ran at the sight of them, suspecting them to be government spies who had come to poison their wells or cause the plague to spread. These fears were not easily removed. The Christians went to Hindu melas where people swarmed to worship at the temple or bathe in holy waters. They often pitched their tents in the shadow of idol temples. Spent and discouraged after pouring out their hearts, they cried to the Lord, "Why no fruit?"

In 1905 a crescendo of prayer with fasting was heard in the Mission that continued for a month. Delia Fistler poured out her burden in her report:

> Oh, that there might be a day set apart when throughout our Yearly Meeting and mission fields God's children would prostrate themselves before Him in deep humiliation for our past weakness and indifference, and send up a mighty cry for a Holy Ghost revival that would not only re-energize the church at home, healing divisions and re-uniting scattered forces, filling empty treasuries and sending forth a host of Spirit-filled missionaries to the dark places of the earth, but would also cause a shaking among the heathen, a dethroning of false gods and an ingathering of multitudes into the fold of our blessed Lord.[53]

By the end of that year, the missionaries concluded that without a doubt some deliberate disobedience to God was the root of the fruitlessness. After much prayer they took vigorous action against unbridled debt, drinking, and hidden sin.

> The Holy Spirit having made clear in our hearts that the church in this place has lost her power and fitness for witnessing to the Gospel of Christ, all village work has been stopped until we as a Church shall receive from on high the promise from the Holy Ghost.[54]

At monthly meeting each member of the Church was called forward to answer publicly these queries:

> Do you know without a doubt that having confessed all your sins you have received forgiveness through the blood of Jesus Christ and that your heart has been cleansed?

> Trusting in the grace of God, do you promise to abstain from all kinds of intoxicants, including liquor, opium, hemp, intoxicating sweetmeats, drugs, tobacco, etc.?

> Will you keep your expenses within your means, and keep from useless expenditure and from debt?[55]

Unclear testimonies brought suspension from membership until fruits of repentance and consecration were manifested in their lives.[56]

Following this, a mighty revival swept through the Friends Church in Bundelkhand. Was it a part of the great awakening that swept through Wales and into the Khasi Hills in Northeast India in 1904? Christians in Nowgong opened their hearts to God with confessions, restitution, and forsaking of sin. After that, village work was taken up again by those who made their peace with God.[57]

Coping with Hardship

"In due season we shall reap, if we faint not."
Galatians 6:9

The Battle for Life

On the heels of revival in the Friends Church in Bundelkhand followed a period of great stress. In 1906 another famine brought more children into the orphanage. With more mouths to feed and skyrocketing prices,[1] the missionaries ran out of money. Delia Fistler and Eva Allen both became seriously ill, and in the orphanage the children had fevers, whooping cough, measles, dysentery, and other severe illnesses. In spite of all Dr. Goddard could do, two of the children died. So heavy became the care of the children that the public dispensary had to be closed. Esther Baird took full responsibility for Harpalpur. How they prayed for more workers!

What they did not know even as they prayed was that help was on the way. When all money was gone, God prompted a servant of His to send a gift.[2] When their strength was spent, the president of the FFMS, Elizabeth Jenkins, arrived.[3] She realized these ill and worn missionaries needed rest. She encouraged Eva Allen to spend a long summer in the hills. Delia Fistler prepared to go on furlough. Elizabeth Jenkins felt she was not well enough to go alone and encouraged Esther Baird to go with her, since she was also ill with malaria. Elizabeth agreed to stay on in Nowgong an extra six months until she returned.[4] Esther and Delia soon got off to America, and Eva to the hills, leaving Dr. Goddard and Elizabeth Jenkins alone in Nowgong. "I can never tell what her prayers and advice have been in the work," Dr. Goddard wrote.[5]

Elizabeth felt handicapped in not knowing Hindi, but she was never-theless a very powerful undergirder for the missionaries and Indian work-ers, who could speak fluently. Charlotte Bai, the blind matron and Bible woman, was often lifted in spirit with Elizabeth nearby. Elizabeth, on the other hand, was amazed at the patience of Charlotte Bai, who arose with the girls before sunrise for the grinding of the grain. "It would surprise you how much she can 'see' with her fingers," Dr. Goddard explained. "The girls bring the flour for her approval. By feeling she can tell at once which girl has ground it."[6]

Charlotte Bai also went twice a week with a group of boys for village preaching and accompanied them to the bazaar on Saturdays.[7] She was a woman of prayer. Once while sitting quietly she felt a tap on her shoul-der twice. She called the children to come see what it was, and to their horror, they saw a cobra coiled with its head raised high enough to strike her on the shoulder. After killing the cobra, a boy said, "You have so many clothes on it could not have bitten you!" Nevertheless, blind Char-lotte Bai believed the Lord had delivered her from death, and she praised Him.[8]

Esther Baird returned on February 4, 1908, bringing Carrie B. Wood of Oregon Yearly Meeting with her.[9] Carrie stepped into Eva Allen's place, who due to illness had to leave for America in April. Elizabeth Jenkins also said good-bye. No one, however, was prepared for what happened next. Dr. Abigail Goddard became ill at the end of July and on August 12, 1908, she died.[10] In only four and a half years her service was finished. "She never seemed like a new missionary," others said. Her mature judgment and readiness to take heavy responsibility caused all to trust her. How they missed her when she was gone![11] She was buried by the side of her friend, Louise B. Pierson, in the Nowgong Christian graveyard.[12]

Esther and Carrie would have been alone then had not another per-son arrived the day before Dr. Goddard became ill.[13] Bertha Cox, a Friend from Oregon Yearly Meeting, had come to India under the Revival-ist Mission, which in 1908 had to close. Though welcomed by the Methodists, she preferred Friends in Bundelkhand, and stayed for four years.

Esther Baird became ill in November and went to the hills to recuper-ate. When she returned to assume full responsibility for the medical work, William Parsad, their first orphan, stepped in to assist her on week-ly trips to Harpalpur. With some training, he had been assisting Dr. God-dard earlier.[14] The building work also was Esther's responsibility. New England Yearly Meeting sent money to build a small hospital in honor of

Dr. Goddard. It was built in the Nowgong compound close to the orphanage and was completed five years later in 1913.[15]

Delia Fistler did not return to India until February 14, 1909. On arrival, she found Esther Baird weary with the heavy medical, financial, and building load; Bertha Cox away to the hills for a much needed rest; and Carrie Wood just recovering from fever.[16] Because of Eva Allen's illness and departure for America, the girls' school in the bazaar had been closed.[17] The orphan girls' school crippled along with most inadequate staff. The boys' Christian teacher died, and rather than continue with a Hindu *pandit*, the missionaries put the older classes in the Nowgong Government High School.[18] Esther Baird struggled to find two or three days a week to keep Harpalpur dispensary open even though she was often ill, the weather hot, and the little cart in which she traveled most uncomfortable. They begged the Mission Board for a light, comfortable buggy to make the trips more endurable.

Bertha worked faithfully among the children in the orphanage. Three babies were brought in and she took them all into her own room to nurture them to health. Two of them died, but one boy was able to go into the orphanage strong and healthy. Almost immediately another one-year-old boy was brought in, opium poisoned. Bertha took over again and brought him through.[19]

No matter how much care was given Rupiya, Pancham Singh's bride, she could not be kept from slipping away. She died of tuberculosis in the summer of 1908.[20] Rupiya was a sister of Balla, Prem Das, Mangalwadi, and Harbibai. These five children had come to the Mission with their mother, Duojibai, eleven years earlier under unusual circumstances. Delia and Esther had gone by cart and elephant to take grain and clothes to distribute in Tikar, a village in Lugasi about seven miles from Nowgong. On arrival there, they saw Duojibai and her five children, who clung closely to one another and waited. Duojibai begged to go to the orphanage, but the missionaries objected. After mounting the elephant and reaching the village gate on the way home, they found the little family still waiting to go. "We have no room for you," the missionaries repeated, and rode on. When they reached home two hours later, they found Duojibai and her children had walked the seven miles through the jungle and were waiting for them on the veranda. The missionaries made room for them and listened to the mother's story.

In the early days of the famine, this family had been well-to-do-farmers. When the wells went dry, eleven crops failed, the animals died of starvation, and everything was bartered from their home, they finally had only a few brass plates and six starving children left. The parents shut the children in the house and took the plates to Nowgong to exchange for food. Returning, they were robbed of their grain, and Duojibai's husband, Bodhan, was killed. Duojibai went for help, but by the time she returned, her husband's body was gone, and she never found it.[21] The oldest son refused to leave his village, but Duojibai and five children came and proved to be true and faithful to the Lord, even to the present fourth generation.[22] Pancham Singh, husband of Duojibai's daughter Rupiya, would have a leading role in the development of the Mission, though in later years would become a disappointment.

The Thieves' Village

Prem Das, one of Duojibai's eldest sons, accompanied Pancham Singh often on preaching trips. One day these two went to the thieves' village of Kanjarpur, about one-half mile from Nowgong Mission.[23] Kanjarpur was a village settled by the Government. The Kanjars (thieving caste) were given houses, land, and animals to help them not to practice their trade. The Government also put them under constant police surveillance. Even so, they continued their thieving, and Pancham Singh and Prem Das felt the Gospel of Jesus Christ was the source of hope for them. Every noonday government officials came to count the residents in the village, making sure they had not gone to some distant village to steal. Prem Das immediately took this opportunity to preach to the people just after roll call while they were still together.[24] The Kanjars listened so well that Pancham Singh and Prem Das went back to monthly meeting to suggest that the Mission open a school there. All agreed. Prem Das and Yakub were appointed as teachers and preachers for Sunday services. Delia Fistler got permission from the P.A. and the work was opened in August 1910, with eight regular students meeting from 3:00 to 5:00 p.m. each day, first on a small veranda and later in a rented room.[25]

Prem Das taught five hours a day in the mission boys' school, and then every afternoon he bicycled or walked to Kanjarpur village and taught ten to thirteen students for two hours. On Sundays he returned to hold an evangelistic service. All this he did without pay in the name of the Church.[26] The P.A., Colonel MacDonald, visited Kanjarpur in May 1911 and was so pleased with the influence of the Christian school on the lives of the thieving Kanjars that he ordered a small school built at government expense for the Church's use.[27]

Prem Das was happily married March 7, 1911, to a Christian girl from Igatpuri, a trained midwife.[28] They had great dreams of serving the Lord together, but their time was short. By August this dedicated man, who would in fewer than four years die of tuberculosis, found no energy to continue his second round of teaching each day.[29] The only monetary reward he had received for his year's work there was an honorarium from the Church of Rs. 5 ($1.50). Tulsi Das was appointed to take his place. A year and three months later the Church also recognized his faithful service in Kanjarpur with an honorarium of a pair of shoes costing Rs. 2.50 (75¢).[30]

All was not smooth sailing in Kanjarpur, however, for when students became so interested that they walked to the chapel to participate in the regular Sunday school, they suffered persecution. One Sunday the headman of the village put the two biggest boys in the stocks to prevent them from going.[31]

This work among the Kanjars continued and took a heavy toll of energy and concern for years to come.

Other Adventures in Education

Carrie Wood stepped into full-time educational work as she finished language study. She reopened the bazaar girls' school.[32] By combining it with the mission girls' school she had forty-five students. Three orphan girls helped her. She had to come to terms with caste. High caste girls refused to take pencils and other items directly from the teachers' hands. Teachers learned to place such items before the girl so that she could pick them up without touching the teacher.[33] At Christmas, Carrie worked day and night wrapping hundreds of gifts and preparing treats for all the children in the orphanage, Sunday schools, girls' bazaar school, Khanjarpur school, and the school for the outcaste Chamars in Nowgong. The Chamar school was their newest educational venture right in the heart of the Chamar settlement. These outcastes were not allowed to go to school anywhere else.[34]

For all these schools more workers needed training. Gore Lal Singh was sent for teacher training to St. John's College in Agra, but he suffered periodic severe headaches, and the doctor advised him to go home. Later, he returned and finished his course. A number of others were sent to Nadiad for training in the Methodist Episcopal Industrial School.[35]

The Priority of Evangelism

Schools, medicine, industrial training, buildings, and budgets all made demands on the missionaries, but the heart and soul of their activity was evangelism. No one sang praises of evangelists, and few understood what they were trying to do. With Delia back in India in 1909, the evangelistic camping was stepped up, and with the help of the Church that year, she covered 134 distant villages, 50 that had never been reached before.[36] Esther Baird wrote:

> We never know when we start out what we will encounter before night, but of one thing we are sure — there are needy souls to be reached with

the Gospel, and God's grace will be sufficient for every difficulty. So we go on giving the message, sometimes to the one woman at the well, sometimes to ten or twelve men by the roadside, and sometimes to whole villages where the headman will call all together—men from their fields, women from their grinding—and cause all to listen attentively."[37]

They never knew what to expect. A Brahmin priest and headman of one village strongly opposed them, then suddenly was so transformed that he followed them to other villages giving glory to Jesus. His testimony was clear, but it faded away.[38]

In 1909 Thakur P. Singh, a high caste village man, brought his starving wife and three children to the Mission. Much to everyone's surprise, this "Kshatriya" caste man ate Christmas dinner with the Christians. The full significance of this act was well understood as a public testimony that he considered himself a Christian. Furthermore, he cut off his *chutiya*, the sacred lock of hair, and openly testified to faith in the Lord Jesus Christ.[39] Early in 1911, Thakur P. Singh died, leaving his wife and three children in the Mission. The two older children, Lachman Singh and Ramkibai, were placed in the orphanage. The mother and her baby, Hira Singh, were sent to Kulpahar Mission, which was set up to care for widows.[40]

In the mission servants' quarters on January 31, 1909, to a recently married orphan couple—Kamal, formerly a Hindu, and Jasoda Bai, formerly a Moslem—was born a son, Stuti Prakash. Kamal earned his living by working as a house servant in the mission bungalow. They could never have dreamed then that their son would grow up to marry the Thakurs' daughter, Ramkibai, and that together they would minister in Bundelkhand for nearly sixty years.[41]

Thankful as the missionaries were for one converted family from the villages, they still prayed for a great turning to God of people not dependent on them. Many seemed extremely interested and often filled the bazaar chapel to the doors, with many standing outside looking in the windows, especially when Delia Fistler portrayed the life of Christ with her new magic lantern. Out in the villages their literature was quickly depleted as the few literates read it all to eager listeners. Hira Lal, as Bundelkhand agent for the Bible Society, supplied Scripture portions and tracts in abundance, and the whole team helped with selling and distribution. At the peak of a successful day in one village, the headman suddenly appeared and demanded to see the literature. As soon as it was gathered in one spot, he burned it all with glee.[42]

Stories circulated that the camping team was spreading cholera and contaminating the wells. Frightened villagers roughly ordered the camping team to leave. The team, however, spread nothing but Good News. At the same time the Hindus believed that *Bhumani* (*Kali*) was spreading smallpox, for the epidemic swept through the country. Only one Christian came down with it—Jagannath's little daughter, Asther. The whole family was moved to a government isolation shelter, where they lived until the baby recovered. All through Nowgong and the surrounding villages people were stricken down *en masse* by this dreadful disease.[43]

In 1910, Delia reported:

We hesitate to submit to you our meager statistics, as numbers often convey a wrong estimate of work done. The secret laying hold upon God, the conflicts with a mighty foe, the bearing of sorrows and burdens that well nigh crush the heart, the disappointments and encouragements in the lives of converts, the weary hours spent in jolting over rough fields and jungle road when taking the message of salvation to scattered villages, the joyful praise for interest shown in the message, the glad forgetfulness of weariness in the privilege of instructing inquirers, the keen pain of spirit when Jesus is scorned and rejected, all these and much more throb behind the statistics, but cannot be revealed by cold figures."[44]

If the missionaries were ever tempted to give up, they concealed it. Their actions evinced a growing faith in God, who had called them. They inspired the Indian Church to develop its own program of village preaching, which did not cease in the hot or cool seasons or during the monsoons. Indian evangelists held three services in the bazaar chapel every week and sold and distributed Gospel portions and other books and tracts. Delia Fistler wrote of them, "They often meet with scorn and ridicule, and sometimes fierce temptations are thrust in their way . . . . Allurements and threats are held out to them to try to induce them to return to the religion of their fathers. But through all God has kept them."[45]

| # Praying Doors Open

*"I will break in pieces the gates of brass, and cut in
sunder the bars of iron: and I will give thee the
treasures of darkness."* Isaiah 45:2b and 3a

Developing Harpalpur Outstation

Pancham Singh was married on May 6, 1910, to Noni Bai, brought to him
from Kanpur. Shortly after their wedding they took up work in Harpalpur.[1] Esther Baird gave herself to the development of this outstation and
made regular trips there every week. People lined the sides of the road as
the medical cart bounced along the nineteen-mile journey. They begged
her to keep all the dispensaries open, all the time. Frequently her own illness, plus the heat, made this impossible. The Church joined the missionaries in sending home requests for more workers,[2] but 1909 was a bad year
financially in the U.S.A., and the Board could hardly scrape enough
money together to meet the budget. Training the older orphans to take
part of the load became a necessity. William Parsad had already received
some training and was sent to Agra for a three-year course in pharmacy.[3]
He would be able to keep the Harpalpur dispensary open when he
finished.

Esther Baird, suffering recurrent headaches and fever, had to leave for
furlough on February 13, 1911. She went grieving over the necessity of
closing most of the medical work and particularly the Harpalpur dispensary.[4] She had hoped to hold out for another year, when William Parsad
would be finished with his training, but she was unable to do so. She
thought of the sore eyes, itch, perforated ear drums, ulcers, abscesses,
rheumatism, and asthma that would go untreated. She wondered who
would recognize the early symptoms of typhoid fever, tuberculosis,
malaria, and leprosy, and who would report the cases of smallpox,

plague, and cholera.[5] She wondered if she was doing the right thing to leave. The second day out at sea on the *SS Arratoon Apcar* removed her doubts as she began shaking violently with chills and fever so characteristic of malaria.[6] On April 19, she wrote, "Made too uncomfortable by the sea to rejoice much at this my 50th birthday." She arrived home via China on schedule April 28, 1911, so ill that it took two years and a half of the best of treatment and some months of rest in a sanatorium before she could rid her blood of malaria and return to India.[7]

The Raja of Alipura who gave the land for the house and dispensary in Harpalpur had no desire to see the outstation closed. Pancham Singh and his wife were evangelists, not pharmacists or teachers, and he feared even they would be removed. To keep the place alive until William Parsad returned he rented another building and requested the Mission to start a really good school there, teaching both Hindi and English. Gore Lall Singh, so eminently qualified, with his new bride, Pyara Bai, was placed there October 2, 1911, to start his school with sixty pupils.[8] Early in 1912 William Parsad returned to Harpalpur, fully trained, to open the dispensary.[9] God had used the Raja to keep the doors of Harpalpur open.

Delia's Grief

Delia Fistler, Carrie Wood, and Bertha Cox—all nonmedical missionaries—sought to meet medical needs in Nowgong as best they could. Delia had to lay aside the work nearest her heart—preaching in the villages—and stay home to care for the 100 orphans and workers. All other medical work in Nowgong stopped.[10] In the midst of the pressure, Delia received two cables. The first brought the news that her mother had died. A few days later a second one came saying that her sister had died.[11] In her grief she identified with the young gardener who had just buried his wife. Her heart broke with his as they returned from the graveyard to an empty house except for the tiny baby left behind in a basket.[12] The monsoon failed, and she mourned with the sufferers of drought and famine as wells dried up and seedlings perished.[13] With inward pain she prayed as she saw one of their own young women grow thin and pale as tuberculosis sapped her strength.[14] The weight of all these burdens no doubt contributed to the almost fatal illness Delia suffered in October of 1911. The Church went on their knees, and God answered their prayer.[15]

Overcoming Prejudice in Chhatarpur

For thirteen years the Mission and the Church, both in the U.S.A. and in India, had been earnestly praying for the capital city of Chhatarpur to open the closed doors to the Gospel. Had this prayer been answered earlier, there would have been no worker available to place there. With

Gore Lal Singh and William Parsad in Harpalpur, Pancham Singh and Noni Bai were free to move to Chhatarpur, where the Lord had called them. The door was opened only a small crack, and they went into a hostile environment. They walked through the streets and alleyways where no Christians had ever lived, and with great difficulty and much prayer they finally found a house.[16] As soon as their neighbors learned they were Christians, they drove them out. Word of the Christian presence spread rapidly, and it became impossible for them to find another house. So they took up residence on a day-to-day basis in the village inn.[17]

By July 1912 Pancham Singh, harassed and weary in the sullen, unfriendly atmosphere, wrote a wistful question to his Church: "Shall I go to some other place, since I can find no house to rent or buy in Chhatarpur?" The Church reassured him of their prayers and encouraged him to remain there as long as the innkeeper allowed them to stay.[18] With this support, Pancham Singh preached with renewed zeal, and Noni Bai worked among the women. Daily they held regular family devotions, and sometimes a few others would join them in their little room in the inn. Out on the street, Pancham Singh was threatened with jail if he preached again, but he courageously went back to the same spot the next day and preached to a large crowd.[19]

God was answering prayer, not only for the Mission, but for Pancham Singh and Noni Bai personally. In the two crowded rooms of the inn amidst antagonistic inhabitants, God blessed them with a son, Satwant Singh.[20] Then after a long period of testing, the Maharaja called Pancham Singh and told him there would be no further hindrance to his securing a house. This was a long step forward.[21]

Welcoming Clinton Morris

Back in America the Board was wrestling with problems unknown to the missionaries. The continued dependence of all Christians on the Mission and the expansion of the work added up to almost unbearable financial burdens. They prayed to meet the inflated budgets and added outstations. From 1910 to 1912, the Board had borrowed $3,500 to meet delinquent obligations. They knew a reckoning day was fast approaching.[22] Yet they continued to move forward, with prayer, and their next step was to send the first male missionary, Clinton Morris, supported by Iowa Yearly Meeting, to India. He arrived in Nowgong February 10, 1912,[23] and the young men in the industrial school hammered their anvils a little harder and buzzed their saws a little faster. All their lives they had longed for such a missionary brother. They had already developed skills and had saved the Mission money. They had repaired the chapel and the building in Harpalpur and made over a room for Yakub and his new bride.[24] With a man to guide them, they looked forward to outside jobs and contract work. They began by supplying the station with fine posts, making over 500 iron tree guards, and setting up and fitting iron carts. They were skilled in making articles of brass, iron, and wood. Most exciting of all, they landed a contract for all repair work connected with the military cantonments.[25] Esther Baird expected great industrial advance, now that a "Sahib" had come. She wrote:

> We want our boys not only to give glad service to the Master by preaching the Gospel as they are now doing, but we want them also to serve Him by being trained workmen, able to teach the poor village converts, as they come into the Mission, how to earn an honest living with their hands.[26]

Clinton lived in a small bungalow built for a native prince located near the Mission. He was exhilarated by the opportunities for service as he plunged immediately into studying Hindi. He made good progress, and in three months was able to undertake the responsibility of supervising the Mission through the hot season in order to allow the three women a much needed vacation. Bertha Cox proceeded to the hills immediately, and Delia Fistler and Carrie Wood planned to leave in two days when the message reached them: "The Sahib is ill!"

He was indeed ill, with smallpox! They had to report this to the government, and he was isolated in a grass hut by the soldiers' hospital. A strong, hot wind brought the temperature in his hut to 116°-120° F. It was impossible to get his accurate body temperature, for as soon as the thermometer was removed from his mouth, it continued to climb. For days his life hung in the balance. He was so thickly broken out that he had to stay in quarantine for a month. So in spite of Clinton's gracious intentions, Delia and Carrie had no vacation that year.[27]

Not only smallpox, but plague, cholera, and another undiagnosed fever raged through the villages. The symptoms of the latter were a three-day high fever followed by a sudden drop to normal, leaving the patient exhausted or dead. Delia Fistler and fifteen of the orphan children suffered from it, but all recovered.[28]

At the end of 1912 Bertha Cox, who had tremendously helped in the work at a crucial time, left to go to another mission.[29] Clinton spent most of two years in the new language school in Lucknow, where he not only had the company of thirty-five other students but also heard regular lectures on the Hindu and Muslim faiths.

Survival of a Mission

With Clinton Morris in school, Delia and Carrie were left again to supervise all the mission work. On January 4, 1913, Delia fell against a wall and dislocated her left shoulder, causing contusion of the nerves. Her sense of touch returned in about a month, but there was no power of motion in hand or arm. Her hand was so painful she could not sleep, and this all greatly interfered with the work and threw the entire burden for a while on Carrie.[30] When news of this reached the Board, they requested Delia to accompany Carrie on furlough at the end of the year.

The precarious health of the missionaries, the rising debt of the Board, and the uncertainty of the future of the work in India with its shortage of personnel led them seriously to consider turning the work over to another mission and pulling out of India. Probably the only thing that prevented them from doing so was Esther Baird's presence in the board meeting, with a clearance from the doctor to return to India. The battle was rough, but Esther was victorious and continued to pack for India.[31] Delia did not feel ready to go on furlough until Esther returned and was well in charge. Carrie's furlough was long overdue, and she left as Esther arrived. In fact, they met in Jhansi on November 4, 1913 – Esther coming and Carrie going.[32]

Clinton's language study was coming to an end and he began to feel restless with no particular assignment in the Mission. He wrote the Board asking when he could expect to be considered a "full missionary." Rachel Pim, the corresponding secretary for the Board, answered that one was counted a full missionary when he had been on the station two years.[33] He still had a few months to go to qualify, but back in Bundelkhand, he plunged eagerly into an evangelistic camp in Bijawar *Mela* – sleeping in a tent, eating *chapatis*, distributing literature, and preaching in Hindi.[34]

Meanwhile, the women wrapped Christmas gifts and prepared treats for the expanding family of orphans, workers, students, and Sunday school children – using warm dresses, quilts, picture books, and school supplies sent out by Ohio missionary societies.[35] Preparation came to a sudden halt on a bright Sunday morning as Esther, Delia, and Charlotte Bai all fell ill. For the first time the Sunday chapel service was canceled.[36] Clinton was still in Bijawar, and there was no one else to preach. Lying in bed that Sunday, they must have given thanks for the orphans, snatched from the jaws of famine, who now carried on the schools, the preaching at Kanjarpur, the dispensary and school in Harpalpur, the witness in Chhatarpur, and evangelism and Sunday schools in all stations.

The Death of Delia Fistler

Delia remained in bed with a bad heart all through December. She sensed her service in India might be over, and her prayer was for someone to take her place. At midnight on December 10, 1913, Margaret Smith arrived.[37] Esther had met Margaret in America and had encouraged her to come to

Bundelkhand. Margaret was not new to India and already knew Hindi.
Here she was, in answer to prayer, to touch hands with Delia.

Esther accompanied Delia to Calcutta. In the company of a woman
of the Methodist Church,[38] she sailed February 7, 1914, via the Pacific,
arriving in San Francisco March 29. She stayed there with a sister and
hoped to recuperate quickly so that she could return to India,[39] but this
was not to be.

In June 1916 Rachel Pim wrote Esther: "I had a letter from Emma Fistler dated May 10 saying that Delia was very poorly and that the doctor
said that unless the Lord undertook for her there was no hope."[40] On
August 21 she wrote again, "We are very much broken up over Delia's sudden death." She died August 6, 1916, at Eagle Rock, California, at the age
of 49.[41] No one grieved more than Esther, who along with Delia had
forged ahead to open the Mission in Bundelkhand. She sought to put her
feelings into words:

> She did not rest satisfied until she was in the heart of this great
> unworked district of Bundelkhand. The Gospel had never been
> preached here until her voice first proclaimed it in 1896.
>
>   . . . . The always frail body had brought a latent heart trouble to
> India, which developed quickly in this trying climate, and her first year
> here she was told by the head of the English medical service that she
> possibly might live five years and she might drop dead any min-
> ute . . . . She realized as few do, the terrible hold the power of idolatry
> has upon the people. Her heart was here and she longed to stay on and
> suffer and pray and end her days amongst the people she loved . . . .
> She went from us two and one half years ago, with hardly a hope that
> she should see this place and the people she loved again. Once she
> wrote, "A little returning strength causes hope to spring up in my heart
> that God may have further service for me in this needy old world and
> perhaps even in India. He will do what is right and best."
>
> Twenty years ago when Delia Fistler came to this district it was all
> in dense darkness, the Gospel message had never been given and there
> was not a Christian. Now thousands have heard, some have accepted,
> a Christian community is letting its light shine in the still dense dark-
> ness, poor orphan children are still taken in and trained for lives of use-
> fulness and service, two dispensaries are relieving the sick and at the
> same time speaking the words of life, schools are being taught, and the
> Gospel is being preached.
>
> She hath done what she could, and her works do follow her.
>
> The music of her life is no-wise stilled, but blended so with songs
> around the throne of God, that our poor ears no longer hear it.[42]

On hearing of her death, the Indian Friends Church members also poured
out their feelings of love and loss. They called her their "beloved *bari*
[greatest of all] *Missahiba*." She had been to them a mother, leader, and

example. "After twenty-four years of loving, self-sacrificing service for India, God has called her to be with himself."[43] They noted she had lived twenty years in Bundelkhand. "Her work in this barren district of Bundelkhand is fully known to us who accompanied her from village to village through the jungles, so that when the news of her death reached here, not only we, her adopted children, wept for her, but those non-Christian people, too, among whom she had preached the Gospel." They spoke of her wisdom and of her compassion. "When any of us became ill, she came to our houses . . . and kneeling by the bed would take our name in prayer, the answer of which many of us have experienced and are safe to this day." They spoke of her frailty. "Even the smallest of us remember how many times she would get up in the Church to deliver the message and would have to sit down from weakness, saying, 'Who will do this work for God in my place?' We love and mourn her as our own mother, and can never forget her great love for us."[44]

Significant strengths disappeared with the going of Delia Fistler, which would not reappear until other missionaries akin to Delia Fistler in spiritual dynamism and leadership would reach India in 1936. All the missionaries were equally dedicated and gifted in their own way, but few people had the incisive discernment to confront a guilty person and help him see clearly the issue being dealt with. The Church spoke of this quality in Delia at the time of her death: "We appreciated [her discernment] when we saw her deciding any serious matter that occurred in the Mission, with such calmness and firmness, and according to the Bible, the guilty one at once repented and left his wrong way."[45] It was Delia who had the courage to close down all work and call all missionaries and Christians together for a time of heart searching and repentance because there was sin found in the Church. The Church was not to be a farce. There was to be a real difference between those who love Christ and those who did not, a difference in character and in witness. There were some who did not respond to the preaching, praying, and fasting that went with this deep time of heart searching. The numbers were so few that it took great courage to disown anyone, but those who did not respond were disowned until such time that they would repent. The Church of Jesus Christ must be a clean Church.[46]

This intensity and spiritual strength of Delia's made it possible for her to hold high the Christian standard for living. Those who lived near her felt this power and were blessed with the *Light* through God's gift of Delia Fistler to the Friends Church.

PART II
ESTHER BAIRD
1914-1938

Clinton Morris

Carrie Wood, Esther Baird, Victor
Mangalwadi, Mangalwadi, Jai Bai,
Shilwanti, Margaret Smith

Merrill, Catherine, Eugene,
Louis and Anna Coffin

Inez Cope Rogers, Dr. Mary
Fleming, Allison Rogers

Louis, Catherine, Eugene Coffin with Esther Baird

Geneva and Walter
Bolitho in Camp

47

The Kanjars   Prem Das

First three Bible
School students:
Moti Lal
(Teacher), Stuti
Prakash, Yohan
Dalsaiya, Dayal
Chand Singh

Shanti, Mother
Harbi Bai,
Grace Jones

Evangelistic camping

48

First Mission Bungalow at Chhatarpur

Dispensary and Chapel at Chhatarpur

Baird Retreat, Chhatarpur

49

The Elizabeth Jane Bell Stephenson Memorial Hospital, Chhatarpur

Dr. Ruth Hull

Alena Calkins

Vicerine Lady Irwin and Esther Baird
followed by other hospital staff

Crown Prince of Chhatarpur
and protector

James and Judith Kinder

John and Ruth Earle

Nell Lewis

Gore Lal Singh

Moti Lal family (Harbibai,
Shanti, and four
of nine children)

Pancham Singh and Noni Bai

51

Doctor's Bungalow, Chhatarpur

Dr. Grace Jones

Dr. Luke

Pharmacist Lachhman Singh

Esther Baird at Harpalpur Dispensary

Enduring War and Retrenchment

"Refrain thy voice from weeping and thine eyes from tears: for thy work shall be rewarded." Jeremiah 31:16

The Friends Foreign Missionary Society appointed Esther Baird as India Mission superintendent in 1916 though she had been acting in that capacity from the time she had taken Delia to Calcutta more than two years earlier.[1] As she returned to Nowgong and to the only other missionary to stand by her side during the war years, she was delighted with what she found. "Miss Smith knows just how to do things as they should be done," she commented.[2]

Margaret Smith and the Kanjars

Margaret Smith, 31, young and energetic, slipped into many niches.[3] She took over the school work in Nowgong, encouraged the church to rent a room and open a Sunday school in Bileri — a town about five miles from Nowgong — and went on tours with the evangelistic camping teams. In the melas at Khajaraho, forty-four miles from Nowgong, she and the team held twenty-one meetings in seven days.[4] That year they spent sixty-five days in thirteen melas, preaching and distributing literature.[5]

When the Political Agent expressed appreciation for the Mission's presence in the thieves' village of Kanjarpur and promised financial assistance for the Mission to teach the women and girls, Margaret responded.[6] She immediately set aside two hours a day for eighteen girls who enrolled and, escorted by police back and forth, attended the sewing classes twice a week at the Mission.[7]

As time went on, Margaret was convinced that living right in the settlement with the Kanjars and creating a loving atmosphere in their midst was the need of the hour. The Salvation Army did this in other parts of

India with success. Before the end of the year, the P.A. promised financial assistance for them to take over the village and start industrial and agricultural projects along Christian lines. What an opportunity to demonstrate the love of God if only the Mission had personnel to do it! Esther Baird was loaded with building, medical work, and administration. Margaret, the educationist, evangelist, and treasurer, could do no more. Clinton Morris, evangelist and teacher in Harpalpur, seemed not to possess aptitude in this line. A couple was needed, but World War I had begun, funds were tight, and at the time no couple was available. With great disappointment they had to decline the P.A.'s offer.[8]

Retrenchment

Loss of the opportunity among the Kanjars was only the beginning of disappointments in 1914. As the Board met to consider prayerfully what they could do about their debts, they admitted, "Human wisdom is not sufficient . . . . We realize more keenly our insufficiency and our dependence upon God."[9] The Cowgill Fund, on which they had depended for a number of years to meet the deficits, was exhausted. The president of the Board wrote Esther:

> This year when the estimates were all summed up we found that those for the fields of China and India and for our home expenses amounted to about $15,000 and our income for several years has averaged between $8,000 and $9,000 . . . .[10]

> The Yearly Meeting directs the Board in order to avoid debt to adopt a policy of retrenchment along any possible line that may seem advisable.[11]

On receiving this news, Esther Baird called Clinton Morris and Margaret Smith for a special mission council meeting on October 13, 1914, to consider retrenchment. They went through the list of all they were doing:

(1) *The schools and Sunday schools in the town and nearby towns for Hindus and Moslems including those among the Chamars and Kanjars.* If they cut off this work, they would eliminate many areas of contact with the town. The cost of keeping the schools open was so small that retrenchment there would hardly be noticed.

(2) *The girls' orphanage.* Already they had support for the various girls. To drop them would mean losing the support money. There seemed to be no saving there.

(3) *The boys' orphanage.* The support was there for the boys, too. Also, they were the key to the future.

Altogether there were fifty children in the orphanage at that time, but not one could be shifted to another mission — not yet — in favor of retrenchment.[12]

(4) *Workshop.* With the outside jobs and contracts, the men in the workshop were almost self-supporting. At one point they had turned a profit of Rs. 300 ($27) back to the Mission."[13]

(5) *Evangelistic work.* How could evangelism be cut? Preaching the Good News of Jesus Christ was the key purpose of the Mission. Deserting the outstations, like Chhatarpur where Pancham Singh was preaching and from which he visited scores of villages, seemed ridiculous. Preaching must go on in the melas, the bazaars, and the far-flung, neglected Bundelkhandi villages where thousands were hearing the Gospel.

(6) *The Harpalpur school.* Some ninety students ranging from kindergarten through high school[14] were taught by only two teachers — Gore Lal Singh with a salary of five dollars a month and Nathu Lall with a salary slightly less.[15] The building — a small native house donated by the Alipura Raja — cost nothing. It was badly in need of repair and most inadequate for the expanding school. Instead of closing out there, the missionaries wanted to make a strong request for a special gift to build a new school — one that could serve also as a chapel for religious services.[16] As a successful foothold in Harpalpur, it must be held.

(7) *Medical Work.* Retrenchment in medical work would cause untold suffering. In Nowgong the whole Christian community was being cared for, as well as other sufferers in the town. In Harpalpur William Parsad treated 6,624 new cases and 4,741 old cases in the past two years.[17] As many as sixty patients a day came to him.[18] Instead of retrenchment, the missionaries wanted to ask for funds to build a veranda onto the dispensary for patients who needed to stay two or three days for treatment.[19]

(8) *Zenana work.* Mary Bai's salary was the only expense in this work. It was such a pittance it would not be noticed on any financial statement.[20] Even if this work should close, Mary Bai could not be spared, for she served as eyes to blind Charlotte Bai, whose services among the children and in the Church were indispensable.

Their findings at the end of a grueling day after exhausting all possibilities were: There was no way to retrench!

Clinton Morris had been silent through most of the discussion, but he was thinking deeply about what retrenchment meant to his future in India. When the discussion ended, he offered his resignation. Since the Board was not able to extend the work as it should be or even carry it on as it was, he felt he was not justified in staying on in India as a missionary.[21] No one tried to persuade Clinton to reconsider. The Board gave him permission to leave India by March 10, 1915, provided they could find the money for his passage.[22] Fifteen days after this council meeting, Clinton had intended to sit for his second Hindi examination, but he was so discouraged he did not bother. As the only man in the

Mission, however, he fulfilled his responsibility as representative to the Mid-India Regional Council of Churches. With missionaries of many different denominations across central India, he helped form policies for cooperation in a number of essential projects. One was the language school, in which there were thirty-six students.[23] Leaving Bundelkhand on March 25, he traveled through dangerous waters and arrived safely in New York on May 15, 1915.[24]

Retrenchment forced the Mission to stop all improvements and repairs and to keep salaries at the level of three to five dollars a month. With inflation running wild, the people had no margin for school fees in the Mission school. So one way or another, the Mission had to pay. The pressure forced them to give eight of their girls from the orphanage to the Salvation Army.[25]

The Effects of the War

Nowgong was a military base where 1,000 or more Indian and some 300 English soldiers were regularly stationed. During the war Nowgong was emptied of all these soldiers.[26]

After October 1914 mail came late as it passed through censors,[27] letters were often lost, and money sent sometimes did not come at all. Funds for all German missionaries were cut off, and had other missionaries not rallied to their aid, they would have suffered much.[28] As the war progressed, they were all interned.

India displayed great loyalty to England. Even the Mohammedans, denouncing their coreligionists of the Ottoman Empire (Turks), fought bravely on England's side. They pledged millions of rupees for the war effort and thousands of men volunteered for military service. All foreigners in India had to get permits from the cantonment before taking any railway journey. Names had to be registered with the consular offices. All had to report to the magistrate.[29]

As rumors spread that the war would last for three years or more, the Bundelkhand Christian community sought to help. Through a supply of materials from the Red Cross, they made 150 pillows, 275 pillow cases, 150 quilts, dozens of handbags, operating aprons, scarves, and shirts.[30]

The industrial school, kept busy with orders from naval and military officers, landed a contract with the famine relief officer for making a number of doors.[31] After the army left Nowgong and there were no more military jobs, they received a contract to put down wells and extensively remodel a bungalow for the Maharaja of Panna State.[32]

Epidemics, Accidents, and Death

War or no war, the usual epidemic of smallpox moved in with fury, closing the bazaar school and laying low eight in the orphanage. They had to be isolated for three months at a time when temperatures soared to 120° F and hot winds blew for twenty-four hours at a time without stopping.[33] Fortunately, all recovered. Hardly had this epidemic ceased when cholera began spreading rapidly and took its toll.[34] The dispensaries in Harpalpur and Nowgong as well as the Goddard Memorial Hospital were used to capacity.[35]

Retrenchment had stopped all repair, but a special gift[36] came to reroof the bungalow. Esther Baird supervised the work and some of the young men in the Mission helped. One day several of these young men were standing on some timbers supporting the ceiling cloth, when suddenly the timbers gave way and Hassanwa fell through and dropped eighteen feet. He died in about three hours without ever regaining consciousness. He was one of the most skilled of the young men.[37]

Such tragedies in the Mission overshadowed all else, even the war. That year Lachiya, Balla's wife and Prem Das's sister-in-law, died very suddenly.[38] Six days later her little baby daughter, Parsi, also died, leaving Balla with two children. Yakub and Gendibai lost two babies, leaving them with empty hearts and arms.[39] The tiniest orphan died in spite of all the care the missionaries could give.[40]

In Chhatarpur, Noni Bai became so ill they despaired of her life.[41] Conditions were too rugged to put her back in Chhatarpur for the present. So they transferred Pancham Singh and Noni Bai to Bileri, where for $40 they had purchased a two-family house and schoolroom.[42]

A Tribute to the Servant of Love

Prem Das, the most outstanding of the preachers and the brightest spiritual light in all of Bundelkhand, died in Goddard Hospital in Nowgong July 10, 1915.[43] During his last months of activity, he lived in the bazaar near the Church and operated a bookstore and continued teaching in the boys' school. He preached in the bazaar and when able joined the village evangelistic camping team. He was a member of the ministry and oversight body. Esther Baird wrote of him:

> Prem Das — a servant of love — that is what he asked to be called when as a little boy the love of Christ came into his heart in such an impelling manner that ever after he wished to spend and be spent in his Savior's service.[44]

He was an ideal student who kept the rules of the orphanage and influenced the other boys to do right. He was the first volunteer to teach in Kanjarpur and the first to go out into the villages to preach. He was an excellent teacher and a wonderful friend.

On March 5, 1915, he left camp work very ill. Six days later he was admitted to the Goddard Memorial Hospital. His brother, Balla, then took him to the Ghawali tuberculosis sanatorium,[45] but a month later they asked for someone to come get him. His youngest brother, Daruwa (Mangalwadi), brought him home to die. He was a quiet, patient sufferer. When he grew too weak to talk, he still clasped his New Testament. He whispered that if it were not for the book and all he had learned from it, he could not bear the pain. Prem Das's suffering drew all who were near him closer to the Savior.[46]

"We cannot make ourselves willing to give him up," wrote Margaret Smith, "for he is so much needed in this dark Bundelkhand where there is so little light of the Gospel of Jesus Christ."[47] He was buried the next day, the fortieth grave in the little mission cemetery.[48] He left behind a very young widow with two little boys, one three years and the other less than ten months. The church in Bundelkhand wrote of him:

> We thank God for the life he lived among us, for his example of godliness, and faithfulness in the service of our Master, and for the clear, definite testimony which he bore to the saving power of Jesus Christ. He counted not his life dear unto himself that he might finish his course with joy, and the ministry which he had received of the Lord Jesus, to testify [to] the Gospel of the grace of God.[49]

Mangalwadi, Prem Das's youngest brother, stepped forward to take his place. He had changed his name to Mangalwadi, meaning Evangelist as in *Pilgrim's Progress*. He finished high school in Jabalpur,[50] and after his brother died, he began teaching in the boys' school and preaching in the camps and in the bazaar. He reopened the Chamar school, which had been closed for some time and soon had twenty students.[51] By 1916, under Margaret Smith's supervision, he took charge of both boys' and girls' schools on the compound and established the first coeducational school in Bundelkhand.[52]

Panga, the Crippled One

Nathu Lall (Panga) was promoted to the position of headmaster of the Harpalpur Mission School, and Jaganath moved to Harpalpur to help him.[53] His appointment was precipitated by the resignation of Gore Lal Singh, who accepted a secular position at $10 a month—just twice his mission salary.

The appointment immediately brought to mind the first day the missionaries had seen Panga. Many years ago Esther Baird and a friend going through the bazaar suddenly became aware of a hopping sound behind them. Panga (the lame one), so disfigured and poverty stricken he could hardly be recognized as human, was following them. Esther Baird took him to the orphanage, where with clean clothes and a bath he was greatly changed. With good food, he gained so much weight his weak legs could not hold him up. The missionaries then took him to the government hospital for an operation, but at night he crawled a mile back to the Mission, the place he had first come to know love. They had to take him back the next morning. The operation was successful, and as years went by, his legs developed. Panga's mind was never crippled. By the time he finished high school in 1912, he was considered the brightest orphan boy. He was converted during a revival and began to support the church regularly. Married two years before being appointed headmaster, by that time he was the father of a son. Headmaster Nathu Lall, father of Komal Das Lall, was never again known as Panga.[54]

Further Afield with Evangelism

The camping team went out every cool season in loaded oxcarts, jolting over jungle roads through rough fields, fording rivers, and covering some two hundred villages. William Parsad joined the team for one stretch and treated 150 needy cases.[55] The first time an evangelistic camping team went without a missionary in charge, they traveled far. Hira Lal was lame, and he rode a pony, but Pancham Singh and Jai Chand walked. In one month they covered 250 miles, distributing Gospel portions and preaching the Good News to 247 villages.[56] They found meeting the simple, eager people hidden in almost inaccessible areas of Bundelkhand an exhilarating experience. Panna, fifty-seven miles from Nowgong, prohibited gospel preaching, but the men sold Gospels and witnessed to any who seemed interested. "Would you like to buy a book?" Pancham Singh asked the Panna police inspector. "No," he answered, "there is so much power in it that whoever reads it once thoughtfully will become changed in his mind."[57]

Before the men returned home in late March, they stopped for several weeks at Khajaraho, thirty miles from Chhatarpur and the home of the Maharaja. A big mela was on there and as soon as Esther Baird heard they were there, she joined them, taking the magic lantern with the life of Christ. Women, not allowed to attend public meetings, watched the pictures behind closed doors. The next day the Maharaja ordered two tents set up as a place for the general public to see the pictures. A Brahmin who attended all four nights came to love Jesus. He openly avowed he wanted to become a Christian, but in the end—as so often happened—he disappeared.[58]

During the coolest month of the year in January the *Hindu Burki Mela* draws thousands to the banks of Jagat Sagar, "Ocean of the World," a lake about five miles from Nowgong on the way to Chhatarpur. The lake was created by earthworks thrown up by one side to catch the drainage from the surrounding hills during the rains.[59] Every year from

4:00 a.m. by every path leading to the lake, streams of humanity converge on the shore of the lake to worship their gods, bathe in the icy waters to wash away their sins, and to enjoy the day at the fair. On a rope bed placed with two legs in one canoe and two in another they sit for pleasant rides on the lake. They buy and sell sweets, brassware, cloth, farm implements, trinkets, and sugar cane.[60] The evangelists set up Christian book stalls and enter into the excitement of selling Gospels. When large groups gather, they preach. Otherwise, they talk seriously to the passersby, witnessing and answering questions. That people listen is the encouragement that keeps them going back year after year.

Happy Times and the Hot Season

Wars, retrenchment, sickness, death, and disappointment were more than endured; they were offered to God. Out of them came vitality and hope as the missionaries entered into the sufferings and joys of those around them. Pyari Bai, a little girl rejected by her family because of her crippled hands, was given a home and care. An operation by the civil surgeon gave her the use of her hands.[61] The missionaries shook off their heavy burdens to take the orphan girls by bullock tonga to Harpalpur. The girls enjoyed the forty-mile round-trip as they saw for the first time a railway station, a cotton gin, and the Dhasan River with the big dam.[62]

Margaret Smith, longing for Carrie Wood's quick return from furlough, taught the girls in the bazaar school and supervised all the other schools. She helped the women set out 240 mulberry trees through which they could make a profit by developing silkworm culture. By 1917 with ninety trees surviving, they sold a few cocoons at a good price. They hoped to add sericulture to their list of industries, but it did not develop.[63] Kanjarpur school continued with thirteen students taught by Har Das; the Chamar school had twenty-two students taught by Din Dayal; Bileri, with thirteen students, was taught by Tulsi Das.[64]

All work slowed as hot winds brought temperatures to 110°-120° F. Esther Baird immediately ordered the servants to put khas-khas grass mats into all the doors and windows of the bungalow. When wet, these mats brought inside temperatures down by ten or fifteen degrees. Travel to distant villages and outside work during the day now became impossible. Evenings, however, brought cooler air than the hot inside of houses, and families spilled out of their houses to take advantage of twilight. The hot season was a family time and most weddings took place then. Nathu Lall married Anand, a girl from the orphanage, April 29, 1914.[65] William Parsad married a girl from the Presbyterian Mission in late May 1914.[66] Din Dayal, the tailor, married Hiriya from the orphanage September 18, 1915; Jai Chand took a second wife in October 1914.[67] In 1916,

Mangalwadi married Jai Bai of the Canadian Presbyterian Mission Girls' School at Neemuch.[68] His brother Balla married Pukhiya; Jaganath married Puniya, Tulsi Das married Maryam — the first child born of Christian parents in the Mission and the first of the second generation to be married.[69]

Following the weddings were the happy occasions of babies being born. Prem Das and his wife had their second son September 30, 1914.[70] The William Parsads had their first son May 23, 1915.[71] Mangalwadi had two children — Shilwanti, and Victor who was born October 6, 1919.

All activities during the hot season took place between 5:00 p.m. and 9:00 a.m. in the comparatively cooler times of day. The Christians entered into each others' joys as schools held closing exercises and students received prizes and promotion. The women and girls displayed embroidered and hemstitched linen handkerchiefs Margaret Smith taught them to make for sale, and the boys from the industrial school showed off their handiwork. They proudly turned back to the Mission some of their profits from their well digging and bungalow building.[72]

War Prosperity

By the end of 1915, funds started coming to the Board, bringing hope of clearing the debts. The Women's Missionary Union of Friends in America also started an *Esther E. Baird Love Fund* to pay for her salary for the next decade or more.[73] In addition to this, $2,500 to India and $3,000 to China was received from Peter Binford's estate.[74] By mid-1916 the Board had received gifts totaling $8,000 for ongoing expenses and their debt had been cleared. Prosperity filled the coffers as money from children's mite boxes brought in $100 above any previous donation. Their interest also grew as they prepared 47 scrapbooks and 3,000 cards with Scripture texts, dressed 65 dolls, and sent 12 quilts to the two mission fields. Dr. Goddard's friend in Lowell, Massachusetts, sent money for a dispensary in Harpalpur where patients who needed more than one day's treatment could stay over.[75] The missionaries built two rooms, 12' x 12'. By using one row of kiln-burnt bricks on the outside, lime-pointed, with sun-dried bricks on the inside, complete with a tile roof, they got the most for their money.[76]

The windowless Harpalpur school building for eighty-nine boys and three Christian teachers was uninhabitable during the rains and unhealthy in all seasons. Gore Lal Singh's return to the staff sparked action, and the Raja of Alipura offered to pay half his salary. This provided him with a substantial raise. Furthermore, the Raja agreed to pay part of the cost of the building if a course in agriculture were added to the curriculum. The missionaries wasted no time. They added some significant gifts to the sum the Raja offered and wrote home to the Board and received permission to proceed with the building. By July 1, 1917, the new school and a small chapel were put to use.[77]

As to the Binford estate, Esther Baird and Margaret Smith recommended it be used to open the Chhatarpur work ($1,500) and to bring another missionary to India ($1,000). The Board, however, did not think it wise to use all the money at once.[78] The missionaries and their co-workers in India, nevertheless, prepared themselves for future spiritual conquests. They were greatly encouraged by the appointment on the home front of Louise Ellett, who as corresponding secretary for the Board would undergird workers on the field with strength, wisdom, and encouragement for the next thirty years.[79]

Eugene Baird — a War Casualty

At the peak of the war, Esther Baird received a telegram stating that at Ypres, West Flanders Province, North West Belgium, her adopted son, Eugene Franklin Baird, 22, had died on the battlefield June 2, 1916.[80]

Esther's next few hours were filled with stunned, memory-filled grief. Eugene, born October 28, 1893, and brought to her while she was still in Muthura, was her adopted son. On her first furlough when Eugene was seven years old, she took him with her to America. He returned to India with her bursting with energy.[81] In 1907 she took him with her again. He was thirteen, and he stayed on with a friend, Mrs. Irvine, to study in Cleveland. Esther saw him again in June 1911 upon arriving in Cleveland for her next furlough. "He has grown to be such a big fellow," she exclaimed.[82] Esther came home ill, and in the next two and a half years while recuperating, she spent much time with Eugene. When on September 17, 1913, she said good-bye to him and started for India, she did not realize she was seeing him for the last time. Out at sea on his birthday she wrote him a tender letter and penned in her diary:

> To Eugene . . .
> My love, could I but take the hours
> That once I spent with thee,
> And coin them all in minted gold
> What should I purchase that would hold
> Their worth in joy to me?
> Ah, Love — Another hour with thee![83]

The next year the world went to war. Eugene never wrote his adopted mother about his convictions concerning war. It should not be surprising, however, that as a British citizen on his 21st birthday he should make the decision to shape his own destiny. Without consulting anyone, he went to Canada and enlisted in the Canadian army. Esther was devastated by this news.[84]

Apart from her faith, her load of grief would have been unbearable. She lost Eugene and Delia both in 1916. On the anniversary of his death she wrote:

> E'en for the dead, I will not bind my soul to grief;
> Death cannot long divide.
> For is it not as though the rose that climbed my garden wall
> Had blossomed on the other side?
> Death doth hide, but not divide!
> Thou art but on Christ's other side,
> Thou art with Christ and Christ with me,
> In Him united still are we.[85]

Three years later, still feeling her loss, she wrote: "I would not have had him fail in duty, as he saw it, even though the sun set in my own life."[86]

After the death of Eugene and Delia Fistler, the Board arranged for Carrie Wood's immediate return to India even though the war was still raging. She arrived on Thanksgiving Day, 1916.[87] She was appointed to edit the *Friends Oriental News*, supervise the bazaar girls' school, and do zenana work with Mary Bai.[88] Margaret supervised the coeducational school, the new handkerchief-making cottage industry, and was appointed as treasurer.[89]

The War Ends

World War I raged on, and on April 6, 1917, the Americans also declared war on Germany, intensifying the bitterness of the fighting. In Bundelkhand, far from the front lines, everyone was made aware of war's cost through seeing fifty Turkish soldiers, prisoners of war — all lame, halt, or blind — loaded into a railway carriage to be sent to Mesopotamia in exchange for the English. A prisoner of war camp, located in Nowgong, gave the people firsthand acquaintance with these unhappy, hungry men. Regiments of Sikh soldiers were stationed at Nowgong, and the Mission sometimes found opportunity to minister both to the soldiers and to the prisoners. Esther Baird cried in anguish, "Four years of war and the awful carnage still continues with more and more slaughter each day. How long, oh God! how long?" Not long after that, signs of peace were seen. On October 7, 1918, the schools had a holiday to celebrate the peace pact with Bulgaria.[90]

No doubt there would have been a very great celebration on November 11 when the armistice was signed had the people not been so weak and ill with influenza. With great fury this worldwide epidemic wiped out whole villages in India, leaving thousands dead. The Mission was not spared. Seventy of the Christian community were laid low. All other work was closed and the three missionaries gave every ounce of strength to caring for the ill. They were able to keep all but two children alive.[91]

Gaining a "Foothold for the Lord"

*"Ask of me, and I will make the nations your
inheritance, the end of the earth your possession."
Psalm 2:8 NIV*

Speeding Ahead with Hope-filled Hearts

With the end of the war, the flu abated. Miraculously not one of the missionaries came down with the disease. During the war years the three
missionaries were especially blessed with health, and this made possible
their relentless effort to build solidly and ask largely for the future. Their
request for an automobile came to the Mission Board as a surprise,[1] but
convinced by the missionaries' arguments for its need to facilitate the
work, they set about to get it.[2] The missionaries picked up the Ford at the
railway station at Harpalpur on September 1, 1919, and with lessons from
the Political Agent, Esther Baird started driving it alone in three months.[3]

From the beginning of 1917 the church, schools, dispensaries, building work, visitation of the women, and evangelistic work all took on new
intensity. The Mission was blessed with a number of young preachers,
grown up in the orphanage, who could speak in meeting. None were
more gifted than the late Prem Das's brother, Mangalwadi, who was not
only headmaster of the school but the unappointed pastor of the little
church. He preached nearly every Sunday, and his advice and spiritual
counsel were sought by both the Christians and the missionaries. Gore
Lal Singh's messages were also deeply appreciated, but usually he
ministered in Harpalpur.[4]

Esther was so impressed with the breadth and intensity of Margaret
Smith's evangelistic work that she wrote, "The Word has been preached
and left with the people and we can now but await the coming of the
Spirit of God to quicken and give life that many may be gathered out of

the darkness of Bundelkhand as they already have been from other parts of India."[5] She referred to a message at Christmastime in 1915 by Sherwood Eddy, a missionary statesman. He had told of wide response in South India. He had stirred the faith of many and brought hope for a mighty awakening, first among the Christians and the churches and then among the non-Christians of India.[6]

Margaret enthusiastically took up Delia Fistler's camping program and year after year in the company of six or seven Indian evangelists toured the area. In 1917, Carrie Wood accompanied her for 36 miles in the horse and buggy, and from there she went on by oxcart with the rest of the party for about 40 miles. They preached as they went, and at night they set up tents. Because oxcarts could not go down through some rough hilly sections, they walked.[7] "We are quite sure God is going to gather a people out of Bundelkhand that shall praise Him throughout the ages," said Margaret. When fruit did not appear, she still held hopefully to His promises, feeling God was saying, "It is your work to witness faithfully and I will take care of the results."[8]

Success, Failure, Sorrow, Famine

Results came one day, but not through the camping team. The church, entering more and more into vital spiritual matters, heard the witness of a high caste Hindu Thakur who came into the service on August 29, 1917. Mihrban Singh publicly confessed his faith in Christ and asked to be a member of the church in Nowgong.[9] The joy of this occasion was tremendous. It was diminished only by the discovery that three Christians had fallen short of the church discipline by smoking and three others by drinking. One was an evangelist. The church admonished them one by one. The evangelist repented for the time being, but no one else did. None were excommunicated, and on these matters a dullness of conscience almost imperceptibly began to creep in. Pancham Singh noted a more subtle danger and exhorted parents not to resort to amulets and fish teeth around the neck and such superstitions in the care of their children, but to trust God for their protection.[10]

At a later monthly meeting, the little church had to cope with sorrow. Word came of the death of Dr. George DeVol in China on December 31, 1917, and the Bundelkhand Church, having just lost Delia Fistler, sent words of consolation to the people of China, and to his widow, Dr. Isabella DeVol, who had written, "The grief of the past few months has put my heart in closer touch with the sorrow that prevails in the world at the present time." Three years later Dr. Isabella DeVol followed her husband in death, leaving three children who would live to bless both India and China.[11]

Sorrow seemed to compound in Bundelkhand at this time. After the very hot summer of 1918, the rains refused to come, the crops failed, and famine followed. The missionaries again took up famine relief, and the Board responded with generous gifts. With the mission workers' help in supervision, Esther Baird organized a work team for the able-bodied men who came with their families for food. By March 1919, seventy-eight men were kept busy earning their food and clothing by smoothing out rough plots, erecting a garage, trimming hedges, digging wells, cleaning the compound, and building a school in Dhorra village.[12]

Breakthrough in Chhatarpur

At such a time the Lord opened the door at last to Chhatarpur. "An answer to twenty years of prayer,"[13] said Esther Baird as on March 31, 1919, the Maharaja of Chhatarpur gave her an outright gift of an acre of land in Chhatarpur State.[14] The map showed this land located just beyond the city limits toward Nowgong. Plans to build were immediately put into effect. With the Ford in which to travel the 14 miles from Nowgong, supervision was easier. The contract for making bricks was given and the foundations laid. With famine coolies to help, the work proceeded apace, all through the hot season.

Everything came to a standstill as the monsoons came. The year before the rains had failed to come; in 1919 they failed to stop. The heavy downpour made it impossible for people to plant their crops. Their mud houses tumbled down, leaving them homeless, wet, cold, miserable, hungry, and often ill.[15] About 100 people a day crowded into the mission compound for refuge. After two months, the sun began to shine again and famine workers returned to their villages to plant their crops. There was a good harvest in March.[16] Famine relief had cost about $2,000.[17]

The project of building a bungalow in Chhatarpur took precedence over everything. The only way to assure its completion before the next rainy season was constant supervision. Pancham Singh, again living in Chhatarpur, and Margaret Smith, who postponed her furlough to see it through, were assigned the task. Margaret moved into a small native room with a mud floor. First, they erected a small house for protection from the sun. Next, they dug a well. The concrete foundation of the building was finished by Christmas.[18] Making the bricks and tile, digging and burning the lime — and then buying a pair of buffalos to grind it — all had to be done before any more work became visible. They hauled in logs from the jungle for the woodwork and they watched as every brick was put straight. Praise to God went up on both sides of the water as funds came in to see this project through. "Our Board has had the best year financially that we have ever had," wrote Rachel Pim.[19] Persistence paid off, and the bungalow exterior was finished before the hot season ended. The interior, safe from the rains, was finished later.[20] "In the foothold the Lord has given us in Chhatarpur," Margaret wrote, "we feel we have moved up into the front trenches, face to face with the enemy."[21] The missionaries considered the securing of the land in Chhatarpur one of the most wonderful victories the Lord had wrought for them and for His glory in Bundelkhand. At last, with the bungalow secure on its foundations, Margaret Smith finally left in September 1920 for a much-needed furlough.[22] During the following year Esther Baird saw the bungalow completed and ready for a missionary doctor.

Harpalpur Work Threatened

Meanwhile, with Margaret in America, Esther and Carrie were the only missionaries left. As Chhatarpur opened, Harpalpur, their other outstation, was about to close. One morning William Parsad from Harpalpur knocked at the door in Nowgong and handed in his resignation. He moved to a nearby town called Mhow.[23] That left the Harpalpur dispensary without a "doctor" and a whole area neglected. Since the Raja of Alipura furnished vital support for both the dispensary and the school, failure of the Mission to keep well-qualified workers on the job might well lead the Raja to withdraw his support. As soon as possible, Esther Baird motored to Alipura. The government worked out a plan for William Parsad to treat the ill once every other week at two government dam sites — Luchura and Pahari — both about seven and eight miles from Harpalpur. They agreed to pay him for this. William Parsad, homesick after being away for six months, accepted this better financial arrangement and returned to work December 6, 1920. Mangal Singh joined him as assistant dispenser and together they were able to manage all the work and keep the dispensary open six days a week.[24]

Nowgong Activities — Esther Baird

Esther Baird cared for medical work in and around Nowgong. Often as many as fifty-five patients a day crowded in for treatment. The rainy season always brought malaria, and often from out in the district people would call her to come. If roads were impassable, she went in the buggy, traveling over rough roads to see poor sick village women. Able to give relief, she returned very tired after fifteen to eighteen miles of jolting.

Living in Nowgong had its advantages. The British Political Agent often invited the missionaries to garden parties; the Raja sent his elephant to take them to a famous fort; they took rides to the colorful palace of His Highness, the Maharaja of Chhatarpur, to see the lake, buildings, and tomb aglow with illumination on special days; they went on trips through tiger jungle, and relaxed with English friends. Missionary friends of various denominations and nationalities often came and stayed a month or more. English soldiers, as many as thirty at a time, came to the bungalow for tea and to stay on for a Gospel message.

Esther always found time for children and made space for another seven-month-old baby boy in the orphanage. On Sunday evenings she delighted in taking the orphan girls and young boys for a walk. On Monday morning the relaxed atmosphere changed, and work began. Handing out seeds and instructions to the gardener, attending to leaky roofs, caring for the ill, planning new buildings, and advising the workmen filled her day. Some days she had "a very tiresome day with the workmen."[25]

Zenana Work—Carrie Wood

Quietly supporting all the work, Carrie Wood carried her end of the load. She was considered too frail for camp work, but she supervised all the schools and trudged daily with Mary Bai, the Bible woman, into the town to visit in the *zenanas*. These women living in joint families had much work to do, but the hour appointed for them to learn reading and hear the Gospel through song and message was the highlight of their day. Sometimes one of the men of the house, unsympathetic and fearful of what his wife might learn, would ruthlessly pull her out of the class and stir up such opposition that visiting in that home had to stop. Carrie's heart broke at the sight of the women's tears. She grieved especially over one Mohammedan lady addicted to opium who begged them to help her free herself from this habit. They were prevented from close contact with her but urged her to seek help from Christ. So many women, bowed to the earth by oppressive customs, looked to Carrie Wood and Mary Bai as their only hope. This desperate need kept them going back day after day and year after year to take these women the message of the love of the Lord Jesus Christ. They were rewarded very seldom with the joy of hearing a woman cry out to the Lord for forgiveness and adoption into the Kingdom. No matter what these "zenana" women felt on the inside, their initiative was so stifled that such an act required tremendous courage. None of them ever dared to come to church or be known to others as a Christian, even when Carrie Wood and Mary Bai were convinced they had been born again.[26]

Because of Carrie's many abilities, she was asked to do accounts and auditing, take minutes at the business meetings, help with the clothes of the orphans, and supervise the entire Mission during hot seasons. She enjoyed hobbies of reading, studying trees and strange customs, and had a terrific sense of humor. These qualities enriched her writing for the *Friends Oriental News* and made her a delightful conversationalist.[27]

New Recruits — Rogerses, Fords

Margaret started packing for furlough in 1920, and filling her shoes seemed impossible. Just then, however, help came from two directions. Alison H. Rogers and Inez A. Cope, both college graduates, applied to the Board and were accepted for India. They were married June 24, 1920, and arrived in India in 1921. Rachel Pim wrote concerning him, "Mr. Rogers speaks with more or less freedom Latin, German, Greek, French, and Norwegian, and is a student of Hebrew." These qualifications did not sound exactly like those desired in a man to take over the industrial school, but the missionaries in India were thankful anyway. The Rogerses came on an annual salary of $600 and the other missionaries also received a similar raise.[28]

From another direction in August 1920 came the Jefferson Ford family on their way from Kenya for furlough. So intrigued with the evangelistic opportunities was Jefferson Ford that he sent his family on home and stayed on in India for the winter camping season. With six evangelists, one an interpreter, he went from village to village, camping at night, selling books, and holding as many meetings as possible. From October 3 to December 20 he preached to 4,000 people.[29] In one of the villages he met a widow who ten years earlier after hearing Delia Fistler preach had cried out, "O Lord Jesus, if Thou art the true God, show thyself to me and help me." From that day she had left idol worship and followed the Lord. She had one cow and two children whom she prayed would not starve. By the time Jefferson Ford met her, she owned ten cows and her children were nearly grown. Jefferson Ford said, "My eyes grow misty as I think of all it has meant for this lone woman to stand against idolatry and all it means away out here with no help even from those who first gave her the Gospel. My heart rejoices greatly at the rare privilege of finding her, and who can tell of the 'seven thousand who do not bow the knee to Baal?'"[30]

Mangalwadi's Disappointment and Death

Kanjarpur was one village from which the missionaries and Indian Christian workers expected fruit. They were not at all prepared for the heartbreaking and shattering event that took place just after Margaret Smith left for furlough on November 7, 1920. The government disbanded the village of the Kanjars, the thieving caste. They were scattered throughout the district without homes or land. What could they do but go back to stealing? They came to the Mission, pleading for help, but found only tears. For more than a decade Margaret Smith had written profusely for the Mission's backing to move in with force, placing a missionary couple right in their midst. Some thirty such settlements had been successfully managed by the Salvation Army in other parts of India. But there was no missionary couple, and the Rogers family had not yet arrived. As the poor people reluctantly picked up their few belongings and began walking away, at least some of the boys who had learned to read had Bibles packed in their bundles.[31]

Mangalwadi wept as he saw the Kanjars go in different directions, hoping to find a place to rest their heads before night. He recalled how his brother, Prem Das, had given his life to them, and how he, Mangalwadi, had stepped in to take his brother's place. Even as he thought about it, he, too, began to cough. The missionaries noticed he was losing weight. Their finest preacher and spiritual leader's skin began to look transparent. They missed his messages as he grew too weak to carry on his former work. Finally he had to give up both his preaching and teaching and go to bed. Those who dared go near enough to talk found him full of the joy of the Lord even though he was suffering much. His wife and their little girl, Shilwanti, and their little boy, Victor, were sustained in these tragic hours by his courage. On February 25, 1921, he died—the third member of that illustrious family of Duojibai to be taken away by tuberculosis. The church mourned deeply, and Esther Baird wrote five months later, "He was our best preacher and chief adviser. He lived very near the Master. We have not learned how to get along without him."[32]

The Twenty-fifth Anniversary of the Mission

Blind Charlotte was as grieved as anyone by the tragic happenings in the Mission, but she refused to forget how trials develop nearness to God and meaning in life. So she shook the missionaries out of their preoccupation with burdens and reminded them that the 25th Anniversary of the Mission had arrived and that it was time to praise the Lord.

Alison and Inez Rogers arrived February 5, 1921, in ample time to attend the celebration—a wonderful time for them to review the whole history.[33] To prepare themselves for the occasion, they visited the stations and studied the field. They learned Bundelkhand had six major and seventeen minor states, each governed by its own native chief under the British Political Agent. The area of 9,861 square miles, very rocky and barren for the most part, sustained a population of 1,300,000. Alison was not too surprised, on observing the roads, that the Ford was still in quite good condition, as most of the roads in Bundelkhand were impassable for automobiles. Only two good roads crossing the district diagonally were suitable for motor traffic. Earlier Delia had written, "Many of the villages cannot be reached by the oxcart and there are very few that can easily be reached by walking . . . . The soil is black cotton."[34]

The Rogerses took time to see the whole layout of the Mission —
Nowgong in the center with arms extended in both directions to Harpalpur and Chhatarpur. Nowgong's compound of twenty-four acres (and
a ten-year lease on twelve more) boasted of twenty-seven buildings and
five wells. It was beautifully kept. Large silk-cotton trees lined the path
leading to the bungalow. Neem, pepul, eucalyptus, and other trees graced
the yard and garden. The hedges were sharply trimmed, and a profusion
of hybiscus, bougainvillea, flowering trees, and vines enhanced the
beauty of the compound. The buildings were laid out in a pleasing manner, even though economically built with brick and lime or mud. There
was the bungalow and the cottage for missionaries; the school building;
Dr. Goddard Memorial Hospital; two buildings for the orphans; the
workshop; three "lines"— separate houses built next to each other where
workers lived with their families; three other houses for Indian families;
one garage; and three sheds for tools, buggy, oxcart, oxen, and horses.

Before going on to Chhatarpur, they saw two small outstations in the
outskirts of Nowgong. At Bileri with its home for two families they
observed a school in progress on the veranda and an evangelist preaching
in the streets. In Dhorra a school put up by famine coolies was in session
in the mission building. The Rogerses heard about the Kanjars and
sensed the tragedy of the closing of that work.[35]

Next they went to Chhatarpur to see the new "foothold for the Lord"
with its bungalow and well. Finally they visited Harpalpur, where they
had first arrived in Bundelkhand at about four in the morning. Gore Lal
Singh's school for boys was going strong with much noise as they all read
their lessons out loud. They stopped next at the dispensary and medical
shelter to meet William Parsad and his assistant, Mangal Singh, surrounded by patients.

By the time the 25th Anniversary celebration took place on April 1,
1921, the Rogerses were well prepared for it. Only the Christian community was invited to the dinner. There were speeches with lots of recalling. One after another the orphans remembered how they came to the
Mission without hope but now attended the celebration with their children, strong and healthy, gathered about them. The missionaries remembered that in 1896 there was not a single Christian in Bundelkhand, while
at the celebration dinner a Christian community of two hundred sang
praises to God.[36] Then there were only three workers or missionaries.
Now there were five missionaries (one on furlough) and twenty paid
workers — teachers, preachers, compounders, Bible women.[37] They lifted
their voices and clapped their hands in praise to God for His great faithfulness for the first twenty-five years. What could they expect in the next
twenty-five years? They looked forward to it with abounding hope.[38]

| # Adjusting to Changing India

"To do justice and judgment is more acceptable to the Lord than sacrifice." Proverbs 21:3

Mahatma Gandhi

The India to which the Friends missionaries went was ruled by the British, and they established their Mission in Nowgong under the shadow and protection of the British Political Agent. But in the 1920s following World War I they entered a period of turmoil and drastic change. Up to that time, in spite of the well-known exploitation of India for the sake of the Empire, the British nevertheless were magnanimous in spirit and provided an English type of education and administration that many Indians deeply appreciated.

Such an education was provided to Mohandas Karamchand Gandhi, who graduated with a law degree as a perfect English gentleman from a London university. He went to South Africa to practice, but there he experienced racial prejudice in a very personal and violent way.

He met a Quaker who introduced him to Christ, pacifism, and the Bible. Gandhi also read Ruskin, Thoreau, and the Bhagavad Gita. The Beatitudes became the foundation of his thinking as he hammered out a strategy including *Ahimsa* (pacifism), *Satyagraha* (soul force), and *Hind Swaraj* (Indian Home Rule) to reach his goal of freedom for his country.

Gandhi returned to India on January 9, 1915, during the bitter World War I beginnings and, as most Indians, he was loyal to the British throughout World War I.[1] But when England did nothing in the direction of freedom and independence to reward the Indians for their faithfulness, Mahatma Gandhi captured the following of the Indian Congress (formed in 1885), who backed him fully in his nonviolent struggles. By 1921 the effects of his work were being felt even in Nowgong, and Esther Baird wrote that Mr. Gandhi, a religious and political *agitator*[2], had arisen preaching noncooperation with the British government as a panacea for all troubles, and that millions were following him blindly. Many had left jobs with the English and walked out of English schools. "All India is pulsing with this new doctrine. In some places the Indian Christians are joining in this new nationalistic feeling and one can but think that the sifting time of the church in India has come."[3] A year later she wrote again of his unwise influence over the people and how he persuaded them to gather together and burn all clothing imported from England. "Another of his unwise teachings is that all Indians should give up working with any kind of imported machinery and should take up the making of cloth by the old-time hand spinning."[4] She dreaded his influence creeping steadily and forcefully even into Christian communities, and she guarded the Nowgong compound with tenacity, even to stopping all evangelistic work in far-reaching outstations unless a missionary could also be present to keep the Christians from being stirred up by the new nationalistic spirit.[5] England, and also Esther Baird, considered Gandhi's teaching as seditious. The government sentenced him to a term of six years imprisonment.[6] Over the next twenty years Gandhi would go in and out of jail many times as he led his country in a nonviolent war against all forms of injustice and oppression. His weapons were long fasts, a policy of noncooperation, and civil disobedience. He knew the conscience of the British was conditioned by many years of Christian teaching, and he turned that conscience against them and brought them down in the end to a willingness to grant India freedom.

Gandhi's fight was not just with the British. He also fought for freedom and unity within his own country. Eventually he gave his life for that unity, and from the beginning he fought bitterly against caste and its restrictions. He called the outcastes *harijans* (Children of God) and worked for their equality. For this reason Margaret Smith's view of Gandhi differed from that of Esther Baird. Out in the villages the workers had often seen people come to the point of accepting the Lord Jesus Christ as their Savior, only to be sucked back into oblivion by their caste. So she wrote, "We thank God things are beginning to move in India . . . . There has never been a time when we have known so much agitation against the injustice of the caste system. Mahatma Gandhi himself says, 'There is no *swaraj* (self-government) for India until the curse of untouchability has been taken away.'"[7] So Margaret Smith, who called caste a "monster,"[8] and Alison Rogers, who spoke of the "the severity of caste,"[9] saw in Gandhi a friend whom God might use to break the strongholds against the Gospel. Later another missionary joining the staff, Merrill Coffin, after being in the field of evangelism for a short while, also underlined Margaret Smith and Alison Rogers' view: "India is the hardest mission field in the world . . . . One thing makes it so: the caste system."[10] Evangelist Moti Lal added his opinion: "The great leaders of India, although they are non-Christians, . . . preach their teachings on political liberty on the basis of the self-sacrifice of 'this same Jesus' for the sake of others."[11] Such a statement hardly seems that of an unthinking person blindly following a rabble-rouser. It does reveal, however, an increasing respect for Gandhi in the heart of one of the most highly trained teachers and evangelists who had come out of the orphanage in Bundelkhand.

Gandhi: a breaker of caste and therefore an indirect friend of Christianity? At least three missionaries and an outstanding Christian leader in Bundelkhand thought so. Their convictions and attitudes were expressed in articles, but one wonders if they were ever read, for the mission superintendent who had been in India for many decades as a wise and dedicated leader thought otherwise: Gandhi—a seditious agitator working against the Empire and therefore the enemy of Christianity. It is this attitude alone that was reflected by officials to the home constituency:

> Peace and quiet appear to have been restored in India. The arrest and imprisonment of Mahatma Gandhi and many of his fellow-advocates for non-cooperation with the British rule has hushed the cry for Indian independence . . . The political situation now seems to offer to the Christian churches of the West a great opportunity for giving India the gospel.[12]

Those who believed Gandhi worked better for Christianity outside rather than inside jail had nothing more to say. Politics, they seemed to feel, mattered little; there was much to be done together for the sake of the Gospel in Bundelkhand. What was not so clear at the time was that everyone involved in the India Mission on both sides of the water, with listening ears tuned to the superintendent only, were quite obliviously following a dangerous course that would lead them in a very few years to a heartbreaking crisis. And God in His great wisdom and mercy, perhaps even for the guidance of people who read this history, was there all the time seeking to teach His called ones lessons that perhaps they could never have learned otherwise.

Regardless of these politically troubled times, the Mission Board was full of hope and reaching out for new candidates. Charlotte Bai was ready to retire and the orphanage needed a new matron. Margaret Smith had been handling industries, farming, and evangelism—work for three people. Carrie Wood needed help in zenana work and supervision of schools. In Chhatarpur the new bungalow stood empty, waiting for a doctor, and Esther Baird as superintendent was burdened beyond measure with the supervision of all stations, workers, the Church, medical needs, buildings, repairs, and upkeep. Help was hard to find and hard to keep. Within the next five years two men and five women would be sent to India by the Friends Mission Board, but before the end of the decade they would all be gone. One stayed only a few days, another only a few weeks, another three years, and the two families each finished out only one term.

The Rogerses

Alison and Inez Rogers arrived in India early in 1921. Louise Ellett wrote of them, "We truly gave you our very best when we sent them."[13] On return from their first year of language study they moved into the little cottage near the orphanage.[14] Delia Fistler had once lived there but had taken her meals in the big bungalow. Only after the family moved in did the missionaries realize how much the cottage needed repair.[15] In just a few weeks Inez had to go to the hospital in Jhansi, where her first child was born November 26, 1921.[16] Alison came down with malaria and could not be with her, but on Christmas day the family was reunited.[17] Little Alice Virginia Rogers with her fair skin, blue eyes, and light brown hair was dedicated at an impressive Christmas morning service in the Nowgong chapel.[18] Seeing the first white baby in the Mission filled the people with joy. To them she looked like an angel. They loved her dearly.

Linguist that he was, Alison Rogers expected to pick up the language quickly and get out into evangelistic work in the villages, but he did not count on the many diseases of India.[19] There is no way of knowing how Alison Rogers felt sitting in the cottage while Margaret Smith, back from furlough, hadn't even unpacked her bags before she was out with the evangelistic team. She took to this work like a duck—and well she might, for rains poured and flooded her tent, leaving nothing dry. It certainly was no place for a sick man.[20] While recuperating he spent time studying the people and philosophies of India, seeking to understand why through all the years the Mission had existed there was such meager response to the Gospel. Shortage of workers was no doubt part of the answer. There was no way of reaching even the nearby villages more than once a year.[21] Lack of enough good Christian models was another. "Our Indian Christians are not a body of strong, active Christians, all filled with the Spirit," he observed.[22] Caste was no doubt the greatest barrier to conversions. A Hindu told him it was impossible to gain Hindu converts through conversion.[23] His point was strong, because the Church was built of the orphans who as children had left their caste behind and had in a sense formed a new "Christian" caste on the compound. In spite of all their preaching, converts in the villages and the formation of little churches was not visible. The searching mind of Alison Rogers continued to ask, "Why?"

On August 2, 1922, the Rogerses lost their baby daughter. "A little white bud God has plucked from His garden," said a tearful Indian at the funeral. The tiny coffin, made of wooden planks and lined with a sheet, cradled the body of Alice Virginia, eight months old, who was laid to rest in the Nowgong graveyard. Indian brothers and sisters wept without restraint, and the Rogerses felt their love. A few weeks later they stood again in the same graveyard sharing the sorrow of Hira Lal, the crippled evangelist, as his little two-year-old daughter was buried.[24] Before the Rogerses left India, they would bury another little one-week old daughter, Margaret Lois, born October 3, 1923. She was their last child, buried in India beside her sister. As the broken-hearted parents left these two mounds in the heart of India, they wrote, "We will be better able to understand the hearts of the people, for almost every family of our Indian Christians has a part in our little cemetery. There are many little mounds out there."[25]

While still grieving, the Rogerses observed Nowgong as it was struck with plague for the first time. Rats were everywhere and hundreds of people caught the disease. Nearly 200 died. All mission work closed — the schools, evangelism, zenana work, Sunday schools, and bazaar worship services. Christians living outside were brought into the mission compound, where they lived several weeks like semi-prisoners. Rats were immediately disposed of. Shops were closed and food was scarce. When it was all over, not a single Christian had caught the plague, and they praised God for His marvelous protecting care.[26]

Death and plague, however, were not the only frustrations the Rogerses experienced. As secretary of the Mission Council, Alison wrote in the minutes many times. "There was no special discussion."[27] Sensing his frustration, the lady missionaries tended to be annoyed by it. They noted he was behind in his language work, slow at taking responsibility, and had other adjustment problems. To help in that adjustment, the missionaries felt the Rogerses would have more freedom of movement if they were stationed in Harpalpur. A new dispensary had been built there and William Parsad had moved to his own house. This released the mission house for the Rogerses. It was not screened, but the Rogerses moved in happily and invited all the missionaries as special guests to tea.[28]

In preparation for working there, the Rogerses studied the town and area. They found the people on the whole miserably poor. Holidays for weddings and religious festivals ate up half the working time in a year. There were few good craftsmen, and in spite of the railway, Harpalpur boasted no industries. Grain was shipped out in all directions and cotton directly to England while many people in Harpalpur were hungry and poorly clad. The Christian dispensary was humming with nearly 10,000 patients a year coming to "Dr." William Parsad for treatment. Noise from oxcarts, crowds, groups beating their "*tablas*" (drums) far into the night and women up at 4:00 a.m. to grind the grain singing in the early morning often kept them awake. But Harpalpur became their home and they threw themselves into the work. Station supervision, teaching in the boys' and girls' schools, evangelism in nearby villages, and zenana work in the towns engaged their time.[29]

To his great surprise, Alison Rogers discovered that Goverind Das, the President of Harpalpur, was a much-traveled man who had met many Christians and had given serious thought to the message of Christianity. He was impressed with their works of social justice, and he wrote a tract concerning Christ, "Why I Believe that Jesus is the Son of God," and another, "Why I Believe that the Bible is the Word of God." Filled with hope, Alison Rogers told Esther Baird about him. She came to talk to the man about commitment to Christ and His Church, but that is where the story ended,[30] until 1934 when the Kinders came, and led him to Christ.

In early 1927, leaving two small graves, Alison and Inez Rogers returned to America. The Board had already decided not to send them back, though in all fairness of course their report would be heard before telling them so. After meeting the Rogerses, they changed their minds. They found no defensive attitude or critical spirit. There was only deep sorrow at not having been able to make a greater contribution and a deep desire to do God's will, even to return to India. The Board gave further consideration to the investment they had already made in the Rogerses and decided to send them back, pending clear word from India.[31] It never came. The Board never knew that the Indian Christians in Harpalpur in the Monthly Meeting fought to get a letter of invitation sent to the Rogerses but did not succeed.[32] So for whatever the reasons, their voices were not heard, and the Rogerses never went back.

Dr. Elizabeth Ward

When Esther Baird returned from furlough in 1923 she took with her some new missionaries: Merrill and Anna Coffin with their three children and Dr. Elizabeth Ward. The key to the whole development in Chhatarpur where a bungalow stood empty and land had been given for a dispensary was the finding of medical personnel. Dr. Ward came from Camden, New Jersey. This young, vivacious graduate of Pennsylvania University seemed the answer to their prayers.[33] The Board called her their "little" doctor and spoke of her childlike simplicity.[34] Money flowed in for her travel and support, but before the journey to India was ended there was trouble. Esther Baird could not sleep all night "thinking of problems with and before us."[35] Dr. Ward spent only two weeks in Nowgong and then left for Ludhiana Medical Hospital, where she soon got employment. She wrote back to the Board that she would not be dictated to by anyone.[36] The Board had no choice at that point but to let her go, and their strong feelings about it are revealed in the words they used to record it: "The gross insubordination of Dr. Ward during the journey to the field and upon arrival there necessitated her immediate dismissal from our service." So the Chhatarpur bungalow remained empty, and Esther Baird, filled with bitter disappointment and some remorse, had to start over.[37]

The Coffin Family

For the Coffin family, November 13, 1923, would always be a memorable day as they arrived in Bundelkhand. The jasmine garlands even for the children made everyone's eyes sparkle. The roses mixed in with the jasmine for Esther Baird made clear to all the high regard the people had for her. When they reached the Mission, Merrill and Anna Coffin were amazed to see the beautiful and well-organized compound. From the front gate they approached the bungalow by a 220-yard road lined with tall silk-cotton trees. Eugene, nine, and Louis, seven, were more impressed by the six-piece band of the orphanage children. Catherine, the one year-old, at the beginning of the cool season enjoyed the familiar comfort and warmth of her mother's arms.[38]

The Coffins settled into the little cottage in Nowgong the Rogerses had vacated for them the week before. They began to get acquainted with the people. The boys could hardly wait for the Christmas celebration. About 200 Christian people came together like a big family. First there was a worship service. Then everyone got a gift from the Mission — blankets for the men, stools for the women, and suitable toys and clothes for every child. It was hard to wait while the eighty pounds of rice and the two goats were cooked into a delicious *palao* with *curry* and *puris*.[39]

Right after Christmas Merrill Coffin felt there should be special meetings while the Christians were gathered together. He had been a pastor and evangelist before coming to India, and his messages through an interpreter came from a burning heart. The people were stirred as they listened attentively and many renewed their covenant.[40] Two months after that Christmas, the Coffin family were received into the Bundelkhand Friends Church, the parents as full members and the children as associate.[41] In March they had to go to Landour, Mussoorie, for language school. They enrolled their two boys in Woodstock school. The language was a challenge and Merrill Coffin earned the highest marks in the class that year in spite of many frustrations.[42] Both boys were seriously ill, but with the wonderful care of Anna Coffin, and two nurses, their lives were spared. When they were finally able to return to Nowgong, Louis was just recovering from pneumonia, and Eugene had inflammatory rheumatism following dengue, which kept him crippled most of the cold season. Apart from whooping cough, little Catherine kept well until later when she came down with a severe case of malaria.[43]

Just as soon as arrangements could be made, Merrill, leaving the family in the care of Anna, went to camp with six evangelists. In six weeks he and the party visited 124 villages, with 8,726 people attending, selling 446 books and covering 576 miles. They traveled at two or three miles an hour, hauling along in their oxcarts two tents, two boxes of cooking utensils and supplies, a big cotton rug to put down for group meetings, one folding table, two folding chairs, one collapsible cot (for the "Sahib"), and the personal boxes and bedding rolls for each man. Hira Lal's pony followed behind. In 1921 Jefferson Ford had reported that of the 4,200 villages in Bundelkhand about 800 had been reached with the gospel message. "One hundred more villages are now added," wrote Merrill. Out in Ajaigarh he found a man with a New Testament. Jefferson Ford had presented it to him. He gave a clear testimony of joy in Christ and declared he and his son read the Testament daily. He also had left his idolatrous worship and customs. He had come so near, and yet so far! The whole Mission longed and prayed for that final step of faith, but until then they would go on preaching the Good News. "It is for this work that we are in India," said Esther Baird.[44]

Merrill was assigned the writing of the history of the American Friends Mission in India, and he worked on it during spare moments out in camp. In March, after Anna took the children back to school in the hills, Merrill in the quietness of his cottage finished his research and checked it out in interviews with Esther Baird. By October he finished it and it was published in India in 1926.[45]

On July 20, 1925, Merrill Coffin with the help of Carrie Wood and Moti Lal, opened a Bible School. Moti Lal was a very gifted young man from the orphanage who had finished theological college and worked for a short time in Chhatarpur. He married Shanti, a niece of Prem Das and Mangalwadi and a sister of Grace Jones, who on October 28, 1924, entered pharmacy training and would eventually become Bundelkhand's first woman doctor.[46] Moti Lal was a faithful and inspiring preacher and teacher who fit well into a Bible school ministry, and he learned much in working with Merrill Coffin as did the three students in the Bible school: Dayal Chand, Stuti Prakash, and Yohan Dalsaiya.[47] Yohan, son of a former evangelist, married Jai Bai, Mangalwadi's widow (and mother of Victor Mangalwadi). She left the Mission January 25, 1927.[48] But Dayal

Chand Singh and Stuti Prakash graduated in 1928[49] and served the Lord in the Friends church in Bundelkhand the rest of their lives.

Merrill Coffin held frequent meetings with the church and the people responded with concern for a deeper spiritual life and a more consistent walk with God. Many of the leaders of later years credited the ministry of Merrill Coffin for their dedication to God. In ministry through the villages, Merrill sought to put into effect Alison Rogers' vision for more concentrated work. Older workers were reluctant to change, but Stuti Prakash, Moti Lal, and Dayal Chand Singh tried out the new method and reported splendid work from this plan, though they did not continue it after Coffins left. Merrill started listing names of those who made some response to their message and sought to enlist specific prayer for each of them.[50] He also put emphasis on music, being gifted himself, and a committee — Moti Lal, Hira Lal, and Nathu Lall — bought two drums, a harmonium, and two other instruments (one violin). This use of music was so effective that from then on it was continued.[51]

The Coffins faced some trials not readily understood by others. They were the first family in the India Mission with children to put into boarding school. The inconvenience and cost of this had not been sufficiently planned for. Not only finance, but extra time off to care for family matters, became points of irritation under which sensitive spirits suffered.[52] Discouragement sometimes led to physical illness. In 1928 Anna experienced recurring illness, which hindered the work. For Merrill, meetings in other parts of India that opened to him more and more frequently as people came to know of his effective ministry, tended to lift his spirits. He served for a time as president of the Yavatmal India Holiness Association. He usually limited these outside speaking engagements to vacation time and during the rains, in order to keep the cooler days for evangelistic camping in Bundelkhand.[53]

Walter and Geneva Bolitho, sent by Oregon Yearly Meeting, came to India in 1928, and the little cottage in Nowgong in which the Coffins had been living was needed for them. The Mission Council suggested that Coffins move to the Chhatarpur Bungalow, which still stood empty. Coffins gladly agreed, for not only was the house more suitable to the size of their family, but also the evangelistic challenge in Chhatarpur was tremendous.[54] But this never happened. They were moved to Harpalpur instead where they occupied the smallest unscreened accommodation in the Mission. Anna Coffin was ill at the time.[55]

Early in the camping season of 1929, Merrill Coffin became ill in camp and came home early one Sunday morning by lorry from Panna. He was suffering from symptoms the medical personnel felt would recur more or less often until he went home. This, with Anna's severe illness of recent months, caused them to suggest the Coffins go home immediately rather than the following year.[56] The Coffins were willing, and the Mission Board agreed. So they called Eugene and Louis from boarding school in Woodstock, and began to pack. Little Catherine, age six, had some concerns of her own. She knew Miss Baird was the one whom people took problems to, and so she wrote:

> "Dear *Nanni* (grandmother):
>
> "If we go to America, Louis and I want to know if you would like to have BUSTER to live with you at Chhatarpur? He is looking nice these days and barks real loud at jackals and other dogs in the night. With love, Catherine."[57]

Gradually everything was cared for and Coffins sailed away from India, April 26, 1929.[58] They expected to return, but arrangements for the children's education proved difficult. The way back never opened again, much to the sorrow of many Indian co-workers who even to this day remember the Coffins with love.

CHAPTER VIII | Building a Hospital

"The God of heaven, he will prosper us; therefore we his servants will arise and build." Nehemiah 2:20

Dr. Mary Fleming

Early in 1924 when Dr. Ward left the Mission, the plans for Chhatarpur were frustrated, and the bungalow remained empty. The Maharaja offered to buy it,[1] but just before his request came, Dr. Mary Fleming arrived January 28, 1925.[2] She had graduated from Johns Hopkins Medical School and worked five years in Persia,[3] then three years in South India. She became the first occupant of the bungalow in Chhatarpur.

While there, she saw many other building projects completed. A new dispensary was built on land given by the Maharaja. This gift made possible a much better building than thought possible. The location was such that a C. G. Duncan Memorial Church was built in front of it and served as both a chapel and waiting hall for patients. Every day the Gospel was preached there.[4]

Just beside the dispensary and church some old ruined palaces and outbuildings caught Esther Baird's eye. With great courage she asked the *Diwan* (Prime Minister) for these also, ". . . which will add much to the value, usefulness and picturesqueness of the place,"[5] and he gave them to her!

But before she could transform these ruins into workers' quarters and another bungalow, the Gusains, a group who bury their dead in a sitting position and then erect large tombs over them, came to call. A number of their tombs were scattered about the area she was about to occupy, and they were concerned that they not be torn down. Esther Baird gladly agreed, for she thought the old tombs very picturesque. The new bungalow she built there came to be known as Baird Retreat.[6] The new dispensary, a gift of Mrs. Elizabeth Taylor of Philadelphia, was opened on September 9, 1925, and on October 3 Esther Baird, in Chhatarpur supervising the building, scrubbed to assist Dr. Fleming in a major operation.

Dr. Fleming felt honored to be in charge of the first dispensary in Bundelkhand for women and children, and said, "Our great problem, as it is our great desire, will be while ministering to their bodies, to so work and speak and to so live and to so love that they shall come to know Him."[7]

But less than two months later it became clear that her high aspirations and desires were not being fulfilled. Things were not right at the dispensary between her and the patients, and Esther Baird went out to admonish her.[8]

Differences arose between the doctor and Pancham Singh, who was overseer of the building projects in Chhatarpur. Through him negative reports about Dr. Fleming found their way to the Mission Council.[9] For reasons not clear from the record, the Mission Council decided even before Dr. Fleming left Chhatarpur not to invite her back. The Mission Board was shocked at this action, but without further investigation agreed not to send her back for another term. They had not yet talked with Dr. Fleming.[10]

Dr. Fleming, meanwhile, wrote her complaints to the Board. She said frankly that there was no point of sending a doctor out "unless you can provide something to work with, an equipped car to do district medical work, etc., and funds to carry on the medical work."[11]

When Dr. Mary Fleming finally did meet the Board, their assessment was, "She seemed a very capable woman to us . . . We liked her."[12] They wanted to return her to the field, but there was no response, and Dr. Fleming never went back to Bundelkhand.

Mary Allen

Another missionary came to join the staff in 1925. Mary Allen was an English Friends missionary and already in India. She had worked in Jamaica, and in 1924 was accepted as a member of the Bundelkhand Friends Monthly Meeting. Her qualifications seemed exactly right to fill the need left by Charlotte Bai, who was retiring. The Mission Board approved, and Esther Baird went to work immediately to transfer Charlotte Bai to her own little retirement house with Mary Bai and to make repairs on the matron's quarters. Mary Allen moved in and worked for three weeks before expressing her unhappiness. Shortly after that she resigned and moved to the English Friends' field in Sohagpur.[13] Margaret Smith stepped in until another matron could be found.

Time Out to Pray — and New Insight

This quick shifting of missionary personnel in India made the Board aware of tensions on the field they did not understand. In dealing with them they became entangled in such aggravating differences of opinion in their own Board that business came to a standstill. Balancing finance and personnel between China and India did not meet approval, and no suggested solution to any problem seemed acceptable. Suddenly one member confessed he was trying to do the work for God instead of seeking to know the mind of God. He reminded the other members that the mission fields belonged to God, but that they had been seeking to work out all these problems in their own strength instead of looking to the Lord. The members of the Board felt with conviction the truth of his words. They laid aside all business and got on their knees. The Lord wonderfully touched them and changed their perspective, and afterwards business proceeded quickly and peaceably. Great faith and courage possessed them as they agreed to send out others to fill the gaps and to raise money for the expansion programs. That year at Yearly Meeting the offering was $3,675, with $1,000 more promised.[14]

The Board also began to think deeply about the future and the organizational structure of the Mission. By April 19, 1931, Esther Baird would be seventy years old. In spite of frequent severe headaches and recurring bouts of malaria, she kept surprisingly fit and carried on a strenuous program, but no mission leader to take over from her was in sight. "Who is going to take charge of the business of the mission and act as superintendent when we don't have you any more?" Louise Ellett asked — a very hard question, left trembling in the air.[15] The Board seemed suddenly to become aware of the fact that they depended entirely on the superintendent's report for India information and were not hearing from any other member of the Mission Council. "In China work is planned at an annual meeting when all workers contribute their ideas, budgets, etc., with prayer and a warm time of fellowship. Such a meeting would be good to have in India," they suggested. The result of this was that Mission Council in India was again resumed on a regular basis from October 28, 1927, but it took some prodding to get copies of these minutes sent to the Mission Board.[16]

Carrie Wood's Leave of Absence

Carrie Wood, a strong undergirder in the work when others came and went, expected a full eight-year term of service when she returned to India in 1923. Instead, because of the death of her mother, her term was cut in half because she was needed at home to care for her father and a brother for the next two and half years. The Board reluctantly allowed her a leave of absence.[17] Until her return in late 1929, the bazaar girls' school had to be closed and someone else had to care for the mission accounts.

The Death of Margaret Smith

Margaret Smith, like Carrie Wood, was an undergirder. She had not hesitated to take over the building of Chhatarpur's first bungalow, of caring for orphans, supervising schools, building up industries and farming, and carrying responsibility for the entire evangelistic program. Months on end she had lived in a tent in far-flung villages. She was an adventurer, too, and when she found a thirteen-acre field with a good well on it, like the virtuous woman of Proverbs, she bought it. She was interested in developing industry and farming to help Christians become independent of debt. She made repeated requests to the Board to send not only teachers and evangelists but also men with ability in industry, finance, and farming. She watched her crops ripen like a seasoned farmer, and at harvest time she would go with the girls from the orphanage, baskets on their heads, and carry back the grain cut with a hand sickle. After the baskets were emptied on the threshing floor, the oxen's tread threshed the grain. The winnowing on a not-too-windy day completed the job.[18]

On May 16, 1928, Margaret Smith, age forty-five, bent over to roll up her bedding for a vacation trip to Darjeeling with Esther Baird. Suddenly a pain in her head blinded her. Merrill Coffin and Esther Baird were in the room with her and quickly called for help, but she was gone at 9:30 a.m.[19] No one expected to lose a missionary like this. Both the Board and Mission suddenly felt the force of Dr. Fleming's complaint about lack of medical equipment, for there was not even a sphygmomanometer in the dispensary with which to check her blood pressure.[20] Margaret had served India for twenty-one and a half years, and all but seven had been in Bundelkhand. She had spent the previous summer on the plains, expecting to go on furlough in 1928, but because of shortage of staff she decided to postpone her furlough. The Church said of her: "In every work which came before her she did it faithfully and with her whole heart . . . . In her character all the Christian virtues were revealed." Esther Baird said, "This is the first time I have known Margaret to choose the best."[21]

Esther Baird—Administrator, Builder

Margaret's death left Esther the only senior missionary on the field. Coffins were leaving. Two new missionaries—Alena Calkins and Ruth Thurston—having just arrived were in language school.[22] How Esther longed for Carrie Wood! Expansion in Chhatarpur created heavy administrative responsibilities and Esther was needed everywhere. Letters to the

Board carried *requests* for water pumps, rat traps, machines, and screens; *thanks* for a new Chevrolet and for parts to repair the old Ford after a crash with an oxcart; and *reports* in detail of a successful baby show initiated by Esther Baird in cooperation with the Agency and the town fathers. Low caste babies participated but were shown at a different time from the upper castes. The mothers learned much about nourishment and treatment of children, and eighty prizes were awarded. The Christian babies all received prizes. So impressed were the town leaders that they asked for the show to be an annual event.[23]

Esther Baird's skill as a builder was already established in Chhatarpur. The bungalow, Indian workers' houses, dispensary, and the beautiful Charles G. Duncan Memorial Chapel dedicated in 1926, and Baird Retreat all gave testimony to wise planning—but this was only the beginning.[24] Taking over the work of the dispensary after Dr. Fleming left, Esther worked with Noni Bai, Pancham Singh's wife, who gave the Gospel every day to waiting patients in the chapel. Pancham Singh occupied one of the new houses built from the ruins.[25] Esther and Ruth Thurston moved into the Baird Retreat in preparation for the building of the hospital.[26] Missionaries from China, Dr. and Mrs. Henry McKee Woods, gave $500—the first "nest egg" toward the project. Esther Baird with Pancham Singh's help immediately built a three-room shelter—and called it "Nest Egg"—where dispensary patients could be admitted for a few days.[27]

While Esther made trip after trip to meet officials, Pancham Singh kept the workers on the job to clear the land, burn the bricks, and bring in the lumber. Nothing slowed him down but a cholera epidemic. He built a garage and completed a nurses' home. The next thing to build was the hospital, and for this Pancham Singh was Esther Baird's indispensable right-hand man.[28]

Esther's trips month after month to the Maharaja and the Diwan were to request another six-acre grant of land for the hospital building. Who can frustrate a Maharaja? The Diwan tried. He was among the opposing forces in Chhatarpur to the Mission's getting a foothold in Chhatarpur. He succeeded in blocking the transaction for almost a year and a half in spite of the Maharaja's repeated assurance that land would surely be given if Esther Baird would build on it a women's and children's hospital. Finally, on February 16, 1929, the Maharaja sent his surveyors and made the settlement, and they were free to build.[29]

By the time the land was granted, the Board had set aside $2,000 for the hospital and had sent more missionaries to India: Walter and Geneva Bolitho, and Dr. Ruth Hull in 1928; Nell Lewis, a nurse, 1929; and James and Judith Kinder, 1930. Carrie Wood returned with Nell Lewis and shared the load of orientation for these six and for two more, Alena

Calkins and Ruth Thurston, who had arrived together October 29, 1927, and had just completed language school.[30]

Alena Calkins

Alena marveled at how God opened the way for her to go to India. Adrian Quarterly Meeting in Michigan had taken a financial burden off her shoulders in the support of her parents as well as supplying her salary.[31] On arrival, she was amazed at what she found:

> The grounds are beautiful and the home much more attractive than I expected. I have the room which was Miss Wood's . . . 17 feet high, 20 feet long, and 14 feet wide. Each of our rooms opens out on a veranda. Off of each room is a bathroom with an outside door. In my bathroom is a chiffonier, a large wardrobe, a tin bathtub which is set up against the wall when not in use. The floor is made of cement . . . with a drain in one corner. There is a large earthen jar of cold water, and also an earthen jar of boiled drinking water.
>
> We have four meals a day like the English: Six a.m. *chhoti hazri* — bread, butter, tea, and sometimes fruit; *hazri* at ten a.m. cereal, vegetables, sometimes meat, eggs, etc., and fruit . . . such as oranges, custard apples, bananas, guavas, papayas and mangoes; three p.m. *tea*, with bread or biscuits, jam, etc., or cake; *dinner* seven p.m., usually three courses — soup, main meal, dessert. *Work* is done between *chhoti hazri* and *hazri*, and tea and dinner. We have three servants, two men and a boy . . . . Our clothes are washed by being beaten on a rock. The middle of the day is rest time because of the heat.[32]

Alena, the nurse, expected to be stationed in Chhatarpur, but Esther Baird chose Ruth Thurston to live there with her and left Alena in Nowgong. She was disappointed in not getting into the medical work, but she applied herself to meeting the needs of the orphan girls. Shocked to learn they had never seen Chhatarpur, she took them. At harvest time, she joined them, as had Margaret Smith, in bringing in the grain in baskets from six fields. She took over the mission accounts, a job no one wanted. She managed the dispensary in Nowgong, assisted by Shitabu, an orphan girl, who planned to become a nurse. Called for a delivery twenty-four miles away, she took a bus through Chhatarpur, picking up Esther Baird on the way. The bus broke down three times, and by the time they arrived, the woman was already dying in a dark, small, dirty room with no windows. Alena's heart was breaking as the bus bumped back to Nowgong late that night.[33]

Alena found spiritual outlet and a place to use her Hindi in conducting the Sunday school in Bileri. She stayed alone in Nowgong all through the hot summer months of 1929 and had a sharp attack of malaria. She passed all her examinations with high marks, and then at the advice of

Esther Baird and Dr. Ruth Hull, went to Madras for a six-month midwifery course. Only when the course was finished did she admit how lonely she had been and how she longed for other than Indian food. She had received the highest marks of all thirty-seven girls in the course, and this sent her happily back to Bundelkhand, where she was again stationed in Nowgong for three more months. She busied herself with teaching five classes in the mission school and doing further Hindi study.[34] Suddenly the Bolithos came down with typhoid, and Alena was on hand to nurse them. After they recovered, she finally got off to Chhatarpur on October 2, 1930. "Henceforth this will probably be my home," she wrote, and it was so. On November 27 that year she was filled with joy to have all ten of the missionaries join her to celebrate her birthday in her home in Chhatarpur.[35]

Ruth Thurston

When the Board accepted Ruth Thurston in August 1926, they did not know of the developing romance with John Earle that soon led to an engagement. John wanted to finish his training in Cleveland Bible Institute and then get a degree from Eastern Nazarene College; so Ruth went ahead in 1927 to serve a term in India while she waited for him.[36] She expected to teach in the Bible School in Nowgong but on finding herself assigned to Chhatarpur, she opened a school for Christian children in the C. G. Duncan Memorial Chapel. When the Bible school opened in Nowgong again with Hira Singh and four women students, she rode the bus back and forth, living in Chhatarpur, but spending three days a week in Nowgong.[37] One advantage of living and working in two places was getting to know many people. Ruth entered heartily into all activities. She was intrigued by the wholesale weddings of eight couples of the orphanage, including the Bible school graduates. Stuti Prakash and Ramkibai were one of three couples married May 10, 1928. Dayal Chand Singh and Dayawanti were one of five couples married October 25, 1929.[38] The engagements took place the previous afternoon as the brides and grooms all sat in a row. The girls gave the boys handkerchiefs and the boys gave Indian sweets, two silver rings, and whatever else they chose. The wedding the next day was followed by a huge feast. Gore Lal Singh, the first Indian Friends minister to be registered in Bundelkhand, officiated in the five October weddings. Ruth Thurston noted the contrasts with these and her own wedding soon to be.[39]

Ruth, like Alena, passed the Hindi examination with high marks and went on to take the first year Urdu examination. She found her greatest challenge in zenana work, visiting about twenty-five or thirty homes a week. On Sundays she gave herself to the Sunday school and soon had

over one hundred children attending.[40] While she was on vacation in
Coonoor, she took advantage of Indian Sunday School Union courses for
Christian education leaders.[41]

When Ruth went on her first furlough, she and John Earle were married June 11, 1931, at Newport, Rhode Island. Ruth remembered her
Indian friends on that day and arranged to have sweets distributed to
them. Even on their honeymoon they made plans to return to India for
missionary work together.[42]

The Bolithos

In response to Margaret Smith's vision for the farm, the Board sent Walter
and Geneva Bolitho to India, where they arrived in November 1928.
Geneva Bolitho was desperately ill on arrival and had to be carried off the
ship on a stretcher. Fortunately, Dr. Ruth Hull was on the same ship and
accompanied her to the hospital. She lost her baby but not her life.[43]

On reaching Nowgong, Walter and Geneva Bolitho settled into the
little cottage vacated by the Coffins. In April 1929, they left for the
Himalayan foothills to study language in Landour. On their way they
stopped at the Allahabad Agricultural Institute to get insights into Indian
farming. With Bible training at North Pacific Evangelistic Institute, they
felt prepared for evangelism, but Walter felt a need of studying the practical problems of farming in the Indian context.

Back in Bundelkhand by September, Walter was glad to find equipment for farming left behind by Margaret Smith: four pair of oxen, country farming implements, a splendid well, and good buildings. Not only
did he inherit the work of the farm, but as the only man in the Mission,
he was expected to care for annual repair, whitewashing, outside color
wash, new ceiling cloth, grass cutting, and fresh red soil for all paths.[44] As
he got into the work, Walter learned about summer crops — kafir corn, oil
seed and hemp; and winter crops — wheat, barley, channa (gram), and
Indian spices. With rich vegetable gardens during the monsoon season,
there seemed many possibilities of making farming pay. He longed for a
pump that could water as much in a few hours as three pair of oxen with
ropes and leather buckets and four men could do in four days.[45] He
requested a grant of $100 toward farm expenses, but he got neither pump
nor money.[46] Rather, he was sent to Calcutta to pick up two pumps for
the hospital,[47] which, on returning, he installed.[48] Then he put in the
hospital a septic tank and the power system. "May I ask," he wrote the
Board, "if hospitals are more necessary than some way of relieving India's
unprofitable means of farming?"[49]

Walter Bolitho sensed that he was failing in the eyes of the superintendent, who was so intent on bringing the hospital to birth that other things had to be pushed aside.

Just after Bolithos arrived in India, a group of some 2,000 farmers swarmed into Nowgong to complain to the Political Agent that the Raja of Tikamgarh had been buying their land for half its value and then oppressing the farmers.[50] Learning of their problems, Walter developed a keen desire to help them. He called the camping teams from the villages to work among these men while they were in Nowgong. They listened to the Gospel intently, and before returning to Tikamgarh some forty miles from Chhatarpur, they invited the evangelists to visit them. In 1930 the evangelists accepted that invitation. Hira Lal, Balla Bodhan, Stuti Prakash, Dayal Chand Singh, Hira Singh, and Moti Lal went, but there is no evidence from their report that they made any contact with the men they had met two years previously. They reported instead strong opposition, harrassment, and an attack by bees.[51]

Walter Bolitho occasionally joined the evangelists in meetings. He also supervised Sunday schools in Bileri and Gaurali.[52]

Geneva Bolitho helped in zenana work and with the orphan children. She also spoke in meeting, as she had a gift in the ministry. On April 8, 1930, she was put through a severe test as she had a very difficult delivery in Jhansi hospital. Little Myron James Bolitho lived only one week, and Walter, alone, had to bring the little body back through the heat to Nowgong to bury him. Later, when he brought Geneva home, Esther Baird observed sorrowfully, "They came back with empty arms and sad hearts."[53]

Geneva continued to suffer after this with many gall bladder attacks. By mid-August she became critically ill with typhoid fever, and Walter came down with it four days later. Dr. Ruth Hull and the Nowgong Civil Surgeon, Major Ledger, attended them while Alena and Nell nursed them. The Lord's provision of this good medical attention probably saved their lives.[54]

Dr. Ruth Hull Bennett

Dr. Ruth Hull belonged to Nebraska Yearly Meeting. She was first accepted by the Mission Board in 1926 to go to China, but the rapid advance of the Nationalists' Southern Army in China stopped her.[55] While waiting for her $600 annual mission salary from the Board, she took work at the Woman's Reformatory of Massachusetts for an annual salary of $2,400 plus board and room. The Board felt sure they had lost her, especially when they heard also that Ruth Hull was considering marriage with Claude Bennett, a Colorado wheat farmer. But with China closed and

Dr. Fleming not returning to India, they courageously asked Dr. Hull to go to India, and she immediately agreed to go. She invested her spare money and gifts, and also an allowance from the Board, in good medical equipment.[56] She arrived in India in late November 1928. Four days later she was on duty in the dispensary with some ninety patients crowding in. Maternity cases, operations, worms, lice, bronchitis, ulcers, opium addiction, and all kinds of infections and infectious diseases had to be dealt with.[57] Medical work was demanding, but she did not neglect her language study and finished with high marks on schedule.[58] She also found time to attend Christian medical conferences in Madras and Calcutta, which kept her abreast of latest developments throughout India.[59]

By 1930 the work had increased to the point that Dr. Hull had to have three assistants, and the "nest egg" was being used as a small hospital. Grace Jones [Singh] with four years of pharmacy training was now in her second year of medical training. She had given invaluable help in the dispensary work in Chhatarpur in 1929 and the summer of 1930. Prospects for the future looked bright, with hope of an Indian doctor and two foreign nurses, Alena Calkins and Nell Lewis, to assist Dr. Hull.[60]

Nell Lewis

Nell Lewis, a graduate of Cleveland Bible Institute and a nurse with five years' experience, came fully supported for her first year by the Salem Friends Church. She was in India only a few weeks before coming down with a severe case of malaria. Her next blow was not passing her first language examination. She kept on studying while working in the Nowgong dispensary, but she longed to get to Chhatarpur, where there was more medical activity. When she did get there in February of 1931, it was not to work but to lie in bed very ill as the first patient in the new hospital.[61]

The Kinders

James and Judith Kinder were from the Methodist Church and were graduates of Asbury College, he with a Greek major.[62] They were accepted for missionary service in India before they were married on May 27, 1929. Finances delayed the Board in sending them, and during that time Esther Baird received many letters about them. "I just feel like Mr. Kinder is the leader we have prayed for." "Everyone loves the Kinders." "He is the deliberate, thorough, firm, kind, as rich a find as Dr. Hull."[63] They arrived in Nowgong October 13, 1930.[64] After becoming acquainted with the various workers and stations, they moved to Harpalpur to live in the small, unscreened house occupied earlier by Rogerses and Coffins. By this time $200 had been appropriated for screens, and they at least would be saved the annoyance of flies and mosquitos.[65]

On arrival, the Kinders found a great deal of excitement in the air as the whole Mission strained with Esther Baird to see the Chhatarpur medical complex completed.

The Erection of the Hospital

Word that the Viceroy and Lady Irwin would visit Nowgong in December 1930 focused Esther Baird's goal to complete the hospital complex by that time, but she still had a long way to go. Considering the development over the past five years gave her hope. Another famine brought more workers to her aid. Two days after receiving permission to start building the new hospital, she broke ground on the new site.[66] Esther Baird, Dr. Ruth Hull, and Major Ledger, the Agency surgeon, drew up the plans.[67] Four of the tombs on the site were in a good state of preservation, and amidst beautiful palms here and there made a picturesque site. The famine relief victims cleared the area of the crumbling temples, tombs, and overgrown ruins. They took out the stones, graded the land, and fenced it. They salvaged much good building material for the hospital. At the end of the day they received a gospel message and money to buy food.[68] The well was blasted to a depth of sixty-two feet and 15,000 bricks were burned. Inherited with the land were five-feet thick foundations from the old ruins on which the hospital superstructure was built—a structure of symmetry, grace, and beauty. Many verandas and walls nineteen-feet high were built to keep patients cool in India's hot climate.[69]

Claude A. Roane, the enthusiastic president of the Mission Board since 1927, who with unflagging zeal and fervent spirit would fire Ohio Yearly Meeting for over half a century, sent repeated requests for plans and estimates of the hospital. In fact, he asked for specific monthly reports. He soon learned Esther Baird had great difficulty at any time in getting to financial and statistical reports, and during this building program all reports were pushed aside until the end of the year. Claude Roane, knowing the importance of fresh news directly from India to reach the 65 percent of the constituency who did not support missions, kept asking. When news finally reached him that around the main population centers in Bundelkhand—Nowgong, Harpalpur, Chhatarpur, Malehra, Bijawar, Ajaigarh, Panna, and Parairia—the missionaries estimated they had reached about half of the total population, he was excited. Further questioning brought him the news that the missionaries felt that twenty-four more workers from the U.S.A. would be needed to staff all the centers. With these facts in hand and fire in his heels, Claude Roane took to the road and saw both interest and giving increase. When the hospital estimates of their needs were received, the Board heartily endorsed them.[70]

With a twinkle in her eye, Catherine Stalker kept money coming
from an unknown source. It was only after the building was completed
that people came to know who gave the money. The memorial slab, set
in place before the dedication, told the story:

In Memory of
Elizabeth Jane Bell Stephenson
of
Bower, Pennsylvania, U.S.A.
January 29, 1841 to August 24, 1893
"Her children rise up and call her blessed."[71]

The hospital was named "The Elizabeth Jane Bell Stephenson Memorial
Hospital," and the building was made possible by gifts from her daughters, Catherine S. Stalker and Dr. Jennie Stephenson.[72]

Many hindrances delayed the building. They ran out of water.
Malaria, heart trouble, tonsillitis, and dysentery put Esther Baird to bed
many times in spite of herself. There were tragic times such as when Stuti
Prakash and Dayal Chand Singh lost their little ones, and when some of
the Christian people became desperately ill. At such times Esther Baird
left everything and went to their side and stayed until they were better.
Such needs always pulled her away from the building work, but once
cared for, she was back at it again. She traveled back and forth between
Harpalpur, Nowgong, and Chhatarpur, to keep an eye on every phase of
the work. "There are plenty of problems to be met. God is able for them
all," she recorded.[73] By November word reached her that the Viceroy's
visit would take place early in December 1930. Her diary conveyed her
excitement:

Nov. 5: Many things about the work to put right. God is helping
wonderfully.

20: Trying to rush the work for the Viceroy's visit. Much hospital equipment came; unpacking, cleaning.

Dec. 2: Rushing windows.

3: Rushing operation room. Men working well. Pancham
splendid.

4: Grand rush — to return to Nowgong in State car.

The Viceroy's Visit and the Kaiser-i-Hind Medal

Esther Baird, on January 1, 1930, had been notified she was being awarded
the silver Kaiser-i-Hind Medal and that the British Viceroy of India would
come to Nowgong and present it to her in person. This medal was a token
of the British Government of India's recognition of her conspicuously
meritorious service in the advancement of education and morality.[74]

On December 5, at a garden party at the Agency, all the missionaries were present to meet the Viceroy and Vicerine and to attend the impressive ceremony as Esther Baird received her silver Kaiser-i-Hind medal. After the presentation, the Viceroy handed her an envelope from the Maharaja of Chhatarpur containing a contribution of Rs. 2,000 ($650) for the new hospital.[75]

For Esther Baird, the climax of the whole celebration was the next day when Lady Irwin personally visited the hospital. Great preparations had been made by the British Indian Government for this trip. Every precaution was taken for the Viceroy's safety, since attempts had been made to assassinate him. The Maharaja himself with state officials met the party one mile out of Chhatarpur and escorted them in. When they came, they found everything in the hospital in readiness. Nell Lewis, Judith Kinder, Alena Calkins, Ruth Thurston, and Dr. Hull had worked hard to see to that.[76]

The Vicerine's visit was over very quickly, and she left about 10:00 a.m. After that, all the men on the place were asked to leave and the Maharani herself came to see the hospital accompanied by the ten-year-old prince.[77] Everyone was delighted to know that a place of healing for women and children was now available in Chhatarpur.

Dedication and Formal Opening of the Hospital

By the end of December, the work on the hospital was completed. Opening day had to wait until Colonel Tyrell, the government's physician for all of Bundelkhand, could come and formally declare it open.[78] The Christian community, however, did not wait for formal opening day. On December 23, 1930, a dedication service was attended by all the Christian Indian men and all missionaries.[79] They observed with awe the foothold in Chhatarpur: the "First Bungalow," workers' quarters, dispensary, chapel, doctor's bungalow, nurses' quarters, and other buildings — all dwarfed now by the splendid women's and children's Elizabeth Jane Bell Stephenson Memorial Hospital. Moti Lal, looking on with wonder and thanksgiving, put their thoughts in words: "WHAT HATH GOD WROUGHT!"[80]

On January 26, 1931, Colonel Tyrell came and officially opened the hospital with a silver key. This time not only were the Christians present, but leading Hindus, Moslems, and the Maharaja as well. Because of caste, tea could not be served to the Hindus though others enjoyed it. Oranges and bananas were provided for those who refused the tea.[81]

With the hospital open, Dr. Ruth Hull and nurse Alena Calkins were alert to receive patients. Nell Lewis came in first, extremely ill, on February 2, 1931. Dr. Hull and Alena, being the only staff, had to take turns doing day and night duty. Six days later Moti Lal's wife came in as the second patient for her third delivery. The demands on the two staff members were almost unbearable. Fortunately, Nell recovered rather quickly and joined the staff.[82]

Everything was functioning well and Esther Baird's furlough was past due. Still, she hestitated to go. A rumor had reached her that the Board expected to retire her when she got home. Even at seventy, she could not believe it, and before leaving India she wrote the Board to find out. Quickly the answer came back that there was no thought but to return her to India unless her physical condition should hinder. On hearing this, she left with a happy heart, sailing home with Ruth Thurston on the SS *President Fillmore* February 25, 1931.[83]

Rumblings of Discontent

"Confirm your love . . . . lest Satan should get an advantage of us: for we are not ignorant of his devices." 2 Corinthians 2:8, 11

When Esther Baird went on furlough in 1931, Carrie Wood was left as general superintendent and Mission Council chairman.[1] The push to complete the hospital had relegated almost every other business to the "back burner"; but with that finished, the neglected issues began to demand attention. On these specific matters, individual missionaries on the field began to write directly to the Board. The dam broke, and no longer did reports go to the Board only through the superintendent. The Mission Board read about differences and discontent they did not know existed and did not want to acknowledge. They were shocked and immediately on the defensive.[2]

Rules that Rankled

One complaint had to do with voting in Council. The Board had ruled that until a missionary had been on the field two years he could speak but not vote. At the end of 1930 they changed the rule, saying that if a missionary did not satisfactorily complete the prescribed language work at the end of two years, it should be *three* years before he voted. This seemed tailored to fit the case of the only man on the field ready to vote, and the timing rankled.[3]

The next matter was more difficult. In a council session before Esther Baird left for furlough, missionaries in Chhatarpur discovered they had innocently "broken contract." Ruth's mother had sent a parcel containing tins of dried beef and suddenly it came to light that written into the contract and deed to the Chhatarpur property was a statement that missionaries would not import or slaughter beef in Chhatarpur. Ruth felt she had done neither, but what did the stipulation mean? The younger missionaries demanded a clarification from the Maharaja. The delicate balance in relationship of a Mission existing in a strongly Hindu culture caused the superintendent to hesitate. She understood the matter was not simple. The younger missionaries agreed to eat no beef in Chhatarpur, but they felt confused and angry. Their reports home about it annoyed the Mission Board, though they were as surprised as the new missionaries to find such a contract existed. Their strong advice to the missionaries was not to offend the Maharaja by eating beef in Chhatarpur, for after all, that was what the Apostle Paul advised.[4]

Written into that same contract another stipulation was that no water baptisms should occur in Chhatarpur State. James Kinder and the other younger missionaries interpreted this as meaning no public confessions to Christianity. Esther Baird explained that she had refused to sign a contract saying there would be no conversions but saw "water baptism" as being no stumbling block to a Quaker.[5] These and other things upset the younger missionaries.

Favoritism or Forgiveness?

The discovery that Dr. William Parsad was an alcoholic was a shock. Because of the high level of his work in Harpalpur, this fact had not been publicized; but as he grew older, the problem intensified. When an examination of the records showed he had also been taking fees intended for the Mission, the Council had to act. The younger missionaries knew of his fine reputation as a medical worker but were shocked to learn that a leading member of the Church in India had been allowed to escape discipline for these faults. Others had been cut from employment and stricken from church records for less serious offenses. James Kinder wrote the Board, "If you desire that we should acquiesce to a situation such as this, and if you desire peace at any price, even the price of holiness standards, then . . . will you kindly accept our resignation."[6] This case, however, was not easy to deal with, for William Parsad was indeed ill, and considering his long, honorable, and sacrificial record of service, any discipline seemed too severe. Six and a half hours in Council slipped by as the missionaries wrestled with this problem, but finally victory came. Esther Baird was leaving for furlough, but the rest agreed that until they had made every effort to save him, he should not be cut from church membership or dismissed from work. William Parsad was then called before the Council, where he begged forgiveness and promised the Lord and the Council not to drink any more.[7] Carrie Wood and the younger missionaries knew they faced a serious problem, but they sought to deal with it in faithfulness and love.

Abortive Steps Toward Independence

Carrie Wood, always active in the business meetings of the Church, realized that as acting mission superintendent she must give attention to the
church's development. She wanted to emphasize a new understanding of
responsibility and authority. She wanted to see greater caring and sharing with the people in outstations. There was a restive spirit in the church
influenced by the political atmosphere in the country and the demand for
freedom. Nationalism under Mahatma Gandhi's leadership had brought
an awakening of self-respect and consciousness of power to the people of
India. The churches also began to clamor for more authority, often
before the missionaries felt they were ready to handle the problems. At
the National Christian Council in Madras in 1929, the Indian leaders
pointed out they wanted changes: They wanted missionaries who would
be *able* to lead but *willing* to follow; who would stand *side by side* with
Indian Christians; and who would be willing to *decrease* while helping the
Indian Church *increase*.[8]

The people in Harpalpur pressed for a greater voice in the disbursement of funds by Nowgong Monthly Meeting. Since this demand was not
satisfied, they set up their own monthly meeting only to find this cut them
off from the missionaries and made them feel orphaned. Their request
that a missionary attend their business meeting each month went unheed-
ed, and they finally joined Nowgong Monthly Meeting again.[9]

Early in 1929 some members expressed the desire for an Indian advisory committee to work in the various stations with the missionaries.
They were asking for a "side by side" approach, but the Mission was not
ready yet for this step.[10]

New Medical and Evangelistic Opportunities in Malehra

Chhatarpur was a bright spot. The new hospital was full of action with
its excellent staff: Dr. Hull, Alena Calkins, Nell Lewis, an Indian nurse,
and Grace Jones home for the summer. Medical, obstetrical, surgical,
and pediatric patients were being treated and made well. As if that wasn't
challenge enough, they took on another. It came about because the Political Agent had been shot at and uninjured. Someone in gratitude and in
his honor gave money for charitable purposes. The Political Agent
turned this to a dispensary at Malehra, a large village eleven miles northeast of Chhatarpur in the midst of betel leaf fields and beside an artificial
lake. He turned to the Christian Hospital and the State Hospital to staff
it. Dr. Hull took charge, and with a Mohammedan doctor from the
Government Hospital, two pharmacists, a water carrier and a sweeper,
she moved in to accept the challenge. They went every Monday afternoon, the big bazaar day, and saw as many as 217 patients before they

went home. Patients who needed treatment more often than once a week were encouraged to go to Chhatarpur. "We hope to make Fisher Dispensary a center for health information and prophylactic propaganda," Dr. Hull wrote home.[11] The Board members on hearing of this new development were cautious. They felt that further outlay of personnel and money was beyond them. Eventually the government took over Fisher Dispensary and Dr. Hull's dream of public health never developed.

The evangelists found that the medical work done in Malehra by Dr. Hull and Alena Calkins provided a very good introduction for evangelism, so they moved in also.[12] The evangelists were the Kinders, Moti Lal, Pancham Singh, Stuti Prakash, Hira Singh, Dayal Chand Singh, and Hira Lal (though Hira Lal had to drop out because he developed ulcerated eyes in camp, and lost one). The Kinders worked with the evangelists to try a system of more *intensive* evangelism as opposed to the *extensive* method the evangelists had been used to. While in language school the summer of 1931, James and Judith Kinder came into contact with Bishop J. W. Pickett and heard of his studies about mass movements in India. Methods of evangelism among Hindus and Mohammedans, results of evangelism, Indian Church organization, self-support of the Indian Church, use of paid and unpaid Indian workers, and educational, medical, and agricultural aids to evangelism were all discussed. With Pickett and his team they investigated the institutional vs. evangelistic emphases. They learned that "miscellaneous touring" or *extensive* evangelism as was practiced in Bundelkhand had borne little fruit during the last decade. A more *intensive* work in a more limited territory was considered superior. Pickett's recommendation was that the evangelists try concentrating where the Holy Spirit was at work, evidenced by a responsive interest on the part of the people.[13]

James Kinder was challenged by all he had learned and longed to try it out. He had his first opportunity at Malehra, where evangelism and medical work went hand in hand. He became convinced that the intensive evangelism and mass movement approach to the outcastes was the way to go, but he also recognized the difficulties.

> Some missionaries now feel the mass movement approach, sometimes criticized as unthorough, is one of the Indian's best approaches to Christ. A low caste person, converted, will face a hard road. Unless he does break caste he is of no value to a militant church; for his hands are tied. Upon breaking caste he will likely be excluded from using the village well, the shopkeeper may refuse to sell him supplies, the *zamindar* (land owner) may cancel his land lease, in times of sickness and death he can expect no assistance. All of this comes into the villager's mind when he is urged to accept Christ . . . . But if a leading man should

become a Christian . . . it is possible that many others will follow
him . . . in a mass movement. However, we have finally to remember
our greatest arch-enemy is not caste or any external barrier; but a
spiritual adversary who met defeat at Calvary.[14]

Further Medical Developments

One of the unstated purposes of opening a hospital in Chhatarpur was to
provide a place for training the orphan girls.[15] So Alena Calkins opened
a nurses' training school affiliated with the N.C.C.'s Mid-India United
Board of Examiners for Mission Nurses.[16] A powerhouse was built, the
hospital wired, and a water pump installed. By June the electricity came
on and water started trickling from the taps.[17]

Dr. Hull went to Calcutta in mid-1931 to study tropical medicine.
Alena and Nell were left in charge of the hospital and dispensary. Alena
also kept up the weekly visits to the Fisher Dispensary and was thankful
that Esther Baird's Chevrolet had been assigned to Chhatarpur, for it cut
down hours on travel. She also took calls as far as forty miles from
Chhatarpur. Her nonmedical activities took in supervision of the
Chhatarpur Sunday school and teaching English two days a week to the
Maharani.[18]

The first patient to die in the hospital was a baby. On the same day,
six months after the hospital was opened, they delivered the first Hindu
baby. Alena thanked the Lord for her midwifery training in Madras,
which helped her to bring it into the world even though no doctor was
present.[19]

While Dr. Hull was away to get more practice in surgery in Kashmir
in 1932, Nell again fell ill and had to go to Miraj for surgery and then on
to Bangalore. It was fourteen months later that she came back to Bundelkhand.[20] Meanwhile Dr. Hull and Alena continued the work, as more
and more patients came. The newness made commonplace happenings
interesting. For example, a sweeper outcaste lady was put in a ward with
two high caste women and one of medium caste. The woman of the second highest caste complained about the sweeper being in the same ward
with her. The sweeper, who needed sutures removed before dismissal,
begged to go home immediately. Dr. Hull discovered the reason was
caste. She explained that God created us all, and not in compartments.
But the high caste and the outcaste both felt it was wrong for them to be
there together. After much persuasion, the Christian way won out — at
least outwardly — and the outcaste patient stayed.[21]

Though most of the women coming to the hospital were illiterate and
very oppressed by their caste and society, they nevertheless came with

plenty of spunk and their own value system. Alena captured a bit of it in this article:

> *Missionary*: What is your name?
> *Patient*: My name? Why, they call me Dweller in Kompna.
> *Missionary*: I'm not asking you where you live; but what is your name?
> *Patient* (to companion): What is my name? You tell —
> *Companion*: Her name is Pyaridulaiya (beloved daughter-in-law).
> *Missionary*: How old are you?
> *Patient*: Ten years old.
> *Missionary*: You are older than that. Tell me how old you are.
> *Patient*: How do I know how old I am? My mother knows, and you can tell by looking at me, you know everything.
> *Missionary* (writes down her guess): Are your parents living?
> *Patient*: No, both are dead.
> *Missionary*: Of what disease did your father and mother die?
> *Patient*: Oh, only my father died; my mother is living.
> *Missionary*: What did your father die of?
> *Patient*: He stopped breathing.
> *Missionary*: Have any of your children died?
> *Patient*: Three have died.
> *Missionary*: Of what disease did they die?
> *Patient*: I don't know. God took them when they were babies.
> *Missionary*: Did they have fever, a cold, diarrhea, or what?
> *Patient*: One died of a drying-up disease, and one of fever. Please give me some fever medicine.
> *Missionary*: Let me take your temperature now under your arm.
> *Patient* (frightened): Oh no, don't cut me!
> *Missionary*: This isn't a knife; it is only a glass to measure temperature.
> (After much persuasion, she yields; but sometimes at this point the patient runs away.)[22]

The Squeeze of Depression in America

Such hospital stories amused Carrie Wood, whose keen sense of humor delighted everyone. But there were times as she served as superintendent when it was difficult to smile. For almost five years the depression in America wrought havoc with the financial situation in the Mission. "Depression is the most common word in our vocabularies," wrote Louise Ellett. "I have certainly never seen times like these, and hope I never shall again. It seems that there are whole churches of our city friends whose members are almost all out of work and have been for months."[23] Bank failure caused missionaries on the field to receive only one third of their salaries, borrowed from special funds. For the duration of the depression, both missionaries and Indian workers took a 10 percent cut in their salaries, stopped all possible expenses such as driving of the motor cars, and still could not make ends meet.[24] Debts piled up and Walter Williams on investigation reported, "Our Mission has established a reputation for debt which is most unenviable."[25]

Discipline of a Missionary

Carrie Wood fought the financial battle bravely even when losing, but she was almost overcome by what happened to Walter Bolitho. On May 13, 1932, a cable from the Board requested him to leave India immediately. This shocked everyone on the field and left Carrie Wood speechless. She had just sent home a report of the good work done that year by Walter:

> Walter J. Bolitho has supervised the installing of the electric light plant, pump, septic tank and piping of water into the Chhatarpur hospital and dispensary. This in addition to his agricultural work and the Now-gong bazaar and village Sunday school has given him a busy year. Geneva has been in charge of the girls' orphanage and continued zenana work and has taken some of the preaching services.[26]

Earlier that year Carrie Wood had dealt with an incident in which Walter was involved. She had reported it to Esther Baird on furlough, who in turn reported it to the Board. It had so happened that in Chhatarpur the mosquitos disturbed him down at the powerhouse, and Walter had moved up to the operating room roof to sleep. Moonlight kept him awake, and he called down to a nurse on duty to bring him a blanket to put over his net. She took it up to him without saying anything to the matron. She was missed and questioned, and she lied about what he said to her. Before Carrie Wood could get the nurses' confession that she had indeed lied, gossip spread. The missionaries knew Walter was innocent, but they rebuked him for being indiscreet in making the request for the blanket. They considered this rebuke sufficient punishment for the offense.[27] But the Board dismissed him for "inexcusable indiscretion" and wrote Carrie: "We find it hard to understand why you should feel clear in deciding these things yourselves in place of bringing them to the Board."[28]

The Bolithos left for America on July 4, 1932. Just before boarding the ship, Walter Bolitho wrote his feelings to Carrie Wood:

> Why could you as chairman of the Council, not contest or try to get the Board to reconsider their action? . . . . It seems the Board made a hasty action without consulting you . . . . You have been in India for twenty years and I would think the Board could depend some upon your advice.[29]

The whole affair brought nothing but agony to Carrie Wood. All she could answer was, "The Board . . . understood that I did not feel that your dismissal was necessary on that charge." But according to her nature, she apologized to the Board and sought to defend their action with a deep sense of loyalty.[30]

Growing Discontent

With the same sense of loyalty Carrie Wood sought to explain or excuse authorities in answering James Kinder's itemized list of complaints. It was noted that all the male missionaries in India so far had shown the same critical spirit.[31] Kinder's implications that missionaries had been lax in consistent discipline irritated them. His urging did, however, cause the Council to minute their recognition concerning "laxness in use of tobacco, liquor, or *pan*" and to agree to take "definite steps to create a conscience in eradicating the evil."[32]

Discipline of an Outspoken National

Carrie Wood also had to face criticisms from a leading Christian. Bram was an orphan of 1904. He took training as a pharmacist and got a job at the government hospital in Nowgong. He and Sahodra Bai, his wife, had four sons: Pyare Lal, Mitra Sen, Mahendra Singh, and Pratap; and a daughter, Padmawati. Since he did not owe his livelihood to the Mission, he felt free to criticize it. He wrote a stinging letter to the Mission Board under the name of D. Brown. The Board returned it to the missionaries. Bram was called on the carpet and ordered to prove the validity of his charges, statement by statement. Though some of what he wrote was true, all attention was focused on the grossly exaggerated and untrue allegations. Under threat of being disowned, he wrote letters of apology to every person and group concerned. He acknowledged that he had no position or right to send such a letter to the Board. Nevertheless, the Monthly Meeting recorded, "It being the wish of the Board"[33] his name was cut from membership. He was never again restored, though he died November 16, 1933, with a clear testimony.[34] The bitterness of his experience, however, would live on through his oldest son, who became a thorn in the flesh to the Mission in the years to come. From then on, the family went by the name of Brown.

The End of a Troubled Year

Carrie Wood rounded out her time as acting superintendent at the age of 52. Esther Baird, on furlough at 72, completed a book called *Adventuring with God*, telling of God's reward of faith in providing the hospital in Chhatarpur. As soon as it was finished, she headed back toward India. John and Ruth Earle preceded her a few weeks and were already nicely settled in the first bungalow in Chhatarpur—empty since Dr. Fleming left. Their own church in Newport, Rhode Island, paid their way to the field

and also underwrote their salaries for six years.[35] They found the bazaar
girls' school closed, for administrative duties and problems — especially
after Bolithos left the farm, workshop, and orphanage work on her
shoulders — took all of Carrie Wood's time.[36] The bright spot was Harpalpur, where Gore Lal Singh and his wife operated two schools — one for
120 boys, and another for 33 girls. They enjoyed the new facilities of a
chapel and another building renovated from quarters given by the Rani of
Alipura.[37] The mission schools in Nowgong, Chhatarpur, and Bileri were
also flourishing.[38]

| # Facing a Time
# of Darkness

*"Follow peace with all men, and holiness, without
which no man shall see the Lord." Hebrews 12:14*

Beloved Esther Baird Returns and Builds

All the missionaries including John and Ruth Earle were on hand to welcome Esther Baird, who arrived late November 1932. She was joyously received with brass bands, torches, garlands, a gun salute, and decorations. In Chhatarpur later Dr. Ruth Hull noted, "She was greeted vociferously . . . with a band playing 'Home Sweet Home' under a sign of WELCOME. But the depth of the welcome is immeasurable and beyond expression."[1]

As Esther Baird took over the Mission again she found herself not as vigorous as in days past and spoke often of being tired. She looked forward to days of rest and uninvolvement. But she came alive when there was some building or repair work to be done.[2] There was a maternity and baby ward to be built with the money the late Maharaja had given.

The Maharaja had died while Esther Baird was on furlough. Right in the midst of the huge Khajaraho mela, as the evangelists were preaching and distributing literature, he breathed his last. Everything was immediately brought to a halt. All ringing of bells, loud talking, and singing came to a stop for two weeks in honor of this man who had ruled Chhatarpur State for sixty years and had donated the land for the Mission base in Chhatarpur. His heart had often been touched by the Gospel. When Jefferson Ford visited India, the Maharaja became quite fond of him and called him often to talk about spiritual things. He asked many questions. One question he asked was whether Jefferson Ford thought his gift to the Mission would open heaven to him. Jefferson Ford felt the

Maharaja loved Jesus but wanted to add Him to his other gods instead of making Him Lord of all.[3] Many honored him, and eight thousand people came to witness his cremation. The eleven-year-old prince came from Indore to be crowned, though the actual power would be in the hands of the Political Agent and the Diwan until he became of age.[4]

The Maharaja's gift had been depleted to pay salaries of workers during the depression, but Esther Baird had other building funds to use for a start. She put pressure on the Board to send another $800, even though salaries went unpaid, in order to have visible evidence that they intended to carry out the Maharaja's purpose. The building was designed to be larger than first envisioned and would exceed the Maharaja's gift. The Diwan, pleased to see the building going up, agreed that when the Maharaja's gift of Rs. 2,000 was gone, the state would pay the balance.[5] These wards were completed and dedicated on December 10, 1934. The dedication was a ladies' affair. The Maharani opened the ward with about seventy-five Indian and a few English ladies from Nowgong in attendance.[6]

The medical bungalow in Chhatarpur needed another room for guests, and also for Alena Calkins. The room she occupied was uninhabitable six months of the year in the hot season. So bricks, mortar, and workmen again were all over the place under Esther Baird's supervision, and the new room was soon completed.[7]

From the Woodheads, an English family who formerly lived in Nowgong, a special gift of money came to buy a *dak bungalow* (travelers' inn) in Gulganj, Bijawar State, twenty-two miles from Chhatarpur on the road to Amarmau. Some opposition had to be overcome to get this property, but Esther Baird was experienced in that. By October the deal was settled, and by the summer of 1934 it was furnished and ready to be occupied. Esther had every intention of placing the Earles there, but policy and personality matters had so deteriorated by then that the Earles, in the end, refused to go.[8]

Esther Baird, bewildered and frustrated, turned back to her building.[9] Reroofing the girls' hostel and repair of the cemetery wall took several weeks. Then during the summer, water ran out in the hospital in Chhatarpur. Fortunately there were four wells on the land given by the State. Two were quite good but not good enough. So a fifth well was leased but was dry by April. The hospital then had to carry water by oxcart for more than half a mile from the first bungalow. This afforded another challenge — blasting for water. So with dynamite and workmen and many days of close supervision, Esther Baird saw the solid rock of the best well blasted seven feet deeper.[10]

Next, Esther Baird pushed on to build a veranda on the house for Dr. Grace Jones. Grace graduated from medical school with an LMP (Licensed Medical Practitioner) degree and joined the hospital full time beginning November 12, 1933, on a salary of $18 (Rs. 60) per month. Of this she paid back $8 (Rs. 25) per month on her medical debt.[11]

Trouble with Pancham Singh

The next big building project was a new nurses' quarters, but the Board put a stop to any more expansion until the financial crisis was past. "We are running into criticism at home that our medical work is top heavy . . . . So we will consider the medical plant finished for the present until the folks back home get in better circumstances," they wrote.[12]

In the midst of all the building and blasting, the Mission Council was having a trying time with Pancham Singh, who with impunity was breaking mission rules. His importance to the building work did not make it easy to deal with him. Even Esther Baird realized something had to be done. So they called him in and laid their complaints before him. Quickly he attempted to show the Mission Council that he was above the law, but they did not accept this and suspended him from mission employment. He did not accept the suspension, for he was clever enough to know that employed by the Mission or not, he would continue to be needed by them. So after 28 years of service (1906-1933) he resigned, or was dismissed (depending on one's point of view). He continued working without a break on a contract basis. He also remained without a squeak of discipline as a very vocal and powerful part of the Church and even a member of the Ministry and Oversight (Rakhwal).[13]

Death of Charlotte Bai

Besides the repairing and building, Esther Baird found time to visit the sick, care for the children, and have happy times among the people. She grieved with the people at the loss of Charlotte Bai, who died singing to a child in her lap on March 30, 1933. Because she was blind, Charlotte had been left in a mela by her parents when she was seven years old. Missionaries found her and taught her the Moon system for the blind. Her whole life was a service of gratitude to God, and she had been a tremendous blessing to the little Christian community in Bundelkhand. "What a wonderful entrance must have been Charlotte Bai's as the glories of the beautiful beyond unfolded before her restored sight," Esther Baird noted.[14]

Disunity and Polarization

Echoed more than anything else during the midthirties was an anguished cry for peace and unity bursting from the hearts of the Bundelkhand missionaries.[15] There is no doubt from the record that the Mission Board in America and Esther Baird in India were agreed that the easy path to such peace was for the newer missionaries to stop criticizing and accept the proven policies of the years and the leadership of Esther Baird, who had served more than forty years in India.[16] But a number of situations already noted were building up to a crisis, and there were grave questions in the minds of the younger missionaries that they freely expressed. Why there was money for building but none for salaries seemed not to have been adequately explained. The matter of special funds was not reported either to the Mission Council or to the Board at home. The accounts were in good order but were never shared with others until the Mission Board asked for them too late.[17] Alena Calkins had gone on furlough in April 1934 before a polarization took place in spite of tears and prayers. Much heartache followed. James and Judith Kinder, John and Ruth Earle, and Nell Lewis were on one side. Carrie Wood in deep loyalty stood with Esther Baird as did Dr. Ruth Hull, who, though one of the younger missionaries, did not agree with the other five. She felt that one cause of the trouble was that James Kinder expected to be made mission superintendent immediately upon passing his second Hindi exam. When that did not happen, she felt, he found it increasingly difficult to follow Esther Baird's advice and orders. So Dr. Ruth Hull made many trips to Nowgong to undergird and encourage Esther Baird in every way she could.[18]

Resistance to Change in Evangelism

Why were no new souls being born into the kingdom of God? This was a question every man who had gone to Bundelkhand persisted in asking. Their questions seemed to imply on one hand that there was laxness of discipline and that Christians were poor examples. On the other hand, the evangelistic methods, long since discontinued in some missions, were blamed.[19] Over the years the men had tried to initiate new methods. James Kinder and John Earle were no exceptions. Early in 1934 each of them took camping teams in different directions — James Kinder to Orcha and John Earle toward Panna. After ten days of intensive camping and pressing for decision, Kinder's party was driven out of the State. Even so, he felt they had experienced the best evangelistic effort of his four years in India. John Earle was enthusiastic when he returned from the Panna area, for there was every indication that this State, so far closed to open preaching, was about to open.[20]

James Kinder sought to broaden the vision for evangelism throughout the area by initiating an evangelistic convention. He called sixteen workers and three missionaries from neighboring missions to join the missionaries and evangelists in Nowgong. They all shared ideas and experiences and were tremendously inspired and bound together in deeper concern for people of the area.[21] The Kinders also initiated training programs including practical work for the evangelists during the rains when it was impossible to go out camping. Moti Lal was so inspired by this that he led evangelistic services in the Nowgong school and saw forty of the children respond to the call of Christ. Stuti Prakash originated the idea of opening a book room in Chhatarpur where he could continue a steady witness.[22]

Apart from Stuti Prakash and Moti Lal, however, the evangelists indicated little enthusiasm for change. Once left to themselves, they reverted to the old pattern of spending a few hours in a village and then moving on with meager effort to follow up or press for decision. Did they feel somehow that change was a kind of disloyalty to their beloved mother and the policies of the past? That seemed to be the way it came across, and James Kinder and John Earle sensed little support for new methods from the superintendent of the Mission. They concluded she was more interested in medical work. Esther Baird would have denied it, for she often drove miles over rough and dusty roads to visit the camps and encourage the workers. Only when it was too late did she clearly offer her support to their new ideas.[23]

Opposition to Change in Harpalpur

Meanwhile relationships deteriorated and came to a head in Harpalpur in 1934. James and Judith Kinder were stationed there for evangelistic work, and he was put in charge of the station.[24] With clear guidelines, they set about making the Mission in Harpalpur more evangelistic and more self-supporting. Bible teaching in the school, a fee system in both dispensary and school, a closer supervision of examinations, and more suitable textbooks were areas that concerned the Mission Council.[25]

It did not take long for Kinders to discover Goverind Das, the magistrate who had almost become a Christian during Rogerses' stay in Harpalpur. They found him sitting alone in his small upper room isolated from his Hindu friends. They preached the Gospel to him again and saw this eighty-year-old man take the scissors and cut off his sacred lock of hair to break his ties with the past and cast his lot with Christ.[26]

Not long after Kinders got into operation in Harpalpur, reactions set in. The first was against the Scripture memorization program. James Kinder wrote, "The magistrates took exception to the Scripture memory course. Gore Lal, the headmaster, appeared and read them passages in the memory course. Some older Hindus said, 'I didn't know the Bible was like that.' At least once the merchants of the town were attentive at a Bible reading." The magistrates hoped the teachers would not be too exacting on the memory course, and later appealed to the Raja, objecting to its being made a requirement for passing.[27] On hearing this, Esther Baird made a trip to Harpalpur to remind James Kinder that Bible had been taught in Harpalpur for twenty years without examination and that it would be better not to give compulsory examinations on it at present. But before the Raja's complaint, the Mission Council consensus had been otherwise, and James Kinder took Council action as his authority and continued with the program.[28]

The next opposition arose against the fee system. James Kinder announced that for the poor the dispensary fee would be one pice (one half cent) and one anna (two cents) per day for the landowners. The Raja of Alipura objected and sent word he would instead give Rs. 100 in addition to his monthly grant. But after some consultation he allowed the new fee system to stand. However, fourteen leading men in Harpalpur banded together against James Kinder and complained among other things that since the fee system had gone in many poor children had left school.[29]

These fourteen leaders then took their complaints to the Raja. Kinder Sahib's lectures in the dispensary and around the school, they said, were against their religion. They also objected to the Friday chapel services and to new textbooks they claimed ridiculed their religion. These books had been introduced by Kinders in place of former books heavily slanted toward Hinduism. These new texts came from a Christian press and were used in other mission schools in North India. Carrie Wood had approved them, too. Neither the Kinders, Carrie Wood, nor any other member of the Mission meant to ridicule the Hindu religion, but the irritated leaders of Harpalpur ordered that the books be removed immediately and the former books restored. They also demanded that Kinders be transferred.[30]

The most cutting opposition, however, did not come from Hindus. Supervision of the station brought the Kinders into very close relationship with the Christian workers in Harpalpur, and the leading one was Dr. William Parsad. They discovered that he had not discontinued his use of alcohol and tobacco as he fervently promised the Mission Council and the Lord in early 1931. They felt it their duty to report this; indeed, the Mission Board demanded it. The Mission Council then had no choice but to dismiss him. Esther Baird and James Kinder were appointed to inform the Raja of Alipura. The Raja and his private secretary begged for a reconsideration and reinstating. Esther Baird spoke afterwards of her humiliation to sit before these two Hindu men who showed so much more sympathy "than we as Christians do."[31] These same faults were punished quickly in others, but William Parsad was a pharmacist/doctor. He was very ill with cancer though no one seemed to know it at that time. And above all, he was the first orphan to be taken in by Delia Fistler and Esther Baird.

The Death of William Parsad

A month later the Alipura Raja, head of the State, offered to take over the Harpalpur dispensary for one year.[32] Esther Baird gave her approval for William Parsad to work for the State;[33] so with the help of his son, he kept the dispensary open. His work stopped, however, on January 13, 1935. Desperately ill, he came to Nowgong, and Esther Baird put him to bed in the Goddard Memorial building, where she tenderly nursed him until February 12. That day he died, she said, with a "clear testimony as to faith in Christ. Great love and sympathy was expressed for the family by men of Harpalpur, Nowgong and Chhatarpur."[34]

Opposition from the School

Back to the Kinders, they had another problem with Christian leaders in Harpalpur. The Mission Council had requested them to check the examinations in order to discover why Christian students failed in other schools when they left Harpalpur. Carrying this through, the Kinders drew fire from the masters, particularly the headmaster, whose daughter's paper had clearly been tampered with.[35] Gore Lal Singh charged the Kinders with insulting the teachers by forcing on them this kind of supervision. He left his work in Harpalpur without permission from James Kinder to report his feelings to Esther Baird. The story he shared with her was far more serious than Kinders knew about, and Esther Baird asked him to repeat it before the Mission Council the next day. All the Harpalpur teachers and dispensary workers were called before the Council to hear Gore Lal charge the Kinders of a critical spirit and inability to understand the Indian Christians "as the older missionaries do who have been in India a long time." Then he outlined in vivid detail the danger of the Alipura State's stopping all connections with the Mission because of the Harpalpur leaders' anger with the Kinders. Kinders until that moment knew nothing of this.[36]

Transfer of the Kinders

When the Harpalpur leaders' complaints reached the Alipura Raja, he immediately requested Esther Baird to take steps to redress their grievances "before it is too late," and to transfer the Kinders at once. "Harpalpur is not a place where such a person is necessary," he said.[37]

In just a few days Kinders had moved from Harpalpur to the little cottage in Nowgong feeling a sense of betrayal by their own Christian fellow laborers. Why had the headmaster not informed them about the rising storm in Harpalpur? Why had he not called their attention to the offensive passages in the textbooks when he first heard it? Why did he go to Esther Baird to discuss school business over James Kinder's head? And above all, why did Esther Baird encourage it? The Council had no clear answers.[38]

The Church was also divided. Stuti Prakash and Moti Lal, the two finest evangelists, were very fond of James Kinder. The day accusations were brought into the Monthly Meeting against the new missionaries, Stuti Prakash was home with sore eyes. (Hearing how the meeting had gone, he was glad to be absent. "It was the will of God," he said.) Gore Lal, Pancham Singh, and Jai Chand were appointed to write the Mission Board. Moti Lal deplored the fact that when such charges were made, the accused were not present. He also tried but failed to stop the letter from going to the Board.[39]

The Reaction of the Board to Friction on the Field

The Mission Board was deeply distressed by the news from India, which led them to prayer and fasting amidst very great sorrow. At the same time they sustained the loss of their treasurer, Herman Cattell, who died suddenly. Claude Roane, the president, was seriously ill, and Louise Ellett, the corresponding secretary, had to undergo major surgery with complications. Two prominent board members, Leona Kinsey and Catherine Stalker, were far away, and burdens weighed extremely heavy on those remaining. Heaviest of all was the trouble in India. Finally in a very strong letter the Board threatened to close the work if unity was not achieved. Time after time their letters admonished the younger missionaries to be patient and to adjust. Seeking to be fair, they pointed out that the problems were rooted in the past. Referring to a letter from John Earle, Louise Ellett wrote, "The letter was presumptuous . . . as were the letters that came from Mr. Kinder, Mr. Coffin, Mr. Rogers and Mr. Bolitho, in the past . . . . If the five letters . . . were laid side by side it would not materially matter which one signed which letter. They are all alike . . . . But . . . there are two sides to the trouble as always." Then in an effort to balance the criticisms, the letter continued, "The Board feels that the principal source of discontent through the years is that Indians have so often been able to get a sympathetic hearing with Miss Baird at the expense of the missionary against whom they complained."[40]

Resignations and the Aftermath

This letter, in the effort to be fair to everyone, succeeded rather in antagonizing both sides. Esther Baird denied the accusations against her and let the Board know she was offended by their suggested solutions.[41] The five, who felt they had never been heard and never would be heard by the Board, gave up. A few days later on October 8, 1934, the Kinders, Earles, and Nell Lewis cabled their joint resignation to the Mission Board.[42]

The Board immediately cabled Esther Baird: "Five resignations received. Cable your and their plans. Board considers sending representative. Roane."[43] Four days after this cable was received the Kinders left.[44] Esther Baird sent her reply to the Board:

> Kinders gone. Lewis, Earles uncertain of fulfilling six months notice. Others planning to carry on. Pray.[45]

Moti Lal and his wife, Shanti, withdrew their membership from the Friends Nowgong Monthly meeting and left. The missionaries trembled for Dr. Grace Jones, Shanti Moti Lal's sister, but evidently she had no thought of leaving. She went right ahead initiating the observance of Hospital Sunday and attending to her duty. Stuti Prakash was sorely tempted, but after much prayer he felt God's renewed call to Bundelkhand. He settled the matter then that he would not run from a hard situation. God graciously gave him a vision of the rocky dry land of Bundelkhand bounded by two mighty rivers, the Ken and Dhasan. Projects were afoot in bordering states to draw off the water of these rivers for irrigation, leaving Bundelkhand still thirsty. The vision awakened him to the realization that if he left, his native Bundelkhand might remain forever thirsty for the Gospel. So he stayed the rest of his life.[46]

Earles stayed on until January 21, 1935, and Nell Lewis until the end of January. Dr. Hull, whose furlough was due, stayed on until July to give Esther and Carrie a chance to have a summer vacation. Then she, too, left and these two senior missionaries—Esther and Carrie—were the only ones left on the field. Carrie was in charge of the schools, the farm, and twenty-four orphans in Nowgong. Esther moved to Chhatarpur to supervise the building and medical work.[47]

Before the five left Bundelkhand, they drafted a letter and summarized their complaints in twenty-two points of DO YOU KNOW. They had no heart to contact the Mission Board again, but they were determined to be heard. So they sent them to the pastors and leaders throughout Ohio Yearly Meeting. Since some of the points were based on partial information and therefore misleading, the Mission Board and the senior missionaries in Bundelkhand were terribly upset. The letter alarmed the constituency, who had always felt loyalty to Esther Baird. So from all sides the five resigning missionaries were condemned for this action, which closed the door to any further consideration of reinstating them.[48]

The Mission Council went over all twenty-two points one by one, pointing out for the Mission Board the errors in it. But there were many errors also in the Mission Council's defense, and later investigation showed the charges were based on facts and conditions that, according to the Board representative's opinion, could not be denied. It seemed clear that the Board had been at fault for not listening more carefully to the new missionaries.[49]

Facing the Issues — Walter Williams to India

The Mission Board faced these matters deliberately and with courage.

> As a Board, we are realizing keenly our responsibility to the yearly meeting, to the missionaries and to God, and our faith is lifted as we remember the precious promises of God, and that the "battle is the Lord's." The great commission of our Lord Jesus Christ and His "Occupy till I come" are not one whit less binding upon the Church because of the failure of any. This work is greater than any Board or any band of missionaries, so we covet that you continue with us in humble petition that there may yet come such order of things that may be well pleasing to God, and to this end we strive.[50]

In spite of the fact that missionaries' salaries were still eight months in arrears, they appointed Walter R. Williams as Mission Superintendent for India and China and determined to send him out to investigate ways they could guide the India Mission toward more stability and effectiveness.[51]

Louise Ellett wrote the two missionaries in India the Board's decision. She added, "He is not coming to tear down the work of the years . . . . He will not be coming to sit in judgment on you, but to work with you."[52]

Esther and Carrie were happy to know the Board was taking this action. That year as they waited, they worked hard at their various stations. They had many visits to and from the homes of English families in Nowgong. They listened to their first radio while visiting the Agency, and they took rides on the first airplane to come to Bundelkhand. They practiced typing on their first noiseless Remington typewriter. They attended the first ceremony for graduating nurses from the Chhatarpur nurses' training school when Shitabu and Jaiwatti donned their caps and joined the staff. Two hundred and seven prizes were given out during Baby Week.[53] The Women's Missionary Union, who supported Esther Baird, sent a letter expressing absolute confidence in her and the work, and Esther Baird recorded her settled conviction, "God has undertaken . . . the work has been saved as by fire."[54]

Walter Williams arrived in Bundelkhand December 2, 1935. That very day Esther Baird sensed the investigation was not going to be easy.

He had already visited Earles in Darjeeling, had spent four days with Coffins, probably had seen the Rogerses in Oregon, and surely must have visited Bolithos in Idaho.[55] Walter Williams must have felt compelled to note that a senior missionary could sometimes be at fault, for later Esther Baird wrote Claude Roane, "Before he slept in Nowgong, he told me that in over four cases out of five he believed the senior missionary to blame if the new missionary did not fit well into the work."[56] He wasted no time in caring for one ticklish matter about the contract signed with the State for the hospital land. He and Esther Baird wrote a joint letter requesting the Rai Bahadur Pandit Champa Ram Misra, Diwan of Chhatarpur State, to delete from the contract the sentence, "There shall be no water baptism of Christianity in the State," but he was not successful.[57]

After visiting Chhatarpur, Gulganj, and Harpalpur, Walter Williams went to Bombay to see the Kinders and Nell Lewis. He visited other places also before returning to Bundelkhand, and consulted five bishops of the Methodist Church, the secretary of India Christian Council, prominent leaders of Canadian and American Presbyterian Mission, Free Methodist Mission, Christian Mission, American Baptist Mission, Christian Church Mission, and the English Friends Mission.[58] Back again in Bundelkhand, he spent time at each station, holding special meetings at Harpalpur, Nowgong, and Chhatarpur and talking with all the workers and the two missionaries. He went into camp with the evangelistic party and spent time every day in Bible study with the evangelists.[59]

Courageous Conclusions

Before he left, Walter spoke seriously and candidly to the Monthly Meeting. He encouraged the people in the Lord, but he also sought to help them know that the people in Ohio Yearly Meeting who supported them were not rich people. "Many of them are not able to give their children as good an education as many of you have been given," he said. Then he underlined the fact that anyone who received salary from funds that came from America should not use liquor or tobacco. If they did, they should be dismissed at once. He asked them not to write letters of request or complaint to the Mission Board in America but rather to address the Mission Council. Finally, he encouraged them to become more financially independent, provide more money for the work of the Church, and prepare for greater responsibility.[60]

By this time it became quite evident that Carrie Wood was failing in health, and as recommended by the English Civil Surgeon of Nowgong, she prepared to go for furlough. Walter Williams immediately cabled home for Alena Calkins to be sent out as soon as possible so that Esther

Baird would not be left alone on the field. Carrie Wood left Bundelkhand on April 7, 1936, and Alena arrived eleven days later.[61]

Walter Williams left Nowgong on March 12 and returned home in May. He must have prepared his report on shipboard, for by May 6, 1936 it was in its final form to be presented to the full Board, which met June 4, 5 for consideration of its implications.[62] Significant points he included reveal an extensive coverage. A few of them are:

(1) *The Financial Situation:* First, the Board must rectify the matter of delinquent salaries of both missionaries and workers. Second, the Mission must be helped to make the Christian community more self-supporting.

(2) *Supervision of India Mission:* First, the report carried a high tribute to Esther Baird:

> To her, more than to any other single person, belongs the credit for the really good material plant which the Mission owns in Bundelkhand — Nowgong's spacious lands, with missionary bungalows, orphanages, etc.; Harpalpur with its bungalow, school and dispensary; Chhatarpur, with two bungalows and an attractive medical unit. Miss Baird has been signally favored in presenting the needs of the work to people of financial strength in the homeland as well as in persuading the native rajas to allow her the use of land for building purposes. It need scarcely be said that her white hair is looked upon by many former Indian orphans, their children and grand children with respect akin to veneration. For many of them, her will has been their law; her favor, their prosperity.

Second, points in supervision that the Board's representative felt contributed to the problems of the midthirties were pointed out:

> I am convinced that Miss Baird has allowed her strong likes for some of her workers to influence her treatment of them to such an extent that, while they have enjoyed her favor, others have felt themselves less appreciated; consequently, their resourcefulness has been inhibited.
>
> She has exercised too great and detailed supervision over the members of her staff. (This does not mean the young people were without fault . . . some have apologized.) . . . *Now let us cover the tragic past with a wide mantle of charity, and concentrate our best efforts toward redeeming the time left us for serving in Bundelkhand.*[63]

When this report reached Esther Baird, she had a sleepless night, for the negative side echoed the resigning missionaries' comments and broke her heart. "Thank you for enquiring about my eyes," she wrote Louise Ellett. (She was developing cataracts.) "Nights of weeping — no time or place for it in the day — must have been good for them. I am so glad my faith and my life does not hinge on pleasant or unpleasant experiences." To the Mission Board she wrote, "I have worked in India forty-three years.

Until two years ago I praised God for it all. The last two years I have accepted as His plan to make me perfect through suffering."[64]

(3) *Retirement*: The recommendation was that Esther Baird be retired by 1937 at the age of 76.

(4) *Staff*: There should be no fewer than eight missionaries on the field.

(5) *Annual Budget*: There must be a steadier plan for income between $12,000 and $15,000 per year.

A Plan for the Future

At the conclusion of his report, Walter Williams said, "If we are to carry forward the work already begun in India . . . I recommend that we put at least one married couple on the field this fall."[65]

Who would that married couple be? Walter Williams had someone in mind. If at that moment he could have skipped over miles to the parsonage of First Friends Church in Cleveland, Ohio, he would have seen that young couple getting into their car with the express purpose of going to Damascus to tell him of their call to India. Their interest in missions dated from childhood. Catherine DeVol Cattell grew up believing she would go to China as had her parents. Everett Cattell went through college praying that God would give him a missionary call.

Neither happened, but the Lord led them to one another and then into three pastorates before a distinct call to India came to each of them. They had already reached the outskirts of the city that day on their way to Damascus when Catherine asked, "How can we assume we will do any better than the five who resigned?" Everett suddenly pulled to the side of the road. "Let's not go," he said as he turned the car around. "Let's wait at home. If they call us, then we'll never doubt God's will in going to India." Catherine agreed. Back home, it was not long until the telephone rang. Everett answered it. "Will you go to India?" asked Walter Williams, and Everett answered, "Yes, we will go."

As they prepared for the journey, they tried to visualize their new home. By reading Walter Williams's report they learned there were 235 Friends in Bundelkhand, including all members of Christian families. They knew they would get off the train at Harpalpur, the only railway stop in Bundelkhand, and travel on from there to Nowgong and then to Chhatarpur. After that would be Gulganj, the newest station. There were schools and a dispensary in Harpalpur; schools, orphanages, farms, and carpenter shop in Nowgong; a school and hospital in Chhatarpur. Nowgong and Chhatarpur each had two bungalows for missionaries, and the other stations one. About 155 pupils attended all the schools, of whom about 45 came from Christian families. At the hospital Dr. Grace

Jones was now in charge and doing well though she missed Dr. Ruth Hull Bennett (who she thought would not be returning since she had married a Colorado wheat farmer).[66] Six evangelists toured the villages, but the work was difficult. In the church, no members tithed, and some 180 Christians were supported by mission funds.

After a thorough discussion on evangelism, Walter Williams concluded, "There is no prospect that we shall multiply our number of Christians rapidly in India . . . . The best methods will have to be employed patiently and long."[67]

The report on the American Friends Mission in India by Walter R. Williams seems to have been the watershed of its history. Before that there was no clear picture either at home or in India of the ultimate direction. Projects there were, but no integration of them into a specific goal.[68] The report brought the Mission into clear focus and presented to the Board a challenge that they met courageously. New missionaries had to be sent.

On September 2, 1936, the Cattells with their son David, five and a half, and daughter Barbara Anne, ten months, were on their way.[69]

PART III

EVERETT CATTELL

1936-1957

Carrie Wood

Alena Calkins

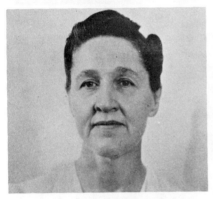

Dr. Ruth Hull Bennett

Everett Cattell

Cattells and Earles (Everett, David, Barbara, Catherine Cattell;
Catherine Jane, Elizabeth, Robert Earle)

Evangelists—Dayal Chand Singh, Stuti Prakash, Hira Singh

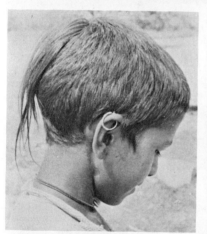

"The Chutiya"—Sacred Lock

Stuti Prakash, Puran Lall, Nathu Lall

Evangelistic Camping Team

Gulganj, the First Outstation

Dayal Chand, Dayawanti, Jonathan, baby, and Amos Singh, first family to move to an outstation

Stuti and Ramkibai Prakash with Khub Chand and family—first convert

Hira Lal with his family second convert

Dimina, Pyare Lal, Khub Chand, Halka — new converts

Hannah, converted mother of Pyare
Lal and Halka of Ghuara

Stuti Prakash preaching at a *Mela*

Halka, the first Ghuara convert

126

Bus travel in India

Rachel Banwar, Nowgong, and school children

Sukh Lal and children

The Mission car

127

Norma Freer

Rebecca, Carol Jean and Milton Coleman

Alena Calkins and Anna Nixon

Mary, Everett, Catherine
David and Barbara Cattell

Missionary children — Bonnie, Evelyn,
Priscilla, Phil, Ron, Mary Carol, Patricia

Missionary children — Joe, Carol, Judy,
Phil, visitor, Anne, Mary; Front: Byron,
Ron, Kathy, Ruth

Robinson family—Anne, Cliff, Betty,
Judy, Byron, Ruth

Banker family—Evelyn, Bonnie,
Bruce, Ruth Ellen, Max

DeVol family—Joe, Dr. Ezra, Priscilla, Phil, Frances, Patricia

Hess family—
Kathy, Ron, Esther,
Bob, Dan, Betsy

Bijawar Church and residence of Pastor

Komal Das Lall,
maintenance superintendent

Christians' homes in Chhatarpur

Ladies' bungalow in Chhatarpur

Goddard Memorial transformed
into a home for Anna Nixon

Office buildings in Chhatarpur

Wedding of Chunni Lall and Manorma Bai with Victor Mangalwadi,
Everett Cattell, and Rebecca Coleman

Ghuara Church

David Cattell
and a Python

Chunni Lall and Manorma Bai with
Ghuara school children

Katherine Skipper Memorial Station

Amarmau Station-Bungalow, Hospital, Chapel and other buildings

Wives and children of Ghuara converts with Frances DeVol and Catherine Cattell

Phillip, Silas, and
Samuel Masih
of Ghuara

132

Prem Das and Nanni Bai and other converts of Dhamora

Evangelist Bhagwati Bai D. Das with Ram Bai—Adult Literacy, Gulganj

Bilwar Christians with Robinson family

Victor and Kusum Mangalwadi family
(three of seven children)

Stuti Prakash and Ramki Bai
and four children

George Masih

Komal Das Lall and family

Daniel and Dr. Grace Jones Singh

Nathu Lall, father
of Komal Das

Interdining

Mission Council 1957 (Everett, Betty, Frances, Norma, Anna, Catherine, Milton, Rebecca, Cliff, Esther, Bob, Dr. Ezra)

Joint Council 1957 with Indian leaders and missionary children

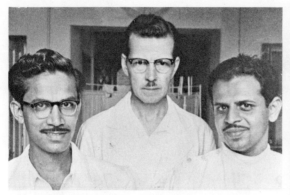

Drs. Mategaonker, DeVol, Shrisunder

Pharmacist
Pratap Singh Brown

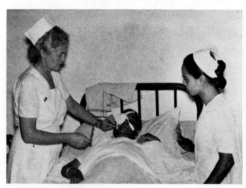

Frances DeVol with nurse and patient

Norma Freer,
Business Manager

Samson and Tabitha
Huri Lal and family,
Navin, Vinod, Sumand
(now headmistress of
Christian English
School)

Operating room — Gabriel Massey, I. William, Sarah Nath, and a male nurse

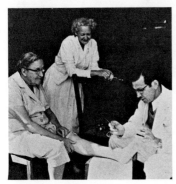

Dr. Ezra and
Frances with
Corrie ten
Boom

Kathy
Thompson
with nurse and
patient

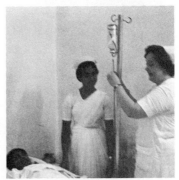

The Hospital Staff

137

DeVols and Fellowship Hall, 1974

Imelda Shaw, who
took Frances' place

Dr. D. W. Mategaonker and family—
who took Dr. Ezra's place

K. D. Lall,

Gabriel Massey

Stuti Prakash,

on way to

U.S.A.

Woodstock School in Mussoorie with Himalayas in the background where children attended and Rebecca Coleman sometimes taught

Rebecca and Orphans—Benjamin, Salomi, Phulmani, Kamlapat Coleman

Visitors Chester G. Stanley and Ralph Comfort "Riding High"

Vishwas Nath and family

Carol Jean, Rebecca and Milton Coleman

Youth Rally 1957 (Sixth row, left to right) Milton Coleman, Vijay Prakash, Victor Crozier, Bob Hess, Pyare Lal Brown, Norma Freer, Helen Rose, Hizikiel Singh; (Fifth row) Eric Massey, Satish Hanuq, Henry Massey, Daniel Bodhan, Yakub Nath, Amos Singh, Satish Lall, Kripal Singh, Prasan K. Prakash, Victor Lal; (Fourth row) Kusum Kumari Prakash, Mrs. Das, Irene Prakash, Anugrah Nath, Dolly, Marina Karsael, Phyllis Das, Jaiwanti Karsael, Adeline Nath, Rajli Singh, Premlata Hanuq, Padmawati Brown; (Third row) Glorious Singh, Shantiel Nath, Benjamin Lall, Wilson Prasad, Harish K. D. Lall, Jonathan Singh, Kamlapat Coleman, Yakub Daniel, Sunil Paul, Jawan; (Second row) Veer Singh Karsael, Vinod Lal, Navin Lal, Vishwas Nath, Jashwant Karsael, Santosh Das, Jawan, Benji; (First row) Pauline Brown, Alena Singh, Salomi Coleman, Hilda Das Lal, Phulmani Coleman, Pauline James, Dorothy Singh, Pramodini Singh, Saroj Das.

Changing the Course

"I have chosen you, and ordained you, that ye should go and bring forth fruit, and that your fruit should remain." John 15:16

Cattells Chosen for India

Everett and Catherine Cattell had some advantages over other couples who had gone to India. They knew the Mission Board well; both of them had grown up in its shadow. Everett Cattell's Quaker ancestry could be traced back to Margaret Fell, and a maternal grandmother far back had been put to death for saying, "No," to the question, "If a mouse ate the holy consecrated bread served at the altar would it be holy?" His parents were active in promoting missions and his father had been the treasurer of the Missionary Board.

Catherine Cattell, the daughter of Ohio Yearly Meeting's missionaries in China, Drs. George and Isabella DeVol, and sister of Drs. Charles and W. Ezra DeVol, was from earliest memories fully aware of the importance of the Mission Board in her life. They felt secure as missionaries of the Friends Foreign Missionary Society of Ohio Yearly Meeting. The Mission Board knew them well and had chosen them for the work to which they felt called. There would never be a time when they would feel, as had the earlier young couples, that they were not at liberty to share their concerns directly with the Board.

The Mission Board had put in writing that Everett Cattell was to be made chairman of the India Mission Council as early as possible.[1] Great faith undergirded their eagerness to get on with the task, in spite of — or perhaps even because of — the difficulties. They approached India cautiously, however, for there was no way of telling just how the Indian people, and particularly Esther Baird, would receive them. To win her understanding was perhaps their greatest challenge. They had prayed many years for India and especially for Esther Baird. She was a member of First Friends in Cleveland. For the past five years Everett Cattell as her pastor was aware of the hurt even though he agreed with the report.[2] His prayer for her was well worded by Louise Ellett in her first letter to the Cattells: "I just hope that you will be able to brighten up her sunset years as if you were her very own dear children, and that much of the bitterness and sorrow of the past years will just be gone."[3]

Esther Baird and Alena Calkins met the Cattells in Harpalpur when they arrived on October 12, 1936, and the people gave them a royal welcome.[4] Later Catherine entertained the two missionaries by recounting the surprises when she boarded the train in Bombay. No long corridors and aisles, but little compartments with four long seats facing in pullman fashion, one above another, was where they were to sleep. "We had reserved two lower seats and one upper. A Hindu man had the fourth seat. It was quite an experience laying our bedding out on the seats for the night with the Hindu right there." It would soon be no shock at all. But settling into the bungalow that night Catherine found other shocking things. "I had quite a time finding bugs and things . . . a poisonous centipede about six inches long and another small one, a toad in our bedroom, and a lizard on a curtain . . . a picture completely riddled during the night with white ants, and . . . a grasshopper in the baby's Karo bottle."[5]

Two days later with relaxation and peace Esther Baird noted in her diary, "The whole family fitting in nicely," and later, "Cattells seem delighted with everything."[6] They all settled down to live in the big bungalow together.[7]

Exploring Possibilities in Evangelism

After being introduced to all the workers and seeing all the stations, Cattells sought opportunity to discuss openly the issue of who was in charge, particularly of evangelism. About a week after arrival the matter came up, and Everett Cattell was quick to recognize in what seemed like casual conversation his opportunity to set things into clear perspective. He quickly let Esther Baird know he was there to learn and that he had no criticism of the past. He looked forward to working out plans for the future under her guidance.[8] This opened the door to discussions that proved to be extremely creative. Their first thought was to concentrate evangelism around Gulganj, but Esther Baird came up with another plan. For many years the Mission had conducted a school and a Sunday school among Nowgong Chamars. A short time before, a Chamar man educated in the former school had come to Esther Baird and offered a room if she would supply a teacher to open the school again. The Church had sent Lachhman Singh to teach there, and he soon had about twenty-three children in the school and fifty attending Sunday school.[9] Esther Baird had been doing a lot of thinking about the revolutionary ideas presented by J. Waskom Pickett, Dr. Donald McGavran, and Mr. Singh from their study of mass movements. She had heard them at a conference earlier that year and came to know that between 7,000 and 15,000 converts were coming into Christianity per month, mostly from the depressed classes. The reports were encouraging, and Esther Baird noted these converts were coming from districts where there had been forty or fifty years of faithful seed sowing. So she was filled again with hope and a sense of responsibility resting upon the Friends Mission. She suggested that there should be a concentrated evangelistic campaign among the Nowgong Chamars—a truly depressed outcaste group—with all evangelists cooperating under the leadership of Everett Cattell.[10]

Everett was both surprised and delighted. The approach was so different from any past mission thrust that one wonders where the idea really originated. The fact that Esther Baird put it into words and laid the plans to carry it out caused all the evangelists to give enthusiastic cooperation.[11]

Fresh hope and earnest prayer swept through the Mission and the Church, and among the evangelists. One can surely understand the heart longing of the newest missionary who wrote:

> I am working and praying to get the evangelists out of a defeatest attitude which is satisfied with having merely faithfully witnessed and does not seem to put people under pressure to accept. If there is no result visible, it will confirm their underlying feeling that nothing can be done . . . . If, however, we should have some genuine converts, or even one solid one who would stand persecution, it would put new life in the whole Mission . . . . I trust my motives are unmixed. If it is God's will that we should wait yet longer through lean years, I trust I may go with Him patiently . . . . I find my heart greatly yearning over these Chamars.[12]

Chamars and the Mass Movement

Chamars were entitled to take all cows that died and use the hides for making shoes. They also ate the carrion. This, and the fact that they drank heavily, added to their depressed condition. Yet those Chamars had just made Everett a pair of shoes he was proud to wear. Everett was amazed to find such skill and artistry hidden in their rough hands and such keen intelligence in their faces. The stench from the half tanned leather and the cramped quarters of their small hovels did not mar their pride in the workmanship of creating each pair of shoes.[13]

In other areas Chamars were the backbone of the mass movement. Everett learned from others who had made a thorough study of mass movements that such outcaste groups as the Chamars made up nearly a third of the Hindu population. Since they were considered too low to be in any of the four caste groups, they had no privileges and were in that sense not really Hindus. Some of them wanted complete severance from the Hindu fold and were looking for another religion guaranteeing equal status.[14]

Dr. Ambedkar, a highly educated lawyer from the Mahar untouchable caste, called upon the 70,000,000 outcastes to come out of Hinduism en masse and throw off the yoke that had held them in bondage for centuries. In 1932 Mahatma Gandhi opposed this with a fast unto death. Dr. Ambedkar, much against his will and conscience, finally gave in to save Gandhi's life.[15] Gandhi wanted to fight against untouchability from within Hinduism. Therefore, he gave the untouchables the name of Harijans — people of God — and clearly sought to lift their status but did not want them leaving the Hindu fold.

Many of the outcaste leaders urging a break with Hinduism, however, showed a strong interest in Christianity. Before precipitating such a movement, however, they wanted at least a million followers.[16]

The Chamars in Nowgong were some of these Harijans, plagued with untouchability and oppression of the worst kind. In them Everett Cattell saw an unparalleled opportunity for Christ and His Gospel.

The meetings held in the Chamar Mohalla for eight consecutive nights in late November were in one sense a great success. The evangelists cooperated with enthusiasm and burden. The messages clearly pointed out the meaning of sin, the life of Christ, the remedy for lostness, and the way of salvation. When the call for decision was given, the issues were clearly understood, and the leaders stepped forward and gave their answer. Nothing like it had ever happened in Bundelkhand before. The leaders stated clearly that they honored Christ and they would even pray in His name; but to break caste was asking too much, and they would not. Even in their depressed state, they preferred to remain as they were, for it was their custom, they said, incorporated into their race hundreds of years before.[17]

Discouraged though the evangelistic party must have been — for they were expecting miracles — Esther Baird was pleased and showed her wisdom and compassion by appointing Everett Cattell in full charge of all mission evangelistic work.[18] The evangelists got oxcarts, tents, and supplies and took off to far-flung villages for the whole month of December, preaching in the manner they knew so well. Later they followed up five Chamar men who showed unusual interest during the campaign.[19] Everett and Catherine, in India less than three months, busied themselves with the study of the language and followed up response among the young people during a recent prayer meeting. Twelve of them had come to the altar, and the Cattells started Bundelkhand's first Christian Endeavor Society to help them grow.[20]

Easter in India

Cattells' first Easter in Bundelkhand was unique in that three holidays occurred simultaneously. The Hindus celebrated *Holi*, beginning with a bonfire and lots of laughter, drinking, and revelry. They followed this with a few days of riotous mud throwing and color spraying until dozens together reeled down the streets with purple, green, and orange faces and multicolored clothing splashed with dye that would not wash out. The Mohammedans celebrated *Moharrum* after a forty-day fast honoring Hassen, a son of Mohammed who was killed in battle. They had spent weeks making beautifully decorated paper *tajiyas* — tombs and horses. At the celebration they carried them in procession with sword dancers and acrobats following, and everyone shouting "Haseen," as they buried the *tajiyas* in the sand at the river bank. *Easter* lacked the noise and glitter of these festivals, and there were very few Christians in Bundelkhand to celebrate. In Nowgong the band of believers climbed to the top of a nearby hill just before sunrise. They reached the top just as the sun peeped over the horizon setting the heavens aglow. Everett played the violin with Catherine at the little folding organ. "He Arose" and "When Morning Gilds the Skies" filled the air. The Indians in their *dhotis* and *saris* looked as if they could have stepped out of Bible times, and something of the excitement of the first Easter morning was captured.[21]

Out in Chhatarpur, Alena met with the people in the corner of the Christian cemetery, where they watched the red glow in the east grow more vivid and sang of the resurrection in the first service of its kind ever held in Chhatarpur.[22] The following year Carrie Wood in Harpalpur led the Christians to a hilltop half a mile away in spite of the fact that even at sunrise the temperature registered 108° F.[23]

Winning through to Greater Independence for the Church

Right after Esther Baird's 75th birthday celebration, Cattells went to Landour for five months of language study. They looked back on their first few months in India with a great degree of thanksgiving. Relationships were good and two deep concerns in Walter Williams's report had been tackled with unity in the Council. The first was persuading some Christians on the compound to go live in the villages, and the second was the need of greater self-support. The total dependence of Christians on the

Mission had alarmed the Board. Everett Cattell, realist that he was, felt that settling the Christians on their own land was absolutely vital for any permanence. He also sensed that until Christians stood on their own feet there could be no hope of developing village churches. Christians had to learn how to earn their own living. Some would be evangelists, but not all.

The Council approved both of the ideas — putting evangelists out in villages and also developing self-support. Many failures in such attempts in the past, however, inhibited the senior missionaries from making any suggestions as to how it could be done. During his first year in language school, Everett wrestled with this problem, talking with other experienced missionaries gathered in Landour. He also read all relevant books at hand and discussed them with Catherine and also with the authors themselves, such as Bishop J. Waskom Pickett and Dr. Donald McGavran.[24]

Setting Priorities Straight

The Cattells surrounded themselves with other missionaries seriously dealing with similar problems. While Catherine coped with the needs of the children — infected cuts, malaria, measles, whooping cough[25] — and ran the household, she also managed to let her "over the teacup" hospitality show in entertaining a host of interesting guests who stayed to discuss these problems far into the night. Everett soon discerned in his discussions and reading two diametrically opposed approaches to missions. One approach was that evangelism has priority and you must evangelize first and then provide social services through the indigenous Church. The other was that evangelism must be coupled with a "ministry of helpfulness." Leaders like Pickett agreed with the first, saying this second approach used social services as evangelistic "bait" and tended to create resistance to the Gospel. He wrote:

> Let it not be understood that we have come from this study with any convictions against a ministry to social and economic needs. Rather, we see more clearly because of this study that no ministry is fully Christian which ignores such needs. But this lesson is written across the whole experience of the Church with India's poorest people, the Depressed Classes, that no ministry to them in Christ's name arouses their hopes, and commands their faith, unless it presents the Gospel of the love of God making full provision for the needs of the soul.[26]

Everett Cattell weighed these two approaches. It would be comparatively easy to start a new mission with "evangelism first." But with schools, an orphanage, a hospital, and a compound Christian community already established, where could a new beginning flourish? Should the Harpalpur school, the orphanage, and the compound be closed out?

These were questions he began to explore not only with leaders in India but also with the Missionary Board.[27]

Walter Williams responded first:

The call of a Christian man or woman to be an Ambassador for Christ to China or India or anywhere else goes . . . beyond tying up bruises, beyond teaching English and western science to boys and girls, beyond building up cordial relationships with suspicious races . . . . The souls of men are dying, lost and without hope and without God. If we are not set for witness to the transforming power of saving faith in Christ NOW in this generation, then, I find in the New Testament commission and Church History no sufficient reason for the sacrifice entailed in setting up Missions to the end of the earth.[28]

Claude Roane echoed the same sentiment:

We are not running a social service bureau — a bread line — or an employment bureau — we are there to serve — but we are there definitely for the conversion and sanctification of those people. Make this your objective always.[29]

The Excitement of Travel in India

After finishing the first year of language study, Everett came back to Nowgong with a few new specific ideas of how to put through changes suggested by Walter Williams and approved by Mission Council. Catherine stayed on in Landour for a few weeks with David and Barbara. Then with courage and no doubt a great deal of pain, she left David in boarding school (as she herself in childhood had also been left many times), and like a veteran packed her things and, choosing eight coolies, bargained them down to a reasonable price for carrying down the hill the bedding rolls, lunch baskets, suitcases, and the baby's buggy. In a basket tied to his back another coolie carried Barbara, her sleepy little head nodding from side to side, as Catherine started her first long trip alone in India. As they passed through Landour bazaar, Catherine noted again the variety of India's people strolling through the mall. There were coolies hardly seen under their unbearable loads; bejeweled rajas and maharajas riding horses or in rickshaws; Punjabi women in baggy pants and knee length dresses with silk scarves about their heads walking a few steps behind their stately bearded husbands, and long hair done up in colorful turbans; Moslem women hidden in *burkahs*; Parsee women with cultured charm in expensive silk saris; *sadhus* — holy men — in saffron robes; Tibetans in grey Buddhist robes. What a variety of people in India, all in need of Christ![30]

The Return of Ruth Hull Bennett and Carrie Wood

Catherine and Barbara reached Nowgong just in time to welcome Carrie Wood and Dr. Ruth Hull Bennett and her ten-month old son, Claude

Fraser, as they arrived September 28, 1937.[31] That Claude Bennett, Ruth's husband, had been willing to allow his wife to return with their infant son for a term of three years amazed everyone. Sitting over cups of tea and enjoying the breeze of a warm Setpember morning, the returning missionaries brought news of Board appointees — John Earle's brother Robert, and his wife, Elizabeth, daughter of Charles and Catherine Stalker, with their four-year old daughter, Catherine Jane. Everett was thrilled with the anticipation of having another man on the field to assist in the work. The others listened eagerly as Everett shared what he had been able to put into effect during recent months.

Dayal Chand Singh in Gulganj

Dayal Chand Singh with two orphan boys very reluctantly consented to move to Gulganj, a point from which they could minister to sixty or more surrounding villages. Living twenty-two miles away from all other Christians frightened them. Dayal Chand was an orphan who had always known the shelter of the compound. In the village he would be in the heart of Hinduism, where caste would separate him from fellowship. No one would eat with him or allow him to draw water from the village wells. Festivals and feasts in the village would all be connected with idolatry and he would not be able to participate. The only playmates for his children would be those who practiced idol worship. Women would ostracize his wife, and the loneliness at times would be unbearable. Even so, he eventually accepted the challenge and moved his entire family to Gulganj. A beginning toward decentralization had been made. Lachhman Singh and family later joined them there and opened a dispensary.[32]

The New Bible School

Carrie Wood listened attentively as Everett told of the new Bible / Vocational School, as she would be teaching there. The idea was to help the students earn part of their fees as they learned a trade, and the school was opened July 27, 1937, with eight students. They met in the Goddard Memorial Dispensary building. Parents were not pleased with too much emphasis on work, and due to lack of teachers the vocational part languished.[33]

The Hospital

Dr. Bennett was delighted to be back in Chhatarpur and pleased with evidences of change she found in the hospital. Hospital Sunday giving had increased 175 percent. The nursing school under Alena Calkins's direction was turning out pharmacists and nurses with the highest grades in all of mid-India. Apart from major surgery, Dr. Grace Jones was managing the work well. Through strict isolation, she had prevented the spread of a cholera epidemic. "It could not be," the city doctors said even though she had a slide to prove it.[34]

Esther Baird's Last Days in India

A gift from the King George V Jubilee Celebration fund, requested by Dr. Bennett during her first term in India to build a darkroom, finally arrived, and Esther Baird went to work. "A busy and enjoyable day. Seemed like old times," she recorded as she got into the bricks and mortar again.[35] Determined to leave everything in good repair, she bustled from place to place to check all properties. In Gulganj she supervised building a dispensary and rooms for two families. With Pancham Singh's help, she put up a wall around Nowgong cemetery and went over all repairs needed in Chhatarpur and Harpalpur. "Pancham Singh most helpful. Work going nicely. Happy in my soul. Busy day here and there amongst the people," Esther jotted down as the days went by.[36]

Early in the new year another honor came to her. The Nowgong Political Agent recommended her name as recipient of the gold Kaiser-i-Hind medal on Coronation day, May 12, 1937. This medal was awarded only by the King on recommendation of the Secretary of State in India. She returned the silver medal received in 1930 and in an impressive ceremony at the Agency was decorated by the Aide-de-Camp to the agent to the Governor of Central India. The gold Kaiser-i-Hind medal was an oval-shaped badge with the royal cypher on one side and on the other the words, "Kaiser-i-Hind for Public Service in India." The gold in it was worth about $60. On her return to the orphanage, the band met her with music and garlands. This honor at the close of forty-six years of service in India seemed most appropriate.[37]

Esther Baird looked forward to taking her last vacation in Kashmir with friends, but unfortunately, her friends became ill. Alena Calkins joined her a month later, but she also became ill. Even so, the beauty of the place would always remain with her. She enjoyed the breathtaking winding road into the valley, as they climbed a tremendous ridge, zigzagging up through mountains, past terraced rice fields, springs, waterfalls, across rivers, past snowcapped mountains and fir trees, and finally through Banihal Pass, which divides Jammu State from Kashmir (both under the same maharaja). Then they plunged into 220 feet of darkness and came out of the tunnel to view the beautiful vale of Kashmir 4,000 feet below. She would never forget Nishat and Shalimar, the Moghul gardens with their playing fountains, built more than 300 years ago by Mohammedan kings; or the brief view of *Nanga Parbat*—the eighth highest mountain in the world, seen from Gulmarg.[38]

The Changing of the Guard

The day set for Esther Baird to step down and for Everett Cattell to become Mission Council chairman was preceded by a lot of groundwork. She was confident that he was the right one for the work.[39] So in a Council meeting October 26, 1937, with no fanfare, Esther Baird expressed appreciation for Everett Cattell's cooperation during the past year of her leadership and passed on the torch. He returned the compliment and, after taking the chair, led the Council in an expression of appreciation for her remarkable accomplishment during her years of faithful service.[40]

When Everett Cattell took over, the Mission was on a sound financial basis. Banking was done through the new Inter-Mission Business Office coupled with the American Express. Giving in America for the first time in ten years had exceeded the budget. Financial dependence of the Bundelkhand Friends Church, however, was as bad as it had ever been. The very next day in monthly meeting under the new mission chairman's prodding, the Church agreed to start taking offerings not just once a month at monthly meeting but rather every Sunday in all the main worship services. This immediately increased the giving 400 percent.[41]

Early in November through Bhakt Singh, a converted Sikh, Bundelkhand Friends Church was revived. All-night prayer meetings and four- to seven-hour services emphasized surrender. The results were very deep and practical. The Mission set up a firm salary scale covering increments, qualifications, and retirement benefits. A number of members began to tithe. Harpalpur and Chhatarpur as well as Nowgong set up monthly meetings — a step that delivered the Church from excessive missionary domination and started them on the way to self-government. The three monthly meetings then met four times a year for spiritual meetings, and in April they gave their annual reports. They developed a new discipline to meet their growing needs.[42] Visitors coming through often spoke at these meetings. At the first quarterly meeting Charles and Catherine Stalker spoke. Next came Jefferson and Helen Ford on their way from Kenya. Jefferson Ford was Kenya's representative to the International Missionary Council held in Tamberam, Madras. The Fords ministered to all the churches in Bundelkhand as they had done eighteen years previously.[43]

Esther Baird's Departure

The changes Esther Baird saw taking place in positive and well-planned ways represented no threat to the work to which she had given her life. Earlier there had been those who sought to bring about the same changes and had failed, but in the new context change represented growth and development, and Esther Baird was pleased. The time had come for her to leave India along with the Stalkers who sailed on March 10, 1938. Farewells covered several days. First, fourteen missionaries of the area surprised her with a day's picnic. English officers and their wives gave a surprise tea.[44] The Church and missionaries gathered in Chhatarpur to honor her. They met in the chapel, and Indian leaders from each station spoke in appreciation. They presented her with a silver vase engraved, "From your dear children." Dr. Ruth Bennett voiced the missionaries' appreciation, which would have contained these thoughts she wrote later:

> In my estimation Esther Baird was one of the most marvelous characters I have had the privilege of associating with. As a nurse she was wise in things medical, she was a capable builder, designing and directing the erection of all the lovely mission buildings, planning charming landscapes, overseeing all the types of work going on in the different mission stations and out in the field, highly respected in the local community and by many missionaries throughout India. She was honored by the British government with a Kaiser-i-Hind medal and was greatly loved by the Christian Indians, as well as by many Indians who were not Christians.[45]

The missionaries presented her with a blue georgette sari and the children gave her a water jug.[46]

Packing was agony, but with the help of others, it was finally finished by early morning the day of departure. There were so many precious things Esther Baird could not take. She did them up in parcels and gave them to her missionary colleagues. She could not wrap the piano given her by Colonel Tyrell of the Agency when he retired, but she did give it to Everett Cattell with the note that she dedicated it to "future harmony in the Mission."[47]

As she departed, the people in Nowgong loaded her down with their love, putting around her neck twenty-five garlands — one at a time. At Harpalpur all the people came to the train, and tears flowed when Puran Lal's little two-and-a-half-year-old daughter, Agnes, prayed that *Nani* (grandmother) would reach home all right.[48]

On the way home Esther Baird celebrated her 77th birthday at Honolulu, was met in San Francisco by the Coffins, and arrived in Los Angeles to be welcomed at the Friends Women's Union Missionary Conference at Whittier, where she sat with thirty-nine other missionaries on the platform and gave thanks to God.[49]

| # Battling for Priorities

*"I have appeared unto thee for this purpose . . .
delivering thee from the people . . . unto whom now I
send thee, to open their eyes, and to turn them from
darkness to light, and from the power of Satan unto
God." Acts 26:16-18*

Surveying the Field

Everett Cattell, firmly in charge, boarded a rickety bus with an inexperienced driver and started on a long journey to attend the Burki Mela at Ajaigarh. Between Panna and his destination, the road doubled back on itself fourteen times, and at one point they had an accident, killing a buffalo. On reaching the top of the 1,000-foot hill, he observed the milling crowds of some 12,000 people who had climbed to this peak to bathe in the small tank made of quarrying stone brought there centuries ago to build a fort.

These were his people, the ones to whom he was responsible for bringing the Gospel, living in that area called Bundelkhand—two hundred miles long and a hundred miles wide. There were no other people to bring them to Christ except the Friends Mission. Camping teams sent into this area of Bundelkhand had found two responsive groups: a tribal group called Gonds, and the low-caste group, mostly Chamars.[1] To reach these people, Everett wondered, what strategy would please the Lord?

Dr. Donald McGavran's Findings

Strategies were drastically changing in India, and the Mission Council agreed to seek advice from one of the key men in the mass movement, Dr. Donald McGavran. He came, and his masterful evaluation of the Friends work, workers, and area both shocked and challenged Friends at home and abroad.[2] He discovered that the promise not to baptize written into the land deed for the hospital in Chhatarpur had been a real stumbling block to conversions. Non-Christians believed that the Mission held a helping, friendly nonconversion policy. Some evangelists, he pointed out, actually feared making a convert, lest he be put out of the State. "There must be a showdown," Dr. McGavran recommended. If not baptism, then some public declaration before the people of the villages that a man had indeed become a Christian.

> The new convert must acknowledge Jesus *publicly* . . . as Savior and Lord, the sinless incarnation of God, the only incarnation of God; the Bible . . . as the only Scripture; and the Church as a sacred brotherhood which every believer must join . . . . Furthermore, [the new convert should publicly promise] to attend Church, to read or hear read the Bible daily, to give [tithes] at harvest, and to marry children to Christians by Christian rites.[3]

The Friends Mission Council accepted this recommendation and agreed on *chutiya cutting* as the act to symbolize the break with Hinduism and *interdining* with Christians the symbol of being joined to the Church.[4]

Dr. McGavran's second recommendation was to encourage more teaching and preaching the Gospel with greater burden for the lost by all members of the Church. The Mission accepted this and joined in a "Week of Witness" sponsored by the Mid-India Regional Christian Council. People entered into this gladly. Even the doctors and nurses in the hospital went out when they were off duty to preach and to sell literature.[5]

The third recommendation called attention to the fact that only about one tenth of the budget went for evangelism. Several suggestions were made for cutting down in less significant areas or making them more self-supporting in order to have more money for hiring at least a dozen evangelists with village background.

The missionaries gulped when confronted with these statistics and suggestions, but they agreed to raise the evangelistic budget from 11 to 25 percent in the next three years.[6]

The fourth recommendation was key: Concentrate on the Chamars, who make up 15 to 20 percent of the population of Bundelkhand. Do extensive evangelism to locate responsive groups, then go into these areas for intensive camping. Spend three fourths of the time evangelizing the Chamars and one fourth the higher castes.

> Their gods, fears, marriage customs, sins, oppressions, relationships should be studied. Funeral feasts, weddings, *sabhas* (meetings) should be attended by Christians . . . . Each evangelist should get to know the names of at least 1,000 of them.

Though only about 120 of the 25,000 Chamars were literate, he felt a good supply of literature should be provided for them. He strongly urged that converts be kept in their villages at their old trades so that the movement would spread and village churches rooted in the land would be born. He expressed great hope that once the Chamars started coming, other depressed groups like the sweepers (Basors) and cowherds (Ahirs) would respond, too.[7]

The Challenge to Change

Everett Cattell, expecting some opposition from the missionaries and evangelists to these recommendations, was more than pleased by their unanimous and enthusiastic approval.[8] They, too, were longing for a move toward God throughout Bundelkhand. Alena Calkins put everyone's thoughts into words:

> The old idea . . . was to concentrate more on high caste people feeling that when they were converted the low castes would be sure to follow. The theory has not worked . . . . It has been found by concentrating more on low castes in many places they are being converted by the thousands and some high castes have followed. It does seem more biblical to work among the lowly and depressed.[9]

"The movement will start," said Dr. McGavran, "only when some man . . . is so convinced of the truth of the Christian message that he is willing to break with his caste and come apart."

Everett Cattell led the evangelistic team out immediately to find that man. Stuti Prakash and Dayal Chand Singh went to mass movement areas for firsthand observation of how evangelists dealt with new converts.[10] Everyone prayed, and they were encouraged in the new direction when the Tambaram International Conference openly backed the new strategy and declared that evangelism was the only sound basis for any missionary strategy.[11]

Death and Illness—Hindrances to Progress

All seemed set for advance, but the Mission had to stop to grieve. Harbi Bai, Dr. Grace Jones and Shanti Moti Lal's mother and Balla Bodhan's sister, died and was buried by her sister Rupiya Bai and brothers Prem Das and Mangalwadi. Nathu Lall's wife died, leaving him with six children. His eldest son, Komal Das Lall, had married that year, bringing a daughter-in-law into the home to help.[12]

Two cables from U.S.A. brought news that Everett's younger brother and also his maternal grandfather both had died suddenly.[13]

On February 14, 1939, Everett Cattell himself started down a path toward death. That day he entered Jhansi Hospital for a simple appendectomy, but with the first breath of anesthesia, the operation turned into a nightmare. Captain Cardis, a military doctor, assisted by Dr. Green and Alena Calkins, discovered an appendix grown fast to the intestine and liver. The operation went on for hours. Within three days Everett developed a dilated stomach from which few ever recover. The following week he hovered between life and death. Dr. Ruth Bennett rushed in from Chhatarpur for consultation, and Alena stayed on for ten days' night duty. The people in Bundelkhand Friends Church with one accord went to prayer.

Dr. Green discerned that more than the physical was involved and took shelter "under the precious blood." After ten days Everett began to eat again, but the battle was not over. The next week he had an abscess, and the week after that, phlebitis in his right leg. Bedsores from heat and pressure tortured him, and finally an intestinal obstruction seemed destined to take his life. The doctors saw no answer apart from more surgery, which they feared would be fatal. But God answered prayer, making surgery unnecessary, and the doctors sighed with hope.

When life was the darkest, Catherine bought two lawn chairs in which she planned to sit on the veranda with Everett as he recovered. She called these her "faith chairs." She watched with thankfulness as Everett began to move freely, then sit up in bed and reach for a pen to write his first letter home in two months. Four days later his temperature struck normal, and a few days later he moved to the bungalow and sat with Catherine on the veranda in the "faith chairs."[14]

Recuperation in Australia

The doctors all agreed that full recovery called for a bracing climate at a lower altitude than Landour, Mussoorie. They recommended a sea voyage to Australia. On May 14, 1939, Everett, Catherine, and Barbara set sail, leaving David in boarding in Woodstock School in Landour. Carrie Wood took over as acting superintendent.

The trip to Australia accomplished more than the Cattells dreamed possible. "He had started out an invalid able only to take a few steps supported with a cane," wrote Catherine. Even on the ship he had gained fifteen of the forty pounds he had lost while ill, and afterwards on a farm inland from Sydney about fifty miles in the exhilarating climate, he continued to gain. The rich milk, eggs, and farm products balanced with light exercise such as horseback riding and tennis brought increasing strength. The quiet atmosphere provided time for Bible study, reading, and writing. Everett summed up the experience in a letter to Claude A. Roane, who himself had just undergone a long illness:

> I know now that the doctors and attendants despaired of life again and again. I believe with all my heart that it was the work of the devil and that my getting well at all is the work of God . . . . The devil does not

like our Mission . . . . I am convinced we are due for a harvest here quite soon in the good grace of God. Some promises:

"But since to live means a longer stay on earth, that implies more labour for me — *and not unsuccessful labour.*" (Philippians 1:22, Weymouth's translation)

"He rescued us from so imminent a death . . . . He will still rescue us, while you lend us your aid by entreaty for us, so that thanksgivings may rise from many on our behalf for the boon granted to us at the intercession of many." (See 2 Corinthians 1:8-11.)

This business of the kingdom is all mixed up with sorrows and patient endurance . . . and a cross. May God keep me steady . . . . I can't forget that I came to India on the grain of wheat text. (John 12:24)

When they came back to India at the end of August, Everett seemed almost entirely himself again. After going to Landour to see David and to round out the doctors' orders, they returned to Bundelkhand October 4, 1939 — eight months after leaving — to a faithful, praying, and caring Church.[15]

The Evangelists' "Thorns in the Flesh"

Everett Cattell was able to get into camp for the first time since his illness on November 12, 1940. They went to Lugasi, a village of about 1,500 inhabitants, but the Chamars were out watching their crops and interest was only fair. So Everett Cattell turned his attention largely to the evangelists themselves, who all had deep needs. Bharos William had just come from the hospital with a bad knee. Hira Singh was absent at first because of fever. Tulsi Das was weak from fever. Stuti Prakash had been ill with dysentery and had been suffering much from opposition of some of the older men, especially Pancham Singh. Dayal Chand had just lost his little boy with tetanus. Johnson's wife was hopelessly insane. Shapan Nath was having trouble with friction between his mother and his wife. So a Bible study in the book of Hebrews brought comfort to them. The village was full of mongrel dogs, and one was mad. They sent a man who had been bitten to the hospital for antirabies injections, and Everett killed the dog.[16]

The Man — Khub Chand

Early in 1939, before his illness, Everett Cattell with Jefferson Ford and a full team of evangelists had gone to the village of Shivpura to start the new scheme of evangelism. They had tremendous response and stayed three weeks. In the end, instead of leaving a friendly village behind, they had left a group to face clearly the decision for or against Christ; and under pressure of a devil worshiper, the people turned Him down.[17] From there the Indian camping team went to Dhamora and again had a wonderful reception with six men vowing to become Christians — but not just yet.

Thirty-six families seemed ready to respond as soon as the leaders moved. The interest was higher than it had ever been, and even after Everett Cattell became ill, the evangelists kept on visiting those villagers. After Cattells returned from Australia, Everett sent the camping team into Dhamora again. Khub Chand, the most hopeful man, had two wives with children by each of them. Hope rippled through the whole Christian community on Christmas day when he, with his first wife, came to eat Christmas dinner with them. Was this their man?[18]

The Conversion of Khub Chand

For a while Khub Chand disappeared from his village but they found him again in Pipra. His second wife's baby had died, and Khub Chand had taken her back to her home in Lalitpur. Henceforth he was a man of one wife. He sat in the meetings the evangelists held in Pipra shaking with conviction. "This is worse than malaria," he said.[19]

The next place Khub Chand turned up was in Bijawar. There was a large group of Chamars there, and he was caught there in trouble with the law. He had uplift for Chamars in mind, but without permission he and two companions had gone into the villages around Bijawar and started collecting money in the name of the Bijawar Chamar leaders without their permission. The State, at the instigation of the Chamar leaders, arrested the three men and found they had collected a sum of Rs. 14 ($4). The Chamars soon came to have confidence in Khub Chand, bailed him out, and tried to have his case, which was set for March 31, 1941, dismissed. About a week before this, the camping team led by Stuti Prakash moved in, and Khub Chand came to the meetings. Stuti Prakash told a humorous story, picturing a man with his feet in two boats, unable to make up his mind which boat to choose. The boats pulled apart and the man fell into the pond. Looking at Khub Chand, Stuti Prakash asked how long he intended to continue in such a condition. Khub Chand jumped up and declared that he wanted both his feet in the one boat, and that was Christ. "Now what else do I need to do?" he asked. Stuti Prakash told him he had better cut off his *chutiya* (sacred lock of hair). He was willing to let Stuti do this, but there were no scissors. A shoemaker produced a knife, but Stuti was afraid he might cut Khub Chand's scalp; so he again asked for scissors.

"Give me that knife!" said Khub Chand. "I can do it myself." As soon as the knife was in his hand, he hesitated. He looked around on the Chamars and the evangelists gathered there, all waiting with baited breath. "Before I take this step, I want to pray first," he said. He bowed his head and asked God's help in making this great decision. Then with one resolute stroke he cut off the *chutiya*. There was a great stir, and about two hundred heads of families started talking at once about following in his steps. "When we come back from harvest," they promised, "we also will become Christian."[20]

Stuti Prakash burned up the twenty-four miles on his cycle to get to Everett Cattell in Chhatarpur with this news. Everett and Dayal Chand had been over in the Amarmau area. What rejoicing there was throughout the Mission! The man was found, or so it seemed. The big temptation that would come again and again would be his desire to be paid for his witness. The line between paying an evangelist to preach and a villager to witness was not always clear. But while Khub Chand waited for his trial, he continued to witness. He opened a night school for Chamars and taught them Bible stories, songs, and how to read.[21]

Three months later at quarterly meeting in Chhatarpur, Khub Chand and his wife with a new baby daughter in her arms received their certificates as probationary members of the Church. They signed the promises, accepting Jesus as Savior and Lord; the Bible as the only Scripture, with the promise to read or hear it every day; the Church as a sacred brotherhood with the promise to attend regularly. They promised to give at harvest and to marry their children by Christian rites.[22]

Khub Chand's Witness in Bijawar

Khub Chand was determined to live with his wife and baby daughter in Bijawar, remake a house there for a chapel, and win the Chamars to the Lord. He had other children still in Dhamora with relatives. His dream was to make his living by his trade as a mason and teach reading to Chamar boys at night. His work was far from easy. Right in the midst of a service hard-looking men with heavy whips representing the State sometimes stamped in and broke up the meeting. One night they demanded that twenty Chamar men come immediately to put out a jungle fire. Another time they took them to carry tins of oil. Being outcaste, they had to go. They received no pay. This system was called *begar* and outcastes had no protection against it. Khub Chand suffered with them, and his plan did not work out. When he and his wife and baby were found to be near starvation, Everett Cattell gave him some mason's work in Chhatarpur, in the building of the nurses' home, and Khub Chand then moved back to his own village in Dhamora only five miles from Chhatarpur.[23] He continued to visit Bijawar with the evangelists, hoping the people present the night of his conversion would turn to Christ. Ten of them did come to Bharos William, who was stationed in Bijawar as a pastor-evangelist. These ten said they would step forward as soon as their leader, Hizari Lal, was ready, but Hizari Lal was full of excuses, and the whole group were still involved in idol worship. They all got drunk at *Dasara* festival and followed the little boys with spears sticking through their cheeks to appease the goddess *Bhumani*.[24]

Khub Chand's "House of Worship" in Dhamora

Back in Dhamora, Khub Chand set his house in order and began paying off his debts in order to gain credibility with some of his fellow caste members.[25] He also built a place of Christian worship. It was only a platform made of mud, 18' x 22', with a wall at one end behind the preacher high enough to block the vision beyond him. On this he painted a red cross. Cattells rode in an ox-tonga the five miles from Chhatarpur to Dhamora for the dedication service of this roofless church.

"The dedication was one of the most impressive services I have ever attended anywhere," wrote Everett later. By the light of flickering *diyas* outlining the platform, Khub Chand played his handmade coconut violin and sang his original Christian songs to fit Chamar tunes. Pastor Roberts of Nowgong spoke of the dedication of Solomon's temple, and Stuti Prakash, using a chanting method dearly loved by villagers, delivered a powerful message. Bhuriya, Khub Chand's eleven-year-old daughter, home from boarding school in Nowgong, read the Scripture. Khub Chand's chest must have swelled a good bit, for he had fought with his relatives — even his wife — to send her to school instead of getting her married.[26]

A great service was held at the "house of worship" in Dhamora on Christmas day. Two hundred Christians from Nowgong and Chhatarpur marched into the village carrying banners, singing, and exalting Christ.[27]

Early in 1942 Khub Chand's father on his death bed repented of his sins and cut off his *chutiya*. Relatives were horrified, for they believed that sacred lock of hair was the only place from which his soul could leave his body, and with it gone he would be condemned to eternal torment. But he died in peace, and his wife also believed.[28]

A Chamar named Siddhu from Nowgong went to Dhamora to see this roofless church and to hunt for a wife for his son. He had known about Christianity for a long time. From the time Everett Cattell was ill, he had started praying, but he did not have the courage to defy his caste and come out as a Christian as had Khub Chand. Siddhu's son, Nathu, attended Nowgong Christian School and secretly determined to become a Christian when he became of age. Siddhu attended a Christian service in Dhamora's roofless church and for the first time saw what Christianity could be like off a mission compound. He made the arrangement for Nathu to marry Raja Bai, the daughter of Khub Chand's elder brother. He knew nothing about the times Raja Bai had listened attentively to Christian stories told by Catherine Cattell or about the time she told Catherine that she would be a Christian when she grew up. Nathu and Raja Bai had never met each other, but their marriage was decided that day.[29]

The Conversion of Ram Dulari

Another convert came knocking at the door of the Mission. Ram Dulari Bai was of the clerks' caste and was an educated and intelligent woman. Her situation, however was deplorable. Her own husband had sold her for $60 to a married man; she had adopted a ten-year-old daughter, and life seemed very mixed up. Alena Calkins befriended her and won her to Christ at Christmas, 1940. The little daughter was put into the Nowgong boarding school, and Ram Dulari took shelter with the missionaries. First with Alena in Chhatarpur, next with Carrie Wood in Harpalpur, then with Catherine Cattell in Camp far beyond Bijawar in Deora, she sought to escape a frustrated search.[30] Later one evening she was abducted from Alena Calkins's house by the man who bought her. The police were called, and Ram Dulari, who had been beaten, chose before the officers to go back to the man. He took her away, and Ram Dulari was never heard from again.[31] The Political Agent took the adopted daughter from the mission school, and in spite of her bright Christian testimony, placed her in an *Arya Samajist* orphanage.[32]

Conversions were few, and the loss of any one of them brought grief to the missionaries like the loss of a loved one. Response was slower than expected, but there was no letting up on plans for church growth in the future. It was clear to the missionaries that preparation for such growth was double-pronged. There had to be new converts and the establishment of strong village churches. But prior to that, the church members, who stood as models of what Christianity actually was, needed to be revived, cleansed, and inspired with vision. The new strategy began, therefore, with revival in the Church.[33]

CHAPTER
XIII

Serving with Love

"May the Lord make your love increase and overflow for each other and for everyone else."
1 Thessalonians 3:12 (NIV)

Dr. Bennett's Dream for India's Villages

Perhaps the best example of Christian love seen and understood by the villagers was the healing service of the hospital and the dispensary in Gulganj. "There are probably few villages in Bundelkhand in which the name of our hospital has not spread," Dr. Ruth Bennett wrote in 1940.[1]

Her vision for the area was broad. She envisioned the permeation of modern medicine into the vast areas of Bundelkhand where superstition and malpractice held sway. She did not object to the practice of *Aryuvedic* medicine, which was an ancient form in India based on Sanskrit teachings and dealing with herbs, or to the *Unani* system based on Arabic medicine practiced by Moslems. But often the *Viad* who practiced these systems in Bundelkhand had received no training and failed to hold up the tradition. In untrained hands these systems deteriorated into superstitious practices.

Dr. Bennett's dream was that while keeping the hospital going in Chhatarpur, she would also train a medical team to work shoulder to shoulder with evangelists and teachers in the villages. To live acceptably with one's neighbors in the villages demonstrating throughout the year the value of simple hygenic measures while taking part in village life would help immensely in winning the villages, she felt. "Withal, our goal does not stop short of bringing each individual to Him who came that they might have life and have it more abundantly." Dr. Bennett backed fully Everett L. Cattell's repeated requests to the Board to send out Dr. Ezra and Frances DeVol for this work.[2]

163

Dr. Bennett's Departure from India

The pull to stay and fulfill the dream was strong, but the time had come for Dr. Bennett to return home. The importance of the medical work can only be measured by the three-year sacrifice of Dr. Bennett and her husband to the work. Claude Fraser, her little son, was neither walking nor talking when he left America. In India, he loved his pony, Dobhin, given him by a French woman, but he could not remember his father. He went through his first two years quite well, but before his third birthday, he fell off a veranda and broke his right arm. Soon after that amoebic dysentery "took away his round, rosy cheeks," Alena said.[3] Then his fever shot up to 105° F.[4] He recovered from that, and back to normal, he fell and again broke his right arm. A month later his cast was taken off, and he fell and broke it again. Under anesthetic he got another cast, which he had to wear as he left for the U.S.A.[5]

That summer Dr. Grace Jones went to study surgery under Sir Henry Holland in Kashmir, and Dr. Bennett managed the hospital alone. One hot night she also became ill. As she sat down on a bamboo stool for a moment to rest, she was suddenly stung by a scorpion—"a painful and stimulating experience," she wrote Alena Calkins.[6]

On July 26, 1940, Dr. Bennett and Claude Fraser, loaded with gifts and gratitude and accompanied by Alena Calkins as far as Bombay, left for the U.S.A. Even to this day people who were in Bundelkhand in 1940 still remember the cheerful helpfulness, skill, love, and Christian example of Dr. Ruth Hull Bennett.[7]

The Development of the Hospital under Dr. Grace Jones

The very next week after Dr. Bennett's departure, Dr. Grace Jones on her own performed her first major operation. Alena Calkins acted as assistant surgeon, and everything went well. Next, they coped with Balla Bodhan's typhoid and pneumonia, and then with each other as in turn both Dr. Grace and Alena came down with serious illnesses. Carrie Wood came down with typhoid and had to be moved from Harpalpur to Chhatarpur, where she stayed three months to recover. Everett Cattell became severely ill twice, and his unusual complications always taxed the ingenuity of the doctors. This time streptococci infection and intestinal trouble plagued him. Catherine also suffered from recurring bouts with amoebic dysentery. Dr. Grace applied her skills to keep them alive and going.[8]

Hospital Sunday donations increased annually. From these gifts the hospital bought a wheelchair, Fairbanks baby scales, and a moveable wash basin rack for the children's ward. They were thankful for the promise of a nurses' home for which Esther Baird raised the money. She sent $390 immediately, but because of the war, they could not begin building immediately.[9] Within two years, however, they had gathered the materials, and then Everett Cattell and Komal Das Lall — assistant in building and maintenance — put in twelve septic tanks and completed a very well-built nurses' home. They connected the hospital buildings with state power and put in fans.[10]

Dr. McMasters, 69, who had developed a 100-bed hospital in Indore, had just retired and came for a year to assist Dr. Grace before leaving India. Like Esther Baird, she also received the Kaiser-i-Hind medal the year she became seventy. She and Dr. Grace Jones did a great deal in preventative medicine and in teaching child care. She nipped a cholera epidemic in the bud. The hospital had more patients than ever and became 28 percent self-supporting. When she retired from Chhatarpur, Dr. Luke of Kerala, a recent graduate of Ludhiana Christian Medical College, joined Dr. Grace Jones.[11]

Personnel for Development of Nurses' Training

Alena Calkins pursued the development of nurses' training. She became an examiner for the mid-India Board of Nurses and in 1941 traveled 1,900 miles by train and bus to examine twenty-seven third-year nurses.[12] Right at the time training opportunities were at a peak, Alena's furlough came due and there was no one to replace her. Arrangements had been made for Elisabeth Earle of OMS International to fill that place during Alena's absence. She left U.S.A. for India and traveled on the same ship as Anna Nixon, a member of Kansas Yearly Meeting of Friends from Colorado who, on graduating from Cleveland Bible College, was asked by the Friends Mission Board to go to India. She had been appointed in June 1940, but because of the war, visa, passport, and sailing problems, she had been delayed until November 9, 1941. Elisabeth Earle and Anna Nixon became friends as they sailed from San Francisco to Honolulu, and from there to Manila in blackout and in convoy with two destroyers and a cruiser. Before their ship left Manila, Pearl Harbor was bombed and war declared. The passengers were asked to leave the ship, and they sent home a cable to their respective mission boards: "Delayed, Manila." The Japanese captured the city and interned all American and Allied citizens in the Santo Tomas University Concentration Camp.[13]

Therefore, Alena was forced to leave with no replacement except one of her own trained nurses, Shitabu. Most of the work fell on the shoulders of Dr. Grace Jones.[14]

In blackout and wearing a life jacket, Alena lived through the next two months as the ship zigzagged through submarine-infested waters and finally arrived safely in the U.S.A. She thanked God that she had taken furlough at this time, for in less than three months her mother died. In India, two other nurses were found eventually to fill the gap while she was delayed in America by the war.[15]

Developing
Independence

> *"I am the true vine and my Father is the gardener. He cuts off every branch in me that bears no fruit, while every branch that does bear fruit he trims clean so that it will be even more fruitful." John 15:1, 2 (NIV)*

Developing Industrial Education through the Earles

The whole purpose of a centralized school in Nowgong was to develop self-supporting churches. The coming of Robert and Elizabeth Earle with their three-year-old Catherine Jane was a giant step in that direction. They had arrived in Nowgong November 18, 1938. Robert had grown up on a farm in Rhode Island and had taken a special agricultural course in Ohio State University. He graduated from Marion College and received a master's degree in Christian education from Winona Lake School of Theology. Elizabeth with her major in education from Ohio State had felt called to India since she was eight years old.[1] They both plunged into language study. They had helped manage affairs while the Cattells were in Australia. Robert also observed farming in India and Elizabeth surveyed Indian education. The presence of these two well-qualified educational missionaries drew better-quality teachers, and by 1941 they had a fully trained staff, thus raising the educational standard.[2] Heavy emphasis was put on self-support. The boys worked a minimum of two hours a day and girls made clothing for the orphans. Each child had a garden to supplement his diet. The level was raised to eighth class.[3] With the aid of the Trueblood Trust Fund, dairy buffalos and cows were added for the training program.[4] The Bible school had been closed for lack of students after the graduation of Stuti Prakash's sister, Ratan, but the industrial side now became prominent.[5] Elizabeth visited Wardha, where she met personally the outstanding, vivacious, ascetic leader of India's Independence movement, Mahatma Gandhi, and observed his Basic Education scheme firsthand. His idea was to select one industry or craft suitable to home production, and through this teach all school subjects. His purpose and the Mission's were much the same. He wanted through his schools to make people economically independent. His scheme did not succeed, nor did the Mission's.[6]

Developing self-support in the Church in Bundelkhand became almost an obsession. The example of strong dependence on the Mission was a great stumbling block to new converts. "If Khub Chand reverts, it will be because of this dependence of Christians on foreign funds. He cannot understand why he doesn't get his share," wrote Everett Cattell.[7]

The Mission followed every possible avenue they knew to bring independence to the Christian families. Everett inquired about posts for teachers, clerks, and pharmacists in various villages. He got meager response. He bought some goats from Khub Chand, hoping he could entice a few Christian families to take them over as a means of earning money, but he was stuck with the goats.[8]

The Sale of the Farm

In the same way Robert Earle did not know what to do with the farm. He discovered that there was no way of making the farm pay. It had been bought many years ago with much hope by Margaret Smith, but every year it had cost the Mission a good sum to keep it in operation. Walter Bolitho had faced the same frustrations as Robert Earle now experienced.

Other missions who had tried the same experiment were no different. Taxes, irrigation costs, labor, seed, storm, and wandering cattle ate away all profits. Finally the young prince, who had studied in the Christian Allahabad Agricultural Institute, became of age and took the throne at the Investiture *Darbar*. His Highness Maharaja Bhawani Singh Bahadur, ruler of Chhatarpur State, set about immediately to activate a large training program in Bundelkhand and wanted to buy the farm.[9] He had the cooperation of fourteen states and would work under the Political Agent. The Mission with Board consent agreed to sell him their farm for $666, feeling this would enhance their self-support emphasis. They also felt safe with the Maharaja as their neighbor.[10]

The money was set aside for helping Christian employees in the Mission build their own houses. First preference was given to orphans.[11] Getting plots of land on which to build was not easy, for the Christians were sometimes asked for a bribe or charged exhorbitant prices. They pushed on, however, and most people not employed in school or hospital were eventually settled off the compounds and in their own or rented houses.[12]

Harpalpur School Turned over to the Government

Since educational institutions throughout India had not been successful as evangelistic agencies for the conversion of non-Christians, the Mission Council finally agreed to stop supporting the Harpalpur school of ninety students, mostly from non-Christian homes. It took years to close out, but finally in September, 1944, Alipura State gave a "thank you" offering of Rs. 6,500 ($1,970) for the buildings and guaranteed to continue employing all the Christian teachers. This meant four more Christian families were on self-support.[13] Even though the State raised the wages of the teachers and the Mission reserved a small plot on which to build a church, the people in Harpalpur who had been reared in the Mission as orphans felt betrayed by the move and have not yet overcome their disappointment.[14]

Hira Singh's Inheritance

The idea of developing self-supporting Christians was coming from every direction. The Tamberam International Conference in Madras attended by Jefferson Ford and delegates from seventy different countries underlined this. "Mission stations must become self-supporting, evangelistic churches," they resolved.[15] So in line with this, the Mission took the first opportunity to help one of its evangelists get located on his own land. Hira Singh had been carried in his mother's arms to the Mission compound when his father, Thakur P. Singh, took the whole family there and declared himself a Christian just before he died. In early 1940 Hira Singh learned that his father owned ten acres of land in Isanagar in Charkhari State. By making out proper papers and paying back taxes, he obtained the property. The town was located in a mango grove on the banks of a lovely lake. Some said there were ten thousand mango trees and that great oxcart loads of the fruit were sent to many other areas of India.[16] Hira Singh was delighted to move out there to improve his land and evangelize the area. He moved in March of 1941 and plastered the village in no time with Bible verses painted on the walls. He and his wife made a solid Christian impact and were greatly encouraged by the visit of many missionaries and Christian leaders who came to help celebrate their first Easter in the village. They had lived in Harpalpur for eight years and in Isanagar they missed Christian fellowship.[17]

Hira Lal's New Home

In Nowgong the oldest evangelist, Hira Lal, the crippled man with the pony, asked to have the mission house in Bileri where he lived. The Mission arranged for him to have it through slow payment over many years

from his part-time retirement salary. They presented him with his seventh
and last pony in 1941.[18]

Resistance to Self-Support

For the most part, all these changes were opposed by the older men, who
from childhood had grown up in the Mission without having known anything but dependence. In some cases there were deep spiritual failures,
which led to their dismissal from mission employment, but they and their
families were still there needing to be fed. They were given work on a day
basis. Eventually the Mission Board agreed to allow the Mission to give
them a pension,[19] and though this was not exactly self-support, it did take
them off the payroll. This striving for self-support among the people who
strongly resisted it was extremely enervating and disappointing work in a
land of poverty. Probably, however, there was no other missionary effort
more vital or necessary at the time.

Headquarters Moved to Chhatarpur

Bundelkhand was a vast area with a population of 1,481,140. The eastern
side, the largest, was beyond the Ken River. The western side, between
the Ken on the east and the Dhasan River on the west, was the most
densely populated. Chhatarpur was in the center between these rivers.[20]
In 1940 the Cattells saw Chhatarpur as the logical headquarters for the
western area. With Earles well in charge in Nowgong, they moved to
Chhatarpur August 15, 1940.[21] They made their home in the First Bungalow built by Margaret Smith about half a mile from the hospital. It had
not been occupied for six years, and Catherine, accustomed to the bustle
of the well-populated Nowgong compound, was at first overcome with the
quietness. No chatter of children's voices, no bells, and no sound from
the city broke the solitude. "I haven't heard a sound for hours," she wrote.
"There is only the sound of distant thunder and the wind whispering in
the palms clustered about the picturesque tombs on the next field."[22] But
as time passed, they found the location ideal. Everett started regular English services attended by many government men and Hindu professors,
who came partly to improve their English. As many as seventy crowded
into the chapel for the services. He also found the villages in closer prox-
imity for intensive evangelism, and supervision of all stations and outstations more easily accomplished.[23]

Introducing the Pastoral System

A further step beyond self-support was also urgent. Because of the war
no one knew when all missionaries and their funds might be withdrawn.
After America became embroiled in the war, the Mission Council drew up

emergency plans for the Church. The Tambaram Report had strongly urged missions to give more responsibility to the Church with missionaries serving as companions and advisers,[24] but it took the war to spur missions in the right direction.

The first step in Bundelkhand to give more responsibility to the Church was the introduction of the pastoral system. This was not done easily. Pancham Singh and some of the other older men opposed it all the way. Pancham Singh, who should have been the pastor of pastors, was so powerful and opposed to the missionaries that he played havoc with the churches. The Ministry and Oversight tried to confront him with his failures: Sabbath breaking, shady business dealings, the use of obscenity, attacking people he opposed with a shoe, using Hindu greetings, holding back wages from his laborers, and chewing tobacco were some of the practices that grieved them. Another was that he had evidently taken a vow not to cut his hair until the pastoral system in the churches had been discredited. Nothing they did or said seemed to touch him.[25] Finally after months of struggle Dayal Chand Singh was installed as the first pastor in Chhatarpur. G. M. Roberts became pastor in Nowgong. He was an ordained minister from the Mennonite Church. He came first as a language pandit for the Earles, but he threw in his lot with the Friends Mission and because of his pastoral background became a positive pastoral model for others.[26]

On April 27, 1941, the Church recorded its first ministers. Gore Lal Singh had been given the right to perform marriages but had not until this date been recorded. With him were Stuti Prakash, Dayal Chand Singh, and Hira Singh. Pancham Singh was so opposed that he threatened to leave the Church and take a following with him to start another church.[27]

Opening Outstations

A new system already underway for evangelists to live out in villages the year round was proving somewhat successful. In Bijawar the Mission purchased a site for a church and parsonage on two lots fifty by fifty feet very near the lake and palace. They built a two-story house—a guest room and place to worship upstairs, and living quarters for the pastor/evangelist below.[28] Bharos William's wife, Jaiwatti, worked in the State Hospital as a nurse while Bharos was free to serve as pastor for the four Bijawar Christian families and also to witness to the Chamars. Shapan Nath and his wife and baby stayed in a rented house in Satai between Bijawar and Chhatarpur. With Lachhman Singh, pharmacist, Babu Johnson replaced Dayal Chand in Gulganj. Puran Chand was stationed thirty-five miles east of Chhatarpur at Pahargawn. Hira Singh faithfully evangelized the area around Isanagar. Another five or more outstations would have been opened had there been evangelists to put in them.[29] Cattells and Stuti Prakash frequently visited each of these outstations as well as Dhamora, ministering to lonely evangelists and their families. The women who had formerly been employed as teachers and Bible women needed a lot of encouragement to witness for Christ, without a salary.[30]

Everett and Stuti sometimes by bicycle took the 75- to 100-mile tour to visit each of them, and encourage them. During the cool season other evangelists would join the local evangelist for an intensive campaign in his area.[31]

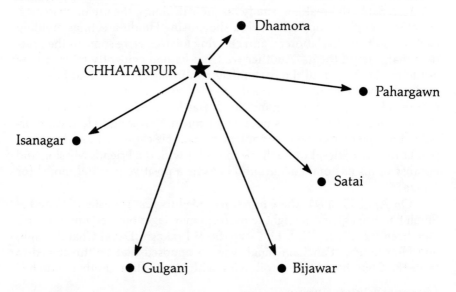

Every time they toured the outstations, Cattells found deep problems. Khub Chand in Dhamora went home from church in Chhatarpur one day to find thieves had broken into his house and stolen his grain. He found it hard to understand why the Mission did not replace his loss. But God had a lesson for Khub Chand. When he had no food left except goat milk, he prayed for a rupee (thirty-three cents) to buy grain. The next day Stuti Prakash and Dayal Chand visited him without knowing anything about Khub Chand's desperate situation. Dayal Chand asked Khub Chand for some *ghee* (clarified butter). Khub Chand had four annas (eight cents) worth. Dayal Chand gave him a rupee and said, "Please supply four annas worth of ghee to me weekly for the next three weeks." That was about all Khub Chand's goats could produce. He praised the Lord as with that rupee he went to town and bought grain.[32]

Out in Bijawar the Bharos Williams family lost their little girl. They grieved deeply and felt very much alone until Khub Chand and the Cattells came for a meeting, and Everett Cattell especially ministered to them in their sorrow. Later the Cattells hitched their new house trailer to a pair of oxen and went to Bijawar for a whole week of revival, with excellent response. They started home after the last evening service and slept as the oxen took them the twenty-four miles to Chhatarpur. They woke up at sunrise safely home.[33] Keeping up the morale of those in far places cost lots of effort but was vital to the effort of winning the lost for Christ.

"War Emergency Proposals"

The mission work had already been set up in seven different boards, but all handled by missionaries: *Evangelism* — Everett and Catherine Cattell and Carrie Wood; *Education* — Elizabeth Earle; *Farm* — Robert Earle; *Medical* — Missionary Doctor and Alena Calkins; *Orphanage* — Elizabeth Earle; *Property* — Everett Cattell; *Administration* — Everett Cattell. The time had come to include Indians. So now under the "War Emergency Proposals" three Indians were elected to each of these seven boards.[34] The top governing body called the Joint Council was comprised of all these boards together. Indian treasurers were appointed for each board. Missionaries continued as chairmen, but Indians were learning how to carry on. Responsibility would gradually be shifted more and more to the church. K. D. Lall became the Quarterly Meeting treasurer responsible for gathering all accounts together in a ledger.

Up until this time the Mission had not taken Indians into confidence in matters of policy, budgeting, or accounting.[35] The Evangelistic and Pastoral Board agreed to assume support of all pastors to a level of Rs. 20 ($6.60) per month through storehouse tithing. Robert Earle had strongly emphasized Christian stewardship in the churches, and forty people had signed up as tithers. Since a rupee was made up of sixteen annas, and not ten, the concession was made that storehouse tithing would mean giving one anna for every rupee and the rest of the tenth would be given as offering to Sunday school and Christian Endeavor.[36] The Mission sought to get churches and parsonages into good condition ready for any eventuality. Both Nowgong and Chhatarpur started funds for their own parsonages. For $150 Nowgong improved the two-story caretaker's quarters attached to the church. Chhatarpur was able to buy a building large enough for three families for $500. The Mission agreed to pay half for rent-free use of the back quarters for ten years.[37]

The Council set up a plan so that in case of withdrawal of funds, the Church could maintain primary schools, the medical work on a fee basis along with a grant from the State, and secure homes for orphans with

Christian families in the area. Already the last baby orphan had been so placed.[38] Evangelists in outstations could be encouraged to find work in the villages where they were stationed.[39] The Mission considered turning over property, particularly churches and parsonages, but apart from the parsonage property in Chhatarpur, the Mission Board at home was not quite ready for this forward step.[40]

Home Support

Amazingly World War II, instead of hindering the work of the Mission, seemed to give it a real spur in the right direction. Walter Williams wrote, "It is my opinion that I have never seen the day when the yearly meeting was more solidly behind the missionary work of both our missions than it is today."[41] The 1,378 members of the missionary auxiliaries kept books and magazines going to the field and promotional materials and calendars of missionaries to the entire constituency.[42] Clifton and Betty Robinson, choice young people in the Church, were accepted as new missionaries for India. Clifton was a keen evangelist and the son of a strong Christian family in Newport News, Virginia. Betty was the daughter of Dr. Byron and Ruth Malone Osborne. Dr. Osborne was professor (and later president) of Cleveland Bible College and Malone College. Both Cliff and Betty had graduated from CBC and felt ready to go.[43] They were held up in the U.S.A. not for lack of money to send them but because of the war. Meanwhile they took a pastorate at West Park, Cleveland, where God greatly blessed their ministry.

At this time Ralph Comfort stepped in to Charles Roberts's place as the new treasurer of the Board at home. The Missionary Board officers, Walter Williams, Louise Ellett, and Claude Roane, Ohio Yearly Meeting Superintendent, moved into the Memorial Building in Damascus, their first permanent office. The following year when Claude Roane resigned due to ill health, Walter R. Williams combined the two superintendencies of the Yearly Meeting and the Missionary Board. Inflation in the U.S.A., increasing wages, and employment encouraged the Missionary Board to aim toward a reserve fund of $100,000.[44]

Steadying the Hands of Indian Treasurers

It may have been heady wine for the new Indian treasurers to learn of the Mission's prosperity at this point, as they had until now been kept in the dark on mission finances. Suddenly the budget for 1942 of $14,759 began to flow through their fingers. The Mission Board did not look with favor on this even though the system had strict accounting safeguards, but they gave reluctant consent. There would be casualties, but the missionaries in India never doubted even in the disappointments that this step was a right one. Before these new treasurers took office, Carrie Wood had been able to work out an arrangement with Inter-Mission Business Office for receiving money from Bombay, thus eliminating long waits for letters to go to America and come back before money was available. Hence, even though mails were often delayed because of the war, the financial situation in the Mission had never been more stable.[45]

The Bundelkhand Christians might have found it very difficult to understand the almost feverish activity of the Mission to prepare for the day when there would be no funds had they not been living with examples all about them. English, German, Danish, Norwegian, and Swedish missions had their funds totally cut off or strictly reduced for the duration of the war.[46]

How near such an emergency came to Friends in Bundelkhand is not fully known, but it was enough for the American Consul to request all American citizens to have valid passports. They never knew when they would be asked to leave. Singapore fell, then Rangoon, and the Japanese marched into Burma. The Cripps talks on India's freedom failed. The political situation in India had gone from bad to worse. The British Government, the Congress Party, and the Muslim League all set their teeth and determined to cooperate only on their own terms. Gandhi's threat of total civil disobedience brought down the heavy hand of English oppression, and they clapped Gandhi and other leaders into jail.[47]

There was a threat of Japanese invasion of India. In mid-1942 the American Consul advised all American women and children to leave India immediately. Elizabeth Earle, Carrie Wood, and Catherine Cattell were in the hills. Robert Earle, still in Nowgong, felt especially that Elizabeth, with Catherine Jane and their new little daughter Nancy Ann, born February 5, 1941, should go. Everett Cattell had not gone to the hills at all, for he felt he needed to guide the Indian treasurers in the new accounting system and steady the people in case of invasion. At this time he had gone to Bombay to find out where to keep $3,000 emergency money the Board had sent. He fell ill there, and no one knew where to contact him. There was great uncertainty. The women prepared to leave. However, just in time, Robert Earle received a telegram from Everett in Bombay and learned that the situation was less serious than supposed. So the sailings were cancelled.[48] Physically speaking, Carrie Wood should have gone, for she had been very ill again through the summer. But back in Chhatarpur in July, she was able to step in beside the new Indian treasurers and give them the help they needed. This included one of many revisions of the Indian salary scale, as inflation in India was going wild.[49]

By taking over one bedroom and dressing room of the doctor's bungalow in Chhatarpur, the new centralized treasurer's office was set up. Carrie Wood and K. D. Lall both had desks in the main room, and Everett Cattell set up his office in the dressing room.[50]

Reviving the Church

*"The nations will know that I am the LORD, declares
the Sovereign LORD, when I show myself holy
through you before their eyes." Ezekiel 36:23b*

Emphasis on Spiritual Life

All through those terrible war years the concern of Bundelkhand missionaries continued to be revival in the Church and conversions in the villages. Revival spilled over onto the missionaries themselves and even onto their children. David Cattell was converted in one of the revival meetings.[1] Many young people, helped through the Christian Endeavor developed through the work of Catherine Cattell, were brought to full commitment in some of these revivals. Genuine conversions took place among the Nowgong school students, the Chhatarpur hospital workers, and in the church families from all stations with a "real breaking through and confessions and seeking forgiveness."[2]

In 1941 they started an annual jungle camp, when there was strong preaching by an Indian evangelist, Mr. E. S. Timothy. Young people responded eagerly. Mrs. Stuti Prakash, who rebelled at being asked to move with her family into a smaller house, repented and said, "Now both my hands are in His." There was clear spiritual uplift throughout the Mission.[3] Speakers like Jefferson Ford of Kenya held revival meetings in all the stations as he passed through. Some well-known Indian converts came and gave effective witness.[4] Experienced missionaries from other missions also came and led revival meetings and preached in jungle camp.[5] The missionaries also, particularly Everett and Catherine Cattell, held frequent meetings of revival in all the stations.

Carrie Wood and Catherine Cattell had been equally concerned about lifting the standard of women's evangelism. They held regular weekly Bible study for all the women concerned. Catherine prepared a systematic method of following up their visitations. The women learned the importance not only of telling the Bible story and preaching, but also of praying with the women, especially hospital patients, working personally with them, teaching them to pray and to memorize Scriptures. Dr. Grace Jones gave active cooperation, and nurses were also given some training in personal work. It became common for nurses to pray for their patients.[6] Earles in Nowgong, while striving to raise the standard of every branch of education, also worked with the students to increase their spiritual vision and commitment. There was a sense of unity among all branches of the Mission around the common evangelistic aim. "I cannot tell how it gladdens my heart," wrote Everett Cattell, "to see the way in which the Lord has helped us pull up the spiritual life and emphasis of the Mission."[7]

It was a constant battle to keep up the spiritual life of the Christians in Bundelkhand. That is why in every evangelistic camp, where the effort to win converts was uppermost, the evangelists took time for Bible study meant primarily not to prepare them for preaching but to feed their own souls and sharpen their commitment. Likewise missionaries met every month for the same purpose.[8] Everett Cattell wrote:

> I have been drawn out to preach on the cross. It is not only the way of salvation but it is a way of life. It is holiness . . . . It is in the grind of these desperate real life situations here that holiness becomes more than an ecstacy. Can one face this baffling power of Satan in caste, preach on and on, pray almost without ceasing and still see no result — and keep trusting without doubt, or bitterness, or overmuch rushing around to try something new, and have the vision of Christ grow larger? . . . One must learn what it means to take up the Cross by faith, for faith is essentially without losing poise, rallying forth in self-defense, or massing arguments in self-justification; and can he be kind to those who treat him ill without feeling like a martyr; then he must know the way of a cross that is more than an experience of ten years ago — he must have learned to "die daily." . . . This has been by all means one of the best years of my life — all praise to God. It has been, I trust, a year of a turning point in our Mission with the conversion of Khub Chand. What will the next bring?[9]

Division Over a Love Feast

Just at the peak of great spiritual growth, the Indian Christians and missionaries were ambushed by the enemy of men's souls at the point of cultural differences. India was struggling for independence from British rule, and this affected Bundelkhand Christians, too. They had just experienced a heady taste in the Mission when the responsibility of accounting for mission money was placed in their hands. Also with the formation of the Joint Council they gained the right to sit down with the missionaries in policy and budget making sessions. Each station got a new place under the sun by the organization of separate monthly meetings, which put more responsibility on their shoulders. When they met in quarterly and annual meeting sessions, each group had a new sense of identity.

Jungle Camp and revival meetings brought individual Christians face to face with the real meaning of being a Christian. The Church was growing spiritually. Now Christmas was near, and for the first time in history, the Indian Christians of Bundelkhand thought of a very Indian way in which they would celebrate it. They borrowed a Hindu practice, stripped it of its reference to idols, and poured into it their own Christian content. They named it a *Prem Sabha* (love feast). All the Christian families in the vicinity brought odd musical instruments (including a *tabla* or drum) and met together in a home to sing, tell stories, and testify from about nine o'clock in the evening until two or four the next morning. Of course the hostess was expected to serve tea.

The very thought of sitting cross-legged on the floor, clapping and singing Hindi *bhajans* over and over night after night was enough to turn off the missionaries, but there were other more serious points to which they objected. They disapproved the dissipation of so much energy, which would detract from the spiritual impact they hoped would be part of quarterly meeting following Christmas. They deplored the financial pressure put on the Christian families, most of whom were too poor to afford the sugar, milk, and tea for such a large group. Also, the little group was so in-grown that if a single person happened to miss one night, the hostess was offended. The missionaries opposed the idea, but the Church won out, compromising only on the point of closing time. They agreed to try to stop by 11:00 p.m. In Chhatarpur, Cattells felt they did not dare begin; so they purposely did not attend.

When quarterly meeting convened before every Christian household had had a turn, the families agreed they would continue to meet every night after the meetings were finished in the Church. The absence of the missionaries was even more conspicuous, and Dayal Chand Singh, Chhatarpur's pastor, felt more and more insecure. Indian though he was, the foreign missionaries were the only parents he had ever known, and his loyalty to them was deep. But the Indians seemed to be struggling for something important, though he knew not what. Some people were clearly using Dayal Chand to get the upper hand over the missionaries, but probably most of them wanted only to celebrate their Indian-ness.

The next afternoon in the business session Robert Earle voiced the missionaries' concern about continuing the *Prem Sabha* during quarterly meeting, and before he could sit down, the tension of the weeks snapped. Pastor Dayal Chand tearfully and loudly accused the missionaries of fostering a divisive spirit and standing off as a party aloof from Indians. In the confusion that followed, Everett Cattell suggested that he, Robert Earle, and Pastor Dayal Chand leave the meeting so that others in a calmer spirit could make a clear decision about what to do. Just as they went out the door, Pancham Singh, a strong supporter of *Prem Sabha*, was passing by the Church. Dayal Chand ran right into his arms.

Hindus, smelling a quarrel, formed a mob around them, and it was only through much prayer and persuasion that Everett Cattell finally got the Christians back into the Church, where they could settle their problems away from the public eye. Pancham Singh refused to go in until Catherine Cattell came out and in tears and on her knees pleaded with him to do so.

Unity seemed to have evaporated, and the Church seemed to have suffered a tremendous spiritual defeat. That night some of the missionaries and a number of the preachers spent most of the night in prayer. Hira Singh remained all night and Dayal Chand went in and out. The importance to the Indian Church of their first innovation of the *Prem Sabha* was not understood, and the enemy used it to split missionary/Indian solidarity and to create havoc in the tiny Christian community for a season.[10]

The Missionaries' Prayer, Soul Searching, and Fasting

The Cattells, Earles, and Carrie Wood were so exhausted after the *Prem Sabha* affair that they were unable immediately to reestablish relationship with each other or with the people.

Soon after the first of the year they put aside everything and came together to pray, fast, and study the Scripture. They opened their hearts, prayed, and made confessions one to another, and God began to speak to them. The books of Ezra, Nehemiah, and Ezekiel began to speak to them about the condition of the Church. Then they read Zechariah and Hebrews and considered their priestly role in ministry among the people. Ezekiel 36, 37 came to be the special message: Sanctifying the name of God in the eyes of the heathen; the cleansing and living again of the dry bones. After ten days of intense searching and laying hold of God, they felt they had prayed through.[11]

The missionaries went home claiming in sheer faith that God would, on one hand, cleanse the Church either through repentance or (God forbid) through judgment; and on the other, that there would be a great ingathering.[12] There was no doubt in their minds that the cleansing and the ingathering were inseparably linked.

Faith Taking Hold

The situation, however, seemed to deny all that they believed. "The Lord opened to me that all the ten commandments are being openly and flagrantly broken in our Church," Everett Cattell noted in his diary the very next day. "The burden of this sin greatly troubles me." The missionaries kept the promises in mind as they entered into the Jungle Camp Meeting in March 1943, but their faith was to be further tried. Evangelist Mital, who had been used to spark such genuine revival at quarterly meeting in October, utterly failed to do so in these meetings six months later. Right in the meetings enmity sprang up between leaders. Khub Chand began pressing for handouts. Stuti Prakash was under fire and terribly discouraged. Everett Cattell also came under temptation. He wrote:

> I just felt I couldn't take another thing. I have always been able to look on the bright and hopeful side of things. I experienced such darkness. I fled to the trailer . . . and fell before the Lord. And there He met me . . . . I came to know what faith is — pure, naked faith unbuttressed by natural optimism. Just sheer casting of oneself on God. And there I found the promises still existed, unchanged and undiminished and undimmed. Indeed a light began to glow and peace that passeth understanding . . . . I had personally struck bottom that evening and from that day forward peace and joy began wondrously to triumph in my heart over all the surrounding gloom.[13]

God was dealing with Stuti Prakash, too. Some of his peers resented his easy access to the missionary and were jealous of his rise to leadership. They were furious with his clear John-the-Baptist-like exposure of sin. So they determined to bring him down. He went home that dark night utterly discouraged and started to throw himself down in despair on an earthen platform around a tree in front of his house. Awareness of subtle movement caused him to draw back, and suddenly he discerned the form of a poisonous snake coiled to strike. He thanked God for saving him. Then in a flash he saw the snake as a symbol of Satan, who through discouragement was seeking to destroy him. As Everett Cattell prayed through in the trailer, Stuti Prakash under the tree in the dark took a new firm grip of faith on the Lord.[14]

A Mini-Furlough in India

Several weeks later when letters from India reached the desk of Walter Williams, he wrote, "It is evident that Cattells and the entire Mission are working under unusual strain."[15] So the Board began to think of ways to ease the load. While they were doing that, the missionaries were finding some relaxation of their own by attending the young Maharaja's wedding. The elephants, horses, glittering red and gold costumes, the crowds of great glamour when the bride and groom passed seven times around the sacred fire were all fascinating. They dined in royal company on the best of the land, and Bundelkhand's sweepers swarmed in to pick up the crumbs.[16]

But bone-weary people found little rest in that kind of diversion. More was called for, and the Board came through with the suggestion that Cattells, whose furlough was due, should take six months away from Bundelkhand as a long vacation in India. This pleased the Cattells, for a regular furlough at that time would have made it impossible for them to get back to India until after the war was over. They felt no freedom in leaving under those conditions, but time away from the pressures was welcomed. So Stuti Prakash took full responsibility for the evangelistic work, Komal Das Lall along with Robert Earle took over property and accounting, and Carrie Wood stepped in as acting superintendent.[17]

As the news spread in India that Cattells had been set free in India for six months, mission groups from north to south sent invitations to them for conferences. To many, this would have been no vacation, but Everett and Catherine both thrived on such ministry, giving much and learning much through the contacts. Everett often spoke for the India Holiness Association and also served as its president. Both ministered at Jhansi and Sagar conventions, and in cities like Bombay, Allahabad, Lucknow, and Landour. Ministering to groups like the Mennonites, where on an average ten to twenty new Christians were being baptized every week, provided opportunities for study.[18]

With both children in boarding school, the Cattells started south by train for Bombay, Kolar, Bangalore, Bangarapet, Tirippatur, and Kerala. The Methodists in Bangarapet and the World Gospel Mission in Kolar had arranged meetings. Catherine went to Bangalore while Everett visited *Christa Kulu Ashram* in Tirippatur to study an effort to combine Hindu temple architecture with Christian worship. He preached there twice a day sitting cross-legged on a deerskin as a sadhu would have done. He felt inspired by the beauty and Christian symbolism that had been introduced, but wondered about the effect of the Hindu symbolism on the Hindu mind.[19]

Together they went to Kerala. There they visited the metropolitan, Abraham, who sponsored the Maramon Convention, the largest Christian gathering in the world attended at that time by more than forty thousand people each year. Everett spoke at this convention, which is in a land of many churches, since one third of Kerala's population is Christian.[20] Two years later he went back again accompanied by David, and spoke at the same convention to fifty thousand Christians — a marked contrast to Bundelkhand.[21] On their way to the Nilgiris Hills, where missionaries from the South spend their vacations, the Cattells stopped at Madurai to see the huge temples. Everett had the Bible studies in three week-long conventions held in the three hill stations—fifteen miles apart—Ootacamund, Coonoor, and Kotagiri.

The atmosphere was bracing, the company stimulating, and the conventions challenging. After this, they stayed on in Kotagiri for three weeks before starting north again. They stopped in various places along the way for sight-seeing and study. In Mysore they saw the glamorous palace and its marvelous carving, silver-plated doors, chandeliers, trophy room with the mounted tiger, panther, buffalo, elephant, and other animals shot by the Maharaja. They went into the great amphitheater where the *Dassera Darbar* was held each year. Set as it is in a land of so much poverty, the wealth of the palace was staggering.[22]

Going on from there to Bedar, Hyderabad, they visited two Methodist mass movement areas where many were turning to Christ. On to Pardi, Gujarat, they visited Floyd Banker of the Wesleyan Methodist Mission, where the mass movement was also successful. On July 1, 1943, the train went directly to Dehra Dun, where they got a bus up the hill to Landour, Mussoorie, and found their children thriving in Woodstock School. For the next two months they involved themselves in the school and hillside activities. At the Mussoorie Convention Bishop Pickett spoke of the pressures of government on those who would seek to convert anyone to Christianity.[23]

In September while Catherine stayed in Landour with the children, Everett went to Kashmir for a convention where he met the rugged missionaries from the Nepal and Tibetan border.[24] From there he proceeded to the Sialkot convention held in the center of a mass movement numbering some 500,000 Christians. "They have just about the only self-supporting work in India," Everett noted. "No pastor in the United Presbyterian Church receives any American money." The convention tent was filled to capacity by two thousand people. There were some things that shocked a Quaker, however, as he moved among the people. "They all smoke the *huka!*" he commented.[25]

From Sialkot, Everett went to Jabalpur to attend the Mid-India Representative Christian Council; from there, to attend Yearly Meeting with the English Friends at Itarsi; then to Yavatmal to the India Holiness Convention. There he and Bishop Badley of the Methodist Church were speakers. Between meetings, these men discussed the matters nearest their hearts—conversions and church growth. Everett shared some of the methods he had observed on his recent tours. There were those who believed that new converts should be taken in when they professed Jesus Christ and left their idols. Right at that point they were baptized and called Christian though the *chutiya* was not cut and there still was much to be dealt with in their lives such as the habits of drinking, smoking, and use of pan. Bishop Badley and Everett Cattell saw eye to eye on the importance of a slower route whereby a tobacco smoker would not be admitted as a full member of the Church, and the *chutiya* would be cut from the very beginning. After that, the constant emphasis on spiritual life through camps and meetings for revival was imperative.[26]

Back to the Heartaches of Bundelkhand

The Cattells got back to Bundelkhand October 24, 1943, having traveled 10,000 miles and preached in a dozen conventions.[27] They had seen in other places what they expected God to do in Bundelkhand. This had brought new hope. New undergirding for missions also came from the home side with the formation of the National Association of Evangelicals. Walter R. Williams, the newly appointed full-time president and superintendent of the Friends Foreign Missionary Society, was also a member of the NAE's Board of Missions.[28] As the Earles and Carrie Wood listened to the experiences of the Cattells, they also felt renewed in spirit, for the work had not been easy for them the past year. Robert Earle could not find a suitable housefather and for several months had himself slept nights in the boys' hostel. Finally Johnson Babu was brought in from Gulganj. But in a short time he was caught in dishonesty and was dismissed.

The coming of Victor Mangalwadi to the staff was a real boon. He married Kusum Gore Lal Singh, a well-trained teacher, and the Earles thought they had one solid couple to count on for a period of time. But to their great disappointment, they found Victor Mangalwadi undermining the faith of the students with his outspoken rejection of inspiration of Scriptures.[29] Robert had to take over the Scripture teaching.

Elizabeth was working hard to complete her thesis based on the Leiter International Performance Scale, a special mental test loaned to her by Dr. Leiter of the University of Southern California. She did complete her master's program for Ohio State,[30] but she was faced with moral failures in the school staff that were heartbreaking.

Carrie Wood was not able to keep the outstation evangelists happy or to prevent disunity in the hospital staff. Political times were changing, the inflated war prices caused untold hardship, and the enemy of souls was doing everything possible to nullify any spiritual advances made through various revival efforts in the Church. The weight of all these problems fell on the shoulders of Everett Cattell on his return. He found crises in every station. The missionaries united in prayer and attacked the problems on a spiritual basis. "I think I have never been so burdened in spirit before in all my life," wrote Everett to Walter Williams.[31] The Cattells started out on an intensive evangelistic tour to all outstations and nearby villages. One center they visited near Bijawar was the village of the Kanjars who had been transferred from Nowgong. Years before the Mission had worked much among them, the only fruit being one girl who came into the orphanage, named Lalli Bai. She went back with Catherine to visit her people and give her witness.[32]

Showers of Blessing

In the spring of 1944 a different kind of jungle camp was planned. Eighty men of the area went into the real jungle, where each chose a quiet spot for prayer and meditation between the morning and evening meetings. This resulted in great blessing. In April at annual meeting, services were held for six days. Then in July during the rains a refresher's course for preachers was held. Carrie Wood, the Earles, Stuti Prakash, and Rev. G. M. Roberts taught the courses in 1943, and Cattells joined them in 1944.[33] Special revival services were held in Chhatarpur, Nowgong, and Harpalpur. With all of these spiritual activities, the missionaries witnessed splendid victories on all fronts. One such victory was the restoration of Victor Mangalwadi and his wife. Everett Cattell had spared him of criticism when he left the Mission but supplied him with books suitable to his problem. The bright young man was an avid reader and he found for himself the wonder of God's inspired Word. He felt a deep calling back to his father's old field of Bundelkhand and begged to come back. He had meanwhile completed some theological training at Leonard Theological College in Jabalpur.[34]

The Conversion of Hira Lal of Bilwar

Another bright spot was to discover that a man from Bilwar village who had come to jungle camp in 1942 was deeply interested in becoming a Christian.[35] Hira Lal's wife had died in 1938 and left him with a little boy named Dariyao. In 1942 he married again, but when his second wife's parents learned of his commitment to Christianity, they snatched his wife away. Hira Lal put his little boy into Nowgong Christian School, and for the next eight years the Cattells paid his fees. Six months later Stuti Prakash went to Hira Lal's wife's village to persuade her parents to let her come back to her husband.[36] After a year of their separation, the parents gave in, and Hira Lal immediately took his wife to Chhatarpur to expose her to Christian teaching from Catherine Cattell, hoping she would also receive Christ. She was not at all cooperative and as soon as possible returned to her parents for another four years.[37]

Finally, Hira Lal could bear the separation no longer. He returned to get a judgment from the Malhera *Panch* (the ruling body in the village). Before a session of one hundred people the rulers said to Hira Lal: "You don't have to leave your new religion; worship God as you please. You don't have to leave your Bible; read it and follow it. BUT DO NOT JOIN THEIR SOCIETY or be numbered among them, or go to them." Then they presented illiterate Hira Lal a very long paper to sign, stating he would not leave their *samaj* (society). He asked one question, "But if my wife agrees to go with me into this new *samaj* (society), what then?"

They felt sure she would never become a Christian; so they said, "Then both of you may go together; don't let your home be broken." Then Hira Lal, full of faith that his wife would eventually become a Christian, signed the paper and left the village with her. When the Christians in Chhatarpur heard of this, they were deeply grieved that Hira Lal had betrayed Christ in order to get his wife back. But after five years of patiently waiting, he again brought his wife to see Catherine Cattell, who led her to Christ. From that time on Hira Lal, the cloth peddler, and his wife joined the society of Christians (Friends) and were numbered among them.[38]

Surviving
World War II

*"I will bring you back to this land. I will not leave
you until I have done what I have promised you."*
Genesis 28:15 (NIV)

Missionaries in Transit

Change constantly marked the life of the Mission, and the next three years
would see vast shifts in missionary personnel. Carrie Wood was in need
of furlough, war or no war. She was suffering from recurrent attacks of
malaria and was extremely weary from carrying the load as superintendent while Cattells were gone. She gave much energy to getting the Mission on a sound financial footing.

No one was happier than Carrie for the founding of an Inter-Mission
Business Office in Bombay through which immediate exchange of dollars
to rupees was possible, thus saving long delays and frequent cables to the
Home Board. The IMBO also helped secure passage home for mission-
aries and provided a home at low rates to missionaries in transit through
Bombay.[1]

Carrie Wood had been at Everett Cattell's right hand as he sought to
put Indian treasurers into position and to introduce other fiscal changes.
She welcomed heartily the introduction of a provident fund and pension
plan for workers.[2] She gave a great deal of energy to training the Indian
treasurers since none of them had training in accounting.

The fruit of her years of work behind the walls of *zenana* quarters
would never be known, not even to herself. The many times doors were
slammed in her face, the heartbreak she shared, the teaching she gave in
many skills, and the witness for Christ on a one-to-one basis for thousands of women in Bundelkhand are all buried in the hearts of the women
who were hidden behind those walls.

Carrie Wood left India August 7, 1944, not at all sure she would ever be able to return.[3] Alena Calkins, meanwhile, had been trying to get passage back to India, even in war time. It was next to impossible, but finally she got a place on a Portuguese ship and traveled under severe restrictions and blackout from U.S.A. to Lisbon, leaving November 25, 1944.[4] She was held up five weeks in Lisbon. Finally she and other passengers traveled on a cold train through snow toward Haifa and stopped at a small village where they were housed in a hotel that had not been used for two years. When the town people understood their plight, they brought bedding for the 128 passengers. They slept on tables, benches, and the floor. They were next transferred to Gibraltar, where Alena came down with bronchitis and was in bed for a week. The whole trip was cold and dangerous as they were shifted from ship to ship. It is not surprising to find Alena claiming as her promise, "Great peace have they which love thy law, and nothing shall offend them." (Psalm 119:165)[5]

The Chhatarpur to Which Alena Calkins Returned

Alena finally arrived in India February 26, 1945, to find Dr. Grace Jones suffering from neuritis in the shoulder and worn out from too heavy responsibility and personality clashes in the staff. While Alena was away, two additional doctors had come in to help — one a retired missionary and the other a new graduate from medical school — but they did not stay. Likewise, two nurses had come. They also found difficulties in adjusting and the last one left as soon as Alena arrived to take over, even before she had unpacked her trunks.[6] So Dr. Grace Jones alone had carried the hospital through the past year with its 437 inpatients and 3,427 outpatients. Alena immediately took full charge and let Dr. Jones go to Jhansi for hospital treatment and care.[7]

Alena found many changes in Chhatarpur. She liked the office system with Indian treasurers at work in the two rooms of the bungalow set aside for a mission office. K. D. Lall's supervision of all the buildings took a great load off her shoulders. She favored a new plan to build family wards just as soon as the war ended. She liked the new pastor, Mr. G. M. Roberts, recently installed in Chhatarpur. The tithing system in the Church was working well, and they paid their pastor in full, as well as Rs. 400 ($120) toward the new parsonage.[8] She was glad some good nurses trained in their training school were on duty, but she was distressed to learn she could not reopen the school because of new rules requiring turnover of nine hundred patients a year. This eliminated the Chhatarpur hospital from the field of nurses' training.[9] She found war inflation had wrought havoc with the economy. Grain and cloth had quadrupled in price though workers' salaries had increased only one third. Often flour, sugar, kerosene, and cloth were totally unavailable, or strictly rationed. The unreliable power system threw them back to the use of oil lamps for the wards and they depended on kerosene to run their sterilizer. Another difference was the frequent presence of Allied soldiers who stopped by for boiled water, a cup of tea, or a snack.[10]

Freedom for Anna Nixon

As Alena Calkins was on her last lap of the journey to India, the American troops had entered Manila and were engaged in fierce fighting to free the city from the Japanese and the American prisoners from the prison camp. On February 3, 1945, just after dark, 1,500 men of the First Cavalry Division fought their way down behind the lines and pushed into Santo Tomas Internment Camp, where Anna Nixon had been held captive since early 1942. Half of the men died in this effort, but the other half remained with the prisoners through the battle for Manila, which took place in the weeks that followed (February 3-23, 1945). The first word to reach home of the safety of Anna Nixon came in the form of a news photo taken by a United Press reporter. During the shelling of Santo Tomas, he had early one morning slipped up to get the names of four rain-drenched women huddled against a stone wall for protection against both rain and the bombardment. This picture was published in the home state of each of the four, one of whom was Anna Nixon.

Letters began to get through, and in their first direct word from Anna for nearly three and a half years, the Mission Board found that God had wonderfully answered their prayers in preserving her from starvation and many other evils. Earlier from Elisabeth Earle, who had been repatriated from that camp in late 1943, they had heard that Anna was teaching in the camp high school and in the Sunday school, and working in the hospital office.[11] At the end, schools were closed and most activities had been stopped to conserve energy for the absolute essentials. Many died of starvation in the camp and many were killed in the shelling. So the fact that Anna Nixon lived caused her to write, "I knew that in the years left to me I would always carry a sense of responsibility to all those who in their youth had been cut off from life for freedom's sake."[12]

Anna arrived home May 2, 1945, on the *SS Eberle*, a ship evacuating some four thousand Americans from the Philippines. She was still suffering from beriberi, and it would be a few months before she would be ready to go to India.

Norma Freer Sails for India

As the ship bringing Anna home pulled into the harbor at San Pedro, another ship was getting ready to leave New York, and aboard was the

Mission's newest appointment, Norma Freer. Norma was from Wal-
bridge, Ohio, and had graduated from Cleveland Bible College in 1944.
The Missionary League of CBC came forward with an offer to pay her salary for her entire first term in India, a beautiful indication of the love and
confidence of her college friends, the ones who knew her best.[13]   Dr.
Walter Williams went to New York to see her off in the company of Mrs.
Angus MacKay, a missionary from Canada returning to Jhansi, India, at
that time. Just as her steamer got underway, the tremendous news of the
end of the war in Europe reached the U.S.A. shores.   On May 7, 1945, the
German High Command surrendered all forces unconditionally at Reims,
and V.E. Day was declared — before Anna reached her home in Colorado
and just as Norma's ship passed the Statue of Liberty.[14]

Norma Freer arrived in India June 21, 1945, and went as far as Jhansi
with Mrs. MacKay, where she repacked some luggage to take on to Landour for language school.   All the other missionaries were in Landour for
vacation to welcome her when she arrived six days later.   Cattells were
about to leave for furlough.   Alena Calkins was just recovering from a
round in the hospital with amoebic dysentery.   The Earles were there, too,
and she got in on the last two days of a long Mission Council meeting.[15]

Mission Council Concerns

The Council had been reviewing the work of the past few months in Bundelkhand. It was with great reluctance that they realized they were trying
to do an educational job with the wrong people. The orphans would
never go back to the villages, nor would their children. They already had
been cut off from the land and had no interest in discovering their roots.
Their highest ambitions were to become pharmacists, preachers, teachers,
nurses, or office workers. "The real solution lies in the training of the children of village Christians," Everett Cattell concluded. "Khub Chand's
daughter and Hira Lal's son are in school now. Our one solution is village
converts."[16]   But before the Council met, Bhuri, the fourteen-year-old
daughter of Khub Chand, had died of typhoid fever. This was the first
death in a family converted from Hinduism, and it was gratifying to the
Christians that there were no Hindu rites performed at her funeral.[17]

There was only one village boy left in the school after that — Dariyao
Hira Lal. The Earles in charge of educational work kept dreaming of the
day when they could have not only many village children in many village
primary schools but also in higher boarding schools scattered throughout
Bundelkhand. Elizabeth Earle felt the whole development keenly as tests
showed many of the orphans lacked the level of intelligence required for
the higher education necessary to meet their dreams.[18]   She was in charge
of the orphans and was deeply concerned about the best education and

marriage arrangements for them. Besides mothering the orphans, Elizabeth had her hands full at home with three children after their young son Charles Robert was born September 8, 1944, to join Catherine Jane, 10, and Nancy, 3.[19] Therefore, she was pleased to get an exchange teacher from Jhansi who later felt called to stay in Nowgong to help lift the load. Rachel Banwar was an outstanding teacher and also a keen Christian worker. She organized the first women's society in Nowgong and inspired Chhatarpur and Bijawar to follow suit.[20]

Stolen from a Bedding Roll

Robert Earle also served as treasurer, a job which would be taken over from him by Norma Freer. Toward the end of January 1945, he went to Bombay to attend the Regional Conference of Mid-India Christian Council and to discuss post-war plans with John Decker, American secretary of the International Missionary Conference. From there he went to Ankleswar to study the very fine mission educational institution, which had an agricultural bias.

He withdrew Rs 6,643 ($2,016.08) of mission funds from the bank to take up-country. He carefully put it in the corner of his bedding roll when no one was looking. At 10:30 p.m. he went to sleep on the upper berth with his coat, pillow, and his head over the securely placed money. When he woke up at 5:00 a.m., the bedding roll had been slit open and the money was gone. This caused him much anguish. The money was never recovered. But after that the Mission opened a current checking account in a bank in Harpalpur to avoid such possibilities in the future.[21]

Colemans Challenged by Village India

When word came that Colemans were seriously considering coming to India, Everett Cattell wrote them about the evangelistic work in Bundelkhand. Milton Coleman was the son of Friends Christian workers in Cleveland, Ohio. Rebecca Heller Coleman came from Avis, Pennsylvania. They met in Cleveland Bible Institute, where Rebecca graduated in music and Milton in theology. He continued his education in Eastern Nazarene College, where he received his Bachelor of Arts Degree. They were married in 1939 and became pastors in Adrian, Michigan, then later in Columbus, Ohio, at Highland Avenue (Westgate).[22]

Everett Cattell wrote the Colemans while recovering from ten days' fever from an infected ankle. The infection had been picked up as he trekked in the jungle with two of the other evangelists for two weeks. They each took a pack of seventy-five pounds on their backs and pushed into the most remote and hilly jungle areas, which were too rough for carts or bicycles. They walked eighty-five miles and rode forty-five by bus. They found the Kishangarh and Gangao areas very responsive to the Gospel.

They slept in the jungle or sometimes on mud verandas of village homes. Though the area boasted of a lot of tiger, panther, bear, and other wild animals, the party saw nothing more than deer. "Come join us," wrote Everett.[23] He felt that seventeen stations in six districts with six district superintendents, four pastors, and thirteen evangelists would be required to do the work of evangelism in Bundelkhand. At the time, there were seven recorded ministers, two outstations, and three pastors. As usual, the annual evangelistic report was impressive with 693 villages visited and 3,370 people witnessed to personally.[24] They were still working toward a mass movement, and Stuti Prakash had again spent three months in the Methodist mass movement area under James L. Kinder, from whom he learned much and received great inspiration.[25]

Rebecca Coleman was challenged by Catherine Cattell's development of the work among women and young people in the Church. She had written out one hundred questions to help the women improve their home life and teach them thrift and handwork. She had prepared a booklet on the lives of missionaries for study in the Christian Endeavor groups. She held classes on witnessing for the Bible women and the women in the Church.[26]

Planning for Post-War Expansion

Pressing his points for a post-war policy that would allow for maximum development, Everett Cattell, backed by the Mission Council, asked the Mission Board for $20,000 to build workers' quarters, an office, and some hill housing for missionaries. He further proposed the continued push toward self-support—in the hospital through rent of rooms, family wards, and a state grant; in the school through fees and scholarship endowments; in the churches through tithing and aid for evangelism (never exceeding 50 percent). The establishment of a full yearly meeting was still in the future, but the Mission Council looked forward to the day when they would work under the direction of the Church.[27] The letter home outlining all these and many more plans numbered seventeen pages, and Walter Williams commented to Claude Roane, "The details of Everett's letter . . . I felt snowed under. My head actually ached before I finished reading . . . . I wish Everett had rested more during the past year, and left off going at so high a speed."[28]

After Nine Years—Furlough for Cattells

Cattells had planned to go on furlough early in the year, but because of war conditions no ship was available. It was during this very Mission

Council meeting when Norma Freer arrived that the telegram was received requesting the Cattells to come at once to Bombay. They sailed on the *SS Gripsholm* on July 10, 1945, and arrived in the U.S.A. August 2, too late for Camp Caesar but in time for Yearly Meeting.[29] During the days while they waited in India, they had experienced some joys and many sorrows. They saw the annual meeting take on new life with a big open tent in the garden and daily evangelistic meetings. The speaker at the last minute could not come, and Everett Cattell took the services. Three Indian delegates came from the English Friends Mission.[30]

But there were deep disappointments at this time as trusted and loved Indian workers failed. One key Christian had been caught stealing; the housefather was caught padding accounts; a teacher failed morally. Most painful of all, Khub Chand threatened to go to the *Arya Samajists*.[31] It had taken less than six months for him to lose his vision of going without salary to Bijawar, where he planned to make shoes for a living while winning people to the Lord. He had undergone severe persecution and had led two relatives to cut their *chutiyas*. He had started a fire that would not die, but he had slipped in the temptation of wanting mission pay for his witness.[32] The missionaries felt that to pay converts to witness would negate the witness. Everett wrote:

> Outwardly it looks like most everything is slipping from us. Only faith in God holds us. We have prayed earnestly for cleansing and have labored with all our strength the past three years to see that cleansing come by way of confession and faith and revival . . . .
>
> It is not the work that wears us out . . . . It is the burden . . . and the frustration that takes our strength. The definitely sinful have been purged; most of the spiritual ciphers are gone . . . . If now the ingathering can begin—both of spiritual workers and of converts—it will be worth all the heartache it has cost.[33]

During those waiting weeks, Everett became ill and lost twenty-five pounds in three weeks. Nevertheless, he continued to push forward in writing a mission manual and completed the first draft of sixty pages in time to present it to the last Mission Council meeting before leaving for America.[34]

Miscellaneous Council Business

Other points reviewed in Norma's first Council meeting and Cattells last before furlough included the grant of the Mission Board to Vellore of $1,000 to be paid over a five-year period for the development of the (Union) Christian Medical College.[35] This was the beginning of a great deal of union work in which Friends in India would have a part. They became members as a Council of the India Holiness Association that year.[36] They also had in their hands a letter from Louise Ellett of September 8, 1944: "I am so happy to tell you that the Board has released a thousand dollars of the emergency travel money . . . which you may use to buy released war materials when it is put on the market . . . we are willing to put another thousand into them—jeep, refrigerator, typewriter—anything on the list to be purchased from war materials according to your own judgment. They are expected to be good buys." The missionaries began to plan, though the materials would not be available for nearly a year.

Finally there was the report on salaries. The Mission Board sought to meet the erosion from inflation. They increased each missionary's basic salary to $800 a year, beginning July 1, 1944; preschool children's allowance to $200, and older children to $250 beginning January 1, 1944. Hill allowance was also given. Home salaries were brought up to the same level. The missionaries in turn struggled with salaries of workers in India to get them onto a more firm and equitable basis.[37]

Missionary Conventions and Furlough Activities

After the Cattells arrived home in early August, they with Colemans, Anna Nixon, and Walter Williams started out after Yearly Meeting on an intensive missionary convention tour. God wonderfully blessed these meetings, and such conventions became a regular yearly promotion feature for the next seven years.

Another development at this time was the men's missionary movement through which many men became active in the promotion of missions. By 1947, thirty-five churches had active Men in Missions groups.[38]

In the midst of the conventions, Colemans' passport arrived and they left for India October 11, 1945, on the SS Marine Raven of the Isthmian Steamship Company. They arrived in Calcutta on November 11 and in Nowgong November 17.[39]

Later that year Catherine Cattell began writing Till Break of Day, a book requested by the Missionary Board. Everett Cattell went to Mayo Clinic for a serious hernia operation, and Catherine went with him, writing as she sat by his bedside.[40]

Before the Cattells returned to India in early 1947, their daughter Mary Catherine was born August 1, 1946. Just before they arranged passage back, Everett had to undergo surgery again, and though Walter Williams feared for his life, Dr. W. Ezra DeVol assisted in the operation October 31, 1946. There was much prayer for him and within three weeks he was on his feet again and packing to leave for India. At the same time in India evangelist Dayal Chand Singh underwent the same operation and recovered well, too.[41]

Carrie Wood, in the U.S.A., also recovered from her malaria, and letters from India as well as the Board convinced her there was still work for her to do in India, helping in the orientation of the many new missionaries. So she sailed from San Franciso on the *SS General Gordon* July 10, 1946.[42]

Welcoming
New Recruits

> *"He stilled the storm to a whisper; the waves of the
> sea were hushed. They were glad when it grew calm,
> and he guided them to their desired haven."*
> *Psalm 107:29, 30 NIV*

War Surplus Supplies and Anna Nixon's Arrival

The war was over! The *SS General Hershey*, on which Anna Nixon
sailed, was a troopship meant to bring soldiers home from India. As the
American army left, they dumped supplies no longer needed, and missions were allowed to buy them. Robert Earle, Milton Coleman, and
Angus MacKay, Canadian Presbyterian missionary from Jhansi, were
together in Calcutta to get these surplus supplies and had MacKay's jeep
and trailer and the Friends Mission's truck, jeeps, and two trailers almost
loaded for the return trip to Nowgong when Anna arrived on Easter eve,
1946.[1] These vehicles, plus two motorcycles, 500 mosquito nets, 200
khaki pants and shirts, 12 alarm clocks, more typewriters than they had
ordered, blankets, duffle bags, water bottles, mess kits, wire, folding
organs, pencils, paper, DDT powder, tents, camp tables, canned fruit,
peanut butter, soap, pins, medicine, medical equipment, stretchers, and a
large kerosene refrigerator — all these things they purchased for a sum of
$4,000.[2] The refrigerator was the second one to arrive in Bundelkhand;
the Maharaja had one in which he stored newspapers. This one had no
instructions and even Milton's ingenuity failed in making it work until an
instruction book was ordered from America. A few items were sold,
including the large gas-eating truck, for $2,700, making the net cost to the
Mission for all the equipment only $415.76.[3]

Anna's luggage was put on the truck, but since the hot season was at
its peak, she was sent up-country by train. Milton accompanied her,
while Angus MacKay and Robert Earle undertook the task of driving

through with all the equipment. Milton and Anna arrived in Nowgong just as the sun rose on April 26, 1946. Rebecca, Norma, Elizabeth, and Alena were all waiting in front of the bungalow to greet her. The school-children welcomed Anna with garlands, songs, and drama. In the cool of the evening she was taken to Chhatarpur in the old mission car, which broke down several times on the way. The people waiting to welcome her became discouraged and went home. Long after dark the horn honked and rallied them again. There were more garlands and songs. The next morning, back at Nowgong, all the missionaries gathered and sang, "Great Is Thy Faithfulness," Anna's favorite hymn, which became the Mission Council's favorite, also. Sunday morning about nine o'clock the truck, two trailers, and two jeeps were navigated into the compound driven by Robert Earle and Angus MacKay. The luggage was unloaded, and Alena joined Anna in quickly repacking. The Colemans, Anna, and Norma left that night in the new jeep for Landour language school, which was opening on May 1.[4] The eighty-mile trip to Jhansi and the nearest train took them across two rivers without bridges, but a ferry took the jeep load safely across. In Jhansi they left the jeep and crowded into an already packed second-class train with no reservations and sat partly on luggage and partly on benches for the night. The hot furnace-like wind and sand blowing in the open windows kept them awake, but there was a long stopover in Delhi before the final all-night train journey to their destination. Too excited and hot to sleep much even during the Delhi stopover, Colemans and Norma shared news with Anna of what had happened in Bundelkhand since they had arrived. A sixty-page manual with all the mission rules was given to Anna to review. Later one of her assignments would be to retype the whole thing and always keep it up-to-date.

Language Study versus Work Assignments

Colemans and Norma Freer talked of feeling in a "strait betwixt two" as they had sought to lend a helping hand to the Earles and Alena but without a working knowledge of the language. Norma related to Anna how with only two months of study behind her she had arrived in Chhatarpur from Landour on September 19, 1945. After a very hearty welcome with garlands, songs, and dramas—for she was the first new missionary for seven years[5]—she barely had time to visit all the Christian families in the various stations until demands of the work began to press in. The Earles were getting ready for furlough, and Norma with some business training was destined to become mission treasurer. Language study suffered and her first language examination had to be postponed until fall.[6] Seven months after arriving in India Norma received word of the sudden death of her father, and the emotional toll of being so far away was great.

However, she worked hard at the treasurer's books and learned early to appreciate the Indian accountants, Komal Das and Nathu Lall, who worked in the mission office still located in the walled-off guest room of the house she lived in.

On March 14, 1946, at 2:30 a.m. Norma awoke suddenly. On the veranda in front of the office, she could see four men stooped over *something* very large and heavy. She guessed correctly that they were stealing the safe containing about $5,000. She quickly slipped out her back door and aroused a carpenter who was sleeping on his veranda. By that time the four burglars were already outside the compound gate with the safe. As the carpenter and Norma started after them, the thieves dropped the safe and ran for their lives. They had twisted off the lock of the office and removed the five-hundred-pound safe, and everyone wondered how they had done it without waking anyone but Norma. But the safe was safe! Nothing was lost but sleep. After that, two men slept all night every night at the office door.[7]

Colemans had arrived in India before this incident and were living in Nowgong. They were a great encouragement to the Earles. On December 1, 1945, Earles' twelfth wedding anniversary, they all celebrated. Robert and Elizabeth repeated their marriage vows and Milton officiated. Elizabeth wore Rebecca's wedding dress and Rebecca played and sang, "I Love You Truly." This took place between Mission Council meeting and a Thanksgiving peacock dinner.[8]

Milton especially felt the pressure of both work and language. As representative to the Mid-India Representative Christian Council, he was immediately responsible for organizing revival meetings throughout the Central India area.[9] He met regularly with the educational and evangelistic boards. Both he and Rebecca were appointed joint advisors for the Senior Christian Endeavor though their main assignment was supposed to be language study.[10] Rebecca's musical ability was immediately useful. Called to assist the thirty children enrolled in the Junior C.E., she was deeply impressed with the leadership of an eleven-year-old child trained by Rachel Banwar, ". . . the finest junior meetings I have ever attended," she said.[11] From Elizabeth, Rebecca took over responsibilities in the educational board, women's work, classroom supervision, and also gradually the care of the sixteen orphans. Elizabeth felt keenly the insecurity of these orphans, compared to her own three little ones. She could hardly bear for them to be passed from one missionary to another. "The history of the children is on paper, but the special problems of disposition, development, and destiny are acquired only by a daily hearing of the particular problem arising."[12] She must have conveyed this feeling to Rebecca, for never again would these children of the orphanage feel parentless. Even on furlough and now into retirement Rebecca and Milton continue correspondence with them. They have taken the name *Coleman* as their family name.[13]

Milton Coleman's Pull to Evangelism

The greatest pull from language for Milton and the driving force back to it was the evangelistic work. Before Christmas, Milton bicycled thirty-six miles to Isanagar. In early March the camping team was sixty-four miles away in Talgaon. Milton drove out to pick them up in the Mission's '34 Ford, "kept running by grace, gumption and Komal [Das Lall]."[14] Talgaon was in Panna State, where preaching was forbidden, but Khub Chand visited there shortly after being restored to a good spiritual experience. Finding deep interest in the Gospel, he called for Stuti Prakash and Hira Singh to come and teach the people. They found one family ready to receive Christ. So Robert Earle joined in an intensive camp there along with Stuti Prakash, Shapan Nath, Khub Chand, and two Bible women — Manorma Bai and Rupa Das.[15] They arrived on Monday and started Bible classes morning, afternoon, and night. By Wednesday they felt the time had come for public declaration of faith and acceptance of Talgaon's Gore Lal and his wife into the Christian community. After prayer at their home the party marched a quarter of a mile to a pond. Khub Chand cut the man's sacred lock of hair and Stuti Prakash baptized the man by immersion and the woman by sprinkling. They marched home singing "Victory to Jesus" and to take part in a communion service in the tent using chapati and boiled raisin juice, with the communion cup being the palm of the hand. The Christians, including the new converts, all ate together that evening to demonstrate there were no caste barriers in Christ. Robert Earle wrote, "I had not expected this ceremony; Stuti . . . [who] had not only never been baptized but had never even seen a baptismal service . . . had planned and prepared for it all."[16] A few weeks later, Stuti Prakash also performed his first marriage ceremony.[17]

Earles' Concern for Evangelism

There was no doubt that evangelism had come to hold top priority in the Mission. When Hira Lal, the convert from Bilwar near Gulganj, left his village to live in Nowgong to get away from his father's persecution, the Earles were deeply troubled.[18] They felt he should stay among his people and win them to Christ. To keep him there they felt they should move to Gulganj to give him spiritual support. So they formed a *panchayat* (committee) to carry on the work in Nowgong, appointing Victor Mangalwadi, chairman; Rachel Banwar, secretary; and other members Reubin Oriel, pastor; David Ganjir, superintendent of grounds. These extremely capable people did not see eye to eye, to put it mildly, on how affairs should be managed. The Mission Board also did not approve the Earles' leaving Nowgong, and no such move matured.[19]

Golden Jubilee Celebration and Vision for the Future

Less than a month before Anna Nixon arrived in India, the Fiftieth Jubilee Celebration of the Mission was held. The program had been planned entirely by Indian leaders. Stuti Prakash was in charge of meetings, Moti Lal came from Jhansi as Bible expositor and evangelistic speaker, and G. M. Roberts arranged for hospitality.[20] Twenty Indians and three missionaries took part in the service expressing their thanks to God, their disappointments, and their hopes for the next twenty-five years. One quoted Delia Fistler: "I have filled in the foundations and now look carefully what structure you build on it." It was clear that the Indians felt ready to tackle the building. Victor Mangalwadi said, "Missionaries must be co-workers with Indians side by side. Older Indians must guide young Indians toward progress."[21] In the U.S.A. at the same time Everett Cattell was saying in the Ohio Jubilee Celebration, "The missionary of the future must more and more 'decrease' while Indian church leaders 'increase.' The new missionary must go out to be not so much a boss but rather a brother and a companion in the work of the Lord."[22]

These attitudes kept step with the national scene, but actions lagged behind, partly because the missionaries did not fully trust the maturity of the Indian leaders, and partly because the Indian leaders did not trust one another. On the matter of having a greater part in decision making, however, they were conspicuously united. They felt quite capable of handling their own affairs. Saturday afternoon the whole church, about two hundred and fifty strong, marched two by two in a procession through the Nowgong streets carrying banners, singing, witnessing, and distributing tracts; but the business meeting that evening was so fiery and bitter that the people went away burning. It did not end there, or hope may have died. Instead, that night many met to pray and a dozen men prayed all night long. In spite of the fact that discussion about water baptism had "created much heat and little light," enough of a consensus was reached so that the next day nine young people were baptized in the fount built earlier at the order of Elizabeth Jenkins, and the jubilee celebrations ended with a great sense of the presence of the Holy Spirit as the people repented, confessed their sins, and asked forgiveness of one another.[23]

Sharing the Field with Another Mission

Indian leaders and missionaries were increasing in number, but from the beginning they had never been able to cover their field east of the Ken

River. Two other missions wanted to occupy that area, and the Mission Board permitted the Council to proceed with turning it over.[24] Early in 1946 Wesley Duewel and Mr. Khanna of OMS International Mission came to see the area. All of the Friends missionaries joined them to explore the field. All eight of them got into the battered Ford, and with Robert Earle at the wheel, successfully negotiated the first thirteen hairpin curves from Ajaigarh to the Panna rest house—except for the last ten miles, when near the summit, the Ford hit a boulder and the lights went out. Flashlights revealed a broken battery box, a broken cable to the starter, and a badly cracked and leaking front cell. Pliers, ropes, a safety pin, Band-Aids for insulation, a hammer, and ingenuity restored the ignition and lights, and they reached the rest house and supper at 9:30 p.m.[25] On the trip home they all visited the diamond mines and met the Maharaja of Panna State.[26] OMS did not come, but the area was later occupied in 1948 by the World Evangelization Crusade, founded by C. T. Studd.[27]

The Spearhead Party and Carrie Wood's Return

With the Earles leaving, Alena Calkins was the only voting member on the Mission Council. Walter Williams, Mission superintendent, went to China with Charles DeVol and Charles and Elsie Matti in what was called the "spearhead party" to reestablish the Mission in China. He had expected to return via India and stay on there until Cattells came back from furlough. Carrie Wood's better health, however, and willingness to take on another short term released him, and he returned to the U.S.A. with a severe streptococci infection of the throat and had prolonged treatment from Dr. W. Ezra DeVol before finally recovering.[28]

Landour Language School

These things and many more were shared by Colemans, Norma, and Anna as they journeyed to Landour, where they immediately upon arrival enrolled in the language school bustling with 150 new missionaries.[29] "Missionary life is a high adventure indeed—at least at the beginning," said Catherine Cattell,[30] and it was that for these four as they viewed the steep beauty of the snowcapped Himalayan peaks from a cottage that seemed to cling to the side of the hill. "Bethany," their new home, was managed by Cathie MacKay, with whom Norma had traveled to India. Amidst pine trees, roses, and the visible snow-covered ranges beyond, they climbed breathlessly up and down to language school.[31]

Alena Calkins came to Landour a month later to be with the new missionaries. She roomed with Norma and Anna. As general superintendent of the hospital, she asked Dr. Grace Jones to be in charge while she was away. As nursing superintendent, she asked permission of Dr. Grace Jones to leave.[32] Through her the new missionaries learned that a new family ward built in 1945 was bringing in rent at Rs. 2 a day and that this money was being put aside to build another.[33] Komal Das Lall had built the ward with money donated by a wife of a merchant and lorry contractor of Nowgong at the cost of $400.[34] She told of the struggle of Dr. Jones, with Alena at her side, to keep alive the Maharaja's young wife when she delivered her baby. Her hemoglobin was only 50 percent. The little prince brought great rejoicing, but she gave her life for him. She was cremated on sandalwood saturated with ghee (clarified butter).[35] Other hospital stories Alena had to tell concerned cholera and plague and the first visit ever of a dentist to the area. He must have been in dental glory with all the cleanings, extractions, and fillings as he worked in a community who had never seen a dentist before.[36]

Mahatma Gandhi's Prayer Meeting in Landour, Mussoorie

On June 6, 1946, all the missionaries in Landour took time to go down the hill to Silverton Hotel to hear Mahatma Gandhi speak. He came wrapped in a wool shawl, leaning on the arm of his great niece, Manu. Other important Congress leaders were with him. Sitting cross-legged on a sheet-covered platform he conducted his prayer meeting with Muslims, Christians, and Hindus all taking part. The crowds were unbelievable. His burden was for the poor living conditions of coolies in Mussoorie. That day he raised $3,030 (Rs. 100,000) to build shelters and resting places for them.[37]

The Earles Leave India

The Earles, who had planned to leave for furlough in May 1946, were delayed again and again. They had not booked a house in Landour and there was no room left. Baby Charles Robert was covered with prickly heat and mosquito bites, and the Political Agent in Nowgong, Mr. Egerton, invited them to come stay in the P.A. bungalow with its *khas khas* (grass) soaked mats at the doors, its electric fans, and its thatched roof. They left Nowgong for Bombay in mid-July but found no place on the ship sailing that month. A postal and telegraph strike stopped communication, but a cable finally came through saying Carrie Wood was arriving on the *SS General Gordon* about August 12. Therefore, the Earles were there to greet her as she arrived. They then boarded the same ship and reached America October 8, 1946.[38]

Robert Earle left India broken in health and utterly discouraged. He had suffered severe back trouble over a period of years. As he sought to prepare the final annual reports to send off to the Board that summer, he came down with malaria and 105° temperature. The whole family was ill with amoebic dysentery. In their weariness it was difficult for the Earles to be encouraged by their accomplishments. They had given themselves to administration, evangelism, the loving care of orphans and support of the Church, and they had made tremendous improvement in the whole educational system. The entire staff were well-trained, there were ninety-six students, and the latest methods of teaching and hostel living had been introduced. They took the students out weekly in village evangelism and scheduled revival meetings regularly in order to bring all to the feet of Christ. Their loving care overflowed at such times as when thirty-five students were all down with malaria at one time and the school had to be closed. They had increased the educational opportunities for all Christians through developing the Bundelkhand Christian Education Society financed by shares from which any Christian young person could borrow funds for his further education. Victor Mangalwadi was the first one to benefit. He returned to Jabalpur to complete his theological training.[39] Robert Earle did not seem to be aware of these accomplishments. His self-doubt at times was overwhelming. He seemed unable to rise above this, and the Board decided he should not return to India.[40] Later, through God's help, Robert's understanding and acceptance of himself brought peace and victory and his remaining years of ministry as a pastor encouraged many. In 1976 he and Elizabeth returned to India for a blessed time with the people. Colemans were visiting India again at the same time, and when Robert's terminal illness cut their visit short, the Colemans accompanied them home. Robert died a few weeks later.[41]

Alena Calkins and Carrie Wood Orient the New Missionaries

Though language study was top priority, the needs of the field pushed the four new missionaries into heavy responsibility as soon as they left language school in the fall of 1946. Norma and Anna returned to Bundelkhand in October after completing their first-year language examinations, but Rebecca and Milton (he being the only man and by profession a pastor) decided to postpone their examination until spring, and returned earlier.[42] They found Alena exhausted. "We notice she is just plodding," they wrote, "hardly any notice or concern for any deviation from routine."[43] Then she turned yellow from hepatitis, a good reason to be weary, and before recovering from that, she suffered a severe attack of amoebic dysentery. Milton visited her often to assist and encourage, riding back and forth on a war surplus motorcycle from Nowgong to Chhatarpur.[44] She had encountered violence on returning to Chhatarpur in July. A well-bandaged *chowkidar-chaprasi* (watchman-peon) met her, and she discovered he had twelve stitches in his head from an injury he sustained from an attack of thieves on the Cattell compound the week before. The thieves had sneaked in at night and found people asleep out under the stars because of the hot weather. Stuti Prakash's wife Ramki Bai, who was born of a warrior caste, awakened with a gun pointed at her heart. She grabbed the gun. They hit her over the wrist and then struck at her ten-year-old daughter. The watchman ran to help and they struck him down and left him for dead while they began searching for treasure. He revived and, dripping with blood, slipped off to the hospital compound a quarter of a mile away and blurted out his message before falling unconscious at Dr. Grace Jones's doorstep. She immediately called all available men who grabbed bamboo poles and ran to Cattells' compound, shouting as they went. Hearing the men coming, the robbers ran away without mortally wounding anyone and without much loot. The next day all the families living there and all the Cattells' valuable articles were moved up to the hospital compound, where they remained until Cattells returned from furlough.[45]

Carrie Wood, who arrived in July, welcomed the four new missionaries for whose sake she had returned to India. She had not previously met any of them except Anna Nixon for a few hours in 1945. "I think she will make a good missionary," she wrote at that time.[46] Later she made similar assessments of the other three. Colemans and Norma Freer were stationed in Nowgong and Anna in Chhatarpur, Carrie Wood explained, because she was more free to help Alena than was Norma with her accounts. "Then we felt that she needed more responsibilities . . . to take her mind off her Manila experiences. She is taking hold just fine in Chhatarpur (housekeeping for herself and Alena, cleaning in the hospital, developing Junior C.E. and studying language) . . . . Taking a selfish view of it, I realize it has worked out well for me, as Anna is still very restless and nervous and excitable and I get tired when I am with her very long at a time. With more regular interests and work and a normal life I think she will soon quiet down and not use up so much nervous energy."[47] Anna seemed to sense the effect of her intensity, for about the same time, after a period of solitude among the Landour pines, she wrote, "Like the pines, we missionaries must needs be close to one another on the steep hillside of India's need . . . . I am aware that without Christ I have possibilities of being a great deal of trouble."[48] That annoying intensity, however, did help her earn distinction in the first-year Hindi examination that fall, the only Bundelkhand missionary ever to accomplish that.

Clifton and Betty Robinson's Stormy Arrival in India

"Except a corn of wheat fall into the ground and die, it abideth alone: but if it die, it bringeth forth much fruit." (John 12:24) This was Everett Cattell's text on Easter Sunday in 1936, just after his call had been sealed to go to India. It was Clifton Robinson's text one Sunday when Perry Hayden, a flour mill operator in Tecumseh, Michigan, was in the audience. Through the inspiration of that message Perry Hayden started a stewardship program, *Dynamic Kernels*, that revolutionized giving throughout Ohio Yearly Meeting (Evangelical Friends Church — Eastern Region) and spread into other areas, even attracting the attention of Henry Ford. It became the life motto of Cliff, who began habitually to write the Scripture reference below his signature.

As Cattells and Robinsons sailed on the SS *Marine Adder* for India just before Christmas 1946, Walter R. Williams reminded them of the significance of John 12:24. In his steamer letter he wrote Cattells, "Frailty and disappointment have disciplined your souls. Your dreams are more truly set in the pattern of the known. The reality of the 'corn of wheat falling into the ground' is better understood than ten years ago."[49]

Robinsons, who had waited five years to be sent to India, now with their three-year-old Judy and nine-month-old Anne looked into a nightmare. "This is my eighth trip on the ocean but I never in all my life saw anything like this," Catherine Cattell wrote. The ship had been pulled out of drydock and the crew hastily assembled. A storm hit immediately and the day after Christmas was so intense that the ship tossed like a cork. Everything not bolted down skated back and forth across the cabin floors; dishes crashed to the floor. People with broken arms, legs, and backs and other serious injuries filled the hospital. One crew member died. At four o'clock the next morning the lights suddenly went out and the engines stopped. Everyone by flashlight dressed in the warmest clothes and some prepared to board the lifeboats. One of the lifeboats was lost in the storm. Suddenly the lights came on again, the engine started, and the storm ceased. It was officially recorded as a "full gale." Unsanitary conditions on the ship contributed to much illness, and Friends missionaries did not escape. "This has been a long trip with almost no nice weather," Catherine wrote from Singapore, "It may be only a symbol of the storm we are to find in India . . . but in the storm at sea, God was very near and kept us quiet."[50]

All nine Cattells and Robinsons arrived in Bombay January 24, 1947, and discovered that the "storm" was not over. Moslem/Hindu unrest upset the city, closing shops and stopping transportation. The trip on to Harpalpur took five days.[51] There they came through another storm, for the annual scourge of bubonic plague, spread by the bite of fleas from rats to humans, impelled the government to enforce strict quarantine, compulsory cholera injections, and widespread sanitation programs. Milton Coleman with a special ration of gasoline and a special concession from the agency surgeon and wearing high boots to protect himself from fleas, drove the truck to meet them in Harpalpur. All were extremely tired, and Cliff had a temperature of 105° F.[52] Norma, Rebecca, Anna, Alena, and Carrie Wood, along with the entire Christian community, welcomed them in Nowgong with palm branches and singing.

The New Mission Council — Filled with Hope

Three days later, Cliff was able to attend the Mission Council meeting, convened February 1, 1947, with all ten members present. Everett Cattell opened the meeting with a devotional session that took the Council back to January 1943, when the promises from God during an intense time of prayer came to them from Ezekiel, chapters 36, 37 — promises of cleansing, judgment, and ingathering. "And the nations shall know that I am the Lord God when I shall be sanctified in you before their eyes."[53] After that, business proceeded smoothly.

Everett Cattell, the new superintendent for a three-year term, commended the missionaries' recommending to the Mission Board a closer and more costly relationship with Woodstock Boarding School in Landour, where two thirds of the 425-member student body came from missionary families. "Woodstock is giving its students a unique opportunity to live and work and play with children of many nationalities, and this is a fact of great significance in the present world situation."[54]

The Mission Board also requested the Council to appoint two other members to act with the superintendent as an executive committee. Carrie Wood and Milton Coleman were the first such appointees to assist in assigning missionaries to work and station.[55]

Carrie Wood's main assignment was orientation of the six new missionaries, but she also served as chief auditor. She was stationed in Nowgong. Catherine Cattell, Chhatarpur, took over from Alena the work of women's evangelism. Milton Coleman, Nowgong, was chairman of the Educational and Evangelistic boards and manager of the Nowgong Christian Institute. Everett Cattell took over from Alena the superintendency of the Mission and hospital, and from Milton the chairmanship of the Board of Trustees. Rebecca Coleman was chairman of the Orphanage Board and a teacher of music in the Nowgong Christian Institute. Norma Freer, Nowgong, was treasurer. Anna Nixon, just then transferred to Nowgong, became Mission Council secretary in place of Milton Coleman and began teaching in the school. The Robinsons in Nowgong were assigned full-time language study, and the other four new missionaries were expected to continue their language study at least half time.[56]

All the missionary men had calls to outside ministry, and everyone accepted local church responsibilities. Alena, for example, was a member of the Ministry and Oversight (*Rakhwal*). She joined the committee in visiting every Christian family in every station and outstation throughout Bundelkhand.[57]

Dr. Grace Jones's Wedding

Alena with Dr. Grace Jones had carried the medical work. Alena dreaded being left alone with the total medical program, but she feared that would happen soon when Dr. Jones's brother-in-law, Moti Lal, suddenly made an arrangement for her marriage to a Methodist chaplain. After meeting her fiance a few times, Dr. Grace felt he was not the one for her. She broke the engagement.

Moti Lal, her brother-in-law, was exceedingly embarrassed. Nevertheless, he knew his duty and was determined not to be frustrated a second time. So he sent out wedding invitations for her marriage to Daniel Singh, brother of her best friend, without informing her. Daniel Singh had been a military engineer for six years. On arrival in Jhansi at the call of Moti Lal, Dr. Grace was introduced to Daniel Singh for the first time. They were engaged formally then and were married the next day, February 12, 1947.

After the wedding Daniel Singh went back to Malaysia to complete his military assignment and Dr. Grace Jones Singh returned to the hospital work. Komal Das Lall supervised the erection of another family ward and Alena and Dr. Grace with their staff did 30,000 treatments that year.

The missionaries' fear of losing Dr. Grace faded when her husband returned from Malaysia and opened a bicycle shop in Chhatarpur, and they settled in to live there for the rest of their lives.[58]

Village Leaders' Conference at Barethi

The most important happenings brought to the attention of the Cattells in the Council meetings those days concerned the new developments in the villages. In late 1945 Khub Chand discovered a hopeful area about fifteen miles southwest of Gulganj. He toured an area surrounded on two sides by branches of the Dhasan River—referred to as an "island"—and visited Chamars of twenty-six villages. These people were dissatisfied with their lot under the caste Hindus and had severed their relationship with them. They were open to anything that could give them relief from oppression.[59]

Before Khub Chand was a Christian, he had toured those same villages to raise money for building a Hindu temple for them. No temple was ever built. As a Christian, he felt convicted for this deceit and went back to confess and to give them the Gospel. He took no food or bedding—only his precious handmade coconut shell violin. He went from village to village, singing songs of Christ he had composed and set to Chamar tunes. The people received him joyfully and fed him freely. Khub Chand called Stuti Prakash and the team of evangelists to bring a camp into the area for intensive teaching.[60]

Never before had the evangelists witnessed so much interest. They decided to hold a conference, calling leaders from all twenty-six villages. The dates set were December 13-15, 1946, when the weather was crisp. Describing the conference later, Stuti Prakash said, "The people which sat in darkness saw a great light." (Matthew 4:16) Together with Khub Chand, Bharos William, and two Bible women — Manorma Bai and Rupa Bai Das — they camped three weeks at Barethi and spread the news. Khub Chand returned to each village, inviting them. The team prayed earnestly.

Opening day, December 13, was extremely cold, cloudy, and windy. No one was on time, but finally one 70-year-old man arrived, leaning on his cane. Slowly through the day, scantily clothed and shivering, 150 men, 35 women, and 30 children arrived from 40 villages and were treated with honor. Classes all day interspersed with games led by Manorma Bai gave them something they had never before experienced. Between classes, biting a guava dangling from a rope with their hands tied behind their backs was not only fun, but it taught them there were no caste distinctions. In class sessions Stuti Prakash taught from Genesis 1-3 the common parenthood of all mankind, the falseness of caste, and God's plan for monogomy. By turn all the evangelists, both men and women, gave lessons from the New Testament about the power of Christ over illness, death, demons, nature, and sin, illustrating with stories of Jesus healing the sick, raising the dead, casting out demons, stilling the storms, and forgiving sins.

Through stories and pictures the people began to understand the meaning of the crucifixion and the resurrection. They memorized the Ten Commandments and Khub Chand's gospel songs. Then the classes got right down to the where, when, and how of becoming a Christian, spelling out the difference this would make in life habits, work, festivals, weddings, and deaths. From Zacchaeus they learned, much to their surprise, that being a Christian did not mean leaving their work and their village to live on the mission compound. They realized idol worship, sorcery, and sinful practices had to go. They also had to receive Jesus Christ as their one and only Savior and Lord. Even their great and courageous leader, Mahatma Gandhi, had refused this last step, saying that he refused to put Christ on a solitary throne. But that is what the evangelists taught, and that is what they believed was the clear teaching of the Bible.

On the third day in worship together an offering was taken, not primarily for the sake of money but rather for the purpose of giving thanksgiving to God. The villagers responded with their *pice* and the offering totaled two dollars — an average villager's two weeks' wages.[61] Before they returned to the villages, all agreed to meet again in Ghuara, ten miles further south, on January 25, 26, 1947.[62]

After hearing all these things at the first council meeting in 1947 with Robinsons and Cattells present, the ten missionaries returned to the various stations and homes to which they had been assigned. The tide of hope had never registered higher.

| Suffering for
Freedom — and
Just Suffering

*"Now this is what the LORD says — he who created you . . .
'Fear not, for I have redeemed you; I have called you by name;
you are mine. When you pass through the waters, I will be
with you; and when you pass through the rivers, they will not
sweep over you. When you walk through the fire, you will not
be burned; the flames will not set you ablaze. For I am the
LORD, your God . . . .'" Isaiah 43:1-3 (NIV)*

The Cost of Freedom

The American missionaries in Bundelkhand in the late forties and early
fifties were eyewitnesses to unprecedented events shaping a new India.
Colemans, Robinsons, DeVols, Bankers, Hesses, Norma Freer, and Anna
Nixon would never experience — as had Cattells, Carrie Wood, and Alena
Calkins — the pomp and splendor of the British Raj.

They were impressed, however, with the twentieth and last viceroy,
Louis Francis Albert Victor Nicholas Mountbatten, 46, and his compassionate and beautiful wife, Vicerene Edwina Mountbatten. The Mount-
battens arrived in India March 24, 1947. Within three days they had
taken control and set about to free India.

In early April Mountbatten called in the leaders of the Interim
Government that had been set up in September 1946. One by one he
talked with Prime Minister Jawaharlal Nehru, Congress Leader Mahatma
Mohandas Karamchand Gandhi, Home Minister Vallabhai Patel, and
Moslem League President Mohammed Ali Jinnah. The consultations continued for weeks, with Jinnah in and out at least six times.
He was the only one who insisted on partition. Gandhi detested it, and
rather than divide India, he proposed appointing Jinnah as prime minister
over the whole. No one else — not even Jinnah — shared his view. So on
June 3, 1947, Mountbatten, with the realism and incisive action so characteristic of him, ordered the division of Pakistan and India. On August 14,
at 9:00 a.m., he stood with Jinnah in Karachi and ushered in Pakistan. At
midnight that same day he was back in Delhi to order the British flag

lowered as the new Indian flag was unfurled amidst tumultuous celebration of freedom.[1] In Chhatarpur Victor Mangalwadi represented Christians and spoke courageously about the foundation for freedom as found in Christ.[2] In Nowgong, the only American present at the ceremony, Anna Nixon, was given the honor of delivering her first speech in Hindi. The Nowgong Christian Institute boys attended the celebration, but the girls and Miss Wood stayed behind on the compound. The following year even the girls would have freedom to celebrate independence.

The saffron, green, and white flag with the *chakra* had hardly fluttered twice over the nation before the hatred and bitterness that led to India's division exploded into indescribable violence and led to the most massive migration in history. Ten and a half million refugees crossed the borders to and from India and Pakistan, leaving at least half a million of their dead and dying strewn along the way — victims of unleashed Hindu-Moslem revenge. Everett Cattell was caught in the crossfire in Delhi on his way for meetings in Kashmir. He proceeded as bloody trainloads of passengers pulled into Delhi station from Pakistan. No one got off. All passengers were dead. Travelers going the other direction met the same fate. Everett watched in terror as he saw a man trying to escape jump off a speeding train and roll down a steep embankment. Cities he traveled through, such as Lahore and Sialkot, were in complete shambles. As many as 100,000 refugees were already herded into makeshift camps for protection. As they sped on north, Hindus and Sikhs killed every Moslem they found. When the train started south with Hindus and Sikhs, the Moslems took their turn to search and kill.[3]

Clifton Robinson went to Calcutta to participate in establishing "Youth for Christ in India." Riots broke out — taking the lives of 6,000 people, and the dead lay neglected in the gutters.[4] Three men were stabbed to death within a stone's throw from the Anglican church where Cliff was speaking, and a bomb exploded in the church compound as Cliff extended the call to accept Christ.[5] "Needless to say, the meeting was interrupted!" Cliff reported.

Police slapped on a seventy-two-hour curfew in Landour and then came right to the home where Colemans, Norma, and Anna stayed and took away the Moslem cook to intern him. Sikhs of the Punjab were leading the riots in Landour, and more than sixty missionaries trying to return home from hot season vacation were stranded until Prime Minister Nehru took the situation in hand and sent an escort for them. India was a boiling caldron. Disaster threatened all and everything within reach. Law and order had vanished from the scene.[6]

Sikhs from the Pakistan side of the Punjab left all their possessions and escaped for the sake of their lives, crowding into India. They flooded into Chhatarpur, forever changing the face of that small city. Moslems of Bundelkhand fled in terror before them, taking refuge in Hyderabad in the South, still a Moslem stronghold right in the heart of India. But it fell quickly, too, and was incorporated into the nation of India by September 1948.

Kashmir, ruled by Hindus but with its 90 percent Moslem population, was another serious trouble spot. Nehru was a Kashmiri Brahmin, and he held his native state with an iron grasp.[7] Kashmir continues to this day as part of India – though somewhat precariously.

The Calcutta riots were so ghastly that Mahatma Gandhi went on a fast unto death to stop them. "I'm not interested in freeing India merely from the English yoke," he wrote in 1923. "I am bent upon freeing India from any yoke whatsoever."[8] On January 13, 1948, Gandhi went on another fast, this time against the wrongs committed by his own people. The key issue was India's injustice in dealing with Moslems in Pakistan. He won his way, but shortly afterwards on his way to a prayer meeting on January 30, 1948, he was assassinated by Nathuram Godse, a fanatical Hindu RSSS party member. Ironically, Jinnah in Pakistan also died that same year.

Before partition, India boasted of some 90,000,000 Moslems, 300,000,000 Hindus, and a few other minorities. Afterward, India was left with 275,000,000 Hindus, 35,000,000 Moslems, 7,000,000 Christians, 6,000,000 Sikhs, 100,000 Parsees, and 24,000 Jews.[9]

The New Constitution and Its Effects

By June 1948, Mountbatten and his wife followed other ruling English out of India, and the Indians were at last on their own. They showed their goodwill to the departing British by choosing to remain in the Commonwealth.

The genius that is in India manifested itself through the constitution drafted and put into effect on the first Republic Day, January 26, 1950. Their goals were to provide:

Justice (social, economic, political),

Liberty (of thought, expression, belief, faith, and worship),

Equality (of status and opportunity),

And to promote:

Fraternity (assuring the dignity of the individual and the unity of the nation).[10]

A secular, democratic state, providing freedom of conscience to each citizen with the right to profess, practice, and propagate his religion, indicated the high statesmanship of those who drafted the constitution. Individual rights were protected with an attempt made to put men and women on equal status and to leave untouchability and caste with no legal backing.

India had as yet an insurmountable task of bringing true freedom to fruition across her land. Their constitution said this freedom included even the 70,000,000 untouchables, who were fired with hope of schools for their children, and the right to enter temples and to draw water from the wells. As time went on, these blessings were slow in reaching them. Instead, inflation pushed prices of food and cloth up 400 percent and kept them in dire poverty.[11] Strict rationing of cloth, kerosene, sugar, and salt opened the door to profiteering so that the rationed articles became available nowhere except on the black market at exhorbitant prices.[12] So even though the untouchable's shadow was no longer supposed to contaminate a Brahmin, outlawing caste — quipped one *Time* reporter — was like trying to make lying unconstitutional.

Backward, benighted Bundelkhand knew little of the national constitution and its rights. The villagers and their petty officials continued to live under the old bondages while a whole nation struggled to understand the meaning of freedom. Ignorance and superstition yet dominated illiterate minds, and moneylenders kept their tight grip on the villagers.

Even so, India was determined to form a democracy and gave the right to vote to its masses in the first elections lasting from October 1951 to the end of February 1952. Eighty-five percent of the voters were illiterate, but each voter was given help to thumbprint and write his name on a paper and drop it into a ballot box marked with a symbol of the party of his choice. To be assured he would not vote again, the back of his/her left index finger was marked with an indelible dye that would not wash off for many days. They elected Congress's Jawaharlal Nehru by an overwhelming majority.[13]

With one sweep the many small Bundelkhandi states ruled by rajas and maharajas were brought into the Union. The rulers were pensioned off and popular government instituted. The beloved young prince of Chhatarpur became just an ordinary man. The old rules of not eating beef or baptizing in Chhatarpur were rendered obsolete.[14] Panna and Orissa states, formerly closed to the Gospel, were thrown wide open. Since Ghuara was in Panna, this was indeed good news. The new province of Vindhya Pradesh, encompassing four districts each of Bundelkhand and Baghelkhand, was formed April 4, 1948, and was given seats for four representatives in parliament.[15] Rewa was chosen as the capital. Goals of the new government were to bring law and order in an area disturbed not only by national problems but also by notorious robber gangs. Great plans were on the drawing board, also, for exploiting the coal, iron, and diamonds in the Vindhya Range. By 1949 they hoped to establish electric power plants and a thousand new village schools.[16] Freedom's dreams were ambitious, but action lagged. A budget had not even been prepared, and deep rivalry for chief posts kept small leaders quarreling. When one Vindhya Pradesh minister was caught taking an $8,000 (Rs. 25,000) bribe, all ministers were ousted and Delhi appointed an administrator.[17] Vindhya Pradesh was later amalgamated with India's largest state, the Hindi-speaking Madhya Pradesh.

Restrictions on Christians and Missionaries

Dr. E. Stanley Jones met with leaders in Delhi early in June 1947 to determine what the new government's attitude toward Christians, missions, and conversion would be. The leaders assured him that there was no objection to conversions that brought about real moral and spiritual changes, but that there would be no toleration of mass conversions.[18]

Constitutional rights of every individual, enforced or not, were so clearly stated that anyone with courage could turn to Christianity without breaking the law.[19] These rights, however, did not go uncontested by radical political parties such as the RSS and Hindu Mahasabha. Their influence was felt through the official communique sent from the deputy secretary of India's Ministry of Home Affairs to all provincial governments and chief commissioners, stating that the Central Government was imposing greater restrictions on admission of missionaries into the country. They insisted that their action was not a violation of the constitution but rather a safeguard for Indianization. Henceforth, they ruled, only foreign missionaries with specialized leadership skills and qualifications would be admitted.[20] Home Minister Sardar Patel, who against strong opposition had fought for inclusion in the constitution of the articles guaranteeing religious freedom, tempered this new rule by asserting again that he stood for religious freedom and a welcome to missionaries ". . . if for no other reason, for their help during the Punjab disorder."[21]

Some missionaries, nevertheless, began to panic with the first refusals of visas. With final word left to local officials, any disgruntled Christian could negotiate such a refusal. The National Christian Council called attention to this fact and requested that local authority not be final.[22] They received a gracious hearing from the Government. Everett Cattell assessed the situation thus:

> It would seem to me that most of our difficulties there are out of sheer ignorance and bungling on the part of clerks and officers who have not yet learned how to handle these kinds of matters rather than any determined opposition . . . . I feel rather we ought to plan to put everything that we have into these ten years to try to establish a Church in Bundelkhand with roots in the soil.[23]

The thirteen new missionaries sent to Bundelkhand immediately after World War II were a part of the largest influx of missionaries to India in history. The language school, larger than ever in 1946, almost doubled in 1947 with some 250 students. There, Bundelkhand missionaries dug into the language, preparing for a lifetime of service in India. "I am finding out," wrote Cliff Robinson, "that all things are possible to him that believeth . . . and studieth!"[24] Catherine Cattell tried to make it easy for the new missionaries to learn the village language not taught in the language school and worked diligently on a Bundelkhandi grammar. This book and a translation of the Gospel of Mark in Bundelkhandi served as valuable guides to the missionaries who agreed with Catherine when she said, "There seems to be no correct way of speaking this dialect, and yet there are many wrong ways."[25]

Carrie Wood's Departure

Carrie Wood's presence had given security and comfort to the Indian people as she guided the new missionaries in adjusting to the culture. The missionaries would later value her patience as day after day she sat with them over a cup of tea, spinning stories of the past as they fidgeted to get out for a game of tennis after a grueling day of language study. She was trying to increase their sympathetic judgment and feelings of tenderness toward the people.[26] She was a bulwark of strength to Alena Calkins, who in Cattells' absence was the only other senior missionary and the acting superintendent. So Carrie Wood stood with her and lifted the load with her wherever possible. She taught English to relieve Milton Coleman in the school; did housekeeping to relieve Rebecca; straightened out school accounts to help Anna; explained how to get legal and financial assistance from the Inter-Mission Business Office in Bombay and how the accounting system was set up to help Norma; played grandmother to Robinsons' Judy and Anne and marveled at Betty as she conquered the charcoal stoves and camp life. "I love the cooking out of doors on the ground and living in the open," Betty said, "but not the flies, the prowling dogs and the howling jackals." Nor did she like 30° F weather when camping in a tent in winter.[27]

Carrie Wood urged all new missionaries to share deeply their spiritual experiences with the Indian people, spend more time with them, and pray more for them. She celebrated her fortieth anniversary in India on February 3, 1948, in Gulganj, and a few days later on February 7, in Nowgong, with all the missionaries. Also in attendance were Violet Peel, an English Friends missionary from Itarsi at the mission for purposes of language study, and visitors—Myra Martin, Friends missionary from Bangarapet with World Gospel Mission, and Esther Shoemaker, Methodist doctor at Kolar.[28]   In the fall Carrie Wood said good-bye.   The last service Carrie Wood rendered before leaving was to arrange a difficult little orphan girl's marriage, which she hoped would last.[29]   Anna Nixon was appointed in her place on the Executive Committee of Mission Council.[30] After beautiful farewell services in Chhatarpur and Nowgong, Everett Cattell accompanied her to Calcutta, where she sailed for the U.S.A. on the *SS Borneo of Java,* a 9,000-ton freighter with passenger space for thirty-two.[31]   "I am just beginning to fully realize the MULTITUDE of little, time-consuming things that she took care of for us, from white-washing a bungalow to dismissing a pastor . . . . She was a blessing and a help in many ways to each of us in orienting us to such a drastically new and different way of living," Cliff wrote.[32]

Max and Ruth Ellen Banker

In 1948 Max and Ruth Ellen Banker were appointed to Bundelkhand. Max came from Wesleyan and Marion College background, where he majored in English and music.   World War II put him in the army and took him to China and India, opening his eyes to the needs abroad.   In Marion College he met Ruth Ellen Henry of Alum Creek Friends Church.   They were married January 30, 1943.   On returning from service, Max completed work on his master's degree at Western Reserve University. After being accepted for India, many delays frustrated them, but finally with their little daughter, Bonnie, they got off and arrived in Bombay May 6, 1949.   From there they went straight to Landour and enrolled immediately in language school already in session.[33]

Dr. Ezra and Frances DeVol

Dr. and Mrs. W. Ezra DeVol with twin daughters Priscilla and Patricia, and sons Joseph and Phillip, started for China in September 1948 – their second attempt in the 1940s.   Dr. Ezra was the third child of Drs. George and Isabella DeVol, missionaries to China.   He had been born in China, and after his father's death, he, Catherine, and Charles DeVol had come to the U.S.A. with their mother.   In 1920 she also died, asking, "Who will go?"   Charles and Catherine, coming near her bed, each said: "Mother, I will go."   Ezra, on the other hand, said nothing.   He had already made up his mind that he would never be a missionary.   When a junior in Marion College, he finally surrendered to the Lord, and three weeks later, after a painful struggle, he too, said, "I will go."

Catherine DeVol Cattell was in India and Charles DeVol in China as Dr. Ezra and Frances DeVol started for China.

Frances Hodgin DeVol was the daughter of Rev. Daniel and Frieda Hodgin.   Her father served many years as pastor and evangelist in Friends and Wesleyan Methodist churches and her mother was a great woman of prayer.

Ezra and Frances met at Marion College. Afterwards, she switched from teaching to a nursing career and took her R.N. at Western Reserve University in order to be a part of a medical team with her husband. Dr. Ezra graduated in 1935 and they were married August 15, 1936.[34]

After selling his medical practice in Ohio and packing to go, news came to Dr. Ezra that there was a shipping strike. They proceeded to California to wait patiently for sailing, staying in the home of Elizabeth Jenkins and later in the *Home of Peace* in San Francisco.[35] By the time the shipping strike was settled, headlines concerning China were ominous. Missionaries were being evacuated, and DeVols were strongly advised not to proceed. As younger missionaries returned, being evacuated from China, DeVols were still on the west coast to welcome them. John and Geraldine Williams came in with their baby, John, critically ill with measles. DeVols' presence eased his pain and comforted the parents.[36]

The DeVols now faced a multi-dilemma. Should they continue to wait for China to open, return to Ohio to reopen a practice, open a new mission for Friends in Japan, or go to India? The Board suggested India. Guided by prayer and Scripture, two promises blessed them: "This is the way, walk ye in it." (Isaiah 30:21) "My God, in His loving kindness, shall meet me at every corner." (Psalm 59:10) They were assured that there was purpose in their delays and that nothing in the circumstances was impromptu or "last minute."[37] They saw in the whole sequence of events God guiding them to India. They applied for a visa. Before they got rid of their heavy coats and other equipment not suitable for India, the arrival of *SS Borneo* bringing Carrie Wood home to America was announced and they booked passage on it.

Dr. Ezra, with Board approval, quickly purchased, packed, and delivered to the docks essential medical equipment.[38] Within a month the visa came through and they were on their way to India after waiting in California for passage from September 1948 to February 12, 1949.

Cattells met the DeVols in Bombay. Customs were easy except for the tedious paper work. "To get the Dodge truck through customs we had to get the signatures of twenty-one officers, then fourteen more signatures to get a license for it," wrote Dr. Ezra.[39] They went by train to Bundelkhand accompanied by Catherine while Everett drove the loaded ambulance. At the gate in Nowgong the school children welcomed them. "We have arrived," Dr. Ezra wrote. "All of the delays, the days of indecision, the problems of the past few months have faded into insignificance, because we are conscious of being in the place of God's choosing." Robinsons were just leaving for the hills and Patricia and Priscilla accompanied them to

Landour, where they entered Woodstock School. Ten days later, after visiting Chhatarpur, Gulganj, Bijawar, and a little village called Ghari, Dr. Ezra penned one more line before heading for Landour and language school: "We are happier than we have ever been."[40] As they traveled along through rocky wastes, expanses of barrenness and brown fields relieved only here and there with patches of green where there was some irrigation, they got their first bitter taste of India's hot season. Hot winds and great clouds of dust buffeted them. If only it would rain, they thought, then the parched ground would respond with a blanket of green and spirits would be revived.[41]

A Royal Welcome to the Bankers

DeVols returned from Landour on October 2, 1949, with the Bankers, who were arriving in Bundelkhand for the first time. As educational missionaries, they received special attention from the school in Nowgong. Rachel Banwar, the headmistress, gave the school a holiday to prepare a suitable welcome. Arriving at night, the first thing the Bankers saw was flickering lights outlining the compound and shining through letters cut through cardboard spelling WELCOME. The whole roadway, lawn, and bungalow were outlined with *diyas*. In front of the bungalow were two more large signs saying WELCOME—one made of *diyas* in English, and another of white cotton on red cloth saying it in Hindi—"swagatam." It was breathtakingly beautiful. The children met them at the gate and marched by their sides waving palm branches, singing and dancing all the way.[42]

Happily, the Bankers and DeVols both settled into the big bungalow, one family on each side. Anna Nixon, in the little cottage, was no longer the only missionary in Nowgong.

Losses

Personal tragedies, illnesses, and loss often were dwarfed by the magnitude of the national agonies and sufferings, but they nevertheless brought pain. Robinsons lost all their luggage containing their wedding gifts, and Betty quoted the verse, "Take cheerfully the spoiling of your goods." Their packing company went bankrupt, and the loss was total. Cattells lost three boxes en route that, when discovered, were so damaged as to merit being thrown into the sea.[43] The home rented by Robinsons and Cattells in Landour was robbed, probably by Sikh refugees. Dishes, curtains, and irreplaceable photographic equipment were taken.[44] A pickpocket relieved Everett Cattell of $170 along with his passport and registration papers. Cliff failed to insure a letter containing $133 for Betty in Landour, and she received the envelope but no money.[45] Robberies and lootings increased with breakdown of law and order. While Hira Singh was attending a refresher course in Nowgong, his house in Isanagar was robbed.[46]

Milton Coleman was caught by a band of robbers one day as he bicycled home through the jungle after a visit to Ghuara. These outlaws had just murdered two policemen; so with a gun in his face and command to dismount, Milton seemed eager to comply. Back in Amarmau Rebecca sensed an intense urge to leave her work and stop to pray for Milton, though she did not know why. Sitting down in the outlaws' circle, Milton sought to be courteous to his captors. This disarmed them, and he caught a remark of one to another, "He doesn't suspect anything." When he discovered some of them needed medicines, he sold them a few pills, and they let him go.[47]

Separations

Missionaries felt separation from their children a special kind of suffering, often more painful to both child and parents than illness or loss. The children could not escape boarding school, but at those special times of heartache or grand success, matrons did not take the place of parents. David Cattell experienced trauma when his parents had to leave him behind in boarding school to go to Australia for his father's recuperation in 1939. So great was his pain that he fell behind in his class. By mission rule, his allowance stopped with his 18th birthday on February 8, 1949. The financial stress of putting a son through his final year of high school with no allowance was great but managed without complaint. Afterwards the rule was changed, but not until David had graduated from Woodstock School in November 1949. He spent three happy months in Bundelkhand with his parents before turning homeward. Then as Catherine wept alone, David's father and his Uncle Ezra accompanied him to Bombay, where on February 23, 1950, there was a painful good-bye as the first missionary child of India sailed away on the SS Strathmore and arrived via England in New York on the RHS Queen Mary. David found himself a foreigner in his own homeland—before cultural shock had been clearly defined or understood.[48]

Illness

Smallpox, cholera, plague, typhoid, hepatitis, malaria, dysentery, tuberculosis, and many other killers took their toll. Stuti Prakash's family seemed riddled with tuberculosis. Two brothers-in-law and one brother died of the disease. His young evangelist brother, Prem Prakash, also, came down with it and probably would have died, too, had Dr. Ezra DeVol not been on hand with the X ray to discover the disease early. Stuti Prakash's own son also might have died, for it was a common belief that

Indians did not have appendicitis. Dr. DeVol diagnosed Vijay's illness and operated. Hira Singh about the same time had a ruptured appendix that Dr. Ezra recognized and cared for by emergency surgery.[49]

Betty Robinson out in camp during the cold season grieved for the village children without a stitch of clothing. She could not resist at times taking them into her lap and letting her tears drop on their pus-filled eyes, red and swollen from their mothers' ignorant treatment with hot spices.[50] One school child died of cholera. Rebecca Coleman wept because poor villagers in ignorance gave up to three days' wages as a bribe to officials to avoid free smallpox vaccinations. She saw some of those same children die of the dreaded disease.[51]

In spite of mosquito nets, boiled water, prophylactic pills, and many inoculations, missionaries were also frequently ill. Milton Coleman suffered severe hepatitis through the year of 1947. Rebecca remained well though she was grief stricken to hear of the death of a sister. Later that year Carol Jean was born on November 11, 1947. The happiness in their home with a little one after eight years of marriage was enhanced by the fact that they passed their final language exam that year, too, in first division. But tragedies and heartaches were also a part of their lives, and just a faint glimmer of this came through in a letter Rebecca wrote to Walter Williams: "We were hoping Carol Jean would have a brother next summer but things didn't go so well as before. These jungle roads can't be trusted. The camp we went to was only seven miles away but what a seven miles! Even the jeep trailer upset . . . . The orphan children will come to Amarmau to spend Christmas."[52]

Norma, Rebecca, and Catherine all had severe and repeated bouts with amoebic dysentery that hospitalized them occasionally and kept them on periodic treatment. On arriving in Landour, Bankers all came down with heavy colds, sinusitis, and diarrhea. Max developed hepatitis and malignant tertian malaria – a real killer.[53] Everett, Max, and Cliff all seemed to major in malaria. Cliff had it time after time. This recurring fever not only incapacitated them but often threatened life itself. In 1949 when Cliff stayed down through the summer, when nights sometimes cooled off to 90° F, he also developed carbuncles.[54]

Rabies became a threat from Bonnie Banker's little dog as it died snapping and biting, and later the Robinsons, too, had to get fourteen injections for their third daughter bitten by their rabid puppy.[55] Carol Jean Coleman's *aya* was discovered to be suffering from leprosy.[56]

Frances DeVol, Phillip DeVol, and Barbara Cattell had major surgery. Phillip also had a greenstick fractured collarbone, pneumonia, dysentery, and tonsillitis.[57] Anne Robinson suffered nine months with steady coughing, unable to keep food down. She had pneumonia and paratyphoid, and ran high fever for eleven days. Judy later suffered a "deep down bronchitis," which proved later to be incipient tuberculosis. She also had a serious case of mumps and measles that soon passed down the line.[58]

On February 10, 1949, Robinsons' third daughter, Ruth Alma, was born — delivered in the Chhatarpur hospital without anesthetic by Dr. Grace Jones Singh. Ruth brought much happiness but also wakeful nights until she got days and nights in order. For about two weeks both of the Robinsons and Anna Nixon, living together in Nowgong at that time, each took four-hour shifts all night long.[59] On June 5, 1951, Dr. DeVol was on hand to deliver Byron Randolph, Robinsons' son, in Landour Community Hospital. He had a difficult time entering the world but within three weeks all was going well.[60]

Betty earlier that summer had experienced heat stroke, and Anna Nixon cycled to the bungalow of the Chief of Police to get ice for her. "Anna, how is it that you never get sick?" she asked. Anna looked at her swollen ankles and thought of her annoying intenseness — but it was true she had not had a fever or spent a day in bed since coming to India.[61]

Alena Calkins Leaves India

Alena Calkins began a series of illnesses in 1947 that truncated her service in India and threatened to incapacitate her for life.

"This is the last year I will have to play doctor," Alena had written her sister as the DeVols finished their language study.[62] She and Dr. Grace Jones Singh had carried the hospital for years, taking over for each other during illness and vacations. Alena looked forward to reverting to her true profession, leaving diagnosis and operations to the doctors. She plunged into training nurses, representing the Mission at the meetings of the mid-India Examining Board meetings and arranging post graduate work for Priobala and Mercy Nath, daughters of Jagannath and Puniya Bai, who later became outstanding in their work as head nurse and pharmacist.[63]

In the spring of 1948 stiffness in the right shoulder began hindering her in getting her arm back farther than the outer side of her right hip or higher than her waistline. The pain spread to her back and soon she needed help in combing her hair. Diathermy, milk injections, iodolacto protein, calcium, and finally daily ultraviolet ray treatments made no impression. In January 1949 she saw Dr. Paul Brand, the orthopedic surgeon in Vellore. He manipulated the shoulder regularly under anesthetic, and Alena slept between times with her arm tied to the head of her bed. Results were good, and back in Chhatarpur, with Norma Freer's help with difficult exercises, Alena returned to work. "I do not accomplish as much as formerly," Alena modestly wrote her sister.[64]

By October she had an attack of neuritis in her left hand and forearm. Vitamin B injections and intravenous shots of typhoid vaccine gave some relief. In May 1950 severe pain in her back and abdomen intensified over a week's span in spite of various treatments. Alena, still "playing doctor" with Dr. Grace away on vacation and the DeVols in language school, had to give up. Leaving the hospital without a director, she went to Jhansi. The doctor there sent her on to Landour for more expert advice in a much cooler climate.[65] On her arrival, Dr. DeVol laid aside all language study and with a team of doctors went in search of the cancer that the tests indicated they would find. Two weeks later, still mystified, the doctors discharged her without discerning the cause of her problem.[66]

By July she was back in the hospital with two stomach ulcers. The doctor put her on a six-month ambulatory treatment and allowed her to go back to work. She returned to the Chhatarpur hospital at the end of August, and two months later Dr. Ezra and Frances DeVol, having finished language school, moved to Chhatarpur to help. Finding Alena's condition much worse, Dr. Ezra operated and found she had regional ileitis (Crohn's disease), which does not respond well to either medical or surgical treatment. After prayer and fasting, the Mission Council was convinced that the mysterious will of God pointed to sending Alena home. She left by air on November 17, 1950, and Frances DeVol, bewildered and alone, shouldered the duties of the nursing superintendent without the benefit of the orientation she was expecting to receive from Alena.

In the U.S.A. the Mayo Clinic made the same diagnosis and performed an intestinal bypass operation. They put her on a lifelong restricted diet, got her back on her feet, and told her she could return to India.[67] Dr. and Mrs. Charles Smith, medical missionary candidates for Bundelkhand who had been forced to give up their dream because of ill health, were studying at Mayos' at this time and graciously extended hospitality to Alena as she recuperated.[68]

Alena joined Vincent's Hospital for part-time duty and part-time refresher course, fully intending to return to India. However, she was stricken with the same trouble in her left arm as she had previously experienced in her right. Ligaments again had to be torn loose under anesthesia. Finally, she wrote Dr. Walter R. Williams, Board president:

> In face of my rather unsatisfactory health in recent years both in India
> and here on furlough, after much prayer and consideration, I feel that
> I should resign from further service in India.[69]

Her resignation was accepted with regret.

Death of Jefferson Ford

Before Alena Calkins left India, Jefferson and Helen Ford visited the Mission on their way to retirement from Kenya. While holding meetings in India, particularly in Bundelkhand, Jefferson Ford began having recurrent fever. In Vellore hospital they discovered that his problem was not malaria, mononucleosis, or some rare tropical disease, but lympho sarcoma.[70] Jefferson Ford responded to treatment and finished his preaching tour. He completed the Old Testament translation for his people in Kenya, having finished the New Testament earlier. He returned to the U.S.A. and died December 16, 1949. He was buried in Friendswood, Texas.[71]

Death of Esther Baird

Before Alena Calkins arrived in the U.S.A., Esther Baird also died on September 1, 1950. For thirteen years before her death, Ethel Eastman, a graduate of Cleveland Bible College, felt it her calling to care for Esther Baird. This she did to the very end, as a daughter would care for her mother.[72]

In India, Victor Mangalwadi preached at a memorial service for Esther Baird from the text:

If my people which are called by my name, shall humble themselves, and pray, and seek my face, and turn from their wicked ways; then will I hear from heaven, and will forgive their sin, and will heal their land.

With tears he confessed his lack of humility and asked to be forgiven. He then asked two men to forgive him for his lack of love for them and for talking about them. As pastor and leader of the flock, he set the example, and others followed.

"We feel revival is near," wrote Catherine.[73]

Everett wrote, "Could Esther Baird have heard the impassioned pleas of this fiery preacher, she would have known that the sacrifices of the years were not in vain."[74]

One could almost hear Esther Baird's response in words she had written just before she died: "Since I have retired, I have no greater joy than to hear that my children walk in truth."[75]

CHAPTER
XIX

Preparing for the Care of a Growing Church

"Keep watch over yourselves and all the flock of which the Holy Spirit has made you overseers. Be shepherds of the church of God, which he bought with his own blood." Acts 20:28

Avenues and Results of Revival

After Cattells first arrived in India in 1936, the axis of mission emphasis radically shifted. Evangelism came to the fore. All social services, valuable though they were, took second place. Carrie Wood and Alena Calkins, who spanned the change from care and nurture of orphans to intensive evangelism, favored the new policy, as did all of the new missionaries who came after World War II.

The change did not take place automatically. Evangelism was purposely, strenuously, and often painfully thrust forward. Such strategy required dedication, cooperation, and unity of an informed body — the Mission Council. To assure this, the superintendent, Everett Cattell, called the missionaries together every month for the study of God's Word, prayer, and business. At times when problems or policy needed special attention the meetings lasted up to four days.[1]

Evening book reviews and reports gave a broad setting to matters under discussion. The missionaries joined eagerly in these meetings, seeking to know, participate, and act. The unity achieved was unique; letters home reflected from all that these meetings were an oasis for the American missionaries scattered in various stations throughout Bundelkhand.

By April 1950 a joint committee drafted a new Discipline: G. M. Roberts, Victor Mangalwadi, Stuti Prakash, G. L. Singh, Nathu Lall, and the Mission Council Executive Committee — Everett Cattell, Milton Coleman, and Anna Nixon. The Discipline called for setting up a provisional yearly meeting, quarterly meetings, and district rallies with the expectancy of maximum growth in a number of village churches. It was agreed that while *chutiya* cutting would remain the public rite for enrolling new converts as probationaries, baptism would publicly signify full membership. Elders, lay leaders, and pastors would be appointed to oversee the work. The whole plan was approved by the Mission Board, and in 1950 after wide consultation, the Mission and Church were both registered with the Government.[2] Though the Mission Council was still in control, the new organization opened the way for more and more responsibility and authority to pass over to the Church. Council meetings, retreats for both men and women, refresher courses, youth rallies, revivals, and all church services were meant to revive the believers. The annual women's retreats initiated by Catherine Cattell not only brought new spiritual life but also a new status and dignity to the women in the Church. All the missionaries were keenly aware that no evangelism was possible if the Church was bypassed. The only way to witness to the non-Christian was through the corporate witness of a revived Church. Therefore, revived Christians, including all the new converts as well as all the missionaries, provided their only hope. Small groups of young people in their Christian Endeavor meetings or women in their *Mahala Samaj* became an avenue for revival. Everett and Catherine Cattell, while making repairs on Nowgong roofs, spent evenings with the boys in the hostel and the women living near the school. At just such a meeting in 1949 Vijay Prakash, son of Stuti Prakash, heard God's call to Christian service and rose up to follow. By 1951 this keen desire to win souls caused the Christians in Bundelkhand, like Korea, to start early morning prayer meetings in every station.[3]

The result was that when Moses David from the Free Methodist Mission came as special speaker in 1951 for Annual Meeting he found the whole area ripe for revival. New Christians from six villages wept at the altar side by side with those who had lived all their lives in the Mission. Adultery, dishonesty, bitterness, gossip, and unclean habits were openly confessed and forsaken. All over the tent (*shamiyana*) people went from one to another seeking reconciliation and forgiveness, with missionaries and Indians all mingling together before God. Staff problems in school and hospital were cleared up. Annual Meeting was always a time of spiritual renewal. Two years earlier Everett Cattell had written, "What joyous days! The Lord has been good to us beyond the telling. Annual meeting was the high peak in our missionary experience . . . the finest annual meeting ever." But in 1951 this was deeper and more far-reaching than even two years earlier. There were three outstanding results. First, witness bands sprang up in every station. Second, Khub Chand again saw the light of witnessing without pay. Hira Lal of Bilwar expressed his contentment to continue on self-support. The Mission Council felt this was an opportune time to form a policy not to employ converts for witnessing, but rather encourage them to serve as local elders in village churches on a voluntary basis. Should they encounter expenses in their work, the local village church they served was encouraged to help.[4] The third result was the organization of the first Youth Rally in Bundelkhand. It was held a month later and attended by more than forty Christian young people. With temperatures soaring well above 100° F, Clifton Robinson was the evangelist. Colemans organized the whole thing in Amarmau, and the Chunni Lalls, Stuti Prakash, and Max Banker helped. Two theological students from Yavatmal also came and witnessed. The blessings of a revived Church held promise in Bundelkhand of "fruit that shall remain."[5]

"Hold the Line" or a Policy of Faith?

The Mission Board, considering their small constituency, agreed in August 1947 to call for a "Hold the Line" policy until economic and political conditions showed definite improvement. Walter Williams wrote:

> There is an element of conservatism in many of the Board actions taken at the recent meetings. World conditions are not conducive to generous spending. This action . . . dims our eyes to near vision just now. *We seek to exercise faith, yet would not practice folly.*[6]

That last sentence caught Everett's attention. Surely, he felt, it was not folly to exercise extraordinary faith at this time when he believed Bundelkhand was, under God, blooming like a rose. So with the hope of jogging loose the whole Church and particularly the Board from their "hold the line" policy, he sat down and wrote an article for publication in the *Friends Oriental News* entitled, "Do Friends Have a Faith Mission?" With the editor of the *Evangelical Friend*, Charles Haworth, urging him to write more articles, Everett, who was famous for his seventeen-page letters, sat down and wrote what he "intended as a brief article," but which "grew into something else . . . a thing which I do not feel clear to offer anywhere for publication without your permission," he wrote Walter Williams. "I have one request. If you feel it should not be published I would appreciate it if somehow it could be brought to the attention of the Board members."[7] In that article Everett urged the Board to follow the principle that

> . . . where young people, obviously called of God and qualified, apply for service, they should be sent forth as rapidly as their outfit and passage is available, *fully trusting God* for their future support. This is a real test of faith . . . To date our attitude has been governed by another principle. It is a principle of limitation . . . . Could it not be also God's will . . . to have us launch out in faith to undertake larger tasks and larger commitments than are reasonable to be supported by

our limited means in sheer faith that God is able to turn resources into our hands beyond the limits of the giving power of our membership?

Everett believed this was exactly what the Board ought to do, for two reasons: (1) The needs on the field; (2) human limitations, which prevent both individuals and boards from knowing the wisest course for the future. "Is it scriptural," he asked, "for us to base our missionary policy on a fear of the future?" Finally, he wrote, "I am pleading that the whole policy be taken off the level of human wisdom — whether conservtive or radical — and based on an act of faith."[8]

The Mission Board's reaction to this article was defensive as shown in Walter Williams's reply. He pointed out that until home membership grew considerably, $75,000 seemed the limit of their total missionary budget.[9] Caught as he was between a conservative Board and the apparent critical audacity of missionaries with no responsibility for raising the funds, Walter Williams dealt with the matter incisively:

> Not one of us felt himself ready to take the position called for . . . . We believe it needs to be brought to your attention that our present policy is one of faith, not of fear. Under our policy we seek Divine light and guidance and often *know* that it is given us . . . . In your concern (for a larger staff) we share, but . . . by unanimous vote we laid the article with its proposals "on the table indefinitely." . . . I believe that the above faithfully reflects the feeling and conviction of the.Board. In a purely personal word I would add that we are with you for souls in Bundelkhand; we cannot go with you in dreams and visionary excursions. That we love you, you cannot doubt . . . . Inasmuch as you requested that the article be brought to all the Board, I request that this letter be shown to all the staff.[10]

Everett was somewhat crushed and felt quite misunderstood, but he did what the Board requested and read the letter to the India staff. With disciplined faith, both the Mission Council and the Board proceeded from this point. A positive result from this encounter was that the Board immediately rescinded its "Hold the Line" policy, and the missionaries in India persisted in their requests for the needs of expansion. The Board warmly responded. Walter Williams wrote, "We recognize that God's work calls for the very best you there and we here can give as we unite our efforts and our judgments along with our prayers."[11] He continued pressing the battle on the homefront. He considered the forty-six intercessor bands, developed by the women under the direction of Edith Salter and Edna Springer, as the "greatest achievement of the past year on this side of the ocean." He continued, "Nowhere have I seen finer loyalty to the missionary task." He pointed to the faithfulness of the women's and men's groups, the Friends youth who fully supported Cattells, the Sunday school classes who supported many workers and students, and Cleveland

Bible College (later Malone College), who paid the salary and travel of Norma Freer. Vacation Bible Schools and Junior Bands gave money for special projects. People eagerly read *Friends Oriental News*, the *Evangelical Friend, Till Break of Day* by Catherine Cattell, *Telling the People of India about Jesus* by Eleanor Chambers, and a devotional booklet of twelve messages by younger missionaries of India and China edited by Marjorie Myers.[12]

Though evangelism held prior place, a growing church needed other phases of work kept in balance. Famine relief had opened the hearts of the people to the Gospel in the beginning, schools had provided leaders, and the hospital had cracked open the tightly closed doors of Chhatarpur. Such programs were not being closed. Rather, with the coming of the Bankers and DeVols, they were given greater significance and blended into the overall purpose and priority of the mission plan of expansion over the next five years.

Improving the Plan and Plant for Education

Until the Bankers got through with language study, Anna Nixon continued to be responsible for the educational program. After language school, she was given time to visit other mission schools throughout the Hindi area. Convinced that the cottage system could be continued and improved, she emphasized the importance of students living in small groups and learning to manage the dairy, grow their own gardens, do their own shopping, plan their own meals, and keep their own accounts. The chief need, it seemed to her, was that of dignifying labor. She ran headlong into student lethargy and parental opposition. By working with the children in the garden each day, she finally won them over. Failure, however, dogged her steps when she tried to spark interest in the dairy training program. No student took the least interest. The caste who knew how to care for the animals also knew how to drain off the milk supply. Figures showed a yearly loss in that department. Finally, hard facts and strong persuasion led the Mission Council to give up their dream and sell the fourteen animals.[13]

An excellent teacher from Earles' time, Rachel Banwar of the Mennonite Mission, returned to Nowgong as headmistress. Not only the academic, but the evangelistic level also, rose in the school. Enrollment went up to about one hundred twenty. Rachel Banwar's uncle served as a Brahmin priest in the *Kali* temple, but before Rachel was born her mother had chosen to herd goats and become a Christian. Anna Nixon was the manager, but Rachel Banwar cared for the internal working of Nowgong Christian Institute. Anna worked out a scholarship plan to cover all students through high school and college so that with the help of the

Bundelkhand Christian Education Society, an educational cooperative Earles had founded, no Christian young person had to stop short of all the education of which he was capable. In 1948 seventeen young people went beyond the eighth grade Nowgong Christian Institute to complete high school. Virginia Singh (1950) and Vijay Prakash (1951) went to Yavatmal to Union Biblical Seminary; Raj Kumari Kamal, sister, and Shyam Kumari, daughter of Stuti Prakash, took teacher training; Christine, daughter of G. M. Roberts, went for medical training.[14] A dormitory was opened for boys who wanted to study in a local college, first in Nowgong, then in Chhatarpur. Finally, when no suitable housefather could be found, the boys were transferred to the United Church of Canada school at Rasalpura. This was not entirely satisfactory.[15]

Friends in Bundelkhand felt a great need to develop education for boys as the Canadian Presbyterian Women's Board had developed for girls. The American Presbyterian Boys' Christian School in Jhansi had long been without missionary supervision and this mission offered their buildings at a rent of Rs. 1 (less than a quarter) a year to the missions of the area if they would take it over and lift its spiritual and academic standard. Clifton Robinson represented the Friends Mission in these discussions and came home enthusiastic. The committee recommended going ahead, and the Mission Council backed the proposition wholeheartedly. The mission boards involved, however, did not. Walter Williams in his reply outlined the reasons for their refusal. The proposition was far too big for the small Friends Mission; too few boys were involved from the Mission; they feared city education would drain off the village Christians and stifle the growth of the Church in Bundelkhand.[16] Apart from this third reason, which showed lack of understanding of a rapidly changing India, most of the missionaries felt, due to lack of funds and for the sake of evangelism's priority, the decision was right. However, the need for just such a school in the area still remains today.

In plans for expansion, the Nowgong compound received its share of attention. Since the big bungalow was occupied first by Robinsons and later divided into two suites for Bankers and DeVols, Goddard Memorial Hospital building underwent transformation to become the home of Anna Nixon after July 25, 1949.[17] New buildings were erected for increased staff and the whole plant was remodeled and brought into efficient shape for the future. Dormitories, chapel, classrooms, and teachers' quarters received new roofs. The former cottage was remodeled for suitable office and classroom space. Either Everett Cattell or Komal Das Lall was on hand to supervise the many workers and to race with the monsoons, which came on relentlessly even though building supplies were delayed. Because of these delays, the chapel walls went down three times in the rains before the roof finally went on.[18] The new asbestos roofing frustrated scorpions who used to hide in the old tile and drop down on sleeping children. Scabies also dried up though it was hard to see how the roof played a part in that. Malaria, paratyphoid, lice, chicken pox, infections, and pinkeye diminished some, too—but probably this was due to the cases of Atabrine, Paludrine, vitamins, dried milk, and other food supplies received through Church World Service. Instead of sixty children down at a time with malaria during the rains, these preventive measures reduced the number to four or five.[19]

In 1949 a new housefather with eight children was employed. His oldest son, Hizikiel Lall, 23, gifted in music and trained in science, became a valuable staff member. However, within two years, spiritual failure and vicious gossip caused such an upheaval that the headmistress, housefather and family, and all but two staff members left. The year ended in mighty revival at Annual Meeting, but not soon enough to keep the staff from leaving. The children, however, went home in a blaze of spiritual victory. Anna was able to have one more very good year after that with a new staff, which she transferred to Max and Ruth Ellen Banker, who took charge in July of 1951. Anna was then transferred to Chhatarpur as treasurer in Norma Freer's place as she went on furlough April 23, 1951.[20]

The Women's Hospital Changed to General

Out in Chhatarpur Dr. Ezra was appalled to find Khub Chand very ill with malaria with no place in the mission dispensary or hospital for his treatment. "A mere man in a *zenana* (women's) hospital is *persona non grata!*" he complained, "but don't put this in the *Oriental News!*"[21] The Board heartily approved moving toward a general hospital, and Dr. Ezra visited mission hospitals in Kachchwa and Bareilley to observe their mode of operation as well as to understand better how to negotiate the change. *Clara Swain* in Bareilley was the first mission hospital built in India and had started off, as in Chhatarpur, as a women's hospital and then changed to general. Dr. Ezra was somewhat amused to learn that at first the head nurse had locked the male patients in their rooms at night until she learned it was not necessary. Back in Chhatarpur again, he found there were no significant transitional problems as they moved forward.[22] He performed his first operation in the Christian Hospital in Chhatarpur November 18, 1950, and was from that time assisted by the first male nurse to join the staff, Samson Huri Lal of Jhansi. The first male patient to be treated in the new general hospital was Har Charan, a Brahmin *pandit* from Isanagar, the village of Hira Singh. The medical people all got together with Everett and worked hours on drawings and plans for the buildings needed for extension of medical services. Until a ward could be built, a tent was set up for men who needed hospitalization.[23]

Expansion in Chhatarpur sometimes frightened the Mission Board, but after the shock waves passed, the forty-six intercessor bands went to prayer in America, and the Mission Board superintendent went public informing the people throughout the churches of the need, challenge, and opportunity. On March 10, 1951, men started occupying their places in the sixteen-bed Williams Ward, named after the Mission Board superintendent. It was dedicated on Easter Sunday with many guests present to hear Victor Mangalwadi deliver a powerful Christian message.[24]

One of the first patients admitted to the new ward was Prem Prakash, just graduated from Allahabad Bible Institute and recently married to a nurse, Shama. His complaint was pulmonary tuberculosis. He was transferred from Gulganj and occupied one of three cubicles in the new Williams Ward, which provided semi-isolation. His wife went to work in the hospital.[25]

While building the men's ward, Everett and Komal Das made a plan for a drug room and a place for storage housed under the same roof. They also built a darkroom, a morgue, a house for the generator, and an X-Ray room. They remodeled the operating suite and dug an underground storage tank to hold six thousand gallons of water for the sterilizer. They enlarged the doctor's bungalow for the DeVol family, connecting Baird Retreat to furnish an office and a guest room for "foreign" patients. They built new quarters for Dr. Grace and a new ladies' cottage attached to Alena's quarters for Norma. The missionaries' tithe fund paid Rs. 5,000 ($1,200) for a new office and workshop. After that was finished, they turned their tithe regularly toward evangelism to set an example for the Church. A large donation from Dr. Charles Smith helped with the new dispensary for men. Any money left over from anywhere was used to build family wards. Next in the main stations, the workers' quarters were enlarged to give every family with children at least two rooms with roofs that would not leak.[26]

New facilities called for additional staff. The former housefather in Nowgong and a trained pharmacist, George Masih, was transferred to the hospital. Shapan Nath, office manager in the school in Nowgong, was transferred to take over as hospital accountant and mission bookkeeper. Norma Freer—mission treasurer, secretary to the superintendent, sponsors' correspondent, and supervisor of the nurses' home (after Alena's departure)—also assisted Dr. Ezra with correspondence. Her medical education broadened and later she took over as business manager.[27] Priobala Nath, daughter of Jagannath and Puniya Bai; Clara Singh, daughter of Lachhman and Ruth Singh; and Catherine Ali from Jhansi all joined the staff as nurses.[28] These lovely young women seemed too small to be postgraduate midwives. Priobala, typical of all, weighed only seventy pounds, but she was so efficient in helping to deliver Carol Jean Coleman that Rebecca said of her, "One would have to travel far to find a better nurse."[29] Bhagwati Bai, the first trained Bible woman in Bundelkhand under Ruth Thurston Earle, became official hospital evangelist among women. Her compassion and ability in presenting Christ to suffering patients endeared her to all. Her husband, Dharm Das, was DeVols' cook and did his part by being especially efficient in handling all the stream of guests who came, sometimes for medical treatment, and always as boarders in the DeVol home while there.[30]

Growing Pains in the Hospital

Frances DeVol was more than busy as head nurse and assistant to the doctors. Before she could get her breath, patients began crowding in. Increased staff and expansion of facilities stepped up the pace to the point where some used to the more relaxed rhythm of the old days experienced cultural shock. There was need for greater sensitivity to Dr. Grace's deep and unexpressed feelings. She suddenly found herself busier than she had ever been but no longer in charge. She missed Alena Calkins, who had departed just at the peak of her career and at a time in her midforties when she needed special quiet understanding. Interpersonal relationships in this fast moving arena were not always smooth.

Missionaries were concerned about the staff problems and handled them with counsel and revival. When Manorma Bai came to help the nurses do a drama called "The Story of the Cross," the nurses became so convicted that before they could portray it, they had to seek reconciliation with one another and with the Lord. Catherine Cattell, ever sensitive to the inner hurts of people, led Bible studies with pointed applications that brought the nurses to the feet of Christ. Thus the focus was kept on big goals and the Christian testimony in the hospital.[31]

People from all different castes for many miles around found their way to the new general hospital. With the mingling of castes, there were often situations in which the Christian had to take his stand on equality. Samson Huri Lal one day was treating a stream of villagers, and suddenly finding it necessary to remove a man's turban, he handed it to the next man in line. The man drew back in horror, exclaiming. "He's a Chamar!"

"So, he's a Chamar!" Samson quickly replied, as he wound the turban firmly around his own neck, making himself an "untouchable." The horrified man did not run away, but one can only guess the struggles going on in his mind.[32]

Medically speaking, the challenges were greater than any Dr. Ezra had seen in the West. For example, a woman with a large ovarian cyst came for surgery. She measured sixty-five inches around the waist and the cyst of 108 pounds weighed her down. When the tumor was removed, she weighed only 83 pounds. She went home well and believing, having heard the Gospel daily from Bhagwati Bai.[33]

The missionaries felt that the hospital ministry went beyond physical healing through the vital witness of every staff member concerning the love of Christ. Only then, they knew, would the hospital evangelists' words be understood.

New Affiliation with EFMA

To increase cooperation between the home front and India, the Mission Board shifted affiliation in 1948 from the Foreign Missions Conference of North America to the newly formed Evangelical Foreign Missionary Association. They not only processed visas and made travel arrangements, but also set up channels for securing equipment: Alladin lamp parts, legal size file folders, spiral screen door springs, whitewash brushes, spring rattraps, bedpans, ether masks, hand-pressure spray pumps for DDT, long-handled shears, buck saws, tools for a jeep, hacksaws, chisels, planes, and claw hammers.[34] The list definitely tilted toward carpenters' tools as Everett, following the trade of his contractor father, dedicated himself to the expansion program.

Expansion and Devaluation

For the next few years, Everett Cattell, the only builder in the Mission, was surrounded with blueprints. Komal Das Lall came to the fore as his understudy and proved to be so adept that he was taken on with additional pay as building overseer in 1949. These two men shuttled back and forth across the field supervising the work, laying in supplies, and mapping out priorities. Keeping within the budget with drastically rising prices was no easy task. Periodic raises in workers' and missionaries' salaries ate into expansion funds.[35]

In September 1949 the rupee was devalued. Instead of Rs. 3.3, Rs. 4.75 was needed to buy $1.00. The Council agreed to cut their own salaries to $1,000 a year and double all salaries of Indian workers plus adding a children's allowance up to the age of eighteen. This new salary scale took care of inflation and lifted mission workers to a higher standard of living. Even beyond this, the total budget in rupees still showed a solid gain. The missionaries requested that all the gain be credited to expansion, and the Board agreed.[36] On both sides of the water, however, there seemed to be a fear of "a half acre of roofs" in Bundelkhand without commensurate evangelistic growth. "Our praying has been taking on a tone of desperation this year as we have pled for souls. This has been the more obvious as we have been confronted with the folly of building programs which do not lead to soul winning," Everett wrote.[37]

Hill Housing

Roofs were increasing in Bundelkhand, and also in Landour. Families on vacation during some of the hot months from April to September needed to be near Woodstock school, where their children attended. With the great influx of new missionaries after World War II, houses were so in demand that it was almost impossible to find places to stay. The Mission Board listened sympathetically to requests for funds to meet this need. Mrs. Wilkie, a college classmate of Walter R. Williams, and her husband had built "Pinepoint" as a retirement home within five to ten minutes' walk from Woodstock, but now they wanted to sell it for Rs. 16,000 ($4,850). The house had a big veranda, kitchen, living room, dining room, two bedrooms, and bath on the main floor; below the veranda was a small dining room, bedroom, and bath with a breezeway that could be used for a kitchen. Quarters for workers nearby were well built with storage and office space as well.[38] The whole estate was thirteen acres with many trees to furnish firewood. The Mission Board approved the proposition heartily.[39] Two families occupied it, but it was not sufficient for all. So three years later the Mission Council recommended clearing land next door to Pinepoint where a house called Suraj Bhavan and occupied by a Pederson family had been swept away a few years before in a landslide. Clearing the land with reinforcements to the hill behind made the site ideal and it was on sale for $5,000. The Mission Council sent home their building plan for two family mirror suites built of reinforced concrete with workers' quarters similar to those in Pinepoint. The Board accepted these plans and by September 1951 building was started. It was completed and dedicated with an open house June 18, 1953, and they named it *Pennington*. The Women's Missionary Societies furnished it. Many people considered Pennington, though simple in design, as the best-built and most desirable house on the hillside.[40]

Equipping the Missionaries and Workers for the Task

Not only buildings, but all kinds of equipment followed the increased number of missionaries and additional Christian workers on the field. As requests came, the Board sought to determine the needful and provide it. The Friends Women's Missionary Societies in 1947 resolved to put a refrigerator into every missionary home even though the missionaries had not requested this. In those days, kerosene refrigerators were available, but kerosene was rationed and often unavailable. To save fuel, the missionaries shared. Colemans' large refrigerator, a gift from Milton's aunt, went to the Robinsons and Anna Nixon in Nowgong, where the missionaries often met for Mission Council. A small one was shifted to the Cattells' bungalow, and Colemans shared the hospital refrigerator with Alena Calkins and Norma Freer. On April 13, 1948, they all enjoyed the first refrigerator-made ice cream in Bundelkhand. Later, DeVols brought a refrigerator, which they shared with the Bankers. The India missionaries were never again without refrigeration.[41]

More than refrigerators, however, the missionaries wanted $4,500 to buy three more military jeeps. The Board authorized one more. The transportation committee—Everett, Milton, and Cliff—quickly pointed out that an oxcart was just as expensive in upkeep as a jeep, but the Board did not hear them. Letters flew back and forth. "This is not an unwillingness to abide by your decision," Everett wrote, "rather it is just a tussling with a huge problem that remains unsolved by your decision." He then went on to say that the missionaries would be glad to give up some of the comforts—even the refrigerators—in order to have these tools with which to work.[42] More than anything else, they wanted to be prepared to care for the ingathering envisioned in the Church in Bundelkhand.

| Breaking Through in Ghuara

"If we are thrown into the blazing furnace, the God we serve is able to save us from it, and he will rescue us from your hand, O king." Daniel 3:17 (NIV)

Colemans in Amarmau District

More significant than any other development at this stage was the stationing of the evangelistic missionaries and Christian workers in strategic centers throughout the area. The purchase of property in Amarmau from the British Bible Churchman's Missionary Society was a move in this direction. The Amarmau purchase included a bungalow, a small hospital, chapel, a doctor's house, four small rooms for patients, a few small fields, and a garden space.[1]

War had so depleted funds in England that the BCMS could no longer keep the station open. Developments in Ghuara made Amarmau an ideal district headquarters — preferred even to Gulganj. Amarmau was only sixteen miles from Ghuara across one river, while Gulganj was twenty-eight miles away and across two rivers. Amarmau was about twenty-five miles from Gulganj, fifty miles from Chhatarpur, and sixty-four miles from Nowgong. The BCMS wanted Rs. 30,000, but the Mission Board felt they could pay no more than Rs. 20,000 ($6,061).[2] Charles Roberts, Mission Board treasurer, ventured, "If we are sure we are in the will of God in this, I would feel like going ahead with it even if we cannot see all the way through."

God honored his faith. E. L. Skipper and daughters, Irene Skipper and Margaret Fox, called the Board on August 29, 1949, and offered to pay for this as a memorial to Katherine S. Skipper.[3] Milton Coleman had been Skippers' pastor before going to India, and they knew the Colemans were planning to live in Amarmau. A cable was sent to India in early September:

BOARD BUYING AMARMAU WONDERFUL
YEARLY MEETING

It was clear that "wonderful" fit both ways.

Providentially, this agreement came just as devaluation was announced, and the BCMS received within $225 of their original asking price for their property.[4]

Milton and Rebecca Coleman, with Rupa Das as Bible woman, Dayal Chand Singh and family as evangelist, and with cook and *aya* moved on September 17, 1949. Later George Masih joined as pharmacist to open the dispensary.[5] Rebecca opened wide the doors of hospitality and welcomed the Mission Council, refreshers' courses, and the second women's retreat.[6] Nearly all the Christian women in Bundelkhand came. The retreats were a means of emphasizing spirituality as central in the home.

With the purchase of Amarmau, the field between the Dhasan and Ken rivers was divided into five districts with a superintendent assigned to live in each district headquarters, supervise two or three outstations, and evangelize the villages around him:

> Amarmau (Ghuara)   324 villages — Milton Coleman
> Bijawar (Gulganj, Bilwar)   314 villages — Clifton Robinson
> Nowgong (Chhatarpur, Dhamora)   264 villages — Victor
>   Mangalwadi
> Ganj (Rajnagar)   287 villages — Stuti Prakash
> Launri   318 villages — to be developed later.[7]

New Interest in Ghuara

Early in 1947 the second village institute like the Barethi leaders' conference was set up in Ghuara. Stuti Prakash, who had picked up this idea of leaders' institutes from James Kinder in Bihar, was in charge. Chamar leaders from as far as twenty miles attended. Later Everett Cattell visited Ghuara and met some thirty men brought in by Khub Chand from nearby villages. The response and interest were beyond anything he had ever seen in Bundelkhand. No fewer than two dozen leaders begged him for a school and for further Christian teaching. Remembering Dr. McGavran's recommendations, he took note of their requests but determined not to start schools or other services until there was a solid body of Christians in the village.[8] On the other hand, something had to be done to keep interest alive.

Villagers always go north for the wheat harvest in the months of February and March to bring home their basic food supply for the year. In 1947 Khub Chand went, too. During that time a group of evangelists did a walking tour through those villages to keep up interest among those who stayed behind. The Mission Council decided that Khub Chand should, upon returning, go to Ghuara for awhile and seek to bring them through to genuine commitment. Since he could not live in Ghuara without provisions, the Mission offered him a stipend to cover this period. He gladly accepted the arrangement. State officials became immediately suspicious and demanded a reason for his presence. He read to them from the Bible: "Let every soul be subject unto the higher power . . . . they that resist shall receive to themselves damnation . . . . Render therefore to all their dues."[9] Hearing this, the officers relaxed.

The Chamars in Ghuara furnished Khub Chand and his family a tiny house. Accompanying himself on his *sarangi*, his own homemade violin of coconut shell and bamboo, he sang his own Christian words to their familiar tunes.[10] Stuti Prakash, at that time the district superintendent of Gulganj and Bijawar, moved from Chhatarpur to Gulganj mid-May in 1947 to be nearer the Ghuara development.[11] He often went to Ghuara and joined Khub Chand to "blow out the Gospel" on his trumpet.[12] As cooler weather came, it became evident that three men in Ghuara were ready to accept Christ, at any cost.[13] They sent word to Everett, and dropping everything, he started by bicycle to Ghuara. Khub Chand met him and guided him over the last unmarked sixteen miles. He arrived at dusk, and the next day amidst throngs begging for medicine he ascertained that truly Pyare Lal and Halka, two brothers, and Dimina, a cousin, with their wives were ready for a public confession of their faith in Christ. On November 25, 1947, because of a gas shortage, Everett Cattell again rode his bicycle the full fifty miles to Ghuara, thankful it was not eighty—because Milton Coleman and the evangelists had recently built a bridge across a stream that cut off thirty miles. Sunday morning was the time set for cutting the sacred lock, granting the certificate, and interdining. Besides these, at least half a dozen other families seemed ready to take the step. Manorma Bai Singh had held classes daily for the children of these families, and six or seven had made wonderful progress in learning to read.[14]

Persecution Begins

Officials, however, were getting restive. They appealed to higher authorities, who explained that there was no legal way they could stop the conversions, but agreed not to interfere in any private action they wished to take. So Saturday morning before the big day (November 29, 1947), local officials incited a mob of some two hundred strong who with staffs, spears, and a few guns descended on the evangelistic team camped about half a mile from the village. Two of the hopeful ones were caught and beaten mercilessly, one until he fell unconscious. With a gun pointed at his heart, Khub Chand expected to wake up in heaven, but the men were stopped from shooting by Everett's agreement that the camp would move by that afternoon.

In a very ugly mood, the mob leaders nevertheless took time to explain that they did not object to the preaching or the school but warned that there should be no conversions. "We will make Khub Chand a Hindu again or kill him," they threatened. Khub Chand answered, "I will make you Christians, or die." On hearing of this persecution, Walter Williams called for a day of prayer. The last day of the year, December 31, 1947, found Christians throughout Ohio Yearly Meeting on their knees. "Prayer changes things." (Hebrews 11:33)[15]

The Hopeful Ones

Pyare Lal, Halka, and Dimina were not beaten that day because the first two were away and Dimina escaped their notice. These three men had already stopped drinking, eating carrion, and worshiping idols. When their test came, would they stand true against the fierce persecution? They differed from the ordinary Ghuara Chamar in their independence and initiative. During World War II, Pyare Lal had worked in an Italian prisoner of war camp near Bhopal and had come home with Rs. 800 ($270) in his pocket. For Rs. 150 ($50) he bought ten acres of land on which he, Halka, and Dimina were at that time living. They produced rice one season and wheat the next. They had been offered Rs. 3,000 ($909) for their land.[16]

Before the Barethi conference, Halka had a dream. He dreamed he was searching for the true God and there was a man pointing to a white figure saying, "There is the true God; follow him." He woke with a sense of awe and consulted a Brahman to learn its meaning. The Brahman priest scoffed, "Can a Chamar have visions?" But Halka could not dismiss the message of his dream. He told it next to a shopkeeper. "I don't know what it means," confessed the man, "but you will know in one month's time and will find the true religion." Within the month Halka attended Barethi conference and there felt within his heart that he had found Jesus, the true God. Repenting of his sin, he forsook idol worship, foul speech, and tobacco. Only later after the Ghuara conference as Halka, Pyare Lal, and Dimina began to declare their interest, did the Christians come to know how God first revealed Himself in Ghuara.[17]

Halka Daniel, the First Christian in Ghuara

Just before Christmas 1947, Halka slipped away from Ghuara and found his way to Chhatarpur. For the first time in his life he sat at a table as a guest along with Victor Mangalwadi in Cattells' home. On Christmas day he participated in the Church's festivities and prayers. That day his name went down as a Christian. Never before, he said, had he known what brothers and sisters were until he found them in his new Christian family.[18]

Early in January, Victor Mangalwadi, Khub Chand, and Everett Cattell followed Halka back to Ghuara, knowing persecution was apt to result from his brave step. They went straight to the leading officer who had been party in the mob violence. Victor Mangalwadi preached a full-length sermon to him and those listening, using much Scripture, and closing with prayer. The delegation took the officer by surprise since he and his colleagues thought their mob violence had settled the matter. They were alarmed to find that even after threats these men were still standing true.[19]

Halka Daniel's Fiery Trials

Cattells camped in Amarmau for some weeks in January, making frequent trips into villages around Ghuara and holding weekly meetings with the Christians there. Manorma Singh was with them, waiting to move in with teaching for both adults and children as soon as it was safe to do so. "I do not expect further violence," Everett wrote as he prepared to leave for two weeks' ministry in Burma, "though some of the young men of the opposition could make a lot of trouble in private ways."[20]

His plane, however, had hardly cleared the runway, and Gandhi's ashes had barely reached the Ganges, before these same town officials arrested Halka and forced him to burn his Christian certificate. He clung to it until they pushed him with it into the fire. They beat him with sticks and forced him to swallow five elements of the cow—dung, urine, milk, ghee, cud—to "cleanse" him of Christianity. To humiliate him they tied a sweeper's broom around his neck. Then they warned him that any contact with Christians would lead to his property being confiscated.

Frightened almost to death, Dimina slipped into the jungle and ran to Chhatarpur for help. Milton Coleman and David Cattell stopped at Gulganj and from there, with Stuti Prakash and Lachhman Singh, proceeded to Ghuara in a jeep.[21] Parking a good distance from the village, David stayed by while the other three men stealthily found their way toward the village. They met Pyare Lal and then Halka, bruised and shaken, but not seriously injured. They proceeded into the village, but the officers refused to see them. A mob gathered and with wild threats ordered them out and warned them never to return.

Meanwhile, out at the jeep, David was engaged in interesting conversation. He had just settled down with his *Farm Journal* when ten men came by. Keeping his eyes on the printed page, he listened intently to their conversation. The men tried to guess who this seventeen-year-old might be in his surplus army fatigues and an overseas hat. David started taking notes in the margin of the magazine, freely translating their Bundelkhandi into English. "It's the mission jeep, surely . . . but he must be a soldier!" David quickly decided to play that role. Since English soldiers did not usually know Hindi, David did not respond to their questions.

One man pushed his face close to David's and yelled, "BAKSHEESH" (alms)!

"No BAKSHEESH!" David yelled back.

Another man tried his English: "Sahib, I want smoke!"

"No smoke!" answered David.

That was the extent of conversational exchange. The men concluded that he was a soldier, that he would surely have a gun, and that other soldiers would be nearby. "That cannon in the back must have ten shots," one ventured. (The "cannon" was a canvas-covered stretcher for taking Halka to the hospital if he had needed it.)

"Get out of here!" ordered the leader, pointing to the road. "This is a dangerous place."

David smiled and waved good-bye to them as if they were leaving.

Defeated, they left, still wondering, as David sat pondering, "Even a fool, when he holdeth his peace, is counted wise . . . ." (Proverbs 17:8)[22]

Stuti Prakash, Lachhman Singh, and Milton Coleman left the village, but not defeated. On the advice of the Regional Commissioner in Now-gong, Milton reported to the political minister of Panna State and put the constitution to the test. Nothing came of it immediately. Halka was not allowed to leave his village.[23]

Halka's baby and wife died and Ghuara villagers rushed in to find him a Hindu wife. His refusal to cooperate brought angry threats. The next great step was to find a Christian wife for Halka, and after a long search the Mission heard about Prabhuwati, an orphan girl in the Industrial School in Sagar. Khub Chand arranged for Halka and Pyare Lal to attend the Sagar convention. The engagement took place immediately and the wedding the next day, October 27, 1948. Manorma Bai accompanied the bride to Ghuara to help her adjust to village life.[24]

Halka's mother was a Hindu until Prabhuwati came and said, "I have been without a mother for years. You shall have her place now. I will take care of you." The mother immediately declared her faith. She left the grain grinding and field work to her new daughter-in-law. Halka was so happy with the new harmony in his home that he began that day to burn bricks to build a little church.[25]

Persecution let up for awhile after that, only later to be intensified. Threats to burn the Christians' houses and confiscate their property caused Everett Cattell, Stuti Prakash, and Halka again to appeal to higher authorities in Chhatarpur in February 1949. They responded by sending a town crier with a drum to march through Ghuara streets and alleyways shouting, "Hear, hear! You are not to persecute, or beat, or harass the Christians in any way by order of the law! Anyone doing so will be fined Rs. 1,000 [$333]."[26]

Pyare Lal's Conversion

A new officer came on the scene and ordered all preaching and baptisms stopped. He knew nothing of the real meaning of the new constitution. Illiterate villagers like Pyare Lal, much more knowledgeable, knew a price had to be paid to live for Christ, and he said, "You may kill me, cut up my body into little pieces and pass it around the village displayed in a basket, but I will never forsake the Lord Jesus Christ."[27] No one doubted his sincerity even though he had not yet gone through a public ceremony to declare his faith. The reason for his delay was that he had already spent nearly Rs. 2,000 (more than $500) to secure a wife for his son, and he wanted to give her family no legal way out of honoring that agreement.

Finally, however, he stepped out on faith and with Stuti Prakash officiating, he made his public declaration along with his wife and son, and was accepted into the Church as a probationary member. The same day Halka and his new wife became full members. This took place in Ghuara just a week before annual meeting in Nowgong, and Pyare Lal wanted above anything else to go, but there was no one to watch his watermelons and cucumbers just ready for picking. Sunday night he dozed off at the wrong time and wandering cows came in and cleaned him out. So he, also, went to annual meeting in the jeep with Stuti Prakash and others from Ghuara, Bilwar, and Gulganj.

As he came into the gate, he threw up his arms and shouted, "*Ham ne kharo!*" ("I did it!") Bundelkhand's first Christian minister, Gore Lal Singh, former high caste Thakur, threw his arms around former Chamar Pyare Lal, declaring him dearer than his own blood brothers and sisters because he had accepted the Lord. In Christ all caste feeling was washed away. That year the center of interest in annual meeting was a row of half a dozen borrowed tents housing village Christians from Ghuara, Bilwar, Dhamora, Khandora, and Maharajpur. Their simple and sincere prayers electrified the atmosphere as God poured out His Spirit once more on the annual sessions of Bundelkhand Yearly Meeting.[28]

Dimina's Conversion

Of all the converts, Dimina perhaps had the hardest time making a clear break. One day with rare courage he resolutely started gathering up the

household idols — clay gods made just in the next village — but, nevertheless, the images he had worshiped for many years of his life. With relatives following and scolding him every step of the way, he took the path
to the river. There, one by one, he threw the gods into the waters and
watched them sink. "Float if you have any power," he challenged.

As he returned, angry villagers shouted at him, "Go live with the
Christians! Take your family . . . your pots and pans . . . leave nothing
to defile us!" But Dimina went into his house with his family and shut the
door. His family fell beside him on their knees. Dimina looked at the
empty places where the idols had stood around the wall. Did he see a ray
of light coming from each place? That is how it appeared to him. The
angry voices died away, and the family slept in peace throughout the
night.[29]

Manorma Bai and Chunni Lall's Marriage and Move to Ghuara

Manorma Bai Singh finally moved to Ghuara, living with the families in
their little shanties on the farm. She taught the men to read and the children in a regular school course. After some time a much better arrangement was made. Chunni Lall, former evangelist with the BCMS Mission
in Amarmau, consented readily to the arrangement of a marriage. Everett
Cattell united Manorma Bai and Chunni Lall in holy wedlock on May 5,
1949.

The honeymoon took place in Ghuara, where they lived in an ox stable since no one would rent them a house. Rocks were thrown through
their roof at night, shopkeepers refused to sell them provisions, and water
carriers refused to bring them water. "But we're not discouraged,"
Manorma Bai declared through her tears, "we will win through."[30] And
win they did, for by the end of 1950 the Mission bought a small piece of
land adjacent to a well for just over $100 and built a house and a church
there.[31]

Silas and Family's Conversion

In 1952 another very poor family braved the storms of persecution and
came to the Chunni Lalls with the request to be taken into the Christian
fold. Manorma Bai gave the man the Christian name Silas. While he and
his wife went out to cut wood, she kept their two boys, renamed Samuel
and Samson, so that they could go to her school. This family were not
only saved from their sins but literally also saved from starvation. Silas
and his wife would return to Ghuara from time to time with their heavy
loads of wood on their backs, which they bartered for grain. After grinding it they would leave a portion with Manorma Bai for their children's
bread and then again would be off to the jungle. Poor though they were,

they brought to the Ghuara Church unusual gifts of dedication and intelligence.

The Colemans, with Ghuara central in their strategy, visited other villages around Amarmau, also, concentrating on half a dozen to get those "chickens that have almost hatched."[32] Milton traveled about one hundred and fifty miles a month by bicycle, preaching and teaching each day. They saw other converts come to the light and then revert again into darkness under the pressure of the high caste moneylender, who thought nothing of charging from 75 percent to 200 percent yearly interest on loans, thus reducing the poor villager to abject slavery for the rest of his life.

Proclaiming Freedom to the Captives

"If you hold to my teaching, you are really my disciples. Then you will know the truth, and the truth will set you free." John 8:31, 32 NIV

Victor and Kusum Mangalwadi in Nowgong District

All over India people were eager to lay hold of their new political freedom.

In Bundelkhand, where spiritual freedom was the Mission's ultimate goal, Victor Mangalwadi often proclaimed the message, "If the Son shall make you free, ye shall be free indeed." (John 8:36)

Victor Mangalwadi, B.A., from Indore and now B.D. from Jabalpur, was stationed in Chhatarpur as both pastor and as Nowgong district superintendent. For the sake of highlighting the villages, however, Dhamora was chosen as the eventual headquarters of the Nowgong District, and Victor and his wife, Kusum, and family looked forward longingly to the day they would move into such a village setting and be able to give themselves wholly to developing village churches.

The Mangalwadis had not returned easily to Chhatarpur after his final Bachelor of Divinity training in Jabalpur. He felt the mission terms were far from adequate and requested changes. The Mission, however, considering him nationalistic in attitude, did not accept his suggestions but regretfully set him free to seek employment elsewhere. Victor was so deeply committed to Bundelkhand that in a retreat where he wrestled alone with God, he came to the conclusion that he would have to return to Bundelkhand regardless of the terms. The missionaries rejoiced in his spiritual victory, and Everett Cattell wrote home:

> There is much immaturity in Victor and much to be learned but with such obviously real dealings with the Lord in his life I am glad to accept him and perhaps suffer with him to make the choice vessel I believe he

can become. He will be appointed to the Chhatarpur pastorate at present.[1]

So Victor and Kusum took up their work in Chhatarpur mid-April 1947. At Christmas they dedicated their children to the Lord Jesus, and at annual meeting in 1949, Victor was recorded as a minister in the *Bundelkhand Masihi Mitra Samaj* (Friends Church of Bundelkhand).[2]

Victor Mangalwadi was in a unique position as pastor of the largest church in Bundelkhand and as Nowgong district superintendent. He committed himself to follow through on the Mission's policy of binding together the "old line" city Christians who came to Christ mainly through the orphanage and the new converts being raised up in the villages, mostly from among the outcaste Chamar group. Church growth studies were just beginning; so the missionaries, though abreast with latest developments, were nevertheless still poorly equipped to understand the deep animosity of some of these orphan-bred Bundelkhandis who considered themselves the first-class Christians and who looked askance at the uncouth villagers coming in to share their benefits and undermine their status. Victor himself was a Bundelkhandi, the grandson of that widowed mother Duojibai who followed Esther Baird and Delia Fistler on their elephant to the Mission in 1897.

Victor was born October 6, 1918. His mother, widow of the late Mangalwadi, left the Mission in 1927, taking Victor and his sister with her to Indore among people of the United Church of Canada from which she came. She married Yohan, a son of Dalsaiya, a former evangelist. By the time Victor came back to Bundelkhand as pastor, his heart had been set on fire with such zeal for all his people that he never seemed to notice any difference between his own former *Kachhi (Sudra)* caste group and the lowest of the low. He "sat where they sat," and sought to win them all to Christ. Later Indore sought every way possible to get him back for work in that area, but Bundelkhand was his call, and nothing moved him from it.[3]

His egalitarian views blinded him to the deep prejudices of those who had never lived outside Bundelkhand, and he easily went along with mission policy in this regard.[4]

Victor Mangalwadi's Work with Congress

Victor's higher education plus his understanding of the people of Bundelkhand soon drew Congress leaders' interest. They adopted him as their counselor to interpret to them the meaning of freedom. Milton Coleman, threatened by Congress agitation with expulsion from a village, called Victor and found that his timely arrival on the scene totally turned the tide. The ringleader of the group, after his encounter with Victor, asked for a New Testament. These Congress leaders then asked Victor to help them organize. He guided them in choosing their own leaders and agreed to meet with them on a regular basis, beginning in Dhamora. Meetings were held in six different villages with attendance ranging from twenty to sixty, and Victor opened each meeting with prayer and Scripture and spoke with openness about Christ as the One who could bring human uplift. Public evils — such as debt, tobacco, expensive weddings, and kindred economic liabilities — he boldly attacked.[5]

Village Work

During the summer Victor rented a small hut in Bakri village seven miles from Chhatarpur. In that 10 x 15 room with no windows and a door 4 feet high and 3 feet wide, he put his boxes, cooking utensils, cot, and bicycle. Then each night he welcomed twelve adults who wanted to learn to read by the light of a petromax lantern. Two of them were Halka Daniel and his son who lived with him. In the morning he held Bible study for boys. In a month's time a great deal had been accomplished. For the next three summers Victor gave a total of nine months to this type of work, returning weekends to fulfill his pastoral duties and to encourage Christians in Dhamora, where persecution was sometimes fierce.[6]

The Dhamora headquarters plan was so strongly opposed by government officials that the idea finally had to be dropped. Village work in Nowgong District, however, became so heavy by 1951 that Victor gave up the Chhatarpur pastorate and concentrated on one village, Goethera, about five miles east of Chhatarpur, where interest was intense.[7]

Stuti and Ramki Bai Prakash in Rajnagar District

Interest on all sides was increasing, and in early 1950 all the evangelistic teams decided to converge on Bilwar for an intensive push. The new Christians from every area were encouraged, and at least one new convert cut his *chutiya* and was enrolled as a probationer.[8]

Bilwar was near Gulganj, the new district center prepared for the Robinsons. Efforts to put them in Bijawar were frustrated; so the Mission enlarged the bungalow in Gulganj at a cost of $5,000 and transferred Stuti Prakash to Rajnagar District. No house could be found in Rajnagar, so they rented a rest house at Ganj, fifteen miles from Chhatarpur, for eighteen dollars a year with an option to buy when expansion funds would allow. Stuti Prakash moved there November 1, 1950.[9] He was marvelously gifted at going into a new area and breaking down prejudice. He went in with Khub Chand and Itwari Lal — a new evangelist with musical ability that appealed to villagers. Khub Chand strummed out the songs he wrote; Itwari Lal with his harmonium did "kirtan" (story-song) presentations, and Stuti continued to "blow out the Gospel" with his trumpet, saxophone, and booming voice.[10]

In earnest about winning the lost in Bundelkhand to Christ, Stuti Prakash was aware of his people's blindness and confusion. They believed in many gods, in the insurmountability in this life of the caste system, and in transmigration. They knew only hopelessness as they looked toward the future. His heart was broken by the prayer of a man who had seen a vision of Jesus and cried out, "Don't give me any more visions, Jesus! I *cannot* follow you!"[11] Stuti was determined to break their chains and help them know the joy of forgiven sins through the blood of Christ, the reconciliation between brothers, the love that only Christ can give, everlasting hope, and eternal life. He carried in his pocket and also shared with others some of the problems needing prayer, especially for those who wanted to come to Christ in Bundelkhand. By the side of the problem he listed an appropriate Scripture with which he could help those converts to keep their minds fixed on the will of God:

(1) A convert loses all right to inherit his father's property (by law). 2 Corinthians 5:1
(2) A wife cannot be forced to live with her husband if he becomes a Christian. Luke 18:19, 20
(3) Villagers annoy Christians and try to put them out of the village. Matthew 5:11, 12
(4) A Christian's relatives are ashamed to live with him. Luke 21:16, 19
(5) Brahmins and *Arya Samajists* seek to turn interested people away. (A message for them: John 3:18; Acts 4:12)
(6) Converts, persecuted, desire to come to the Mission for refuge. Encourage them to go back to their villages. Luke 8:39
(7) There are not enough workers. Romans 10:13-15[12]

Clifton and Betty Robinson in Gulganj District

As Stuti Prakash moved out and the workers moved in to renovate Gulganj, Lachhman Singh stayed on in the dispensary treating up to 2,000 patients and performing 100 operations a year as well as entering into evangelistic work.[13] Gulganj bungalow, more workers' houses, and improvement on the dispensary were all finally completed, and Robinsons moved in on October 16, 1950. "While in the rush of the Cleveland metropolis," Betty wrote, "I never dreamed I would ever live in such an isolated and solitary place."[14]

The mission station was just outside the village and somewhat lonely. But down in the village one saw women peeping through their saris, not daring to show their faces, moving stealthily down village lanes with huge ankle bracelets clanking while they carried heavy loads of grass or pots of water on their heads. Children ran naked in the streets, some covered with untreated sores. Men, with painted foreheads showing the god they worshiped, bent low to get out of their little mud huts. Bells in the temples rang as people offered their sacrifices, and light burned in hollow places in a huge pepul tree in honor of a loved one whose ashes were being carried to the Ganges.

When the bearer of those ashes returned to the village, the light could go out. Goats and cows competed for right of way in the streets as over and over again the missionaries found their way to the homes of the 4,000 people in Gulganj village, telling them the Good News of Jesus Christ.[15]

The area of real action, however, was three miles from Gulganj in the little village of Bilwar. Stuti Prakash had done a tremendous job in bringing to birth a little church in Bilwar sparked by Hira Lal, the second convert, whose wife came back to him and to Christ at annual meeting in 1948. After Hira Lal, an early convert, was Nanna whose Uncle Bharosa, a powerful Chamar leader in many villages, became the chief persecutor. He threatened to kill any Christian who came into his village.[16] In a very short time his nephews, the brothers of Nanna and their wives, began to show interest. Hallu, Mansukh, and their wives made the break in 1949, putting their thumbprint signatures on the certificates and cutting their *chutiyas*. Next came Ranjaola, next to the oldest. The youngest, Har Das, was put off by persecution and held back by his wife. Finally even Bharosa was convicted of his sins and seemed to be on the verge of becoming a Christian.

The witness spread from there to other villages, and a few others braved the storm and came out for Christ. Even the high caste men of the area, Brahmins, Lodis, Ahirs, became interested. Ten of them came from Rajpur village and told Cliff they were ready to become Christians. The time for the ceremony was set, but they never showed up. However, by August, six more probationers were enrolled in the Church and there were four Christian families in Bilwar, two in Pipara, and one in Pathapur village. All these villages were near Gulganj.[17]

In Bilwar when the people decided to build a church, the women's society of the Church in India agreed to put the roof on it. There was a great battle as opposition rose against the builders, and only through the prayerful intercession of Stuti Prakash did the work continue.[18]

Catherine Cattell, with flannelgraph and simple Bible stories, spent much time in these villages along with the Robinsons. She witnessed the *chutiya* cutting ceremony of a man from the weaver caste who gave a strong testimony amidst the turmoil of some one hundred people. Four Brahmin families in a nearby village were thinking seriously. It was refreshing to see that villagers realized the Gospel was not only for Chamars, but for all people.[19]

Bilwar Conference for the New Converts

February 3-5, 1950, were dates set for all the camps to converge on Bilwar for a big gathering of all the villagers of the area who were interested in Christianity. The new Christians from Ghuara, Bilwar, Dhamora, and other villages were there to give their testimonies. Victor Mangalwadi and Stuti Prakash were in charge. A villager from near Delhi who cared for 250 Christians without pay was there to sing and give his testimony. "When we become Christians," he said, "we do it to get our sins forgiven, not to get a better job."

Nanna's Uncle Bharosa, chief persecutor of the area, was there twenty-four hours early. Bilwar, Ghuara, and Dhamora Christians came singing. Fifteen non-Christians who were "almost persuaded" came, and Panchu came through, signing his name laboriously on the register. Others not so courageous said to him, "You have done a great thing; we are coming."[20]

Deliverance from the Power of Satan

God's ambassadors continually sought to bring true spiritual freedom to the oppressed, the sinful, the bound, and the possessed. Within the church in Nowgong there was a woman who disrupted meetings, talked with two voices, and claimed to be possessed of the devil. Hanging on to life by a thread, she lay on the bed day after day saying, "He won't let me up, and he won't let me eat." Then sometimes pacing the floor, she would add, "he's making me walk." Word about this tormented woman spread through the area, and there seemed no hope for her, until the Christians meeting in their early morning prayer meetings came under a deep burden for her deliverance.

Finally with fasting they went to prayer with her and after the third day saw her gloriously set free. It did not last, however, and Anna was alone with her when she screamed that the demon was returning. "Don't let him come again," she begged, clutching Anna's arm. She began pacing the floor as before, and was soon right back where she started.[21]

Was Satan indeed stronger than God in this land? This was a question tormenting Anna, and the question with which she tormented all her colleagues for days afterwards. Peace came, however, with the assurance that the woman in God's time would be delivered.

A few months later word came that Dr. E. Stanley Jones's dream of a psychiatric center in Lucknow for the healing of troubled Christians had come into being. Early in 1952 Nur Manzil was opened with a Christian psychiatrist and staff, and Anna sent the woman there, where she was again set free from bondage.

Deliverance from Opium

Out in Bijawar a veterinary pharmacist, named Brij Kishor, lived in a similar kind of bondage. He became the first Brahmin convert in the area, but while Catherine Cattell was holding meetings in Bijawar, she noticed him and prayerfully sought to get to the bottom of his problem. He confessed to her that he was addicted to opium and that all efforts to leave it only drove him to it. His life was in shambles. His wife had left him because the opium cost him so much he could not support her.[22] The Christians began to pray for him, and Clifton Robinson, B. Z. Smith, evangelist, and Dr. Ezra DeVol made up the team that God used to deliver him. Dr. Ezra, remembering his father's practice in China and using Russell Glazier's principles developed in the University Hospital in Nanking, asked Brij Kishor to come to the hospital voluntarily and stay for at least a week. Clifton Robinson and B. Z. Smith agreed to take turns staying with him twenty-four hours a day.

The relatives, not at all concerned that Brij Kishor was destroying himself with opium, were exceedingly alarmed that he was becoming deeply involved with Christians. They promised him all the opium he wanted for the rest of his life if he would not go through with this plan. Brij Kishor was in earnest, however, and the procedure started February 22, 1951. His violence and mental anguish did not respond to advice, but when Cliff and B. Z. went to prayer and called on the name of Jesus, he quieted down and went to sleep.[23]

Before the week was up Brij Kishor walked out of the hospital a free man, praising God. Soon after that he disappeared. Searching diligently, B. Z. Smith finally found him in a distant city holding secret Bible classes with a group of young Hindus, more than fifteen in number, still free from the habit that had put him into bondage.[24]

In 1952 a missionary from another town pricked up his ears as a casual conversation with a Hindu turned to the subject of conversion. "You know," the Hindu said, "there is a veterinary pharmacist and his wife who live in [our town] and they are wonderful Christians. They have both been after me to give my heart to Christ. And I have been thinking about it seriously."[25] Three years later an evangelist again saw Brij Kishor still in victory. After that all contact was lost.[26]

Conversions in Bilwar

Persecution never lagged far behind the conversion of these people. Dozens came and then reverted. Probation was always a long, testing time. But in the fall of 1951, Cliff baptized—and by that sign took into full membership—Nanna, Hallu, Mansukh, and their wives. In a brief message before the baptism, Cliff noted Nanna look over his shoulder and saw his face freeze. Turning, Cliff also saw a long line of village men, lathis raised, standing on the ridge above. Cliff asked if they should go on. Nanna answered, "We've come this far, let's go all the way." And they did. Afterwards Cliff learned that these village men had threatened to beat the new converts senseless if they went through with the baptism, but nothing happened except the fact that the new Christians sensed they had won a great victory and had become the first baptized Christians in that jungle area — an act that would distinctly and forever separate them from the surrounding Hindus.[27]

Further tests were yet ahead, for these families were all hopelessly in debt to the high caste village moneylender. The economic bondage of these outcaste villagers was so deplorable that it baffled the minds of the most astute missionaries. "Even the Muslim kings couldn't break it," a CID (FBI) officer commented.[28] As these people came to Christ, they tended to look to the missionary to step in for them where the money-lender had been. "One never knows quite what to do," confessed Cliff, "at least I'm sure I don't . . . . It does make you feel terrible when the report comes that the Bilwar folks have had nothing to eat all day."[29] He concluded that the Mission had rules that none of them could live with, and in the pressure of it all, the political, economic, social, and satanic tentacles of evil held these poor people in their grip.

Concerns for the Newly Converted

Besides the need of bringing these people to repentance and faith, there were three other major concerns that kept the missionary and Indian workers awake at night in prayer and searching: (1) The need to deliver them from the power of the moneylender; (2) the need to find spouses for their children; and (3) the need for education.

Victor and Milton went to work on developing cooperatives. They consulted the mid-India Regional Christian Council and enlisted Komal Das Lall and Everett Cattell on their committee. The Joint Council suggested a cooperative for consumers, for building houses, for buying stock for cottage industries, and for providing education. The Mission Council worked out a scheme for loaning provident (pension) funds for building homes.[30]

The marriage problem, acute only in Ghuara, had been wonderfully settled for the time being in Prabhuwati's willingness to marry Halka Daniel, and Pyare Lal's daughter-in-law being willing to join his son and become a Christian. There was no other convert with a child of marriageable age. Therefore, this problem could be postponed.

Education without a doubt was the most crucial concern. The Mission feared starting a system that would stifle the growth of the Church by subsidizing education so that the number coming to Christ would be limited to the number of children whose education they could pay for. Ghuara had already caused a great deal of heart searching with the Chunni Lall couple placed there at Mission expense. Bilwar, Pipara, Dhamora, and Pathapur also were expecting such a couple to be placed in each of their villages. In all other villages where there was one Christian family, there was the wistful hope for a mission school.

Probably Victor Mangalwadi more than anyone else saw the inconsistency of the mission policy in seeking on the one hand to bind together the old and new Christians, and at the same time trying to keep village children rooted in their own village way of life.[31] Victor had grown up with a suspicion that missionaries wanted to keep Indians in an inferior position and in reality, he felt, were opposed to higher education. Any policy faintly suggesting this attitude stirred him deeply. As in Amarmau and Gulganj districts, he had witnessed in Nowgong District in scattered villages a number of conversions from different outcaste groups — sweepers, *basors* (keepers of pigs), and chamars. The Mission's fixed policy, with the exception of Ghuara, was that where there were ten children ready for school, a teacher would be placed until a boy from that village could be trained to take over.[32] The Mission Council seemed to feel this pressure would be an incentive to new village Christians to win more converts. Also through such a policy expansion would not be stifled and the Church could keep on growing.

Victor Mangalwadi did not approve the Mission's educational policy. He saw and felt the frustrations of new Christians in a sea of Hinduism being pushed under by persecution, about to drown for lack of understanding and opportunity. He advocated taking all the village children into a primary boarding school immediately until mission policy could work. Other Indian leaders must have felt much as he did, but knowing the strong policy of the Mission, they kept quiet. The Mission Council clung tenaciously to their rules, struggling against being pulled under in a sea of dependence.

In this grim battle for survival, village pressure was so great that the missionaries, in meeting after meeting, agonized over the educational needs, and inch by inch made changes. They decentralized all primary education up to fifth grade in order to be consistent in establishing primary schools throughout in connection with local churches. Nowgong and Chhatarpur were immediately challenged to assume responsibility for paying the bills and caring for their primary schoolchildren. Ghuara, to survive, had to be an exception, and the Mission continued to struggle with that.

Primary boarding schools, over Victor's strong objections, became a thing of the past. The whole plan was aimed toward release of funds for village schools until they, too, would become strong enough to bear their share of the financial load and keep on growing.[33] Anna drew from her own experience as a child of pioneer parents in Colorado. She had attended an eight-grade, one-room, one-teacher school up to seventh grade, and she felt the system would work very well in India's new village schools up to the fifth grade, and that Chhatarpur would be a good place to start the experiment. She hired Mrs. Samson Huri Lal, wife of the male nurse in the hospital. Mrs. Lal was a well-trained teacher and eager to give the new system a try, but Victor Mangalwadi, backed by most of the parents, opposed the plan vehemently. Since Chhatarpur Church could really afford nothing else without mission help, the plan went forward in spite of opposition.[34]

Middle schools were planned for Nowgong, as usual, and also for village children in district centers like Amarmau and Gulganj. Students from villages around these centers were encouraged to bring their food with them for the week and return often to their villages. Mangalwadis were transferred to Amarmau when Colemans went home for furlough in 1952, and Kusum managed such a middle school for the village children from Ghuara along with her own and other children in Amarmau. A brief attempt was also made in Gulganj. These district middle schools did not prove to be practical, however, and were soon closed. Finally the Mission Council decided Nowgong Christian Institute under the Bankers would continue as the boys' boarding middle and high school for missions in the whole area, and that the middle and high school girls would go to Jhansi Canadian Presbyterian boarding school.[35]

The village school problem was still far from settled, and it was evident that new village Christians felt keenly that education for their children was the crucial step to full freedom for which they longed.

Such were the mission educational policies when Max and Ruth Ellen Banker took charge of that work in 1951.

CHAPTER XXII | # Extending the Boundaries

> *"I have other sheep that are not of this sheep pen.
> I must bring them also. They, too, will listen to my
> voice, and there shall be one flock and one shepherd."*
> John 10:16 NIV

Unity of Purpose

In the early 1950s the building expansion program was nearing an end with the completion of dispensaries, hospital wards, workers' quarters, houses for fifteen missionaries and additional Indian staff, plus complete repair and reroofing of all the school and all older buildings. Everett Cattell had succeeded in challenging the expanding staff with a vision of the needs in Bundelkhand. There were the opportunities of presenting Christ to the educated in the cities, the discipling of new converts; the ministry in *melas* attended by millions of people from all over the area, and above all — village evangelism. The gaping social needs were not forgotten — the ill, wounded, illiterate, malnourished, and oppressed, caught in a system that would not let them rise.[1] While in some areas social service and medical missionaries fought with those in evangelism for the greater share of the budget, Everett Cattell had fostered in the Friends Mission agreement on priorities and "a beautiful spirit of cooperation between Indians and missionaries and a common sharing of responsibility and burden."[2]

Furloughs

This sense of unity was so felt by every missionary that there was a reluctance to break the close fellowship even for furlough; but the time came in 1951 when Norma Freer had to pack up and go home. The custom was to leave for furlough about April and return the end of September the following year, making it possible for the missionary to attend two sessions of Ohio Yearly Meeting and miss two hot seasons in India. The Mission Board had provided a new home for the missionaries in Damascus, Ohio.

The Women's Missionary Society had completely furnished it even to a small electric organ.[3] Colemans and Anna Nixon were the first returning India missionaries to occupy it in 1952. Robinsons returned to the U.S.A. in 1953, Cattells in 1954, and DeVols and Bankers in 1955.[4] Their reports in conventions and various churches in the U.S.A. inspired people who prayed regularly for the converts in India by name and loved and welcomed their missionaries like returning family members.

Arrival of Robert and Esther Hess

In 1952 just before Colemans and Anna Nixon left India for furlough, Robert, Esther, and Kathleen Ann Hess, age one-and-a-half, arrived bringing joy and hope to all. Robert, usually called Bob, came from a large family of five boys and one girl. They lived in Hughesville, Pennsylvania, and the Ecroyd sisters there influenced him greatly in his early spiritual pilgrimage. While in the Air Force during World War II, he commited his life to Christ and later felt called to India. Chester Stanley, pastor at Highland Avenue (Westgate) in Columbus, and his wife, Evangeline, introduced Bob to one of their keen young members, Esther Garner, who with one sister and a widowed mother worked to help support the family. She also had missionary service in mind. Both attended Asbury College and were married one year before Bob graduated. They then served in a pastorate in Marysville while Bob completed his master's degree at Ohio State University.

By the time Bob and Esther Hess applied to the Board, India's policy for admission of missionaries had begun to tighten, and their visa was refused. Having already packed and closed their house, they became the first residents in the new missionary home provided by the Yearly Meeting and furnished by the Women's Missionary Society. Deputation work filled the next six months as they reapplied for a visa and waited.[5] Finally it came through in January 1952, and the Board rushed them by ship to London and on to India by plane in order to beat the "stork." They arrived in Nowgong February 21, 1952.[6] In her first letter home, Esther wrote, "Walter Williams told [Bob] that he wouldn't really be a part of the India Mission until he learned to use the word 'desperate' . . . I feel a full-fledged member [since] the ride from Harpalpur to Nowgong in the Dodge station wagon! It shimmies . . . almost gets out of control—actually going from one side of the road to the other. [There was the] possibility of a serious accident, either rolling into the ditch or killing someone along the road . . . Milton's jeep behaves the same way . . . a rather 'desperate' situation."[7]

After a quick trip over the stations in Bundelkhand, the Hesses proceeded to Landour. Their luggage containing all the baby's clothes, because of unusual delays, did not arrive from America for six months, but Ronald Wayne was born on April 14, 1952, in the Landour Community Hospital and survived well without these essentials, thanks to Catherine's thoughtful purchases at the annual barter sale in Landour.[8] On the same day Ron was born, a cable from Columbus crossed with the one from Landour telling of two other births in the spiritual realm, that Esther's mother and sister had been born again.[9]

Khumb Mela Tragedy

Hesses were the first two Friends missionaries to have the advantage of a full-year language school — summer season in Landour and winter in Allahabad, U.P. Joyce Bryner was the third. A college graduate and a nurse, she also completed Cleveland Bible College and was the fifteenth missionary sent out as requested by Everett Cattell in 1945.

Joyce set sail November 24, 1952. She was born in Monongahela, Pennsylvania, but got her training in Ohio and lived in Ashtabula. She plunged into language study — and into a treacherous illness, hepatitis, which kept her on her back for some weeks. This did not impede her language progress, but as time went on, adjustment problems developed that caused her to question whether or not she could remain the full six-year term.

She was still in Allahabad in February 1954 when the large *Khumb Mela*, which occurs only once in twelve years, was held. Such a mob was present that a stampede occurred in which several hundred people were trampled to death. Joyce went to work on the *mela* grounds caring for the wounded. Darkness settled in and they were without flashlights. She tripped over a tent rope and fell. She slipped a disc, broke a rib, and injured the muscles in her back. There was nerve injury and partial loss of use of the right leg. The adjustment problems and the injuries led to Joyce's return home.[10] The peak of fifteen missionaries would never again be reached.

The Call Beyond Bundelkhand

The downhill trend in personnel for Bundelkhand, however, did not begin with Joyce Bryner, but with Everett Cattell. In spite of himself, in spite of Mission Council, and in spite of the Mission Board, he never did get back to intensive village evangelism. Conversions had already begun to slow down, and the concern about how this all might turn out showed up in his letters. "It would be an utter tragedy if we are to have expansive buildings and staff without commensurate growth in the Church. We are determined by God's grace that this tragedy is not to happen."[11] But inexorable changes in India were closing the doors to village evangelism for Everett.

In 1950 Clyde Taylor of the Evangelical Foreign Missions Association and Elwin Wright of the National Association of Evangelicals were sent to India to encourage evangelical cooperation on an India-wide basis. "I hope it may be possible for you to contact the other leaders in our section and aid these men in their efforts," Walter Williams wrote Everett.[12] Following through on this, Everett learned that their itinerary from November 21 to December 19, 1951, covered Bombay, Nagpur, Akola, Madras, Calcutta, Allahabad, Kanpur and New Delhi. He immediately made train reservations for a trip to Nagpur, Akola, and Allahabad, the three centers that were the hub of groups forming the context in which an Evangelical Fellowship of India would eventually emerge.

In Nagpur, Everett was with Taylor and Wright as they met officers of the National Christian Council, a group made up of nearly all Protestant missions in India. This council represented missions to government. He went with them from there on to Akola, the hub of the Berar-Khandesh Christian Council made up entirely of evangelical missions. This B. K. Christian Council group would be the springboard for the evangelical movement in India. Because the NCC could not by constitution enter into church union and was committed to no statement of faith, all the BKCC groups felt comfortable in their relationship with NCC, as did the Friends Mission in Bundelkhand. In fact, Everett Cattell and other evangelical leaders served as members of the NCC executive committee.

Clifton and Betty Robinson and Catherine Cattell also joined Everett at the meeting in Allahabad,[13] where two other significant groups of evangelicals were present: the India Bible Christian Council and a small group known as the Evangelical Fellowship of North India. The India Bible Christian Council, formed in 1950, was a branch of the International Christian Council led by Carl McIntyre. Leaders of this group were located in Kanpur. Their rules made it impossible for an individual or a group to belong to both NCC and IBCC at the same time. Therefore, many evangelicals who were members of NCC were excluded. The Evangelical Fellowship of North India sought to underline the importance of prayer, revival, and sound doctrine. Friends were members of this group. Some of these evangelicals objected to membership in NCC because there were those in it who were also members of the World Council of Churches, but the EF in North India did not exclude others as did the IBCC.

The organization of the National Association of Evangelicals in 1943 and its recognition of the IFMA and EFMA, including a broad spectrum of evangelical groups, was not an exact counterpart of what was needed in India because many of the strongest Indian evangelical leaders were from the large and often liberal denominations. These leaders needed to be included in any evangelical movement of significance in India. Everett Cattell felt that any new fellowship should be broad enough to include all evangelicals, both individuals and groups, regardless of their association by denomination with any other group.[14]

The Birth of the Evangelical Fellowship of India

Clyde Taylor and Elwin Wright were quick to see that India should be an autonomous body and not merely a branch of an American NAE.[15] The cleavage in India was not between denominations, but between liberal and conservative theology. For that reason, evangelical leaders in India had a strong responsibility not to divide denominationally, but to unite on the basis of a statement of faith that would give strong support to every individual in such groups as the NCC as well as in their own various denominations.[16]

Most evangelical groups in India wanted exactly this, and as delegates to these meetings, they heard their ideas expressed so clearly by Everett Cattell, the superintendent of the American Friends Mission, that they unanimously wanted him to lead in the formation of the new Evangelical Fellowship of India.[17]

Cliff Robinson went on to Calcutta with the Taylor-Wright team to assist in the meetings there. He reported that in Calcutta, also, the person focused on as leader for the new movement was Everett Cattell. They considered him the one with the experience, background, and position to bring about the cooperation needed for founding such a movement. Cliff, back home from Allahabad and Calcutta, played a vital role in convincing the Mission Council to release their superintendent for this work. He spoke convincingly to the Mission Council of "the need for such an all-India evangelistic medium uniting spiritually with the national evangelical movements of the world, to sound an alarm and stir men to find Christ before night falls and hope is forever gone . . . . [In] these meetings we were fired with the new hope that at long last the evangelical burden in this land was to be cooperatively borne . . . . Everett Cattell [was] used to give direction at these important meetings. People look to him for future leadership."[18]

Milton Coleman also gave his support: "The establishment of the Evangelical Fellowship of India offers a large measure of hope for the future of the Christian Church in this land," he said. The attitude of Mission Council gradually changed from "we can't spare him" to "we must bow to the inevitable."[19] Resolutions, passed at Allahabad to be acted on by groups present at these meetings with Taylor and Wright, were approved by the Mission Council and acted upon January 1, 1951:

Resolved that this conference, with a sense of the urgency of the present hour, request all evangelical missions in India to approach their Home Boards at once, emphasizing

(1) the present need for unity of evangelical work and witness

(2) as a consequence, the provision of adequate finance and personnel to carry forward the work of the all-India Fellowship of Evangelicals now being formed; and

(3) the high priority of this project and the resultant necessity for all possible sacrifice of local and mission needs in order to face the total challenge.[20]

The foundational meeting was called for at Yavatmal, January 16-18, 1951. At that meeting the fifty members present mapped out their strategy as prayer and their priorities in this order: (1) Revival, (2) Literature, (3) Theological Education.

The Friends Mission immediately accepted these proposals and became members of EFI.[21]

In spite of himself, Everett Cattell was appointed as the chairman and executive secretary. "I went to Yavatmal without a flicker of uncertainty that my call was to Bundelkhand," he wrote. "That lasted half way through. On the one hand my burden for Bundelkhand has not abated one whit . . . I have no sense of release from our work . . . ." Yet the new EFI position was already placed on his shoulders! "But I have misgivings . . . . By acknowledging that the all-India call for me takes precedence over Bundelkhand, I fear it will open the doors for a wider exodus [from Bundelkhand] for . . . our mission has more than its share of all-India calibre. My struggle is between an acute need for revival in all of India . . . and my call to Bundelkhand."[22]

Quickly came back a letter from Walter Williams pressing the alarm button at the thought of a Bundelkhand exodus. Reminding Everett of the Board's backing in expansion and in sending his fifteen missionaries, he further added:

Has the vision you had in '46 dissolved? It surely has not been realized, except in token form. Would it mean that you could face the Christian forces in India as a leader, when we have only 150 Indians enrolled as members of the Church thus far? . . . that our staff in India is sufficiently seasoned to carry on without you? . . . Do we scrap or reduce plans for covering the entire field while the door is open?[23]

Clyde Taylor also wrote to Everett Cattell. "Frankly, I think you are the man to head this movement in India."[24]

Walter Williams, in a final protest, wrote Clyde Taylor, explaining, "On the field right now we have no [other] second termer. [This would be] like removing the keystone from an arch while the building was in the process of construction."[25]

Meanwhile like an avalanche the burden for all of India — still including Bundelkhand — rolled onto the shoulders of the American Friends Mission, particularly its superintendent. They realized that for revival to come to Bundelkhand, it had to come to all of India, and for it to come in India it had to begin in Bundelkhand. So Everett wrote Walter Williams, "The most necessary contribution that I can make is to get the Church going in Bundelkhand."[26] The outcome was that the EFI office was set up in small, remote Chhatarpur and Anna Nixon, the DeVol twins — Pat and Pris — and Barbara and Catherine Cattell all helped with mailing lists and dispatching.[27]

Having Cattells stay in Chhatarpur pleased both the Mission Council and the Board at home. So long as the Cattells remained in India, Chhatarpur remained their base. Catherine continued to give full time to evangelistic work, and even as Everett was away nine months out of twelve, he still kept Bundelkhand's future in focus, though he never did get back to village work.

The Birth of Union Biblical Seminary

The first project undertaken by EFI was the formation of the Union Biblical Seminary. As far back as 1948, Catherine Cattell had brought home from the Holiness Convention in Yavatmal this resolution passed by that convention:

WHEREAS, independent India affords a new and greater challenge to the Christian Church and,

WHEREAS, the need of the new can only be met by a Spirit-filled, wholly sanctified, and adequately trained leadership of all grades, and

WHEREAS, the present several Theological Colleges are not sufficient for the meeting of the growing needs of India in the B.D. Grade,

BE IT RESOLVED that the India Holiness Association in its 1948 Annual Meeting through a widely representative Committee implore the Mission Boards of all groups holding the definitely holiness emphasis to appoint official representatives on a common Commission to explore the prospects for creating a union "Asbury Seminary" type of Institution in India.[28]

Dr. Frank and Betty Kline, of the Free Methodist Church and principal and teacher in the Free Methodist Bible School at Yavatmal, had great dreams of a Union Biblical Seminary in India formed along evangelical and holiness lines, qualified to grant a B.D. degree.[29] A *Ransom Commission*, appointed by the NCC, did an in-depth study of three categories in theological education: (1) Bible schools such as started by William Carey where admission was to students below matriculation (high school) and usually taught in the various regional languages (fourteen of which were recognized by the new India); (2) Theological schools, in regional languages, requiring middle school and matriculation for entrance and granting an L.Th. degree (Licentiate in Theology); (3) The Theological College, usually in English medium, requiring matriculation, higher school, or college graduation, and granting G.Th., B.Th., or B.D. degrees (Graduate of Theology, Bachelor of Theology and Bachelor of Divinity).

Ransom's dream was for the development of the third category, and Frank Kline picked it up, adding to the name "Theological College" the word "Evangelical." Since the new EFI encompassed evangelicals from churches of many countries of the world where some knew very little about Arminian and Calvinist controversies that had polarized the West, the leaders felt a responsibility to foster spiritual unity between all evangelical groups.[30] Before proceeding with this, two polarized Americans, Everett Cattell and Dr. Norton Sterrett, met in Chhatarpur to discuss these evangelical differences in depth. Norton was Everett's trusted friend, a noted missionary, a Doctor of Theology of the Reformed Presbyterians, and a former classmate of the late Dr. Francis Shaeffer. Agreeing to use only well-defined biblical terms, they discovered that though they represented the watershed of the two schools of theology, yet, at the peak they were profoundly united on the great doctrinal issues, such as the sovereignty of God and free will of man, the need for instantaneous cleansing and the further need for daily cleansing by the blood of Christ, and on other issues that seemed to divide them.

Their firm belief in the Bible, "the fully and uniquely inspired Word of God, the only infallible, sufficient and authoritative rule of faith and practice," bound them together in such a way as to convince them not only of the possibility of working together in one evangelical institution, but also the responsibility for doing so in order to declare the whole counsel of God.[31] Everett Cattell then wrote to Walter Williams: "Our school in Union Biblical Seminary must be based on the broader evangelical base for reasons of leadership, for reasons of laying down 'shiboleths,' [remembering that the Calvin/Wesley controversy was rather new in Church history], and for reasons of producing the highest academic standard possible."[32]

Dr. Frank Kline, the Free Methodist principal and chief architect of Union Biblical Seminary, was asking for the best scholars in the country as teachers, and for an enlargement of the library. His goal was to turn out deeply spiritual and evangelistically minded ministers. "Just think, if evangelicals could really rise to it," wrote Everett, ". . . we could, if God gives us another twenty-five years here, change the complexion of the leadership of the whole Christian movement in India."[33]

The Mission Board got right behind this on recommendation of the Mission Council and sent $200 June 13, 1951—the beginning of their annual grants that still continue to this day.[34] By March 1953 the Mission Council also accepted the draft of the organizing committee of UBS and agreed to become a cooperating mission and to appoint a member to the Board of Governors. This was ratified by the Friends Foreign Missionary Society at Yearly Meeting that year. In 1950, Gore Lal Singh's daughter, Virginia Singh, and in 1951 Stuti Prakash's son, Vijay Prakash, joined the Seminary as students. Everett Cattell not only assisted in drafting the constitution, but also served as the first chairman of the Board of Governors. He wrote:

> We . . . will admit to the Bachelor of Divinity course men who have a B.A. or a G.Th. . . . . Our B.D. course will be three years and we hope eventually to give graduate theology degrees, also to obliterate the necessity of men going abroad. The standard of work which we envisage will be in advance of anything being given in India today.[35]

At the National Association of Evangelicals' Convention in Cincinnati in April 1953, eleven mission board leaders of U.S.A. and Canada considered the implications of such a venture and became incorporated as The Cooperating Home Boards of Union Biblical Seminary, Inc. Their purpose was to cooperate with the UBS Board of Governors in doctrinal and financial matters.[36] At that time, the $140,000 needed for development seemed an insurmountable obstacle before even their combined efforts, but faith compelled them to move forward.[37]

Discussion both in U.S.A. and in India brought forward questions about location. Yavatmal, located in a provincial area, seemed inadequate for dreams of the future. Three considerations, however, led to the decision to build in Yavatmal rather than to move at that time:

(1) There were not sufficient funds to move.
(2) The rural setting seemed better suited for the training of leaders for the Cooperating Home Boards' students who were predominantly from rural settings.
(3) Yavatmal was surrounded by sympathetic missions.[38]

The UBS Board of Governors received official government authority to grant theological degrees.[39] Everett Cattell was present for convocation in March 1956 and wrote:

> I saw six young men graduate with the G.Th. degree . . . . and had tea . . . with five students who have entered our first B.D. class . . . . Amongst all our needs in India today THIS IS IT! We must go beyond the Cooperating Home Boards for grants of money.[40]

Later Harold Kuhn with his wife, Anne, taught in Yavatmal for a term and agreed with what Everett Cattell had written. All this confirmed his earlier expression of faith at the beginning:

> To my mind there is no doubt that in the long range view that, if the Lord should tarry, and the doors remain open, this is the most strategic move that evangelicals can make.[41]

The Executive Committee of EFI led by Everett Cattell held the second EFI conference in Akola January 1952, with Dr. Paul Rees and a layman missionary from Australia, Norman Burns, as speakers. A mighty revival took place among the 100 delegates attending. If any vestige of doubt remained in any Friends missionary's mind about the significance of their contribution to EFI, it was swept away in the flood of blessing that spread to every corner of India, including the Union Biblical Seminary. The Friends students there, Vijay Prakash and Virginia Singh, felt the impact of it and walked in the light.[42] Thus out of revival both the EFI and its first project, UBS, was born.

Trouble in Bundelkhand

While in EFI's context Everett Cattell was seeing revival fires kindled from one end of India to another, back home in Bundelkhand everything was not quite in order. Pancham Singh, that powerful man who once knew the Lord but was now backslidden, led a movement in Chhatarpur to establish a "free" church—free to drink, smoke, go to the movies, chew pan (betel nut), work on Sunday, and live with no restraints. Fourteen disgruntled members joined him in his "free church" and another fourteen who had been disowned rallied under his banner. He tried to win the new converts in Ghuara, Bilwar, Dhamora, and other villages, but he got none of them. He called a man who had formerly been dismissed from mission service as their pastor—ironic indeed, since Pancham Singh had at one time vowed not to cut his hair for months to prevent the acceptance of the pastoral system in the Church. This group established themselves as a separate body on July 20, 1952. Failing to get permission to use the church building, they met in Pancham Singh's house.

Four days later the certificates of registration with the India Government of both the Mission and the Church as legal bodies, able to hold property, were received. The new discipline had been accepted by the Government and was now put into effect. One clause in it stated: "Those joining another church . . . shall automatically forfeit membership with us from that day." So all who had joined the "free church" were stricken from the church roll.[43]

The group did not last. The pastor, whose support became a burden, soon stopped coming. Within two months the "free church" had already split a second time with half of the members applying to come back.[44] At the annual meeting in 1953, those who seemed truly to have repented were received again into membership of the BMMS (Bundelkhand Friends Church). Gradually Pancham Singh lost all of his following. Since he was no longer a member of the Church, peace reigned in the quarterly meetings. No longer could he oppose every forward move, discount every testimony of others, and oppose every change suggested.[45]

The Battle to Hold Converts

In spite of this trouble in Chhatarpur, preparative meetings were developed in various outstations along financially feasible lines. For example, Amarmau District held its first rally or preparative quarterly meeting in a jungle, halfway between Ghuara and Amarmau. Each individual from these respective preparative monthly meetings was responsible for his own transportation, food, and shelter. Stuti Prakash was the special speaker. The people walked for miles to the place, slept under the trees, and ate their own *chapatis* and *sag* (Indian bread and spinach). Twenty people came and had a spiritual feast. Such meetings were established also in Bijawar, Bilwar, and Gulganj.[46]

In late 1952 Clifton Robinson was overjoyed to see eight more villagers bow at the feet of Jesus in the face of strong opposition. Before they became established enough to be taken in as full members, however, persecution claimed them all. Cliff and his co-workers did not give up easily. By going after them, he was able to bring some of them back and also gain a few others. Then followed a furious battle. Catherine Cattell joined them in it, working with the women while living with Kusum Mangalwadi and Rupa Bai in a mud house far from any medical help.[47]

When Kusum was suddenly stung by a scorpion, the village women heard the groaning and rushed in to see Kusum in agony. They heard Catherine and Rupa Bai praying, confessing their helplessness and asking God to show His power for the sake of His great name. The village women noticed there were no idols before them. They also sensed the love and faith with which the Christian women addressed the Almighty, with faces upturned, eyes closed, and tears streaming down their cheeks. Caught in the wonder of it all, they hardly noticed that the groaning had stopped. Usually, that pain would have lasted three days. As it subsided, the praying turned to thanksgiving. Catherine quickly took advantage of the opportunity afforded by the gathering. Taking her Bible, she read to them of the healing of the woman with the issue of blood. The women, wiping away their own tears and vigorously nodding their heads from side to side, said, "We believe it. Haven't we seen His healing power with our own eyes?"[48]

Following this, another surge of interest brought converts in from many villages — but not for long. Nanna, recorded as elder the same day as the dedication of the new Bilwar chapel, November 7, 1952, soon lost his victory. Bitterly he turned the little chapel into a stable for his oxen. The reason was that a year earlier Cliff had loaned Nanna seed grain on terms that a specific portion of the crop at harvest time would be returned. Mansukh, another recent convert, had received the same kind of loan under the same terms. Mansukh kept his side of the bargain; Nanna did not. Actually this was just one of a number of times Nanna failed in this kind of agreement. Planting time again arrived, and both Nanna and Mansukh came back for more seed. Cliff gave Mansukh what he asked for but refused Nanna. The Council firmly backed Cliff.[49] The discipline was agonizing for everyone, but especially for Cliff, who later reflected that it was the most difficult personal confrontation he had ever had to make.

Shortly after this James and Judith Kinder, now superintending fruitful Arrah and Ballia districts of the Methodist Church in India, visited Chhatarpur again and brought answers to some of their questions. The Kinders were involved in village work in North India where there were many conversions of unusual spiritual depth. "Our mission certainly lost two very outstanding missionaries when they left," wrote Everett Cattell.[50] "They were very helpful to us . . . we have learned our lesson and are trying to mend our ways." He referred here particularly to economic assistance given to converts by missionaries in Bundelkhand. Kinders had the advantage of seeing so many conversions in their area that they could not possibly have given such aid.

To Friends, however, the conversions were so few it seemed sheer cruelty not to give. Thus the converts came to feel that becoming a Christian was a sure way out of financial difficulties. To correct this, the missionaries tightened their charity and loans to the new converts and this resulted in reversion.[51] Robinsons grieved as they saw these people they had learned to love slip away.

The final year of their first term in India was indeed filled with many disappointments. Judy, just getting over tuberculosis, came down with the mumps as did the other three children. Complications from measles, which also soon ran its course, included pneumonia for Anne, rickets and intestinal infection for Byron, and earache for Ruth. Cliff suffered his usual bouts with malaria complicated with an ear infection.[52] Then as they were packing in Nowgong, they were robbed. Applying to Rewa through one of the newer missionaries for their "No Objection to Return" certificate, they were refused, and even Everett Cattell's personal intervention was fruitless.[53]

Robinsons' Departure from Bundelkhand

Not only were Robinsons thinking deeply about the future of their India ministry in light of the struggle in the Gulganj area, but the new cooperative movement of evangelicals for all of India was appreciated more by them perhaps than any other of the missionaries in Bundelkhand. They stood firmly back of the Council's decision to release Everett Cattell nine months out of twelve to this work. Before leaving for furlough Cliff came to the conclusion that he also was called for evangelism to the heavier populated centers of India rather than primarily to the villages of Bundelkhand. There were too many missionaries in Bundelkhand, he suggested.[54] This set the other missionaries reeling, and Everett called Cliff for a frank talk. Everything was laid on the table and Cliff suggested a change in mission policy from the present view that a certain number of missionaries was needed to saturate Bundelkhand to the view that the Mission should now release the personnel to go outside where needs were pressing and wait for the present converts and Christians to produce others. As the move got underway in Bundelkhand, they could return.

The idea at first sounded absurd, but a light flashed into the mind of Everett Cattell. Accepting the suggestion as Spirit-revealed insight, he urged Cliff to present his thoughts to the next Council session. Cliff did so and though discussion sometimes would have been said to shed more heat than light, in the end it was recorded, "God cleansed us of suspicious attitudes," and restored unity. Everett rejoiced to hear, however, that while recognizing the validity of Cliff's desire for and Everett's appointment to expanding the boundaries, all the others vowed they would redouble their efforts for fruit in Bundelkhand.[55] Dr. Ezra DeVol was appointed chairman of Mission Council at this meeting though Everett Cattell maintained the superintendency.[56]

Reversions and a Changed Course

The greatest blow came to the Robinsons, however, when after they left the shores of India the first word to reach them was that all the converts in the Gulganj-Bilwar area had reverted to Hinduism — a religion that condemned them all as outcastes and untouchables. When the news reached the Colemans and Anna Nixon in the Damascus missionary home, they, too, grieved as for beloved relatives. In India an emergency Council meeting with Victor Mangalwadi and Stuti Prakash was called to decide what to do to stem the tide. They feared losing Ghuara, too. Had their "tightening up" policy not removed the Chunni Lals from Ghuara to avoid the criticism that favoritism had been shown there?

Hira Singh and his family, put in their place, kept the preaching going, but, with Manorma Bai out, Ghuara's educational hopes were dashed to the ground and they, too, were exceedingly unhappy. Hira Singh and his family were also unhappy. He felt his lack of acceptance and isolation, huddled as he was with his family in the one-room mud house with its lean-to kitchen and tile roof, and the only latrine at the end of a long jungle trail under a scrub tree behind a rock. Vegetables available in Ghuara bazaar were extremely limited and very expensive. Their food consisted of spinach, dried potatoes, beans or peas, and chapatis or rice. It was all unpalatable to a man appointed — and not called — to such a place.[57]

The Chunni Lall's were equally as unhappy in Gulganj, but what could the Council do? They did not dare "furnish" a teacher to Ghuara again at this stage, they felt. Manorma Bai solved the problem for them by agreeing at their request to return to Ghuara without salary.[58] Perhaps she, more than anyone, deserves the credit for keeping Ghuara on course for the Lord. With the transfer of Mr. and Mrs. Chunni Lall back to Ghuara and Hira Singh's family to Gulganj, other stationing changes were also made. Hesses were assigned to Gulganj, Victor Mangalwadi to Nowgong as pastor, Anna Nixon to Chhatarpur to live with Norma Freer, and Stuti Prakash to Chhatarpur as pastor, though continuing also as district superintendent of Rajnagar District.

The heartbreak of these months put the Christian leaders in Bundelkhand on their knees. What went wrong? Who was to blame? What could be done to recover that which was lost? In his comprehensive way, Everett Cattell listed all the reasons one by one in an eight-paged, legal sized, single-spaced, elite-typed document with suggested courses of action. Clifton Robinson's earlier suggested outline of a new policy was clearly taking root in his mind. On October 30, 1953, he submitted his paper for study to all the missionaries, the Indian leaders, and the Mission Board.[59]

The paper rejected at the outset any thought of giving up, but questions asked included all phases of mission policy in regard to conversions. Had it been wrong to give Khub Chand a stipend for spending time in Ghuara — or had the mistake been in continuing him on salary — thus making his employment the envy and goal of every new convert? Should they have refused to accept a convert until he had come with a group large enough to help him stand? Was it the giving of relief to these suffering new converts so ostracized from their society that caused the problem, or was it the inconsistency with which it had been done? The "orphan Christians" enjoyed the privileges of education, nice homes, mission employment, medical privileges, and close fellowship with missionaries for which the village converts longed but were of necessity denied. "We have been betrayed [by whom he does not say] into the position of withholding from the new Christians privileges which we guarantee to the older Christians (who are still not indigenous)." This, Everett emphasized, was the primary cause of reversion. If only there had been a movement large enough to have survived on its own in the villages! Obviously it was impossible to bring new converts into the same privilege as the "orphan Christians."

On this issue the Mission had fumbled, and the burning question now to be answered was: "Why then do we perpetuate a system which we are unwilling to indefinitely enlarge?" There was obviously no easy answer to this. Schools and hospitals to demonstrate the love of God (though sometimes admittedly they do not demonstrate it) surely were not wrong. Nor was it wrong, surely, to pay adequate salaries to the employees. However, back to Pickett, the development of institutions beyond the ability of a growing church to take the responsibility for them was no doubt a wrong course to follow. It had caused even the hiring of pastors and evangelists to be as institutionalized and dependent on foreign funds as were the hospital and schools.

The profound struggle in which the Mission now found itself was the freeing of the tiny existing Church in Bundelkhand — whether they wanted it or not — from the domination of the Mission so that their stewardship before God would be meaningful and they could come into their own.

At the next Mission Council meeting over a period of eight days the missionaries and Indian leaders began struggling with this huge problem.[60] With new insight, as sure as sunset, the end came to an era in mission history as God helped the heartbroken Bundelkhand Christian leaders pick up the broken pieces to start anew — beyond the boundaries, yes — but also including always at its heart the Church in Bundelkhand.

CHAPTER
XXIII

Grappling with Change

"The vision is yet for an appointed time, but at the end it shall speak, and not lie; though it tarry, wait for it, because it will surely come, it will not tarry."
Habakkuk 2:3

Changes on the Home Front

While the Mission struggled for survival in Bundelkhand and revival in India in 1952, the Mission Board sent Charles Matti and Chester Stanley to explore the possibilities of opening work again in China or Taiwan (then called Formosa). They recommended headquarters in Chaiyi, and Charles and Elsie Matti and Ella Ruth Hutson were chosen as the spearhead party.

India would no longer be the sole focus of attention of Friends of Ohio Yearly Meeting. This was a healthy development, for while results came slowly in India, Taiwan blossomed, developing churches that have become a joy of their parent body in the U.S.A. This success gave the constituency courage to stand by India while missionaries entered cooperative endeavors to produce church growth in India as a whole, but not primarily of the Friends denomination.[1]

On their return trip — from December 27, 1952, to January 24, 1953 — Charles Matti and Chester Stanley visited Bundelkhand. Dwight L. Ferguson and his wife, well-known evangelists from Ohio and uncle and aunt to Ruth Ellen Banker, visited at the same time, and all brought revival and blessing. News of the forty-six intercessor bands with 503 members and of the Women's Missionary societies and the Men in Missions groups all helped the people in Bundelkhand realize they were not alone. Many cards, letters, and parcels also kept them aware of that.

As word came that in Ohio $83,249.19 had come in — $500 beyond the budget — the missionaries recognized that Walter Williams's regular

273

letters to pastors and Arlene Kelbaugh's work with juniors in revising Eleanor Chambers' book, *Telling the People in India about Jesus*, had worked together to keep home interest at a peak.[2] The transition of leadership from Walter Williams to Chester G. Stanley as mission superintendent in August 1954 went smoothly because the new superintendent had been on the Board many years, had been to India, and was informed and dedicated.[3]

Though Everett Cattell was traveling for EFI at least three fourths of the time, he had not lost sight of Bundelkhand. However, he found to his sorrow the same pattern of dependence and deep need of revival in other parts of India as in Bundelkhand. On the other hand, he became aware of the high quality of Indian leaders Bundelkhand had produced. He was glad the Board authorized the enlarging and reroofing of all workers' quarters. This, and the building of three more new family wards and a shelter for relatives of patients in the hospital, could only be done because Komal Das Lall carried on while Everett was away.[4]

The United Mission to Nepal

As the Evangelical Fellowship of India (EFI) became known, calls for meetings increased. An EFI team from the revival area of Ruanda, Africa, was invited to all the hill conventions in North and South India. Everett was called for the summer in 1953 as the pastor of Landour's Kellogg Church, attended by 250 language students as well as an equal number of vacationing missionaries.[5] Many mission councils called him for advice on their plans for the future.

He also took part in the forming of the United Mission to Nepal, established under the auspices of the National Christian Council. The Government of Nepal, though opposed to conversion, opened its doors to united missions:

> . . . to minister to the needs of the people in Nepal in the Name and Spirit of Christ, and to make Christ known to them by word and life . . . to care for the sick; educate; develop agriculture and industry, etc.; and to . . . train the people of Nepal in professional skills and in leadership.[6]

The UMN opened its doors in Nepal March 18, 1954. The American Friends Mission was a part of this outreach, giving a token grant of Rs. 100 ($22).[7] In a short time Friends would also send personnel, but for the present, all the missionaries were still so focused on Bundelkhand that the thought of leaving was impossible. Even Everett still looked on outside developments through the eyes of a Bundelkhandi. "I somehow feel that it may be working for the best interests of Bundelkhand. I trust it may be so."[8]

The Indo-American Agreement

Meanwhile, amidst heavy administrative and medical responsibilities, Dr. W. Ezra DeVol struggled to grasp firmly both reins of responsibility—that of hospital superintendent and chairman of the Mission Council.[9] On the medical front, as operations increased in one year by 300 percent, problems also arose he had never faced before, even in China. "The awfulness of not being believed has hit us in the face," he wrote.[10] "It has been harder to start in medical practice here than anywhere else—and this is the fourth time for me."[11]

An Indo-American Agreement, however, lightened his load. Through it food, hospital equipment, and medical supplies were admitted to India duty free. The U.S.A. Government paid the ocean freight, and the Indian Government charged no duty and paid the internal freight. Church World Service, American Friends Service Committee, Care Inc., Mennonite Central Committee, and the National Catholic Welfare Conference made their services available for this.[12]

Through this plan the hospital secured a new four-wheel drive Willys-Jeep station wagon. Dr. Ezra then established what he referred to as his "milk route." Each week he with a medical team from Chhatarpur went the fifty-five-mile route through Gulganj to Amarmau, supervising the dispensaries in these two outstations and stopping anywhere along the road where a villager in need of medical treatment might flag them down.[13]

Christian Hospital Staff

Medical treatment was greatly enhanced, not only by better equipment, but also by the coming of a highly qualified laboratory technician who knew how to use it. Norman Whipple, an American, had been dismissed from his mission because he dared to flaunt mission policy and marry a Christian Indian teacher. He took laboratory technician training in Bareilley, India, and the Christian Hospital in Chhatarpur eagerly took this Christian family into their fellowship and this dedicated man onto their staff.

Villagers soon learned the value of a microscope during his two years with the Friends Mission, as he took them into his laboratory and showed them—wide-eyed and wondering—the microbes cavorting before their eyes. That microscope began discovering diseases, like filariasis, formerly believed not endemic in the Chhatarpur area.[14]

Dr. Franklin of the English Friends joined the staff for a short time. With Dr. Ezra and Dr. Grace and an increasingly good staff of nurses under Frances DeVol's supervision, the excellence of treatment at Christian Hospital became established. Phyllis Das came as matron of the nurses' home. Five young men enrolled in the pharmacy course. Priobala Nath as head nurse, and her sister, Mercy Nath, in the dispensary at Gulganj — two of Bundelkhand's own — added to the strength of the medical work.

Mary Barton, an English nurse who came on a small inheritance from England with a clear call to Vindhya Pradesh, found her way to Chhatarpur. Such a staff drew the District Medical Officer to the Christian Hospital for treatment, and that opened the door for the Christian team to join medical workers in the city in a public health exhibition for the prevention of some of the more common diseases such as tuberculosis, leprosy, cholera, typhoid, eye diseases, hepatitis, and malaria.[15]

Norma Freer became more and more involved in the hospital, and by 1955 she took over as office secretary and business manager as well as continuing as supervisor of the nurses' home.[16]

Even doctors, however, became casualties. Dr. Franklin left. Dr. Grace found the stepped-up pace was getting out of hand, and she developed such high blood pressure that she was requested to take leave for many months. During that time Dr. Ezra came down with a severe case of hepatitis and later suffered severely with giardia, typhoid, and shingles. Frances at such times — as Alena Calkins had before her —"played doctor" until the doctors recovered.[17]

Accidents and illness of missionaries and Christian workers in both Friends and other missions nearby always got first attention from the DeVols, who believed their first work was to preach the Gospel and to keep all others who did that fit for the task. So when tuberculosis of the kidney and filariasis, one after the other, attacked Komal Das Lall, the medical team members were there to see that he not only did not die, but that he spent the minimum amount of time in bed.[18]

Mary's Accident and "That They May Know"

When Mary Cattell rolled seventy-five feet from the top of Pennington all the way to Tehri Road, Dr. Ezra, preceded only by her father, flew down the hill to give her immediate attention. "I lost my shoe," she said. The examination at that time revealed nothing further.[19] It was four years later in 1956 that a tiny spinal fracture showed up that put her in a brace, took her out of school, and kept her mother in the Landour hills because the heat on the plains would have been unbearable for Mary.

At that time, Catherine remembered and wrote about a lesson she had learned going through dark mountain tunnels. The mountains afterwards had been so beautiful that she had almost forgotten the tunnels. Tunnels were short cuts, sometimes the only way across. She wrote about them at this time when the way seemed dark.[20] As doctors pondered what to do to help Mary, a nurse from World Evangelization Crusade

Mission, Connie Lyne, working in the other side of Bundelkhand, came to live with Catherine.

Then miracles began to happen in each of their lives. Connie, always longing to be an artist, found Catherine writing a book needing pictures. By the time they finished with the illustrated book for teaching salvation to villagers entitled *That They May Know,* the publishers snatched Connie from the villages to become their full-time artist; Catherine discovered she had just produced a best-seller in demand all over North India, and Mary was well and ready to throw away her brace and return to school.[21]

Missionaries — Ill

Dr. Ezra got up from bed with hepatitis to deliver little Evelyn Ruth Banker on October 11, 1952. At the same time he had to prescribe treatment for Bonnie, who was isolated in the guest room with measles. He stopped on the way to care for Betty Robinson with an ear infection as she stayed in the ladies' bungalow with Anne, down with a kidney infection, and Ruthie, with bronchitis.[22] Esther Hess followed these with pneumonia, hepatitis, and an ear infection.[23]

One after another after that, Everett Cattell, Norma Freer, and Bob Hess took turns with hepatitis.[24] Worse still, Everett, over a period of four months, developed three clots in his leg and had to be rushed to the hospital in late July 1953, where Dr. Ezra was able to remove the clot just before it got past the groin, when it would have been too late to operate.[25]

The Results of a Donation for Mullen

The DeVols' reputation spread locally as they took interest in a crippled fourteen-year-old boy. Some of his friends had thought it a good joke to pour gasoline on Mullen and set him afire. After that, unable to walk, he scooted around begging. A public donation of Rs. 50 ($10) was taken at the bus stand at Dr. Ezra's suggestion, a token fee toward Mullen's treatment. This was in line with hospital policy that if possible people should pay for their medicine.

After DeVols performed several skin grafts, Mullen started walking again.[26] Such victories did not go uncontested, however, and some of the lesser medical officials in the town started a running barrage of adverse propaganda charging that the Christian Hospital was no longer a charitable institution and, therefore, should be heavily taxed. A strange fact about these complaints was that they came from the well-to-do and not from the poor.

The complainers, however, had not taken into account that in the *Seva Sadan* (home of service — the shelter for relatives) there was a free ward where anyone could get free treatment, and especially those who often possessed nothing but a loin cloth, a brass jug, and a little piece of rope for drawing water from the well.[27] The medical board also had instituted an insurance plan on the basis of family income to care for all Christians and employees. The hospital clearly was open to all, but the rich were paying, and by 1955 the hospital was seventy percent self-supporting, excluding foreign personnel.[28]

The Placement of Workers and Their Work

Dr. Ezra's responsibilities as chairman of Mission Council encompassed all phases of mission work in Bundelkhand, and although the hospital continued to expand, leaders in evangelism and education sensed a great deal of uncertainty. Winds of change blowing across India increased with government's tightening policy and greater antagonism toward missionaries. Everywhere missionaries began to ask, "Just what is the place now – if any – of the foreign missionary?"

Colemans, questioning, went back to Amarmau with Dayal Chand Singh and George Masih and their families. They supervised Ghuara with the Chunni Lall family back, she having voluntarily foregone salary to give the people their teacher again. After she suffered awhile, the conscience of the Mission Council, in spite of all rules, could no longer tolerate exploiting her burden and paid her retroactively.[29]

Colemans, however, felt some frustration in seeing Ghuara Christians gradually cease to tithe and become more and more dependent and demanding. "Having labored for six years against such formidable darkness and sin with limited numerical results," wrote Milton, "discouragement naturally was leering around the corner." Nevertheless, he encouraged himself, there did seem to be greater interest among all castes, and the appeal of Christ seemed to be steadily rising in Bundelkhand.[30]

Hesses, just out of language school, were stationed in Gulganj with reversions all around them. They wondered where to take hold. Mercy Nath was in the dispensary and Hira Singh was the evangelist.[31] Bob took time off to sponsor citywide meetings in Nowgong and Chhatarpur with Dr. Abdul Haqq, a well-known Moslem convert. He ran into deep prejudice and misunderstanding and was disappointed that there were no converts.[32]

Victor Mangalwadi was transferred from Amarmau to Nowgong, but not before the Mission had honored his concern to buy a little farm in the village of Goethera, five miles from Chhatarpur, where he had fostered so much interest in the Gospel. The Mission loaned him money against his salary to make the purchase. Victor dreamed of one day retiring there.[33] The tragedy that occurred in 1980 when he did will unfold later.

Stuti Prakash was transferred to Chhatarpur as pastor with the clear understanding that he would continue as Ganj District superintendent, and also would be free for evangelistic camps during the cool season. The impact of his preaching was soon felt in Chhatarpur[34] as he began a ministry that would last, year after year, for a quarter of a century through the renewed invitation of his own people. Each year the vote was taken, however, he faced such fierce opposition from disruptive elements in the Church that only a deep sense of call held him steady. He prayerfully confronted people living beneath their spiritual privileges, and sometimes this was not appreciated.

In Chhatarpur, Pancham Singh constantly pushed to get into the Church without repentance, but Stuti held his ground. In Nowgong, Pyare Lal Brown was the "thorn in the flesh," and no one there seemed strong enough to stand up to him.[35] Sometimes Stuti became very discouraged, but visits from outside ministers, like Dr. Harold and Ann Kuhn of Asbury Seminary, lifted him and set him on course again. Renewed vision of God's Church in India and the world helped him put local problems in perspective.[36]

Anna Nixon shared a home with Norma but worked out in the villages with one or two Bible women. Rebecca, Esther, and Catherine also went to camp at times, but Catherine felt that "a full-time woman missionary evangelist without family responsibilities to pull her back" was an asset.[37] Anna, however, found she had time on her hands. So she filled in the empty spots by writing her first book about village life, entitled *More than Shadow*, which was published in many languages and distributed through the EFI book clubs.[38] Together Catherine and Anna worked on flannelgraph lessons, equipping the hospital evangelists and village workers with carts and kits. Rebecca, Esther, and Anna worked on quarterlies for leaders of the women's groups, and Ruth Ellen helped with the typing.[39]

The Camping Seasons of 1953-55

Never in history had village camp work been done more intensely than the two cool seasons from 1953 to 1955. After much juggling, two jeeps and two motorcycles were available for transportation.[40] In spite of the winds of change, evidence of deep interest in Christianity was abundant. Dr. Ezra in his new ambulance used for the "milk route" started going regularly to the camps to visit patients. "I . . . have found a refreshing response," he wrote. "If we can get another doctor I hope to give more time to village work."[41]

Eight women and twelve men participated in at least sixty campaigns those years. Each campaign lasted from one to three weeks, depending on the interest, and hundreds of villages were touched and thousands of people were dealt with personally.[42]

Stuti Prakash initiated Bob Hess into camp work. "His burden and love for the villagers," Bob wrote, "coupled with sound, clear gospel preaching on their level is a real encouragement. Out of his thirty years of experience in this area he gave correction and advice. I appreciate his leadership in camp very much."[43]

Camp work those winters, however, brought no conversions, nor did frequent visits to the former converts around Gulganj. The only visible fruit was the conversion of a Tibetan soldier stationed in Bundelkhand and led to Christ by Bob Hess in Gulganj, and Colemans' cook and his wife in Amarmau.[44] The reversions to Hinduism in the Gulganj area, the slowness of converts in Ghuara, and the general inertia that characterized even the Christians in Bundelkhand ate in on Bob's faith until he was on the verge of losing hope. Across the whole of mid-India from 1949 to 1953 there were just 412 conversions from among non-Christians.[45]

Watching villagers — high castes and low — spin twine all day long with the aid of their hands and two little sticks and lift water from one irrigation ditch to another with the aid of rope and home-woven baskets, Bob realized that one or two very small machines could put the whole village out of work. As he watched the Chamars strike solid rock four feet down in digging a well, he wished for a pneumatic drill. There wasn't one, of course, and the Chamars took turns a day at a time digging by hand and planting ten cents worth of dynamite until they found water. "Their inertia in responding is our greatest trial," Bob observed, "but their stability may someday be used to build a steady church in Bundelkhand."[46]

When Everett's illness with hepatitis put the burden for Annual Meeting in 1954 squarely on Bob's shoulders, he had to come to grips with his wavering hope. He felt impressed to speak from Habakkuk 2:2,3: "Write the vision, and make it plain upon tables, that he may run that readeth it. For the vision is yet for an appointed time, but at the end it shall speak, and not lie; though it tarry, wait for it; because it will surely come, it will not tarry." Afterwards, Bob wrote Walter Williams, "To preach on this message I had to be willing to accept it and I do — what it means I do not know, not being the son of a prophet."[47]

More Authority and Responsibility for the Church

By the time the Cattells left for furlough following Barbara's graduation in June 1954, the Church was beginning to feel the impact of the Mission's plan to put more responsibility on the Indian Church. Dr. Ezra, chairman and now acting field superintendent, sought to guide them. This new authority seemed like heady wine to the Church leaders as three of their representatives began to sit with the Mission Council, the highest policy-making body in the Mission. In January, they had chosen Dr. Grace Jones Singh, K. D. Lall, and Victor Mangalwadi.[48]

At the annual meeting in April, Stuti Prakash was chosen to take Dr. Singh's place. The responsibility coming with authority was more difficult to accept, and they agreed reluctantly to try to raise all pastors' support after April 1954 and to be responsible for evangelism in the Nowgong District. Henceforth, no missionary would sit on a nominating committee and not more than one would be appointed as an overseer in any local meeting.[49] Their faith was strengthened, however, as the very next year twenty-five new members were accepted into the Church, including Prem Das and family of Dhamora, converts of Victor Mangalwadi. Tithers increased from fifty-one to seventy-four.[50]

Educational Policy Changes

Educational policies during this period were whipped from left to right by the winds of change. Bankers faced many disappointments as they labored to fit their vision into the total mission plan of putting education into the hands of the Church. As the Bankers took over this field in 1952, the boys' high school was instituted and all girls above fifth grade were sent to Jhansi, where they continued their education all the way through high school in the Canadian Presbyterian Mission Girls' School.[51]

That year Shyam Kumari, daughter of Stuti Prakash, married K. D. Lall's brother, William, and went to live in Chhatarpur, where she began teaching in the Chhatarpur primary school.[52] A year later the Bankers lost three more of their key teachers. Stephen Moti Lal and his wife, Mabel, decided to go to the U.S.A. to study.[53] Later the principal, a highly respected man and able leader, became very ill, and while taking treatment at Nur Manzil in Lucknow, he suddenly disappeared and later was found dead. This—added to the fact that other missions were not sending their boys to the Nowgong school as Bankers had hoped—led the Mission to withdraw their application for recognition of the high school.[54]

The seven boys in high school stayed on in the dormitory and took government high school exams.[55] Middle and high school education for Bundelkhand's boys would have to be grappled with later, but primary education, the Mission felt, should be placed in the hands of the Church. Primary schools were reduced to four classes in Ghuara, Amarmau, Chhatarpur, and Nowgong.[56] To help the Church hold up a standard, Max Banker developed tests that were given to all.[57]

The Mission Council in its eagerness to push the Church in its program of self-support sometimes lost sensitivity, as in the case of a convert's son who had been many years in boarding school supported by a missionary. The father, by no means rich but able to do something, was quite content to abandon his son to the missionaries. The Mission Council felt the time had come for him to wake up to his responsibilities. To awaken him, they advised the missionary to withdraw his support for the son. The teenage son, not understanding the intricacies of mission policy, felt the sting of their disapproval and suffered greatly. Bankers suffered with him as they sought to give the young fellow work to make up for this father's continued delinquencies.[58]

Missionaries Ordered Out of India

Ruth Ellen, seeking to undergird Max in every facet of education, and in the family, suddenly got word that her mother had died. The long distance deepened the grief, but Walter Williams comforted her by writing that she died with a light on her face "not seen on land or sea."[59]

Just a year before the Bankers' furlough, the Vindhya Pradesh Government, intending to eventually rid the area of all missionaries, refused to grant the extension of their residential permit and ordered them out of the country. Shortly after that, Norma Freer—in bed with hepatitis—received the same order. The Mission appealed to the NCC, who sought to intervene. They sought audience with Prime Minister Nehru and the Deputy Home Minister.[60]

As Max, Ruth Ellen, and Norma anxiously waited, they saw their time running out. More than a month went by and a sense of frustration gripped all the missionaries until suddenly one day a patient of the DeVols' mentioned his brother was coming to Chhatarpur. His brother, Mahendra Kumar Manav, a member of the Congress party and Secretary of Social Affairs, was also a friend of the Mission. Dr. Ezra dropped everything and went to see him. Mahendra Kumar quickly arranged an interview with the Governor in Rewa. Accompanied by Max Banker, Dr. Ezra rushed the 120 miles for the appointment—at 7:00 a.m.—before the Governor began the day's legislative session.

As soon as the two men met, the angry Governor snapped, "What are you missionaries doing up there in Chhatarpur? Why do you persist in making converts?" Dr. Ezra was astounded. What could he say to this powerful, irate official? Recalling the experience later, he said, "I sent up a telegraphic prayer for the Holy Spirit's guidance. Then I said to him, 'All of us who are Christians are witnesses.'"

The governor's mood instantly changed. "That is absolutely right," he answered. "You have as much right to be a Christian as I have to be a Hindu. I will write to the superintendent of police in Chhatarpur and tell him to stop harrassing you. No—I'll *telegraph* him so he will get the message immediately." Dr. Ezra and Max returned home that day with a heart full of praise and a new understanding of the meaning of God's promise in Luke 21:12-15.[61] Later, orders came down from the very top to the Rewa officials to leave the missionaries alone, and after that Prime Minister Nehru often encouraged his people everywhere to "get the missionary spirit." Bankers and Norma Freer were allowed to stay.[62]

Breaking Down Prejudice Against Christianity

Out in Victor Mangalwadi's camp between Nowgong and Chhatarpur on December 7, 1954, Virginia Singh, recently graduated from Union Biblical Seminary, and Anna Nixon were working hard at evangelism. Their first camp together had been in Tindini village, the birthplace of Virginia's father, Gore Lal Singh, and his first wife. The people there were awed and courteous as they came to realize who this vivacious, highly educated, and beautiful young woman was, but no one accepted Christ.

Virginia and Anna went from there to other villages, but this last camp before Christmas was the most difficult. The women were either disinterested or afraid, and on seeing Virginia and Anna, they would dash into their houses and close the door.

The cup of discouragement had almost reached the brim when suddenly a jeep turned off the main road and into the camp, and Max Banker jumped out. "Are you coming from Chhatarpur?" asked Anna, full of curiosity. "Is everything all right?"

"Yes, everything is fine," answered Max, trying to control his voice. "I took Ruth Ellen to the hospital in Chhatarpur and now I am going back to Nowgong. We now have a son named Bruce Craig born this morning at 1:00 a.m." *A son is born!* The news spread as villagers gathered in from every direction. "Shabash!" shouted an old village man, grabbing Max by the arm and whirling him around. Questions, laughing, and shouting filled the air. As soon as possible, Max said good-bye and proceeded on his way, but the villagers, both men and women, stayed to ask more questions — not just about the baby boy born in Chhatarpur, but also about the Babe in the Manger, born in Bethlehem. Virginia and Anna's discouragement ended as they led the villagers in Hindi Christmas carols.[63]

Bankers had less than half a year left in India as they plunged in to help make the fourth All-India Evangelical Fellowship Conference held in Jhansi in 1955 a success. More than three hundred delegates came. Milton was in charge of the music, and the women missionaries helped with the catering and sang special numbers. Many people from Bundelkhand attended also, and all returned home thankful for revival spreading across India and touching their own lives as well.

The whole movement increased the sense of being a part of something God was doing throughout the world, and such a vision made joy ring through the valleys of Bundelkhand. That year Everett Cattell in America was still very much on the team, meeting other Friends groups, traveling more than 38,000 miles delivering messages and consulting leaders of all evangelical groups on behalf of EFI and UBS.[64]

Bankers' Departure from India

After the conference, Max got all the school records in order. He recommended Hizikiel S. Lall, son of the former housefather, as the new headmaster. Hizikiel S. Lall had been a frequent visitor in Victor Mangalwadi's camp that winter, and the result was that Anna Nixon lost her companion, Virginia Singh, to him as his bride. They would through the years make outstanding contributions in education both in Bundelkhand and beyond.

Ruth Ellen, editor for home publications, turned that work over to Rebecca Coleman.[65] After that, packing and the care of her two daughters and baby son took most of her time. When Bankers left Bundelkhand for furlough on April 4, 1955, they were refused their "No Objection to Return" certificate.

Their hearts sank, for they knew it would be difficult to return without it.[66] Rapid changes in mission policy during the next two years led the Bankers, the Mission Board, and the Mission Council to feel that God's will for them pointed in another direction, though all wished it could have been otherwise.[67]

Hospital Care During DeVols' Furlough

The DeVols also left for furlough in June 1955 after the completion of the school year for Joe and Phil and the graduation of their daughters, Patricia and Priscilla. Their "No Objection to Return" was securely stamped in their passports.[68] Norma Freer, treasurer and also since January 1, 1954 the hospital business manager,[69] was ready to step in as acting superintendent of the hospital between DeVols' departure in June and Cattells' return in November. The medical burden fell heavily on the shoulders of Dr. Grace, who in spite of poor health and high blood pressure was determined to keep everything going, including the "milk route." Mary Barton of WEC mission came over to fill the nursing gap left by Frances.

With no male surgeon on hand for the operation theater, patients began to drop off. The staff became frustrated with lack of challenge and before long, tempers flared. The situation made one think of the time Dr. Ezra had gone hunting and with one shot wounded two black bears.

They both roared so loud that the tree in which he was sitting shook violently. The bears turned on each other and began to fight, giving him an excellent aim, and he brought them both down. *"Why did they blame each other, when their real enemy was sitting in the tree?"* Dr. Ezra questioned. Immediately he applied it to himself and the Church: "From whence come wars and fightings among you? . . . Resist the devil, and he will flee from you." (James 4:1, 7)[70]

Norma's task was made heavier by the necessity of constantly pouring oil on troubled waters. It is no wonder she dreaded coming home from vacation after the DeVols left, but she drew courage from these scriptural passages: "My grace is enough for you; for where there is weakness, my power is shown more completely," and "My prayer for you is that you may have still more love — a love that is full of knowledge and wise insight." (2 Corinthians 12:9; Philippians 1:9 — Phillips translation)[71]

The Niyogi Report

Colemans missed the school in Amarmau, which had been closed after the Bankers left. Opposition to missionaries in Madhya Pradesh was on the rise. Since Milton Coleman had been appointed acting superintendent between the departure of DeVols and arrival of Cattells, he was constantly on the road commuting the fifty-five miles to Chhatarpur, caring for property matters, representing the Mission at important meetings, and keeping an eye on all the stations.[72]

Rebecca Coleman, mother of orphans, found her place at that time as the mother for the missionary children attending Woodstock.[73] Milton continued to live in Amarmau to stabilize conditions there as opposition to missions continued to rise. Military aid to Pakistan by the U.S.A. had not helped.[74] Attempts to put missionaries out of the country and restrict their activities had not been confined to Vindhya Pradesh. By the end of 1954, Commonwealth citizens, as well as Americans, were requested to apply for residential permits if they were involved in missionary work.[75]

A number of missionaries for no evident reason were requested to leave. In Madhya Pradesh (Central Provinces), where the Colemans lived, opposition was most intense. A high court judge, M. B. Niyogi, headed the *Christian Missionary Activities Enquiry Committee of M. P.* and was commissioned to investigate (a) unethical practices of missionaries to make Christians, and (b) harassment of Christians. Extensive, intimidating investigations of the first point were made and published in a 182-page report. The records indicate, however, that not one question was asked on the second point.[76]

Later, the Indian Government condemned the Niyogi report as being biased and unfair, but it had succeeded in blocking the entrance into India of many missionaries, particularly from the U.S.A. Of the fifty-one new candidates entering language school the following year, only eighteen of them came from the U.S.A.[77]

Prime Minister Nehru, accompanied among others by his daughter, Indira Gandhi, visited Chhatarpur and Nowgong in September 1955. He took a considerable portion of his time speaking to record-breaking crowds in counteracting the Niyogi report. The Christian religion, he pointed out, belonged to India long before it reached Europe or America. Discrimination, therefore, was not at all in line with India's constitution. To underline this, his committee had invited Milton Coleman to sit on the platform as he spoke.[78] Nine other Indian leaders from across the nation later issued a statement asserting that they had not found any instance of missionaries trying to "undermine patriotic and national loyalties," as had been alleged in some reports.[79]

One exposure of the Niyogi Report, however, which made Christians up and down the land burn with shame was their heavy dependence on foreign funds. The NCC was whipped into action under the sting of their accusations that while other religious groups in India supported themselves, Christianity alone depended on the West. At the NCC Triennial in 1956 the statement was registered that any church depending on foreign aid for its own inner life was in an unhealthy condition. They called on all churches to become self-supporting within the next three years.[80]

Victor Mangalwadi's Departure from Bundelkhand

Victor Mangalwadi, hurting as much as anyone over the reverses in Bundelkhand, became more and more unhappy with the trend in mission policy and finally asked and was granted a leave of absence to take up work in the Christian Retreat and Study Center in Rajpur.[81] Unfortunately, confusion resulted from relationships with other Indian workers, whom he sometimes blamed for the fact that his ideas were not accepted. The Mission Council eventually followed his idea of allowing village Christians to come to district headquarters when there were not ten students in a village,[82] but the action was too late to save the reversions around Gulganj.

Another keen disappointment was Khub Chand's rising bitterness against Victor and the Mission. This was caused by his frustration over mission salary. Since most of the converts had come through his witness, he felt he was worth more to the Mission than Victor Mangalwadi or any other paid evangelist. His flirtation with certain Hindu practices, seemingly to annoy the Christians, caused great pain. Perhaps this very ambivalence in Khub Chand caused him not to vaccinate his new baby in spite of many warnings. The baby died of smallpox.[83]

Victor's heart broke the day he discovered an eight-page pamphlet, mostly Scripture, printed and distributed by Khub Chand and entitled, "Rai Das Ramayan." In front was a picture of a cow and the Indian flag. Inside, the name of Rai Das had been inserted in the place of Jesus.[84] After that, Khub Chand's bitterness increased, and in such a spirit he left the Mission. After eighteen years as a Christian he reverted to Hinduism. That he did it with the promise of a high paying job by the enemies of Christ made it no less painful for the Christians, who still loved him dearly.[85]

Focus on Gulganj

After Bankers and Victor Mangalwadi left Nowgong, Hesses were transferred there from Gulganj, and Bob was appointed chairman of the board of education. Kathy Hess came down with a light case of polio, and two months later Bob underwent major surgery at Kachhwa.[86]

After Virginia's marriage to Hizikiel Lall, Anna Nixon was transferred to Gulganj, still stinging from the valid criticism, agreed to by her co-workers in camp, that her presence with an Indian team in the camp program made the villagers think she was pulling the puppet strings and the Indian workers were dancing.

Was there a place in Bundelkhand for a single woman missionary apart from educational and medical work? This question began to plague missionaries up and down the country. However, Anna was permitted to try again in the village of Gulganj with its nearly four thousand inhabitants of whom not one woman could read.

Along with her went DeVols' capable cook, Dharm Das, and his wife, Bhagwati Bai, and Stuti Singh, a woman evangelist. Mercy Nath in the dispensary and Hira Singh, the Gulganj evangelist, welcomed the new members of the team. Together they set their goals to make maximum contact, gain confidence, convince, convict, and convert. Their methods would be gospel preaching, health education, and literacy.[87] An earlier literacy team for the village participated in by Hesses and Anna had ended in failure as men of the village blocked the way to the women's quarters and rubbed stinging nettle all over the team's jeep.

Persistence, however, finally won as a total of thirty women enrolled, and the first Bundelkhandi women in the history of the Mission received adult literacy certificates. Every week as many as six hundred patients crowded into the dispensary. On Sundays children flocked to the compound to learn Bible verses and receive a reward of an old Christmas card as each repeated the verse without error and explained its meaning. Daily, Hira Singh walked Gulganj's alleyways, preaching the Gospel and distributing tracts.[88] Even so, the team never reached its goal of conversion.

Resistance to change at that point seemed insurmountable. Finally, for the Mission, time ran out.

Robinsons Return to New Delhi

When Robinsons left Gulganj in 1953, the missionaries knew of their desire to return to the larger population centers of India.[89] Therefore, in July 1955, they came back, with Cliff under appointment from the Board as "Minister at Large" to India. They were, as other missionaries, subject to the India Mission Council but not to the Bundelkhand Friends Church.[90] They chose to settle in New Delhi. Betty arrived first with the four children since Cliff was delayed in Bombay to go through customs and clear their car, which he drove up later to Delhi. Anna went from Gulganj to Delhi to help Betty, who found a modest little home in the Nizammudin area.

Just around the corner lived an English missionary family, the Dennis Clarks, who immediately came to call. "Your coming to Delhi is an answer to our prayers," they said. To Betty, surrounded as she was in an empty house with suitcases and children, sweltering in Delhi's oppressive heat, this greeting brought great encouragement. Clarks had recently come to Delhi to set up *Masihi Sahitya Sanstha*, a Christian literature publishing and distribution center.

They were extremely helpful with suggestions as to where Anna could get mattresses stuffed with cotton and buy *charpais* (wooden and rope beds), and where Betty could find food, cooking utensils, and charcoal in a nearby market.[91] As soon as the house was made livable and Cliff had arrived, the Robinsons went to Chhatarpur for council meeting and on to Gulganj to pick up the household items they had left behind in 1953.[92] On their return to Delhi, they wasted no time in getting their new work started.

Cliff and Betty had pioneered before, building up West Park Friends as their first pastorate in Cleveland, participating in revival services in many states, serving as executive secretary in the interdenominational Christ for Greater Cleveland campaigns, and promoting Cleveland Bible College, as well as having eight and a half years' experience since first arriving in India in 1947.[93]

Cliff almost immediately headed south at the call of large, established churches for conventions with attendance ranging from 2,000 to 32,000 resulting in more than 1,000 seekers. Betty got Anne and Ruth off to Woodstock school in Landour, though Judy had to finish out her year of study in Delhi. Byron was still too young for boarding school. Within months of arrival, they accepted the challenge and started a regular Youth for Christ rally in Delhi, and joined Don Rugh and others in forming a

Union Church attended by some Indian leaders but largely by Americans, and Betty became the superintendent of the Sunday school and headed up a lively women's work in the church and community. Prayer groups met with the Robinsons, and missionary and Indian friends found warm hospitality in their home.

The Return of Cattells to Chhatarpur

Everett, Catherine, and Mary Cattell returned to Chhatarpur in November 1955. Barbara had married John Brantingham July 8, 1955; David was engaged to Jane Coons.[94] They returned with a profound sense of the need to finish the task God had called them to in India.[95]

The reversion of Khub Chand was like the death of a son, but Catherine started Bible studies for two other converts — Hira Lal, their first, and Halka Daniel of Ghuara, who was at that time working in Chhatarpur Civil Hospital.[96]

Everett picked up the reins of leadership and by Christmas, with Catherine, had visited all the missionaries and workers — to the last outstation. Then he wrote to Walter Williams, "I believe it is fair to say that our whole staff is in a very deep sense of frustration . . . a heavy sense of uncertainty . . . from the government angle, but what is worse is the lack of sureness as to just what we should be doing in the light of all our circumstances."[97]

Later, as he went to clear luggage in Bombay, he explained to customs officials the purpose of the pressure cookers the Women's Missionary Society at home had sent out for the new hill houses. As he did so, he began thinking of the purpose of pressure. Surely, the Mission had plenty at the moment — from Government with tightening restrictions, from radical Hindu parties who harassed the new Christians and disturbed the evangelistic camps (Stuti Prakash had said their opposition was "like throwing dust at the sun — the dust just comes back on you but the sun goes on shining"), and most of all, the pressure of time. Would there be time to stabilize the Church before all foreign funds and personnel were barred from India? Over all was the pressure of the Spirit for the salvation of those for whom Christ died.[98]

As he traveled to other areas of India, he found workers as frustrated as his own. Cliff's suggestion three years earlier, that there were too many missionaries in Bundelkhand, by now had settled into a deep conviction. The missionaries all came to feel that for a truly Church-centered strategy to develop, there would need to be considerable reduction of mission personnel.[99] Everett began to pray for unity in the Mission Board, the Mission Council, and the Church as plans were formed in line with this deepening conviction.

Billy Graham's Visit to India

The work of the Evangelical Fellowship of India, however, swallowed up all attention through the early months of 1956. The Church throughout India stood on tiptoe to welcome Billy Graham's team. They flew into India with a full supply of bottled drinking water to last the tour and settled into the best hotels. Many other precautions were taken, too, and the press had conflicting things to say. Billy Graham's lifestyle differed considerably from that of Evangelist Hira Singh in Gulganj, but his message was the same.

His sincerity soon won the hearts of the Indians, and by the time he had coped with language riots in Bombay, where public meetings had to be canceled, and held meetings in Madras with 30,000, Palamcottah with 40,000, and Kottayam with 120,000 — twice the population of the city and the largest Christian gathering ever held in Asia up to that time — the press had begun to take notice of the sign, "GOD CALLS THE CHURCH," emblazoned above the entrance to every convention. For the first time in India the Church had become vibrantly visible.

"I have been tremendously impressed with the scope of the preparation in this part of the land for the coming of Billy Graham," wrote Clifton Robinson when he was pulled into the team to take Cliff Barrows's place in Madras. Cliff Barrows's delay left two choirs of 300 voices each, one in Tamil and one in English, and a 75-piece orchestra band needing a conductor. Cliff Robinson took over after much persuasion. "In Madras they have secured the Municipal Stadium . . . The services will be three-way: that is, in English, Tamil, and Telugu languages."[100]

Key in the preparations for these meetings in India was EFI's newest secretary, Imchaba Bendang Wati Ao. ("Just call me Ben," he said.) He came as a secretary of the EFI in September 1953. He was from Northeast India, and his grandfather had been an Ao Naga headhunter before his conversion. Ben had graduated from Wheaton College and Northern Baptist Seminary in Chicago. Blocked from serving his own people at that time because of political unrest, he had accepted EFI's invitation to become one of its secretaries.[101] Everett was still on furlough, and Lincoln Watts, the administrative secretary, had retired.

R. H. Smith of the Christian and Missionary Alliance, who had been appointed to step in, was suddenly requested by the Indian government to leave. Therefore, Ben shouldered the full responsibility and astutely arranged for the next EFI conference to meet in New Delhi prior to the Billy Graham meetings there in early February 1956.

Determined to bring Indians to the fore, Ben invited half a dozen keen Indian evangelists and pastors to speak on the subject, "My Burden for the

Church." Missionaries had never heard their equal. Delegates at the EFI conference that year numbered 350. They stayed on to serve as counselors and to pray for the Billy Graham meetings.

Robinsons in Delhi were on the welcoming committee and arranged morning and night prayer meetings. After 10,000 people were welcomed by Raj Kumari Amrit Kaur, an Indian Christian and India's health minister, Billy Graham rose to say that in no other country had he received as warm a welcome. By the time he had finished his twelve main rallies in India, 16,000 decisions for Christ, one tenth of them in Delhi, had been registered. About sixty percent were conversions of people from nominal Christian background, but there were also numbers of Hindus, Moslems, Buddhists, and Sikhs.

India held the distinction in the world of covering all local expenses of Billy Graham's meetings in the country. No other country where he had spoken had even done that. Missionaries who deplored the dependency in small local churches could hardly believe this. Their concept of the Indian Church as a whole rapidly changed as they realized its mighty strength once it was revived. No less than thirty of the missionaries and Indian workers from Bundelkhand attended the EFI conference and Billy Graham meetings in Delhi, and their vision, too, was lifted.[102]

EFI leaders were well aware that the excitement would soon be over, and they were concerned about a follow-up program that would keep the witness alive. "Along with revival, there must come a mighty up-surge of tithing. It is not on the horizon yet," Everett noted.[103]

Sensing that EFI had come into being for such a time as this, the executive committee in Delhi set about to capitalize on the new impetus given the Church through Billy Graham. They faced squarely the fact that the central problem of evangelicals was not merely the need to emphasize sound doctrine, but rather the need to lay hold of spiritual power, which comes only from the fullness of the Holy Spirit.[104] They were impressed with Billy Graham's interpreter, Dr. Akbar Abdul Haqq. Billy Graham was also impressed and invited him to a campaign to be held in Louisville, Kentucky. This led to a permanent association between these men as Dr. Haqq became a member of the Billy Graham team.

Anna Nixon Transferred to New Headquarters for EFI

Part of EFI's follow-up plan included finding such men to hold campaigns in major cities throughout India. Basic to carrying out these plans, however, was the establishing of an EFI headquarters. The large Canadian Presbyterian Mission Compound in Jhansi, eighty miles from Chhatarpur, seemed ideal because (1) it was near the home of Everett Cattell, (2) all the Canadian Presbyterian missionaries were committed to EFI and would give office space for only a token rent, and (3) since C. P. wives were not assigned to mission work, capable Mrs. Angus MacKay with her expertise in accounts would make an ideal treasurer.[105]

One drawback was that the MacKays were just leaving for furlough. The Indian Government had refused to grant EFI's request to bring a person as office secretary from the U.S.A.; therefore, Everett Cattell, knowing the situation in Gulganj, recommended Anna Nixon for the post.[106] The rapidity with which all these recommendations passed through necessary channels overwhelmed Anna. She wrote:

> I did not realize until then how hard it would be to release what I consider a front-line position in the battle of Bundelkhand. Yet peace of heart indicates that this leaving is not a step of retreat but rather one of obedience — and that's what brought Lazarus from the tomb and what caused Peter and the disciples to get a net full of fish. Need it be less for Bundelkhand?[107]

National Leadership in Bundelkhand

Leaving Gulganj in early February, Anna was concerned about what would happen to the work she was deserting. She went first to fill an emergency in the Union Biblical Seminary at Yavatmal. The Seminary also presented a challenge with its 73 students representing 25 denominations from 11 states and 16 language backgrounds,[108] but the needs in Bundelkhand still held priority in her mind. Back in Chhatarpur for annual meeting at the end of March, Anna expressed her concern for the Vacation Bible Schools. Gabriel Massey, a UBS student home for the summer, and eleven other volunteers agreed to take that responsibility.

Three VBS teams went out and covered the whole of Bundelkhand for the first time.[109] Dharm Das and his wife went back to the DeVols, and Mercy Nath and Stuti Singh of Gulganj both got married, as did Vijay Prakash, who had graduated the year before from UBS. He married Irene Hoffman from Indore, and moved to Amarmau, working with Colemans.

When Milton was transferred to Chhatarpur, Vijay often assisted his Uncle Hira Singh in evangelism in Gulganj, and Anna gave him her filmstrips and projector to use in his village evangelistic work. He was also keenly aware of social needs and succeeded in getting two college students, three hospital ward boys, a mechanic, a watch repairman, a private dispensary pharmacist, and a preacher to help him dig a well for Dimina, one of the Ghuara converts. They returned singing, mission accomplished, proud of every broken blister and enlarged callus.[110]

Out in another direction, Mercy Nath's younger brother, Yohan, had taken a pharmacist job in the government hospital at Tikamgarh. He found other Christians in the town on government jobs and organized a worshiping group of about thirty people.[111] In Nowgong, Pastor Dayal Chand Singh received ten teenage young men into the membership of the Church. The women's groups and the local Church — not the Mission — made it possible for the young men each to buy a new Bible and songbook for half price.[112]

The sixty young people at the youth conference that year made their own arrangements under the leadership of Vijay. The Church — not the Mission — at its annual meeting gave an offering to pay the bill, and the young people shouldered the remainder of their expense.[113] These evidences of the Church's willingness to rise to the challenge made Anna feel right about leaving Bundelkhand, though she was thankful that Jhansi was scarcely farther from Friends headquarters than the Colemans had been in Amarmau. She continued going back for all special meetings and kept her membership in the Bundelkhand Friends Church in Chhatarpur.

EFI's Council of Evangelists and Follow-up Plans

By December 1957 EFI had taken over half a former industrial school men's dormitory building in Jhansi where the Ben Watis, Azariah Benjamins, Sukh Lals, Rose Nawalkar, and Anna lived, and where the EFI office was spaciously settled. MacKays and Selfs of the C. P. Mission returned from furlough and threw their weight into the work of EFI —"an organization with a difference," wrote Anna, noting that the emotionally taxing lack of response to efforts in the village had suddenly been replaced by eager interest on the part of many groups. But her first prayer was still for Bundelkhand.[114]

Follow-up work for EFI crystalized into a definite plan at a meeting calling together fourteen evangelists from all parts of India to form a Council of Evangelists. Twelve were Indians, including one woman. Everett Cattell and Anna Nixon were present as EFI secretaries. Most of the evangelists had not met before, but they came to agreement on a strategy to follow up Billy Graham meetings.

Their plans included (1) *Preparation:* A team to go to a city and hold pastors' retreats, classes for counselors (in which the active spiritual Christians would be found and organized), and conduct family visitation. EFI would lend help also in organizing a city campaign; (2) *Campaign:* EFI would recommend evangelists for the campaign: — whether citywide or church by church would depend on the local situation; (3) *Follow-up:* EFI would furnish personnel to stay as long as necessary to conserve the converts. EFI would not favor pulling converts out to start new churches, but where churches were dead, they planned to foster cell groups for spiritual growth through fellowship, Bible study, prayer, witnessing, giving, and loving service in the Church.[115]

When Dr. Akbar Abdul Haqq returned from the Billy Graham Louisville campaign, he was invited to speak at the 1957 EFI conference in Calcutta. If any missionary present still doubted the ability and dedication of India's sons to stir the churches, he was not heard from again. Clifton Robinson led the singing, and Dr. Haqq laid a doctrinal basis as had never been laid as a brief for EFI's existence.

> A Christian is the one who is in touch [with God's plan for His world]. Upon the Mt. Everest of his life there is a receiving antenna — the antenna of faith — which he pulls out into this great unknown. The world does not know why this antenna is rising. It seems silly, foolish. But when divine music comes down and makes itself known, they know there *must* be something else! Woe unto the Church if it becomes a radio-receiving set from outside but inside mechanism be gone! The Church is the mediator between Jesus of all ages and the world.[116]

Dr. Haqq was chosen to lead the first EFI evangelistic campaign following Billy Graham. The city chosen was Kanpur, U. P. Everett Cattell was personally responsible for preparation and follow-up, and Clifton Robinson led the singing. Catherine joined in the counseling as 874 people bowed at the feet of Christ in the fourteen-day campaign. One of them was Irene Prakash, who in spite of her beautiful personality testified to the fact that she had never been born again. After that, invitations from other cities began coming in for Dr. Akbar Haqq and Clifton Robinson.

As a "Life in Christ Team," they held campaigns in a number of cities with similar results.[117] Members of EFI's Council of Evangelists in other areas of India, following the EFI plan, conducted citywide campaigns and saw thousands converted. Word began to flow into the EFI office of changed lives, new churches, revived pastors, and an increase in church attendance, Bible sales, and the volume of prayer and concern for revival. The Church was on the march in India. Stirred from its deadness through the call of Christ heard during the Billy Graham crusade, the Church of Jesus Christ in India faced a new day that would bring far-reaching change to the remotest corner, even Bundelkhand.

Rooting the
Church in
Bundelkhand

*"Once more a remnant . . . will take root below and
bear fruit above . . . . The zeal of the LORD
Almighty will accomplish this."* 2 Kings 19:30, 31 NIV

Pruning

After sixty years, the Friends Church in Bundelkhand was still so dependent on the Mission that it had little identity of its own. The missionaries were convinced that this dependency was the root cause of failure to grow. The reversion of two thirds of the converts, the increasing governmental pressure, the ingrained prejudice and hostility of the people toward conversion, and the lack of response even among formerly open groups awakened the missionaries to their tenuous position and the impossibility of carrying on as formerly. These facts converged to spur them toward pushing the Church forward by cutting back the Mission, which seemed to overpower the Church.[1]

A Five-Year Plan

The Government of India had succeeded with its first five-year plan and had launched its second with $54,000,000 earmarked for the area in which the Mission was located. A new government hospital in Chhatarpur was a part of that plan.[2] Sweeping changes had already been negotiated. Boundaries of states made to coincide with language areas put an end to Vindhya Pradesh on October 2, 1956, and threw the whole of the American Friends Mission into Madhya Pradesh, with Bhopal as the new capital.[3]

India was in the vanguard in the changeover to the metric system and then to the decimal system in its currency.[4] Cooperative farms using tractors were developed in a number of places. Modern busses, on macadam roads, began going through Chhatarpur and Nowgong. By 1960

Air-India International, with four 707 jets, started air flights from India to London and New York.[5]

Following the lead of the Government, the Mission also drew up a Five-Year Plan designed to shift authority in the Church from missionaries to Indian nationals in the Church. By 1961 they would become an autonomous yearly meeting, organizationally equal to the one in America that had brought them forth. Mission financial aid would gradually be cut back and the Church encouraged to increase its support. Educational and evangelistic work would come under the control of the Church and would be reduced to what they could handle except for scholarship grants. Medical work, on the other hand, would continue to be completely controlled by the Mission with only an advisory committee from the Church.[6]

The Trial and Victory of Dr. Grace

Some failures in the Government's five-year plans had not caused them to give up, and it became clear very soon that the Church's five-year plan would not always succeed. The earliest crisis occurred in the hospital. With DeVols on furlough and a shortage of staff, Dr. Grace Jones Singh's attempt to carry on as before ended in failure. She had previously managed the women's hospital efficiently, but in the years between as the work had grown, she had lost control of the staff. Her physical problems now added to the strain, and relationships deteriorated beyond repair.

A woman of strong discipline, she sought to bring the staff into line; but the sharp directives tended rather to breed insecurity, fear, and sometimes rebellion. Frustration turned outward on patients, and adverse reports were gossiped through the villages. As evangelists sought to tell of Christ's love, their mouths were shut by the villagers' complaints. Polarization and distrust took root, and there seemed to be no hope of healing.

Finally, the new Executive Committee of the Provisional Yearly Meeting took the matter in hand. Pinpointing the cause of the problem as basically spiritual, though aggravated by strain, they stopped all trips to the outstations, closed the hospital for two months to give Dr. Grace a much-needed rest, and agreed to transfer her to Amarmau as soon as the DeVols returned. The small hospital there, they felt, would be more suitable to her physical strength where she could be in complete charge with a staff of her own choosing.[7]

Dr. Grace might have viewed this action as kindness if there had been no drop in salary, but since that also was a part of the package, she was convinced that those against her out of jealousy had manipulated the missionaries into this action. That there was a bit of glee on the part of some, there could be no doubt. She was a prestigious and highly respected woman in the community, Church, and Mission, and there were some people even in the Church who seemed to delight in bringing down anyone in authority. Had not the missionaries experienced much of this? Added to Dr. Grace's status was the completion of her spacious brick bungalow built just across the street from the hospital.

As far back as 1952 the Mission had made provision through the loan of provident funds for Christians to build their own homes.[8] She had taken advantage of this and had built well. Having been born a child of the Mission in Bundelkhand, she had no other plan but to continue working in the hospital until she died. Waves of bitterness threatened to engulf her, and would have, had she not found a place to kneel at an altar with Christian friends beside her to pray for deliverance and peace. This Bundelkhandi woman doctor, rising from among the 95 percent who were still illiterate in the area, had developed a tough faith. Calls for her services came from many directions, but she decided to stay on in her own home with her husband and adopt a son.

Resigning from the Mission as of August 1, 1956,[9] she set up her own private practice in the bazaar. Through the remaining years of her life, the place where she always sat in the Church on the left near the window was seldom empty, and her true-pitched voice continued to start the singing. Gradually, the people in the Church began to realize that in Dr. Grace's life the Church had truly come into its own. No one could ever again accuse her of serving the Lord for what she got from the Mission, and a new awe and respect for her developed among the people.

In spite of a search throughout India for someone to take Dr. Grace's place, the Christian Hospital in Chhatarpur remained without a doctor until DeVols returned. Meanwhile, Esther Hess stepped in as treasurer to relieve Norma, who was too heavily loaded and who continued to suffer recurrent bouts of hepatitis. Mary Barton became ill and had to leave, and the hospital would have closed had not Beth Bruenimier, a nurse from the Woman's Union Missionary Society in Jhansi, come to help. Her cheerful work and witness held the staff together.[10]

DeVols' Return and the Coming of Drs. Mategaonker and Shrisunder

The DeVols arrived the morning of October 6, 1956, and went to work that afternoon. The hospital soon filled again and work became so heavy that requests went home for another American doctor.[11] But God had other plans. Clifton Robinson in meetings at the Christian Medical College in Vellore met two born-again graduating doctors, both sons of archdeacons in the Anglican Church who on graduation were in search of a place where they could witness and learn surgery at the same time. They had never heard of Chhatarpur, but after talking to Cliff, both decided to come.

Dr. D. W. Mategaonker, whose mother tongue was Marathi, could speak Hindi, also. He arrived May 7, 1957, and started a Bible study immediately for the young people.[12] A few weeks later Dr. Shrisunder arrived, and his expertise in anesthesia brought into full service a new machine DeVols had just brought back with them.[13] The hospital bed capacity increased from 58 to 65 beds. Requests for an American doctor ceased.[14] Though in the Five-Year Plan the hospital remained under the Mission, securing an Indian staff who could eventually continue it without foreign aid was a definite aim. With the coming of two national doctors, the possibility of reaching that goal seemed nearer than ever before.

The Board Commission's Assistance in the Five-Year Plan

At the request of the Council, the Mission Board sent out a commission — Chester G. Stanley, missionary superintendent, and Ralph Comfort, treasurer — to assist the Mission and Church in the radical changes proposed in the Five-Year Plan. They arrived in mid-December 1956 and for the next five weeks visited all the stations and outstations as well as calling on the Robinsons in Delhi and attending the EFI Conference in Calcutta. They brought news of the evangelical Friends in America drawing closer through the publication of the new magazine, *Missionary Voice*, with a circulation of 6,000, and the formation of the Evangelical Friends Alliance in 1956.[15]

They dropped a bombshell, however, by letting everyone know that on Walter Williams's retirement in 1957, Everett Cattell had been requested to return to the U.S.A. as general superintendent of Ohio Yearly Meeting (now Evangelical Friends Church — Eastern Region). The decision presented an acute dilemma to Cattells, for both the EFI and the India Mission were most reluctant to release them.[16]

Though temporarily pushed to the background in order to get on with the Five-Year Plan — now at the end of its first year — this news clouded all actions from that time on. The very heart of the plan, calling for deployment of missionary personnel, made their going almost inevitable. Other missionaries except Norma Freer and the Colemans would go to work elsewhere, but there was no thought at that time of any of them except Cattells actually leaving India.

Therefore, education of the missionaries' children still remained an item on the agenda, and affiliation with a group of other small missions with children in Woodstock school in Landour was necessary to prevent prohibitive fees.[17]

The changing of the Woodstock school year from July to June also made five-year terms with one-year furloughs a necessity — replacing six-year terms with one-and-a-half-years in the U.S.A.[18] Implicit in the Five-Year Plan was the understanding that as soon as a mass movement took place in Bundelkhand, all these missionaries, if needed there, would return.

Besides deployment of missionary personnel, the Five-Year Plan called for the sale of all their residences except those being used by the hospital, which would be turned over to a trust. Curtailment of evangelistic and educational programs led to further property sales except for churches, parsonages, and cemeteries, which would be turned over to the Church. The high school and also the middle school were closed. The Mission agreed to assist in setting up a dormitory for boys going to the technical school in Nowgong or the college in Chhatarpur, whichever place was chosen by the Church. They chose Chhatarpur.[19]

The three remaining primary schools — Ghuara, Nowgong, and Chhatarpur, by the end of the plan, were to be completely under the direction and support of the Church.[20] The Plan presented a scheme for putting evangelists on self-support. The hope was that voluntary witness would have more authority and remove the stigma of "witnessing for pay." Also, the missionaries were concerned about leaving evangelists with some means of livelihood when foreign funds would no longer be available.

All the evangelists were given an option of a sizable capital grant for starting a business venture in lieu of salary to the end of the Five-Year Plan. All of the evangelists except Stuti Prakash accepted the grant, which was to be paid from sales of the properties.[21] Vijay Prakash and Gabriel Massey, UBS-trained men, were not given this option since their training equipped them for positions easily found in other areas of India even if the door to Bundelkhand closed.

A perceptive listening to the Indian viewpoint revealed many doubts as the Five-Year Plan was reviewed. Bob Hess and Milton Coleman, noticing the conflict, called together a group of the employed and nonemployed by the Mission in order to deepen their understanding of the meaning of the Church. Four of the nonemployed men were asked to discuss the topic, "My Place in the Church." Reubin Oriel, a government hospital employee with strong feelings about the Mission's abandoning its workers (his view of the self-support plan) led the discussion.

Bitter feelings reaching far back into the past were expressed, but in the end positive good came from the conference. Old wrongs were made right. A spirit of independence was fostered and underlined by the visiting speaker, Dr. K. Thirumalai, a Christian doctor with his own private practice in Sagar near Amarmau. Dr. Thirumalai was a highly respected leader in India and was the one chosen to be chairman of EFI year by year for more than a decade.[22]

Stuti Prakash, sensing that the missionaries were discouraged, gave a powerful message to the Provisional Yearly Meeting's Executive Committee as the three Indian Leaders, former Mission Council, and the Board Commission — Chester Stanley and Ralph Comfort — met together. "I wish I were an artist to declare the work that has been done in this field in these sixty years," Stuti Prakash began. Recalling the care of orphans, the early evangelistic work, and the birth of the Church, he emphasized the point that a great work had already been done. "But," he declared, "a greater work is still needed to be done."

Turning to the Bible, he read: *"We would have healed Babylon, but she is not healed: forsake her, and let us go everyone into his own country."* (Jeremiah 51:9) After a brief pause, he continued: "Let our minds be cleared." Urging each one present to think about his call, he reminded them that a mango seed, when planted, did not bring forth a tree with fruit in a year. Then he continued:

> When our Church was divided, the Lord gave me a vision of our Church before the altar, praying. Then the Lord led me to this Church as pastor and I was guided to carry this kind of work. I have had to bear many things because the Lord gave me this vision . . . . All my life has been a life of tears . . . . If any are called elsewhere, let him go with blessing. If any are called to stay, let us suffer, let us stay, let us surrénder and labor in unity . . . with great patience . . . and last of all, let us leave the fruit in the hands of the Almighty![23]

Deep heart searching, prayer, and tears resulted from this message. The course on which the Mission and Church had already started was also set in prayer, and there was a profound sense of the presence of God leading some to go and some to stay. Colemans, for instance, were under pressure from Council to open a work in Calcutta with Vijay Prakash to plant new churches. They did not feel clear to leave Bundelkhand.

Milton Coleman, more than any other, seemed to sense the additional work involved in negotiating the new Woodstock school affiliation, in helping evangelists establish their new business ventures, and in clearing titles, transferring and selling the properties. Dr. Ezra DeVol, the new mission superintendent, with a hospital also on his hands would need assistance.[24] So no Calcutta work was opened, and Vijay Prakash stayed in Bundelkhand another year to work in evangelism.[25]

Departure of Cattells

The Cattells prepared to leave Bundelkhand at the end of July 1957. They had seen I. Ben Wati appointed as EFI's new executive secretary in Everett

Cattell's place. The Five-Year Plan was well underway with all lines of responsibility clearly delineated. Packing was nearly done, and then a series of tragedies began to strike that would test their faith to the limit.

Early in the year, Itwari Lal, the singing evangelist in Mission employ, had come under discipline for a violation of evangelistic principles in his district. Refusing to accept correction, he lost his job. When the Ministry and Oversight (Rakhwal) took up the matter, Itwari Lal refused to appear before them and was disowned. During the summer his daughter married Pyare Lal Brown, who was at the time in a suit against the Church for not allowing him — as a matter of discipline — to partake in a wedding dinner. He withdrew the case only when the Church gave in, dropped their discipline, and made him a member of the Church.[26] Even so, Pyare Lal Brown seemed to enjoy court cases. Therefore, he encouraged his father-in-law to sue the *Rakhwal* Committee members — Everett Cattell, Stuti Prakash, and Samson Huri Lal — for defamation of character. This was a criminal charge.

Knowing that within two days the Cattells were set to depart, a friendly officer slipped by to warn them. By leaving immediately, he advised, they could avoid being caught in India, involved in a long, drawn-out case of which no one could ascertain the end. The Cattells, however, with twenty-one years of service in India, did not want to run away. They stayed on for their farewell, and just before they were to leave, the summons came on August 5, 1957.[27] Their home in Chhatarpur had already been closed, and for the sake of Mary, they proceeded on their journey as far as Jhansi, where she could celebrate her eleventh birthday on August 1 in an atmosphere of peace.

Catherine and Mary stayed on with Anna while Everett returned to Chhatarpur to prepare for the court hearings and go on to Allahabad for previously scheduled meetings.[28] Returning the next day from Allahabad, Everett was met at Harpalpur by DeVols, telling him the court hearing for the day was canceled and that he must go with them to Jhansi immediately. As soon as they arrived, they broke the tragic news to Catherine and Mary of the cable received the day before from Chester Stanley — that the Cattells' son David, his wife, Jane, and tiny baby girl Lisa, had all been killed in a car accident on Sunday, August 4, 1957.[29]

Catherine and Mary returned with Everett to Chhatarpur, where so many who loved David comforted them. Khub Chand, deeply involved in the court case on the other side, found himself with a special agony. Finally he could bear the pressure no longer, for he loved David and wept to see his spiritual mother suffering as she was. "Khuba," Catherine said as he came to her, "I have lost two sons — David who was my physical son, is dead — you, who were our spiritual son — are dead also."

Khub Chand, brushing away his tears, answered, "Memsahib, someday I will do the work of David and me both. He was my true brother.
I will come back."[30]

The missionaries sought to guide the Cattells in how to handle their
tragic situation. Finally it was decided that Catherine and Mary would
proceed to Calcutta and take the flight already booked for Taiwan.
Everett would stay until the case was finished, and if possible, catch up
with them there.[31] The court cooperated, scheduling hearings nearly
every other day. The missionaries and Christian leaders of the India
Church met often to pray. The Holy Spirit gave them wonderful promises
that so precisely met the situation that even the lawyer, Mr. S. N. Khare,
a Hindu, was greatly impressed.

The opposition had nine lawyers working to defend them. Mr.
Khare alone displayed rare courage in defending Christians when their
cause was not popular. The power of the Church in prayer was in evidence when, on the final day of hearings, Khub Chand took the stand as
the star witness for the opposition and — to their consternation — told the
truth.[32]

On September 2, 1957, as they waited for the verdict, the Christians
continued to pray. Frances DeVol received as God's special promise for
that time 2 Chronicles 20:17: "Ye shall not need to fight in this battle: set
yourselves, stand ye still, and see the salvation of the LORD with
you . . . fear not, nor be dismayed; *tomorrow* go out against them: for
the LORD will be with you." The next morning, September 1, 1957, at the
breakfast table, Everett Cattell in the regular morning devotions read
Jeremiah 40:4: "And now, behold, I loose thee this day from the chains
which were upon thine hand . . . . whither it seemeth good and convenient for thee to go, thither go." Right after that the lawyer came and
asked, "What is your verse for today?" When he heard it, he, too, was
assured along with the missionaries that victory was theirs.

A few hours later the court delivered its verdict that the case had been
thrown out of court. The Church was told that every organization has
the right to discipline its own members. Twenty-five minutes after that,
Everett left for Calcutta.[33] Catching up in Taiwan with Catherine and
Mary, they arrived together in the U.S.A. on Sunday, September 13, 1957.
On the following Monday morning, Everett went to his office in
Damascus, Ohio, as general superintendent of Ohio Yearly Meeting, and
Mary entered grade six in Damascus elementary school.[34]

Court Cases and Other Trials

The Friends Mission felt keenly the absence of the Cattells in India, yet
God's promises and presence during and after the trial were like a shaft of

light shining in their lives. "We have won the legal battle," Dr. Ezra noted, "now we pray that the Lord will cleanse the Church and give us a real spiritual victory."[35] His prayer was answered, not as expected, but with darkness falling again all too soon. The opposition appealed the case against the Rakhwal Committee to the high court and once again Stuti Prakash and Samson Huri Lal took their stand, proceeding from court to court, judge to judge, and city to city, for over a period of three years.

Personal tragedy also had not ended for the missionaries. Frances DeVol and Rebecca Coleman both came down with typhoid fever and had a long battle back to health. Rebecca then had a relapse and nearly lost her life. Before fully recovering, she received word of her father's death.[36] As this sad news was on its way, the DeVols and their medical team were battling for the life of Esther Hess, who nearly died following the birth of her stillborn son on October 2, 1957. The baby's funeral was held at the graveside.

As Bob looked around that day on those who were present, he realized that nearly every family had one or two little mounds in the graveyard now receiving his son. Three other small mounds were there marked with the name of Bolitho and Rogers. That day in the midst of grief there was a melting together of hearts, whether missionary or Indian. Such moments as these — probably far more than all the plans in the world — helped root the Church in the hearts of the people of Bundelkhand.[37]

As the Five-Year Plan continued to unfold, so did the court cases. No Christian or missionary was spared from agony as the process unwound. Samson Huri Lal and Stuti Prakash manifested grace and patience as they prayed for the judges and for those who opposed them. Time after time they were called to the courtroom to stand for long, weary hours as they waited for the judges to appear or as they listened to the barrage of false accusations. To give them moral support, Dr. Ezra DeVol or Milton Coleman often stood with them.[38] Finally, the strain took its toll as early in January 1958 Samson Huri Lal came down with a heart attack. In spite of the fact that the court case seemed to be going against them, Samson soon rose up in good spirit and was able to be back on his feet on the witness stand.[39]

As the year of 1958 turned into its second month, another court case threatened the Mission. Two men in highly trusted positions in the hospital, both sons of fine families whose fathers had been nurtured through the Friends Mission orphanage, were caught stealing medicine from the Christian Hospital dispensary and selling it to another. Investigation brought the younger man to a place of confession and forgiveness; but for the other, it revealed other areas of embezzlement and dishonesty amounting to thousands of rupees. His persistent and inconsistent lies to cover up eventually left the Mission no alternative, and they dismissed him from service.

The Church then took up the case, and in spite of being on trial for another discipline case, they dealt with him face to face. Getting nowhere, they courageously dropped his name from the membership roll. Immediately he drew many to his side who dearly loved his family, and with their support threatened to take the Church and Mission to court. The Church did not look upon getting advice from the best lawyer in Chhatarpur as any lack of trust in God. Rather, they acknowledged the need of this as a step of humility and obedience as they continued to pray for God to guide them and to glorify His name. Faith to them was in no way equated with presumption. Through these trials, which had not at all been written into the Five-Year Plan, Dr. Ezra began to notice a depth, stability, and unity coming to those who were seeking to lead the Church forward.[40]

Though that case never materialized, another did. A teacher who had lost his job because the middle school closed brought a civil suit against Dr. Ezra DeVol, Milton Coleman, and Chairman of the Board of Education George Masih.[41] Cutting back the work in the Mission had hurt a number of people who were thus thrown out of work. Hizikiel Lall, headmaster of the high school, was one such person, but he took an office job in Jhansi until another school opportunity in a village eight miles from Chhatarpur opened to him.[42]

The Mission was conscious of the need of these people and sought to find other jobs for them. Three such jobs had been found for the suing teacher, but he refused all of them.[43] When this case started, Dr. Ezra was in Landour, and his lawyer, Mr. Khare, wired him this simple message: "Exodus 14:14" ["The Lord shall fight for you, and ye shall hold your peace."] Dr. Ezra rejoiced not only in the message of the verse but even more in the evidence that Mr. Khare had been reading the Bible and was discovering God's promises himself. That case was soon dropped as there was no real basis in fact.[44]

When property began to go, more court cases seemed inevitable. Pyare Lal Brown put his own lock on the Nowgong property gate, and many godly people in the Church for sentimental reasons did not oppose him. Even Stuti Prakash, though loyal to the Mission, was moved to tears at the thought of the birthplace of the Mission going into the hands of non-Christians.[45] Pyare Lal Brown furthermore went to the district court and announced that he was now in charge of all property in Nowgong.

A letter from the Mission's general superintendent quickly clarified that matter by pointing out to the officers that Komal Das Lall was the official representative of the Church.[46] The Mission broke the lock and the property was sold, not only in Nowgong, but in Amarmau, Ganj, and Gulganj, and no court case followed.[47] Churches in many areas of India, caught up in similar situations, could only marvel that the properties were disposed of without another court case. It seems God was keeping His promise not to allow the little Church to be tempted above what it was able to bear.

The Itwari Lal vs. Rakhwal case was destined to continue from court to court for more than three years. It seemed to come to an abrupt end with the acquittal of Stuti Prakash and Samson Huri Lal in the Chhatarpur Civil Court under Judge Goswami. With great joy they quoted Psalm 37:33 (RSV): "The Lord will not abandon him to his power, or let him be condemned when he is brought to trial."[48] However, within two months Pyare Lal appealed the case to the Sessions Court and the decision was against the Church under Judge Baijpai, an Arya Samajist. The case then had to be taken to the High Court in Jabalpur.

It was difficult at times not to question the wisdom of God as money for lawyers, court fees, and travel went down the drain, and as time disappeared in seemingly wasteful hearings at court that could have been better spent in the hospital saving a life or in villages preaching the Gospel. Through it all, Stuti Prakash and Samson Huri Lal retained their courage, and lawyers and even judges began reading the Bible and asking questions related more to life than to the cases.

On November 21, 1960, Stuti Prakash received the promise found in Isaiah 35:10: "And the ransomed of the LORD shall return, and come to Zion with songs and everlasting joy upon their heads: They shall obtain joy and gladness, and sorrow and sighing shall flee away." Finally, patience and prayer won the day. At last, the High Court in Jabalpur sent the following written notice to the Church in Chhatarpur:

> Criminal Appeal No. 73 of 1960
> No. 169 of 1958, 20.5.59 (appeal)
> The appeal, on 21th day of November, 1960, fails and is dismissed.[49]

By this action of the High Court the right of the Church to discipline its own members was clearly upheld. Then followed rest to the Church in Bundelkhand, and to Christians throughout India who had joined in prayer for victory and for the right of churches everywhere to set the standards for their members.

Hesses' Departure from Bundelkhand for Furlough

The Hesses, as all the Friends missionaries, left India before the court case was finished and heard the news with great joy. Before they left India, the call for training Indian leadership in Union Biblical Seminary was beginning to come so loudly that Hesses' leaving Bundelkhand for Yavatmal was as inevitable as the departure of the Cattells for America. In 1958 they, with DeVols and six Indian delegates from Bundelkhand, attended the EFI Conference in Vellore.[50] Anna Nixon was there as one of the EFI secretaries, and the *Life in Christ* team, Dr. Akbar Haqq and Clifton Robinson, were in charge of the evening evangelistic meetings. Great blessing attended the EFI meetings under the leadership of I. Ben Wati, and the motto over the entrance was fulfilled: "TO GOD BE THE GLORY!"

Refreshed in spirit, Hesses returned by way of Yavatmal to see the seminary. They observed that no railway served the small city and that rains often cut off travel for days. Esther considered the thousand miles that separated Yavatmal from Landour, where their children attended Woodstock boarding school. The language of the area was Marathi, not the Hindi they had learned. Yet the call was clear, and Bob wrote their decision to the Board. They would return from their furlough to serve in Union Biblical Seminary.[51] That meant time in America for further study, and Bob received permission for this with the Board's encouragement at his own expense. Hesses left India for furlough April 25, 1958, and Bob enrolled in the University of Pennsylvania for his doctoral studies.[52]

The Ministry of the Colemans

As the final year of the Five-Year Plan began, furlough came due for Colemans and Anna Nixon. Though Anna was living in Jhansi, she still came back at least six times a year to assist as an elected member of the Church on both the Board of Education and the Executive Committee of the Church.[53] Colemans' departure, however, would leave greater responsibilities to be picked up by the DeVols and Norma Freer. Major repairs for both hill houses due to landslides, as well as all other property matters, fell on the shoulders of Dr. Ezra.[54]

After Cattells left, Colemans had moved into their house in Chhatarpur. Rebecca found a wide-open door for women's work and hospital visitation.[55] As mother of orphans, she had fostered a brother-sister relationship among them, fully aware that they would need each other in the days ahead. Four of them were permanently handicapped. Rebecca was delighted when Prio Nath with a job in Delhi sent part of his salary to help his orphan brother Lachhman, who was ill with tuberculosis.[56]

Milton negotiated the sale of the Amarmau property soon after moving away from there, and then began dealing with all the legal matters involved in transfer and sale of properties as outlined in the Five-Year

Plan. Ghuara, Nowgong, and Chhatarpur churches and parsonages, Nowgong grass plot, the cemeteries in Harpalpur and Bijawar, and the Boys' Dormitory building in Chhatarpur were registered in the name of the Bundelkhand Masihi Mitra Samaj. Of the four mission properties, only Amarmau had been sold. Milton had the privilege of attending the ground-breaking ceremony for the Friends' house in Yavatmal, where the Hesses would live. It was paid for from the proceeds of the Amarmau property.[57]

During the summer of 1959, a three-month illness diagnosed as pylitis took its toll, but Milton continued with his property responsibilities, helped repair all the jeeps, ministered in the churches, appeared in court, and represented the Mission on the Woodstock Board, the Mid-India Regional Christian Council, and at Union Biblical Seminary. When Norma went on furlough in January 1959, Milton also took over as Mission treasurer until she returned just as Colemans were leaving in May 1960.[58] The self-support plan for the evangelists ate up the rest of his time as he sought to advise them. Inexperienced as they were, they either could not or did not take his advice, and he watched each of them eat up his capital and fail. He wrote:

> The changes which God is bringing into the life of Bundelkhand Masihi Mitra Samaj are affecting strenuously nationals and missionaries alike. At one and the same time to be a spectator, to be an instrument in divine hands and to be one of the objects under discipline, is truly a humbling and profitable experience.[59]

Hope through the Young People

The young people offered more encouragement. Colemans had initiated the rallies in 1950 in Amarmau, and they had become a yearly event. The young people had developed a growing concept of every layman as a vital witness in evangelization. They did not draw back from self-government or self-support. These young people were well educated, two of them with master's degrees. Many of them had life-giving contact with God.

If only some of these young people would feel called to Bundelkhand! This was the constant prayer of Stuti Prakash, who sometimes pointed out:

> Bundelkhand had two rivers. On one side is the Ken River and on the other . . . the Dhasan. But really these two rivers are doing no good to Bundelkhand. The dams that were built send water to [the next state].
> Now our people go [there] to cut the harvest. Why could not they have had harvest here in their own Bundelkhand from these rivers?[60]

Gabriel Massey was an answer to this prayer. After graduating from UBS in 1959, he came back to work most effectively in both the hospital and the Church.[61] Stuti Prakash's own son, Vijay, UBS graduate of 1955, was also an answer. He and Irene, his wife, entered heartily into the young people's work. Irene was dearly loved by all who knew her. Her helpfulness and cheerfulness were constant and uplifting.

Vijay was the president of the Youth Fellowship, and his UBS training served him well as he led them in a number of very constructive projects. Vijay and Irene had to move from Amarmau when the mission property there was sold, and the Mission offered both of them scholarships—Vijay for Bachelor of Arts and Bachelor of Divinity Training, and Irene for Montessori teacher's training—in Yavatmal. Their studies were interrupted by Irene's severe illness following an earlier eclampsia pregnancy.

When they returned to Yavatmal in July 1959 they took with them their baby son, Vineesh, born on Christmas Day, 1958.[62] Both were making remarkable progress in their studies, and Irene stood at the top of her class, when she again became desperately ill and died December 7, 1959, leaving her beloved husband and baby boy less than a year old.[63] Vijay dropped his B.D. studies but finished his B.A. He then accepted work in the Bible Society before returning to Bundelkhand.[64]

DeVols and Norma Freer were the only missionaries left in Bundelkhand after Colemans left, and anticipating such a time, Dr. Ezra had earlier written Walter Williams:

> I have just passed through a very dark time . . . . Regardless of how few or how many missionaries we have, how many stations that we are operating, how many preachers, evangelists we have had, the result is all the same. Practically a rejection of the message by the people of this area. They have a certain curiosity about the message but they have no intention of breaking with their Hinduism as they acknowledge that Christ is a wonderful person and many acknowledge Him as divine . . . . In spite of all the efforts and prayers of years it seems that our outreach to the Hindu public is at a standstill . . . . I realize that we have a message to give, whether they will hear or whether they will forbear. Furthermore, I feel that there will be fruit sometime, somehow, somewhere in this area, whether we see it or not.[65]

The Place of the Hospital

These hospital missionaries knew their calling was not just to heal, but also to build the Church. Therefore, with the development of greater medical services in the government hospital in Chhatarpur, they reviewed and recorded their purpose: To set a standard of loving personal care and a more specialized service than could be found generally, especially in rural areas.[66] "Not merely to pass out medicine . . . nor to make good will and friends . . . but a staff of medical people working together in the love of Christ giving a clear-cut demonstration—not merely of good surgery and the most modern medicines, but a demonstration of the love of Christ . . . . We must see that the staff measures up to that."[67]

The coming of two new Christian doctors and additional nursing staff brought hope that the hospital could help the Church and make a strong spiritual impact. Dr. Shrisunder was committed eventually to return to his own mission, but Dr. Mategaonker decided to stay. On March 5, 1958, he brought his membership to Chhatarpur.[68] Two months later on May 14, he married a Chhatarpur nurse, Sosan Singh, the daughter of Lachhman Singh. Both new doctors were young men and enjoyed the cricket, tennis, and badminton on the hospital compound after hours. They were also spiritual men and appreciated the weekly staff Bible studies in the DeVols' home, the morning prayers at the hospital as they began duty, and the time of prayer before every major operation.

Many times they saw God answer prayer by giving insight to the doctor about what to do next in crucial moments. Such was the case when Parwati, pulseless, was brought to the hospital for a caesarean section. She needed a blood transfusion, but no one could be found to give it. The operation proceeded, and as blood was removed from the abdominal cavity, it was citrated, filtered, and put back into the veins. Thus the woman received two pints of her own blood, and by the end of the operation, her blood pressure was up to 90/70. The next day she was sitting up in bed. "We have a great God," said Frances. "He is able to help us in time of need."[69]

Dr. Mategaonker was an eager student and learned quickly. The last three months of 1958 he went to Mungeli to learn eye surgery from Dr. Rambo, known to many through Dorothy Wilson's book, *The Apostle of Sight*. Before he returned, under the Indo-American agreement, $6,000 worth of drugs and also a gift of eye instruments from a Massillon, Ohio, doctor were received.[70] Dr. Mategaonker performed his first cataract operation on a woman who later came into the dispensary wearing her new glasses and smiling broadly, "just like a little girl with a new doll!" Dr. Ezra commented.[71]

An efficient laboratory technician, Pratap Singh Brown, the youngest son of the late Pharmacist Bram, joined the staff. He had been trained first by Norman Whipple and then in a Methodist Hospital by Hannah Gallagher, a member of First Friends Church, Cleveland, Ohio, and a Sunday school teacher of Betty Robinson there.[72]

Visitors

Though missionaries in Bundelkhand were becoming much fewer in number, visitors were more plentiful. During these years of the Five-Year Plan, they brought a lot of encouragement. Sylvia Pipkin, a Quaker evangelist from Bellefontaine, Ohio, visited the various stations.[73] Ellen Velma Edwards of Chicago also spent a month with the Colemans. Dr. Harold and Anne Kuhn of Asbury Seminary taught a term in Union Biblical Seminary and afterwards visited the missionaries in Delhi, Jhansi, and Bundelkhand.[74] Waldo Johnson of Adrian, Michigan, followed, producing films for the Missionary Board's use in the churches in the U.S.A.: "White Unto Harvest" for Taiwan, and "Ere the Night Cometh" for India.[75]

Dr. Byron Osborne came to visit his daughter, Betty Robinson, and family. President Eisenhower visited India at the same time, and Dr. Osborne was impressed with the friendly reception he received. He took part in the annual Christmas pageant Betty produced in New Delhi, and then went with Robinsons to Chhatarpur for Christmas and ministered to all the churches in Bundelkhand.[76] Pastors Clarence Sekerak from Ohio and Gerald Dillon from Oregon also visited all the missionaries. Accompanying Gerald Dillon was a businessman, Everett Heacock.[77]

DeVols' First Ministry in Nepal

The hospital work was humming, and in the midst of all this activity an urgent call came from the United Mission to Nepal for a surgeon. The DeVols' interest in Nepal was well-known, and the Mission Council agreed that they should go since the two young doctors in Chhatarpur were taking hold of the work so well.

So the DeVols went to Nepal for the month of February 1959.[78] During their absence, a very difficult operative case was thrust upon the two new doctors. Recognizing it as beyond them, they sent a message across the street to Dr. Grace Jones Singh, who graciously came into the operating room, giving them the necessary encouragement and advice and helping them succeed.[79]

Drs. Shrisunder and Mategaonker got along so well in Chhatarpur and the need in Nepal was so great that DeVols went time and again to fill in for emergencies. In the three months they spent there the following year, with Frances' assistance, Dr. Ezra performed 250 operations, while Dr. Mategaonker, alone since Dr. Shrisunder left, carried on in Chhatarpur with only a slight diminution in the work.[80]

The Board approved the DeVols' going to Nepal for a month or so each year, but when on April 10, 1959, the United Mission to Nepal (UMN) requested the American Friends Mission to release them not just for emergencies but full time, the reaction was one of alarm.[81] The Mission Council viewed the request with favor but requested that DeVols continue until their furlough to give half time to the hospital and Church in Chhatarpur.[82]

The Hospital Standing by the Church in Time of Trouble

DeVols did not carry through these plans. They stayed on in Chhatarpur, but not because of lack of approval, or because of any failure in the Chhatarpur hospital. The government hospital's higher wage scale did take off five nurses and a compounder,[83] but still more patients flocked to the hospital and showed greater friendliness than heretofore known. Income in 1961 exceeded expenses by $1,070.[84] Rather, DeVols had to let Nepal go because of increasing unrest in the Church due to the agitation of Pyare Lal Brown.

The court cases were over, but Pyare Lal Brown remained a member of the Nowgong Church. The Quarterly Meeting *Rakhwal* and the Mission Council both at various times had urged the Nowgong pastor, Dayal Chand Singh, to deal with Pyare Lal Brown and try to get him to submit to the Church discipline. They called him and dealt tenderly with him, but he spurned their efforts and continued to remain a member with a vote of ten to nine.

At annual meeting and spiritual life meetings through the year, many of the Christians were revived. Khub Chand and his wife and family were among them. Pyare Lal Brown, however, missed most of these, though he was almost always present at all the business meetings where elections were scheduled. That Stuti Prakash was chosen as assistant general superintendent both in 1959 and again in 1960 was a testimony to the fact that a majority of the people did not follow Pyare Lal Brown.[85] From 1960, with the Nowgong property being sold, Annual Meeting sessions were held in Chhatarpur. This gave the hospital stronger influence than ever on the Church.[86]

The enemy of men's souls was not content just to stir up trouble in Nowgong. Division in the Church in Chhatarpur was caused by the marriage of Pastor Stuti Prakash's youngest daughter to a Punjabi bus driver. She had already finished training and held a position in a school in the district. At the time a suitable marriage arrangement would ordinarily have been made for this daughter, she came down with tuberculosis.[87] Marriage plans had to be postponed. As she recovered and started back to her school, riding the bus, she met the young driver and married him according to the rites of his religion without the knowledge or consent of her parents. They were, of course, heartbroken. Many people in the Church, shocked and ashamed, were easily led to join the forces calling for the resignation of Stuti Prakash as pastor on the grounds that he had not demonstrated control of his own household.[88] Stuti Prakash in all humility accepted their blame but did not resign. A majority of the members stood with him. One man who spoke out on his behalf was the secretary of the Executive Committee, Hizikiel Lall.

Hizikiel taught in a school eight miles from Chhatarpur and commuted from Chhatarpur, where he and his wife lived in the housing unit providing the dormitory for the young men going to high school and college. Virginia Lall, his wife, was officially appointed in charge of arrangements for them, but Hizikiel voluntarily tutored them and taught them music so that they could use their talent in the church services.[89] When Pyare Lal Brown could find no other way to undermine the influence of Hizikiel Lall, he reported to the government officials that Hizikiel was holding two jobs. Without investigating, the government transferred Hizikiel to a distant village. Missionaries wrote home to the intercessors bands to pray for the reversal of this action.[90]

Return of the Hess Family

Amidst this trouble and heartache in the Church, Hesses returned to Bundelkhand after an absence of two and a half years in the U.S.A. They arrived in November 1960 and would not go on to the Union Biblical Seminary to teach until the new term began in July, 1961.[91] Bob was able to help get a reversal on the government's transfer of Hizikiel Lall, at least for the time being. He entered wholeheartedly into mission affairs and went to camp with Stuti Prakash. Other missions called him for special meetings, and he ministered in three of them.

Esther cared for Betsy, born in U.S. on July 4, 1959, and taught Kathy and Ronny to prepare them for entering Woodstock school at the end of February. She also assisted Norma Freer by auditing her books.[92] The presence of Bob and Esther was an encouragement to both Church and Mission and was felt immediately. As they all looked forward together to the end of the Five-Year Plan in April 1961, Bob's suggestion of a Three-Year Plan to conserve all that had been gained was readily agreed to by the Council. This plan called for grants from the Mission of some $4,000 being gradually reduced about $400 a year to increase the continued growth in self-support.[93] In March 1961 the Church in Chhatarpur realized that, as they came to the end of the Five-Year Plan, they would be required to take on the full support of their pastor. In spite of all the controversy of the year before, they chose Stuti Prakash again but reduced his salary from Rs. 200 ($42) to Rs. 125 ($24) a month. He graciously accepted this with only one condition, and that was to be allowed to continue evangelism in the villages as a part of his church responsibilities. They agreed to allow him 105 days for this work.[94]

The Hesses reported organizational changes in America in 1960 and 1961 that put Chester G. Stanley in as general superintendent of Ohio

Yearly Meeting (Evangelical Friends Church—Eastern Region) as Everett Cattell became Malone College president. The office of missionary superintendent was replaced by the office of administrative assistant, and Sherman Brantingham in that post took up the missions portfolio.[95] These changes postponed the Board's action on India's Five-Year Plan, but in March 1961 the FFMS and the Executive Board of OYM (EFC—ER) unanimously agreed to set up an autonomous yearly meeting in Bundelkhand.[96]

The Battle for Survival of BMMS

In its annual meeting sessions in 1961, the Bundelkhand Masihi Mitra Samaj (BMMS) became a full yearly meeting. This meant that from henceforth it would be self-governing. Self-support would still be a goal for the distant future, though at that time they continued to receive a sizable grant from the Mission. Self-propagation would depend on how seriously they took their responsibility in the coming years.[97]

The Church and Mission in Bundelkhand had gone through traumatic times. The court cases, the deployment of missionary personnel — including the DeVols' call to the United Mission to Nepal — and the sale of the four large mission properties had undermined their prestige and destroyed their security. They were, after all, a very small group of only 247 members.[98] They lived in a sea of Hinduism with its centuries-old caste system, which still held half the population of Bundelkhand as outcastes.

In spite of India's constitution outlawing observance of caste and guaranteeing all citizens religious freedom, the area's provincialism put up a strong wall of hostility that very few converts had been able to scale and that forced Christians into their own "caste group." Not fitting exactly into any society, the tiny Church, nevertheless, had willingly accepted the Five-Year Plan and assumed responsibility for producing fruit where the Mission with all its vast resources had failed. What greater testimony could be given to the birth of the Church in Bundelkhand than that!

Annual Meeting sessions went well with Bob Hess as the speaker and with Dr. Ezra DeVol, mission superintendent, announcing their autonomy granted by the Mission Board in the U.S.A. "The spirit of cooperation between Indian and foreign personnel these past years has been a cause of rejoicing to all of us," he told them.[99] When the Friday afternoon business session set for 2:00 to 4:00 p.m. convened, the Church would have the privilege of electing their new officers.

Just as the business meeting began, Pyare Lal Brown brought a bus load of people from Nowgong who followed him into the meeting and voted according to his lead on all matters of business. This group succeeded in putting Stuti Prakash off every committee and then fought to put him out of the Chhatarpur pastorate on the grounds of his daughter's marriage with a non-Christian. The business session lasted five hours. The missionaries became alarmed when they noticed that even some of the mission hospital employees aided Pyare Lal in this, giving him a majority and making him virtually the leader of the new BMMS.[100]

After the meeting was over, the missionaries were so stunned by the turn of events that they used the only weapon left in their hands — the complete withdrawal of the offer of future grants. They stopped the building of hospital staff quarters then in progress to make this fact visible. Then in a letter to Komal Das Lall, the new superintendent of the BMMS, the Mission Council stated their unwillingness to recommend continuing aid so long as Nowgong Church under Pyare Lal Brown's leadership continued to disregard the discipline of the Church.[101]

Komal Das Lall called the other seven elected members of his committee — Dr. Mategaonker (elected chairman), Hizikiel Lall (secretary), George Masih, Gabriel Massey, Pratap Singh Brown, Robert Hess, Norma Freer, and Dr. W. Ezra DeVol. The committee decided to get separate, written reactions from each of the churches in Nowgong, Chhatarpur, Ghuara, Bijawar and Harpalpur. With the exception of Nowgong, all desired that the discipline of the Church be upheld. Nowgong sent a letter refusing to be disciplined by the BMMS Executive Committee. They rejected the letter from the Mission Council.

This led the BMMS Executive Committee to take the only action open to them of severing connections with Nowgong. The new Quarterly Meeting *Rakhwal* almost defeated them by its vote of only ten out of nineteen in support of the Executive Committee's suggestion. With this majority the BMMS Executive Committee made copies of their letter to Nowgong — with its eighty members — for all the churches. The letter stated that as from April 27, 1961, Nowgong Church affiliation with the BMMS would cease and that they would be free to form their own discipline.[102]

As soon as this happened, some of the people from Nowgong and nearly all from Harpalpur, who were registered in Nowgong, joined Chhatarpur Church.[103] Nevertheless, the total membership of the new BMMS was now only 176 as in faith they claimed the promise: "The surviving remnant shall again strike root downward and bear fruit upward." (Isaiah 27:31)

Dr. D. W. Mategaonker, BMMS Executive Committee chairman, wrote to the clerk of Ohio Yearly Meeting in session in 1961:

> Though we are now an independent yearly meeting we still look forward for your prayers and also for the help in the way of finance and the labourers.

> As we have embarked on this new responsibility, with a heavy heart we
> had to snap our ties with the Nowgong Monthly Meeting due to the
> constant breach of discipline in them. That was a necessary step and
> we took it.
>
> The hearts of the people in the villages are still responsive to the
> Gospel . . . . We hope to carry on this work in the villages.[104]

In line with this action, the Mission Council withdrew its ultimatum and
continued with the Three-Year Plan.[105]

"It still seems to many of us," wrote Bob Hess at the time the Mission
first started its missionary deployment and appointed him to Yavatmal,
"that there are areas we must help the Church here, but let it be help,
wisely and prayerfully administered, in areas where they cannot do it
alone."[106] So the Mission from that day still stands by, believing that it
helps more than it hinders.

Hesses' and DeVols' Departure from Bundelkhand

Hesses left Bundelkhand in July 1961 to take up responsibilities in the
Union Biblical Seminary. They lived in the Katherine Skipper Memorial
Station now transferred from Amarmau to Yavatmal. Bob began teach-
ing classes in philosophy, church history, apologetics, Hinduism, and
Isaiah. Esther taught English expression and assisted her husband as secre-
tary. Dan was born February 26, 1962, in Umri Hospital, near
Yavatmal.[107]

Joe graduated from high school and Phillip from eighth grade just
before the DeVols left for furlough in 1962. By that time healing already
had begun in the Church. The new Yearly Meeting elected Stuti Prakash
as its general superintendent for a term of three years.[108]

By the end of the year Nowgong Church was set up as a preparative
meeting under the Chhatarpur Church with thirty names on the list. They
continued to worship in Nowgong, on probation, and the Church
proceeded with the advice of a lawyer in order to avoid difficulty through
Pyare Lal Brown, who with his party was still stirring up opposition.[109]

In spite of the DeVols' occasional absence in Nepal, the Chhatarpur
hospital had an annual increase in outpatients by 18 percent, inpatients by
12 percent, treatments by 25 percent, major operations by 22 percent, total
operations by 45 percent, deliveries by 25 percent, and laboratory tests by
13 percent.

The hospital broke a record that year by taking in more income than
they spent (excluding missionary salaries). "We feel we should plan to
continue," Dr. Ezra wrote, greatly encouraged.[110] With full plans to return
from furlough to work in Nepal,[111] the DeVols were nevertheless given a
great send-off from Chhatarpur community and Municipal Council at

their farewell April 21, 1962. The chairman paid them the following tribute:

> Your devotion to the cause of humanity and its service can well be envious for any man in this country. The persons who got a chance to come in your contact as a patient . . . are the living examples how good you had been to them . . . . I don't feel that the gap will be filled in, till you take over the charge of this hospital again.[112]

Though the people knew the possibility, they did not accept the fact that DeVols, on return, would go to Nepal. Like all the other missionaries who had gone, they would serve elsewhere with the hope that the Bundelkhand Masihi Mitra Samaj, left on its own amidst many stormy blasts, would nevertheless take deeper root in Christ and flourish as never before.

PART IV

FRIENDS IN FELLOWSHIP

1954-1984

Dr. I. Ben and Nirmala Wati

Everett Cattell
with Billy Graham

Cliff Robinson directing Madras choir at Madras Billy Graham meetings

319

Robinsons (right) with Anne and Milton Lipes at an ICL Meeting

CEEFI Executive Committee, 1971. Three in the center took over from Anna Nixon: Alma Kludt, Theodore Williams, M. M. Das, Administrative Secretary

Anna Nixon explaining the new CEEFI curriculum

Charles Warren, Chairman, examines new Youth Fellowship Guides

M. M. Das, CEEFI Secretary; Vijaya Charles, Telugu Secretary; Theodore Williams, Chairman

Marie Moyer, Hindi VBS & Youth Fellowship Guide Editor

Virginia Lall, co-editor and translator

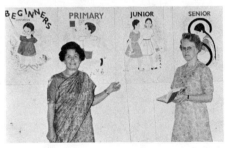

Dorothy Gruber, Hindi SS Editor (with Vijaya Charles)

Ethelyn Watson, Cathie MacKay, co-CEEFI Secretaries 1965-66

321

Church in Nepal

Dr. Ezra and Frances DeVol and
Jamie Sandoz, Nepal

Shanta Bhavan Hospital

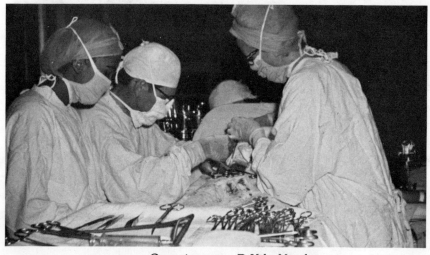

Operating scene, DeVols, Nepal

UBS Graduating Class 1984

Anil Solanki, Saphir Athyal, Bob Hess

Prabhu Dayal Prasad and
Ratnakar Rao, present
Friends Students, UBS

Sakhi Athyal, Esther Hess, Shaila Solanki

Virginia and Hizikiel
Lall and sons,
Hemant and Harshit.
Virginia was Friends'
first UBS student

323

Monica Rao, UBS
newest Friends student

Vijay Prakash and family, second UBS graduate

Ratnakar Rao '85

Gabriel Massey and family, third UBS graduate

Phillip Silas Masih '80 at graduation

Ravinder Nath,
evangelist in Ghuara

The Friends Church in Chhatarpur

Catherine, Barbara and Everett Cattell with Dayal Chand and Dayawanti
Singh in 1971. Dayal Chand was the first pastor in Chhatarpur.

Converts — Nathu and Raja Bai Prasad and
family with Catherine Cattell, 1971

Pancham Singh, a man
who truly repented

Christian Hindi School calisthenics

Shyam Lall, Principal, with student

William and Shyam K. Lall
and family

A — Ruth Mangalwadi B — Vishal Mangalwadi C — Victor Mangalwadi: ACRA

Christian English School Staff with Norma Freer, Principal

The "School Bus"

Phyllis Das, Asst. to the Principal

Norma Freer and Sumand Singh, Headmistress, with students

Dr. D. W. Mategaonker and
FFMS President Charles Robinson

Vijay S. Prakash

Mr. Lalchungliana,
Ex. Director of EHA

Dr. Anne Cherian,
the new doctor in charge, Chhatarpur

Eye Camp sponsored by ACRA under Dr. Mategaonker, Chairman

328

| # Leading the
Leaders to Christ

*"Except a corn of wheat fall into the ground and die,
it abideth alone: but if it die, it bringeth forth much
fruit." John 12:24*

The Friends Mission in India grew to include the areas into which Robinsons, Anna Nixon, Hesses, and DeVols were deployed. The budget set up to accommodate this new arrangement reflected the breadth of the work of the American Friends Mission:

1. Aid to BMMS Branch (grants to all the work of the Church and
    Colemans' support)
    Administration Branch (pensions, orphans, and office expense)
    Hospital Branch (all mission medical work, and Norma Freer's—
    and later Kathy Thompson's and DeVols'—support)
2. Delhi Branch (Delhi project grants and Robinsons' support)
3. Jhansi Branch (EFI and CEEFI grants and Anna Nixon's support)
4. Yavatmal Branch (UBS grants and Hesses' support)
5. Nepal Branch (United Mission to Nepal grants and DeVols'
    support)[1]

No one at the time could foresee the significant contribution to the growth of the Church in India these various cooperative ventures would make. Yet a phenomenal bond held the scattered missionaries together and kept them praying for one another and especially for the Church in Bundelkhand. No matter where they worked, they all came "home" to Chhatarpur for Christmas and encouraged one another with news of what God was doing throughout India. They also kept their doors open to any Bundelkhandi visitors, watched the mail for news of the area, and accepted every invitation back to operate, or to speak at workshops, retreats, yearly meetings, or youth rallies. Meanwhile, they plunged into the stream of great missionary opportunity throughout India and beyond its borders.

Following Billy Graham in Evangelism in Delhi

Robinsons chose to live in the capital city of Delhi because of the availability of transportation to all parts of the country for evangelistic services. It was also less than overnight to Landour, where the children were in school. They discovered it to be a city of few Christians and in need of a strong evangelical witness. Strategically, it offered fields of service they had not dreamed of when they first set up housekeeping in their small home in Nizammudin.

Delhi proved to be the ideal center for fulfilling their concern to stimulate revival and spiritual quickening in the Church throughout India. "Personally," they said, "we have never been more assured that we were in the center of the divine will — right where we ought to be."[2] When they spoke these words, they had no idea that a month later they would be pulled into a major role in the 1956 Billy Graham campaign. Cliff Robinson not only filled in for Cliff Barrows in the Madras campaign, but was on the welcoming committee in Delhi. Betty opened their home to the large delegation from Chhatarpur who came to attend the meetings. In spite of a painful attack of sciatica, she also arranged and attended the all nights of prayer that supported the campaign.

When the meetings ended, Robinsons were deluged with following up more than 1,600 people who had found their way to the altar during the ministry of Billy Graham in New Delhi. The youth rallies they had started boomed, and their home became a meeting place for groups for prayer on a regular basis.

Christian leaders in Delhi government and business had for the first time been awakened to the power of the Church in India. Cliff, already alert to this challenge of awakening these leaders to their responsibility in Christian witnessing, capitalized on their new insight. Even before the campaign, he had written for advice in starting prayer breakfasts for such leaders to Abraham Vereide, the executive secretary of International Christian Leadership Council and in charge of Fellowship House in Washington, D.C. With minor adaptations, the movement under Cliff's dynamic leadership began in New Delhi in December 1955 with a tea — not a breakfast.[3] By 1957 it had spread to twelve cities of India.[4] The next goal was to open a fellowship house in Delhi, but the cost seemed so prohibitive to the Mission Council that their dream had to wait for awhile.[5] While the idea developed, Cliff kept on the road in evangelism with Dr. Akbar Haqq and his father in the "Life in Christ" Team. In their campaigns in Akola, Vellore, Ludhiana, and Bangalore, they witnessed over one thousand decisions for Christ. When in Delhi, Cliff conducted professional and business men's prayer groups and preached in a number of the churches. He also developed an idea of "Bands of Fifty" young men who conducted open air meetings and handed out tracts as they witnessed throughout the city.

While Cliff was on the road, Betty kept up the Delhi prayer groups and encouraged the young people in their planning rallies, and fanned the flame of evangelical faith in the International Church through her position as superintendent of the Sunday school. Occasionally she was called out of the city to Landour to be with the children, or to various cities to speak at women's conferences. Usually, however, she was on hand to assist in planning for ministry in the city.

As a resident of Delhi, Betty was concerned that a solid Christian impact would be made on the whole city. To do this, at Christmas each year she mobilized the Christian forces in the Delhi churches to produce in the Fine Arts Theatre or other suitable location a cantata or pageant that carried a solid gospel message.[6]

In mid-1958, the Mission Council tightened their seat belts when they heard suggested a budget of up to $100,000 for developing a fellowship house in Delhi. This was followed with news of Cliff's planned trip to Noordwijk, Holland, in the company of two Indian men — a lawyer and an assistant superintendent of a bank — to attend the World International Christian Leadership Conference. They began breathing again when they realized ICL in Washington was paying the travel bill.[7] The conference, held in early September 1958, was attended by 300 delegates from all parts of the world. Through the courtesy of IBM and World Vision, Inc., they heard simultaneous translation in French, Dutch, and English — a novelty at that time. Drs. Paul Rees, Robert Pierce, and Richard Halverson were the main speakers. The final session was held at the World Exposition in Brussels. Clifton Robinson and his two Indian colleagues were given a fifteen-minute audience with Queen Juliana, who evinced a lively interest in the Church in India.[8]

The Holland conference gave great impetus to the development of ICL in India. The only cloud was the battle for finance. Great care had to be exercised to keep up the work in Bundelkhand and peel off enough to make a dent in the need in Delhi.

As if to further underline the precarious situation, Chester Stanley, the missionary superintendent, wrote, "The Board since the days of depression have not faced such financial difficulties as we are facing today. Therefore, we see no light in the Fellowship House or the purchase of a center in Delhi."[9] The follow-up of this letter was a cut in the entire India budget.

Developing a New Strategy through ICL

Shortly after that, a Paul and Barnabas situation arose in the "Life in Christ" Team that sent Akbar Haqq ministering in one direction and Clifton Robinson in another. This shattering blow, along with the cut in the budget, led Cliff to the brink of resigning. The Mission Council, however, on hearing it, were so concerned for the Robinsons' work that they called a special prayer and council meeting. They agreed to squeeze from the budget some money for a secretary and supported Robinsons' request for a larger house in which to carry on their ministry.[10]

Cliff, rethinking his priorities, felt he should give up citywide evangelism and confine his ministry to Christian conventions and ICL, through which he could inspire Christian leaders to witness. While looking for a larger house in Delhi, he continued ministering in such places as E. Stanley Jones's Sat Tal Ashram, in large conventions in Kerala, and in Chhatarpur's youth rally.[11]

Assistance to Youth for Christ

The next confirmation that Delhi was the right base of operations for Robinsons came when the Youth for Christ Tenth World Congress of Christian Youth planned its meeting in India. All was set for the meeting in Madras January 4-10, 1959 — when suddenly all Americans planning to attend discovered their visas had been canceled.

All eyes turned to Cliff, who left no stone unturned in getting all facts before India's top policy makers since Prime Minister Nehru himself was the only one who could reverse the decision. With 2,300 Indian registrations, the leaders sighed with relief when the visas were granted and in time.[12] The Robinsons attended with their two older daughters. Stuti Prakash's daughter, Kusum Kumari, also attended. Delegates came from fifteen Indian states. At the closing rally more than 8,000 came to hear Dr. Paul Rees, Dr. Ted Engstrom, and Rev. Sam Wolgemuth speak. There were 1,200 decisions for Christ.[13]

Back in Delhi, Betty Robinson again through the year entertained guests from the YFC Congress, world evangelical leaders on their way to EFI, Corrie ten Boom on a tour of India, visiting Friends like Clarence Sekerak and the David Le Shanas, and Rev. Mel Miller of Campus Crusade.[14] Young people from Youth for Christ in Delhi gravitated to the Robinson home, holding choir rehearsal, prayer meetings, and their Christmas party with forty-seven present.[15] There was no doubt about the need of a larger place for these activities, and the Mission Board gave permission, so long as the move did not increase the budget.[16]

Through the year Cliff continued follow-up of the YFC meetings in a number of centers in India. Even though YFC rallies did not grow as expected in Delhi, Cliff noticed that five churches in the city previously with no youth work now sponsored large rallies.[17]

Deepening Ties with ICL and Opening of Fellowship House in New Delhi

Early in 1959 at a second conference in Holland, Cliff was accompanied by a former member of Parliament and Indian ambassador to the Sudan, C. P. Mathen. He was the first ICL member in Delhi and had been one who took his Christian faith rather lightly until on this trip. After prayer one day, he said, "Cliff, the Lord has heard our prayers. He's done it. He has come into my life."

After the conference came to an end, he stayed behind in Europe on business and wrote Cliff in London: "There is now but one thing on my mind — to return to India and see ICL spread from man to man and place to place. If we succeed in getting across the idea that with Christ at the center of our lives Christianity is workable and practical, we shall have begun a new day for our Lord in India." Tragically, C. P. Mathen never returned to India. He died suddenly in Paris just a short time after posting the letter.[18]

On a three-day stopover in Russia, Cliff snatched up every opportunity to observe and witness. In later years Robinsons would visit Russia many times and assist in getting Bibles into the country. This time he talked meaningfully to a priest of the Orthodox Church and also with a leader of the Baptist Church in Moscow. His greatest opportunity to witness, however, came when an atheist customs official challenged Cliff to tell him what Christ had done for him. Cliff grabbed the man's hand and began talking about purpose and design, as shown in the marvel of a hand. Many other points followed as he shared his personal experience of peace and assurance. "Mr. Robinson," the official said as they parted, "I want you to know that you have opened up an entirely new world to me."[19]

Dr. Abraham Vereide, general secretary of ICL from Washington, D.C., visited India at the time of the first All-India ICL meeting in Madras.[20] Pleased with the growth of groups in 12 cities, he agreed to assist Robinsons in opening Fellowship House on the ground floor below the quarters in which they lived.[21] There at Christmas 1960 they celebrated ICL's fifth birthday,[22] thanking God for the groups now to be found in thirty-two cities and towns in India. To accent the celebration, Betty's father, Dr. Byron Osborne—visiting them at that time—addressed the entire ICL group in the city. Then, in the largest hall in the city of Delhi, he witnessed his daughter's production of the cantata *For God So Loved the World.*

Fellowship House became the center for the weekly prayer meetings and Bible study groups. Sikhs from seventy miles away came for classes, seeking their way to Christ. Betty opened a women's chapter of ICL. With daughter Anne's help she undertook the responsibility of preparing a fifteen-minute weekly program for Far East Broadcasting Company entitled *Home and Happiness.* Women from America sent bookmarks and money to buy Scripture portions for listeners.[23] The *Times of India* through a survey encouraged her, for they found out that only 3 percent of their readers owned refrigerators, 12 percent had access to a telephone, but 52 percent owned their own radio.[24] Fellowship House ministry by air reached many thousands.

After furlough following Judy's graduation in 1961, Robinsons returned to India in June 1962 with ICL's underwriting of the lion's share of their budget. ICL took on the costs of the work and the Mission Board the responsibility for personal support.[25] In no time at all they were back into the deep waters, letting down their nets for the draught. When they met in Calcutta in late 1963 for their third all-India Biennial ICL Conference with 157 delegates present, they recognized they were dealing with very serious matters: "The choice of the latter part of this Twentieth Century: Pentecost or Holocaust."[26]

The blessing of the conference exceeded expectations. Dr. Halverson's ministry along with that of twenty other American business and professional supporters underlined one of his key statements: "When we seek unity, it usually evades us; when we seek Christ, we find ourselves drawn together in unity."[27]

Preventing an Anti-Conversion Bill from Passing

Cliff experienced this unity when a key leader who had been opposing him at every step was drawn to Christ through the sincerity of the testimonies he heard in Calcutta. One by one the lives of India's leaders in government, business, and professions began to take their Christian witness seriously. Perhaps Cliff's greatest confirmation of this came the day he learned a leading Christian parliamentarian had courageously confronted the Hindu author of the "Anti-Conversion Bill," which threatened to undermine evangelism throughout India. Encouraged by Cliff in ICL, he rallied forces, including Prime Minister Nehru, and saw the bill defeated at Pandit Nehru's own call on the floor of the parliament. Later at an ICL conference this parliamentarian testified:

> Had it not been for that morning in my living room, standing with Clifton Robinson in surrender to Jesus Christ, I would never have had the power either to conceive or to implement the plan that put an end to that wretched bill — a bill which would have meant the end to a distinctive Christian outreach in my country.[28]

Family Matters

In mid-1964, Robinson's second daughter, Anne, graduated from high school in Woodstock, and Robinsons — who after that attended the Seventh Biennial World Conference of the International Council for Christian Leadership in Bad Godsberg, West Germany — said goodby to her July 2, 1964, at London airport.[29] Soon after arriving in America, Anne sent back a nostalgic note expressing feelings of many a missionary child who has had to leave parents behind:

> I heard someone shouting in a nasal voice the other day and immediately was transported back to an Indian railway station and the vendor was shouting, and the people were bustling past with all their bundles, and the train was starting to chug off and someone was taking a bath at the tap and monkeys were on the roof . . . I was right there . . . .
> Ever since that experience I've had sort of a nagging longing to return. I never thought I would feel this way, especially since I find the States so beautiful, clean, friendly, and exciting. But there seems to be a part of me that is in India.[30]

Betty, with two of her children gone and Cliff away in ministry the whole winter except for three and a half weeks, kept her home open for a stream of guests and boarders. For three months she cared for two boys who could not get to their parents in Burma because of barriers against visas. They enjoyed being with Ruth and Byron, and Ruth was able to lead one of the boys to Christ. Betty next took in a sixteen-year-old Tibetan girl while her parents went to Yale University to write a book on Tibetan history and she entertained Joe and Mae Mosher, friends and loyal supporters visiting the mission from Ohio. While Joe was speaking at an ICL group of forty leaders, the Defense Production Minister, who had launched the first jet trainer aircraft built in India, rushed in.[31] Four days after Moshers left, Milton and Anne Lipes came. The same Defense Production Minister chaired the meeting as Milton, Space Research

Engineer with NASA, spoke at the 10th anniversary Christmas celebration at Fellowship House.

By that time ICL had small groups in thirty-two cities, and the Robinsons were witnessing the whole of Southeast Asia being opened to them for developing further ICL groups. At the same time, however, they were facing a life crisis. The educational experts in India in both Delhi and Landour strongly advised them to seek special education in the U.S.A. for their son Byron. After much prayer, they were able to accept all the circumstances touching their lives as an indication of God's leading them to establish a base in Washington, D.C., area from which Cliff could continue his ministry in Southeast Asia, including India, as Betty provided a stable situation for the children's education.

A U.S.A. Base for Asia ICL

The task was great and the vision was clear. Clifton Robinson wrote to the Mission Board:

> I need most from you . . . continuing support in prayer and in faith which you have given us through the years . . . . I do not mean to convey we do not need your financial backing . . . . I want you to continue your support of us in this new approach because I know of no more dedicated and prayer conscious people on earth, and I would be greatly encouraged in undertaking this new and enlarged venture to know that you are with us in it all the way. And what more can I say to you who have, as a Church, from infancy led me into the family of God, nurtured me in the faith, recognized in me the gift of the ministry, commissioned me to go forth to the "uttermost part of the earth" and to this date have stood with me through thick and thin? Ephesians 3:14 (J. B. Phillips): "As I think of this great plan I fall on my knees before the Father . . . and I pray that out of the glorious richness of his resources he will enable you to know the strength of the Spirit's reinforcement."[32]

The struggle that followed was traumatic for both the Robinsons and the Mission Board. No one wanted to lose the Robinsons, who had served faithfully in India for eighteen and a half years, but the Mission Board could see no way financially to carry on foreign missionary work overseas from a U.S.A. base without seriously jeopardizing the other overseas work to which they were committed.[33] They supported the idea if ICL would furnish the base and take over the full support. They wrote Dr. Halverson the same day, "We feel that he [Clifton J. Robinson] is perfectly fitted for the type of work carried on by your organization."[34]

Acknowledging this decision, Cliff wrote:

> Although it brings a wrench down deep in the heart to realize you cannot continue, yet it helps to know that you have decided thus after much discussion and waiting before the Lord.[35]

If I were not sold that this approach was so desperately needed in our world today, I certainly would not think of leaving the "security" of a concerned Board like Ohio Yearly Meeting [EFC–ER].[36]

The Robinsons worked diligently to plant their burden in the hearts of people who would carry on after them. Many laymen and persons in responsible leadership positions responded to the challenge. During the large Maramon Convention held in February 1965, Cliff delivered eight messages under the great *shamiyana* erected over a sandy dry river bed. An estimated 50,000 people attended. On request of Bishop Athanasius, Cliff preached the missionary service on his life text: "Except a corn of wheat fall into the ground and die, it abideth alone: but if it die, it bringeth forth much fruit." (John 12:24)

Giving a bit of the background of the "Dynamic Kernels" project launched in Michigan by Perry Hayden, Cliff challenged the people to good stewardship and dedication of their lives to the Lord Jesus Christ. Before leaving that convention, the ICL area secretary brought Rs. $1,000 for the ICL India budget. "This is Kerala's contribution for two months to see the work in India go forward . . . . By no means must we let this work lag."[37]

Though the all-India organization as such continued for only three years after Robinsons left,[38] the impact on leadership is still felt today in India and can only be measured when the final books are open. Local groups continue to function and send representatives each year from India to Washington National Presidential Prayer Breakfasts.

The India missionary arrangement with Robinsons was concluded on June 30, 1965, as they moved on to Washington, D.C., to work with International Christian Leadership. With a focus on Southeast Asia and India,[39] they continued together in Leadership Ministries until Cliff's death on May 12, 1985. Betty now plans to carry on this ministry.

| # Pioneering in Christian Education

"Go and make disciples of all nations . . . teaching them to obey everything I have commanded you. And surely I will be with you always to the very end of the age." Matthew 28:19-20 NIV

The Ministry of the Evangelical Fellowship of India (EFI)

When Anna Nixon moved to Jhansi in 1956, she proceeded to set up the EFI office in the large Canadian Presbyterian Mission bungalow while two families of that mission were on furlough. A token annual rent for the whole plant cost less than $20. This, plus the fact that all the missions around Jhansi thoroughly supported EFI, brought the new organization into the "black" for the first time.

By mid-1956 Azariah Benjamin and his wife moved to Jhansi. Azariah had worked as accountant and secretary for EFI in Ootacamund and Mysore and was well versed in what it was all about. He brought all the EFI files and attempted to settle into the Hindi area even though his mother tongue was Tamil. By December, I. Ben Wati with his wife and two daughters arrived. Ben was EFI's first national secretary. Cattells left India in mid-1957 and the mission car they had driven was assigned to Anna Nixon in Jhansi. Along with the car came the driver, Sukh Lal and his family.

The C. P. missionaries on furlough began coming back, and the big bungalow had to be vacated by EFI personnel. So during the year they arranged with the C. P. Mission to move the entire staff and office to a former boys' dormitory for an industrial school. The C. P. Mission was happy to have the building used and at very low cost made the necessary basic improvements under the direction of Rev. Russell Self.

By late 1957 the Watis, Benjamins, Sukh Lals, Anna Nixon, and Rose Nawalkar, a young secretary from Calcutta, all moved in, living side by side. Ben Wati put out a bulletin for pastors to spur revival in the churches. It went out from the Jhansi office in four languages to thousands of pastors. In 1959 Ben with the help of World Vision also held sixteen pastors' conferences all over India. Through these conferences revival began to touch churches vitally. Ben also handled the Radio Portfolio, the Evangelical Radio Fellowship of India — ERFI — established October 15, 1957, in the Jhansi headquarters. The Far East Broadcasting Corporation offered ERFI a six-hour block of time, beginning November 1, 1958.[1]

Hill Convention planning fell to Anna Nixon. Each year during the months of May and June when missionaries vacationed in the high hills, overseas speakers — particularly from England's Keswick Convention — gave their summers to spiritual ministry in these conventions.

The Evangelical Literature Fellowship of India (ELFI)

The MacKays of the C. P. Mission returned in 1957, and Catherine MacKay immediately took over the treasurer's work. This freed Anna to give more time to editing the magazines and supervising the book clubs, now in seven different languages with 6,000 subscribers.[2] In 1958 she replaced Rev. R. F. Couture of The Evangelical Alliance Mission (TEAM) as secretary of the Evangelical Literature Fellowship of India (ELFI), a department of EFI opened in 1954.

Priority at that time was setting up bookstores and publishing houses in at least eight major language areas. ELFI also sought to stimulate new writing and facilitate the sharing of scripts and artwork. They sought to motivate writers through writing contests and encouraged Bible correspondence courses, libraries, and reading rooms.[3] Dennis Clark, chairman of ELFI and Hindi publisher in Delhi, succeeded Anna as literature secretary as she was leaving in 1960 for furlough. ELFI requested the Friends Mission Board to return her to India after furlough to train Indian writers. "I feel," wrote the ELFI chairman, "she must receive much credit for the success of ELFI over the last year."[4]

Jhansi headquarters, though ideal financially, proved to be too provincial for the India-wide organization of EFI. One by one the Indians who did not know Hindi began to move away. The Benjamins returned to the South to assist in the Tamil ELFI publishing agency. Rose Nawalkar returned to her home in Calcutta to assist the pastor of Carey Baptist Church. Ben Wati and family moved to Delhi, which immediately became the official EFI headquarters with a suboffice in Jhansi in which all files were kept and from which all mailings were posted.[5]

In early 1960 the Christian and Missionary Alliance Mission released Gladys Jasper for a period of three years to assist EFI. She first came to Jhansi to take over the office and soon became the new literature secretary.

EFI was pleased to obtain the services of this second-term missionary, already known for her astute financial ability and keen business sense. With the Friends Mission's permission, Anna turned over to Gladys most of her work and also her car with the driver and her furnished house with the cook, and Anna left for furlough in April 1960, knowing everything was cared for.[6]

The Christian Education Department of EFI — CEEFI

In January 1960 at the Tenth Anniversary of the EFI Conference in Deolali, EFI recalled its initial meeting in 1951 when Dr. Frank Kline, a Free Methodist missionary, later appointed as the first principal of the Union Biblical Seminary, presented a paper entitled "Some Evangelical Tasks and Why They Must Be Done." One of the tasks he listed was that of developing Christian education for the churches, and he felt this could best be done through the cooperative efforts of many missions through EFI.

As early as 1952 the EFI published Sunday school notes in its magazine. The United Mennonite Literature Committee used these same notes to produce *Bal Shiksha Mala* in Hindi, and EFI became the sponsor for this series of primary Sunday school lessons. At its tenth conference, EFI seriously considered ELFI's recommendation that a Christian education department — sister to ELFI — be opened.[7]

The United Mennonite Literature Committee's beginning in Hindi primary lessons and VBS materials and the World Gospel Mission's Vacation Bible School movement in the South were small beginnings. WGM had started VBS in India in 1955 with 3,600 children attending. By 1960 the attendance grew to 22,000.[8] EFI hoped to enhance and encourage these movements and develop others.

In 1958 Rose Nawalkar and Anna Nixon were requested to survey the field and present recommendations. They found no complete evangelical materials in any language. Fewer than half the Christian congregations in India had Sunday schools. In a land with more than half the population under twenty-four years of age, there were no Sunday school books in any language to put into the hands of students.[9] Rose and Anna found no lack of need but rather a total lack of personnel and finance to carry the project forward. However, EFI thrived on faith and went bravely forward. They appointed Russell Self of the C. P. Mission in Jhansi to choose a committee and explore possibilities of development.[10]

Russell Self found great interest in such a project, and throughout the following year enthusiasm mounted for opening such a department in EFI. Michael T. Ray, of the American Baptist Mission in Nellore, had just written a book called *A Sunday School Teacher and His Pupil.* He planned to publish it in Telugu for his own church, but instead he gave the book to CEEFI along with the copyright. It was published with the CEEFI imprint as its first publication. EFI's only hesitance lay in the fact that it was already committed to theological education, conferences, literature, radio, evangelism, pastors, and hill conferences, and missions. To undertake the vast task of Christian education curriculum, they knew, would double their commitment.[11]

As Anna Nixon returned from furlough for her third term in India in September 1961, EFI appointed her to this new development in Christian education instead of their earlier assignment of teaching writing. "Where do we get the people to do the job? Where do we get the money? It will take at least ten years. Do we have the determination to see it through?" she questioned. The full curriculum for Sunday school would have to be written first in English within an Indian context. This would be used in English-speaking churches throughout India and would also serve as the basis for translation in other languages in India. "And Asia," Russell Self reminded them.

EFI granted Anna three months, or until EFI Conference in Hyderabad 1962, to consider the appointment. In those three months she received strong confirmation that God's time had come.[12] Gospel Light in U.S.A. gave EFI permission to use their Sunday school curriculum for adaptation and to make any change necessary so long as evangelical doctrine was not undermined. The next step was to find writers and adapters. "Will you help us?" Anna asked Betty Pritchard, an Irish Quaker and first prizewinner of an ELFI writing contest.

"I will," Betty Pritchard answered, choosing the Junior course. Esther Hess chose the Beginners, and one after another volunteers came forward, offering their services.[13] Just at that time the United Mennonite Committee's Vacation Bible School materials in Hindi, with books for the students as well as for the teacher, came off the press. Anna arranged some workshops in Jhansi and nearby cities. A team including Marie Moyer and Helen Kornelsen, two of the producers of the course, came to assist.

When the 150 teachers at the workshops saw the students' books produced for the VBS courses, their response drove away all remaining doubt about including students' books in the new Sunday school materials.[14] The vision grew, and with it a sense of the audacity of little EFI's undertaking such a costly project.

Anna attended a session of the World Council of Churches in Delhi in November 1961. The 620 representatives of major churches from all over the world strode about the place in flowing bishop's robes and a sense of great authority. *Surely this is the group who should do this work,* Anna thought. There were many, however, who lacked the evangelical vision that had produced the EFI. In the only complete Sunday school course — with books for teachers but none for students — there were serious doctrinal flaws. No one could have foreseen then the renewal of evangelical faith that would occur in the coming decades and the demand this would create for just such evangelical Christian education materials as EFI felt necessary.[15]

By January 1962 every development had confirmed that EFI should go forward with the CEEFI project. At their annual conference that year, attended by more than a thousand, they formally opened the Christian Education Department of the Evangelical Fellowship of India (CEEFI). On January 4, 1962, they ratified the CEEFI constitution and appointed Anna Nixon as the departmental secretary.[16]

CEEFI's Task

CEEFI's task was (1) to build Sunday schools, (2) to inspire teachers to teach and win students for Christ, (3) to produce evangelical Sunday school materials and other helps considered necessary, (4) to promote the use of all evangelical Christian education tools and organizations already in the field.[17] As they opened this department, however, the EFI Executive Committee stipulated that CEEFI should not solicit funds from any EFI member organization.. Fortunately, the Friends Foreign Missionary Society already had slipped $2,000 into their budget for literature that was directed toward Sunday school publishing. Also, the very day CEEFI was established a letter was received by Anna that contained a $100 check toward CEEFI publishing.[18]

CEEFI's organizational meeting took place January 6, 1962. A committee of eight was appointed and chose Rev. Charles Warren of TEAM Mission as the chairman.[19] Later a writer of VBS Materials from Bangarapet, Theodore Williams, joined the committee as an editor and later chairman. Nine writers were at work by January 10.[20] With guidance and approval of the EFI, Anna drew workers for CEEFI from all over India. They planned with prayer. Charles Warren, chairman, said, "Let's make our plan according to the need. Then let us work according to our resources."

Studying past failures, Anna realized that one problem in completing such a project had been that very busy people were asked to take on more than they could handle. She deliberately chose Christian educators who were wives and mothers to join the teams as adapters. When children went to boarding school, these missionary wives often had time on their hands and a desire to use it profitably. Busy theologians and professors did not mind taking a week or two now and then to get away from their other work and meet with the CEEFI committee to edit the finished manuscripts, but they were too busy to meet writing deadlines. Every writer and adapter had a national co-worker. When their work was finished, it was edited by the CEEFI secretary and three others, two of whom were Indians. Only missionaries with at least ten years' experience in India were chosen.[21] Connie Lyne, the World Evangelization Crusade missionary artist who had worked with Catherine Cattell in producing *That They May Know*, did the artwork for the fifteen-year Sunday school curriculum. She never missed a deadline.[22]

Publishing Sunday School Curriculum

The plan worked beautifully. By January 1963 the CEEFI department announced that the first five years of Sunday school materials — both teachers' and students' books — were ready for the press.[23] The first course went to press January 15, 1963, paid for with the $2,000 literature budget from the Friends Foreign Missionary Society.[24] Anna had edited a magazine in India and published a few bulletins. The publishing of a Sunday school curriculum in Calcutta was something else. The printers owned old-fashioned letterpresses and often knew not a single word of English. They had been taught to recognize letters only.

Patience was nearly exhausted by the time the first 32-page student's book came off the press June 9, 1963. The full first-year Junior course was completed on August 10.[25] By the end of 1963, through donations totalling $9,000 and help from 70 volunteer workers who had given the project a total of ten years time, five courses had gone to press.[26] At the Madras EFI Conference in January 1964, first-year books in the five departments — Beginner, Primary, Junior, Intermediate, and Senior — were displayed along with one dozen of fifty teaching pictures — another first for India.[27]

The Emmanuel Methodist Church in Madras was the first to departmentalize their Sunday school and to begin using all five books in 1964. In six months they had doubled their attendance.[28]

"A dollar more in sixty-four," was Anna's challenge to her own Mission Board — a request that each Sunday school department in each of the Friends churches give an additional dollar for the next year to get Hindi translation going. The Friends Mission Board responded by budgeting $2,000 a year for three years — enough to print one whole department of books in one language.

EFI withdrew their ban on CEEFI solicitation for funds from its members, and forty other missions responded to the same challenge.[29] A girl from Australia gave up her watch, a high school graduation present, and sent the money for the Marathi translations. This started the translation fund. Work on the Hindi edition began in April 1964; Tamil was started in July; Marathi and Telugu editions were begun in September.[30] Capitalizing one language edition required at least $30,000. The hope was eventually to do ten languages.

Billy Graham on his television program featured Ken Taylor's *Living Letters*, and as the money came in, Ken Taylor sent $8,000 to CEEFI.[31] Within three years twenty-one missions, churches, and groups had contributed toward publications, and a number of foundations and other groups agreed to match these contributions. Therefore, David C. Cook Foundation provided funds for teacher training and conferences; *Back to the Bible* helped finish the English publications; Tyndale Foundation gave a further matching grant for various language publications.[32]

The Jhansi office through these years became a beehive of activity. As many as nineteen editors representing various parts of India and different theological viewpoints converged on Jhansi to spend one to three weeks scrutinizing the scripts and making corrections — educationally, theologically, and culturally. Missionaries, even after fifteen years in India, were amazed to learn for the first time that girls do not fly kites, boys do not jump ropes, children do not say "thank you" to parents, and teachers do not greet children when they come into the class (instead, the children greet the teacher).[33]

Joe and Ethelyn Watson of the Reformed Episcopalian Mission just sixty miles west of Jhansi were on call, at the drop of a telegram, to assist on committees for editing and translation. Ethelyn gave attention to preparing teacher-training packets, Cathie MacKay of the C. P. Mission worked on publicity, and Virginia Lall became Anna's assistant in preparation of the scripts for press in English and also as Hindi translator. Virginia previously worked with Anna in the Bundelkhand villages and was in Jhansi with her husband, who was teaching in the city. Her brother, Mahendra Singh, joined the staff as secretary, accountant, and typist.

Chhatarpur Hospital's first male nurse, Samson Huri Lal, was glad to see his son, Navin, take up work with CEEFI Hindi translations. Chandra Leela Solomon, an Indian graduate of Wheaton College from the Woman's Union Missionary Society, also joined the staff. Three Gospel Recording workers also made their base in CEEFI's guest room and assisted in CEEFI when they were not out in far-flung places recording the Gospel for unreached areas in rare languages.[34]

By January 1965 second-year courses were off the press in English and a few books in Hindi and Marathi. As the EFI Executive Committee considered the rate of development in this department, they recommended that Anna take an early furlough on completing the English courses at the end of 1965 in order to raise funds in U.S.A. for regional translations and be back early in 1967 for promotion and training.[35] Ethelyn Watson and

Cathie MacKay were on the spot to step in as Co-CEEFI secretaries. Dorothy Gruber of the WEC Mission joined the staff also to spend the next five years working with Virginia Lall on the Hindi translations. Joe Watson relieved Anna of editing the *Evangelical Fellowship* magazine, and from July on to furlough Anna had time to plan the CEEFI First Triennial Conference and complete the Sunday school curriculum.[36]

First Triennial Conference and Growth of CEEFI

The conference took place in Nasrapur, Maharashtra, August 13-15, 1965, and was attended by eighty delegates from eleven states in India. By that time CEEFI's "honor roll" of volunteers who assisted in production of materials and promotion of CEEFI exceeded 100. Twenty-three missions, churches, and foundations had given $40,000 toward publication, and the Sunday school curriculum was in the process of being translated in seven languages.[37]

In October Anna had to go to bed for the longest period of illness she had ever experienced. Afterwards, the doctor realized her allergy to the medication was more at fault than the amoebic dysentery for keeping her down for a full week. In any case, when the medicine was stopped she felt fine and was off to a workshop in Gorakhpur with Virginia Lall and Ethelyn Watson. From there she went straight to Calcutta and spent the rest of her time before furlough completing the English courses. On November 19, 1965, at 3:30 p.m. the first Sunday school curriculum of fifteen years with books for students as well as the teachers was completed in India and the last script put in the press.[38]

Gladys Jasper was again on hand just at the right time, having come to take over as publisher for the Evangelical Literature Depot in Calcutta. She agreed to finish the proofing of courses still at the printers, and Anna left India for furlough December 13, 1965. Representing the EFI and the Friends Foreign Missionary Society at the Congress of the Church's World-Wide Mission in Wheaton and at a number of conferences, she met many groups who were interested in Christian education who gave a total of $24,000 to expedite the work.[39] On her return to India in December 1966 she found CEEFI moving forward at a fantastic rate and great improvements made in the office and living quarters. Training workshops had revitalized Christian education in many areas and the curriculum was going into its ninth language.[40]

Right after the EFI Conference in Bangalore early in 1967, as Anna escorted Gospel Literature in National Tongues' (GLINT) representative Eva Cornelius through nine teacher-training workshops set up by CEEFI, she was amazed to see the growth that had occurred the year she was away.[41] The next big task was to hold a workshop in Nagaland and help the leaders set up the publishing program for former headhunters who had heard the Gospel first in 1872, and through the hard work of I. Ben Wati, EFI executive secretary, had just received the first copies of the Bible printed in their own Ao Naga language.

The hills were filled with the sound of the "Hallelujah Chorus" as delegates walked as far as thirty miles to get to the workshop. Nagaland is the only state in India that boasts of a majority of Christians. Through their own donations supplemented by Bible Literature International and a $1,000 gift from Blanche and Willard Pim, the complete Sunday school curriculum and other materials also went into the Ao Naga language.

Daffodils for God

The gift from the Pims stirred the people in Nagaland more than any other. Pims were farmers and members of Damascus Friends Church. They had been tithers and loyal supporters of the missionary work of their church for many years. On retiring, they found they did not have as much money to give to missions as before, and this was a concern to them as they planted spring flowers in their yard. They enjoyed flowers. The pastor came along one day, asked for a bouquet of gladiolas and daffodils from the Pims' garden, and handed Willard Pim a dollar for it.

Willard Pim objected, but the pastor insisted, and that dollar drew interest. It became the first dollar of thousands that went to India from bouquets sold from the Pims' flower garden. For the next fifteen years half the Friends Foreign Missionary budget for Christian Education — $1,000 each year — was met through the Pims' bouquets at $1.00 each. When they heard of the need in Nagaland, they worked a little harder and sent an extra $1,000.[42]

Emphasis on Indian Leadership

As CEEFI soon grew into what EFI's historian called "one of the most impressive EFI activities,"[43] EFI became concerned about rooting it in Indian soil under Indian leadership. As they considered this in a meeting in September 1967, a newspaper came into their hands with these head-lines: "ALL FOREIGN MISSIONARIES WILL HAVE TO QUIT." It was gratifying to look over the fifteen EFI Executive members and secretaries present and see only two foreigners — Russell Self and Anna Nixon. CEEFI had the help of at least eight full-time missionaries who came "free"— supported by their various missions. All funds coming in were quickly devoured in publishing programs. So the matter of getting an Indian to take over CEEFI not only concerned personnel but money.[44]

At CEEFI's second triennial conference, March 29-April 5, 1968, the answer began to unfold when through the testimony of M. M. Das they were made fully aware of untapped resources. Das was an employee in the electric company in Ahmedabad, Gujarat. Each day as he closed his office at four o'clock he returned to his small house, pulled out from under his bed a box of notes and manuscripts, and until sleep stopped him, he continued to work on translations for his Methodist Church. Head of the Sunday school work, he worked with other churches in getting the CEEFI curriculum into their churches. No one paid him for this.

Theodore Williams, CEEFI's new chairman, was supported by his Indian church and set free to serve wherever he felt God would lead him, and he gave much of his time to CEEFI. Such support in India, however, was exceptional. CEEFI felt that churches just beginning for the first time to buy Sunday school books were in no position to be challenged to support a full-time salaried Christian education worker. So they faced the alternative of closing the work if missionaries were pulled out, or developing a policy of using a greater number of volunteers like M. M. Das. The first man on his feet in support of the policy was Das. After him delegates from all over India rose to their feet, offering to take some responsibility.

One was Vijaya Charles, a teacher. She felt God was calling her to turn her full time to Him to develop Christian education in the Telugu area. So she stepped out on faith — and to this day she continues to serve in this capacity. Lova Bush, a Telugu area missionary of the Ceylon and India General Mission, continued full time, also, using her skills in art, electronics, publication, and organization to promote CEEFI.[45] With the help of these Indian and missionary leaders, CEEFI set up committees in ten languages and closed the conference with the election of a completely Indian executive committee. Missionaries still in leadership were requested to search for an Indian volunteer associate to train in the work.[46]

Youth Work Development

At the close of the conference Anna, with the help of her family, went to the U.S.A. to celebrate the sixtieth wedding anniversary of her parents. It was a happy time, and the last opportunity for such a reunion. It proved to be a profitable trip for CEEFI, too, as Anna was able to arrange for further publication of youth materials adapted from Scripture Press and gain a promise from the Conservative Baptists to return Alma Kludt, completing her master's degree in Christian education, to India for a third term to serve as CEEFI's training secretary.[47]

On returning to India in June, Anna made an extensive tour throughout the country, visiting the regional committee secretaries in their various states and participating in workshops along the way. Also, as she traveled, she discussed the feasibility of CEEFI's development of Youth Fellowship guides with groups already working among youth, such as the Youth for Christ, Child Evangelism, Children Special Service Mission, Vacation Bible School movement, Pioneer Girls, and others.

These groups not only approved but gave support to the project.[48] Nirmala Cain, a 1968 graduate of Union Biblical Seminary, joined Anna in the adaptation and writing of these materials.[49] By the time materials were ready for translation, Marie Moyer, editor of the United Mennonite Committee's VBS series, joined the staff in Jhansi to assist in many fields and particularly in the Hindi CEEFI promotion and publication program.[50]

Phenomenal Growth in CEEFI on Many Fronts

At Bhubeneswar, Orissa, in January 1969 EFI stepped out on faith and at CEEFI's recommendation appointed M. M. Das as the first Indian full-time EFI Secretary in Christian education. He moved to Jhansi with his family on July 4, 1969, to take up promotion and learn all the areas of work being conducted through the headquarters office. That was an exciting year, as Sunday school curriculum translation went into its thirteenth language. Teacher training materials were in five languages, and Youth Fellowship materials were just going to press.

The phenomenal growth in CEEFI had opened and encouraged Christian educators in the U.S.A. and Canada to assist. Dr. Howard Hendricks, accompanied by Charles Warren, held eight training conferences in key centers, increasing awareness among church leaders of the importance of Christian education.[51] Rosemary Turner of Moody Bible Institute assisted in one all-India training workshop and half a dozen others across the northern part of India.

Dr. Cyrus Nelson of Gospel Light Publishing House visited three main centers. Lillian Swanson of Canada Scripture Press came later, demonstrating new Christian Education methods and how to use the Youth Fellowship guides. She and Rosemary were each accompanied by the training secretary, Alma Kludt. Anna wrote, "Our work in Christian Education is expanding so rapidly that we can hardly get time to sleep. It is thrilling to see . . . but nearly killing us to keep up with it . . . . It draws people of the highest training."[52]

An order from Africa for $5,000 worth of CEEFI's English Sunday school curriculum alerted CEEFI to inflation as nothing else had. Determined to protect capital, CEEFI had set prices to cover expenditures but had not allowed enough margin for rising costs. Overseas orders threatened to deplete supplies and force CEEFI to reprint at inflated prices. So a higher price was set for overseas sales, and the question was raised as to whether the profit should go to the publisher or protect the CEEFI capital investment.[53]

Problems began to arise as the ELFI publishers of CEEFI material, one after the other, began to realize that CEEFI publications were crowding their warehouses and dominating their distribution to the point that other areas of publishing were being neglected. This happened at a crucial time in the C. P. Mission in Jhansi as missionaries were leaving, and the property used there by CEEFI was on the verge of being turned over to the Church of North India. On CEEFI's recommendation, EFI bought the whole building, of which CEEFI had been using only half, for a sum of $13,000.

Every member of the EFI, CEEFI Executive, C. P., and Friends Mission agreed with this move. The Friends Foreign Missionary Society signed a note with *Back to the Bible* Broadcast, who loaned CEEFI $10,000; the C. P. Mission donated $3,000, and a gift of $1,000 from a missionary paid the registration fee. While in Singapore at a workshop and to attend an All-Asia literature conference, April 6-11, 1970, Anna got word that Ben Wati had signed the final papers and the property was secured for CEEFI's use.[54]

Knowing the property matter was finally settled, Anna enjoyed the Singapore conference attended by ninety-seven representatives from fifteen Asian countries. The conference had been arranged by Evangelical Literature Overseas and David C. Cook Foundation. The coordinator was Gladys Jasper of the C. and M. A. Mission. Most of the representatives were nationals though a few full-time missionaries in the field of literature were present. "Forward through dynamic literature," had been the theme of the conference, and high expectations emerged for the future as in the final session the delegates all agreed to continue to keep in touch with one another through an Asian Evangelical Literature Fellowship. Before parting they all stood and declared:

> By God's grace . . . and under God's guidance . . . we determine to move forward together . . . in a major breakthrough . . . with dynamic Christian literature . . . . May God help us . . . and to Him be all glory. Amen.[55]

On returning from the Singapore conference, Anna found that the Dorothy Gruber-Virginia Lall team had completed the translation and manuscript preparation of the full Hindi Sunday school curriculum — five years from the time they started. Virginia Lall had been responsible not only for translation, but copying corrected scripts by hand — a five-foot stack of them.[56] M. M. Das with his staff began to prepare the new quarters to receive both English and Hindi publications as a beginning of a new CEEFI supply center.[57]

In preparation for turning over the new CEEFI quarters to M. M. Das, who would soon be stepping into leadership, Anna Nixon moved into the bungalow on the hill rented from the C. P. Mission by the Friends Mission.[58] With MacKays retiring and the Selfs being stationed elsewhere in Asia, there was plenty of room in their bungalow for other CEEFI workers, too.

Though Nirmala left to get married and Dorothy Gruber returned to WEC headquarters in Lucknow, having completed the Hindi publications, Marie Moyer of the Mennonite Church, Nell Gibson of Gospel Recordings, and Eldeana Dunlop of Ceylon and India General Mission from South India moved in with Anna. They helped pay the rent and stayed on to continue with CEEFI work under M. M. Das's leadership after Anna left for furlough in 1971.

The Visit of the Cattells

Early in 1971, Everett and Catherine Cattell, accompanied by their daughter Barbara Brantingham from Taiwan, were again in India. Everett had been called to speak at the twentieth all-India EFI Conference in Vellore.[59] He could hardly believe the advance made in the EFI work in all phases. He was impressed with the attendance at the conference with three out of four being Indians. Registered delegates numbered 550 and attendance was more than a thousand. He remembered that fewer than fifty had attended the first conference in 1951. He highly approved the forming of the property trusts — the Evangelical Trust Association of North India (ETANI) and of South India (ETASI), which Friends and many other missions had joined, turning over properties in 1968 such as bungalows, hospitals, and schools, thus protecting them for the use of building the Kingdom.[60] Reporting on EFI later, he said:

> Seeing the high caliber of Indian leadership who carry on the EFI came to me as a seal of my leaving India when I did . . . . It was a thrill . . . to hear reports of the affiliated commissions:
>
> Literature [ELFI],
>
> CEEFI [The Christian Education department of EFI],
>
> The Evangelical Theological Commission, 1962 — a new society for the study of theology at the grass-roots level [ETC],
>
> [Theological Education by Extension] to upgrade work of pastors [TAFTEE]
>
> Council of Evangelists, and
>
> the new missionary society sending missionaries, the Indian Evangelical Mission [IEM], . . .
>
> a tremendous legacy being left to the Indian Church.[61]

M. M. Das, CEEFI's New Leader

CEEFI planned its third triennial conference in Jhansi February 27-March 2, 1971, with the theme "FOCUS ON YOUTH." There was high expectancy in the air as delegates came to see CEEFI's new spacious quarters and the CEEFI Supply Centre being developed, to be formally opened on April 15. Sunday school and Vacation Bible School curriculum materials were on display in fifteen languages and Youth Fellowship guides in four. Youth workers from various groups in India discussed ways CEEFI could further assist in reaching young people.

Alma Kludt, the training secretary, reported on a series of workshops held in ten cities of India throughout January. Looking back over her time in CEEFI she said, "I would estimate that we have reached at least 5,000 leaders during the past three years though our workshops . . . . These inevitably lead to growth — in numbers *in*, as well as numbers *of*, Sunday schools . . . . In one area, I know, workshops led to forming 13 new Sunday schools."[62]

On March 2, 1971, in a formal service under the chairmanship of Theodore Williams, Anna Nixon formally turned over the leadership of CEEFI to its first Indian secretary, M. M. Das.[63] Recommended by CEEFI and appointed by EFI, M. M. Das felt secure with his CEEFI Board of ten members and four associate secretaries. Beyond that an office staff and twenty-five other regional assistants including five missionaries stood ready to assist. Eighty-seven groups and many individuals had supported CEEFI financially and would continue to do so.[64] Much remained to be done. CEEFI was only half through its publishing program, and beyond lay the vast field of Christian education development throughout India and Asia.[65]

Before leaving for furlough in July, CEEFI requested Anna Nixon to complete the Youth Fellowship guides and print a CEEFI manual containing all the rules and job descriptions.[66] On finishing the latter in early April and taking the twenty-one lesson topics to be completed with her, she took the train south to the Mennonite area to meet her former co-worker, who had left Jhansi to get married. Nirmala Cain Johnson came in from her village to Dhamtari, where they set up office and got to work. They were nearly finished with the full second year when on May 4, 1971, at midnight, a telephone call came telling Anna that her father had died.[67]

By four a.m. on May 6 with manuscripts in a briefcase, Anna boarded the train in Raipur and finished the second year Youth Fellowship guides by the time she reached Jhansi. Papers for leaving the country were cleared as soon as possible, and she waved goodbye to M. M. Das and his staff in Jhansi. She felt deep gratitude in recalling a letter from

Nagaland on the completion of the first Ao Naga Sunday school materials:

Lips are often silent though the hearts are full. Our people are full of gratitude to CEEFI for the Unique Contribution. Time may pass away and a new generation may come in but the blessed contribution will never fall into oblivion from the hearts of our people. May God bless CEEFI and all the personnel used of God as a channel to flow His blessings to us.

— (Signed) Evangelist T. Alem-Meren Ao
Impur, Nagaland[68]

Cooperating in Theological Education

*"The things you have heard me [Paul] say in the
presence of many witnesses entrust to reliable men
who will also be qualified to teach others."
2 Timothy 2:2 NIV*

Katherine L. Skipper Memorial

The Hess family left Bundelkhand in July 1961 for Yavatmal — one thousand miles by bus and train from their two older children, Ron and Kathy, who were in Woodstock boarding school in Landour. They moved into *Mitra Niketan* (Friends House), just at the left of the entrance gate. Gleaming in fresh whitewashed splendor, the house was built around a courtyard with a wide inner veranda. On entering, one could see the shiny brass plaque — inscribed as a memorial to Katherine L. Skipper. The plaque had been removed from the Amarmau bungalow and placed on this UBS campus building that had been paid for by $6,300 from the sale of the Amarmau property.[1]

Students Hesses met at Union Biblical Seminary

The first term at Union Biblical Seminary opened in early July. Among the 104 students from India and other Asian countries was one from Kathmandu, Nepal, named Ram Bahadur Shrestha. The story of how he got there is impressive. Three graduates of Yavatmal Biblical Training School, C. K. Athialy, George John, and C. G. George, had gone as missionaries to Nepal. They were members of the Mar Thoma Church, which dated its beginning back to Thomas, the disciple of Jesus. Before C. K. Athialy was born, his mother heard the great saint Sadhu Sunder Singh tell of the tremendous need of preaching the Gospel in Nepal. She had at once dedicated her unborn son to serve the Lord in Nepal.

While in seminary, the other young men studying with him were also challenged with a concern, and as soon as Nepal opened its doors, the three young men trekked into Kathmandu with bundles of books, and with burning hearts they began a mission. The Mar Thoma Church gave them some support, but not enough. They supplemented it by doing dry cleaning, tutoring, and typing. Sometimes they were hungry. They did not, however, neglect their chief purpose of spreading the Good News of Jesus Christ. Shrestha of Kathmandu was their first convert, baptized April 29, 1957. He was the first Nepali student to enter UBS, sent there by C. K. Athialy.[2] Shrestha joined students from India, Burma, Japan, and Africa, representing a total of 22 different languages from 36 denominations.

Birth of Union Biblical Seminary and Its Growth to 1961

Amazing growth had taken place from the time Frank and Betty Kline of the Free Methodist Mission had set up the Biblical Training School in 1937. After World War II, member missions and churches of the Berar-Khandesh Christian Council and the India Holiness Association joined in plans to enlarge the scope of the Bible School to include students from other parts of India. They agreed on English as the medium of instruction, replacing Marathi, and made plans for expansion of the operating plant.

This opened the door for C. K. Athialy and his friends from Kerala. By September 4, 1953, when the EFI brought together eleven groups to form the Union Biblical Seminary, attendance had increased to 54 students, and by 1961 there were 256 graduates who had gone out from UBS into Christian service. Students present in the seminary when Hesses arrived formed eight evangelistic teams who went out preaching during vacation, between terms, and also on weekends.[3] Eleven full-time and seven part-time faculty and staff from eight denominations and four nationalities were at work, and twenty-one missions and groups sent representatives to the UBS Board of Governors.[4]

By 1961, twenty-three students graduated—twelve with Bachelor of Divinity degrees (M.Div. equivalent). This was the largest number ever in India, the principal reported, to have been awarded the three-year B.D. graduate degree.[5]

When Hesses arrived in Yavatmal, they found not only their house finished, but also added to the campus were a number of other new buildings: a chapel; three other bungalows; four married students' quarters; an international house; students' quarters; a radio studio. Still under construction were an administration/library/classroom complex called the Ad-Lib building, men's dormitory, and two more staff bungalows. A five-year building program had been started in 1954 and revised in 1958 to a total of $105,000.[6] Free Methodist and India Holiness Association buildings on the campus were already in use as classrooms, library, and living quarters.

The new houses being put up for faculty members were donated by the General Conference Mennonites, American Mennonites, Conservative Baptists (2), Friends, and Bible and Medical Missions Fellowship; Bob Pierce arranged for funds for the men's dormitory named Pierce Hall; cooperative giving paid for the Ad-Lib building; the I.H.A. put up the chapel.[7] After their arrival, the Hesses saw further improvements in the men's dining hall and a 3,000-foot pipeline installed to bring needed water from a distant well. Friends also gave $2,000 toward the addition of quarters for married students and allowed the use of funds left in UBS Branch for landscaping and fencing.[8]

Robert Hess Appointed Principal of Union Biblical Seminary

Robert Hess continued in vital touch with the Mission and Church in Bundelkhand, serving as the superintendent of the Mission and visiting the area at least three times a year. In the Seminary, he taught church history, philosophy, and biblical studies. On weekends and during vacations he was called upon for Christian conventions in various parts of India. He ministered in Kodaikanal hill station, in the Assam hills, and in a number of mission gatherings.

One convention that impressed him deeply was among tribal people in Orissa. At the invitation of the British Baptists, he spoke to all the missionaries in the area, where there had been phenomenal growth after years of rejection of the Gospel as had been the pattern in Bundelkhand. Since 1955, however, they had been experiencing some 1,000 converts every year and had formed 163 churches.[9]

There were so many opportunities to minister to students and speak in conventions that Bob found it impossible to finish the doctoral dissertation on which he was working. UBS, concerned that he complete it by mid-1964 when he would be taking over as the second principal, released him a term to study with one of his professors who was teaching for a short time in Pune. When summer vacation drew near, his brother Max gave financial assistance to bring the whole family home so that Bob could have all the facilities at hand that he needed to complete it.

Esther, in spite of battling mononucleosis, helped with the typing and organization. Before the summer was over she, too, was feeling on top physically again.[10] Bob worked hard but did not complete the work in time to get back to India by June 8 in time for the beginning of the new Woodstock school term for Kathy and Ron. They flew on ahead and Bob, Esther, Betsy, and Dan left New York June 23, with the work—except for the final typing—behind them. Six people offered help in the final details and Bob's Ph.D. degree from the University of Pennsylvania was mailed to him on August 19, 1964.[11]

When Hesses arrived in Bombay, it was pouring rain. They were grateful, for terrific heat during the summer in Yavatmal had aggravated a water shortage that threatened to keep the seminary from opening. But it opened on time, with its new principal present. Showers of blessing also fell during the opening spiritual life conference for the students and during the faculty retreat.[12]

This beginning reassured Bob Hess, who at times wondered how he had ever received such an appointment. A trainer of pilots in the U.S.A. Air Force during World War II, then in turn a university student, a pastor, an evangelist in India's remotest villages, and a convention speaker, he suddenly found himself chosen to head up the leading evangelical graduate seminary in Asia. The challenge was great, with the international character of the student body, the Bible-centered curriculum, and the unique combination of intense evangelistic-missionary zeal and academic excellence.[13] Esther assisted in the teaching in the fields of English and bookkeeping, managed the household, hosted conventions, and catered to many guests.

Drought, Financial Difficulties, and Stress

The Hesses along with other faculty members found they had to exercise great faith each month as operating expenses always went to about $1,200. Some relief came from a grant of the Theological Educational Fund shared by Serampore, Jabalpur, and Yavatmal,[14] but it soon evaporated.

Like George Mueller, they learned to scrape the bottom of the barrel every month. *Time Magazine* featured articles about India's drought that year, for after the first rain, the monsoons failed. *"Too Many People, Too Little Food,"* was their caption on a feature article. The loss of crops was very serious in Maharashtra and prices doubled.[15] Lines at ration shops became almost endless. Esther was stirred to the depths when three women who had waited in line for more than six hours through the heat of the day became so dehydrated that, one after the other, they fainted and fell face forward into the dust. This, just to get four pounds of grain![16]

Sometimes the fevers and strains of India coupled with the constant demands of students and guests made it necessary for Hesses to leave the compound for a day and get out to a quiet place for rest. One such time right after hosting the India Holiness Convention in 1964 they went to a nearby semihill station in Chikalda. Just after tucking in the mosquito net for a good night's sleep, Esther suddenly screamed with excruciating pain and fainted. Before Bob could find the cause, a scorpion had stung her five times. No doctor, drugs, or medical help were available except for an English homeopathic nurse who applied something from her supplies that seemed to give some relief.[17]

The heavy demands on time at the seminary and the long distance to Landour made the Hesses search for opportunities to be with their children. Christmas in Chhatarpur always had priority. During a summer vacation, Bob, Kathy, and Ron went with the DeVols to the Kulu Valley.[18] Kathy went with her father on a business trip to Kerala. Ron, during winter school holidays, roamed the meadows around Yavatmal studying birds. Betsy enjoyed many playmates on the campus and was unmoved by the cobra that slithered over her foot one day as she stepped off the path into the grass near the front gate. Dan, born February 26, 1962, at Umri Free Methodist Hospital thirty miles from Yavatmal, was getting a good start.

Sometimes life became very difficult, due to lack of supplies, transportation, and medical facilities in Yavatmal. During the rains, rivers cut them off from their nearest large city. When Dan had an acute bronchitis attack and was allergic to the antibiotics provided locally, he nearly died before they could get him to the hospital.[19] The summer of 1965 brought many trials. Esther was ill with hepatitis. Ron missed twenty-six days in school and was hospitalized for ten days with paratyphoid.[20] When time came for the new seminary term to begin, Esther was unable yet to travel back to Yavatmal from Landour where the family had been together part of the summer. She stayed on in the hills with Kathy, Ron, and Betsy, who were in school.

Bob took Dan down with him, hoping for a lot of help from Baina Bai, the *aya* who cared for the children. He was called back in less than three weeks because Esther had to undergo major surgery. Kathy and Ron went into boarding and Mary Bauman took Betsy to Yavatmal with the promise to keep an eye on her and Dan. That same month word came that Bob's sister Doris, who had visited them a few times in India, was seriously injured in an auto accident in Mozambique and was hospitalized and in traction with two broken ribs, a possible dislocated vertebra, fractured left collarbone, and a head injury.[21] Bob also lost his father that year.[22] The excellent cooperation of the faculty helped Hesses survive these times of stress.

Union Biblical Seminary Staff

In 1963 Dr. Saphir Athyal had joined the staff. A former student of South India Bible Institute of the World Gospel Mission, a graduate of Allahabad University, and a magna cum laude graduate of Princeton

Theological Seminary, he had returned to India in August with his Ph.D. in Old Testament. He was the only Indian in the country to hold such a degree. While working on his doctorate, Bob had been in touch with Saphir and they had become good friends.[23]

Saphir taught the Old Testament classes. As the nephew of C. K. Athialy, who had gone to Nepal, he also was from Kerala and a member of the Mar Thoma Church. Three other staff members — K. M. Mathew, who supervised the grounds and building, K. C. Mathew on sabbatical leave for a year, teaching in Asbury, and A. S. Mathew, the librarian — were all of the Mar Thoma Church.

Mr. Samudre, a Free Methodist, taught Indian Church history and was the senior member of the faculty. The maintenance man, typist, matron, night watchman, and dietician were all Marathi-speaking Free Methodists.

American missionaries on the staff besides the Hesses were Stella Patoukas, Conservative Baptist, treasurer; and Ken and Mary Bauman of the General Conference Mennonites. They taught homiletics, Christian education, and Bible; New Zealand Baptists Ian Kemp and Bruce Nicholls taught Greek and New Testament studies; Ian's wife, Elizabeth, the nursery school, and Kathleen, Bruce's wife, English. Peter O'Brien of the Australian Anglican Church taught Biblical Theology, and his wife, Mary, was headmistress of the nursery school.

Daryl Cartmel, an Australian with the Christian and Missionary Alliance, taught Church history, and his wife, Bea, an American, Christian education. Alexis Cameron, a Canadian Anglican, was studying for her doctorate; Zoe Anne Alford, an American from Texas Disciples of Christ and a member of TEAM Mission was returning to assist in the library and the Christian education department. "With such a variety of backgrounds geographically and educationally, it is no wonder that faculty discussion hours on Monday mornings can be lively times," Bob wrote.[24]

Striving for Personnel and Financial Stability

When the seminary closed for the summer in 1966, the Hesses left for furlough and Kenneth Bauman was appointed as principal in his place.[25] Before they left, twenty more students graduated and went out to serve as pastors, evangelists, and teachers in Japan, Indonesia, Ceylon, and to many parts of India.[26] Back in America, Bob Hess met with the Cooperating Home Boards of UBS, Inc., and worked out plans for a program on Church Growth with Donald McGavran. He was also requested to represent UBS at the World Conference on Evangelism in Berlin, October 26-November 4, 1966.[27]

Hesses at that time were prayerfully going through the valley of decision. They felt the time had come to discontinue their overseas missionary service. On one hand there were family concerns,[28] and on the other, the deepening conviction that the time was near for installing an Indian principal in UBS. The Seminary Board, however, was not yet ready to appoint an Indian principal, and Ken Bauman, who was due for furlough in 1967, was asked to continue for a period of three years after his return in 1968. The intervening year, the Board felt, required Bob's presence. The Cooperating Home Boards helped EFC – ER pay the travel bill, and the Hesses agreed to return for one year.[29] They arrived in India via Taiwan on June 30, 1967, for a final and very significant year.

Not only were students by that time pushing out the walls of dormitory and classroom space, but graduates at work in the Church throughout India and Asia were making a difference in the quality of Christian living. Church leaders looked on UBS with respect. An acute internal need, however, was financial stability. Ken Bauman reported as he left for furlough, "Finances have not been a major problem this year. This is due to the sound financial policies laid down by Dr. Hess before he left for furlough last year. Contributions towards the Seminary have continued throughout the year." He also noted that some $10,000 was still needed for building, and that beyond that, ". . . we want to keep uppermost the need for endowment."[30]

Ken in the U.S.A. and Bob in India became two hands reaching out to gather in from everywhere the support UBS needed in endowment. Among the Cooperating Home Boards Ken raised funds for the completion of the men's and the building of a ladies' dormitory and purchase of a car. But beyond promises, he had not been able to secure endowment.[31]

When the government refused his request for Barry Ross, a Wesleyan missionary of U.S.A., to join the faculty, Bob Hess, back in leadership, became abruptly aware of the urgency to develop both endowment and Indian leadership in the seminary. Clouds of such restrictions had long been hovering over missions. This made abundantly clear that survival for a theological institution in secular India demanded both Indian personnel and funds. Bob wrote the Board of Governors:

> We believe that Union Biblical Seminary has a strategic place in contemporary India. The Holy Spirit has signally blessed our institution with a rich spiritual endowment of praying people in all parts of the world. Capable teachers have trained students, some of whom are returning to teach for us. We are making definite plans for adequate Indian leadership in each department of the Seminary — academic, business, and maintenance.

Now our major need is for financial endowment to adequately implement the program which God has entrusted to us.[32]

Projected goals reached before the Hesses left India in 1968 were (1) acceptance of an organizational chart and job descriptions for the entire seminary; (2) increase in the number of Indian faculty members; (3) enlargement of the nursery school; (4) better servants' quarters; (5) completion of the dormitories; (6) appointment of Dr. Saphir Athyal as vice principal of academic affairs.[33]

Other projected goals striven for but not quite reached until later were (1) the appointment of an Indian principal, though the Board set their eyes on taking this step in 1971;[34] (2) tube wells for an adequate water supply on campus, started in 1968 but had to be dug so deep they were not completed until 1970;[35] (3) increased grants for the operational budget. Friends increased theirs from $200, their first grant, to $2,000 beginning in 1969.[36] They also began considering turning hill houses, Pennington, and Pinepoint, to endowment.[37]

Many applications flooded the seminary in those days, requiring careful selection of candidates. UBS wanted young men who were sincerely committed to Christian ministry and not those merely looking for professional training. In order to increase this sensitivity to the call of God, UBS began sponsoring "Days of Challenge," a time when young people from the churches over India came to UBS for a weekend retreat. Students on campus planned the program to introduce the young people to what UBS was really like and also to challenge them to commit their lives to Christ. Sixty guests came that last year the Hesses were in India, and many of them received Christ as their Savior and Lord. Some of them returned in later years as students.[38]

Anil Solanki's Training by Friends

A significant relationship began that year as Bob Hess appointed as prayer secretary a student who had joined the seminary during his furlough. Anil Solanki had considered himself well settled in life. He had already married Shaila and had received his diploma in engineering. God's call to Christian ministry came after that, and they came to Union Biblical Seminary, where their first daughter, Elizabeth, was born at the end of their first year of studies. Anil frequently visited the Hesses, bringing his family, as he and Bob discussed the weekly prayer needs on campus.

Anil's abilities and scholastic record caused the UBS Board of Governors to request him on graduation to continue studies with a view to returning to UBS as a teacher. He chose United Theological College, Bangalore, rather than a graduate school outside India, to complete his M.Th. degree in Old Testament. In 1968 a second daughter, Missy, was born, and in 1970 Madhur completed the family. Anil returned to UBS as a faculty member in 1972 and was later appointed registrar. In 1978 the Board of Governors sent him for further study in administration. Though he was a Methodist, Friends in EFC—ER agreed to sponsor him for further study in Ohio State University. Solankis arrived in Columbus in September 1978. Westgate Friends Church in Columbus took them in as part of their church family and gave them a house.

Four years (not two as first agreed) were required for Anil to complete his Ph.D. in administration, but the house furnished by Westgate with the help of others, plus an assistant professorship in Ohio State and teaching opportunities in Lutheran Theological Seminary helped Anil carry his financial load the last two years.[39] On June 11, 1982, he graduated with honors and immediately returned as academic dean of UBS for the 1982-83 academic year.[40] He remains an ordained minister in his own denomination but represents Friends at UBS as well. Had Hesses not returned to India for the 1967-68 year, Friends might have missed this rich opportunity.

Hesses' Departure from India

That final year in India for the Hesses was significant to their family. In November 1967 as cool weather set in, Bob took warm clothes to the children in Woodstock school and spent a few days with them. Ron took him on a favorite hike. Bob wrote:

> He wanted me to see the sunrise on one of the snowcapped mountains, so we left Pennington at 4 a.m. and arrived at our destination before the sun did. It was most interesting to walk across the Himalayas with the stars above glittering so brightly. We even spotted a satellite skimming its way across the heavens. We did get some good pictures and Ron and I had a good visit when we stopped in a pine forest to build a fire and eat. We also rode a bus about twelve miles farther into the mountains. This was interesting from several points of view—there were steep rock cliffs on the left side of the unpaved road and nothing but eternity on the right side.[41]

Back in Yavatmal, Bob nearly always found guests at his table. That year Dr. and Mrs. Ralph Earle of the Nazarene Seminary in Kansas City; the Rt. Reverend Marcus Loane, Archbishop of Sydney; C. & M. A. Area Missions director, Rev. G. T. Manghum; and the Christian Institute for the Study of Religion and Society's professor, Dr. M. M. Thomas, were among the visitors who challenged both the Hess children and the students in the Seminary with spiritually and mentally exercising ideas. M. M. Thomas, uncle of Sakhi Athyal and chief arranger of her marriage to Saphir, though of a different theological stance, graciously gave everyone things to grapple with mentally.

One student was heard to say, "My head aches from thinking." Esther Hess's head and hands also ached at times in trying to cope with power and food shortages and yet keep her guests happy. Electricity was allowed on their campus only three days a week. Only the library had a small generator for the dark days.[42] Food rationing produced only tokens of sugar, rice, and brown, wormy flour. The only vegetables available through many months were potatoes and pumpkin. They had to send to Bombay to get any variety.[43] Yet, somehow, she managed to care for all the guests and serve seventy staff and board members at the Board of Governors' dinner at the end of the academic year.[44]

On their way to the hills in April for their last summer together in Pennington, both Bob and Esther Hess were ill. Fever plagued Bob, and Esther had since January been in and out of the hospital. As soon as they reached Landour, she went in again, this time for major surgery.[45] She quickly recovered, and they had a pleasant summer. Since Kathy was graduating on July 12 and Hesses planned to leave for U.S.A. directly from Landour on July 16, Bob returned to Yavatmal at the end of June to meet Ken Bauman coming in from U.S.A. Baumans, however, were delayed in coming because their children came down with mumps.

As Bob regretfully left Yavatmal without meeting them, he was indeed happy ninety miles away in Nagpur to see them coming in on June 30, the last possible moment for such a meeting. Information was shared quickly between plane and train, and with a handshake and a prayer, the torch of leadership in UBS passed back to Ken Bauman.[46]

Back to Yavatmal to meet his board as Hesses turned their faces to U.S.A., Ken Bauman reported: "The Seminary owes a deep debt of appreciation to Dr. and Mrs. Hess for their efficient and consecrated services. Dr. Hess will be remembered for his contributions to the Seminary of sound business procedures and academic policies."[47]

Ken Bauman, Principal of Union Biblical Seminary

Advances were made in the next three years on several fronts. The Association for Theological Education by Extension (TAFTEE) was formed under the guidance of the seminary.[48] Union Biblical Seminary Board of Governors agreed that their property should be registered with the Evangelical Trust Association of North India (ETANI). The English-medium primary school on UBS campus received government recognition.[49] The Research and Communications Institute (TRACI) was set up with these goals:

(1) A serious in-depth study in any field of the various theological disciplines.

(2) Creative theological thinking related to Asian thought and culture.

(3) The publication of the most needed evangelical literature in the form of books, articles, and monographs.

Staffed and housed by UBS and in the first instance directed by a UBS professor,[50] the TRACI students used the library facilities and sought guidance from UBS professors. This organization was funded by the Theological Assistance Program for Asia (TAP), Theological Education Fund, a gift from the Bible and Medical Missions Fellowship, and some funds from the Friends Mission.

Endowment, by then set at $500,000,[51] was being taken seriously by the Cooperating Home Boards. Friends voted to give its first $5,000 in 1970.[52] By 1974 they authorized another $20,000.[53] The Cooperating Home Boards of UBS agreed to seek matching funds from foundations for half the funds as they each took responsibility for the other half. The chairman and secretary along with Robert Hess, Everett Cattell, and Wilbert Shenk, Mennonite, were appointed as a committee of five to work out this plan.[54]

Saphir Athyal was on sabbatical leave in 1970-71. He taught in Asbury Seminary as his wife, Sakhi, completed her Master of Religious Education degree. It came as no surprise to anyone except Saphir that he had been requested to serve a three-year term beginning June 1972 as the first Indian principal of UBS. After prayerful consideration, he accepted, sensing the weight of responsibility and requesting prayer support of the Board of Governors.[55]

Two years earlier the UBS Board of Governors appointed I. Ben Wati as the first national chairman, and in 1970 his alma mater, Wheaton College, conferred on him an honorary Doctor of Divinity degree. Recognized throughout India as an outstanding leader in EFI, UBS, and the Church, he was chiefly recognized for the translation of the Ao Naga Bible.[56] That same year Anna Nixon was appointed to the Executive Committee of the Board of Governors[57] and requested to represent UBS on her furlough in 1971-72.[58] Malone College in 1972 and later Friends University in 1978 similarly honored her for the work done in CEEFI.

This recognition opened the way for Principal Athyal to request the Evangelical Friends Church — Eastern Region to loan Anna's services to UBS.[59] Need in the Friends Mission kept her in Chhatarpur for a year, but she joined the staff in 1973, teaching Christian education, English, psychology, and related subjects for the next seven years. On the death of Lexie Cameron, she was appointed as head of the Christian Education Department.[60]

Elmer R. Parsons, Free Methodist Area Missions secretary, commented about UBS at that time, "During its nearly 20-year history UBS in

Yeotmal [Yavatmal] has established itself as a leading theological seminary in the Orient."[61]

Saphir Athyal, First Indian Principal of Union Biblical Seminary

As soon as Dr. Saphir Athyal took charge as principal of UBS, there was a quickened pace. Anyone doubting the ability of Christian nationals to lead mission-founded institutions was left trailing in the dust as I. Ben Wati, the grandson of a former Northeast tribe headhunter, and Saphir Athyal, son of a preacher of the tradition who dated his Christianity all the way back to Jesus' disciple Thomas, joined hands to see theological education through UBS in India reach its highest peak.

Almost immediately Saphir requested a feasibility study. Endowment, it was agreed, had to stand first, but in long-range strategy, he suggested, the seminary should be relocated to a more cosmopolitan center.[62] Programs were projected for granting the Master of Theology degree in both Old and New Testament with Serampore affiliation in 1973, and a Master's degree course in missions in 1974.[63] By 1974 the Board voted unanimously to affiliate its Bachelor of Divinity degree courses with Serampore.[64]

Students were pleased, for Serampore now gave its colleges freedom in their own curriculum but set academic standards acceptable to all denominations. UBS students, sometimes accused of being long on prayer but short on academic ability, surprised the country by winning all the top academic awards in the first year they sat for Serampore examinations.

The influence of UBS was increasing as its graduates entered Christian service. The student body by 1976 had increased to 174 — 111 in the graduate section and 63 undergraduates. They represented thirty-nine denominations, seven countries, and all but two of the twenty-two states of India.[65] At EFI's Silver Jubilee Conference in Hyderabad January 5-9, 1976, one hundred of the 650 delegates were UBS alumni, faculty, or students.[66]

That same academic year the first student representation appeared on the Board of Governors and UBS Administrative Council. Two student-elected members with full voting rights began to change the viewpoint of the controlling powers.[67] An immediate change was a shift from the semester system to the quarter system.[68] Another was the recommendation to open an M.Th. in Pastoralia, Mission, and Christian Education affiliated with Serampore.[69]

At the first board meeting with the student representatives present, priorities for the seventies were outlined in this order: (1) A stable core faculty who are outstanding evangelical scholars; (2) financial stability;

(3) launching out on an extensive program to theologically train lay leadership of both urban and rural churches by a nonformal program; (4) the defense of the historic evangelical faith by warning the church of subtle, false teachings that prevail within Christendom; (5) and most important of all in every step, guarding against the danger of gradually cooling down in ardor and conviction.[70]

At this same meeting sincere consideration was given to developing a Hindi-Marathi B.Th. college, perhaps on the Yavatmal campus after UBS relocated to Pune. The idea grew and by the time Narendra John returned from completing his doctoral studies in the U.S.A., the Board shared his vision for such a development with great excitement.[71] By 1985, 40 students wre enrolled in this mission-bias Yavatmal College of Leadership Training, opened July 1984.

Another outstanding development was UBS's inauguration of the Center of Mission Studies on October 24, 1982. This was a first for India.[72] Perhaps the greatest achievement of these years was a well-planned training program, through the help of supporting missions and friends, to develop Indian faculty members for leading administration posts as well as teaching.

Relocation Plans

In line with findings on the feasibility study, by 1974 the Board of Governors moved forward on relocation.[73] The study clearly indicated Pune as the nearest-to-ideal location, but the distance of four hundred miles as compared to only ninety to Nagpur brought in all votes except one for Nagpur.[74] It took a year of further study, prayer, and negotiation to convince the Board of Governors that Pune was the right place.[75] A tremendous struggle then began as the missionary boards who had cooperatively brought into being this great institution saw it slipping out of the central area nearest their constituency.

To support the Pune move, both I. Ben Wati and Saphir Athyal flew to the U.S.A. from India to be present at the next meeting of the Cooperating Home Boards of the seminary in U.S.A. and Canada. Not only would there be better transportation, with air and bus service and ten trains a day between Pune and Bombay, but improved educational and medical services as well. Service opportunities in the forty-three established churches and evangelism among the 18,500,000 people in a reachable radius of Pune representing all major languages of India would enhance practical work experiences for the entire student body.

Pune offered a balanced training opportunity for both urban and village ministry. There were twenty colleges and large libraries, one containing up to 100,000 volumes, in which students could do research. The climate was mild and would give opportunity for the buildings to be used all the year. "The move to Pune is in every way a move that will strengthen the church in India," said Saphir.[76] Everett Cattell had earlier pointed out that one of the great challenges to the early founders had been that of providing leaders for the larger churches as well as for the supporting missions. "The small evangelical bodies sponsoring UBS should see the enormous contribution they are making to the total church in India," he wrote.[77]

At this time Free Methodist Charles Kirkpatrick resigned as chairman of the Cooperating Home Boards of UBS, Inc., but stayed on to cooperate. His successor was Wilbert Shenk. Twenty-four missions, churches, and groups sent representatives to the Board of Governors of UBS at that time.[78] A majority of them were from the Cooperating Home Boards of UBS in U.S.A. and Canada, and they agreed they would attempt raising $1,150,000 for relocation.[79] Heavy loads now rested on both shoulders, as by 1974 the UBS Board of Governors' request for endowment, to keep up with inflation, had gone up to $1,250,000.[80] To protect this endowment, UBS set up a separate Educational Endowment Trust registered with the government as a separate society on January 19, 1974.[81]

In 1975 relocation took priority over endowment, and the Cooperating Home Boards of UBS sought assistance from Russ Reid and Company in raising $1,000,000 for the project.[82]

While Bob Hess was in India for a visit in 1975, the Women's Missionary Fellowship of EFC—ER responded to a lesser but urgent need in UBS by providing $4,000 toward the purchase of a minibus. *Back to the Bible* matched their gift.[83]

As Bob rode the fifty-five miles from Wardha to Yavatmal with the man who would drive that minibus, he learned that UBS had been offered in Pune a 22-acre property by the Catholic Medical Mission Sisters for $100,000.[84] After thirty sites were considered, it is of interest that this one, among the first to be considered, was the one finally chosen.[85] The Friends Mission Board wanted a part in this move and pledged $25,000 over the next three years. They also committed themselves to continue the annual grant of $2,000 toward the operating budget for the next ten years.[86]

A most unexpected gift came through a pencilled note found in the drawer of Willard Pim, who died in 1978. He and his wife had sent more than $15,000 to India for Christian education from the sale of gladiolas and daffodils. She preceded him in death and he had retired. His probated will called for his estate to be divided between his three children and the Damascus Friends Church, but his daughter-in-law, Melissa Pim, found a note that changed everything.

At the time of his death, he had been in the process of willing his entire estate to Union Biblical Seminary. Melissa quickly consulted the three Pim children and also Damascus Friends Church about their wishes in light of this note. They all agreed to follow his dying wish and turned the entire estate of $23,056.69 to UBS relocation.[87]

The Missionary Board hoped to get the rest of the relocation money from the sale of Pennington and Pinepoint properties in Landour. However, land freezes in U. P. and registration problems had held up negotiations even when there were buyers. Anna Nixon had been working on the sale of Pinepoint since 1972 and Pennington since 1975. But by 1979 everything came together. The land freeze was lifted, registration problems ironed out, government evaluations approved, income-tax clearance granted, and permission of the Missionary Board given to deposit the whole amount in rupees in UBS relocation account.[88]

At last buyers appeared with pounds and dollars, which, according to the Reserve Bank of India, had to be negotiated and paid in rupees. When this was assured, the last hurdle — permission of the Reserve Bank — was received.[89] On June 19, 1979, Pinepoint sold for Rs. 40,000 ($5,000); on September 17, 1979, Pennington sold for Rs. 100,000 ($12,500).[90] After all expenses were deducted, UBS received Rs. 132,000 ($16,500).[91]

The money to buy Pennington arrived from U.S.A. on September 6, 1979 — the very day UBS was hoping that the permission to own the campus in Pune would come through. Already in August 1978 a groundbreaking ceremony had proclaimed their faith. Paul Miller, the director of relocation for UBS, was in Pune to negotiate the transfer, after overcoming many delays caused by strikes, change of officials, and even corruption.[92] People all over India were praying that there would be no further delays. After five years of negotiations, at 12:30 p.m. September 6, 1979, the agreement was signed. Twenty days later the deed for the new campus bought for Rs. 700,000 ($87,500) was registered in the name of UBS.[93]

Departure of Anna Nixon from India

The selling of the hill houses in Landour and seeing UBS moving forward was a challenge to Anna Nixon, who hoped to see the move to Pune before she retired from India. But all was not well. As early as 1974 she wrote to the Missionary Board:

> In spite of cyclic floundering in Yavatmal when often I was ready to give up, the principal kept the door open . . . . At Christmas in

Chhatarpur [1973] our missionaries [Dr. W. Ezra and Frances DeVol and Norma Freer] gave undergirding with further medical advice, spiritual understanding, and prayer. I left Chhatarpur January 6, 1974, and on the way [back to Yavatmal] read this promise from one of my course books: 'In returning and in rest shall you be saved. In quietness and trust shall be your strength.' (Isaiah 30:15) Aware of that promise, I completed the term . . . and am ready for the next.[94]

Three years later Anna wrote, "If I can continue to cope with the work, there is no place on the earth I would rather be to finish out my years with the Mission than right here at UBS."[95] But early in 1978 the "cyclic floundering" became so intense that on medical advice she left early for furlough. After receiving clearance from her doctor to return that fall, she wrote again:

I have 107 different students in the three classes I teach and we have a student body of over 200. We have 17 students in B.R.E., the largest class ever in B.D., and B.Th. is holding well. I have one class in each of these sections. I like that for it means that eventually I have every student in the seminary in at least one class.[96]

By the end of the 1979-80 term, however, this cyclic depression became more intense, and led to Anna's resignation. On accepting this, the UBS Board of Governors recorded:

She has brought to the Seminary her rich experience of an all-India organization, namely, The Evangelical Fellowship of India, and particularly her leadership in the Christian Education Department of EFI. Her extra-curricular activities especially in publicity will always be remembered with gratitude. We wish Dr. Anna Nixon the blessing of God as she leaves the Seminary at the end of the academic year in April, 1980. We would like her to represent the interests of the UBS when she is away in the USA.[97]

The Move of Union Biblical Seminary from Yavatmal to Pune

Back in Union Biblical Seminary the pace did not let up after the property was registered, but lack of steel and cement held up building plans for more than a year. By March 1981 the sum of about $1,000,000 was on hand from contributions.[98]

On December 31, 1981, the seminary received an import permit for cement. At the same time, A. R. Antulay, the Chief Minister of Maharashtra, who had been involved with allocating cement in the State, got into trouble and had to resign. The case against him still continues, but cement was immediately released and building at a rapid pace got underway.[99] By early 1983 hope was alive that the seminary would move to begin the 1983-84 term in Pune.

"God has done some marvellous works before our eyes," Principal Saphir Athyal reported. "The permission to sell and buy the property under the restrictions of the Urban Land Ceiling Act, getting the land for perhaps one percent of its value today, the Municipality putting up a water tank just above us and building a long access road to it which will be primarily our road, the major part of the finance raised coming from entirely unexpected sources, etc., are but a few to mention . . . . As we reach Pune, we have not finished the race, we have only just begun it."[100]

To beat the rains, the library was moved first while everything else was packed for shipping. The principal and academic dean held their breath while in Pune masons, carpenters, and plumbers worked overtime. Only half the campus was ready for occupancy.[101]

The new term was set to begin with inauguration day on June 30, 1983. Just before the students stepped onto the trains and buses for Pune, telegrams came from the principal instructing them to return to Yavatmal. As they entered their old campus, they found the library empty and faculty houses barren. However, a truck with books for the courses of first term returned from Pune where gas, water, electric, and sewer connections were yet to be made before students could be accommodated.

In Pune four hundred guests arrived on June 30, and the scheduled inaugural was changed into a thanksgiving and farewell service. S. Paul and Vesta Miller, having spent more than 40 years in India, were ready to retire. S. Paul Miller had served capably and faithfully as director of development and was ready to turn over to his successor, Archie McMillan. The principal spoke of Paul as a "modern Nehemiah."[102]

Inauguration day was postponed until October 10, 1983, when in spite of rubble, dust, noise, and heat — and the fact that gas connections still needed to be made — the 220 students arrived, attended the Inaugural, and immediately began classes. Food was cooked outside over open wood fires for three weeks, and faculty members had to share houses while some students slept in classrooms, waiting for dormitories to be completed. The atmosphere was one of challenge more than hardship, and Dr. Saphir Athyal kept the goal in focus by pointing out, "What really counts in the training for Christian ministry is growth in depth."[103] In line with this, a new Master of Arts in Religion degree course was opened as a specialized two-year training program in Mission and Evangelism.

At the UBS Association Board of Governors' Meeting in March, 1984, Dr. Saphir Athyal was again appointed for a three-year term as principal to guide the seminary into the new beginnings to which the Lord is leading it in the new cosmopolitan center in Pune.[104] Some years will yet be required to complete the nearly $3,000,000 campus, but meanwhile every year God is increasing through UBS the breadth and depth of ministry to the churches it serves in India and throughout the world.

CHAPTER
XXVIII | # Healing
in Nepal

> *"Then the angel showed me the river of the water of
> life . . . flowing from the throne of God and the
> Lamb . . . . On each side of the river stood the tree
> of life . . . . And the leaves of the tree are for the
> healing of the nations." Revelation 22:1, 2*

The Opening of the United Mission to Nepal

In October 1959, eight months after his first month in the United Mission
to Nepal, Dr. W. Ezra DeVol in Chhatarpur received a letter from Dr.
Edgar Miller of Shanta Bhawan Hospital, Kathmandu. Dr. Miller, a
cardiologist, who with his wife, Dr. Elizabeth Miller, a pediatrician, after
completing a thriving practice in the U.S.A., had joined the Flemings as
they returned from their furlough. Dr. Miller wrote:

> We are in trouble . . . at least twenty people [are] on vacation
> now . . . . Again we are asking for your help in our surgical problems.
> We lost two cases of peritonitis last week . . . . Right now we have an
> acute gall bladder, an intestinal obstruction, a goiter . . . and these all
> need surgical help . . . . We would love to have you and Frances come
> up again. If not . . . perhaps you could send one of them [Dr.
> Mategaonker or Dr. Shrisunder] . . . . [We have] just three doctors
> and none of us are surgeons. It is hard for us to watch them die . . . .
> We are looking forward to the time when someone will come to be with
> us and to stay with us. We are hoping and praying that will be you.[1]

Nepal, so recently opened to the Gospel, is a beautiful country of about
56,000 square miles sandwiched like a hot dog between the Tibetan
plateaus and fertile Indian plains. Kathmandu, the capital, city of
wooden temples and many gods, is nestled in a 4,500-foot-high valley surrounded by Himalayas' snowcapped peaks.

Medical needs there in 1959 were five times greater than in India. In
the whole country there were only 600 hospital beds and 50 doctors for a
population of 8,500,000.[2]

The chief religion is Hindu-Buddhist. Great changes have come since the Ranas were overthrown in 1951. His Highness King Tribhuvan Bir Bikram Shah (1911-1955), followed by his son, King Mahendra Bir Bikram Shah (1920-72), threw the doors open to the outside world. Nepal became a member of the United Nations in 1955 and the same year launched a five-year plan to improve its transportation, agriculture, industry, and education.[3]

Majestically beautiful was the way God "on the wings of a bird" opened the heart of Nepal to the Gospel when His time was ripe. Dr. Robert Fleming, the first ornithologist to enter Western Nepal to find rare specimens, had become so burdened for the needs of the people that on returning he told his doctor wife, Bethel, about it.[4] She and her children went with him the next trip, as did also Dr. Carl and Betty Friedericks and their children (1951-52). While Betty cared for the children and Bob Sr. and Bob Jr. studied birds, Drs. Bethel and Carl conducted clinics in Tansen.[5]

Before leaving to return to India, they were requested by town leaders to return and open a hospital in Tansen. Other requests also came, and after their return, Flemings and Friederickses met to pray and consider the matter. They felt God, not just the people, was calling them. So Bob Fleming wrote a letter to the King in February 1952, offering to do what the people requested.[6] At the same time they wrote their missionary boards: Flemings, the Methodists; Friederickses, the American Presbyterians.[7]

Another bird trip and one year later, February 13, 1953, they wrote another letter to the King, including the offer also to open clinics in Kathmandu Valley. Eventually, His Majesty replied through proper channels on May 18, 1953, granting permission under these four restrictions: that the missions bear all expense, that Nepalese be employed, that in five years their establishments become Nepali Government property, and that medicines and treatments be free.[8] The missionaries felt "the hour had come."[9]

Bob and Bethel Fleming were the first to go in, transferred from Woodstock School to Kathmandu in October 1953 by the Methodist Church of Southern Asia. Dr. Bethel Fleming opened five clinics and began work immediately.[10]

In Nagpur March 4-5, 1954, the administrative structure of the United Mission to Nepal (UMN) was set up and missions were sent invitations to join.[11] Six months later the missions who signed up sent representatives to Delhi to a second meeting, September 22-23, 1954. Eight missions were approved as charter member bodies.[12] By 1979 there had been forty member bodies,[13] but eight had withdrawn, probably for financial reasons.

Dr. Carl and Betty Friedericks moved into Nepal that same year, to open work in Tansen in Eastern Nepal. Other missions also moved in on the wave of Nepal's new open door. In 1951 the Nepal Evangelistic Band, working on the border since 1940, moved into Pokhra and opened a hospital made of aluminum, called the Shining Hospital. Catholics opened schools in 1951, and Seventh-Day Adventists arrived in 1957.[14]

However, Nepal's new constitution, announced on February 12, 1959, proclaimed religious freedom but allowed no conversions. Two Christians were put in jail that year for no other offense than seeking to lead a soul to Christ.[15] On their first night in prison, they led three other prisoners to Christ, and the next day, seven more.[16]

The Need for Healing in Nepal

On their first month to Nepal in February 1959, DeVols saw the tremendous need of the land, which pulled them with cords of compassion to that country. The people had very little training in the meaning of sanitation and health. At the end of Kathmandu Valley, for example, there was a town called Bhatgaon. In that ancient Asian city with century-old buildings lived some 40,000 people — sometimes some hundred in one house. Livestock stayed in the same shelter at night. Inside the inner courts were open wells. Their sewers emptied into the streets. Tuberculosis was rampant.

Temples and numberless gods drew countless pilgrims from Tibet and the higher reaches of Nepal. Bodhnath, built on a small hill, had the all-seeing eyes of Buddha looking out from the four sides as below all around the temple base were hundreds of prayer wheels kept spinning as the pilgrims walked around it.[17] Dr. Ezra DeVol wrote:

> The need is tremendous. We operate three days a week — Monday, Wednesday, Friday . . . . Frances is helping me in the operating room and Joe and Phil have been helping out where they can — painting the X-ray room, etc. — and Joe has been doing some typing for the hospital office.[18]
>
> . . . . Shanta Bhawan [Hospital] has 65 beds — constantly filled to capacity plus places on the floor, in the halls and kept on the emergency table for want of space . . . . This has been one of the happiest months of our lives.[19]

That they would be welcomed back after that first trip was made amply clear by the UMN staff through a letter signed by Dr. Bethel H. Fleming, Executive Director of Shanta Bhawan Hospital, and forty-two others:

To Dr. and Mrs. DeVol, Joe and Phillip:

Because we don't know exactly how to say "Thank-you," and because we want you to know how grateful we are to you
for all you have done for us
for your willing spirit in working with all of us,
for your fellowship in the things of God,
for the service, rendered in love, to so many patients,
for the reality of your witness among us,
for your sense of humor,
and because, along with this, we want to express our desire and hope that the Lord may find it in His will to lead you back again into our fellowship, we have signed our names in token of these things.

"NOW MAY THE LORD OF PEACE PERSONALLY GIVE YOU HIS PEACE AT ALL TIMES AND IN ALL WAYS. THE LORD BE WITH YOU ALL." II Thessalonians 3:16.[20]

DeVols Called to Nepal

This new challenge in Nepal over against the hard pull in Bundelkhand created tremendous tension for the DeVols, who still felt keenly the responsibility of a Church needing to be more firmly rooted and the Chhatarpur hospital's desperate need for his professional skill.[21] By May 9, 1961, UMN Board Chairman E. E. Oliver finally gathered the courage to request the DeVols to come full time. "We believe that you have the gifts of leadership as well as professional ability, and that you would be a great asset to our work here," he wrote.[22] Dr. Mategaonker's willingness to carry the Christian Hospital in Chhatarpur under Mission supervision released them to accept.[23]

While on furlough, Dr. W. Ezra DeVol took courses in medical administration at the University of Pittsburgh in preparation for his new appointment as director of Shanta Bhawan Hospital, following Dr. Bethel Fleming.[24]

Restrictions Against Conversion

On the DeVols' return to India, the American Friends Mission became the twenty-third member of the UMN.[25] They released the DeVols with the request that UMN permit them to visit Chhatarpur twice each year for the next three years. Bob Hess, at that time serving as general superintendent of the American Friends Mission, was appointed as the Friends' representative of UMN.[26]

No sooner had the DeVols arrived than a new law went into effect on August 17, 1963, specifying that no person should propagate Christianity or convert any adherent of the Hindu religion into any other faith, under penalty of imprisonment for three years for an attempt to convert, and six years for conversion. If such a case were brought against a foreign citizen, he would also be expelled from the country. Should a person attempt to convert himself, he would be fined Rs. 100. If he did not return to Hinduism, he would be imprisoned for a year.[27]

Respecting the law of the land but being committed to the One who said, "And as ye go, preach," the DeVols made their witnessing a matter of constant prayer. They made regular visits to Prem Pradhan, a Christian serving his six-year jail sentence for converting. In 1964 the wife of the officer who jailed Prem Pradhan was converted, and her family started reading the Bible.[28] Though the law was very strict, people continued to become Christian.

Only those reported were brought to trial. Up to the end of 1964, Prem Pradhan and only four other cases had been reported.[29] After four and a half years, Prem Pradhan's release was announced on the King's birthday, June 9, 1965, and he joined his wife and children in a happy reunion two days later.[30] "The Church is growing and is truly indigenous," Frances wrote.[31] Soon after that, the Nepali Christian Fellowship sponsored a Christian camp with seventy-five people present. Their purpose was to encourage short-term Bible schools, and they were successful in holding several. Though UMN as a mission did not sponsor these efforts, as individual members of the congregation, they assisted.[32]

Directing the United Mission Medical Center

As director of United Mission Medical Center, Dr. Ezra was interested in clearing lines of responsibility, raising fees to help cover a greater percentage of the running expenses, organizing the staff for steady duty, and building a free ward for the poor.[33] He continued with days for operations as well, while tightening security, encouraging those in charge of improving electrical equipment and transportation, and gaining His Majesty's Government's recognition of the UMN school of nursing.[34]

There were, by that time, eighty missionaries in the United Mission to Nepal from twenty denominations and ten separate missions. The medical work had expanded to include two hospitals and clinics in nine centers, a literature work, a thriving educational program, and agricultural development.[35] Dr. Ezra wrote, "There are a lot of battles but we know that our Lord is bigger than all our problems put together."[36]

Christmas offered a rich opportunity for Christian witness, as related by Dr. Ezra:

> The Hindus in India and Nepal have many holidays and they celebrate them with considerable expense and gusto. So when the staff at the United Mission Medical Center asked me, "How are we going to

A CENTURY OF PLANTING

celebrate Christmas?" I replied that we would celebrate Christmas in every way possible for at least ten days.

The staff took great delight in putting up pictures, copying texts relating to Christmas on posters and displaying them on the walls of the wards, hallways, and in the foyers. We transcribed carols on tape and played them at intervals for the ten-day period. For two nights the staff and members of the little Nepali Church presented a drama of the manger scene, acting out the events of the holy season while the pastor read from the Bible the words of the participants.

The space available did not allow for larger animals, but we did have some sheep and lambs with the shepherds.

On Christmas Eve, the staff visited every ward with a candle-light procession. We had so many in the group that they had difficulty finding room around the walls and between the beds. Carols were sung with great joy. A message from the Word was read, and the short service was concluded with prayer. The patients and their relatives really seemed to appreciate it.

We glorified the coming of Christ into the world as fully as we knew how with the full knowledge that we might be called to account for conducting a religious service with the patients — but the only reaction that came to our ears was that of approval. Some of the patients' relatives stood with us and sang the Christmas songs which were unfamiliar to them, but which nevertheless seemed to strike a joyous chord! I remember that the gentleman who stood and shared the hymn book with me was of the royal family. After all, the Wisemen did come from the East![37]

During the next year, the pace did not slacken. The DeVols faithfully spent two months in Chhatarpur twice a year, assisting in surgery with Dr. Mategaonker. In Nepal UMN decided a new hospital should be built to replace the old palace, Shanta Bhawan. Dr. Ezra went to Lahore to see a hospital built there according to the latest architectural planning. He and the board then presented their plan for a 250-bed hospital to His Majesty's Government, but it took a year to get permission to build.[38] Meanwhile, Surendra Bhawan, a five-minute walk from the Shanta Bhawan hospital, was in use for maternity cases and children. Building did not go forward immediately, but plans were laid for increasing Shanta Bhawan to a 250-bed capacity.[39] The new hospital was destined not to come into being until 1982.

Frances served as hostess and conciliator. By August 7, 1965, she had entertained 494 guests, including Indians, Nepalese, and Europeans all at once. Norma Freer, Anna Nixon, Jane McNally, Joe and Mae Mosher, Cliff and Betty Robinson, Ann and Milton Lipes, Clyde Taylor, Archbishop Marcus Loane, and others were among those who visited them.[40] Frances also assisted in surgery each Thursday, mostly with orthopedic and urological cases. She was impressed by two boys coming for operations — one so knock-kneed he could not walk, and the other so bowed he could barely walk. Both were put in casts and came out with straight legs.[41]

Northwest Yearly Meeting cooperated with UMN, first of all, by contributing $1,500 to DeVols' salary and backing the mission with wholehearted interest and prayer support.[42] On June 30, 1965, Jamie Sandoz of·Oregon arrived to do his alternate service in the UMN Medical Center as a medical technologist in charge of Shanta Bhawan's clinical laboratory. By September, Jamie had a Mennonite companion, Jerry Nietzsake, of Lincoln, Nebraska.[43]

Cataracts and a Time of Stress

As the third year of the DeVol's term in Nepal neared the end, Dr. Ezra was prepared to face surgery on his eyes. Three times during his previous furlough he had found it necessary to change his glasses because of the development of cataracts. So on October 9, 1965, in Ludhiana, under the care of Dr. Franken of Holland, he had his first operation on his right eye.[44] By the time DeVols came to Chhatarpur the end of that year, it was evident that the condition of the left eye was steadily deteriorating.

Eye difficulties were not the only troubles the DeVols faced that year. There was opposition to some of the financial policies Dr. Ezra, with the backing of the Board, felt essential to promote. He was successful in bringing the percentage of self-support from 39 percent to 68 percent.[45] Other problems of a similar nature began to cluster about that one, and there was some striking of steel on steel as policies were hammered out. At the same time, the missionaries in Chhatarpur, feeling they had been generous long enough, began to clamor for the DeVols to return so that Dr. Mategaonker could get a postgraduate degree in surgery while Dr. DeVol was still able to relieve him.[46] DeVols, also, began to sense that their work in Chhatarpur was still incomplete.[47]

Before returning to Kathmandu from Chhatarpur on January 17, 1966, Dr. Ezra was able to get his new contact lens for the right eye. The DeVols left Chhatarpur with happy hearts, not only for the improved sight in that eye but also because the hospital work in Chhatarpur under Dr. Mategaonker had not diminished during their absence of the past two and a half years, but had steadily increased.[48]

Ministry to Russians in Kathmandu

By the time the DeVols reached Kathmandu, the Indians in the city were making plans for the celebration of India's Republic Day on January 26 at the expansive Indian Embassy grounds. DeVols were invited and, along with other people from all the foreign communities, attended the gala occasion. Across the crowd Dr. Ezra noticed a former Russian patient surreptitiously glancing his direction. He recalled the first time he saw the Russian and some of his colleagues in the Russian Embassy. Since they had only paramedics and no doctors in Kathmandu, they often came to the Shanta Bhawan hospital for treatment.

It occurred to Dr. Ezra that he could silently witness to these Russians as they came into his office by placing on open copy of the Bible in their language on the corner of his desk. The first Russian who came in to see him after that was drawn to the book like a magnet. "You have a Russian book here," he said as he picked it up and examined it. After a few moments he asked, "May I take it with me?" Of course he could! That same man was now edging his way through the crowd toward Dr. Ezra at the Indian Embassy. He kept looking behind, as if to make sure no one was following him. When he got close enough to speak, he said softly to Dr. Ezra, "There are several of us at the Embassy who are reading your book."

Your book! Dr. Ezra thought about that. Yes, it was his book — to share with *all* people. So he placed Bibles at the bedside in the private rooms used by Russian patients. These, too, were taken home.[49]

DeVols' Departure from Nepal

While the DeVols were still balancing their future service in Kathmandu against Chhatarpur, Dr. Ezra, on March 6, 1966, suddenly realized he had a retinal detachment in his right eye. As soon as the cable reached the Mission Board office, arrangements were started for his hospitalization. He and Frances flew to the U.S.A., where he entered Cleveland Clinic and on March 18 underwent surgery repair with scleral buckle.[50] The laser beam could not be used, for by the time he reached Cleveland, his condition had deteriorated to the point that there was danger he might not see again. The Church was praying, and God touched the hands of the surgeon. When the bandages were removed, Dr. Ezra could see. He left the hospital on April 1, 1966.[51]

After his second cataract operation on the left eye July 12, 1966, sight improved and the DeVols returned to India, arriving in New Delhi March 10, 1967. Dr. Ezra was appointed as general superintendent of the Mission and of the Christian Hospital, and Frances as nursing superintendent.[52] He continued to represent the Friends Mission on the UMN Board until 1971. At that time, due to a marked increase in the membership fee, the Mission Council referred the matter to the Mission Board in the U.S.A., and they felt they could no longer remain a financial partner in UMN.[53]

The work in Nepal, however, did not end there. A 135-bed hospital envisioned during DeVols' term came into being in 1982. It functions as a general hospital, providing service for obstetrics, gynecology, general surgery, medicine, and pediatrics. It has a large outpatient department open five days a week, and a staff of 250. His Majesty's Government and the United Mission to Nepal shared the cost of building.[54]

In spite of restrictions, the Church has continued to grow. In 1979 Ramesh Khatry, a Nepali B.D. graduate of Union Biblical Seminary, Yavatmal, returned to Nepal and built the first Bible school, which was opened May 14, 1981, with eleven students. He arranged for two more couples to go to UBS with a view to their returning to teach in the Nepali Bible Institute. On December 16, 1982, there were four graduates of N.B.I.

Then on January 17, 1983, the government closed the Bible school building and put fifteen people in prison for converting or being converted. The nameless Bible school still continues, and the Church in Nepal has increased five times in four years. There are now more than 15,000 Christians and some 250 church groups meeting all over Nepal. Each of these groups has its own outreach program and they are planning soon to send out from their churches the first Nepali missionary. The love of Christ, channeled through the United Mission to Nepal, is broadening. Through Dr. Ezra and Frances DeVol, the American Friends Mission in India also had a small but vital part in imparting life there for the healing of a nation.

CHAPTER
XXIX

Keeping Watch
Through the Night

"I have posted watchmen on your walls. [O Bundelkhand:] they will never be silent day or night. You who call on the LORD, give yourselves no rest, and give him no rest till he establishes [Bundelkhand] and makes her the praise of the earth." Isaiah 62:6, 7

Most people in Bundelkhand live in small villages surrounded by their farms. As harvest time approaches, the men build shelters on stilts in the midst of their fields and stay there all night, keeping watch over their crops. If possible, two men stay together, and one watches while the other sleeps. A band of wandering cows can devastate a field in a matter of minutes, and sometimes both men are awake, using their slingshots and yelling wildly to chase them away.

The Role of the Hospital in Keeping Watch

As the new church-centered policy went into effect in Bundelkhand, the Mission felt they should continue to man the area with the hospital, supporting and protecting the spiritual crop that had taken root in Bundelkhand against the wiles of the devil. Amazing grace was bestowed on the hospital staff in the 1960s as they labored through the transition from a mission-centered program. With DeVols assigned to Nepal, Norma Freer, from 1962 to 1965, was the only American Friends missionary stationed in Chhatarpur. In the absence of the hospital superintendent, she assumed that role, though DeVols came regularly from Nepal and kept the avenues of correspondence open.

Bob Hess, the mission superintendent, also came four hundred miles from Yavatmal when needed. Anna Nixon dropped down from Jhansi occasionally to audit or deal with problems in education. Norma Freer, however, had to make the daily decisions and interpret the new policy to the people. The care of the elderly and the orphans, the keeping of mission accounts, the discipline in the nurses' home, and the responsibility of troubleshooting and oiling the administrative operations rested with the daily, wise decisions of this lone missionary. Mission Council stepped in to deal with larger issues, such as the transfer of remaining mission property to ETANI Trust,[1] yearly budgets, furloughs, and review of each missionary's work.

The Mission Board kept in close touch, and each individual missionary in India was made aware of their caring through hundreds of cards and parcels regularly received from the missionary societies.[2] So no missionary in India, not even Norma Freer, felt alone. During such crises, however, as the China-India War in 1963 and the Pakistan-India War in 1965, not only the Mission Board but the American Government drew near with guidance and directives to all American citizens in India, preparing them for any emergency.

As the missionaries and the church leaders in India struggled to put into practice the new policies, the Mission Board in U.S.A. also sought to clarify their goal in missions. In 1963 they restated their aim — to be carried out through the ministry of preaching, teaching, and healing:

> The supreme and controlling aim of Foreign Missions is to make the Lord Jesus Christ known to all men as their divine Savior, to persuade them to become His disciples, and to gather those disciples into the Christian churches which shall be, under God, self-propagating, self-supporting, and self-governing; to cooperate as long as necessary with these churches in the evangelization of their respective countries.[3]

"To cooperate as long as necessary" was the statement requiring judgment needed day by day. Over a period of many decades the Church had learned patterns of dependence and the Mission habits of paternalism. Years would pass before all the necessary changes in action and attitude could catch up with the printed and ratified minutes.

Hospital employees were all subject to the Mission. Norma Freer was the business manager, assisted by Komal Das Lall. Dr. Mategaonker was the medical superintendent. When there was no nursing superintendent, he also supervised that department. Constantly on the alert for more workers, both Norma and Dr. Mategaonker were relieved by the loan of Betty Geissler of the Woman's Union Missionary Society in Jhansi. Betty came for four months, beginning January 7, 1963. She served as nursing superintendent and lived with Norma, fortunately in time to take over while Norma was down six weeks with hepatitis.[4]

But on August 13, 1963, no missionary was with Norma when she received word that her mother had died. As soon as Anna heard of it, she immediately boarded a bus in Jhansi and went to Chhatarpur for a day.[5] Norma's many Indian friends, however, drew near and comforted her deeply at this time.

The Mission Board was working hard to find a missionary nurse in the U.S.A. to join forces in Bundelkhand. Kathryn Thompson volunteered her services and arrived in Chhatarpur on March 22, 1964. She entered the missionary language school in April to prepare for her new assignment. Kathy was a member of a solid Quaker family in the Willoughby Hills Friends Church, a church known for its missionary vision. After completing her nurses' training, she worked as nurse in Malone College.[6]

While in language school, she became ill and was not able to get her luggage in Bombay. Norma went to get it, only to discover that duty charges were listed as $2,000 or more due to new laws and requirements not previously known to the missionaries. Rather than pay that huge amount, Norma took a train to see Hesses in Yavatmal, a plane to Delhi to argue with officials, and another train and bus to Landour to get Kathy's signature on certain necessary documents, and then by bus, train and plane, back to Bombay. In spite of her cost of travel, she saved $1,620.[7]

Surgery did not correct Kathy's problem, and Anna accompanied her to Ludhiana, and finally to Lucknow for special treatment. Dr. and Mrs. James Stringham had recently come to Nur Manzil Hospital in Lucknow, and they took Kathy into their home and into their hearts. By the time their furlough was due in 1965, she was serving as staff nurse and acting head nurse in Nur Manzil.[8] The Methodist Board requested Friends to allow her to continue in Lucknow and serve in Nur Manzil for a period of two years as nursing superintendent and hostess.[9] She was permitted to continue her language study in order to be ready to return to Chhatarpur in 1967 for the completion of her term.[10]

In 1965, because the government ruled that nurses had to have some training in a general hospital, the WUMS Mission arranged for one year of their training to be conducted in Chhatarpur. A supervising missionary nurse moved in with Norma while fourteen students and a matron occupied the "first bungalow," the former Cattell home. Their coming gave incentive to the Mission to wire that bungalow with electricity.[11] This provided essential nursing help in Chhatarpur and led eventually to the two missions entering a cooperative venture in nurses' education. They drafted articles of incorporation and the WUMS Mission built a student nurses' center near the hospital in Chhatarpur under the supervision of Komal Das Lall.[12]

Dr. Mategaonker carried on for the most part as the only doctor. This was by no means easy with the rush of patients, the X-ray in need of repair — and when repaired, no film available.[13] There was also harassment of petty officials charging him with no longer running a charitable institution, thus forcing him to pay high taxes on denatured alcohol. Still he kept on and was not afraid of accepting difficult cases whom other local doctors refused to touch.

The public came to trust him as they witnessed his skill and compassion, and they filled the hospital.[14] The need of more ward space was evident to all, and permission to add a twenty-bed ward to Williams' Ward, bringing capacity to 75, was approved. The new ward was opened March 1, 1965, but it soon became inadequate for the average 85 daily census. OXFAM gave a grant of $6,000 for building a relative shelter, a pediatric ward, and a water tank.[15]

Dr. Mategaonker also wanted a hospital chaplain. Gabriel Massey, a UBS graduate, pharmacist, and anesthetist seemed to fit that need. He had married Suzanna, a nurse, in October, 1963, and both were working in the hospital. He was appointed as chaplain in 1965.[16] In his usual competent and orderly way, Gabriel requested a room in which to develop a reading room. He kept it open three hours daily and used it as his office, from which he supervised the work of the lady evangelists who ministered in the hospital and followed patients to their homes for ministry in their communities. He visited the male patients and conducted prayers for non-Christian employees each day. On Saturday evenings he held an open meeting for all patients and their relatives. More than a hundred people regularly attended.

Once a week Gabriel conducted health lessons and sold books among them — 23 Bibles, 26 New Testaments, and 180 Gospels the first year. He distributed Bibles to graduates and signed people up for Bible correspondence courses. Soon he had several people deeply interested in Christ who came to him on a regular basis for Christian teaching.[17] After visits from Eugene and Jean Coffin and later Louis and Betty Coffin, sons, and their wives, of Merrill and Anna Coffin, who had served in India, a gift from the Coffin Memorial Funds came to increase Gabriel's efficiency. A sound system, with speakers in each ward, was installed so that Gabriel could play gospel music and give short devotionals; the medical staff also found the system extremely helpful in getting messages through to doctors on rounds.[18]

Activities continued to increase in reaching the patients with the Gospel, but there was only one doctor to treat them. Dr. Mategaonker's annual report showed he had performed 406 operations. The two months a year Dr. DeVol came from Nepal, the two doctors would operate together for five or six days a week, performing as many as 84 operations — 51 major — in a month.[19] Dr. Mategaonker appreciated Dr. DeVol's cutting short his vacation to come to Chhatarpur for the casarean delivery of the Mategaonker's baby daughter, born May 7, 1964.[20]

The necessity of having a second doctor in Chhatarpur was acknowledged by all, but the problem of finding one who would stay continually dogged their steps. An older lady doctor came first and stayed for nine months.[21] Two young single doctors with good recommendations, just out of medical school, arrived next. Each stayed only three months. Then came an older man with questionable recommendations. He stayed eleven months. A year went by before they got another young man, Dr. Yohan, with keen ability. Dr. Mategaonker was yearning to go for some further training in surgery and had been accepted for January 1, 1967. He hoped Dr. Yohan would be the one to hold the hospital together and assist Dr. DeVol on his return, but the army, with greater pay, stole him away.[22]

The Return of the Colemans to Bundelkhand

The Mission Board, facing these difficulties, suggested that perhaps the time had come to close the hospital. Norma was astounded. She thought of the patients crowding into the dispensary and hospital and the growing enthusiasm in hospital evangelism. "The news of your letter concerning closing up here came to me on Christmas day . . . " she answered. "It surely put a shadow over my day."[23]

The Mission Council, however — Hesses, Kathy, Norma, and Anna — suggested a better plan. They requested the Board to return Colemans for a five-year term. Colemans arrived August 5, 1965, a month after Norma left for furlough. Because the visa process was delayed, Carol Jean had to come alone ahead of them to enroll in Woodstock School. Esther Hess in Landour somehow managed both mission accounts and emergency surgery between Norma's departure and Milton's arrival and still was able to turn balanced books over to Milton.[24]

Colemans took over all of Norma's work. Milton acted as treasurer, hospital business manager, and general supervisor. Rebecca assisted in medical orders, paying bills, supervising the nurses' home, and stepped back in place as mother of the growing "Coleman" orphan family. She arranged for the future education and training of the young people, and as the custom was, chose suitable marriage partners for those who were ready. She nurtured one orphan boy through severe illness until he died. She gave loving support to two other handicapped ones. Carol Jean — as did Phillip DeVol also — left them on graduating from Woodstock in July 1966. Both found their way to U.S.A. to attend Malone College.[25]

The heart of the ministry of the Colemans in India was through the use of their pastoral gifts. Rebecca worked with the children and young people. She established a group for Pioneer Girls and encouraged Gabriel Massey in developing Junior C.E. She supported the Sunday schools for both Christians and non-Christians and guided the women in retreats and activities. She learned that with the disowning of Nowgong, the primary school there had been closed. When Nowgong meeting was reestablished, the school remained closed because the Church felt it did not have funds to keep it open.[26]

In 1963 Chunni Lalls moved from Ghuara to Amarmau, due to lack of support when the Church took over; so that school closed, too. Rebecca knew that the way to children's hearts now lay through the churches and the Chhatarpur primary school. She helped distribute UNICEF milk and clothing to the needy children.[27]

Milton often preached as invited, and sometimes prodded the reluctant Church into becoming more independent. The three-year plan had come to an end in 1964. The Mission refused to initiate another plan, and the Church, seemingly too timid to rise to its privileges, failed to take the initiative to make a new plan. The only promise the Mission made was to give a matching grant up to $1,500 for all the Church would give. This became established practice as time went on.[28] The Christian leaders, lacking vision, cut scholarships and evangelism. Missionaries and Stuti Prakash wept, but many of the leaders answered, "We are not able to meet the standard as before."

Some were not that pessimistic. Dr. Mategaonker jumped to his feet in the meeting and said, "I will not stop any medical person from going to camp at any time to help in evangelism." He insisted evangelism was the most important job being done.[29] Even so, when Milton returned to India he found that evangelism, without paid workers, was moving at a slow pace. Anti-Christian forces working against conversions did not help.

The death of strong, fair-minded Prime Minister Jawaharlal Nehru in May 1964 shook the country. Yet surprisingly, conversions continued. Khub Chand was back with a vital testimony, and he, his son-in-law, and Prem Das of Dhamora were regularly in church. Nathu and Raja Bai (his niece) and family in Chhatarpur came out openly for Christ. Out in Ghuara a new couple came out and adopted Christian names: Bishwas (Faith) and Premkumari (Princess of love) and little daughter and mother Nonni Bai (good woman).[30]

The most hopeful place of response Milton found was among the youth. Attending the rally he had started fifteen years earlier, he found one hundred eager young people thinking hard as Victor Mangalwadi of the Bible Society led them in discussing "Today's Youth Problems and Their Christian Solutions."[31] Another avenue in which he felt the Church could be helped was through a different approach to the villages. He set about developing evangelism with literature work under the name of "Bibles for Bundelkhand."[32] Milton missed Vijay Prakash, who had moved away. Vijay, a UBS graduate, after his wife's death, had, in the early sixties, made his base in Chhatarpur. His mother took care of his little son, Vineesh.

Vijay did evangelism and opened a Friends Book Room near the Maharajah's College, where he could engage college professors and students in meaningful conversation about the Gospel of Christ. He arranged a pleasant reading center and library and also carried books for sale. With assistance, he spread this ministry to religious fairs in the area and in his first year sold seven times more literature than had ever been sold previously.[33] One of the books Vijay found useful was *The Spirit of Holiness* by Everett L. Cattell.[34] It was later beautifully translated into Hindi by Victor Mangalwadi.

During the camping season, Vijay always arranged to get to the villages. His warm friendliness drew villagers, but success in winning them to Christ did not exceed the evangelists who had preceded him, and he was often discouraged. Missionaries living in Rewa asked Vijay to come take over their station while they went to U.S.A. for a year's furlough. So on May 15, 1964, Vijay married Prema, a nurse in the Christian hospital, and with his little son, Vineesh, and his new bride, he moved to Rewa. The Friends Mission closed down the book room and decided to open another near the hospital.[35] When the missionaries returned to Rewa, *Jiwan Prakash* (Light of Life) Correspondence School in Jhansi begged Vijay to join them, and the Railway Hospital in Jhansi employed nurse Prema and gave living quarters.

Since Jhansi was only 80 miles from Chhatarpur, Vijay found it convenient to join Milton occasionally in literature campaigns. There, trips took them and volunteer teams as far as sixty-one miles into the jungles, where they sold Gospels, distributed tracts, and signed up people for the Bible correspondence courses. A peak day for sales took place when Gabriel Massey with thirty-two of his intermediate C.E. members signed up to go out after school. In two distribution workshops they sold 1,800 Gospels.[36]

After five years in U.S.A., Milton found the mechanical equipment in the Mission antiquated: a fourteen-year-old Jeep, a fifteen-year-old Dodge, and the hospital ambulance about to fall apart. He requested and eventually got a new jeep and a jeepster with a four-wheel drive.[37]

After Hesses left in mid-1966 for furlough, Milton also became acting mission superintendent. Norma Freer returned from furlough in late October and relieved the Colemans of some of their work.[38] They then turned more attention to the Church.

When Mangal Singh, compounder in Bijawar, died on December 15, 1965, the Church lost one of the few who really understood and practiced tithing.[39] The Church seemed to carry on, somewhat bewildered and lost without its Mission identity, maintaining the status quo. It did, however, take initiative under the leadership of Dr. Mategaonker to revise its discipline.[40]

Three Church Leaders Visit America

In 1966 the Church leaders received an invitation directly from the secretary for the Fourth World Conference of Friends, meeting in Greensboro, North Carolina, July 24-August 3, 1967. Included was a promise of $1,500 for their chosen delegate to that conference.[41] Politics were not absent from the voting process, but nominations showed the wisdom of the Church: Stuti Prakash, Chhatarpur pastor and senior Church leader; Komal Das Lall, the general superintendent; and Gabriel Massey, theologically trained in UBS, young, and most fluent in English, were nominated; and Gabriel was chosen.

Many, however, were not entirely happy about the decision, and the missionaries felt the answer was to send all three of the nominees to the U.S.A. to attend the conference and remain for some deputation work up to two months.[42] The Friends World Committee supplied an additional $1,000 and the FFMS gave the rest.

The conference was attended by 900 delegates from 27 countries. Everett Cattell presented a paper, and for the first time the press truly recognized the position of Evangelical Friends.[43] To the three men who went to U.S.A., the greatest reward seemed to be seeing former missionaries, or the graves of those missionaries, who had worked in their midst. For Stuti Prakash the highlight was a trip to Newberg, Oregon, to see Carrie Wood, Merrill and Anna Coffin, and Ethol George, who had supported him in Bible School and prayed for his ministry since it began.[44] People in the U.S.A. were refreshed by their ministry. ". . . the best proof that missions surely paid off," said Anna Cobbs. "We'll never forget them."

Back in Chhatarpur, the three men all started contributing more to the Church. Their awakened sense of responsibility caused them to stir the Church in giving neglected Christian families pastoral care. Money came in to send the Chunni Lalls back to Ghuara.[45] They all contributed to the VBS sponsored by Gabriel, making it possible for him to buy the new CEEFI-sponsored VBS books in Hindi.[46] The Municipal Board took notice of them and elected Komal Das Lall as a member — the first time in history a Christian had been on Chhatarpur's Municipal Board.[47]

Bibles for Bundelkhand

Colemans then turned their attention more to "Bibles for Bundelkhand." The year-end tally of 7,319 Gospel portions and 134 Bibles sold was encouraging,[48] though the plan itself was being challenged from three directions. First, Milton sensed a growing doubt about the value of a foreign missionary's presence in village distribution when there were Indian leaders around like Vijay and Gabriel. Second, he began receiving persistent calls to help in relief of drought-stricken India suffering from three years of monsoon failure. Third, they felt a growing concern for their daughter in the U.S.A. with no home, and for Rebecca's nearly 100-year-old mother.

With DeVols, Norma Freer, and Kathy Thompson back in Chhatarpur by 1967, the acute need of their presence was no longer felt.[49] They did not rush in making a decision, but in March 1967 quickly and happily moved to their old home in the "First Bungalow"—now provided with electricity—to make room for the return of the DeVols.[50]

When the DeVols returned to Chhatarpur on March 16, 1967, they appreciated Milton's initiative in the construction of the relatives' shelter; the installation of an X-ray, electric sterilizer, and unit for making pure distilled water; and the negotiation with OXFAM (Oxford Committee for Famine Relief) for a sum of £1,800 to build the pediatric ward and water tank. A new suction machine had been provided by the Women's Missionary Societies.[51]

Relief Work in Bihar

Recognizing the continued pressure on Colemans to alleviate the need in Bihar, Dr. Ezra endorsed heartily Milton's desire to take part of his vacation to assist EFI's Committee on Relief (EFICOR) in that terribly devastated area.[52]

Milton left for Bihar April 29, 1967, with the jeep. When the Board in U.S.A. heard of the need and asked what they could do to help, Dr. Ezra replied:

> The best contribution that you can make is to loan Milton and Rebecca Coleman to the work for the duration of the acute emergency. They seem to have plenty of grain on hand to distribute—it is the oversight of the very demanding responsibility of distribution that is so sorely needed.[53]

Monsoons had not been normal in Bihar for seven years, and water was scarce.[54] Of the fifty million people in Bihar, over six million would have died without relief. EFICOR was one of forty volunteer relief agencies who joined to avert the tragedy.

Palamau District in South Bihar revealed the most severe conditions, and EFICOR placed Milton in that area with the Mennonite Central Committee to oversee the work. He established jungle feeding kitchens for 2,000 preschool children, nursing mothers, and the aged; and supervised food for work projects for 6,000 of the able-bodied, who dug thirty-five wells and built roads and dams.

The daily wage was four pounds of grain, or three pounds plus seven cents cash.[55] Cattle, as well as people, also suffered. A network of "cattle camps" was set up. The largest was one for 202 villages with 130,275 cattle.[56] Commenting on a newspaper account of the "unsmiling children receiving a glob of tasteless mush," Milton pointed out: "But with love added, the smiles are returning. Ribs are being covered with flesh. Legs and arms are filling out again . . . children [are] running and playing to and from the kitchen."[57]

The work involved movement of hundreds of tons of grain supplies. During May, Milton drove the jeep 1,800 miles in this relief work, unloading 220-pound bags of wheat from Canada, milo from U.S.A., rice from Thailand, fish tins from Germany — then finding storage space free from impending monsoons, rats, insects, and thieves.[58]

In July Rebecca joined Milton in the Bihar work until the end of September.[59] EFICOR received over $20,000 for emergency relief, and the Colemans administered one fifth of it, all in small notes, "and not one was 'lost,'" Milton reported. "One was constantly conscious of being just one part of a multitude of dedicated servants of God and of humanity, continually receiving strength from unseen sources to carry on sixteen to eighteen hours daily . . . . I got thinner . . . and healthier."[60] So did Rebecca, who nevertheless felt deep concern about the pace Milton was forced to keep up, often without time to eat or sleep. In the midst of it all, too, was personal sorrow. Milton received news of the death of his saintly mother early in July.[61]

Lavish appreciation was expressed by EFI for the Colemans' five months in Bihar and their patient, compassionate, and understanding ways. Milton was commended for his knowledge of Hindi, his capacity for hard work, and his leadership among his Indian colleagues —"and all this in weather above 100°F."[62] The local block development officers and the Deputy Commissioner of Daltonganj also commended them for the equitable and efficient handling of relief without discrimination.[63]

Colemans' Departure from India

When the emergency was over in Bihar, EFI requested the Mission to release Milton Coleman on a permanent basis to EFICOR as its secretary. Bob Hess also sought their help in Yavatmal. Colemans expressed willingness to go but there was no compulsion within.[64] Clearly, their hearts were in Bundelkhand, but that door seemed to be closing to them. By the end of the year they felt clear to return to pastoral work in U.S.A., and the Board and Mission Council backed them in this move. Their departure on April 10, 1968, however, left transportation problems, Woodstock school representation, orphans' care, property matters, and many pastoral and evangelistic concerns to be cared for by others.[65]

The Precarious Personnel Situation — Frustrations and Encouragements

Just a month after Milton Coleman had gone to Bihar in 1967, Dr. Ezra DeVol, back in the operating room with no trouble from his eyes, felt it was time for Dr. Mategaonker to get on with his masters degree in surgery.[66] So Dr. Mategaonker left Chhatarpur with his family on June 29 for Ludhiana. But a month before Colemans returned from Bihar, Dr. Mategaonker was back in charge of the hospital in Chhatarpur and Dr. Ezra had returned to the U.S.A. He wrote about the experience: "I had to stop work on account of bilateral retinal detachments. I called Dr. Mategaonker, who came from Ludhiana. He is like a son to me. Norma arranged for the 'No Objection to Leave/Return' Certificates and income tax clearance in 24 hours . . . Anna arranged a retirement room between trains in Jhansi. Ben Wati helped us get out of Delhi."[67]

Dr. Ezra was operated on at St. Luke's Hospital in Cleveland on September 1, 1967, for retinal detachment on the left eye, and ten days later, on the right eye. The right eye did not respond; he had to return to the hospital in October, and again in January 1968. By April there was definite improvement, and on May 8, DeVols were back in India, arriving just a month after the Colemans left. Hesses, also, were leaving India. Frances, observing the missionary staff left — Norma, Kathy, Anna — commented: "Ezra feels bereft, especially being the only man now."[68]

Feelings of loneliness were soon pushed aside, however, as everyone thanked God for Kathy Thompson's success in all language requirements and her return to Chhatarpur for full-time service in December 1967. She brought with her a fund of knowledge and experience from her work at Nur Manzil.

Her expertise in scheduling soon took a load off the shoulders of Dr. Mategaonker, and by the time DeVols had returned, she was already planning a procedure manual, which turned out to be seventeen pages in mimeographed form when it was finished.[69] Heartening, too, was the presence of a new doctor, Dr. Mathew, on the staff.[70]

The Mission Board's full support of hospital expansion was encouraging.[71] Through monsoon floods for 700 miles from Bombay to Chhatarpur, Dr. Ezra took turns with Komal Das Lall in driving the new ambulance the Board had provided. When all shipments had arrived, they not only had a new ambulance but also an air conditioner for the operating room, a new operating table from Germany, a colorimeter, incubator, analytic scales, an emergency light for the operating room, and some oxygen equipment.[72]

When everything was cleared, Dr. Mategaonker left with his family again for Ludhiana. DeVols, with the new doctor and Kathy Thompson assisting, went to work. Dr. Ezra wrote, "We hope we can settle down for a long, steady, profitable stretch of service."[73] But that very summer Frances began having heart difficulties.[74] Being a doctor and the son of missionary doctors, Dr. Ezra was alerted to pray even more earnestly for an Indian staff, strong in faith and competent to carry the Christian hospital into the future.

Furlough soon rolled around for Kathy Thompson, and the Mission had to bid her goodbye. They did so with sorrow, but with thankfulness to God for her positive contributions to Nur Manzil in Lucknow and the Christian Hospital in Chhatarpur.[75] Shortly after that, they said goodbye to Dr. Mathew, who left at the end of 1970. Had Dr. Elizabeth Pothan of South India not come to take up work in January 1969, Dr. Ezra would have been alone again. She had just graduated from Ludhiana Medical College, and she plunged into the work of the hospital and church right from the start with such enthusiasm that she soon won the love and admiration of the whole community.

Betty Geissler of WUMS came back early in 1970 also to guide the student nurses and supervise the building of their new quarters in Chhatarpur.[76] The building was completed and dedicated December 9, 1970. Other events bringing encouragement included a visit of Dr. Ray Knighton, president of the Medical Assistance Program, which gave help to 1,000 hospitals in 81 countries. Chhatarpur Hospital was one of them.[77] DeVols also were glad to have their son, Joe and his family, join the staff at Woodstock school. They arrived December 7, 1969, and spent vacations in Chhatarpur. Many friends in U.S.A. gave lavishly to supply hospital equipment, and OXFAM offered another $12,000 to remodel some of the hospital buildings.[78]

A Visit from Mission Board Officers

In 1969 Sherman Brantingham, administrative assistant, and wife, Dorothy, and Herbert Burch, FFMS president, visited India. "What a thrill to see national and missionary personnel working together," wrote Sherman, ". . . the 80-bed hospital with 100 patients, the 24-hour prayer service — part of EFI's 100 days of prayer . . . . We have a live Church in India!"[79]

The Birth of Emmanuel Hospital Association

Encouraging as all of these events were, they were not enough to keep a hospital going. There was need for a thoroughly Christian Indian organization, medically oriented, to whom the hospital would be responsible when the Mission no longer existed and missionaries were no longer present. Dr. Ezra began working on this locally with the formation of an internal advisory committee of seven members meeting every other week to share with the general superintendent in the guidance of the day-to-day affairs of the hospital.[80]

At the same time, he and fifteen other concerned leaders in the EFI drew together a plan for the Emmanuel Hospital Association. At its first meeting November 19, 1970, the Christian Hospital in Chhatarpur was one of five that joined.[81] Other groups supporting EHA were the EFI, Vellore and Ludhiana medical centers, and the Christian Medical Association of India.

EHA's purpose was to develop a distinctively Christian India-based medical association under Indian leadership to bring spiritual, physical, mental, and social healing to the poor and needy rural areas like Bundelkhand. They planned to maintain and develop Christian hospitals and dispensaries in such areas. Through retreats and chaplains, they hoped to train and challenge Christian doctors and administrators to fill these posts. They wanted to insure that not only the doctors, but the entire hospital staff, would see spiritual ministry as one of their primary responsibilities and would cooperate with and help establish local churches.

They agreed to offer staff members opportunities to develop their skills and to guarantee educational opportunities for their children. They determined to stress the importance of fiscal responsibility and adequately train spiritual administrative officers. They recognized the importance of continued relation through EFI with all other all-India Church and medical organizations.[82]

Dr. Ezra DeVol was vice chairman and a member of the executive committee of EHA. By June 1971 the Christian Hospital in Chhatarpur became affiliated with EHA. Dr. Mategaonker, still studying in Ludhiana, took time to attend the June 1970 executive committee of EHA.[83] Commenting on this new organization, Dr. Ezra wrote the Board:

> As long as we have men like Dr. Mategaonker here and other men like him in other medical centers I do not think we need to worry about whether the plan will work or not. The important thing is to have men of integrity and real spiritual life in these key positions. If that fails, no amount of rule-making is going to bolster up an organization no matter how well conceived.[84]

That EHA continues to this day to further its purposes through the states of Maharashtra, U.P., M.P., and Bihar is testimony to the fact that such men of integrity were found.

Failure in the Church

Chhatarpur Friends Church, however, faced a severe testing at this point
of integrity through the years of 1970-72. Temptation, always present
when huge sums of money pass through the hands of those who have
known severe poverty, overcame one of the Church's strongest leaders.
Komal Das Lall had worked with the Mission from his youth. In his positions as member of the municipal board, superintendent of the Church,
medical accountant, builder of the student nurses' center, and superintendent of maintenance, he commanded great respect. Mechanic, driver,
builder, accountant, manager—he was a businessman with keen judgment, humor, and ambition.

In early 1971 those who lived and worked near him began to notice
disturbing changes. "I feel things aren't what they ought to be," Norma
wrote as she asked for prayer.[85] The Church also began to question, and
at annual meeting they replaced him as superintendent by electing the
hospital cashier, George Masih. George Masih was awed by the responsibility placed on him and requested people to pray that he might be a real
blessing and help to the Church. He was known for his integrity and his
broad political concerns. He came into position at the time India was
being flooded with 100 million refugees from Bangladesh, and he
encouraged the Church to pray and give to this need.[86]

As time went on, the new student nurses' center began to give way
and exposed the use of inferior materials in the building. A keen auditor
uncovered evidence of forgery and embezzlement. Komal Das Lall was
given opportunity to resign. Kamal Prasad, his assistant, stepped in to
take the load of maintenance. All the accompanying emotion, anger, confusion, and polarization drove bitterness deep and shook the Christian
community from top to bottom. He rebelled against church discipline
and was dropped from membership, though Pastor Stuti Prakash sought
to keep the door open for him to "come home."[87] The family's dearest
friend and his closest co-worker, Norma Freer, suffered deeply through
the heartbreak of the situation plus the almost unbearable work load that
fell on her shoulders when he resigned. The judgment fell just before
Christmas and took the heart out of everyone.

Hope Restored and Anniversaries Celebrated at Christmas

Priorities, nevertheless, had to be brought back into order, and in spite of
the deep spiritual struggle, Dr. Ezra mobilized the whole hospital staff in
celebrating Christmas more significantly than they had ever done before.
They planned a pageant showing the purpose of Christ's coming as well
as a commemoration of the seventy-fifth anniversary of the Mission and
the fortieth anniversary of the building of the hospital in Chhatarpur. The

pageant came first, held in the open in the L-shaped courtyard of the hospital, with scenes in the various archways of the veranda. Nazareth, King Herod's Court, Bethlehem, the shepherd's field — and this year on the steps of the new outpatient department Komal Das had just finished building — a temple scene for the dedication. At a little distance was the home of Zechariah and Elizabeth. Costumes and decorations were authentic, as was the setting under the genuine star-studded sky.

The focus was the manger scene at Bethlehem and its nearby field, where shepherds huddled around a fire watching their real sheep. At the appropriate time a spotlight revealed the singing angels suspended against the sky (though they were actually standing on the hospital roof). Another spotlight showed the startled shepherds, and then their dash with lambs in their arms to Bethlehem. All the animals in the drama were real ones — the sheep and goats, pigeons for the offering, horses for the Roman soldiers, and camels for the three kings. Even the cry of a baby just born was real, coming from inside the hospital. Dr. DeVol directed and operated lights; Dr. Pothan decorated; Frances and Norma helped with costumes; many others set up props and took part, and Chaplain Gabriel Massey from the rooftop read the prophecies from Isaiah, Micah, and the account from the New Testament as the pageant proceeded.

Many people from the city crowded in to see it and at the end everyone sang, "O Come All Ye Faithful." In previous productions, the pageant had ended there, but this year something more was added. After Gabriel gave a terse but powerful summary of the whole life of Jesus, pointing to the purpose of His coming, at the mention of His death, a large, rough cross appeared against the sky above the whole setting and the angels sang, "There was one who was willing to die in my stead."[88]

Three days later the people throughout the area gathered for the celebration of the seventy-fifth anniversary of Friends in Bundelkhand, and the fortieth anniversary of the hospital in Chhatarpur. The Maharaja of Chhatarpur was the guest of honor. Civil Surgeon Dr. G. S. Saxena officially opened the new outpatient department built through a gift of OXFAM. "What hath God wrought!" again echoed through the Christian community as it had in 1931, and everyone rejoiced. "It was a happy time for us, a time of rejoicing when we truly say, 'Hitherto hath the Lord helped us.' "[89]

Victory in the Church

No one would ever be the same again — not even Komal Das Lall — or his predecessor, Pancham Singh.

Pancham Singh had grown old in his bitterness against the Mission and had split the Church. Disowned at that time, he had taken his wife and family with him. When his wife died in mental and physical agony, the Church, full of pity for her, deliberately set aside the letter of the law and gave her a Christian burial, mourning for her as their sister in Christ. Pancham Singh became ill and was taken to the hospital he had helped to build forty years earlier.

Stuti Prakash made frequent visits to him, sensing his end time was near, and urged him to come back to the Church before he died. Each time Pancham Singh refused. Sensitive to the possible hostility against himself, Stuti stepped aside, requesting two other Christian hospital patients to deal with Pancham Singh as they had opportunity. They also had no success until after Pancham Singh lost consciousness for three days. Then they approached him again and found him different. Pancham Singh said to them, "I don't want to fill out a form. I have something to say to the Church."

What would Pancham Singh say? No one knew, but on June 4, 1972, the first day he had been able to be in Church, Stuti Prakash with great love and courage gave him the pulpit. Leaning on his cane and wobbling weakly forward, Pancham Singh reached the pulpit and carefully placed his cane at the side. Tense silence reigned as he looked out over the congregation of men, women, and little children sitting breathlessly before the august presence of this lion of a man.

Slowly, he brought his two hands together as in prayer and said, "God has been speaking to me while I have been ill. I am sorry I split the Church. I have been a stumbling block to so many of you. I ask your forgiveness, and I pray the Church may become *one*." He stopped for a moment to get his breath, then with husky voice repeated his confession again — and then again.

"It was sincere, clear and tender, before even the women and the children," Stuti Prakash reported later. Hearts were melted, and Pancham Singh was taken back into the bosom of a loving and forgiving Church.[90]

From that day until the day he died six months later, January 1973, his life was transformed. Superintendent George Masih said, "His last days were sweet in the fellowship with the Lord and with the members of the Church. His last words of encouragement and challenge still ring in our ears."[91]

There were many tears at Pancham Singh's funeral, more of joy than of sorrow, for one who had been lost and was found. One man there, however, shed no tears. Komal Das Lall went out from that funeral through a side door — and it was night. A missionary there saw the despair on his face as he left and thought of Judas. Fearing for his life, she followed him and sought to point him also to the God who forgives. Months and even years passed by; then Komal Das, too, found his way back to the place of repentance and, like Pancham Singh, was taken back into the Church.

When he died suddenly five years later of cerebral hemorrhage on January 16, 1977, hundreds, both Christian and non-Christian in the city, mourned his death. Peace and serenity marked his funeral. Norma Freer had observed his consistent response to light through the latter years of his life. She worked more closely with him than any other missionary since Everett Cattell, who had trained him. She said of him: "He walked in the light and learned things he said that would stay with him his whole life . . . . I feel perfectly at rest . . . that he is with the Lord . . . . I have lost a brother. I will miss him greatly. He has been a good advisor and was helpful to all."[92]

Visit of Russell and Marjorie Myers

From December 1972 through January 1973 Russell and Marjorie Myers came to India and were present in Chhatarpur for Pancham Singh's funeral. They had attended EFI Conference in Lucknow, but Russell's illness forced them to cancel a trip to Union Biblical Seminary. Recovering in Chhatarpur, they settled in to give their full remaining time to helping the Friends Church in Bundelkhand. As one general superintendent to another, Russell met George Masih, who arranged for meetings with other church leaders.

Noting that the Church was still bound by the habit of looking to the Mission to take initiative, Russell did what he could to build a sense of identity in the Church. Attending services, ministering, counseling, meeting in committees and business sessions, Russell found the three weeks went by all too quickly. The last week was spent in Mission Council sessions and to welcome Norma Freer back to India.[93]

Relieved to see EHA functioning well and the mission property being turned over to ETANI, Russell agreed also that the time had come to sell and reinvest the proceeds of the two hill properties that six years later enriched UBS. He sanctioned the plans for the building of a reading room and assembly hall near the hospital and the continued subsidy to the hospital after the DeVols retired in 1974. He brought to the Mission Council what he had learned through meetings with the church leaders. They pled for schools again in Ghuara and Nowgong and a boys' hostel in Chhatarpur. They also still felt their need of help in evangelism. A letter signed by thirteen non-Christians in Rakshapura underscored this need.

> If only there could be some man sent to help us . . . who can teach us the Bible. Some can read . . . but don't understand. Some of us

cannot read . . . . We are again praying to God that our lives (our situation) will be set right. This is our prayer to God.[94]

Russell Myers was quick to see a mighty band of young people who should be challenged by the Church for evangelism and the need for the Church to take initiative in meeting the needs in education for which they had trained leaders. Initiative and stewardship were still problems in the Indian Church. Russell and Marjorie Myers joined the Mission Council in assuring them of love and concern and continued support from sending churches, but encouraged them also to take their responsibility. Their empathy and enthusiasm had deep effects both among the church leaders and among the missionaries.

Dr. Mategaonker Succeeds DeVols as they Depart from India

The Emmanuel Hospital Association affiliation definitely helped in raising the standard of the hospital and in getting doctors, but it did not seem to help in keeping them. Two doctors came early in 1971 but left for Africa at much higher salaries eighteen months later.[95] EHA helped supply a business manager, too, who stayed only a year.[96] Dr. Pothan's resignation was a real blow, but her parents in South India needed her.[97]

Dr. Mategaonker planned to return to stay in April 1972, but when only one in three passed the final examination, he was not one of them. DeVols for health reasons left for the summer, and with the resignation of the three other doctors, Dr. Mategaonker was left with the whole burden of the hospital and no time to study for a retake in September. Dr. Pothan, understanding his plight, agreed to return in August to give him six weeks free for study before the final attempt. She was present to help two more new doctors with orientation in the hospital. She stayed on until Dr. Mategaonker, with his degree and his wife with a postgraduate nursing administration degree, returned victoriously to Chhatarpur in mid-November 1972.[98]

Miss Imelda Shaw of Lucknow, an Anglo-Indian woman of many years' experience and proven capabilities, joined the staff as head nurse and later as nursing superintendent in April 1973. Another doctor just out of medical school also came, but he and the other two new doctors all left in just a few months.[99]

What made Dr. Mategaonker different? Why did he come to Chhatarpur and continue, year after year? He had suffered poliomyelitis as a child, which affected the muscles in his left leg. All through life he had known the humiliation of a physical handicap. His mother sold her ornaments to get money to send him to medical college. During his last year a staff member led him to personal faith in Christ, and on graduating, he felt called to Chhatarpur. Fourteen years later as he finished his work on his master's degree in surgery, he met the same staff member again and thanked him. With the same deep sense of call he returned to Chhatarpur.[100]

Dr. Ezra and Frances DeVol thanked God for answered prayer in providing Imelda Shaw and Dr. Mategaonker to take their places. From the first heart attack, Frances had not been able to return to the high altitude of the cool hills; so each summer DeVols had to find rest outside of India. Before leaving for their last vacation in 1973, Dr. DeVol with the Mission Council's approval set up a "Bethesda Hospital Society" to manage the operation of the Christian Hospital under the Societies Act of 1860. This had become necessary because of new income tax laws.[101] Written into the constitution was a provision placing it under EHA.

The new board that took over from the Mission Council was formed and approved April 24, 1973, and took in medical workers from other hospitals in the region.[102] DeVols expected to be in the U.S.A. a very short time that summer, but Frances developed further heart problems and Dr. Ezra had retinal trouble again in his right eye. The doctor had to use argon laser to seal the retina in about twenty-five places. This detained them in America until November, where they were cared for by the Hines sisters, Marie and Alice, in their home in Cleveland. During this time while Dr. Mategaonker continued alone, Russell Myers wrote him a letter of appreciation. Dr. Mategaonker replied:

> It is just human to feel a little happy when somebody appreciates the labour done . . . . I am doing little. I wish I could overcome my shortcomings and weaknesses. Still I get the satisfaction that the One whom I trust will never fail. So many times I have felt the helping hand of the Lord over me during very difficult operations and complicated situations.[103]

Only six months of service remained for the DeVols when they returned, and the hospital staff was anxious that the new book room and hall be built before they left. As it was being built, Dr. Mategaonker suggested, "We should call it DeVol Fellowship Hall." And so it was.[104] On April 17, 1974, after twenty-six years of service in India and Nepal, Dr. W. Ezra and Frances DeVol returned to the U.S.A. They, with Colemans, Norma Freer, and Kathy Thompson, had watched through the night in Bundelkhand. With their going, a grand era in missions in Bundelkhand came to an end, and a new day dawned.

| # Bearing the Heat of the Day

> "Be strong, do not fear; your God will come . . . . The burning sand will become a pool, the thirsty ground bubbling springs." Isaiah 35:4-7

Norma Freer, the Only Foreign Missionary Left in Bundelkhand

In 1974 the mission era came to an end—almost, but not quite. The Friends Foreign Missionary Society of EFC—ER at first thought so and requested Norma Freer to plan to leave Chhatarpur with the DeVols,[1] though she felt no such leading. The Board seemed to have been prompted not so much by a desire to be consistent with mission policy as by compassion for a single woman being left the only missionary in a dangerous, robber-infested area.

Seemingly for the moment they had forgotten that Norma had often been alone in Chhatarpur, even before the famous and innovative politician, Jai Prakash Narain, had somewhat successfully tackled the robber problem. He had introduced a scheme that brought about the surrender of 400 notorious outlaws who had been terrorizing the villages. In 1972 he persuaded the government to help rehabilitate the children of these outlaws as a reward for their surrender. The plan worked miracles for a time, though many gangs remained in hiding.[2]

Whether a missionary remained or not, the people were reluctant to let mission resources go. Victor Mangalwadi, fearing the work would stop, offered to resign his post with the Bible Society and return as treasurer and evangelist. He longed to help the Church in Bundelkhand as his father had done before him. He wrote a comprehensive letter with plans for the work, including a modest plan for remodeling the "first bungalow" to establish an English-medium school where first-rate education could be

403

provided for both the rich and the poor. "All of this may be a new dream of a visionary," he wrote, "but if it is the will of God, and if Evangelical Friends trust me and my family to help give concrete form to their dreams, the Lord may yet conclude the dark night and bring about a new dawn for Bundelkhand."[3]

In spite of Victor Mangalwadi's great caring, his letter revealed the concept of continued dependence on mission funds. That may have been the reason the Board failed to give consideration to his plan. However, this letter may have awakened them to the fact that they had been too abrupt in their plan to close the Mission, so they permitted Norma Freer to remain in Chhatarpur until W. Robert Hess, FFMS Board president, could come to India to assess the situation.[4] A year later, the executive committee of the Friends Church in India (BMMS) also sent a request for the Board to open an English primary school and appoint Norma Freer as the manager.[5]

Robert Hess's Visit to India

In September 1975, Bob Hess returned after seven years and noted many changes in India.[6] In spite of criticism by the Western press of India's Prime Minister Indira Gandhi and her "emergency government," he found tighter discipline and a higher standard of public service in the country. Varieties of produce on sale in the bazaar amazed him, such as an abundance of apples in Delhi. He also heard of and felt some of the tragic happenings of the years in between. In Ghuara, for example, people continued to grieve the loss of Mr. and Mrs. Chunni Lall, who had spent twenty years there before they died in 1970.[7]

The Church had not been able to find another such couple for Ghuara. Work in Jatara and other villages was bearing fruit and there were a few new converts. Brightest among them was Khub Chand's niece, Raja Bai, and her husband and family. Raja Bai had already won some of her relatives to Christ, including her brother and his family.[8] Church giving had increased six times, and Bob happily renewed the promise of matching funds from the Mission. The hospital, under Dr. Mategaonker's leadership in EHA, was continuing treatment distinctly Christian and serving the poor.[9]

Some unrest was in evidence under hospital administrative changes. Gabriel Massey, for example, had to choose between a medical career or Christian ministry instead of continuing to balance the two. He chose full-time Christian ministry.[10] Another change came as auxiliary nurses' training was started and the hospital needed all available space in the nurses' home. Responsibility for arranging a home for Dulli and Karuna, two elderly orphans living in the nurses' home, fell on Norma's shoulders and emphasized the need of the Mission still in Chhatarpur. Only the Mission had funds to provide a house and compensation to the matron, Mrs. Phyllis Das, who agreed under this arrangement to care for Dulli and Karuna as long as they lived.[11]

The Opening of the Christian English School in Chhatarpur

In February 1976 Norma received permission from the Board to open the new English-medium school. Milton and Rebecca Coleman were visiting in India when the news arrived, and they rejoiced with her for this new door of service in Bundelkhand. In conveying the Board's permission, Bob Hess outlined the guidelines:

> We will want you, Dr. Mategaonker, Mr. S. N. Khare, and the superin-
> tendent of BMMS to work out an agreement for a three-year
> experimental period for the use of the "first bungalow" for the English
> Primary School.[12]

As soon as EHA found a replacement for the position of hospital business manager, Norma Freer, in compliance with the Board's request, resigned from her work in the hospital and on the Bethesda Hospital Association Management Committee and moved to the "first bungalow." She had been given permission to use money from the sale of the mission ambulance, jeep, and other supplies to fund the project and buy rickshaws for trans-portation of the students.[13] The women's "least coin offering" in 1977 went to provide her with a small car.[14]

Norma expected to begin with a kindergarten of about 25 students. She hired two English-trained teachers and claimed as her promise for the year Ephesians 3:20: "He is able to do exceeding abundantly above all that we ask or think." However, not even she was prepared for the ava-lanche of applications that came for admission that first year. She accepted eighty-six of them between the ages of three and a half to six and placed them in nursery, KG I and II.[15]

The officials in Chhatarpur, a city of 35,000 population were delighted. A member of parliament, Vidhyawati Chaturvedi, came as chief guest for the opening, and Lawyer Shri Narayan Khare also spoke. The children in their brown and gold uniforms, black shoes and white socks, made quite an impression on the town. They rode to and from the school crowded twelve together in the rickshaws clearly marked, "Chris-tian English School." Often they went singing their school song, "Learn-ing and Growing Together."

With each year, a new class was added so that by 1977 Norma had to rent a big tent for classroom space. The tent worked beautifully in 1977, but in 1978 the monsoon season was the worst the people in that area had seen. Norma said:

After 14 tries I finally got the candles burning—also after 48 hours of constant rain—and I mean rain! No electricity . . . . The tent classroom (rotted by the rain and torn in shreds by the wind) is almost beyond repair. Six containers in my office are catching the leaks. Many houses have fallen . . . . Still it rains. No school until Thursday.[16]

While the Board was passing minutes to the effect that the school should be registered, put under Indian leadership, and made self-supporting within three years,[17] Norma was struggling to keep enough teachers on the staff to cope with the growth, and planning how to get more classroom space on property still under the EHA. A first step was to get the school under the control of a registered society and the property directly under ETANI. With Dr. Mategaonker's approval, EHA let go their claim on the property.[18] The school was registered as the "Shalem Society" and placed under an administrative board according to FFMS Board approval and directed by Norma Freer, their representative on the field.

On June 26, 1979, the certificate of registration for the Shalem Society was issued.[19] The new administrative board was comprised of nine members, including Norma Freer, manager; S. Paul Miller, UBS director of relocation; Leah Moshier, director of Kulpahar Mission; Mabel Lal, teacher in Lalitpur Mission; Pratap Singh Brown, homeopathic doctor and lay member of BMMS in Chhatarpur; Victor Lal, pharmacist in the Christian Hospital; Shyam Kumari William Lall, principal of the BMMS Hindi Primary School; and Sunand P. Singh, the newly appointed headmistress.[20]

S. Paul Miller's presence on the committee was a great help as the building began. Damascus Church gave their Easter offering of $6,000 to get it started.[21] Early in 1979, Cliff and Betty Robinson took a tour group to India. Other visitors also stopped. The FFMS Board sent their president, Charles Robinson, and his wife, Anne, and W. Robert Hess on another trip to give encouragement and guidance. Impressed by what they saw, many of these visitors gave substantial financial assistance to build the school.[22]

Among the visitors was a representative of TEAR (The Evangelical Association on Relief, Evangelical Alliance, England), who granted all that Norma requested—a sum of $18,820.99—to put up a two-story, eight-classroom building. It was dedicated on November 16, 1980, in an impressive service attended by 800 people from the city. The District Commissioner, the main speaker, cut the ribbon. However, by that time, the building was already too small. Double sessions had to be held to accommodate the 215 students. A Gestetner from Michigan, a projector and playground equipment from other friends, and schoolbooks from women's societies helped Norma equip the school. COMPASSION, a group with TEAR for helping children in need, also granted scholarship funds to assist in paying fees for eleven children from poor families. By 1983 their funding paid for ninety-six scholarships, enhanced teachers' salaries, and helped purchase playground equipment.[23]

The first large Christmas program was attended by 600, but by 1983, more than 1,000 came. On special occasions for Christmas and Easter each year the children presented Christian broadcasts on Chhatarpur radio station. Though only 25 of the 375 students in 1983-84 were from Christian homes, all were enrolled in Bible classes and many attended Vacation Bible School.[24]

The need to build pushed them beyond the boundaries of the land owned by the Mission, and Norma in 1981 on furlough requested the Board to allow her to purchase property adjoining the compound. By mid-1983, Norma was able to negotiate the purchase of land 50' x 92' just beyond the back wall of the compound. Again, through a donation from Damascus Friends Church, they built four more new classrooms. With the addition of an assembly hall and two more rooms on the first floor with more rooms on top of them, the plant continues to expand.[25]

At the beginning of the 1983-84 academic year in July with fourteen teachers and 375 students, the 7th class was added. Already recognized by government through 5th class, the Shalem Society seeks to secure government recognition through 7th. By the 1984-85 academic year, 8th class was added and with that, they applied for affiliation with the Indian School Certificate Examination from Delhi.[26]

Though education of children has never been a primary means of evangelism in India, it is too early to ascertain what the result will be in this new day of democracy in India. Independent choices on the part of such young people may one day change the face of India. Meanwhile, the English Christian School has become a key missionary strategy that the Board hopes to continue.[27] As a confirmation of that, they sent two short-termers December 27, 1983, to March 29, 1984, with the hope that Ruth Johnson and Judy Nutt, or others like them, may one day turn short term into long term, like Norma Freer who has served in Bundelkhand since 1945.

The Christian Hindi School

The Christian Hindi School under the Chhatarpur Church has been managed over thirty years by Mrs. Shyam Kumari William Lall, daughter of Stuti Prakash, mother of four children, and a leader in the Church. Shyam Kumari teaches as her husband, William, farms and repairs watches. In 1976 the Hindi school had over 100 students and a distinguished record in the district.[28] In 1981 Australian Friends sent a gift of $300 toward enlarging the Hindi school building, and Clifton Robinson, in Leadership Ministries, also sought to raise funds for this worthy project. James Morris of EFM also supported the request for a new school building.[29] Meanwhile, the Hindi school, fully recognized by the government, filled their facilities to capacity with 212 students and nine teachers, and added the sixth class in 1983-84.[30]

The Ministry of Gabriel Massey and Vijay Prakash

The Church was on its own; the Hindi school, under the Church; the hospital, under EHA. None reported directly to the Mission Board in the U.S.A. The Christian English School and its administrative council, however, was directly under the FFMS Missionary Board. Though no one intended it to be so, the Indian leaders in other phases of the work could not avoid noticing the U.S.A. constituency's tendency toward a loss of interest in the work to which they gave grants but no foreign missionary personnel. Gabriel Massey must have felt this keenly as he resigned his post to go full time into ministry. He had been recorded as a BMMS minister at Annual Meeting held March 31-April 5, 1970.[31]

The total membership in 1977 was 273, with worshiping groups in five places.[32] Nowgong and Chhatarpur were the only churches large enough to afford pastors, and Dayal Chand Singh and Stuti Prakash were serving them acceptably. Gabriel wrote, "I have great love for the Church . . . and great hope . . . . My heart is here in the Church and I shall continue to uplift the Church as long as I am here."[33]

But the penetration plan for evangelism he had sponsored through which converts were coming had to be laid aside. Regular cottage prayer meetings, ministry in VBS, CE, and Sunday school, literature distribution at melas, and many other areas of voluntary service for which he was responsible in the Church stopped as he left for a three-year term in the Bible Society. Gabriel's home, however, was in Chhatarpur, and his wife, Suzanna, kept the two sons and a daughter in Chhatarpur while she worked in public health through the Christian Hospital. Long hours and heavy responsibility may account for her high blood pressure developed in 1983.[34] When home on weekends or for special times, Gabriel often preached in the churches.[35]

Bob Hess's visit to India in 1975 came just as Gabriel's term with the Bible Society was nearing an end. Sensing a need for a coordinator in Bundelkhand, Bob talked the matter over with Gabriel, but the time was not ripe.[36]

Vijay Prakash, since 1970, had been involved in developing a Hindi Evangelical Fellowship to which the Mission gave support. His term also was at an end, but he, like Gabriel, shunned an administrative post in Bundelkhand. His burden was to develop a laymen's movement in the Hindi area through genuine and voluntary witnessing. He received support from Asia Evangelistic Fellowship and chose to continue in that ministry at this time.[37] Based in Jhansi, Vijay traveled widely in ministry, though he was somewhat limited when his wife, Prema, began having acute coronary difficulties.[38]

Federation of Evangelical Churches in India (FECI)

Gabriel found his niche in a new organization called the Federation of Evangelical Churches in India (FECI) launched November 3, 1974, in Nagpur, India, under EFI auspices.[39] Church Union schemes had brought about the Church of South India and then the Church of North India. Though many large denominations did not join, small evangelical churches, when cut off from western churches that had given them birth, were left adrift in a sea of Hinduism. EFI was a broad fellowship encouraging evangelicals in all denominations, but FECI brought evangelical churches into a federation patterned after the ideas of Dr. E. Stanley Jones. Dr. Donald McGavran, the apostle of church growth, also favored this development as it began in 1970.[40] Mr. P. T. Chandapilla, general secretary of the Union of Evangelical Students of India and a member of the very large St. Thomas Evangelical Church in South India, accepted appointment as the FECI general secretary. Sixteen denominations representing more than 500 congregations with a community membership of about 80,000 covenanted to work together for the evangelization of India and the defense of the historic biblical faith. The BMMS was one of the founding members.[41] Gabriel Massey was chosen in October 1977 as the associate secretary, and the FFMS Board agreed to support this organization with a small yearly grant.[42] By 1983 FECI had grown to forty-two full and nineteen associate members representing more than 1,000 evangelical congregations from Episcopal, Congregational, Brethren, Friends, and Mennonite forms of government. Members come from fifteen of India's twenty-one states, and eleven languages.[43] Their fundamental purpose was stated as seeking to involve every congregation directly in evangelism and church planting.[44] Gabriel Massey ministered constantly, even when ill, in as many as twelve states of India a year. He suffered from hepatitis and also while in Assam, he fell and fractured his right arm. He experienced famine and drought and showed compassion on the blind by developing a ministry among them. He served on the BMMS evangelistic board and on CEEFI committees, often holding workshops for them.[45] Somehow he also found time to work on his bachelor of divinity degree by extension through UBS, with the young man he had

led to Christ in Junior C.E. as his tutor—Phillip S. Masih.[46] More and
more responsibility fell on his shoulders, due to poor health of the general
secretary, who resigned in 1982. On September 9, 1983, at FECI's ninth
assembly, three representatives from Chhatarpur were present to witness
the appointment of Gabriel Massey as the general secretary of FECI. The
headquarters office was moved to Nagpur into rented quarters until funds
can be secured to build.[47] Gabriel Massey and his family continue to live
in Chhatarpur. Gabriel commutes from there to all the churches making
up FECI, giving close attention also to his own church in Bundelkhand.
He seeks to achieve new depths of cooperation and consecration throughout the evangelical churches in India.

Founding of the Association
for Comprehensive Rural Assistance (ACRA)

Vishal Mangalwadi is the fourth child and second son of Victor and
Kusum Singh Mangalwadi, grandson of the first evangelist called Mangalwadi and Jai Bal, and great grandson of Bodhan and Duojibai. Vishal
was born December 20, 1949, in Bundelkhand and was only six years old
when his parents left that area for Rajpur and later Allahabad. He knew
little of his birthplace except through his father's constant prayers for
deliverance of the people of that area.

Vishal at first rebelled against his father and against the Lord, but
during college years he had a dramatic conversion experience that turned
his life around. He then became a leader of early morning prayer in his
college and was known to be willing to "put his life on the line" when matters of justice were at stake. His older brother, Vinay, and he held midnight prayer sessions, asking God to lead them into significant Christian
service. Vinay came to Chhatarpur and worked in the hospital while living on the Mangalwadi farm in Goethera. Unfortunately, he developed
eye hemorrhages, which required long treatment and pointed to a less
strenuous life.

Vishal, however, had been deeply touched at the 1973 EFI conference
when Sam Kamaleson pointed out the greatest evangelistic message would
be preached to secular man, not by an individual evangelist but by a living Christian community. Vishal completed his work on his master's
degree in philosophy at Indore University, studied three months with
Francis Schaeffer in L'Abri, and afterward published his book, *The World
of Gurus*, emphasizing Christ as the true *Guru*.

All this time he kept Sam Kamaleson's words in mind. He met and
married Ruth Frey, a young woman of equal dedication. Ruth was an
army colonel's daughter, born in Jullundhur, Punjab, March 1, 1951. She
held a B.A. from Lucknow, a B.S. from Florida Southern, and an M.A. in

theology from Wheaton. She is also an accomplished writer both in English and in Hindi.

Convinced that God was calling them, Vishal and Ruth came to Chhatarpur in 1976. They claimed Ezekiel 24:27 as their promise—"You will be a sign . . . then they will know that I am the Lord." They proceeded to set up a *sashram*—a community to demonstrate the love of God through their love and service.[48] "We must guard against individualism which destroys relationships; and on the other hand, collectivism that robs the individual of his identity," said Vishal.[49] "We want God to make us a demonstration that He exists and that Christ is the answer to the tough problems of India," he wrote Russell Myers. Vishal believed Christ was the answer to the problems of hunger, poverty, injustice, ignorance, sickness, and corruption. "This claim, however, is yet to be demonstrated clearly by *Indian* Christians," he added.[50]

The Mangalwadis' advent into Chhatarpur produced a few shock waves. No one had invited them. Both were dynamic, vocal, and pro-Indian. Ruth wore a tilak and red streak in her hair to show she was culturally Indian. Christians in Bundelkhand tended to identify this mark with Hinduism and were confused. However, they accepted the Mangalwadis as members in the Chhatarpur Church.[51] In January 1978 the Mangalwadis moved from Chhatarpur to their family farm in Goethera, five miles east of Chhatarpur, with the hope of further developing their community.[52] They registered their new society as ACRA (Association for Comprehensive Rural Assistance) and set about to bring a better way of life to the oppressed and poor in Bundelkhand.

Buying land at Kadari up and across the road from the small Mangalwadi plot of Goethera, ACRA began building simple village living quarters subject to white ants and the ravages of weather. Their community settled on acreage large enough to demonstrate modern farming methods. Supported by a board with Dr. Mategaonker of the Christian Hospital as chairman and six leaders from other areas of India, ACRA's early services included digging latrines on the one hand and holding eye camps on the other. Dr. Mategaonker wrote:

> Vishal Mangalwadi is doing a wonderful work . . . contacting non-Christians. His house is always open . . . . I only hope and pray that his work [may] not be misunderstood by the nominal Christians in the community as a competitive work. It is far from it. On the other hand, his work is acting as a catalyst to stimulate the sleeping people here.[53]

In 1978 forty students from various Indian seminaries including UBS joined all the Christians in Bundelkhand in a program of saturation evangelism called "Project Harvest." This was a part of a broad program coordinated throughout North India by Discipleship Center in Delhi under the theme, "I Will Build My Church." This produced eleven converts from Bundelkhand's villages and stirred interest in many more.[54]

One of the great joys at this time was the return of former Bilwar Christians and their children to Christ. "The harvest is started and I don't want to miss it," Norma Freer wrote.[55] Dr. Pratap Brown, remembering the educational problem in earlier days, took some of the children into his home and put them in school.[56] Through the years more converts came, a few at a time, and God blessed the Church in spite of times when the enemy of men's souls attacked them from within through church politics, jealousies, and misunderstandings that threatened to tear them apart.[57]

By February 1979 thirty-five workers lived in the ACRA *sashram* in Kadari. Village Christians like Raja Bai, Khub Chand, and Halka Daniel were revived and began witnessing more vitally for the Lord. By early 1979 three more converts came and were baptized by Stuti Prakash. "I am not trying to imply we are fully one," wrote Vishal, whose guidelines for accepting converts were not as strict as those of the Church.[58] Bob Hess, commenting on this difference, cautioned Vishal to be aware of a danger of overdependency of new converts and to seek to establish people who were grounded in their own culture, with their own initiative, and developing their own integrity.[59]

As members of the Theological Research and Communications Institute (TRACI), Vishal and Ruth were also encouraged to continue with their writing. Ruth found this difficult as she provided hospitality to the many village guests, who constantly came and went through their doors, and cared for their two little daughters, Nividit and Anandit. However, TRACI arranged for a grant from TEAR to send them to fifteen countries to do research on Vishal's second book.[60]

In February 1980 Vishal's father, Victor Mangalwadi, and his doctor wife retired and moved to Goethera to serve the villages in Bundelkhand. While in Allahabad, Victor had lost his first wife, Kusum, and had later married Dr. Luke, who much earlier had served in the Chhatarpur Christian hospital. Victor joined ACRA, who appointed him as their honorary pastor.[61] While Vishal and Ruth were away, Victor Mangalwadi took charge of ACRA.

Violence in the Christian Community

Not long after Vishal and Ruth Mangalwadi left for their tour, violence shook the Christian community. Terrorism, beatings, robbery, kidnapping, and murder were a part of it. First, masked outlaws came at night, brutally attacked a helper on the farm, beat Victor Mangalwadi and his wife, and robbed them of their possessions including all their life savings except one hundred dollars. Driving them from their home, the robbers threatened to kill them if they ever returned. Reports to the police and even letters to the Prime Minister brought no action.[62]

In Nagod, where the new Christian group of converts was forming, violence struck also, leaving a worker nearly dead from the blow of an ax. In Chhatarpur Christian Hospital, later, he recovered.

Then the greatest blow of all! Coming home from a service held during women's retreat in Chhatarpur Church at 7:30 p.m. on November 5, 1980, Dr. Grace Jones Singh, Victor Mangalwadi's first cousin, said goodnight to Norma Freer and entered her house. Early the next morning Daniel Singh was found knifed to death just inside his door; his bloodstained watch had stopped at 8:27. Dr. Grace was dead in the bedroom, sitting on a *mordha* (stool), strangled by a red blouse, with knife wounds on her head. The radio was blaring, and the house had been emptied of treasures.[63]

The funeral was hardly over before Dr. Mategaonker received a threat of the kidnap of his son if he did not pay Rs. 20,000 ($2,000).[64] The Mategaonkers prayed about what to do. A boy had disappeared from the Christian English school and was returned only after a large ransom was paid. Later the boy's father was murdered.[65] As once before when his life was threatened by a robber, Dr. Mategaonker and his wife sought God's help and were led to send their son away for a time.

"The ghastliest of months," Vishal commented as he and Ruth, on hearing the news, cut their trip short and sped back to India. Arriving November 22, 1980, they were detained in Delhi by friends who feared for their lives. Vishal, however, was not to be kept back. Ruth also insisted on going with him. "I will either follow [Christ] all the way by faith or quit the facade of 'Christian work' altogether," she said as she picked up her two daughters and boarded the train with Vishal.[66] Vishal wrote:

> I am not too much concerned that God would not allow us to suffer or die, but that whether through our lives or death He will be glorified (John 12:27-28) . . . . Therefore . . . I want to invite you, too, to join in this battle. I am not asking for casual praying. That won't do . . . Pray all the time . . . plead with Him . . . keep praying earnestly! (Ephesians 6:18)[67]

Bruce Nicholls, director of TRACI, could not bear to see Vishal and Ruth return to Kadari in the midst of all this violence without support. So he permitted his secretary, Liz Brattle of Australia, to go with them to assist Vishal with his book and to keep Ruth company. A U.S.A. student from Wheaton, Ruth Kay Kudart, also joined them to study a research project for her college courses.[68]

Victor Mangalwadi's Departure and Death

The shock of this violence was too much for Victor Mangalwadi. Understanding the strong Hindu belt through those regions where Hindu communalism held sway with the Jan Sangh and Rashtrya Sewa Sangh fanatacism that killed Gandhi, he knew his presence in Goethera would no longer help. Still, hope burned in his heart, and he said:

> The Lord convinces me that His day has already dawned in Bundelkhand and that God's will shall be done . . . among those who are at present groaning under wickedness and sin.

> It is true that men with their weaknesses and sins can slow down or even close the work of God for some time. But where the true SEED has been sown, the Power of God shall bring it forth out of the dirt and the dust, and shall multiply it thirty-fold, sixty-fold, even a hundred-fold.

> The Brahmins and the Thakurs . . . now perpetuate their neo-colonialism. These people rule with the power of their guns and lathis . . . and suppress the masses until the suppressed are rescued by the God Almighty. Only God knows how and when. But till then we have to pray and wait and suffer patiently. We may have to leave Chhatarpur and even Bundelkhand.[69]

For the sake of his wife, who suffered shock from the violence, they returned to Allahabad. There, on April 25, 1981, Victor Mangalwadi died, with a broken heart.[70] Hospital Chaplain T. C. Cherian stepped into his place in ACRA and baptized six Hindus and one Muslim before the end of 1981.[71]

Other Problems in ACRA

"ACRA is the hottest topic of discussion in the corridors of power." This was a message carried by grapevine. Whether true or not, eyes of many Christian groups were riveted on Kadari at this time, and wheat and rice by the truckloads poured in to them for disbursement to the poor.[72]

Support for the work came from World Vision and various other prominent organizations. Vishal and Ruth, however, had a rude awakening when staff of high integrity began resigning in protest to dishonesty within their community. "We were far too ambitious and naive," Vishal confessed after having a thorough audit. "We should have done it before . . . . We have been vulnerable to the greed and thefts of evil men"– their own employees. "This has been an area of glaring failure . . . . But the goals are not unachievable . . . . Even though we have not succeeded we have not failed."[73]

To support this claim, Vishal cited the existence of their experimental farm, the seed bank, and plans for a fish tank, poultry farm, and dairy.

Most successful of all was the carpet and blanket industry, employing more than 300 men, women, and children. Schools were in operation in twelve villages, giving help in gardening, tailoring, goat and chicken raising, and health. He also claimed converts or interested groups in ten villages.

Polarization and distrust between ACRA and the Church grew even though all evinced a desire for the conversion of the lost and the planting of churches. At the urging of EFM Director James Morris, the Ministry and Oversight body of the Church met with ACRA leaders and agreed to cooperate and keep the Church together in Bundelkhand.[74] This agreement, however, was destined to be strained because of differences in viewpoint. ACRA tended to accept people at face value; the Church wanted a testing time to prove sincerity.[75] Stuti Prakash explained:

> We have the condition that converts are to apply in the Church . . . and then we will baptize after some teaching can be given. We like to see both . . . man and wife come together, though they may have to wait for one another. When [one recent ACRA convert's wife] heard [her husband had been baptized] she fell in a well and died.[76]

Nevertheless, the Church loaned the services of Evangelist Ratnakar Rao to assist ACRA from May 1 to December 30, 1982. Ratnaker was married on May 7, 1982, to Monica.[77]

When it was reported that ACRA had received some $30,000 to repair village houses severely damaged in a hailstorm on March 22, 1982, people in power — fearing Vishal might use it as a political weapon — put him in jail. As soon as he was released, he took out a procession through the hail-affected villages and gained a good bit of praise, on one hand, for his concern for the poor and blame, on the other, for turning to the Janata party. He was supported by some Christians, and especially by ACRA chairman and workers. When the additional collector ordered ACRA not to distribute the money, they ignored the order. Vishal was again arrested on a series of false criminal charges. Disgruntled workers played into the hands of the accusers, and these court cases against Vishal continue to drag on.[78]

Invited to Wheaton '83 Consultation to deliver a paper on the subject "Christian Response to Human Need," Vishal, Ruth, and their two daughters came to the U.S.A. "Jesus, the Trouble-Maker," was the title of a paper he presented along with a scheme to develop Bundelkhand through building up a fund against which poor farmers could borrow. He pointed out that development is an issue of justice, not charity. Out of that developed the *Kisan Sewa Samiti* (Society for Service to the Farmers). The Centre for Development Studies, Bombay, has examined the plan and supports it.[79]

After the conference, Vishal and Ruth took the initiative to come to Ohio to meet with the FFMS Board. They stayed in North Olmsted with Neil Orchard who had recently visited India to encourage the Church and better understand the problems.[80] The meeting with the Board was not altogether pleasant and revealed strong differences of opinion within the Board as well as between the Board and ACRA. After reflecting on that meeting Vishal wrote back:

> I can never be too grateful for what FRIENDS have meant to my family. If not for you all, we would still have been living in the darkness of Hinduism.

Then as "a son come of age," he proceeded with a critique of the Mission hard indeed to hear. In conclusion, he made his plea:

> Some leaders in your church need to make up their minds whether I am Satan's instrument in Bundelkhand or a genuine heir to your spiritual-ity, call and mission to Bundelkhand.

Then he appended the verse he had used as his text when speaking in a number of the Friends churches in Ohio:

> Behold, I am doing a new thing. Now it springs up. Do you not per-ceive it? I am making a way in the desert and streams in the wasteland. (Isaiah 43:19-21)[81]

W. Robert Hess, no longer merely a lover of Bundelkhand and a former missionary, but now also the EFC—ER general superintendent, had the responsibility of responding to this letter, discerning the truth, and guid-ing in future relationships at present polarized in Bundelkhand. He found himself not in full agreement with some of Vishal's specific recommenda-tions and judgments. He wrote:

> To what extent the mantle has fallen on you for Bundelkhand will be determined by the way you seek first Christ's kingdom. Solid Christian work, as good ethics, involves a serious consideration of motives, means and consequences, so you as well as we must pay attention to all three. Christ instructs us not to judge one another's motives and I won't criticize yours . . . . Many have confidence in you and in your potential. I have tried and will continue to try to develop this trust.[82]

Back in India, Vishal and Ruth Mangalwadi took time to write and reflect. Vishal had to return to Chhatarpur from time to time to appear in some of the court cases against him. Overcome there by the continued injustice, corruption, violence, and oppression, Vishal and Ruth Mangal-wadi determined to take a course that would lead them into even more fierce conflict, for they have become convinced that the people in Bundel-khand live in a system firmly in the grip of evil:

> So much so that when a man of courage and integrity stands up against [it] he destroys not the evil, but himself. We in India indeed live in the

kingdom of Satan. The social evils that we confront are almost invincible because they have a supernatural dimension to them . . . . The battle is cosmic . . . . That makes it possible for you to stand with us . . . . Your prayers can make the difference.[83]

The Burden of Dr. Mategaonker

Dr. Mategaonker was encouraged by the coming of ACRA to the Chhatarpur area, and he gave support to this concept from beginning to end. In 1975 the shock of the death of his leading male nurse, Samson Huri Lal, and other changes almost inevitable following a shift in leadership, were difficulties he faced as he took firm charge of the hospital. The Christian Hospital became incorporated in EHA in 1976 and Dr. Mategaonker was one of its officers.[84]

EHA assisted in finding an administrator, a chaplain, and nurses; they also helped set up the auxiliary nurses' training school and a public health program.[85] Dr. Mategaonker was honored with enrollment in the International College of Surgeons in September 1974.[86] A continual stream of patients indicated community confidence had survived the departure of Dr. DeVol.[87] The Mission Board showed their confidence by budgeting $20,000 for 1977.[88]

The interests of Dr. Mategaonker, however, went far beyond the practice of medicine. He had been chairman of the discipline revision committee of the BMMS Executive, quarterly and local ministry and oversight chairman, and assistant general superintendent. After taking complete charge of the hospital, pressure of work had forced him to drop these responsibilities and encourage appointment of others of the hospital staff, who made up ninety percent of the Church attendance in Chhatarpur.[89] Their performance often disappointed him, but the possibility of working through ACRA was exciting.

In late 1976 the Christian Hospital joined ACRA in eye camps, first in Goethera, where Dr. Mategaonker operated on ninety-seven patients as the villagers took responsibility for feeding the whole crowd for many days. The team preached and showed the love of Christ. A year later they held a similar camp in Jatara village, where there had been converts. They witnessed as they examined some 500 patients, operated on 130 eyes, and surveyed some 800 children.[90]

Christmas was celebrated that year by a tableau mounted on a truck trolly with the kings following on camels. In twelve different places throughout the city they stopped to give the Christmas message and hand out tracts. The Church and hospital, invited by the local Congress party, sang carols and witnessed in the city hall.[91]

The Church, however, continued to disappoint Dr. Mategaonker, though his faith in a great ingathering remained. To push the Church, he accepted the post of evangelistic chairman. "I have got full faith that very shortly there is going to be an explosion around this area, a spiritual explosion! I am not at all discouraged," he wrote.[92]

Hospital staff continued to turn over rapidly as it always had. With help from OXFAM they built a covered ramp between wards. Doctors no longer had to carry umbrellas to protect themselves from the heat and rain as they went on rounds. I.C.C.O. Netherlands financed the building of a new ward, duplex staff house, and an administration building. Christofel Blinden Mission in West Germany gave money for a storeroom for medicines and financed the eye camps.[93]

All the three Mategaonker children—in boarding school in Jabalpur—Mala, Dinesh and Shobha—were growing up and entering high school and college. Sosan, their mother, began battling for her life through six major operations, one after the other. God wonderfully answered prayer for her and restored her to good health.[94] Dr. Mategaonker, in his positions in the hospital, ACRA, and the Church, was grieved as were others that these groups were pulling against each other. With a firm hand he tried to control this, but his efforts seemed to have an opposite effect.[95] The reduced number of patients coming into the hospital was a new disappointment as was also the cut in the hospital budget to $17,000 from the FFMS Board.[96]

Departure of Mategaonkers from Bundelkhand

On May 7, 1982, Dr. Mategaonker completed twenty-five years of service in the Christian Hospital in Chhatarpur. "I do not think I should stay here much longer," he decided at that time. "I do not want the work to suffer. It is the Lord's work and I want to see it progress . . . . I am under a depression that I could not help the hospital, Church and ACRA to come under one umbrella."[97] On September 8, 1982, he resigned. After securing a replacement in the coming of Dr. Anne Cherian, he left in April 1983 to take a new post in Muir Memorial Hospital in Nagpur.[98]

"Do not think that Mategaonkers' term in Bundelkhand is over," wrote Vishal Mangalwadi. "Their children have caught the faith and the vision of Dr. Mategaonker in the same way as we have caught my father's vision. And I believe that Mategaonkers' ministry in Bundelkhand has just begun."[99]

James Morris's Visit to India and His Recommendations

In early 1982 James Morris of EFM made a trip to India to help the Mission Board decide whether or not to continue their Mission in India or look for other fields. Though the suffering and frustration in India appalled him, Jim was filled with hope through the Christian testimony going out clearly through the work in which Friends had been significantly involved in India: EFI, CEEFI, UBS, FECI, ACRA, EHA, the hospital, the English and Hindi schools, and the Church – BMMS.

The friction between the hospital and Church, and ACRA and the Christian English School pointed up the need for an overall coordinator. He hoped a few more missionaries also could be sent, for the need in Bundelkhand was still great and he saw no light in abandoning a foundation so solidly laid. He found as many as nineteen young people had been coming to church membership classes conducted by Stuti Prakash[100] and that five young men were entering the ministry – surely a sign that the Church was very much alive. Vishwas Nath went to Delhi to work for "Back to the Bible" and minister in a Hindi church, where many found the Lord. Ravindra Nath, his cousin, took training in a Hindi school in North India and returned to BMMS as an evangelist. Ratnakar Rao served as an evangelist, and after his marriage, he and his wife went to UBS for further training. Nathu and Raja Bai's son Prabhu Dayal Prasad (great nephew of Khub Chand) entered UBS, just a year after Phillip Silas Masih of Ghuara graduated and returned to Chhatarpur as an evangelist and assistant pastor.[101]

The Church in Chhatarpur also had a new building. A legacy from a former orphan, Mr. Mathew, got them started. The new church building with adequate space was ready for use by the time people gathered to celebrate Stuti and Ramkibai Prakash's 50th wedding anniversary on May 8, 1978.[102]

Stuti Prakash's Retirement and His Replacements

On April 4, 1982, Stuti Prakash retired as pastor of the church. He had served the Lord in Bundelkhand for 59 years and as pastor of Chhatarpur for 30. It would not be easy to find a person to take his place. Phillip Masih found the situation far too difficult and accepted a post in Delhi. Another young man stayed only a few months.

At the yearly meeting in April 1983, some less respected leaders in the Church made a radical, drastic, and totally original proposal. They moved and the church accepted, that all the cumbersome boards and committees – set up by the mission for a very large church expected to be born in the 1950s – be canceled. In their place one board of eleven members was chosen: from Nowgong, Harpalpur, and Tikamgarh together, five members; Chhatarpur, five; Ghuara, one.[103] Their first task was to get a pastor to replace Stuti Prakash. They found one, Sukh Lal, the son of a former evangelist, Darru Lal.

Another position held by Stuti Prakash had been that of coordinator and BMMS general superintendent. As such, Stuti Prakash was appointed to go to Kaimosi, Kenya, in July 1982 as representative of one of sixty-seven yearly meetings at the World Friends Conference. Pratap Singh Brown also went as a representative of BMMS.[104]

Seeking God's guidance for the future of Bundelkhand, EFC—ER General Superintendent W. Robert Hess went to the historic International Conference for Itinerant Evangelists in Amsterdam in July 1983. Gabriel Massey and Vijay Prakash were two of the 4,000 third-world delegates from 130 countries who attended.[105] New inspiration and understanding of today's role for missions encouraged Bob to continue underlining Jim Morris's suggestions that the Bundelkhand Mission continue to be held in focus.

So the invitation was renewed to Vijay Prakash to become the representative consultant for the FFMS of EFC—ER in India. His task would not be administration but discussion with such groups as BMMS, UBS, EFI, FECI, EHA and CEEFI, and exploration of opportunities for further mission development.[106] Vijay accepted and began work January 1, 1984. His wife, Prema, though suffering of heart ailment, as of mid-1985, was still working as a nurse in the Railway Hospital in Jhansi; the son, Vineesh, married April, 1985, was employed in medical supplies, and the daughter, Vineetha, was enrolled in college.[107]

Even before Stuti Prakash left for Kenya, on June 11, 1982, he lost his life-long companion, Ramkibai.[108] "She never held me [back] or hindered me in my ministry. [Rather,] she had a great part in His ministry," Stuti wrote concerning her.[109] The year ahead for him would have been very difficult had not his daughters, Shyam Kumari William Lall and Kusum Nanda, rallied to care for him. Kusum was the nearest since her family lived in one side of Stuti Prakash's house. She had long since repented of her early rebellion in leaving the Church to marry Nanda, a Punjabi.

Through the years Kusum had attended services, taking her children with her. The two oldest boys were by 1983, like their father, driving their own buses. The daughter was in college and the two youngest boys were in primary school.[110] All wanted to join the Church. Legalism won the day when they applied in 1980, as the leaders—against their Quaker heritage—demanded she submit to baptism as one from non-Christian background. Some even insisted she should not come at all until her Punjabi husband was also ready.[111]

As difficult as this was, Kusum finally received the written permission of her husband, took baptism with her children from her father, and asked the Church publicly for forgiveness.[112] On Sunday, March 25,

1984, Stuti Prakash had the joy of seeing Kusum and her children formally received as full members of the BMMS.

It was his last Sunday in the Church he had served without interruption for nearly sixty years. He began that week to plan ways to witness to passers-by and on March 29, 1984, wrote friends in Oregon about a large *mauwha* tree in front of his house under which he intended to build a platform where he could sit and "give his Christian assurance."[113] Three days after writing this, on April 1, 1984, Stuti Prakash, 73, died. His heart's cry expressed nine months earlier will continue to echo through Bundelkhand:

> How I wish now some young man would get the vision for this part of Bundelkhand. I remember when I was young God dealt with me and showed me the need to surrender to Him for this needy area. It was not a dream; I will call it a vision. A man was suffering and facing death and the voice came to me asking if I was willing to give my blood that this man may not die. I said, "Lord, here I am." This is the secret of my surrender. God so faithfully has led me through.[114]

"I tell you the truth, unless a kernel of wheat falls to the ground and dies, it remains only a single seed. But if it dies, it produces many seeds." (John 12:24 NIV) This is the hope in Bundelkhand.

Appendix

Table of Contents for Appendix

Presidents of Foreign Missionary Society of Ohio Yearly Meeting

Sarah E. Jenkins	1884-1895	Chester G. Stanley	1951-1956;
Elizabeth Jenkins	1895-1913		1958-1960
George E. Kent	1913-1915	Elden Snyder	1960-1967, 1972
Elmer Wood	1915-1927	Herbert Burch	1967-1972
Claude A. Roane	1927-1943	Robert Hess	1972-1978
Walter R. Williams	1943-1951	Charles Robinson	1978-1984
Edward Escolme	1956-1958	Roger Wood	1984 —

Superintendents, Corresponding Secretaries, and Assistants to Mission Superintendents

Emma Lupton	1894-1901	Sherman Brantingham	1961-1975
Rachel Pim	1913-1920	W. Robert Hess	1977-1979
Louise Ellett	1920-1948	(Evangelical Friends Mission)	
Walter R. Williams	1935-1954	James Morris	1980 –
Chester Stanley	1954-1961	(Evangelical Friends Mission)	
Anna Cobbs	1955-1984		

India Missionaries

Delia Fistler	1892-1916	Walter and Geneva Bolitho	1928-1932
Esther Baird	1892-1938	Dr. Ruth Hull Bennett	1928-1940
Martha Barber	1892-1898	Nell Lewis	1929-1935
Mary Thomas	1892-1895	John Earle	1932-1935
Eliza Frankland	1897-1902	James and Judith Kinder	1930-1935
Anna Edgerton	1899-1904	Everett and Catherine Cattell	1936-1957
Dr. Abigail Goddard	1903-1908	Robert and Elizabeth Earle	1938-1946
Eva Allen	1905-1908	Anna Nixon	1941-1984
Carrie Wood	1908-1948	Norma Freer	1945 –
Bertha Cox	1908-1912	Milton and Rebecca Coleman	1945-1968
Clinton Morris	1912-1915	Clifton and Elizabeth	
Margaret Smith	1913-1928	Robinson	1947-1965
Alison and Inez Rogers	1921-1927	Max and Ruth Ellen Banker	1949-1956
Dr. Elizabeth Ward	1923-1924	Dr. W. Ezra and	
Merrill and Anna Coffin	1923-1929	Frances DeVol	1949-1974
Dr. Mary Fleming	1925-1927	Robert and Esther Hess	1952-1968
Mary Allen	1925	Joyce Bryner	1952-1954
Alena Calkins	1927-1952	Kathryn Thompson	1964-1969
Ruth Thurston (Earle)	1927-1935		

Friends Indian Leaders in Bundelkhand

Served	In Mission or Church	In the Area	In Other Areas
Charlotte Bai	1886-1933		
Pancham Singh	1906-1933		
William Parsad	1908-1935		
Prem Das Bodhan	1909-1915		
Mangalwadi (Daruwa)	1915-1921		
Gore Lal Singh	1911-1960		
Nathu Lall	1912-1965		
Lachhman Singh	1920-1970		
Mangal Singh	1920-1940	1940-1965	
Moti Lal	1922-1935		1935-1980
Stuti Prakash	1924-1983		
Dayal Chand Singh	1925 –		
Hira Singh	1926-1958	1958 –	
Grace Jones Singh (Dr.)	1930-1956	1956-1980	
Komal Das Lall	1937-1971	1972-1977	
Victor Mangalwadi	1943-1955	1980-1981	1955-1980
George Masih	1947-1979		1940-1947
Hizikiel Lall	1949-1961	1984 –	1961-1984

Shyam William Lall	1951–		
Samson Huri Lal	1950-1974		
Phyllis Das	1954–		
Virginia S. Lall	1954-1961	1984–	1961-1984
Vijay S. Prakash	1955-1964; 1983–		1964-1983
Gabriel Massey	1956-1974; 1984–	1974–	
D. W. Mategaonker (Dr.)	1957-1983		1983–
Pratap Sing Brown (Dr.)	1958-1970	1970–	
Vishal Mangalwadi		1976–	
Ruth F. Mangalwadi		1976–	

Important Events

1892	Delia Fistler and Esther Baird along with Martha Barber and Mary Thomas sail to India
1896	Friends Mission opened in Bundelkhand – Delia Fistler, superintendent
1897	First school for girls in Bundelkhand
1902	Friends Church in Bundelkhand founded with 31 full and 18 probationary members
1905	Men are included on the Mission Board
1906	Harpalpur station opened Louise B. Pierson Chapel built in Nowgong
1909	Thakur P. Singh – first village convert
1910	Kanjarpur School opened
1912	First evangelist stationed in Chhatarpur – Pancham Singh First male missionary sent to the field – Clinton Morris
1913	Goddard Memorial Hospital (dispensary) built in Nowgong
1914	World War I
1916	Esther Baird appointed superintendent First coeducational school established by Mangalwadi
1919	Chhatarpur station opened – "A foothold for the Lord"
1921	Twenty-fifth Anniversary with 200 Christians present First married couple sent to the field – Alison and Inez Rogers
1925	Chapel and dispensary opened in Chhatarpur Bible school opened in Nowgong
1931	First hospital for women and children in Bundelkhand opened Esther Baird awarded Kaiser-i-Hind silver medal
1934	Five missionaries resign
1936	Walter R. Williams's report – "The Watershed of History of the Mission" Everett and Catherine Cattell arrive in India First Christian Endeavor organized
1937	Everett Cattell appointed superintendent Decentralization begins – Dayal Chand Singh and Lachhman Singh and families move to Gulganj Esther Baird awarded Kaiser-i-Hind gold medal Bible-industrial school opened – Nowgong Christian Institute

1938   Tamberam International Conference, Madras
           Esther Baird's retirement

1941   Conversion of Khub Chand of Dhamora
           Conversion of Hira Lal of Bilwar
           World War II
           Introduction of the pastoral system — Dayal Chand Singh first pastor
           Jungle camps introduced

1942-43   A church coming of age — Prem Sabha

1943   National Association of Evangelicals formed

1945   World War II ends

1946   Golden Jubilee Celebration of the founding of the mission

1947   India gains independence (midnight, August 14)
           Halka Daniel, first Christian from Ghuara

1948   First women's retreat
           Mahatma Gandhi assassinated

1949   Purchase of Amarmau and hill properties
           Devaluation of rupee (3.3 to 4.75)

1950   Women's Hospital made a general hospital
           India's first Republic Day, January 26 (members of the Commonwealth)

1951   Evangelical Fellowship of India formed

1953   Union Biblical Seminary founded

1954   Fifteen missionaries on the field
           Mass reversion of new converts begins

1955   Khub Chand's reversion

1956   Beginning of the Five-Year Plan to make the Church independent

1957   Dr. W. Ezra DeVol appointed superintendent
           Dr. Everett L. Cattell appointed superintendent of Ohio Yearly Meeting

1957-60   Court case in which Church won right to discipline its own members

1961   Bundelkhand Friends Church (Bundelkhand *Masihi Mitra Samaj* — BMMS)
               becomes an independent yearly meeting

1976   Christian English school opened in Chhatarpur
           ACRA — Association for Comprehensive Rural Assistance founded

1983   Appointment of Vijay Prakash as Representative Consultant of EFC — ER

1984   Assassination of Prime Minister Indira Gandhi
           Appointment of Prime Minister Rajiv Gandhi
           Several buildings in ACRA burned at time of Sikh Massacre
           Bhopal Tragedy

1985   Indian missionaries of Friends Missionary Prayer Band join BMMS in
               "Project Harvest."

SHIFT FROM BUNDELKHAND TO WIDER MINISTRIES

1954   Clifton and Betty Robinson to Delhi
           Development of International Christian Leadership (ICL), 1955

1956   Anna Nixon to Jhansi
           Development of the Christian Education Department of the Evangelical
               Fellowship of India, opened in 1962

1961   W. Robert and Esther Hess to Yavatmal
         W. R. Hess served as Union Biblical Seminary principal 1964-1968

1963   Dr. W. Ezra and Frances DeVol to Kathmandu, Nepal
         Dr. W. E. DeVol served as director of United Mission Medical Center in
         the United Mission to Nepal, opened in 1954

1967   Milton and Rebecca Coleman to Bihar for work in the Evangelical Fellow-
         ship of India's Committee on Relief (EFICOR)

1970   The founding of the Emmanuel Hospital Association

1973   Anna Nixon to Union Biblical Seminary

1974   The founding of Federation of Evangelical Churches (FECI)

Selected Bibliography — Primary Sources

DIARIES

Esther Baird	1911-1937	Anna Nixon (letters)	1946-1980
Alena Calkins (letters)	1927-1951	Alison and Inez Rogers	1920-1927
Catherine Cattell	1942-1946	Carrie B. Wood	1911-1948
E. L. Cattell	1942-1947		

INTERVIEWS

Dr. Ruth Hull Bennett	Hira Lal
Alena Calkins	Ruth F. Mangalwadi
Catherine Cattell	Vishal K. Mangalwadi
Milton and Rebecca Coleman	Olive Osborne
Dr. W. E. DeVol	Vijay S. Prakash
Elizabeth Earle	Clifton Robinson

Vijay S. Prakash also translated interviews of the following and recorded them (1972-1973):

Kush Lal Bodhan, Pratap Brown, Sahodra Brown, Kamlapat Coleman, Phulmani Coleman, Halka Daniel, Bhagwati Bai, Dharm Das, Phyllis Das, Puniya Bai Jagannath, Hira Lal, S. Huri Lal, Sukh Lal, Hizikiel Lall, Mabel M. Lal, Shyam K. William Lall, Virginia Lall, Victor Mangalwadi, George Masih, Mrs. George Masih, Gabriel Massey, Dr. D. W. Mategaonker, Monica Nath, Salomi Reubin Nath, Ramkibai Prakash, Stuti Prakash, Vijay S. Prakash, Kamal Prasad, Kampta Prasad, Pyari Bai K. Prasad, Shitabu Prasad, Kamal Sardar, Dayal Chand Singh, Mrs. G. L. Singh, Gendi P. N. Singh, Dr. Grace D. Singh, Hira Singh, Jashwant Singh, Mangal Singh, Pancham Singh, P. N. Singh, Priobala Nath Singh, Bharos William, Jaiwanti Bai William, Hannah Williams

LETTERS

From Mission Board to the Field		(Abbreviations used in footnotes)
Sherman Brantingham	1961-1975	ShB
Emelyn J. Cattell (Emma Lupton)	1894-1901	EL
Carrie L. Chambers	1914	CLC
Church World Service	1949	CWS
Anna Cobbs	1960-1984	A.Cobbs
Louise Ellett	1920-1948	LE
W. R. Hess	1976-1984	WRH
Elizabeth Jenkins	1895-1949	EJ
Sarah Jenkins, first president Mission Board	1892-1894	SJ

George Kent	1914	GK
Leona Kinsey	1928-1929	LK
Russell Myers	1971-1983	RM
Rachel Pim	1913-1920	RP
Claude Roane	1927-1936	CAR
Catherine Stalker	1929-1930	CS
Chester Stanley	1946-1960	CGS
Walter Williams	1936-1946	WRW
Elmer Wood	1923	EW
Mary B. Wood	1897	MBW

From Field to the Mission Board

Esther Baird	1892-1937	EB
Max Banker	1949-1956	MB
Ruth Ellen H. Banker	1949-1956	REB
Dr. E. Ruth Hull Bennett	1934-1940	RHB
Walter Bolitho	1932	WB
Bram	1932-1935	B
Catherine D. Cattell	1936-1957	CDC
Everett L. Cattell	1936-1957	ELC
Merrill M. Coffin	1929	MMC
Milton Coleman	1945-1968	MEC
Rebecca H. Coleman	1945-1968	RHC
Frances H. DeVol	1949-1974	FHD
Dr. W. Ezra DeVol	1949-1974	WED
Elizabeth S. Earle	1939-1946	ESE
Robert Earle	1939-1946	RE
Delia Fistler	1892-1916	DF
"Five Missionaries"	1934	Five Missionaries
(James Kinder, Judith Kinder, John Earle, Ruth Earle, Nell Lewis)		
Norma A. Freer	1945-1984	NAF
Dr. A. E. Goddard	1908	AEG
Esther G. Hess	1952-1968	EGH
W. Robert "Bob" Hess	1952-1968	WRH
James Kinder	1932	JK
Ruth F. Mangalwadi	1976-1984	RFM
Victor Mangalwadi	1950-1981	VM
Vishal K. Mangalwadi	1976-1984	VKM
George Masih	1973-1979	GM
Gabriel Massey	1980-1984	GaM
Dr. D. W. Mategaonker	1974-1984	DWM
Anna Nixon	1941-1980	AN
Stuti Prakash	1946-1984	SP
Vijay S. Prakash	1973-1984	VSP
Clifton J. Robinson	1949-1965	CJR
Elizabeth O. Robinson (Betty)	1949-1965	EOR
Alison Rogers	1921-1927	AR
Inez C. Rogers	1921-1927	ICR
Gore Lal Singh	1932-1935	GLS
Pancham Singh	1932-1935	PS
Carrie Wood	1908-1948	CBW

MINUTES

		(Abbreviations used in footnotes)
American Friends Mission Superintendents' Annual Reports	1896-1974	AFM Annual Report
Bundelkhand Friends Church Monthly Meeting Minutes	1902-1936	BFCMM Minutes
Bundelkhand Masihi Mitra Samaj Executive Committee Minutes	1957-1973	BMMS Ex. Com.
CEEFI Executive Committee Minutes	1962-1971	CEEFI
Evangelical Fellowship of India Executive Committee Minutes	1951-1971	EFI Minutes
Evangelical Friends Church— Eastern Region Minutes	1976-1983	EFC—ER Minutes
Friends Foreign Missionary Society Minutes	1945-1984	FFMS Minutes
India Mission Council Minutes	1903-1983	MC Minutes
Joint Council Minutes	1954-1961	JC
Ohio Yearly Meeting Minutes Personal Reports of All Missionaries	1884-1975	OYM
Union Biblical Seminary Association Board of Governors Minutes	1953-1983	UBSBdG
Union Biblical Seminary Executive Board (Governing Body)	1953-1983	UBSEX

Selected Bibliography—Secondary Sources

BOOKS

Baird, Esther. *Adventuring with God.* Mt. Pleasant, Ohio: Friends Foreign Missionary Society, 1924, 48 p.

Cattell, Catherine D. *Till Break of Day.* Grand Rapids, Mich.: Wm. B. Eerdmans Pub. Co., 1962, 214 p.

_____. *From Bamboo to Mango.* Newberg, Oreg.: The Barclay Press, 1976, 218 p.

Cattell, Everett L. *Christian Mission: A Matter of Life.* Richmond, Ind.: Friends United Press, 1981, 160 p.

Coffin, Merrill M. *Friends in Bundelkhand.* Mysore, India: The Wesley Press, 1926, 53 p.

Collins, Larry and Dominique Lapierre. *Freedom at Midnight.* New Delhi, India: Vikas Pub. Hse. Pvt. Ltd., 1976, 500 p.

Fletcher, Grace Nies. *The Fabulous Flemings of Kathmandu.* New York: E. P. Dutton & Co., Inc., 1964, 219 p.

Ford, Helen and Esther. *The Steps of a Good Man.* Pearl River, N.Y.: Africa Inland Mission, 1976, 202 p.

Griffiths, Percival. *The British Impact on India.* New York: Archon Books, 1965

Lindell, Jonathan. *Nepal and the Gospel of God.* New Delhi, India: Masihi Sahitya Sanstha, 1979, 279 p.

McMahon, Robert. *To God Be the Glory.* New Delhi, India: Masihi Sahitya Sanstha, 1971, 76 p.

Niyogi Report. Christian Missionary Activities Enquiry Committee, Madhya Pradesh, 1956, Vol. 1 Nagpur: Government Printing. M.P., India, 1965, 182 p.

Pickett, J. Waskom. *Christ's Way to India's Heart*. Lucknow: Lucknow Publishing House, India, 3rd edition, 1960.

Spear, Percival. *India*. Ann Arbor: The University of Michigan Press, 1961, 491 p.

Williams, Walter R. *The Rich Heritage of Quakerism*. Grand Rapids, Mich.: William B. Eerdmans Pub. Co., 1962, 279 p.

Wolpert, Stanley A. *A New History of India*. New York: Oxford University Press, 1977, 471 p.

ENCYCLOPEDIAS, DICTIONARIES

Concise Dictionary of the Christian World Mission. New York: Abingdon Press, 1971, 597 p.

Encyclopedia Americana, Vol. 29, 1978

BIBLES

Amplified Bible   *Living Bible, The*
King James Version   *New International Version* (NIV)

MAGAZINES

		(Abbreviations used in footnotes)
AIM		–
Bulletin of Association for Comprehensive Rural Assistance		ACRA
CONTACT		–
EFM World		–
Evangelical Fellowship Magazine		EFM
Evangelical Friend (EFA)	1968-1984	EF
The Evangelical Friend (Ohio)	1955-1967	EF
Federation of Evangelical Churches in India Bulletin		FECI
Friends Missionary Advocate	1889-1908	–
Friends Oriental News	1908-1954	FON
Light of Life		–
Missionary News Service		MNS
Missionary Voice	1955-1967	MV
UBS Challenge		–
UBS Contact N.A (formerly UBS Contact U.S.A.)		–
UBS Up-Date		–

PAMPHLETS

"A Brief Historical Statement – The FECI," Nov. 3, 1974.
Bundelkhand Friends Church Membership Record (1902-1927)
CEEFI Triennial Report, 1965
CEEFI Triennial Report, 1968
CEEFI Triennial Report, 1971
"Greetings from Nepal." Mari Printing House, Darjeeling, 32 p.
India Mission Manual
India Missionary Directory, 1948
Interviews recorded by Vijay Prakash (1973)
Jubilee Report, 1946
McGavran Report, 1938
Mahatma Gandhi Centenary Report, n.d. Paramount Bldg., Englewood, Ohio 45322

Missionaries in the Making
Report to Cooperating Home Boards of UBS, Frank J. Kline, Principal, 1961
Reports to Missionary Board — Walter R. Williams, 1936
                              E. L. Cattell, 1971
                              W. R. Hess, 1975
UBS Report to World Vision — Saphir Athyal, 1976

UNPUBLISHED THESES AND ARTICLES

E. L. Cattell — unpublished article "Do Friends Have a Faith Mission?" 1948
E. L. Cattell's Report on Missions, 1971
Milton Coleman — unpublished articles
Rebecca Coleman — unpublished article, July, 1972
Ella Escolme — unpublished article, n.d.
W. R. Hess's Report on Missions, 1975
James Morris's Reports on Missions, 1983
Anna Nixon — "Advance on Sixteen Fronts"
Anna Nixon — Guidelines for Adapters and Editors of CEEFI
G. Edwin Robinson — "History of the Policy of the American Friends Mission in
    Central India," 1978

Notes

Preface/ Acknowledgments

1 Delia Fistler, Report to FFMS, July 12 1904
2 Luke 10:2; John 4:35
3 DF, Report to FFMS, July 23 1901
4 Ideas compared with P. D. Forsythe as quoted in *Friends Missionary Advocate*, Dec 1908, p 8
5 Assurance given to Everett Cattell at a time of great darkness; cf. ELC Diary, Apr 20-26 1947
6 Residents of Friendsview Manor and others in Newberg, Oregon, who assisted were Elen Bowman, Jean Bradley, Esther Brougher, Edith Campbell, Betty and Louis Coffin, Gertrude Hibbs, Marjorie Higgins, Alice Hines, Bonnie Hollinshead, Esther Klages, Elsie Meeker, Elva Neifert, Ilene Osgard, Joseph Reece, Alice Ross, Edna Springer, Gwen Winters, and Beryl Woodward.

CHAPTER 1
Occupying a Field

1 Delia Fistler, "Our Missionaries in the Making" pamphlet series
2 *OYM Minutes*, 1898, p 31
3 MMC, *Friends in Bundelkhand*, pp 9, 10
4 *OYM Minutes*, 1893, p 36
5 *Ibid.*, 1892, p 53
6 SJ to DF, Sep 14 1892
7 MMC, *Friends in Bundelkhand*, p 11. (Bishop Thoburn came from St. Clairs-

ville, Ohio. The church there is named for him and he is buried there.)
8 SJ letter, Nov 4 1892
9 *OYM Minutes*, 1893, p 36
10 *Ibid.*, Nov 21 1892
11 *OYM Minutes*, 1893, p 46
12 SJ to EB and DF, Jan 19 1893
13 *OYM Minutes*, 1893, pp 45-47
14 EC(L) to DF, July 6 1894. (The other two missionaries were supported by the Loomis family.)
15 EC(L) to DF, May 15 1894
16 CA Swain to DF and EB, Mar 4 1896; cf. EC(L) to EB, Mar 12 1894, and unpublished article, n.d., of Ella Escolme
17 *Ibid.*
18 *OYM Minutes*, 1894, p 31
19 *Ibid.*, 1895, p 41
20 *Ibid.*
21 EC(L) to DF, July 6 1894
22 *OYM Minutes*, 1894, p 48
23 *Ibid.*, 1895, pp 38, 49
24 ECL to DF and EB, May 31 1895
25 *OYM Minutes*, 1895, pp 37-39
26 Women's FFMS, Aug 22 1895; cf. EJ to DF and EB, Sep 4 1895
27 *OYM Minutes*, 1897, p 70
28 EJ to DF, Apr 28 1896
29 MMC, *Friends in Bundelkhand*, p 11
30 *OYM Minutes*, 1896, p 45 (Mary Thomas withdrew from the Mission in 1895 to ease the financial burden of Mrs. Loomis. She remained with the Methodists.)
31 MMC, *Friends in Bundelkhand*, p 12
32 *OYM Minutes*, 1896, p 45
33 *Ibid.*, p 46

34 ER Thesis, quoting from Percival Griffiths, *The British Impact on India* (NY: Archon Books, 1965), p 188 and from *Imperial Gazateer* of India, 1908, p 72
35 EJ to DF, Jan 11 1897
36 *Ibid.*, Nov 9 1896
37 *OYM Minutes*, 1897, p 33
38 EB, *Adventuring with God*, pp 22-24
39 MMC, *Friends in Bundelkhand*, p 15
40 *OYM Minutes*, 1897, pp 34, 36; 1898, p 37
41 MMC, *Friends in Bundelkhand*, p 16
42 *OYM Minutes*, 1897, p 35
43 ECL to DF, Apr 13 1897

CHAPTER 2
Planting a Church

1 *OYM Minutes*, 1897, p 36
2 EJ letter to DF, Jan 11 1897
3 *OYM Minutes*, 1897, p 27
4 ECL to EB, Sep 28 1897
5 Mary B. Wood to EB, Nov 8 1897
6 ECL to EB, May 24 1898
7 *Ibid.*, Sep 8 1898
8 *OYM Minutes*, 1897, p 27
9 *Ibid.*, p 34
10 *OYM Minutes*, 1899, p 33 Note: Anna Edgerton went out for her first term of six years. Delia Fistler, going for the second time, signed an eight-year contract.
11 ECL to DF, Oct 14 1900; cf. DF to ECL, Mar 29 1899
12 *OYM Minutes*, 1899, p 41
13 *Ibid.*, p 42
14 *Ibid.*, pp 37, 45
15 ECL to DF, July 16 1900 & Sep 5 1901
16 DF to Board, July 12 1899
17 *OYM Minutes*, 1901, p 48
18 *Ibid.*, 1902, pp 49, 50
19 MMC, *Friends in Bundelkhand*, p 21
20 *OYM Minutes*, 1903, p 44
21 *Ibid.*, p 60
22 BFC MM Minutes, Dec 11 1902
23 *OYM Minutes*, 1904, p 56; cf. 1903, p 60
24 *Ibid.*, 1903, p 60
25 *Ibid.*, 1899, p 42
26 *Ibid.*, 1900, p 44
27 *Ibid.*, 1901, p 35
28 BFC MM Minutes, Nov 4 1902; cf. June 1902
29 BFC MM Minutes, Mar 13 1903
30 *OYM Minutes*, 1903, pp 60, 63
31 *Ibid.*, 1930, p 56
32 MC Minutes, Nov 9 1903
33 *OYM Minutes*, 1904, p 38; 1905, p 49
34 *Ibid.*, 1902, p 43; 1903, p 60; cf. DF to ECL, July 30 1903
35 *OYM Minutes*, 1904, p 56
36 *Ibid.*, 1905, p 64
37 *Ibid.*, 1906, p 19
38 *Ibid.*, 1905, p 64
39 *Ibid.*, 1907, p 49
40 *Ibid.*, 1904, p 56
41 *Ibid.*, p 55
42 MMC, *Friends in Bundelkhand*, p 24; cf. *OYM Minutes*, 1906, p 37
43 *Ibid.*, 1904, p 38
44 *Ibid.*, 1906, p 37; cf. BFC MM Minutes, Dec 12 1906. Note: This place would be filled eventually by Pancham Singh, who became a Church member in the fall of 1906 (BFC MM Minutes, Aug 1906)
45 *OYM Minutes*, 1903, p 46
46 *Ibid.*, 1904, p 41
47 *Ibid.*, 1905, p 48
48 *Ibid.*, pp 63, 79
49 *Ibid.*, 1904, p 56
50 *Ibid.*, 1904, p 57; cf. BFC MM Minutes, Nov 10 1903
51 FON, Vol 1, No 4, 1908, p 3; *OYM Minutes*, 1903, p 38; 1906, p 36
52 MMC, *Friends in Bundelkhand*, p 23
53 *OYM Minutes*, 1905, pp 63-65
54 BFC MM Minutes, Dec 13 1905; cf. Joshua 7:19, ff.
55 *Ibid.*
56 *Ibid.*
57 *OYM Minutes*, 1906, pp 35, 36

CHAPTER 3
Coping with Hardship

1 OYM Minutes, 1905, p 38
2 *Ibid.*, pp 37, 38
3 BFC MM Minutes, Jan 9 1907
4 *OYM Minutes*, 1907, pp 46, 48
5 *Missionary Advocate*, Apr 1908, p 8
6 Dr. A. E. Goddard to Mrs. Hathaway, Apr 9 1908
7 *Missionary Advocate*, Feb 1909, p 16
8 FON, Vol III, No 5, Feb 1911, p 6
9 *OYM Minutes*, 1908, p 46
10 BFC MM Membership Record, p 1
11 *OYM Minutes*, 1908, p 47
12 MMC, *Friends in Bundelkhand*, p 26
13 MC Minutes, July 8, Nov 9 1908
14 MMC, *Friends in Bundelkhand*, p 26
15 *Ibid.*
16 *OYM Minutes*, 1909, p 42
17 *Ibid.*, 1910, p 55
18 MC Minutes, May 7 1909; cf. Mar 10 1909
19 *Ibid.*, Mar 10, Apr 14, May 7, Oct 5 1909
20 BFC MM Minutes, Jan 9 1909
21 FON, Vol VIII, No 2, 3, Oct 1915, p 6
22 EB, *Adventuring with God*, pp 22-28; cf. India Mission Directory, 1948
23 MMC, *Friends in Bundelkhand*, p 27
24 FON, Vol VI, No 6, Sep 1914, p 6
25 BFC MM Minutes, June 10, July 4, Oct 12, Nov 9 1910
26 *OYM Minutes*, 1911, p 53
27 BFC MM Minutes, May 10 1911
28 MC Minutes, Mar 7 1911

29 BFC MM Membership Record. He died July 10 1915.

30 BFC MM Minutes, May 10, Aug 9 1911; Apr 11 1913

31 FON, Vol IV, No 6, Apr 1912, p 7

32 MC Minutes, Nov 10 1910

33 OYM Minutes, 1911, p 53; cf. FON, Vol IV, No 4, Dec 1911, p 6

34 MC Minutes, Mar 7 1911; cf. OYM Minutes, 1910, p 73

35 OYM Minutes, 1910, p 73; cf. MC Minutes, Jan 5, Nov 8 1910. Note: Gore Lal Singh had been brought to the Mission as a very small boy in 1896. His mother left him in order that he might not starve. While she was arranging for his stay, Gore Lal spotted a loaf of bread cooling on the table in the mission bungalow. By the time they found him under the table, the last of the bread was disappearing. A year later when his mother returned, Gore Lal hid, fearing she would take him away. Instead, she stayed on and became a faithful Christian and splendid worker, and Gore Lal became the first Friends minister in Bundelkhand.

36 OYM Minutes, 1909, p 55

37 MC Minutes, Jan 5 1909

38 Ibid., Feb 10 1909

39 OYM Minutes, 1910, p 72; FON, Vol III, No 6, Apr 1911, p 7

40 OYM Minutes, 1911, p 64

41 Interviews collected through Vijay Prakash, Fall, 1972

42 MC Minutes, Jan 15, Feb 2, and Apr 6 1910

43 Ibid., Apr 14 1909; Apr 6 1910, May 9 1910 and FON, Vol III, Aug 1910, p 10

44 OYM Minutes, 1910, p 71

45 FON, Vol IV, Nos 1 and 2, June-Aug 1911, p 7

CHAPTER 4
Praying Doors Open

1 MC Minutes, May 9, Oct 6 1910

2 OYM Minutes, 1909, p 42

3 Ibid., 1910, p 72

4 MC Minutes, Mar 7 1911; EB Diary Feb 13 1911

5 FON, Vol V, No 3, Oct-Dec 1912, p 6; cf. Vol III, No 6, Apr 1911, p 1

6 EB Diary, Feb 20 1911

7 Ibid., Apr 19, 28 1911, Nov 6 1913, p 7; BFC MM, Oct 11 1911

8 FON, Vol IV, No 4, 1911

9 OYM Minutes, 1912, p 41

10 Ibid., 1911, p 54

11 Ibid., p 52

12 MC Minutes, Mar 7 1911

13 FON, Vol IV, No 3, Oct 1911, p 7

14 Ibid., No 7, June 1912, p 6. Note: Pyari Bai was the oldest orphan and very dear to all, especially to Gore Lal's mother. After a year in the Almora sanatorium, she recovered and in March 1912 married Gore Lal.

15 OYM Minutes, 1912, p 41; BFC MM Minutes, Jan 17 1912

16 BFC MM Minutes, Feb 14 1912

17 FON, Vol V, No 1, Aug 1912, p 7

18 BFC MM Minutes, July 12 1912

19 Ibid., Apr 11, Aug 14, Oct 9 1912

20 OYM Minutes, 1913, p 51

21 BFC MM Minutes, Sep 10 1913. Note: Prayer was not reserved just for big issues. Christians thanked God for answers in smaller matters, also, such as the time Dalsiya, Bhagwan, and Balla were chosen to go to Delhi to see King George, in Delhi Dec. 12 1911, proclaimed Emperor of India. This set the stage for the seat of India's Government to be moved from Calcutta to Delhi on Dec 23 1912. Other orphans, at the same time, toured Bundelkhand – seeing Bela Tal and Harpalpur for the first time, and being introduced to their first sight of a train. FON, Vol IV, No 5, Feb 12 1912, p 6; Vol V, No 2, Oct 1912, p 7; No 3, Nov-Dec 1912, p 7.

22 OYM Minutes, 1912, p 38

23 BFC MM Minutes, Feb 14 1912

24 MC Minutes, Mar 7 1911

25 OYM Minutes, 1913, p 51

26 EB in Missionary Advocate, May 1908, p 9

27 FON, Vol V, No 1, Aug 1912, pp 6, 7

28 Ibid., Vol V, No 2, Oct 1912, p 7; No 3, Nov-Dec 1912, p 6

29 OYM Minutes, 1912, p 42

30 FON, Vol V, No 4, Feb-Apr 1913, pp 6, 7

31 EB Diary, July 30, Aug 5 1913

32 Ibid., Nov 4 1913

33 Rachel Pim to EB, Dec 16 1913

34 EB Diary, Nov 24 1913

35 FON, Vol V, No 4, Feb-Apr 1913, p 7

36 EB Diary, Nov 30 1913

37 Ibid., Dec 10 1913

38 MMC, Friends in Bundelkhand, p 31

39 OYM Minutes, 1914, p 44

40 Rachel Pim to EB, June 7 1916

41 Ibid., Aug 21 1916

42 FON, Vol IX, No 1, Dec 1916, p 6

43 BFC MM Minutes, Nov 8 1916

44 FON, Vol IX, No 1, Dec 1916, p 7

45 Ibid.

46 BFC MM Minutes, Dec 13 1905

CHAPTER 5
Enduring War and Retrenchment

1 Rachel Pim to EB, Aug 21 1916
2 EB Diary, Feb 18 1914
3 MC Minutes, Mar 3 1914
4 BFC MM Minutes, Apr 8 1914; Sep 9 1914
5 *OYM Minutes*, 1914, p 44
6 Margaret Smith wrote, "The women tell us there's no use to try to do anything with them — they are born Kanjars and to steal — but we tell them God is able to save them and to so change their hearts they will not want to steal."
7 FON, Vol VI, No 6, Sep 1914, p 6
8 *Ibid.*, p 6, 7; cf. *OYM Minutes*, 1914, p 48
9 *OYM Minutes*, 1914, p 42
10 George E. Kent, Pres., & Carrie L. Chambers, Sec., to EB, Sep 7 1914
11 The Board requested the workers on the field to make their own reductions. The one bright star in a very dark sky was that the gifts and pledges given at that same yearly meeting totaled $3,421.
12 *OYM Minutes*, 1914, p 48
13 *Ibid.*, p 47
14 *Ibid.*, 1915, p 55
15 *Ibid.*, 1914, p 47
16 FON, Vol VIII, No 1, July 1915, p 6
17 BFC MM Minutes, Feb 18 1914
18 *OYM Minutes*, 1915, p 51
19 *Ibid.*, 1914, p 48
20 BFC MM Minutes, Sep 8 1915
21 MC Minutes, Oct 13 1914
22 Rachel Pim letter to Esther Baird, Dec 15 1914
23 FON, Vol VI, No 3, Jan 1914, p 7
24 Rachel Pim to EB, Mar 24 1915; cf. *OYM Minutes*, 1915, p 44
25 EB Diary, Feb 1 1915; cf. MC Minutes, May 18 1915. Note: The diary says eight orphans and the minutes report seven were transferred to the Salvation Army, where they would take industrial training.
26 FON, Vol VII, No 3, May 1915, p 6
27 EB Diary, Oct 29, Nov 16 1914
28 FON, Vol VII, No 2, 3, Oct 1915, p 6 (A sum of $7,000)
29 EB Diary, Aug 25 1914
30 *OYM Minutes*, 1915, p 54. Note: The Red Cross later even insisted on giving some remittance to those workers whose income was extremely low.
31 FON, Vol VII, No 1 and 2, Jan 1915, p 8
32 *OYM Minutes*, 1915, p 56; cf. FON, Vol VIII, No 1, July 1915, p 6
33 EB Diary, May 16 1915; cf. *OYM Minutes*, 1915, p 55
34 *Ibid.*, Sep 9, 26 1914
35 *OYM Minutes*, 1915, p 56

36 A gift came from J. M. Hole, his daughter, Gertrude Cattell, and her husband, in memory of his wife, Ella Hole.
37 *OYM Minutes*, 1915, p 57; cf. FON, Vol VIII, No 1, July 1915, p 6
38 EB Diary, Oct 6 & 12 1915
39 FON, Vol VIII, No 4, Midwinter, 1915-1916, p 7
40 FON, Vol VII, Nos 1 & 2, Jan 1915, p 8
41 EB Diary, June 29 1915
42 *Ibid.*, Aug 5, 27 1915; *OYM Minutes*, 1917, p 43. Note: Bileri, a village of about 3,000, about five miles from Nowgong.
43 EB Diary, July 10 1915
44 FON, Vol VIII, Nos 2 & 3, Oct 1915, p 6
45 EB Diary, Apr 7 1915
46 FON, Vol VIII, Nos 2 & 3, Oct 1915, p 6
47 *Ibid.*, No 1, July 1915, p 6
48 *Ibid.*, Nos 2 & 3, Oct 1915, p 6
49 BFC MM Minutes, Sep 8 1915
50 *OYM Minutes*, 1915, p 55
51 BFC MM Minutes, Sep 8 1915; cf. FON, Vol VIII, Nos 2 & 3, 1915, p 7
52 MC Minutes, Dec 6 1916
53 FON, Vol VIII, Nos 1 & 3, Oct 1915, p 7
54 *Ibid.*, No 6, Summer 1916, p 8
55 *OYM Minutes*, 1915, p 55; cf. BFC MM Minutes, Jan 13 1915
56 *Ibid.*, 1916, p 43
57 FON, Vol VIII, No 6, 1916, p 7
58 *Ibid.*, pp 7, 8, 9
59 The Hindus had another story. They believed that hundreds of years ago, as there was no sacred river in this area, Brahmins brought water in their drinking vessels from the holy Ganges to make this lake. A wise priest, they believed, had proclaimed it a religious rite to bathe in the lake at least once during the cold season. (*OYM Minutes*, 1927, p 41)
60 FON, Vol VIII, No 5, 1916, p 6
61 EB Diary, Nov 30, 1915
62 FON, Vol VIII, No 5, 1916, p 7
63 *Ibid.*, Nos 2 & 3, Oct 1915, p 7; cf. *OYM Minutes*, 1917, p 31
64 FON, Vol IX, No 1, Dec 1916, p 7; cf. *OYM Minutes*, 1916, p 45 and BFC MM, Aug 9 1916
65 EB Diary, Apr 29 1914
66 FON, Vol VII, Nos 1 & 2, Jan 1915, p 8
67 *Ibid.*
68 *Ibid.*, Vol VIII, No 6, Summer 1916, p 9
69 *Ibid.*, Vol IX, No 1, Dec 1916, p 7
70 EB Diary, Sep 30 1914
71 FON, Vol VIII, No 1, July 1915, p 6
72 *OYM Minutes*, 1916, p 45
73 Rachel Pim to EB, Sep 2 1915; cf. MMC, *Friends in Bundelkhand*, p 32
74 Rachel Pim to EB, Oct 26 1915
75 *OYM Minutes*, 1916, p 31
76 MC Minutes, Jan 27 1916

77 *OYM Minutes*, 1916, p 44; MC Minutes, Dec 6 1916; cf. Rachel Pim to EB, Mar 28, 1916 and *OYM Minutes*, 1917, p 31
78 Rachel Pim to EB, June 7 1916
79 *OYM Minutes*, 1917, p 27
80 EB Diary, June 2, Oct 28 1917
81 ECL to DF, Oct 14 1900
82 EB Diary, June 5 1911
83 *Ibid.*, Memoranda, 1913
84 Ella Escolme Personal Paper, n.d.; EB Diary, Nov 9 1915
85 EB Diary, June 2 1917
86 Rachel Pim to EB, June 7 1916. N.B.: After Delia's death, but before the Board knew of Eugene's death, EB received a letter from the Board concerning FFMS policy regarding adoption of children by missionaries. As new superintendent, it was her duty to inform others that she could not permit the adoption of children. Terms for missionaries were again stated as 6 years for first term, eight years after that. Salaries continued $500 per year on the field and $200 on furlough, unless the missionary had no relative with whom she could stay, in which case it might be $400.
87 FON, Vol IX, No 3, May 1917, p 6
88 MC Minutes, Dec 6 1916; cf. Rachel Pim to EB, Aug 21 1916
89 *Ibid.*; FON, Vol VIII, No 5, Spring 1916, p 6; Rachel Pim to EB, Aug 1 1916
90 EB Diary, Jan 19, Apr 12, Aug 4, Sep 28, Oct 7 1918
91 *OYM Minutes*, 1919, p 35; EB Diary, Oct 20, 29 1918

CHAPTER 6
Gaining a "Foothold for the Lord"

1 Rachel Pim to EB, Sep 3 1917
2 Rachel Pim to EB, Sep 2 1918
3 EB Diary, Sep 1, Dec 1 1919
4 *Ibid.*, Oct 4 1919
5 *OYM Minutes*, 1917, p. 42
6 FON, Vol VIII, No 6, Summer No., 1916, p 6
7 *Ibid.*, Vol IX, No 3, May 1917, p 6
8 FON, Vol XI, No 1, Jan 1919, No 1, p 2
9 BFC MM Minutes, Aug 29 1917
10 *Ibid.*; cf. Jan 19 1919
11 BFC MM Minutes, Jul 31 1918; *OYM Minutes*, 1917, p 29; 1921, p 34
12 EB Diary, Aug 15 1918; Feb 21, Mar 14, 29
13 *Ibid.*, Mar 31 1919
14 *OYM Minutes*, 1919, p 35
15 EB Diary, Aug 1, 4; Nov 3, 18, 28, 29, 1919
16 *Ibid.*, Oct 8 1919; FON, Vol XII, No 1, Feb 1920, p 6
17 *OYM Minutes*, 1921, p. 50
18 EB Diary, Feb. 9 1920; FON, Vol XII, No 3, Aug 1920, p 6
19 *OYM Minutes*, 1921, p 45; cf. Rachel Pim to EB, Sep 6 1920
20 *OYM Minutes*, 1920, p 35
21 FON, Vol XII, No 3, Aug 20, p 6
22 *OYM Minutes*, 1919, p 38; EB Diary, Sep 13, 14 1920
23 EB Diary, Apr 24, 1920
24 FON, Vol XII, No 4, Nov 1920, p 6; EB Diary, Aug 26, Dec 15, 1920; *OYM Minutes*, 1921, p 45
25 EB Diary, Mar 11 1919; Oct 6, 8, 9, Dec 10 1920; Feb 10, Mar 30, 31; Apr 19, Sep 28 1921; cf. Aug 20, Nov 17 1920 and Nov 6 1921
26 FON, Vol X, No 6, Nov 1918, p 4
27 BFC MM Minutes, Dec 29 1920; EB Diary, Mar 14 1921; *OYM Minutes*, 1921, p 40; cf. FON, Vol X, No 2, Mar 1918, p 11
28 Rachel Pim to EB, May 31 1920; *OYM Minutes*, 1921, p 35
29 EB Diary, Aug 3, 31 1920; BFC MM Minutes, Sep 29, Dec 20 1920; EB Diary, Oct 3, Dec 20 1920
30 *OYM Minutes*, 1921, p 43. Note: Response-starved Christians took to their hearts the grave of one who declared himself Christian. Kuman had come to the Mission during the famine in 1897 and was sent to the Salvation Army in Gujarat. After ten years, he returned to his relatives and married a Hindu girl. He never identified himself with the Christians in Nowgong. One day while visiting his villages, one of the Indian Friends evangelists discovered he had died in the influenza epidemic. Before he died, he gave a clear testimony and urged his relatives not to cremate him but bury him as a Christian. The family honored his request. They showed the evangelist Kuman's well-read Gujarati Bible. When the Church heard this, they hunted up his burial place and put a tombstone on his grave.
31 EB Diary, Nov 7 1920; FON, Vol XII, Feb 1921, p 6; *OYM Minutes*, 1921, pp 43, 44
32 EB Diary, Feb. 25, cf. 14-26 1921; *OYM Minutes*, 1921, p 44
33 *OYM Minutes*, 1921, p 45; EB Diary, Feb 5 1921
34 FON, Vol XII, No 7, Aug 1921, p 2
35 MMC, *Friends in Bundelkhand*, p 34
36 EB Diary, Apr 1 1921
37 *OYM Minutes*, 1920, p 40
38 FON, Vol XII, No 7, Aug 1921, pp 1-3

CHAPTER 7
Adjusting to Changing India

1 Collins and Lapierre, *Freedom at Midnight*, pp 44, 45, 46
2 Underlining added
3 *OYM Minutes*, 1921, p 42
4 *OYM Minutes*, 1922, p 53
5 EB Diary, Nov 3 1921
6 *OYM Minutes*, 1922, p 53
7 *OYM Minutes*, 1923, p 39
8 *Ibid.*
9 FON, Vol XIV, No 4, Dec 1923, p 8
10 *The Friends Herald*, Vol V, No 7, Apr 1926, p 8
11 FON, Vol XXI, No 1, Mar 1930, p 6
12 FON, Vol XXIII, No 1, Mar 1932, No 1, p 6 (editorial)
13 LE to EB, Feb 31 1920
14 EB Diary, Sep 5 1921
15 *Ibid.*, Sep 15 1921
16 FON, Vol XIII, No 3, Aug 1922, p 7; cf. CB Diary, Nov 26 1921
17 EB Diary, Dec 4 1921
18 FON, Vol. XIII, No 1, Feb 1922, pp 6, 7
19 *Ibid.*, p 7
20 FON, Vol XIII, No 2, May 1922, p 6
21 FON, Vol XIII, No 3, Aug 1922, p 6
22 FON, Vol XIV, No 4, Dec 1923, p 2
23 FON, Vol XIII, No 1, Feb 1922, p 7
24 FON, Vol XIV, No 1, Feb 1923, p 6
25 Alison and Inez Rogers to F. J. Cope, Aug 2 1922
26 FON, Vol XIV, No 1, Feb 1923, p 6; cf. BFC MM Minutes, Oct 27 1922
27 MC Minutes, Sep 27 1921; Feb 20, Jul 23, Oct 18, 19, 25 1922
28 LE to EB, Jan 15 1925; FON, Vol XV, No 1, Feb 1924, p 3; *OYM Minutes*, 1923, p 39
29 FON, Vol XVI, No 4, Aug-Nov 1925, p 7; MMC, *Friends in Bundelkhand*, p 37
30 FON, Vol XV, No 2, June 1924, pp 5, 6; EB Diary, Mar 16 1924
31 LE to EB, June 2, July 6 1926; cf. May 26 1927
32 BFC MM Minutes, Apr 27, June 29, July 27 1927
33 *OYM Minutes*, 1923, p 36. Note: The Maharaja specifically requested a woman doctor.
34 Elmer Wood to EB, Aug 2 1923; LE to EB, Sep 21 1923
35 EB Diary, Nov 5 1923
36 LE to Elizabeth Ward, Feb 21 1924
37 *OYM Minutes*, 1924, pp 25, 27; LE to EB, Aug 14 1924
38 FON, Vol XV, No 1, Feb 1924, pp 1, 2, 6
39 FON, Vol XIII, No 1, Feb 1922, p 6; Vol XIV, No 2, May 1923, No 2, p 6
40 EB Diary, Dec 26-31 1923; BFC MM Minutes, Jan 30 1924
41 BFC MM Minutes, Feb 27 1924
42 LE to EB, Oct 18 1924
43 FON, Vol. XVI, No 2, May 1925, p 5; Vol. XVIII, Dec 1927, p 3
44 *Ibid.*, pp 5, 6; *OYM Minutes*, 1925, p 45; BFC MM Minutes, Feb 22, 1922
45 LE to EB, Sep 8 1924; *OYM Minutes*, 1925; p 45; EB Diary, Apr 10 1925; MC Minutes, Oct 18 1925; LE to EB, Aug 31 1926
46 EB Diary, Oct 24, 28, 1924
47 FON, Vol XVI, No 4, Aug-Nov 1925, p 6
48 EB Diary, Jan 25 1927; Mission Directory, 1948, No 5
49 EB Diary, May 2 1928
50 Interviews for AN by Vijay Prakash, 1973; BFC MM Minutes, Dec 27 1926 and Jul 25 1928; Mar 27 1929; LE to EB, Feb 8 1928
51 BFC MM Minutes, Apr 28, Jul 28 1926; FON, Vol XXII, No 1, Mar 1931, p 9
52 LE to EB, Apr 17, Jul 6 1926; LE to MMC, Feb 2 1926
53 FON, Vol XVIII, No 4, Dec 1927, p 3; MC, Nov 3 1928; Leona Kinsey to EB, Dec 31 1928
54 MC, Jan 2 1928
55 AC letters, Nov 11 1928; Leona Kinsey to EB, Dec 31 1928
56 EB to MMC, Feb 29 1929
57 Catherine Coffin to EB, Mar 10 1929
58 MMC to EB, Mar 30 1929

CHAPTER 8
Building a Hospital

1 MC Minutes, Dec 21 1927
2 EB Diary, Jan 28 1925. Note: A young Indian woman, Catharine Kassoon, living in the U.S.A. let the Board know that she wanted medical training and was willing to take part of it in India. The Board required a twelve-year contract from her. She was unwilling to sign it but came on her own, spent Christmas at the Mission but never returned as a doctor. (LE to EB, Oct 11 1925; EB Diary, Dec 23 1925)
3 FON, Vol XVI, No 2, May 1925, p 1
4 *OYM Minutes*, 1925, p 44; Memorial gift by Sarah Duncan of Russiaville, Ind.; cf. FON, Vol. XVI, No 2, May 1925, p 1
5 EB Diary, Mar 27 1925
6 *Ibid.*, Apr 15 1925; *OYM Minutes*, 1925, p 44
7 EB Diary, Sep 8, Oct 3 1925; FON, Vol XVI, No 4, Aug-Nov 1925, p 6
8 EB Diary, Nov 9 1925
9 Pancham Singh to EB, Jan 3 1928
10 MC Minutes, Dec 21 1927; LE to EB, Feb 8 1928
11 LE to EB, Feb 8 1928
12 *Ibid.*, Sept 12 1928

13 BFC MM Minutes, Nov 26 1924, Nov 24 1926; EB Diary, Sep 28, Oct 30, Nov 23 1925; Jul 19 1926. Note: At this time the orphanage, built to house 50, sheltered 75, as families sent their children back to boarding school; cf. OYM Minutes, 1922, p 54

14 LE to EB, Aug 31 1926

15 Ibid., Nov 2 1925

16 Ibid., May 26 1927; LE to Margaret Smith, Apr 14 1928

17 LE to EB, June 5 1927; BFC MM Minutes, May 25 1927

18 BFC MM Minutes, May 20 1923; OYM Minutes, 1924, p 37 MMC, Friends in Bundelkhand, p 52

19 AC Letters, May 16 1928. Note: Diagnosis — heart attack

20 LE to EB, July 8 1928

21 Ibid., Jan 4 1928; BFC MM Minutes, June 27 1928; AC Letters, May 16 1928

22 EB Diary, Oct 29 1927

23 LE to EB, 1922-28; EB Diary, Jan 7, 17, 18, 28, Apr 18, Dec 10 1924; cf. FON, Vol XVI, Aug-Nov 1925, p 9

24 OYM Minutes, 1926, p 38

25 EB Diary, Apr 29 1927

26 LE to EB, Mar 5 1928; EB Diary, Jan 10 1928

27 OYM Minutes, 1926, p 38; cf. EB Diary, Oct 5 1928

28 EB Diary, Jan 11, Feb 25, Sep 22 1930; Aug 3 1928; AC Letters, Oct 22 1928

29 EB Diary, Oct 21 1927; Mar 10, May 7 Oct 6, Nov 18 1928; Feb 16 1929; OYM Minutes, 1928, p 43

30 LE to EB, 1928; EB Diary, Nov 24 1928; Dec 17 1929; Oct 29 1927

31 LE to EB, Aug 31 1926 and May 26 1927

32 AC Letters, Nov 1 1927; Feb 26 1928

33 AC Letters, Jan 15, 29, Mar 27-29, Oct 22 1928; Feb 20, 27 1929

34 FON, Vol XX, No 3, Oct 1929, p 4; AC Letters, Nov 28 1928; June 26, July 27 1930; EB Diary, Sep 21, Dec 7, 30 1929

35 AC Letters, Sep 24, Oct 2, Nov 30 1930

36 LE to EB, Aug 31 1926; Aug 31 1928

37 LE to EB, Aug 31 1926; EB Diary, Jan 9, 17, Mar 16 1928; AC Letters, Nov 15, 28 1928; FON, Vol XX, No 4, Dec 1929, p 6

38 EB Diary, May 10 1928; Oct 25 1929

39 AC Letters, Oct 21, 29 1929

40 FON, Vol XXII, No 1, Mar 1931, p 7; Vol XXI, No 4, Dec 1930, p 12; BFC MM Minutes, Sep 24 1930; EB Diary, Jan 19 1930

41 Dr. and Mrs. Annette, English Quakers of the India Sunday School Union, taught the course. They were known all over India for their excellent work in Christian education. Later, Alena Calkins took the same course and followed through on

Ruth Thurston's beginnings; cf. EB Diary, May 14 1930; AC Letters, May 11 1931

42 AC Letters, July 20 1930; FON, Vol. XXII, No 3, Sep 1931, p 8

43 LE to Margaret Smith, Apr 14 1928; AC Letters, Nov 28 1928. Note: Carrie Wood, Bertha Cox, Alison and Inez Rogers, and Walter and Geneva Bolitho were all of Oregon Yearly Meeting.

44 FON, Vol XXII, No 3, Sep 1931, p 6; Vol XX, No 3, Oct 1929, p 5; Nov 4, Dec 1929, p 6

45 FON, Vol XXI, No 2, June 1930, p 1

46 LE to EB, May 6 1930

47 EB Diary, Dec 17, 19 1930

48 EB Diary, Jan 29 1931; FON, Vol XII, No 4, Dec 1931, p 8

49 FON, Vol XXII, No 2, June 1931, p 1. Note: Walter Bolitho had difficulty with the language. In Landour, he discovered that his being deaf in one ear was a serious handicap in learning the language; cf. LE to EB, June 2 1928; cf. LE to CBW, May 14 1931 — he passed his first examination in 1931; LE to EB, Aug 31 1928, Oct 11, Dec 13 1929; May 6, Sep 3 1930; LE to Missionary Staff, Mar 12 1931

50 AC Letters, Dec 16 1928

51 FON, Vol. XXI, No 1, Mar 1930, p 5; BFC MM Minutes, Mar 26 1930

52 Gaurali was a village about six miles from Nowgong with a population of about 5,000 people; cf. FON, Vol XXII, No 2, June 1931, p 10 and BFC MM Minutes, Jan 29 1930

53 BFC MM Minutes, June 24 1931; AC Letters, Apr 16 1930; CBW Diary, Apr 16 1930; EB Diary, Apr 21 1930

54 AC Letters, July 20, Aug 24, Sep 3, 24, Oct 2 1930; CBW Diary, Apr 30 1930; EB Diary, Sep 10 1930

55 The Nationalists Southern Army stormed into Nanking destroying the churches and buildings. The Christians suffered much, and all the missionaries had to flee. Cf. LE to EB, Jul 6 1926; FON, Vol. XVIII, No 2, May 1927, p 4

56 LE to EB, May 26 1927; Jan 4, Feb 8, Aug 31 1928

57 EB Diary, Nov 28 1928; AC Letters, July 29, Aug 2 1931. Note: A pathetic case she had to cope with was a girl with maggots in her nose and sinuses. They had eaten a hole through the bridge of her nose and had invaded her ears, glands, eyes, and sinuses. Esther Baird came to Dr. Hull's assistance and after hours of work they saved her life. Cf. AC Letters, Jan 17 1931

58 FON, Vol. XX, No 3, Oct 1929, p 4

59 EB Diary, Feb 1 1929; FON, Vol XXII, No 1, Mar 1931, p 7

60 *OYM Minutes*, 1930, p 56; EB Diary, Feb 2, Dec 17 1929; Sep 26 1930; Leona Kinsey to EB, July 5 1939; AC Letters, Dec 15 1929
61 EB Diary, Mar 11 1930; LE to EB, Nov 28 1930; MC Minutes, Dec 26 1930
62 AC Letters, Oct 13 1930
63 Catherine Stalker to EB, May 27 1929; Leona Kinsey to EB, July 5 1929; LE to EB, July 14 1929; Nov 28 1930; Catherine Stalker to EB, June 7 1930, Apr 29 1929
64 AC Letters, Oct 13 1930
65 CBS Diary, Dec 11 1930; LE to EB, Sep 3 1930
66 EB Diary, Feb 6, 16, 18 1929. Note: The final papers with map came through on Apr 29 1929 and were a cause of great thanksgiving.
67 EB Diary, July 19 1929
68 EB Diary, Mar 20 1929; FON, Vol. XX, No 2, June 1929, p 1; *OYM Minutes*, 1929, p 47
69 FON, Vol. XX, No 3, Oct 1929, p 5. Note: Louise Ellett in her letter to Esther Baird, May 6 1930, mentions special gifts of the Irvine heirs to put a shade over the well with benches around for a place where patients can rest. Mrs. Irvine took care of Eugene; cf. *OYM Minutes*, 1930, pp 56, 57; FON, Vol. XXII, No 1, March 1931, p 1; Vol XX, No 4, Dec 1939, p 6
70 Leona Kinsey to EB, Mar 25, 26, May 13 1929; *OYM Minutes*, 1912, p 81; 1927, p 81; 1957, p 78; CAR to EB, Sep 23 1927; to "Our Mission Staff," Sep 3 1929, Sep 26 1930; FON, XXII, No 4, Dec 1931, p 5; Vol XXI,No 1, Mar 1930, p 8; MC Minutes, Feb 25, Apr 27 1931; LE to CBW, May 14 1931; LE to Mission Staff, Mar 12 1931; LE to EB, Feb 14 1929
71 Catherine Stalker to EB, July 24 1929
72 *OYM Minutes*, 1931, p 41. Note: The hospital in recent years has been known simply as the Christian Hospital.
73 FON, Vol. XXI, No 3, Sep 1930, p 6; EB Diary, Sep 22 1926; Sep 11, Nov 10-15 1929; Mar 17-19, May 12, July 4, Aug 11-22 1930
74 FON, EXTRA, May 1930, p 6
75 AC Letters, Dec 7 1930
76 *Ibid.*, Nov 30, Dec 3 1930
77 *Ibid.*, Dec 7 1930
78 *Ibid.*, Nov 11 1930. Note: Col. Tyrell had been the one who influenced the Diwan to give up his opposition to the Mission and sign the papers for the Mission's possessions in Chhatarpur, and last of all, the hospital site.
79 All missionaries were present except Judith Kinder, who was ill, and James Kinder, who stayed with her; cf. AC Letters, Dec 28 1930
80 FON, Vol XXII, No 1, Mar 1931, p 7
81 The silver key later was given to Catherine Stalker, and her daughter Elizabeth Earle now has it; cf. AC Letters, Feb 1 1931; *OYM Minutes*, 1931, p 51
82 AC Letters, Feb 4, 10, 18 1931; FON, Vol XXI, No 1, Mar 1930, p 3
83 LE to EB, Sep 3, 1930; FON, Vol XXII, No 1, Mar 1931, p 7; EB Diary, Feb 25 1931

CHAPTER 9
Rumblings of Discontent

1 LE to CBW, May 14 1931
2 LE to Mission Staff, Mar 12 1931
3 MC Minutes, Dec 24 1930; LE to Missionary Staff, Mar 12 1931
4 MC Minutes, Dec 26 1930; LE to Missionary Staff, Mar 12 1931
5 EB to FFMS Board in session June 4, 5 1935; cf. MC, Feb 2 1935
6 James Kinder to Missionary Board, Jan 7 1932
7 EB Diary, Jan 17 1931; cf. LE to MC in India, Feb 18 1932
8 *OYM Minutes*, 1931, p 43; 1929, p 43. Note: A significant NCC meeting was held in Madras where John R. Mott was the keynote speaker in 1928. Esther Baird attended. The burning topic was the indigenous Church. Clamoring for power, the Church was also being reminded of its responsibility as well. It was Esther Baird's deep conviction that the Indian Church still needed the assistance—and to some measure the control—of Western missions; cf. *OYM Minutes*—1928, p 48; EB Diary, Dec 26 1928
9 BFC MM Minutes, Feb 26, Apr 27, 30 1930
10 *Ibid.*, Jan 30 1929
11 FON, Vol XXII, No 3, Sep 1931, pp 2, 8, 6
12 BFC MM Minutes, Mar 25 1931
13 FON, Vol XXII, No 3, Sep 1931, p 7; AC Letters, Jan 17 1931; FON, Vol XXII, No 4, Dec 1931, p 5
14 *Ibid.*, XXIII, No 1, Mar 1932, p 11
15 AC Letters, May 31 1931; Mar 1 1931. Note: Harbi Bai, mother of Grace Jones, daughter of Duojibai, sister of Prem Das, Balla, and Mangalwadi, was the first matron for the four student nurses.
16 FON, Vol. XXIII, No 2, June 1932, p 7
17 AC Letters, June 16 1931
18 FON, Vol. XXII, No 4, Dec 1931, p 8; AC Letters, Mar 1, Jul 13, Oct 8 1931; *OYM Minutes*, 1931, p 51
19 AC Letters, Aug 8 1931
20 CBW Diary, Aug 27 1932; AC Letters, Nov 11, 30 1932; Apr 19, June 15 1933; EB Diary, Oct 26 1933

21 FON, Vol XXV, No 2, June 1934, p 11
22 *Ibid.*, XXIII, No 4, Dec 1932, p 7. Note: Women in Bundelkhandi villages do not consider it proper to take their husband's name. The name they go by is usually in relationship—such as "Mother of Sosan," or as in this case, simply daughter-in-law.
23 LE to CBW, Jan 1932
24 CBW Diary, Oct 14 1931; cf. AC Letters, Jan 17, Nov 2 1931; Apr 19 1933
25 WRW Report, May 6 1936 to FFMS Board
26 *OYM Minutes*, 1932, p 43
27 CBW to EB, Feb 25 1932
28 LE to Mission Staff in India, May 13 1932
29 Walter Bolitho to CBW, July 1932
30 MC Minutes, July 13 1932; CWB to Walter Bolitho, July 20 1932
31 LE to Mission Staff, May 13 1932; cf. James Kinder to FFMS Board, Mar 24 1932
32 MC Minutes, Mar 11 1932; cf. BFC MM Minutes, Apr 6 1932
33 D. Brown to FFMS Board, n.d., 1932; LE to Mission Staff, May 13 1932; MC Minutes, June 17 1932 (recorded July 12 1932); Membership record of the BFC; Bram (D. Brown) letters to FFMS Board, Miss Baird, Miss Thurston—which were all read to the Missionary Committee and also to the M. & O.
34 CBW Diary, Nov 16 1933
35 AC Letters, Sep 1932; *OYM Minutes*, 1932, pp 30, 31
36 CBW Diary, Jul 11, 1932 Note: The girls' school in the bazaar had already received a death blow when the government passed a law against child marriage, setting the age of 14 as the limit. Before the date became effective, 30 school girls between the ages of 10 and 12 were taken from the school and married—to beat the law.
37 *OYM Minutes*, 1931, p 51; FON, May 1930 EXTRA, p 3
38 EB Diary, Dec 10 1929; Apr 30 1930, Sep 29, Nov 5 1923

CHAPTER 10
Facing a Time of Darkness

1 EB Diary, Nov 25 1932; FON, Vol XXIV, No 1, Mar 1933, p 12
2 EB Diary, 1933; cf. Jan 26, Feb 4 1933
3 Helen Ford and Esther Ford Anderson. *The Steps of a Good Man*, p 68
4 FON, Vol XXIII, No 2, June 1932, p 4; No 3, Sep 1932, p 12
5 EB Diary, Apr 13 1934; cf. AC Letters, July 23 1933; MC, Jul 18 1933; LE to Friends in India, Aug 18 1933; EB to CAR and LE, Nov 30 1933
6 EB Diary, Dec 10 1934
7 AC Letters, Dec 10 1933

8 MC Minutes, July 18 1933; AC Letters, Dec 10 1933; MC Minutes, July 13 1934
9 EB Diary, July 14 1934
10 EB Diary, Jan 27 1933; July 10 1934; FON, Vol XXIV, No 4, Dec 1933, p 3 Note: There was no hope of water until the rains, but when the blasting was finished, Dr. Hull went to inspect. Since she was not know for doing a thing half way, she grabbed a rope and went 75 ft. down to the bottom. It was cool down there, a wonderful place in the hottest part of the summer.
11 EB Diary, Mar 5 1935; *OYM Minutes*, 934, p 41 (LMP means Licensed Medical Practitioner.) Cf. MC Minutes, Oct 30 1933
12 EB Diary, Aug 11 1933; LE to Friends in India, June 15 1934
13 MC Minutes, Oct 30 1933; July 13 1934; BFC MM Minutes, Oct 31 1931
14 EB Diary, Jan 31, Feb 12, Mar 30, Apr 1 1933
15 EB Diary, June 29 1933
16 LE to Missionary Staff, May 11 1933; LE to EB, May 11 1933; Sep 1, 1934; EB Diary, Jul 18, 1934
17 LE to EB, Feb 23 1935 Note: The Board requested the contracts with the Maharaja, translated, and the Chhattarpur building account in detail. The account, found by Carrie Wood in good condition, was sent April 11 1935. Cf. EB Diary, Apr 11 1935
18 AC Letters, Apr 4 1934; MC Minutes, July 24 1934; Robinson's Unpublished Thesis, pp 72, 73; cf. EB Diary, Sep 5 1934; Nov 29 1934 as examples of this point.
19 LE to Friends of the Staff in India, Sep 1 1934
20 MC Minutes, Feb 1934
21 FON, Vol XXIV, No 2, June 1933, p 10; No 1, Mar 1933, p 3
22 *OYM Minutes*, 1934, p 31
23 E. Ruth Hull and CBW to LE, Oct 20 1934; EB Diary, Jan 27 1934
24 FON, Vol XXIV, No 3, Sep 1933, p 4
25 MC Minutes, Mar 29, Jul 18, 1933; Jul 17, Aug 3 1934; Mar 29, 1935
26 BFC MM Minutes, Sep 28 1932; cf. FON, Vol XXIV, No 1, Mar 1933, p 2
27 FON, Vol XXIV, No 4, Dec 1933, p 2
28 MC Minutes, Aug 3 1934
29 *Ibid.*
30 *Ibid.*
31 *Ibid.*, Jan 17 1931; Jul 17 1934; Aug 3 1934
32 *Ibid.*, Sep 9, Oct 27 1934
33 *Ibid.*, Aug 3 1934
34 EB Diary, Feb 12 1934
35 MC Minutes, July 24 1934
36 *Ibid.*, July 17 1934
37 *Ibid.*, Aug 3 1934

38 EB Diary, July 27, 28, 31, 1934; MC
   Minutes, July 24, Aug 3 1934
39 BFC MM Minutes, Aug 29 1934; cf. Sep
   26 1934; EB Diary, Aug 29 1934
40 LE to Friends of the Staff in India, Sep 1
   1934
41 EB to LE, Nov 4 1934; MC Minutes, Feb
   27, May 4 1935; EB to FFMS for meeting
   June 4, 5 1936
42 Five missionaries to FFMS, Oct 8 1934
43 Cable received in India, Oct 12 1934 from
   FFMS
44 EB Diary, Oct 16 1934
45 MC Minutes, Oct 27 1934
46 BFC MM Minutes, Dec 26 1934; Interviews by Vijay Prakash c. Stuti Prakash,
   1973
47 MC Minutes, Jan 25, Feb 2 1935; EB
   Diary, July 10 1935; CBW Diary, Dec 25
   1935
48 Robinson's Unpublished Thesis, p 71
49 MC Minutes, Feb 4 1935; WRW Report,
   summarized, May 6 1936
50 *OYM Minutes*, 1935, p 35
51 EB Diary, Sep 9 1935; *OYM Minutes*,
   1935, p 35
52 LE to EB, Mar 27 1935
53 EB and CBW diaries, 1935; CBW Diary,
   Feb 25 1935; EB Diary, Feb 20, 25, 27
   1935; MC Minutes, July 7 1935
54 EB Diary, June 25, Jul 17, Jul 24 1935
55 CBW Diary, Dec 2 1935; FON, Vol XXVI,
   No 4, Dec 1935, p 1
56 EB Diary to CAR, Apr 19 1936; Dec 2
   1935
57 MC Minutes, Jan 8 1936 Note: Later
   records show this was not done and would
   lead to misunderstandings until freedom
   of India would wipe out the agreement.
   Cf. McGavran Report, 1938
58 WRW Report, May 6 1936, presented to
   FFMS June 4 1936
59 *OYM Minutes*, 1936, p 51
60 BFC MM Minutes, Mar 12; MC Minutes,
   Mar 13 1936
61 FON, Vol XXVII, No 1, Apr 1936, p 10;
   OYM Minutes, 1936, p 39; AC Letters,
   Apr 23 1936 Note: Her early return was
   costly, for shortly after that she heard of
   the death of her father. AC Letters, May
   28 1936
62 FFMS Board Minutes, June 4 1936; WRW
   Report, May 6 1936
63 WRW Report, May 6 1936
64 EB Diary, June 19 1936; FON, XXVII, No.
   4, Dec 1936, p 5; EB to LE, Apr 20 1935;
   EB Statement for the FFMS for June 4, 5
   1936
65 WRW Report, May 6 1936
66 Dr. Ruth Hull was married Feb 17 1936 to
   Claude Bennett of Ovid, Colorado.
67 WRW Report on American Friends Mission, May 6 1936
68 Robinson, Unpublished Thesis, p 82
69 FON, Vol XXVII, Sep 1936, No 3, p 6

CHAPTER 11
Changing the Course

1 FFMS Minutes, Aug 25 1936
2 ELC to CAR, Nov 19 1936
3 LE to ELC and CDC, Nov 4 1936
4 AC Letters, Oct 12 1936
5 FON, Vol XXVII, No 4, Dec 1936, p 1
6 EB Diary, Oct 14, 17 1936
7 ELC to CAR, Oct 22 1936
8 *Ibid.*
9 *OYM Minutes*, 1936, p 51; BFC MM
   Minutes, Oct 31 1936
10 EB Diary, Feb 12 1936; FON, Vol XXVIII,
   No 1, Mar 1937, p 8; ELC to CAR, Oct 22
   1936
11 MC Minutes, Oct 29 1936
12 BFC MM Minutes, Nov 12 1936; ELC to
   CAR, Nov 2 1936
13 ELC to CAR WRM and Mother, Nov 1936
14 FON, Vol XXVII, No 1, Apr 1936, pp 8, 10
15 FON, Vol XXVII, No 3, June 1936, p 6
   Note: cf. *OYM Minutes*, 1948, p 45. For
   this, Gandhi gave Ambedkar a part in
   drafting the constitution. Later in 1956
   Ambedkar and 200,000 followers became
   Buddhists. Cf. Robinson's unpublished
   thesis, p 94.
16 FON, Vol. XXVII, No. 1, Apr 1936, pp 8,
   10
17 MC Minutes, Dec 2 1936
18 *Ibid.*
19 *Ibid.*, Dec 30 1936
20 ELC to WRW, Dec 24 1936
21 FON, Vol XXVIII, No 2, June 1937, p 10
22 *Ibid.*
23 CBW Diary, Apr 17 1938
24 ELC to CAR, June 1937
25 EB Diary, Apr 16, Dec 20 1937; Jan 19, 25
   1938
26 J. Waskom Pickett, *Christ's Way to India's
   Heart*, p 45
27 ELC to WRW and CAR, June 1937
28 WRW to ELC, July 14 1937
29 CAR to ELC, Aug 20 1937
30 FON, Vol. XXIX, No 1, Mar 1938, pp 7, 8
31 EB Diary, Sep 28, 1937
32 FON, Vol. XXIX, No 2, June 1938, p 10;
   Vol XXVIII, No 2, June 1937, p 5; MC
   Minutes, Oct 8 1937
33 ELC to CAR, Sep 30 1937; MC Minutes,
   Mar 5, Apr 14 1937; EB Diary, July 26
   1937; FON, Vol XXVIII, No 4, Dec 1937,
   pp 1, 8
34 FON, Vol XXVIII, No 2, June 1937, p 10;
   No 3, Sep 1937, p 13; ELC to CAR, Feb 11
   1937; AN Interview with Dr. RHB, Feb 5

1981; MC Minutes, Oct 26 1937. Note: The Mission was glad to make a new contract with Dr. Jones as she completed all her financial obligations for her training. She signed up for another year at Rs. 75 ($23) a month.

35 FON, Vol XXVIII, No 2, June 1937, p 12; cf. No 4, Dec 1937, p 2. The Jubilee Fund was made up of gifts of the rajas and maharajas to the Emperor, who returned their gifts for charitable purposes. EB Diary, Mar 12 1937

36 MC Minutes, Oct 2 1937; EB Diary, Mar 11, 15, 16, 18, Apr 6, Aug 19, Sep 16 1937

37 AC Letters, July 8 1937; CBW Diary, Jan 11 1938; EB Diary, Jan 11 1938; FON, Vol XXIX, No 3, Sep 1938, p 2

38 AC Letters, June 7, 11, 13 1937; EB to ELC, May 10 1937

39 EB Diary, Oct 25 1937

40 MC Minutes, Oct 26 1937. Note: In Esther Baird's Diary was the quote from Gandhi: "Offices have to be held lightly not tightly. They should be crowns of thorns not ever of renown."

41 MC Minutes, Jan 15 1937; OYM Minutes, 1937, pp 46, 47; BFC MM Minutes, Oct 27 1937

42 EB Diary, Nov 5-9 1937; OYM Minutes, 1938, p 62; MC Minutes, Nov 15 1937; BFC MM Minutes, Nov 24, Dec 29, 1937; ELC to CAR, Mar 17, 1938; MC Minutes, Apr 11 1938

43 EB Diary, Dec 30 1937; MC Minutes, Jan 28 1938; ELC to CAR, Dec 1 1938

44 ELC to CAR, Mar 3, 17 1938; EB Diary, Feb 4 1938; AC Letters, Mar 8 1938

45 Dr. RHB to G. Edwin Robinson, Mar 3 1972, and printed in his unpublished thesis, pp 72, 73

46 AC Letters, Mar 1 1938

47 ELC to CAR, Mar 17, 1938; EB To Whom It May Concern, Feb 12 1938

48 FON, Vol XXIX, No 3, Sep 1938, p 8

49 EB Diary, Apr 19, 25, May 18-22 1938; FON, Vol XXIX, No 1, Mar 1938, pp 5, 7; cf. ELC to LE, Jan 13 1940; ELC to WRW, Apr 21 1938

CHAPTER 12
Battling for Priorities

1 FON, Vol. XXIX, No 1, Mar 1938, pp 5, 7; cf. ELC to LE, Jan 13 1940

2 ELC to WRW, Apr 21 1938

3 McGavran Report, 1938

4 ELC to CAR, Nov 3 1938

5 AC Letters, Apr 14 1938

6 MC Minutes, Aug 23 1938

7 McGavran Report, 1938

8 ELC to CAR, Nov 3 1938

9 AC Letters, Sep 5 1938

10 ELC to CAR, Nov 3, Dec 1 1938

11 FON, Vol. XXX, No 2, Mar 1939, p 4

12 AC Letters, Mar 9, Aug 7, 29 1938

13 ELC to CAR, June 1 1938

14 ELC to LE, Feb 13, Apr 11 1939; AC Letters, Feb 23; Mar 2, 9, 21, 26; Apr 17 1939; CDC to WR & M Williams, Feb 24 1939; CDC Personal Report, 1939; ELC to FFMS, Apr 11 1939 Note: Dr. Green was a WUMS missionary, in charge of Jhansi Hospital.

15 CBW Diary, May 4 1939; CDC to Friends, Sep 3 1939; FON, Vol. XXX, No 3, Sep 1939, p 3; ELC to CAR, June 27 1939

16 ELC to LE, Feb 13 1939

17 AC Letters, Jan 23, Nov 14, Dec 28 1939; FON, Vol. XXX, No 2, June 1939, p 2

18 Ibid., Nov 7 1940; ELC Diary, Nov 12, 24 1940

19 FON, Vol. XXXII, No 4, Dec 1941, p 1; ELC Diary, Dec 9, 15 1940

20 ELC Diary, Mar 24 1941. Note: From that time it became the custom for the convert to cut off his own sacred lock. Thus the evangelists were clear before the law of accusations of forcible conversions.

21 Ibid., Apr 30 1941

22 McGavran Report, 1938

23 ELC Diary, Mar 28 1941; ELC to EB, Nov 25 1940; Jan 18, 19, May 22, Jul 6 1941

24 ELC to EB, Sep 28 1941

25 FON, Vol. XXXII, No 4, Dec 1941, p 1

26 ELC to LE, Sep 9 1941; Dec 10 1942; ELC Diary, Nov 24 1942

27 AC Letters, Dec 30 1941; ELC Diary, Dec 26 1942

28 ELC Diary, Feb 14 1942

29 Ibid., Dec 12 1942

30 AC Letters, Jan 3 1941

31 ELC Diary, Jan 31 1941

32 AC Letters, Sep 29 1941

33 ELC to CAR, Oct 28 1940

CHAPTER 13
Serving with Love

1 RHB Personal Report, 1940

2 FON, Vol XXI, No 4, Dec 1940, p 16; ELC to CAR, June 1, Aug 8 1938; ELC to WRW, Jul 28 1938

3 AC Letters, Aug 29 1939

4 Ibid., Mar 15 1940

5 Ibid., June 27, Jul 21 1940

6 Ibid., May 6, 23 1940

7 Ibid., Jul 25 1940; MC Minutes, Aug 24 1940. Note: Dr. Bennett returned to Chhatarpur in December 1976 with her son, daughter-in-law, and two grandchildren, and was amazed that people of the town again honored her with a special celebration.

8 AC Letters, Aug, Sept 28 1940; Jan 3, July 15, Nov 12 1941; ELC Diary, Sep 21 1942
9 AC Personal Report, 1940; ELC to LE, Jan 13 1940. Note: $390 = Rs. 1,300
10 ELC Diary, Jul 24, Sep 22-28 1941. Note: With careful planning they built the nursing home for $2,000 — ⅓ less than first estimates. By replacing bulbs they were able to use their former wiring system at a great saving. KDL did the work, and for his efficiency he got a permanent raise in salary of Rs. 10 p.m. ($3). The old electric plant was sold to a mining engineer for $359 (Rs. 1,150); cf. ELC Diary, Apr 27, May 9, June 28 1941; ELC to LE, Aug 16 1941; MC Minutes, Aug 8, No 12 1941; ELC Diary, Feb 14 1942; MC Minutes, Mar 27 1942
11 OYM Minutes, 1942, p 70; CBW Diary, Oct 17 1942; OYM Minutes, 1943, p 67
12 AC Letters, Mar 24 1941
13 Ibid., May 25, Dec 5 1941; LE to ELC, Apr 14 1941; Oct 25 1942; LE to Friends in India, Dec 16 1940
14 AC Letters, Jan 24 1942
15 Ibid., Mar 28 1942; June 18 1942 Note: L. K. Raynor, and English nurse from Lalitpur, came for nearly a year. (ELC to LE, Apr 20 1942) Miss P. Phelps of the Free Methodist Mission followed her. Her language was Marathi, and Catherine Cattell had to interpret for her in the nurses' training school; cf. ELC Diary, Feb 25 1943

CHAPTER 14
Developing Independence

1 ELC to CAR, Sep 3 1943; CBW Diary, Nov 18 1938; FON, Vol. XXIX, No 3, Sep 1938, p 1
2 RE—ESE Personal Reports, 1939
3 ELC to EB, May 22 1941
4 OYM Minutes, 1941, p 70
5 OYM Minutes, 1941, p 62
6 FON, Vol. XXXI, No 2, June 1940, pp 9, 10
7 ELC to CAR, Sep 3 1943
8 Ibid.
9 CBW Diary, Dec 20 1942
10 ELC to LE, Dec 24 1942
11 MC Minutes, Feb 1, 25 1943
12 ELC Diary, Feb 3 1943; cf. ELC to LE, Feb 8, Jul 29 1943
13 OYM Minutes, 1942, pp 68, 69, 72, 73
14 ELC to LE, Dec 10 1942
15 FON, Vol. XXXI, No 1, Mar 1940, p 2
16 Ibid., No 2, June 1940, pp 14, 15, 16
17 ELC to CAR, May 24 1940, Mar 17 1941; Apr 15 1941; CBW Personal Report, 1941
18 ELC to LE, Aug 10 1940; MC Minutes, Sep 5 1941
19 ELC Diary, Mar 17 1942; LE to ELC, June 22 1944
20 FON, Vol. XXXI, No 4, Dec 1940, pp 1, 2; ELC Diary, Nov 12 1940; Mar 28 1941
21 AC Letters, Aug 20 1941
22 FON, Vol XXXI, No 4, Dec 1940, pp 6, 11
23 ELC to LE, Aug 10 1940
24 ELC Diary, Feb 20 1942
25 Ibid., Sep 7 1932
26 MC Minutes, Apr 20 1943, No 2; ELC to LE, Jan 13 1940
27 ELC to LE, May 22 1941
28 ELC Diary, May 24-June 1 1942; Feb 13 1943; cf. ELC to WRW, Dec 1 1944
29 Ibid., Jan 21, Mar 21, Jul 19 1941; OYM Minutes, 1942, p 65; ELC to CAR, May 14 1942
30 CDC Personal Report 1942
31 ELC to EB, May 22 1941
32 ELC Diary, Sep 24 1942
33 CDC Personal Report, 1942; ELC Diary, Feb 23, Dec 17 1942
34 MC Minutes, Apr 7, 8 1941
35 ELC Diary, Mar 16 1942
36 MC Minutes, Mar 17, Apr 17 1942; JC Minutes, Apr 11 1942; ELC Diary, May 13 1942
37 ELC to LE, Feb 8 1943; MC Minutes, Feb 1 1943; MC Minutes, Nov 4 1943; ELC to WRW, Feb 3 1944
38 ESE Personal Report, 1942-43
39 MC Minutes, Apr 17 1942
40 ELC Diary, Mar 24 1942; LE to ELC, Oct 25 1942
41 WRW to ELC, Sep 4 1941
42 OYM Minutes, 1941, p 52
43 AC Letters, Jul 22 1941
44 LE to ELC, Apr 14 1940; OYM Minutes, 1944, p 55; WRW to AC, Aug 3 1945
45 ELC to LE, Jan 13 1940; cf. ELC to CAR, May 14 1942
46 AC Letters, Oct 30 1940
47 ELC Diary, Mar 10, Jul 6-Aug 25 1942
48 ELC to CAR, May 14 1942; AC Letters, Mar 24 1941; ELC Diary, Apr 17, 18 1942; CDC and ESE Personal Reports, 1943
49 CBW Diary, July 27 1942; MC Minutes, Dec 3, 4 1942
50 ELC Diary, Aug 26 1942

CHAPTER 15
Reviving the Church

1 CDC Personal Report, 1941
2 AC Letters, Sep 28 1940; CBW Diary, Jul 28, 29 1940
3 ELC Diary, Mar 7, 15 1941
4 Note: Mr. Chakravathy of Brindaban (ELC, Jul 2-4 1941) and Mr. Mittal of Agra (ELC Diary, Nov 29 1942)
5 ELC Diary, Feb 28 1942. Note: C. L. Wood of the C. P. Mission, who first started jungle camps as a means of

reviving the Church in India, held meetings with great blessing.

6 CDC Personal Report, 1941; *OYM Minutes*, 1941, p 65; FON, Vol. XXXII, No 4, Dec 1941, p 4
7 ELC to WRW, June 4 1941
8 ELC Diary, Feb 23 1942
9 *Ibid.*, Dec 1941
10 *Ibid.*, Dec 28-31 1942; Jan 3 1943
11 *Ibid.*, Jan 6-16 1943
12 *OYM Minutes*, 1943, pp 62-64
13 ELC Diary, Mar 20-26 1943
14 *Ibid.*, Mar 28 1943
15 WRW to CAR, Nov 16 1942
16 CDC, *Till Break of Day*, pp 67-74
17 ELC Diary, Mar 29 1943; MC Minutes, Mar 27 1943
18 ELC Diary, Oct 13, 18; Nov 6-10 1942; Jan 5 1942
19 CDC Report 1944; ELC Diary, Mar 30-Apr 14 1943
20 CDC Personal Report, 1944
21 AC Letters, Mar 18 1945
22 ELC Diary, May 22-June 14; June 16 1943
23 *Ibid.*, June 26, July, Aug 1943
24 CDC Personal Report, 1944
25 ELC Diary, Sep 1943. Note: The *huka* is a water pipe with tobacco, smoked throughout the villages of North India.
26 ELC Diary, Sep 1943
27 *Ibid.*, Oct 27-30 1943
28 MC Minutes, Nov 4 1943; NAE Program, Apr 1952
29 RE Personal Report, 1944; *OYM Minutes*, 1944, p 65
30 ESE Personal Report, 1943
31 ELC to WRW, Feb 3 1944
32 CDC Personal Report, 1944
33 *OYM Minutes*, 1944, p 64
34 ELC to WRW, Feb 3, Dec 1 1944
35 Testimony to A.N. by Hira Lal, dated Jan 1973; cf. ELC to LE, Jul 29 1943
36 AC Letters, May 27 1945
37 ELC to LE, Apr 15 1944
38 Interview with AN of Hira Lal, Jan 1973

CHAPTER 16
Surviving World War II

1 CBW to WRW, Dec 17 1944
2 ELC to WRW, Feb 3 1940; LE to ELC, June 22 1944
3 CBW Diary, 1944
4 WRW to Charles Roberts, Nov 21 1944
5 AC Letters, Jan 7, 25 1945; *OYM Minutes*, (?) 1933, p 53
6 AC Letters, Mar 18 1945
7 *OYM Minutes*, 1945, p 74; WRW to FFMS, Apr 4 1945
8 ELC to WRW, Feb 3 1944
9 AC Letters, May 14 1945
10 *Ibid.*, Mar 18, Apr 16 1945; *OYM Minutes*, 1945, p 69
11 WRW to Pastors of OYM, Jan 6 1944
12 AN *Delayed, Manila*, pp 90, 92
13 WRW to FFMS, Nov 9 1944
14 *Encylopedia Americana* #29, 1978, p 529; cf. NAF Personal Report, 1946
15 AC Letters, June 24 1945; WRW to Charles Roberts, Jul 3 1945; Cablegram from ELC, Jul 1 1945
16 ELC to WRW, Feb 3 1944
17 AC Letters, June 14 1945
18 RE to WRW, Feb 17 1944
19 *OYM Minutes*, 1944, p 67; R & ESE to MEC, Nov 27 1944
20 AC Letters, Apr 16 1945; AC to WRW, Apr 21, Oct 4 1945
21 RE Personal Report, 1945
22 WRW to FFMS, Apr 4 1945
23 ELC to MEC, Nov 23 1944
24 *OYM Minutes*, 1945, pp 69, 71, 72
25 ELC to WRW, May 1 1945
26 CDC Personal Report, 1945
27 ELC to WRW, Feb 3 1944
28 WRW to CAR, May 6 1944
29 WRW to Charles Roberts, Jul 20 1945; WRW to MEC, Feb 28 1945
30 AC Letters, Apr 16 1945; FON, Vol XXXIV, No 5, Sep 1945, p 3
31 ELC to WRW, May 1 1945
32 *Ibid.*, Dec 1 1944; ELC Personal Report, 1945
33 *OYM Minutes*, 1945, p 69; ELC to WRW, May 1 1945
34 AC Letters, May 14 1945; ELC to WRW, June 3 1945
35 WRW to Dr. Potter, Mar 31 1945
36 MC Minutes, June 22-28, No 6, 1945
37 LE to ELC, June 22 1944; WRW to Charles Roberts, Aug 27 1945; MC Minutes, Feb 1 1945
38 *OYM Minutes*, 1945, p 60
39 WRW to ELC, Nov 27 1945; MC Minutes, Dec 1 1945; MEC Personal Report, 1946
40 WRW to FFMS, Dec 19 1945
41 WRW to Charles Roberts, Nov 2, 20 1946; RE to LE, Jan 18 1946
42 WRW to FFMS, Dec 19 1945; CGS to WRW, Jul 2 1946

CHAPTER 17
Welcoming New Recruits

1 RE 50th Annual Report of India Mission, 1946
2 AC Letters, Oct 21 1945
3 MC Minutes, Mar 8 1947 2(a); MEC to WRW, Oct 3, Dec 4 1946
4 AC Letters, May 1 1946
5 RE 50th Annual Report of India Mission, 1946
6 AC Letters, Oct 3 1945; LE to WRW (Nanking), Feb 5 1946

7 FON, Vol. XXXV, No 3, May 1946, p 14; AC Letters, Mar 16 1946; ESE to LE, Mar 14 1946
8 AC Letters, Dec 1 1945
9 MC Minutes, Dec 1 1945
10 RE to WRW and ELC, Dec 15 1945
11 FON, Vol XXXV, No 3, May 1946, p 11
12 FON, Vol XXXV, No 5, Sep 1946, p 5
13 FFMS Minutes, Aug 21 1946 (When the Church of Christ opened a "Kulpahar Kids Home" just 22 miles from Nowgong, the Friends orphanage was phased out and homeless children were sent there.)
14 FON, Vol XXXVI, No 1, Jan 1947, pp 5, 8; MEC Personal Report, 1946; FON, Vol XXXV, No 2, Mar 1946, p 6
15 AC to WRW, Oct 4, Dec 6 1945
16 AC Letters, Dec 16 1945; RE to WRW and ELC, Dec 15 1945
17 Ibid., Aug 1 1945
18 MC Minutes, Aug 16 1945, No 4
19 RE to WRW, Aug 18 1945; WRW to RE, Sep 20 1945
20 RE 50th Annual Report of India Mission, 1946
21 Jubilee Report edited by Victor Mangalwadi and Stuti Prakash, Apr 27 1946
22 FON, Vol XXXV, No 3, May 1946, p 16
23 JC, Apr 4 1946, No 11; AC Letters, Apr 15 1946
24 FFMS Minutes, Jul 23 1946
25 FON, Vol XXXV, No 3, May 1946, p 12
26 AC Letters, Jan 25 1946
27 OYM Minutes, 1948, p 54
28 WRW to Edith Salter, Aug 9 1946
29 AN Letters, Oct 21 1946
30 CDC EF, June 1983, p 7 "Missionaries, Depressed"
31 AN Letters, May 2 1946
32 RE 50th Annual Report of the India Mission, 1946
33 MC Minutes, Aug 16 1945
34 FFMS Minutes, Aug 21 1945; RE 50th Annual Report of the India Mission, 1946
35 AC Letters, Aug 1 1945
36 Ibid., Aug 25, Nov 17 1945
37 Ibid., June 6 1946
38 Ibid., May 16, July 31 1946; WRW to Charles Roberts, Sep 20 1946
39 RE to WRW, May 13 1945; RE Personal Report, 1946; RE 50th Annual Report of India Mission, 1946; ESE Personal Report, 1946; AC to WRW, Sep 23 1946; MC Minutes, Sep 14 1945; Feb 14 1946, No 8
40 WRW to EL, Nov 1945; WRW to AC and ELC, Dec 12, 28 1946; RE to WRW and the Ex Bd, Dec 24 1946
41 MEC to AC, Apr 6 1976
42 AC Letters, Apr 17 1946
43 MEC to WRW, Oct 23 1946
44 Ibid., Oct 31 1946; AC Letters, Dec 29 1946; cf. MEC WRW, Oct 23 1946
45 AC Letters, July 1946
46 CBW to WRW, Jul 8 1945
47 CBW to WRW, Dec 1 1946
48 AN to WRW, Sep 17 1946
49 WRW to ELC, Dec 15 1946
50 CDC on SS Marine Adder, Jan 1947
51 ELC to Gertrude Cattell, Jan 16 1947; FON, Vol XXXVI, No 2, Mar 1947, p 5
52 MEC to WRW, Jan 26 1947
53 Ezekiel 36:23b NIV; cf. MC Minutes, Feb 1 1947. Note: Pastoral appointments confirmed at this time: Dayal Chand—Bijawar; Glen Warsingh—Chhatarpur; Shapan J. Nath—Harpalpur; Reubin Oriel—Nowgong. Outstation evangelists: Hira Singh—Isanagar; Bharos William—Gulganj; Daru Lal, Khub Chand—evangelists; cf. FON, Vol XXXV, No 1, Jan 1946, p 5; AC Letters, Aug 28 1946
54 Woodstock School Principal to RE, Dec 14 1945
55 FFMS Minutes, Aug 12 1946; MC Minutes, Feb 1 1947
56 MC Minutes, Sep 14, 21 1946; Feb 1 1947
57 AC Letters, Sep 1 1946
58 RE to LE and ELC, Jan 18 1946; OYM Minutes, 1947, pp 81, 82; 55
59 RE 50th Annual Report of India Mission, 1946
60 OYM Minutes, 1947, p 79
61 FON, Vol XXXV, No 2, Mar 1947, No 2, pp 5, 6, 8
62 MEC to WRW, Jan 5 1947

CHAPTER 18
Suffering for Freedom— and Just Suffering

1 Collins & Lapiere, Freedom at Midnight, pp 234-252
2 AC Letters, Aug 15 1947
3 ELC to Friend, Sep 9 1947
4 AC Letters, Sep 1 1946
5 FON, Vol XXXVI, No 5, Sep 1947, p 2
6 Ibid., No 6, Nov 1947, p 8; AC Letters, Sep 28 1947; OYM Minutes, 1948, p 45
7 AC Letters, Oct 27 1947; Sep 26 1948; FON, Vol XXXVII, No 1, Nov 1948, p 6
8 Mahatma Gandhi Centenary Report
9 Collins & Lapiere, Freedom at Midnight, p 49
10 Wolpert, A New History of India, p 358
11 FON, Vol XXXVII, No 7, Sep 1948, pp 1, 2
12 OYM Minutes, 1950, p 35
13 ELC to WRW, Apr 26 1951; OYM Minutes, 1952, p 49
14 MC Minutes, Mar 24, 25, No 9. Note: Oxford-educated Mr. Balbir Singh Grewal, Bundelkhand Commissioner, sent his red-uniformed government servant to

Cliff Robinson, his new American friend, with a cryptic note: "Please come sit with me this afternoon when Sardar Patel or his representative reads the bad news to the rulers." Thus Cliff, in his Nehru jacket, which made him look like one of the rulers, became the only foreigner to be present at one of Bundelkhand's (and Baghelkhand's) most historic moments. After the delivery of the message and departure of most of the rulers, His Highness of Chhatarpur stayed as the Commissioner requested Cliff to read something from his Bible. Cliff read Matt. 6:33.

15 AC Letters, Nov 28 1949
16 ELC to WRW, June 19 1948
17 ELC to WRW, May 24 1949
18 AC Letters, Aug 17 1947
19 Wolpert, *A New History of India*, pp 109, 319; cf. Spear, *India*, pp 382, 385
20 CJR to WRW, Aug 9 1949
21 FON, Vol XL, No 1, Jan 1941, p 8; cf. ELC to WRW, Feb 3 1950
22 ELC to WRW, Feb 3 1950
23 *Ibid.*, Feb 14 1950
24 WRW to Pastors of OYM, Oct 2 1951
25 MC Minutes, Mar 28, Apr 2 1949. Note: Dr. Charles Smith paid for the translation of the Gospel into Bundelkhandi—the only book written in that language.
26 CBW Personal Report, 1946-47
27 EOR Personal Report, 1949-50
28 MC Minutes, Oct 20-23 1948; CBW Diary, Feb 3 1948; cf MC Minutes, Feb 6, 7 1948
29 CBW Diary, Oct 26 1948
30 MC Minutes, Oct 20-23 1948, No 1
31 FON, Vol XXXVIII, No 2, Feb 1949, p 6
32 CJR to WRW, Nov 14 1948. Note: Her most valued gift on leaving was hearing and reading Cliff's first Hindi sermon.
33 Biodata from parents of MB, 1949 and RHB, 1949; FON, Vol XXXVIII, No 6, Jul 1949, p 8
34 "Missionaries in the Making" pamphlets
35 WRW to Members of FFMS Board, Feb 17 1948; to FFMS Ex Bd, Sep 6 1948; WED to WRW, Nov 2 1948
36 WED to WRW, Dec 14 1948
37 WRW to CGS, Nov 24 1948; cf. WRW to Ex Bd FFMS, Nov 11 1948; WED to WRW, Nov 6 1948;
38 WED to WRW, Jan 3, 25 and Feb 6 1949. Note: By Feb 7 1949, five days before sailing, Dr. WED had packed and delivered to the docks a kerosene refrigerator; X ray $1,400; dark room equipment ($600); Dodge carry-all four-wheel drive for ambulance ($1,050); one-ton metal trailer with canvas top (his donation); 2.5 KW gasoline generator ($400) operating table and rubber pad ($275); supplies ($461.21);

drugs especially needed in India such as Diodoquin, streptomycin, sulfadiazine, and Aralen from Church World Service. Dr. Charles Smith sent a mimeograph; the Board sent Aladin lamps.

39 AC Letters, Apr 7 1949; WED to WRW, Apr 14 1959
40 FON, Vol XXXVIII, No 6, Jul 1949, p 2; FON, Vol. XXXVIII, No 9, Nov 1949, p 6; WED to WRW, Apr 21 1949
41 FON, Vol XXXVIII, No 6, Jul 1949, p 2
42 AN Letters, Oct 9, Dec 2 1949
43 ELC to WRW, May 31 1948; cf. Aug 8 1947
44 AC Letters, Sep 26 1948; cf. MEC to WRW, Sep 1948
45 *Ibid.*, Jul 18 1949
46 *Ibid.*, Aug 7 1949
47 RHC Personal Report, 1950-51
48 ELC to WRW, Mar 16 1950; cf. AC, Feb 21 1950
49 *Ibid.*, Apr 13 1951
50 EOR Personal Report, 1949-50
51 FON, Vol XXXIX, No 2, Feb 1950, p 3
52 NAF to WRW, Mar 22 1947; RHC to WRW, Dec 16 1949
53 WED to WRW, Jul 9 1949
54 CJR to WRW, Oct 30 1949; cf. CJR Personal Report, 1949-50
55 AC Letters, Nov 5 1950; CJR to WRW, Feb 8 1952
56 RHC Personal Report, 1950-51
57 WED to WRW, Aug 17, Sep 8 1950
58 EOR to WRW, Jul 16 1948; CJR to WRW, Aug 26 1952; cf. ELC to WRW, Nov 14 1952
59 *Ibid.*, Feb 16 1952
60 CJR to WRW, June 29 1951
61 AN Letters, Apr 4 1949; Aug 20 1950
62 AC Letters, Apr 18 1950
63 *Ibid.*, Oct 2 1949
64 *Ibid.*, Apr 27 1947; Aug 24, Sep 26, Nov 12 1948; Mar 9 1949
65 *Ibid.*, Oct 30, Nov 28 1949
66 WED to Harriet Calkins, May 24 1950
67 WRW to FFMS Board Members #3, Dec 15 1950; #8, Jan 15 1952; AC Letters, Aug 22 1950
68 WRW to ELC, Nov 24 1948; AC Letters, Oct 31 1950
69 WRW to FFMS, Jan 15 1952, No 8; FFMS Board Minutes, Aug 26 1952. Note: Alena Calkins continued to work in U.S.A.—school nurse at Cleveland Bible College, Houghton College, and nurse at Western Reserve University Hospital. She retired in Adrian, Michigan.
70 AC, Jan 30 1949; cf. June 8 1949. Note: The Fords' daughter Clara was at the same time dying of cancer in Dearborn.
71 FON, Vol XXXIX, No. 1 Jan 1950, p 5

72 FFMS Board Minutes, Aug 22 1950
73 CDC to WRW, Sep 1 1950
74 FON, Vol XXXIX, No 9, Nov 1950, p 4
75 *Ibid.* Note: cf. FON, Vol XXXVIII, No 9, Nov 1949, p 8; *OYM Minutes*, 1951, p 102. Just a year before Esther Baird's death her pony-riding evangelist, Hira Lal, preceded her. On Mar 26 1951, Elizabeth Jenkins—"Miss Lilly"—who followed her mother, Sarah Jenkins, as second president of the W.M.S., died just three weeks short of her 98th birthday. Her active service with the Mission Board spanned 66 years.

CHAPTER 19
Preparing for the Care of a Growing Church

1 MC Minutes, Oct 20-25 1948
2 ELC to WRW, Apr 13 1950; Elizabeth Jenkins to WRW, Apr 22 1949; WRW to ELC, Sep 13 1950
3 FON, Vol. XXVIII, No 4, Apr 1949, p 6; ELC to WRW, Jan 23 1951; cf. Nov 2 1950
4 *Ibid.*, No 5, May 1949, p 1; ELC to WRW, May 5 1951
5 *Ibid.*, Vol. XL, No 6, July 1951, p 7; *OYM Minutes*, 1951, p 46
6 FFMS Minutes Full Board, Aug 25 1947; WRW to ELC, Sep 12, Dec 20 1947
7 ELC to WRW, Apr 30 1948
8 Unpublished article by ELC, "Do Friends Have a Faith Mission?" 1948
9 WRW to ELC, Jan 25 1950
10 WRW to ELC, June 11 1948
11 FFMS Minutes, June 9 1948; WRW to ELC, Aug 20 1948
12 WRW to ELC, Aug 12 1949; *OYM Minutes*, 1948, pp 46, 50. Note: Marjorie Myers was Supt of Missionary Ed for women.
13 AN Letters, Nov 17 1947; ELC to WRW, Oct 6 1948; MC Minutes, Apr 2 1949
14 *OYM Minutes*, 1949, pp 54, 55; FON, Vol XXXVIII, No 8, Oct 1949, p 6; MC Minutes, June 21 1947, No ?; ELC to WRW, Aug 8 1947; MC Minutes, Aug 31, Sep 1 1948; Mar 26, 27 1950
15 AC Letters, July 18 1949; MC Minutes, Nov 1, 2, 3 1949
16 MC Minutes, Aug 10, 11 1950; ELC to WRW, Aug 14, 30 1950
17 ELC to FFMS Ex Bd, Dec 20 1948; AC Letters, Mar 9 1949
18 ELC to WRW, Sep 15 1950. Note: ELC was so busy his letters home ceased. WRW wrote, "I am spoiling for a letter from you." So while standing under a tree supervising a large force of laborers, ELC dictated letters to NAF reporting all the activities and dreams of the future. His first single-spaced and no margin letter filled nine pages with a promise of more to come. A week later he sent a "caboose"—another no-margin single-spaced epistle of 11 pages. Back came the reply from WRW: "Hold everything! I am not spoiling now for a letter from you."
19 AN Letters, Feb 9 1950; Jul 24 1950; FON, Vol XXXVII, No 2, Feb 1948, p 3; AC Letters, Oct 30 1949; Church World Service to WRW, Aug 8 1949. Note: Later, widespread use of DDT under WHO greatly reduced cases of malaria throughout India.
20 AN Letters, Sep 9 1949; FON, Vol. XXXIX, No 6, Jul 1950, p 3; MC Minutes, Oct 27, 28 1950; ELC to WRW, May 3 1951
21 WED to WRW, Oct 16 1949
22 FON, Vol XXXIX, No 6, May 1950, p 2
23 *Ibid.*, Vol XL, No 1, Jan 1951, p 6; cf. Vol XXXIX, No 10, Oct 1950, p 2; AC Letters, Apr 18 1950; WED to WRW, Jan 14 1951
24 WED Personal Report, 1951
25 CJ Robinson Personal Report, 1951; WED to WRW, Mar 25 1951
26 *OYM Minutes*, 1949, p 50; 1951, p 42; ELC to WRW, Dec 20 1948; Nov 15 1949; Apr 13, June 22 1950; Apr 26 1951
27 NAF Personal Report, 1951
28 AC Letters, Jan 14 1959; FON, Vol XXXIX, No 3, Mar 1950, p 4
29 FON, Vol XXXVIII, No 3, Mar 1949, p 5
30 *Ibid.*, Vol XXXVII, No 10, Dec 1948, p 5
31 WED & FHD Personal Reports, 1951; AC Letters, Jan 15 1948
32 WED to WRW, May 2 1951
33 WED to WRW, Feb 18 1951. Note: The 108 lb. cyst consisted of 88 lbs. of fluid and 20 lbs. of tumor.
34 WRW to Wynn C. Fairfield FMC of NA, Jul 9 1948; ELC to WRW, Oct 2, 30 1948
35 MC Minutes, Jul 29, 30 1949, No 7; MC, Mar 23, 27 1948
36 CJR to WRW, Sep 28 1949. Note: By 1949 missionaries' salaries had increased 100% in the preceding decade to $1,200 a year and the minimum wage for any mission employee was $20 per month. There may have been a tinge of pride in the missionaries' letters home on decreasing their pay and increasing the salaries of workers, for Walter Williams' answer was somewhat stern: "The money which we handle and which is sent to you is sacred. Before God we and you stand or fall and to Him we are answerable . . . should you feel it right to revise your allowances downward then we should expect you to do that."
37 ELC Personal Report, 1951; ELC to WRW, Feb 18 1950

38 WRW to FFMS Ex Bd, Jan 26 1948
39 WRW to ELC, June 11 1948
40 MC Minutes, Sep 14, 15 1951; ELC to WRW, Sep 29 1951, June 17 1953; WRW to CGS, May 26 1954
41 AC Letters, Apr 3 1948
42 MC Minutes, Mar 31, Apr 1 1947; *OYM Minutes*, 1947, p 68; ELC to WRW, Aug 8 1947. Note: When ELC casually mentioned the government wanted to turn over the civil hospital in Nowgong plus a grant to the Mission to run it, WRW wrote, "You have handed us two or three jumbo packages for consideration, as for example the extensive motor transportation suggestions, the purchase of British property in Nowgong, and *mirabile dictu,* another hospital to staff! There my hat blew off!"—cf. ELC to WRW, May 13 and WRW to ELC, May 30 1947

CHAPTER 20
Breaking Through in Ghuara

1 AC Letters, Sep 18 1949
2 MC Minutes, Nov 8 1947; AN Letters, Dec 20 1949; ELC to Canon H. Welsh, Sagar, Aug 8 1949
3 FON, Vol. XXXVIII, No 7, Sep 1949, p 5
4 WRW to ELC, Oct 11 1949. Note: The agreement had been made to pay in rupees but the Board sent $6,061 and let it stand.
5 AC Letters, Sep 18 1949; MC Minutes, Sep 9, 10 1949, No 1
6 The first women's retreat was held in Gulganj in 1948.
7 FFMS Board Minutes, Aug 22 1950; ELC to WRW, Feb 8 1949
8 ELC to WRW, Feb 3 1947; *OYM Minutes,* 1947, p 80; FON, Vol XXXVI, No 4, July 1947, p 3
9 *OYM Minutes,* 1947, p 80; cf. Rom 13:1, 2, 7
10 FON, Vol XXXVI, No 4, July 1947, p 3
11 *Ibid.,* p 8
12 AC Letters, May 13 1947
13 WRW to Elizabeth Salter, Oct 30 1947
14 ELC to WRW, Dec 1 1947; AC Letters, Nov 25 1947
15 WRW to Pastors, Dec 18 1947
16 FON, Vol XXXVII, No 1, Jan 1948, pp 2, 3
17 *Ibid.,* No 2, Feb 1948, p 4
18 *Ibid.*
19 WRW to FFMS Board Members and OYM Pastors, Jan 28 1948; AC Letters to Mrs. Nixon, Jan 24 1948
20 AC Letters, Jan 15 1948; WRW to FFMS Board Members and Pastors OYM, Jan 28 1948
21 AC Letters, Feb 25 1948
22 FON, Vol XXXVII, No 4, Apr 1948, p 8
23 *Ibid.,* No 5, May 1948, p 6
24 ELC to WRW, Oct 30 1948
25 FON, Vol XXXVIII, No 1, 1949, pp 2, 3
26 AC Letters, Mar 9 1948
27 ELC to David Cattell, June 27 1950
28 FON, Vol XXXVIII, No 5, May 1949, p 3
29 *Ibid.,* Vol XLI, No 9, Nov 1952
30 55th Report India Mission, 1951; FON, Vol XXXIX, No 3, Mar 1950, p 2
31 FON, Vol XXXIX, No 10, Dec 1950, p 2
32 MEC Personal Report, 1951

CHAPTER 21
Proclaiming Freedom to the Captives

1 ELC to WRW, Mar 21 1947
2 FON, Vol XXXVI, No 4, Jul 1947, p 8; Vol XXXVII, No 2, Feb 1948, p 3; AC Letters, Apr 7 1949
3 ELC to WRW, nd, 1950; FON, Vol XXXIX, No 4, Apr 1950, p 6. Note: Camps under the leadership of Victor, Cliff, Milton, and Stuti fanned out through the district. Evangelists Hira Singh from Isanagar, Dayal Chand (already having served 20 years in the Mission), Amarmau; E. H. Massey, Amarmau; Chunni Lal, Ghuara; Itwari Lal with special music ability recently from the Disciples Mission, Ganj; B. Z. Smith, Gulganj—also worked with them. Bible women and missionaries also joined in the thrust: Rupa Bai Das and Rebecca Coleman from Amarmau; Bhagwati Bai Das and Catherine Cattell, Chhatarpur; Betty Robinson, Nowgong; Manorma Bai C. Lal, Ghuara. Other volunteers went from time to time, and Everett Cattell joined on weekends when not inundated with building work. Victor followed the Mission's policy of giving attention to the Chamars first, but he also kept his eyes open for interested people from other groups and deliberately went in search of his own relatives of the *Kachhi* caste. This led him to camp at Tikar, his grandfather's birthplace.
4 MEC to WRW, June 1, 3 1948; cf. AC Letters, Jan 28 1948; FON, Vol XXXVII, No 8, Oct 1948, p 8
5 FON, Vol XXXVII, No 8, Oct 1948, p 8; Vol XXXIX, No 6, July 1950, p 8; *OYM Minutes,* 1949, p 49; AC Letters, Aug 8 1948
7 ELC to WRW, May 11 1951; FON, Vol XL, No 3, Mar 1951, p 6
8 FON, Vol XXXIX, No 4, Apr 1950, p 6
9 *Ibid.,* No 10, Dec 1950, p 2; Vol XL, No 8, Oct 1951, p 6
10 ELC to WRW, Feb 18 1950
11 FON, Vol XXXIX, No 4, Apr 1950, p 2

12 *Ibid.*, XXXVII, No 7, Sep 1949, p 6; Vol XXXV, No 2, Mar 1946, p 8
13 *Ibid.*, No 9, Nov 1948, p 6
14 EOR Personal Report, 1951
15 FON, Vol XXXVIII, No 3, Mar 1949, p 6
16 *Ibid.*, Vol XXXIX, No 2, Feb 1950, p 2
17 CJR to WRW, July 24, Aug 3 1951; EOR to WRW, July 29 1951
18 FON, Vol XXXIX, No 6, July 1950, p 6. Note: Stuti Prakash rode, instead of a donkey, his motorcycle to the place of controversy and there persuaded the persecutors to put down their sticks. See Neh. 4:1-6.
19 EOR to WRW, Dec 11, 1951
20 FON, Vol XXXIX, No 4, Apr 1950, p 2
21 ELC to WRW, Jan 23 1951
22 *Ibid.*
23 EOR to WRW, Feb 25 1951
24 CJR unpublished article nd 1951. Note: Shortly after this, B. Z. Smith heard a rumor that Brij Kishore was in Rewa. Cliff went immediately by jeep and staying with an Anglo-Indian official, he simply walked through Rewa streets, seeking Brij Kishor. He finally got into his jeep to return to Gulganj when a clean dressed Indian came up to him and said, "I knew you were here. It is best I not declare myself with the foreign Christians. But I am living for Christ and will serve Him forever." With that, he turned and walked quickly away. Cliff said he wanted to call after him, but thought better. Someone asked Cliff why he had not done more to hold him. Cliff said, "I couldn't. It was almost as though I sensed he was in the safest place of all. He was in God's hands." (Interview CJR)
25 CJR to WRW, Feb 8 1952
26 WED to CGS, Mar 29 1955
27 EOR to WRW, Dec 11 1951
28 FON, Vol XXXVIII, No 7, Sep 1949, p 3
29 CJR to WRW, Feb 25 1951
30 MC Minutes, July 3 1950, No 11; J C Minutes, July 1, Oct 7 1949; MC Minutes, Dec 31 1949; Jan 1 1950; Jul 28, Oct 8 1951
31 ELC to WRW, Feb 18 1950
32 MC Minutes, Sep 14, 15 1951, No 15 (4)
33 AN Letters, Sep 21 1951
34 AN Letters, July 24 1950
35 ELC to WRW, Nov 16 1951; MC Minutes, Dec 29, 30, 31 1950; Sep 14, 15 1951

CHAPTER 22
Extending the Boundaries

1 FON, Vol XXXIX, No 7, Sep 1950, p 3
2 ELC to WRW, Oct 30 1950
3 Alice Marsh to WRW, Jan 16 1951
4 CBW to CGS, June 15 1955
5 WRW to Ex Com of FFMS, Jan 8 1952
6 WRW to Pastors of OYM and FFMS Bd Members, Jan 25 1952; ELC to WRW, Feb 27 1952
7 EGH to CGS, Feb 23 1952
8 EGH to CGS, May 25 1952
9 WRH to CGS, Apr 14 1952
10 Bryner Personal Report, 1954
11 ELC to WRW, Sep 15 1950
12 WRW to ELC, Oct 11, 1950
13 ELC to WRW, Feb 3, Aug 14 1950; CJR to WRW, Feb 8 1952
14 FFMS became a member of EFMA in 1950
15 ELC to WRW, Jan 31 1951
16 *Ibid.*
17 WRW Bi-Monthly Letter to Pastors, #5, May 24 1951
18 CJR Personal Report, 1951
19 ELC to WRW, Jan 31 1951
20 MC Minutes, Dec 29, 30, 31 1950; Jan 1 1951
21 *Ibid.*, Mar 30, Apr 10 1951
22 ELC to WRW, Jan 31 1951
23 WRW to ELC, Feb 16 1951
24 Clyde Taylor to ELC, Mar 2 1951
25 WRW to ELC, Apr 8 1951
26 ELC to WRW, Mar 4 1951
27 ELC to WRW, Apr 26 1951; WRW to ELC, June 22 1951
28 MC Minutes, Oct 20-23 1948
29 *Ibid.*, Mar 10, 11 1950, No 2
30 ELC to WRW, Jan 31 1951
31 The EFI Statement was drawn up as follows: We believe in: (1) The Holy Bible, which is the fully and uniquely inspired Word of God, the only infallible, sufficient, and authoritative rule of faith and practice. (2) One God, eternally existent in three persons: Father, Son, and Holy Spirit. (3) The deity of our Lord Jesus Christ, His virgin birth, His sinless life, His vicarious death and atonement through His shed blood, His bodily resurrection. His ascension, His mediatorial intercession, and His personal return in power and glory. He is the only Saviour of mankind. (4) The salvation of lost and sinful men through regeneration by the Holy Spirit. Salvation is by grace through faith. (5) The indwelling of the believer by the Holy Spirit, enabling the Christian to live a godly life. (6) The resurrection of both the saved and the lost; they that are saved unto the resurrection of life, and they that are lost unto the resurrection of damnation. (7) The spiritual unity of all believers in our Lord Jesus Christ, who comprise the Church, the body of Christ.
32 ELC to WRW, Jan 31 1951
33 *Ibid.*
34 FFMS Minutes, June 1951
35 FFMS Minutes, Aug 25 1953; ELC to WRW, Mar 9 1953

36 Coop Hm Bds of UBS Ex Com Minutes, Apr 14, 15 1953
37 WRW to Ex Bd of FFMS and to Full Bd, May 5 1953
38 Organizing Committee minutes of UBS, Feb 24-27 1953, ELC Chm FJK Prin. Note: The Seminary in India voted to use such terms as *convocation* instead of *commencement*; *term* instead of *semester*; and *principal* instead of *president*. Cf. UBS Board of Governors Minutes, Mar 12, 13 1956 #556
39 ELC 1956 report to EFMA
40 ELC to Dr. Clyde Taylor, Mar 18 1956
41 ELC to WRW, Mar 9 1953; MEC to FFMS, Oct 21 1957
42 FON, Vol XLI, No 4, Apr 1952, p 5
43 ELC to WRW, July 25 1952; BMMS Discipline, 1952, first printing, p 27
44 CJR to WRW, Aug 26 1952
45 ELC to WRW, July 18 1953
46 *Ibid.*, Apr 13 1951; *OYM Minutes*, 1952, p 48
47 CJR Personal Report, 1952
48 CDC to WRW, Mar 12 1952
49 EOR to WRW, Oct 18 1952
50 ELC to WRW, Dec 12 1950. Note: Alipura State Raja's criticism of Kinder had been: "He preaches too vehement; he preaches as though he expected us to become Christians right away." WRW's comment was that this was a very high recommendation for James Kinder. Cf. WRW to ELC, Dec 24 1952
51 *OYM Minutes*, 1953, p 32
52 CJR to WRW, Aug 26 1952
53 ELC to WRW, Apr 30 1953
54 WRW to ELC, Mar 2 1953
55 ELC to WRW, Mar 9 1953
56 MC Minutes, Feb 20 1953
57 ELC Diary, July 16-23 1952; ELC to WRW, July 18 1953
58 MC Minutes, June 5, 6 1953
59 Paper prepared by ELC for study by Mission Council Oct 30 1953
60 MC Minutes, Dec 28 1953-Jan 14 1954

CHAPTER 23
Grappling with Change

1 Charles Matti to WRW, Jan 15 1953; FON, Vol XLII, No 2, Feb 1953, p 2; and FON, Vol XLII, No 3, Mar 1953, p 2
2 *OYM Minutes*, 1955, p 40; WRW to Mrs. Earl Kelbaugh, Sep 30 1953
3 WRW to Pastors, Missionary Committees and Missionary Bd Members, July 26 1954
4 *OYM Minutes*, 1951, p 54
5 ELC Personal Report, 1953-54
6 From the Constitution of the United Mission to Nepal, formed Mar 6 1954
7 MC #3 Annual Meeting Sessions, 1954

8 ELC to WRW, Apr 30 1953
9 FON, Vol XLII, No 5, May 1953, p 2
10 WED Personal Report, 1951-52
11 WED to WRW, Feb 18 1952
12 ELC to WRW, Jan 7 1952
13 *OYM Minutes*, 1952, p 49; WRW to All Pastors, May 27 1952
14 ELC to WRW, Oct 8 1952
15 WED to WRW, Oct 12 1952
16 *OYM Minutes*, 1955, p 43
17 WED to WRW, Sep 26 1952; Oct 12 1953
18 ELC to WRW, Nov 14 1952, Dec 12 1952, Mar 9 1953
19 CDC to WRW, July 7 1952
20 FON, Vol XLV, No 6, 1956, p 5
21 MC Minutes, Aug 18 1957 #6; AN Letters, Sep 10 1956; ELC to WRW, June 25, Oct 18, Nov 5 1956
22 WED to WRW, Oct 22 1953
23 WRW letter #16 to pastors, Oct 2 1953
24 WED to WRW, Apr 17, 19; WRH to WRW, Apr 26 1954
25 ELC to WRW, July 23, Aug 19, Oct 3 1953
26 FON, Vol XLII, No 6, 1953, p 7
27 *Ibid.*, Vol XLIII, No 5, 1954, p 3
28 59th Annual Report of India Mission, unedited, 1955
29 MC Minutes, Dec 27, 28 1953; Jan 4 1954
30 MEC Report, 1953-54
31 EGH Report, 1953-54
32 WRH Report, 1953-54
33 MC Minutes, Feb 14 1952
34 ELC to WRW, Jan 6 1954
35 ELC to CGS, Bankers, DeVols, Apr 20 1956
36 WED to CGS, Nov 28 1957
37 CDC Personal Report, 1954
38 AN Letters, June 6 1955; Feb 18 1957
39 *Ibid.*, Oct 31 1954
40 WED to WRW, Nov 9 1953
41 *Ibid.*, Feb 27 1954
42 FON, Vol XLIV, No 4, Sep 1955, p 4
43 WRW Report, 1953-54
44 MC Minutes, Dec 10-12 1953; FON, Vol XLIII, No 5, May 1954, p 5
45 FON, Vol XLIII, No 1, Jan 1954, p 3
46 *Ibid.*, Vol XLIV, No 5, May 1955, p 7
47 WRH to WRW, Apr 26 1954
48 Executive Committee, Jan 1954; AN Letters, Jan 7 1954
49 ELC to WRW, Jan 6 1954
50 *OYM Minutes*, 1955, p 45
51 MC Minutes, July 1 1952
52 FON, Vol XLI, No 7, Sep 1952, p 6
53 ELC to WRW, July 22 1953
54 MC Minutes, Dec 27, 28 1953; Jan 4 1954
55 FON, Vol XLIII, No 8, Oct 1954, p 5
56 MC Minutes, June 5, 6 1953
57 MEB Personal Report, 1954
58 MC Minutes, June 5, 6 1953
59 WRW to REB, Mar 3 1953
60 WED to WRW, Aug 7 1954

61 NIV Luke 21:11-15: But before all this, they will lay hands on you and persecute you. They will deliver you to synagogues and prisons, and you will be brought before kings and governors, and all on account of my name. This will result in your being witnesses to them. But make up your mind not to worry beforehand how you will defend yourselves. For I will give you words and wisdom that none of your adversaries will be able to resist or contradict. (Interview with Dr. WED, Feb 18 1984)

62 WED to WRW, Sep 18 1954

63 AN Letters, Dec 12 1954

64 ELC Report, 1955

65 MEB Report, Mar 23 1955; Prov Y.M. Ex Com Mtg, Feb 18 1955 #2; REB Report, 1955; RHC report, 1956

66 WED to CGS, Mar 29 1955

67 MC Minutes, Mar 9 1956, No 2

68 WED to CGS, Mar 6 1955

69 *Ibid.*, Nov 30 1954

70 FON, Vol XLI, No 6, July 1952, p 8

71 NAF Report, 1956

72 MEC Report, 1955

73 RHC Personal Report, 1956

74 AN, Apr 4 1954

75 WED to CGS, Jan 20 1955

76 Ex Com of Prov Yr Mtg Minutes, Nov 22 1955; cf. Niyogi Report, 1956

77 AN Letters, Sep 10 1956

78 *Ibid.*, Sep 18 1955

79 Missionary News Service, Dec 17 1956

80 Ex Com of BMMS, Nov 15 1956; ELC to CBS, Oct 18 1956

81 WED to CGS, Jan 20 1955

82 ELC to WRW, Jan 6 1954

83 AN Letters, Aug 8 1954

84 WED to CGS, Feb 26 1955

85 *Ibid.*, Mar 29 1955

86 CGS to WRW, Nov 1 1955; WED to CGS, Apr 8 1955; WRH to CGS, Aug 17 1955

87 AN to CGS, Aug 4 1955

88 AN Letters, Sep 4 1955; AN to CGS, Sep 2 1955

89 CJR to Mission Board, Feb 5 1957

90 ELC to CGS, Mar 21 1956

91 AN to CGS, Aug 4 1955. Note: Robinsons had arranged with Don and Joy Rugh of the Methodist Church for this house earlier.

92 MC Minutes, Aug 15 1955

93 CGS to Rev. James Lambert, Lansing, Mich, Apr 26 1955

94 CGS to WRH, June 25 1955; Note: He was married Aug 17 1956

95 CDC form letter, Nov 25 1955

96 CDC Personal Report, 1956

97 ELC TO WRW June 16 1956

98 FON, Vol XLV, No 1, Feb 1956, p 6

99 MC Minutes, Dec 29 1956

100 FON, Vol XLV, No 1, Feb 1956, p 8

101 EF Magazine, Vol I, No 3, 1957, p 7

102 ELC in MV, Vol II, No 2, Apr 1956, pp 4-5

103 ELC Report to EFMA, Mar 1956

104 *To God Be the Glory*, p 25

105 ELC to CGS, Feb 16 1956

106 ELC, Ex Sec EFI to AFM, Chh, VP, Feb 10 1956

107 AN Personal Report, 1956

108 MV, July 1957, Vol 3, No 3, p 6; UBS Brochure 1957

109 FON, Vol XLV, No 4, Sep 1956, p 4

110 MV, Apr 1956, Vol II, No 2, p 9

111 FON, Vol XLVI, No 1, Feb 1957, p 5

112 *Ibid.*, No 2, Mar 1957, p 2

113 *Ibid.*, Vol XLV, No 4, Sep 1956, p 6

114 AN Letters, Sep 22, Dec 1 1957; AN Personal Report, Mar 25 1957

115 MV, Vol II, No 4, Oct 1956, p 9

116 EF Mag, Vol V, No 1, 1957, p 7

117 CDC Personal Report, 1957; MV, Oct 1957, Vol III, No 4, p 6. Interview CJR. Note: CJR had been instrumental in the choice of Akbar Haqq as an interpreter and worked with him in Kanpur and other campaigns for over three years. During that time Akbar Haqq learned to trust God for the harvest and his meetings were signally blessed.

CHAPTER 24
Rooting the Church in Bundelkhand

1 *OYM Minutes*, 1956, p 43

2 ELC to CGS, Aug 6 1956

3 *Ibid.*, Dec 14 1955; AN Letters, Oct 3 1956

4 MC Minutes, Oct 7 1957; From 12 pies = 1 anna, and 16 annas = 1 rupee, to 100 paise = 1 rupee

5 MV, Vol VI, No 2, Apr 1960

6 *OYM Minutes*, p 43; cf. Ex Com of Provisional Yr Mtg, Mar 19, 20 1956

7 Ex Com of Prov Yr Mtg, Apr 19 1956

8 WRW Bi-Monthly Letter #8 to Pastors, Jan 15 1952

9 ELC to CGS, May 13 1956; Prov Yr Mtg Ex Com, Jul 6 1956

10 *OYM Minutes*, 1957, p 38; FON, Vol XLV, No 4, Sep 1956, p 8

11 WED Personal Report, 1957

12 FON, Vol XLVI, No 4, Sep 1957, pp 4, 7; DWM to RM, Sep 8 1982

13 WED to CGS, Oct 2 1957

14 *OYM Minutes*, 1957, p 35

15 Marjorie Myers to M Council Sep 11 1956; *OYM Minutes*, 1956, p 42; WRW to ELC, Feb 21 1956 — organizational meeting in Denver Conference, July 11-15 1956

16 MC Minutes, June 24, 25 1957, No 14; EFI Ex Com Min, Jan 11 1957
17 WOODSTOCK SCHOOL, printed pamphlet, 1957; MC Minutes, Apr 4, 5 1958
18 WED to CGS, Dec 31 1957
19 MC Minutes, May 25, 26 1959, No 2; cf. June 16, 29 1959
20 *OYM Minutes*, 1956, p 43; Ex Com of Prov Yr Mtg, Mar 19, 20 1956
21 MC Minutes, Apr 23, 24 1957; Ex Com, Apr 1, 2, 5 1957
22 FON, Vol XLV, No 5, Nov 1956, p 5, and *To God Be the Glory*, p 21
23 FON, Vol XLVI, No 2, Mar 1957, p 8
24 CGS to WED, Sep 3 1957
25 MC Minutes and Prov Ex Com of Yr Mtg, Dec 18, 12, 21, 22, 29-31 1956; Jan 21, 22 1957; MC Minutes, Apr 23, 24 1957
26 ELC to CGS, June 25; July 9 1956
27 WED to CGS, Aug 8 1957
28 AN Letters, Aug 4 1957
29 FON, Vol XLVI, No 4, Sep 1957, p 5
30 *From Bamboo to Mango*, pp 185, 186
31 AN Letters, Aug 25 1957
32 WED to CGS, Aug 25 1957
33 WED Interview, Feb 1984; WED to CGS, Sep 2 1957
34 CGS to WED, Sep 20 1957
35 WED to CGS, Sep 2 1957
36 *Ibid.*, Aug 14, Sep 3, 28 1957; AN Letters, Oct 8 1957
37 WED to CGS, Oct 2 1957; WRH to CGS, Oct 8 1957
38 WED to CGS, Oct 2 1957
39 *Ibid.*, Jan 31 1958
40 *Ibid.*, May 9 1958
41 *Ibid.*, Apr 5 1959
42 AN Letters, July 27 1958
43 WED to CGS, Mar 13 1959
44 *OYM Minutes*, 1961, p 29
45 WRH to CGS, Jan 28 1958
46 WED to CGS, Mar 7 1958
47 Nowgong compound was sold for a Training Center for Rs. 70,000 ($14,736); [WED to CGS, July 19 1961]; Amarmau to the District Collector for Rs. 45,000 ($9,474); [WED to CGS, Mar 14 1958]; Ganj to the police department for Rs. 30,000 ($6,316); [WED to CGS, July 19 1961]; Gulganj to the police department for Rs. 26,200 ($5,516); [WED to CGS, Sep 26 1961]
48 WED to CGS, May 26 1959
49 *Ibid.*, Nov 22 1960
50 FON, Vol XLVII, No 2, Mar 1958, p 2
51 WRH to CGS, Jan 28 1958
52 CGS to WED, Sep 21 1959; Item 20 of Board Minutes; CGS to Asst. Dean Univ of Pa, Oct 9 1958
53 AN Letters, Apr 3 1958
54 WED to CGS, July 29 1960
55 *Ibid.*, Sep 15 1958; RHC Personal Report 1960
56 RHC Report, 1959
57 *OYM Minutes*, 1958, p 34; MEC Personal Report, 1960
58 MEC Personal Report, 1959; RHC to CGS, May 6 1959; MEC to ELC, July 10 1959; *OYM Minutes*, 1960, p 27
59 MEC Personal Report, 1959; cf. WED to CGS, Oct 7 1959, Sep 18 1958
60 FON, Vol XLVII, No 4, Sep 1958, p 6; Vol XLIX, No 6, Dec 1960, p 2
61 MEC to ELC, Apr 18 1960
62 VSP to WRH, June 3 1959
63 WED to CGS, Jan 7 1960
64 MEC to ELC, Apr 18 1960; FON, Vol XLIX, No 6, Dec 1960, p 2
65 WED to WRW, Sep 14 1958
66 *OYM Minutes*, 1958, p 35
67 ELC, *The Self-Giving Missionary*
68 WED to CGS, Mar 7 1958
69 FON, Vol XLVII, No 4, Sep 1958, p 5
70 WED to CGS, Jan 3 1959
71 *Ibid.*, Mar 5 1959
72 FON, Vol XLVII, No 3, May 1958, p 2
73 *Ibid.*, No 21, Mar 1958, p 2
74 MC Minutes, Apr 9, 10 1958
75 *OYM Minutes*, 1960, p 25
76 FON, Vol XLIX, No 1, Feb 1960, p 3
77 *Ibid.*, Vol XLVIII, No 6, Dec 1959, p 4
78 WED to CGS, Dec 23 1958
79 *Ibid.*, Mar 5 1959
80 *OYM Minutes*, 1960, p 28
81 CGS to WED, Sep 21 1959
82 MC to FFMS, Mar 12 1959
83 WED to SHB, July 16 1961
84 *Ibid.*, Sep 26 1961
85 WED to CGS, Jan 14, July 16, Oct 7 1949; WED to WRW, Aug 4 1960; WED to CGS, Apr 19 1960; MV Vol V, No 3 1960, p 13
86 FON, Vol XLIX, No 3 1960, p 3
87 WED to CGS, Oct 1 1959
88 I Tim 3:4; cf. *OYM Minutes*, 1960, p 26
89 FON, Vol XLIX, No 6, Dec 1960, p 2
90 EGH to Edith Salter, Feb 19 1961
91 FON, Vol XLIX, No 6, Dec 1960
92 *OYM Minutes*, 1961, p 29
93 MC, Mar 28 1961
94 WED to CGS, Mar 6 1961; WED to SHB, July 16 1961
95 *OYM Minutes*, 1960, p 25; 1961
96 Ex Board of Yearly Meeting, Mar 23 1961; cf. FFMS Board Meeting Minutes, Mar 10 1961
97 Sixty-Fifth Field Annual Report, 1961
98 *Ibid.*, WED, 1961
99 WED to CGS, Apr 12 1961
100 *Ibid.*, Apr 12, 23 1961
101 MC, WED Chm, to BMMS Ex Com, K. D. Lal, Supt, Apr 10 1961
102 WED to CGS, Apr 30 1961
103 WED to SHB, July 16 1961

104 Dr. DWM, Chm BMMS to Clerk OYM, Aug 7 1961
105 MC, May 4, 5, 9 1961
106 FON, Vol XLVI, No 6, Dec 1957, p 7
107 OYM Minutes, 1962, p 39
108 WED to SHB, Apr 11 1962
109 WRH to SHB, Dec 4 1962
110 WED to SHB, Feb 21 1962
111 MC Minutes, Dec 27 1962
112 NAF to SHB, Apr 25 1962

CHAPTER 25
Leading the Leaders to Christ

1 OYM Minutes, 1957, p 39; MC Minutes, Apr 9, 10 1958, No 10
2 MC Minutes, Dec 29 1956
3 OYM, 1959, p 36
4 MC Minutes, Apr 4, 5 1956; News Release, p 2, 1955; MV, Jul 1957, pp 9, 15, Vol III, No 3
5 WED to CGS, Dec 31 1957
6 OYM Minutes, 1958, p 35
7 WED to CGS, June 1958
8 FON, Vol XLVII, No 6, Dec 1958, pp 3, 4
9 CGS to WED, Sep 10 1958
10 WED to CGS, Nov 4 1958
11 CJR 1959 Report
12 OYM Minutes, 1959, p 33
13 FON, Vol XLVIII, No 2, Mar 1959, p 5
14 Ibid.
15 EOR Personal Report, 1959
16 CGS to WED, May 19 1959
17 OYM Minutes, 1959, p 36
18 MV, Jan 1961, Vol VII, No 1, pp 5, 6; CJR Report, 1960
19 FON, Vol XLIX, No 4, Sep 1960, pp 4, 8
20 Ibid., Vol XLVIII, No 6, Dec 1959, p 6
21 OYM 1960, p 27
22 EOR: FON, Vol L, No 1, 1961, p 5
23 EOR Report, 1963-64
24 EOR in MV, Oct 1960, Vol VI, No 4, p 6
25 CJR to SHB, May 3 1960; Mission Board Ex Com to CJR, May 10 1962
26 CJR to CGS and SHB, Nov 5 1963
27 Ibid.
28 CJR to FFM, Aug 17 1964
29 CJR to Mission Board, Aug 17 1964
30 Betty R. to SHB, Oct 31 1964, quoting Anne's letter
31 EF, Apr 1965, p 8
32 CJR to FFM, Aug 17 1964
33 Missionary Board minutes to CJR from Missionary Board, Mar 23 1964, Minutes 64-18
34 CGS to Dr. Halverson, Mar 23 1964
35 CJR to FFMS, Sep 25 1946
36 CJR to SHB, Oct 26 1946
37 MV, Apr 1965, p 16
38 MEC to Mission Office, Nov 2 1966
39 OYM, 1965, p 24

CHAPTER 26
Pioneering in Christian Education

1 FON, Vol XLVII, No 6, Dec 1958, p 8
2 OYM, 1957, p 35
3 FON, Vol XLVII, No 4, Sep 1958, p 8
4 Dennis Clark to CGS, Sep 10 1959
5 AN Letters, Nov 25 1958
6 Ibid., Nov 30 1959. Note: Only one portfolio was left—Someone else had to become the Examination Secretary for the Hindi Language School, for Gladys knew only Marathi. For a number of years Anna had been a Hindi examiner and was responsible for arranging the setting of examination papers, choosing the centers, appointing the examiners, and recording and reporting the grades of all missionaries in language study throughout the Hindi area. (AN Letters, Nov 25 1958) The work became lighter year by year because of India's policy concerning admission of new missionaries. In the fall of 1951 there had been 147 candidates for the Hindi examinations; in 1959 there were only 40. (AN Personal Report, 1959) During the March examinations a replacement was found.
7 AN, Advance on Sixteen Fronts, 1972. Note: At the ELFI Triennial Conference in 1959, Russell Self had proposed that a Religious Education Department of EFI be formed and called REEFI. Ethelyn Watson questioned, "Would we call this Religious Education or Christian Education?" Marie Moyer said, "We should be definite, and I suggest we call it Christian Education from the start." Zoe Anne Alford, UBS professor in Christian Education, then settled it with, "I suggest we call it CEEFI."
8 AN Notes, 1960
9 AN Letters, Nov 30 1959
10 EFI Ex Com Minutes, Jan 1960, Deolali
11 FON, Vol XLIX, No 2, Mar 1960, p 8.
12 AN, Advance on Sixteen Fronts, July 1972
13 AN Letters, Nov 25 1961
14 AN Form Letter, June 1962
15 AN, Dec 3 1961
16 EFI Ex Com Minutes 1062b
17 FON, Vol LI, No 1, Feb 1962, p 6
18 AN, Advance on Sixteen Fronts 1972
19 EFI Ex Com Minutes 1062b
20 AN, Jan 10 1962
21 Guidelines for Adapters and Editors, CEEFI, 1962
22 To God Be the Glory, p 35
23 OYM Minutes, 1963, p 23
24 MC Minutes, Apr 1, 5 1963
25 AN, June 9, Aug 11 1963

26 MV, Apr 1964, p 14
27 AN, Dec 6 1963
28 CEEFI Triennial Report, 1965
29 AN, Jan 24 1964
30 AN to SHB, Apr 1, July 31 1964; AN, Sep 13 1964
31 AN Letters, Nov 1964
32 First CEEFI Triennial Report, Aug 1965
33 MV, Apr 1964, p 14
34 AN Personal Report, 1964
35 AN to SHB, Feb 22 1965
36 Ibid., Mar 25 1965
37 CEEFI Report, Aug 1962-65
38 AN Letters, Nov 19 1965; AN to SHB, Oct 27 1965
39 EF, Apr 1971, p 21
40 AN to SHB, Sep 18 1967
41 Ibid., Dec 31 1966
42 EF, Apr 1971, p 12
43 To God Be the Glory, p 35
44 AN to SHB, Sep 18 1967
45 CEEFI Report, 1971, pp 20, 22
46 EF, Dec 1968, p 12; AN to SHB, Apr 7 1968
47 AN Personal Report, 1968; AN Letters, Dec 2 1968
48 AN, July 22 1968
49 AN, Nov 25 1968
50 AN General Letter, June 1969
51 AN, Feb 18 1969
52 AN to SHB, Apr 26 1969
53 Ibid., Feb 14 1970
54 Ibid., Apr 5 1970
55 AN Personal Report, 1970
56 AN, Apr 27 1970
57 MC Minutes, Feb 13, Mar 13 1970; AN Letters, Apr 19 1970
58 WED to SHB, May 6 1970
59 AN, Jan 1 1971
60 SHB to WED, Sep 9 1968; Mission Board Minutes, Mar 13 1970; WED to SHB, Aug 13 1970
61 ELC Report to the Mission Board 1971, pp 13, 14
62 CEEFI Report, 1971, p 22
63 Ibid., p 14
64 AN, Advance on Sixteen Fronts, p 12
65 AN to CEEFI Ex Com, Nov 20 1970
66 WED Annual Mission Report, 1971
67 AN to Berneita Nixon, May 5 1971
68 From "A Brief Report of Ao Naga CEEFI Materials and Sunday School work" sent by AN through BLI Columbus, OH to FMMS and Mr. and Mrs. W. Pim, Mar 29 1971

CHAPTER 27
Cooperating in Theological Education

1 CGS to WED, Apr 1 1959; MC Minutes, Apr 6 1962, No. 9

2 FON, Vol L, No 5, Nov 1961, p 5
3 Ibid., No. 6, Dec 1961, p 5
4 In order of joining, they were: The Free Methodist Mission; Berar-Khandesh Christian Conference (which included the Church of the Nazarene, Christian & Missionary Alliance, Norwegian Free Mission, Conservative Baptists, and Swedish Alliance); India Holiness Association; C. & M.A.; Wesleyan Methodist Mission; Central India Baptists; OYM (Evangelical Friends Church — Eastern Region); EFI; General Conference Mennonite Mission; Mennonite Church of India; Free Methodist Church; Alumni Association of UBS; United Missionary Society; Bible and Medical Missions Fellowship; Woman's Union Missionary Society; Indo-Burma Pioneer Mission; World Vision; Youth for Christ; Assemblies of God. From F. J. Kline report to Cooperating Home Boards, July 5 1961
5 FJK Report to CHBUBS, July 5 1961
6 Missionary Information Service, Free Methodist Church, Winona Lake, IN June 19 1958
7 FJK Report o CHBUBS, July 5 1961
8 WRH to SHB, July 22 1962
9 EF, Jan 1965, p 8; WRH to SHB, Nov 18 1964
10 OYM, 1963, p 23; AN Letters, Mar 22 1964; EGH Report, 1965
11 EGH to SHB, Aug 19 1964
12 EF, Sep 1964, p 7
13 EF, Mar 1964, p 3
14 FJK to ELC, Nov 13 1962
15 EGH to Adrian Q.M., Sep 21 1964
16 EH to SHB, Feb 9 1965
17 WRH to SHB, Nov 18 1964
18 WED to SHB, July 2 1965
19 EGH Report, 1965
20 EGH to SHB, Apr 27 1965
21 Ibid., July 30 1965
22 SHB to WRH, Nov 12 1965
23 FJK to ELC, Nov 13 1962
24 EF, Oct 1966, pp 5-6
25 WRH to SHB, Sep 21 1965
26 EF, Oct 1966, p 6
27 June 13 1966 CHBUBS meeting 66.S.13
28 WRH Personal Report, 1968
29 CHBUBS, Mar 24 1967, #67-12, Oct 6 1967
30 Ken Bauman, Principal's Report, Mar 1967
31 Ibid., July 1968
32 Dr. WRH to UBS Board of Governors, Sep 7 1967
33 WRH Personal Report 1968. Note: At least one person on Campus immediately learned the significance of this new appointment. Five-year old Danny Hess sat on a brick wall surrounding a very

deep well dangling his feet inside and leaning over to see his reflection in the water. "Danny, get off that," Saphir ordered. Danny, turning slightly, replied, "Do you know who my daddy is? He's the principal of this school." Saphir answered, "Maybe you don't know who I am. I'm the *vice*-principal of this school, and you'd better get off." Danny did, at once.

34 WRH to SHB, Sep 29 1967
35 K. Bauman to Charles Kirkpatrick, May 8 1970
36 MC Minutes, Apr 13 1969
37 FFMS Minutes #68, Mar 22 1968
38 WRH to SHB, Nov 18 1967
39 EFC−ER Mission Board Minutes #81-12
40 FFMS, June 1, 2 1982
41 WRH to SHB, Nov 18 1967
42 EF, May 1968, pp 8, 17
43 EGH to Anna Cobbs, Aug 19 1967
44 WRH to SHB, Mar 17 1968
45 EGH to SHB, Apr 18 1968; WRH to SHB, Apr 19 1968
46 *Ibid.*, June 24 1968
47 K. Bauman, Principal's Report to the UBS Ex Com of the Board, July 15 1968
48 K. Bauman to Charles Kirkpatrick, May 8 1970
49 K. Bauman to CHBUBS, Apr 8 1972
50 For six months in 1973 Anna Nixon served with TRACI preparing to take over as acting director in the absence of Bruce Nicholls. TRACI, however, opted to move off the UBS campus and have its own board rather than to continue under the UBS Board of Governors. In October Anna resigned in order to remain at UBS as a full-time faculty member
51 ELC Report to Missionary Board, 1970
52 FFMS Minutes, 1970 #70-3
53 *OYM Minutes*, 1974, p 31
54 UBS Coop Hm Bds 1.12.73 3-73
55 Ex Com of Bd of Governors of UBS Minutes 45-3-71
56 AN to SHB, Apr 18 1970
57 Ex Com Bd of Governors Mtg, Nov 4, 5 1970
58 MC, Apr 5 1971, 7-f
59 UBS Ex Com 40-E-72, Oct 11, 12 1972
60 AN Letters, July 4 1974
61 Elmer E. Parsons to Dr. Charles Kirkpatrick, Mar 3 1972
62 CHBUBS Ex Com, May 5 1972
63 Bd of Gov Minutes, 101-B-72
64 *Ibid.*, 24-B-74
65 EFC−ER Minutes, 1976, p 36; WRH Report
66 UBS Bd of Governors (UBS Assn) Minutes, Mar 26, 27 1976; Principals Report, p 4
67 UBS Assn Minutes, Mar 26, 27 1976

68 Bd of Gov Minutes, 30-B-76(a)
69 *Ibid.*, 30-B-76(b)
70 Bd of Governors, Mar 26, 27 1976, 4-B-76
71 *Ibid.*, 40-B-76; AN to WRH, Mar 25 1979
72 Principal's Report, p 3; UBS Assn Board of Governors, Mar 8-10 1982
73 Bd of Gov Minutes, Mar 18, 19 1974
74 AN Personal Report, 1974
75 CHBUBS Minutes, May 30 1975
76 Paper presented to World Vision, Nov 10 1976
77 ELC Report to Mission Board, 1971
78 From the Annual Gen Mtg UBS Assn Yavatmal, Mar 21, 22 1975: (1) American Friends Mission (EFC−ER); (2) Baptist Church Assn (CIBM); (3) BMMF; (4) C&MA; (5) Ch Miss Soc Australia; (6) Ch of God in India; (7) Churches of Christ in Western India; (8) EFI; (9) Fr Methodists; (10) Gen Conf Mennonite Mission; (11) India Fr Meth Church; (12) India Holiness Assn; (13) Mennonite Bd of Missions; (14) Mennonite Ch in India; (15) Mennonite Br Mission; (16) Methodist Church in South Asia's Gujarat Conference; (17) North East India General Mission; (18) OMS International; (19) Partnership Mission Soc; (20) South Asia Bible College; (21) UBS Alumni Assn; (22) The Wesleyan Church; (23) Woman's Missionary Union; (24) Boys Christian Home
79 CHBUBS, Nov 14 1975
80 *Ibid.*, Dec 10 1974
81 Ex Com of UBS Bd of Gov, Aug 19, 20 1974
82 CHBUBS, May 30 1975; Nov 14 1975; WRH Report, 1975
83 WRH to AN, Sep 8 1976; Herbert Coons to Karl Kose, Dec 28 1976
84 Hess Report to Board, 1975
85 UBS Assn Bd of Gov 37-B-76 (f), Mar 26, 27 1976
86 Russell Myers to AN, Dec 15 1977
87 M.B. Minute 77-29, Wed, Aug 24 1977
88 Russell Myers to AN, Dec 15 1977
89 AN to WRH, Sep 4 1979
90 AN to Carl and Berneita Nixon, Sep 28 1979
91 UBS Assn Bd of Gov No 48-B-80, Mar 17, 18 1980. Note: The joy of completing these sales was not only because of the funds released to UBS, but also because the houses so dear to Friends missionaries in India had gone into the hands of Christians. Pinepoint became home for a family of five; Pennington was bought in the name of ETANI by missionaries Joseph and Marietta Smith, who transformed it into a "Himalaya L'Abri."
92 AN to Russell Myers, Jan 18 1978
93 AIM, June 1980 p 9

94 AN Personal Report, 1974
95 AN to WRH, Oct 9 1977
96 AN to Anna Cobbs, Oct 26 1978
97 UBS Assn Bd of Gvnrs, Oct 8 1980; Mar 17, 18 1980; Note: Arrival in the U.S.A. did not change the cycle, but Anna was kept on mission salary and assigned deputation work and the writing of the mission history while seeking medical help. In line with the expressed desire of UBS, she also served as Communications Liaison for Cooperating Home Boards of Union Biblical Seminary, Inc. In early 1982 the basic cause of her illness, through the cooperative and prayerful care of a number of Christian doctors, was discovered and treated successfully. She retired in good health from mission service in 1984.
98 These contributions were as follows: Cooperating Home Boards – $300,000; German sources – $370,000; U.S.A. Funds raised by Principal Athyal 1979-80 – $290,000; TEAR, World Vision, Knox Church, Canada – $133,000; Indian Sources – $16,600. Principal's Report to Board, Mar 16-18 1981
99 SAPHIR P. Athyal to WRH, Jan 15 1982
100 Principal's Report to Bd of Gov Mtg, Feb 24-Mar 2 1983, pp 5, 7
101 EFM WORLD, July 1983, p 2
102 UPDATE, Oct-Dec 1983
103 UBS CONTACT USA, p 4
104 Anil Solanki to AN, Mar 1984

CHAPTER 28
Healing in Nepal

1 Dr. Miller UMN to Dr. W. E. DeVol, Oct 20 1959
2 WED, Feb 22 1959
3 FON, Vol XLVIII, No 3, May 1959, pp 6, 8
4 Lindell, pp 136, 141
5 Ibid., pp 137, 138
6 Ibid., pp 138, 139
7 Ibid., p 140
8 Ibid., p 142
9 John 12:23-24. Note: The ban on charging fees within reason for medicines and treatment seems to have been waived, and up to 1975, no property had been turned over to the government. See pamphlet, "Greetings from Nepal," n.d. printed by Mani Printing House, Darjeeling, 32 pages, pp 13-15.
10 Lindell, p 152
11 Ibid., p 154
12 Ibid., p 157. Note: They were Regions Beyond Missionary Union, Church of Scotland, American Presbyterian Mission, Methodist Church in Southern Asia,

Zenana Bible and Medical Mission (later called Bible and Medical Missionary Fellowship – BMMF), World Mission Prayer League, Swedish Baptist Mission, and United Christian Missionary Society. The Anglican Churches participated in the formation of UMN, as did American Friends Mission and the Evangelical Fellowship of India. American Friends Mission was represented by Everett Cattell, and a token grant was given, but they did not become a member until 1963.
13 Ibid., p 269
14 Ibid., pp 128, 156, 171
15 FON, Vol XLVIII, No 3, May 1959, pp 6, 8
16 WED to CGS, Feb 22 1959
17 EF, Aug 1965, p 4
18 WED to CGS, Feb 1959
19 Ibid., Feb 22 1959
20 Dr Bethel H Fleming and staff of Shanta Bhavan Hospital, n.d. 1959
21 MEC to CGS, Sep 28 1959
22 Oliver to WED, May 9 1961
23 SHB to FFMS, Feb 1963
24 SHB to Members of Missionary Board, Feb 7 1963
25 AN to Delhia Webb, Colorado, Oct 31 1964
26 WED Personal Report to Missionary Board, Aug 1 1964
27 EGH to SHB, Aug 17 1963
28 WED to SHB, Apr 14 1964
29 EF, Dec 1964, p 11
30 EF, Sep 1965, p 4
31 FHD to SHB, Aug 7 1965
32 EF, Sep 1965, p 6
33 WED to SHB, Oct 13 1963
34 WED to Missionary Bd, Aug 1 1964
35 MV 1966, pp 13, 14
36 WED to SHB, Oct 13 1963
37 Interview, Mar 15 1984 AN with WED
38 WED to SHB, Aug 7 1965
39 Ibid., Apr 14 1964
40 FHD to SHB, Aug 7 1965
41 MV, Jan 1965, p 8
42 FFMS President's Report, 1964
43 WED Annual Report, Aug 7 1965; WED to SHB, Sep 9 1965
44 WED to SHB, Oct 8 1965
45 1965 Annual Report UMN Medical Center, p 4
46 WED to SHB from Kathmandu, Nov 25 1965
47 Ibid., Jan 14 1966
48 MEC to SHB, Jan 31 1966
49 WED Diary, Jan 26 1966
50 WED notes, 1966
51 AN Letters, Mar 31 1966
52 SHB to WRH quoting minute 66-1, Apr 29 1966
53 Ray Windsor to Chm of UMN Bd, Mar 29 1971; MC Minutes, Apr 5 1971, No 2

54 *The Rising Nepal* newspaper, Vol XVII, No 234, Kathmandu, Nov 10 1982, p 1. Note: NB The cost of construction alone was $5,000,000.

CHAPTER 29
Keeping Watch Through the Night

1 MC, June 26 1963, No 14
2 EGH to SHB, Jan 11 1963
3 Missionary Board Minutes, Aug 20 1963
4 NAF Personal Report, 1963
5 AN, Aug 20 1963
6 EF, Apr 1964, p 9
7 NAF to SHB, Sep 22 1964 and AN, Sep 30 1964
8 KT Personal Report, 1966
9 MC Minutes, June 28 1966, No 3
10 *Ibid.*, Dec 27 1967, No 6
11 MEC to SHB, June 22, Nov 5, 30 1965
12 SHB letter of Mar 30 1967 to WED quoting Mission Board Minute 67-9; WED to SHB, May 3 1968 (New York)
13 NAF to SHB, Aug 2 1962
14 OYM, 1963, p 22
15 EF, June 1965; MEC to WRH and AN, Sep 9 1966; NAF, Nov 19 1966
16 EF, Mar 1965, p 10
17 Hospital Chaplain Report, Feb 1965 to Jan 1966
18 WED to SHB, Feb 7, Mar 15 1976
19 NAF Personal report, 1964; WED to SHB, Aug 7 1965
20 WED to SHB, Feb 27 1964
21 NAF to SHB, Sep 6 1962; cf. MC, Apr 1, 5 1963
22 WRH to SHB, Apr 14 1965; MEC, Jan 31 1966; MEC to Mission Office, Oct 19 1966
23 NAF to SHB, Feb 13 1965
24 WRH to SHB, July 21 1965; AN Letters, July 2, Aug 5 1965
25 RHC Personal Report, 1966. Note: This year the Missionary Board voted help to missionaries with college tuition of their children — $725 for the first year — Apr 12 1966, SHB to WRH.
26 OYM *Minutes*, p 39, 1963
27 RHC Personal Report, 1963
28 MC Minutes, Feb 22, 23 1964, No 12; Apr 3, 4 1965, No 2
29 AN to WRH, Apr 15 1964
30 EGH to SHB, Aug 17 1963; WRH to SHB, Oct 10 1963; WED to SHB, Apr 6 1965; Unpublished article RHC, Jan 21 1966
31 MEC unpublished article, May 28 1966
32 Mission Council letter to Foreign Ministry Office, New Delhi, Mar 8 1965
33 OYM *Minutes*, 1962, p 39
34 MC Minutes, June 26 1963, No 10
35 WED to SHB, May 18 1964 and NAF Report, May 1964; WRH to SHB, Feb 26 1964
36 EF, Feb 1966, p 6; MEC to SHB, Oct 5 1966; MEC to SHB cable, Dec 16 1966
37 MEC Personal Report, 1966; MEC to SHB, Oct., 1966
38 MEC to Anna Cobbs, Nov 1 1966
39 MEC unpublished article, Dec 17 1965
40 OYM *Minutes*, 1963, p 32
41 MEC to SHB, May 15 1966
42 FFMS Minutes, Mar 24 1967
43 OYM *Minutes*, 1967, pp 19, 20
44 AN to SHB, Sep 18 1967; Note: Carrie Wood died Mar 1 1968; Merrill Coffin, July 22 1970; Anna Coffin, Aug 4 1983; and Ethol George, May 5 1973.
45 MEC to WRH, Nov 14 1967
46 EF, Nov 1967
47 NAF to SHB, Dec 14 1968. Note: At the same time, Pyare Lal Brown was elected to the board in Nowgong!
48 MEC to SHB, Jan 30 1964
49 MEC to Missionary Supt, Nov 2 1967; EF, Apr 1966, p 6; MEC to SHB, Sep 12 1966; MEC to SHB, Dec 8 1967; Ex Com FFMS Minutes, Dec 15, 16 1967
50 MEC to SHB, Mar 11 1967
51 *Ibid.*, Mar 16 1967; to Mission Office, Jan 18 1967; Cable Jan 19 1967; and cable from SHB to MEC, Feb 1 1967; WED to SHB, July 12 1967
52 WED to SHB, Apr 29 1967; cf. MC Minutes, No 11, Mar 25, 27 1967
53 WED to SHB, May 29 1967
54 FHD to SHB and Dot, Sep 29 1968
55 ELFI Bulletin No 3, 1967, p 1
56 MEC's file, newspaper clipping n.d. 1967
57 MEC Article "Evangelical Churches in Bihar Relief," Jan 30 1967
58 MEC to SHB, June 6 1967; Russell Self to WED, July 4 1967
59 WED to SHB, July 12 1967
60 MEC in EFI News Letter, Oct 9 1967
61 RHC to SHB, July 13, Aug 9 1967 from Chandwa, Bihar
62 Russell Self to WED, July 4 1967
63 ELFI Bulletin, No 3, 1967
64 EFI Ex Com Minutes, No 35-67, 1967; MEC to Mission Board, Dec 8 1967
65 MC Minutes, Dec 26 1967; R. E. Mission Annual Mtg, 68 — 16, Feb 17 1968
66 WED to SHB, May 20 1967
67 WED Personal Report, 1968
68 FHD to SHB, May 28 1968
69 FHD to Dot and SHB, Sep 29 1968; K. T. Personal Report, 1969
70 NAF, Jan 4 1968; Note: Two doctors had come, but through the tragedy of suicide, one had died May 29 1968, WED to SHB, June 1 1968.

71 Ex Com Minutes FFMS, Dec 16 1967, E-67-17, 19
72 WED Medical report, 1968
73 WED to SHB, June 26 1968
74 FHD to Dot and SHB, Sep 29 1968
75 MC Letter to KT, Apr 13 1969
76 NAF, Dec 2 1969
77 EF, Feb 1971, p 13
78 WED to SHB, Nov 19 1970, Feb 14 1969
79 SHB Gen letter from Chhatarpur, Oct 28 1969; EF, Apr 1970, p 12
80 MC Minutes, Apr 13 1969; WED to SHB, Apr 23 1969
81 WED to SHB, Nov 19 1970
82 EHA Brochure, updated in 1984; OYM Minutes, 1970, p 26
83 WED to SHB, Apr 13 1970; FFMS Minutes, Mar 13 1970-70-3; WED to R Myers, June 19 1970
84 WED to SHB, Mar 31 1970
85 NAF to SHB, May 30 1971
86 WED to SHB, July 29 1971
87 Ibid., Dec 15 1971; AN to ELC and CDC, July 10 1972
88 Ibid., Dec 29 1971
89 WED Indian Annual Medical Report, 1971, p 2
90 WED to SHB, July 1 1972; AN to WRH and ELC, June 25 1972
91 GM to Russell Myers, Aug 7 1973
92 NAF to FFMS Board, Jan 18 1977
93 MC Minutes, Jan 25, 26 1973
94 Ibid., Jan 25, 26, 27 1973
95 Annual Medical Report, 1971; cf. Annual Report, Aug 2 1972
96 NAF to RM, Dec 10 1973
97 WED to SHB, Apr 6 1972
98 Ibid., Sep, Nov 1 1972; NAF to SHB, Nov 19 1966; AN to Board Gen Letter, Nov 13 1972
99 WED to RM, Apr 23 1973
100 Dr. DeVol's notes, nd, c 1972
101 MC, Apr 11 1973
102 WED to RM, Apr 23 1973
103 Dr M to RM, June 13 1973
104 WED to SHB, Feb 12 1974; cf. NAF to SHB, Jan 15 1975

CHAPTER 30
Bearing the Heat of the Day

1 WRH to NAF, Sep 14 1974
2 AN to ELC and CDC, June 29 1972
3 VM to NAF, 1974
4 RM to NAF, June 19 1974
5 Ex Com to RM and WRH and SHB, July 14 1975·
6 OYM Minutes, 1975, pp 40, 41. Note: He made a trip around the world at this time on behalf of the Evangelical Friends Mission just in the process of being set up by EFA.
7 OYM Minutes, 1971, p 29
8 EF, Mar 1971, p 15
9 WRH Report to Mission Board from Lyss, Switzerland, Nov 1 1975
10 NAF to SHB, July 15 1974
11 Ibid., Jan 20 1975, MC, Sep 29 1975. Note: MC was a meeting of NAF, AN and WRH. There was no longer a Mission Council because the law in India required at least five members for it to function and only two missionaries of the American Friends Mission were in India.
12 WRH to NAF, Feb 19 1976. Note: WRH also wrote NAF, Jan 8 1976: "Sherman Brantingham will soon be leaving us (for general superintendent post in Indiana) and that will leave a gap in the office and in our emotions . . . . He has done a lot to sell missions to the churches."
13 WRH to NAF, May 11 1976
14 FFMS Bd Mtg 77-39, Aug 26 1977
15 EF, Dec 1977/Jan 1978, pp 8, 9
16 NAF to WRH, Sep 4 1978
17 FFMS Ex Com Minutes, Aug 23 1978 E-78-107
18 WRH to NAF, Nov 21 1978
19 NAF to WRH, June 28 1979
20 Ibid., Apr 10 11 1979. Note: Sunand is the daughter of the late Samson Huri Lal, the first male nurse ever to serve on the Christian Hospital staff, and married to the grandson of the late Pancham Singh.
21 EFC — ER Minutes, 1979, p 56
22 NAF to WRH, Feb 5 1979
23 NAF to A. Cobbs, Aug 13, Sep 24 1980; NAF to AN, Sep 24 1980; NAF to AN, July 1983
24 NAF to RM, Jan 27 1978; NAF to AN, Jul 1983
25 EFC — ER Minutes, 1981, p 45; NAF Report, May 1983; cf. Gen Letter NAF, Apr 1984; NAF to AN, July 1983, cf. NAF Gen Letter, Apr 1984
26 NAF Gen Letter, Apr 1984; NAF to AN, July 1983
27 FFMS Minutes, May 31 1983, 83-32
28 WRH OYM Minutes EFC — ER, p 36
29 WRH to NAF, Jan 1982; JM to NAF, June 23 1982
30 Shyam K Wm Lal to AN, Feb 20 1984
31 WED to SHB, Apr 13 1970
32 GaM Article, 1977
33 GaM to SHB, Jan 15 1975; July 20 1976
34 GaM to James Morris, Jan 16 1983
35 NAF to SHB, July 8 1975
36 WRH Report to Mission Board from Lyss, Switzerland, Nov 1 1975
37 VSP to RM, Apr 8 1976
38 Ibid., June 13 1976
39 Pamphlet—"A Brief Historical Statement— the FECI," Nov 3 1974, p 8
40 EF, Feb 1971, p 13

41 EF, Feb 1975, p 13, cf. FECI Pamphlet, 1974, p 6
42 AN Article to *Facing Bench* Sep 22 1980
43 GaM to RM, Dec 13 1980
44 FECI Bulletin, Aug 13-16 1981
45 GaM to Rev and Mrs R Myers, Dec 13 1980
46 EFC—ER Mission Board, Aug 12 1981
47 GaM to AN, Sep 21 1983
48 Undated paper of VKM to a few friends, 1976. Note: India knew well the meaning of *ashram*—a place of retreat; Vishal and Ruth were beginning something new on this old foundation.
49 VKM to a few friends—nd paper written in 1976
50 VKM to RM, Oct 11 1976
51 VKM to AN, Aug 20 1976
52 Gen Annual Report, ACRA, Feb 1 1979; cf. VKM to AN, Aug 20 1976
53 DWM to RM, Sep 1 1977
54 VKM to RM, Mar 30 1978; DWM to RM, May 12 1978; EFC—ER Minutes, 1978, p 56
55 NAF to RM, Apr 7 1978. Note: Bilwar's first convert, Hira Lal, had died in 1977 and would not see the fruit of his prayers.
56 NAF to RM, Apr 7 1968, cf. letter of PB to AN, July 1982
57 NAF to RM, Nov 14, Dec 15 1977
58 VKM to WRH, Feb 13 1979
59 WRH to VKM, Mar 28 1979
60 Gooddeeds general letter, Apr 1984
61 VM to AN, Sep 25 1980
62 *Ibid.*
63 *Ibid.*, Nov 6 1980
64 ACRA Gen Letter, Nov 26 1980
65 NAF to WRH, Jan 8 1981
66 ACRA Letter, Dec 23 1980
67 *Ibid.*, Nov 26 1980
68 *Ibid.*, Dec 23 1980
69 VM to AN, Jan 13 1981; VM Interview with AN, Nov 27 1972; VM Gen Letter to AN, Jan 26 1981
70 EFC—ER Minutes, 1981, p 45
71 ACRA General Letter, Feb 1982
72 ACRA Newsletter, Feb 1982; NAF to WRH, Feb 21 1980
73 ACRA Annual Report, 1981
74 JM to NAF, June 23 1982
75 NAF to Mission, May 12 1982
76 SP to WRH, Feb 4 1982. Note: BMMS, a Friends Church, does not believe that baptism brings salvation to a person. Baptism was entirely optional to children of Christian parents. It indicated, however, a break with Hinduism and the entrance of a new convert into the Christian faith, and was almost always followed by strong resistance and persecution.
77 JM to NAF, June 23 1982

78 ACRA Letter, June 21 1982. Note: He went to jail May 4 1982; NAF to WRH, May 12 1982
79 VKM and RFM General Letter, Feb 3 1984, cf. Wheaton Consultation paper, June 1983: "You Can Serve the Poor Without Giving Away Your Money."
80 Ch. and Anita Warren, Gen Letter to AN, Jan 1982. Note: A fringe benefit to Neil was being in Delhi to see ASIAD '82, when athletes from all over Asia came to compete in Olympic sports.
81 VKM to Charles Robinson, President Mission Board, July 18 1983
82 WRH to VKM, Aug 9 1983
83 VKM and RFM Gen Letter, Feb 3 1984
84 DWM to RM nd, 1977
85 *Ibid.*
86 NAF to SHB, Sep 28 1974
87 NAF to RM, Nov 17 1976
88 RM to DWM, Mar 10 1977
89 DWM to RM, Mar 12 1977
90 *Ibid.*, Jan 10 1977, Dec 27 1977
91 *Ibid.*, Dec 27 1977
92 *Ibid.*, May 5 1978
93 *Facing Bench*, Sept 22 1980; DWM to AN, Nov 2 1981
94 DWM to AN, Jan 18 1984
95 NAF to WRH, Feb 5 1979
96 WRH to Dr. DWM, June 12 1980
97 DWM to AN, Nov 2 1981
98 DWM to AN, Jan 18 1984
99 VKM to Board President, July 18 1983
100 FFMS, Mar 18, 19 1982 JM Report; SP to AN, Oct 13 1980
101 Phillip Masih to AN, Apr 22 1981
102 VSP to RM, May 8 1978
103 NAF to WRH nd, 1983; GaM to AN, Apr 13 1983. Note: Elected were Norma Freer; Dr. Pratap Brown Singh, son of Bram, chairman; Yaqub Nath, son of Puniya Bai and Jagannath; Pratap S. Singh, grandson of Pancham Singh; Pradeep W Lal, grandson of Stuti Prakash; Jayanti Parsad, grandson of William Parsad; S J Nath, brother of Yaqub; Benjamin Lal, son of Din Dayal; John Peter D Singh, Veer Singh Karasel, and Silas Masih, father of Phillip Masih. Pyare Lal Brown, back into membership after 18 years, insisted that no minister be elected. This barred Gabriel Massey, Dayal Chand Singh, Stuti Prakash, and Hira Singh. The effectiveness of this committee for guiding the Church is yet to be tested.
104 EF, 1982, p 28
105 UBS Update, Oct-Dec 1982, p 2
106 WRH to VSP, Oct 31 1983
107 VSP to AN, Mar 12 1974
108 TC Cherian to AN, June 11 1982

109 SP to AN, Aug 2 1983. Note: Many other members of the older generation had also died. Among those who have died recently were Dr E L Cattell, 1981; Pyare Lal of Ghuara, 1979; Sardar Ji Kamal and his wife (parents of Stuti Prakash), 1975 and 1977; Lachhman Singh and his wife, 1982, 1983; Khub Chand and his wife, 1980, 1982; Hira Lal, 1977; Pramodini, daughter of Hira Singh, 1983; Godfree Parsad, son of William Parsad, 1984; Dharm Das, 1982; Bahadur Singh, 1983; Robinson Lal, 1983; Doel Prasad, 1983; Bharos William, 1982.
110 SP to AN, Aug 12 1983
111 *Ibid.*, Oct 13 1980
112 *Ibid.* and Oregon friends, Feb 13 1984
113 SP to CDC and Oregon Friends, Mar 29 1984
114 SP to AN, Aug 15 1983

Glossary

A

ACRA Association for Comprehensive Rural Assistance (Kadari, Bundelkhand)

AEL Asian Evangelical Literature Fellowship

AFM American Friends Mission

Ahimsa Nonviolence

Ahirs A group of the Sudra caste, milkmen – not outcastes

Anna An old coin, before devaluation and change to decimal system, worth about two cents

Ao Naga An animistic tribal group in Northeast India, now mostly Christian

Arminian Follower of the Wesleyan theological position

Arya Samaj Reformed and radical Hindu group seeking to purify Hinduism

Aryuvedic Type of medicine practiced with the use of herbs

B

BA Bachelor of Arts Degree

BCMS Bible Churchmen's Missionary Society – of the Church of England

BD Bachelor of Divinity Degree (three years beyond college education)

BLI Bible Literature International

BMMF Bible and Medical Missionary Fellowship (a British missionary board)

BMMS Bundelkhand Masihi Mitra Samaj (Bundelkhand Christian Friends Church)

BRE Bachelor of Religious Education Degree (two years beyond college education)

B.Th. Bachelor of Theology Degree (equivalent to college graduation)

Baksheesh Alms (a term used in begging, but it also means a gift)

Basors Keepers of pigs, an outcaste group like the sweepers

Begar The forced labor of outcaste groups without pay

Bengali The people originating in Bengal, an eastern section of India

Beriberi A malnutrition disease caused by lack of Vitamin B

Bhagavad Gita A holy book of the Hindus, the book admired and read by Mahatma Gandhi

Bhajans Songs, like Gospel Songs, in Hindi, etc.

Bhumani The smallpox goddess; related to Kali

Brahmin Priests and teachers; the highest caste in Hinduism

Buddhist A follower of Buddha, an Indian; the religion of Buddhism is followed by only a minority in India but is prominent in other Asian countries

Bundelkhandi One born in Bundelkhand, a designation for a certain portion of central India where the Friends Mission was established.

Burkah A garment completely covering a woman when she goes out of her *zenana* (ladies) quarters. Worn by Moslem women, not by Hindus.

Burki Mela A large fair held in January at a lake or river where people bathe to wash away their sins. Jagat Sagar was the place for this between Chhatarpur and Nowgong

C

C & M A Christian and Missionary Alliance Mission Board

CBC Cleveland Bible College

CEEFI Christian Education department of the Evangelical Fellowship of India

CHBUBS Cooperating Home Boards of the Union Biblical Seminary, Inc.

CID Central Intelligence Department (Like the USA's FBI)

CIGM Ceylon and India General Mission

CISRS Cultural Institute for the Study of Religion and Society

CMA Christian Medical Association

CP Canadian Presbyterian (Mission, School)

CSSM Children's Special Service Mission

Calvinist Follower of the John Calvin theological position

Cantonement A military base

Carrion Meat of an animal that has died

Caste The social stratification from outcaste to high caste, into which a Hindu is born; it regulates all of life, what one does, eats, wears and whom one marries. Present Indian government does not support it.

Chakra The symbol in the center of the India flag, suggesting eternity, or deliverance from the "wheel of things"; an ancient symbol

Chamar An outcaste group of leather workers. Dead animals belong to them for both leather and carrion

Chapati A bread made of whole wheat or whole grain and water without leaven; the chief bread of the villages and all of North India

Chaprasi A peon or message bearer

Choti Hazri An early light breakfast

Chiffonier An antique piece of furniture

Chowkidar A watchman

Chutiya The sacred lock of hair through which a man's spirit is supposed to depart this life when he dies as a near relative cracks his skull to release the spirit after he is placed on the funeral pyre

Compound The large yard of the mission houses where many families lived together

Curry The seasoned food, meat or vegetable, prepared to eat with rice or chapati

D

Darbar Court or place where people appear to meet people of distinction

Dassera (or Dasara) A ten-day festival usually in September glorifying Ram and Sita

Diya A small clay lamp, with a string for a wick in a dish of oil

Diwan The prime minister

E

EFA Evangelical Friends Alliance

EFC – ER Evangelical Friends Church, Eastern Region

EFI Evangelical Fellowship of India

EFICOR Evangelical Fellowship of India Committee on Relief

EFM Evangelical Friends Mission

EFMA Evangelical Foreign Missions Association

EHA Emmanuel Hospital Association

ELD Evangelical Literature Depot (Publishers of CEEFI in English)

ELFI Evangelical Literature Fellowship of India

ELO Evangelical Literature Overseas

ERFI Evangelical Radio Fellowship of India

ETC Evangelical Theological Commission

ETANI Evangelical Trust Association of North India

ETASI Evangelical Trust Association of South India

Eurasian Europeans and Anglo-Indians who make their home in Asia

Extensive Evangelism Contrasted to Intensive Evangelism; a rapid "sowing the seed" from village to village without concentrated follow-up

F

FEBC Far East Broadcasting Company

FECI Federation of Evangelical Churches in India

FFMS Friends Foreign Missionary Society

G

G.Th. Graduate of Theology Degree (four years beyond high school)

Ghee Clarified butter

GLINT Gospel Literature in National Tongues

"God Calls the Church" The theme of Billy Graham Campaign in India, 1956

Gujarati A person living in the state of Gujarat, or a thing showing the customs or traits of people of that state

Gussains A Hindu group in the Chhatarpur area who bury their dead in a sitting position and erect tombs over them

H

Harijan "Child of God"—the name Gandhi used to describe an outcaste man

Hazri Breakfast (literally, "presence")

Hindi The national language of India, the language of Madhya Pradesh (Hindi—and Hindustani and related languages—is spoken by more people than any other in the world except for Mandarin, English, and Russian)

Harmonium An instrument like an organ with bellows, and keys, played with one hand and pumped with the other

Homeopathy A form of medicine using herbs and matching foods to body system

I

IBCC India Bible Christian Council (a group in India affiliated with Carl McIntyre's theological stance)

IBM International Business Machines

ICL International Christian Leadership

IEM Indian Evangelical Mission

IFMA International Foreign Missionary Association

Intensive Evangelism Contrasted to Extensive Evangelism. Intensive evangelism concentrates on a certain group in a certain place and teaches over a period of time in depth in order to gain converts

Interdining People of different caste groups eating together to show that they accept one another equally. A symbol to the new convert that he is accepted fully into the Christian community on becoming a Christian

J

Jagat Sagar A lake between Chhatarpur and Nowgong where Burki Mela is held, and also the place for many youth rallies

K

KLS Khristya Lekhan Sanstha or Writing Institute

Kali A goddess who demands human sacrifices; her famous temple is in Calcutta next door to Mother Teresa's "Home for the Dying"

Kshatriya The Second caste in Hinduism; warriors and rulers

Kanjars A thieving caste among whom the Mission worked

Kaiser-i-Hind Medals, silver and gold, given for education and uplift

Kachhi A group of the Sudhra (fourth) caste in Hinduism—gardeners

Kirtan A presentation of the Gospel by means of song

Khumb Mela A large mela held every twelve years when the stars are right and the Jumna and Ganges rivers meet and overflow

Kanada The language of the people living in that area and state of Kanataka

Krore Ten million

L

Lakh Ten thousand

Lathi A large stick men carry to ward off thieves or animals

Lodis A low caste group of the fourth caste (Sudras)

Loo A hot wind that blows in March and April

LMP Licensed Medical Practitioner, a qualifying degree for a medical doctor

O

Old Line Referring to Christians who came out of the orphanage, not from the conversions of villagers

Oriya The language of Orissa

Outcaste The many people who do not have any part in the four caste groups of Hinduism. There are many outcaste groups who observe caste among themselves.

OXFAM Oxford Committee for Famine Relief

P

Paisa One hundred paise make a rupee, like 100¢ make a dollar

Palao A rice and meat dish (called viriyani in the south). Used for feasts, weddings, Christmas

Panch The ruling party (usually meaning five) in a village

Pandit A Brahmin teacher

Pandita A lady Brahmin teacher

Pice Old coin used before devaluation and going to decimal system; value 1/12th of an anna

Pies Plural of pice

Plague Bubonic plague is caused by a flea that bites a rat with the plague and passes it on

Political Agent (PA) The highest officer in the area during the time of the British

Prem Sabha A love feast

Puris Whole wheat bread, unleavened, cooked in hot oil; used for feasts

R

Raja A ruling prince or king

Rakhwal The ministry and oversight

Ram An incarnation of Vishnu, one of the Hindu gods

Ranas The ruling party in Nepal before the revolution

RE Reformed Episcopalian Mission

RSSS Rashtriya Sewa Sangh Samiti (A rabid Hindu political party — one of their number assassinated Gandhi)

Rupee The monetary unit of India, equivalent to about 10¢

S

Sabha A meeting

Sadhu A man who denies himself everything and travels in the name of religion — a Hindu usually, though Sadhu Sundar Singh was a Christian

Sag Vegetables

Sahib An English, or Caucasian gentleman

Samaj Society

Sanskrit Ancient language of the Vedas, on which Hindi is based

Sarangi A musical instrument made with a coconut shell and played with a bow

Sashram A retreat for service

Satyagraha Soul Force. A term used by Gandhi as a means of fighting with peaceful means

Sewa Sadan A home of service

Shamiyana A tent-like structure for large meetings, to give shade and protection from rain

Shiboleth A saying without meaning (taken from the Bible)

SIBI, SIBS South India Bible Institute, or South India Bible Seminary

Sikh A religion of a group of people in India, especially in the Punjab, who do not worship idols but who follow Guru Nanak and worship the Granth, their holy book

Sudra The fourth caste group in Hinduism

Swaraj Home rule, or self rule (Freedom)

T

Tabla An Indian drum

Tajiyas A paper castle Moslems make for a feast day and bury at a lake or river

Tamil The language of Tamilnadu

TAP Theological Assistance Program

TEAR The Evangelical Alliance Relief Fund (England)

TAFTEE The Association for Theological Education by Extension

TEF Theological Education Fund

Telugu The language of Andhra

Thakur A group from the Kshatriya Hindu caste

Tilak The caste mark worn on the forehead; now sometimes called a beauty mark

U

UBS Union Biblical Seminary of India

UESI Union of Evangelical Students of India (Counterpart of Campus Crusade and Inter-Varsity Fellowship)

Uttar Pradesh Northern Province — a state in India (U.P.)

UMN United Mission to Nepal

Unani System A system of medicine used in India by Moslems

Urdu Language based on Arabic, not Sanskrit, spoken in North India

UTC Union Theological College, Bangalore

V

Vaisya The Third Caste group in Hinduism

VBS Vacation Bible School

GLOSSARY

Vindhya Pradesh The name of Bundelkhand area in transition from the English rule to the present rule (Now the area is in Madhya Pradesh, or M.P.—central provinces)

Viad A doctor of the Aryuvedic or Unani system of medicine

W

WCC World Council of Churches

WEC World Evangelistic Crusade Mission

WGM World Gospel Mission

WUMS Woman's Union Missionary Society

Y

YFC Youth for Christ

Z

Zamindar Land owner

Zenana Women's quarters; women who were isolated in these quarters and cut off from society

Index — Places

Bold face *indicates photograph.*

Index—
Persons/Proper Nouns

Bold face *indicates photograph.*

INDEX – PERSONS / PROPER NOUNS 477

Brahmin(s) 31, 34, 59, 214, 231, 240, 250, 251, 253, 414, 436
Bram *See D. Brown*
Brand, Dr. Paul 222
Brantingham, Barbara *See Barbara Cattell*
Brantingham, Dorothy 394
Brantingham, John 289
Brantingham, Rev. Sherman 313, 394, 424, 427, 459
Brattle, Liz 413
Brij Kishor 253, 450
British Baptist Mission 357
British Empire xvii, 73, 75
British Flag 211
British Government 32, 40, 70, 73-75, 94, 95, 151, 175, 178
British Impact on India, The 429
British Raj xvi, xvii, 211
British (English) Regiment, Soldiers 12, 16, 17, 20, 22, 40, 56, 63, 69
Brougher, Esther 433
Brown, D. 104, 310, 428, 441, 460
Brown, Mahendra Singh 104
Brown, Mitra Sen 104
Brown, Padmawati 104, **140**
Brown, Pauline **140**
Brown, Dr. Pratap Singh 104, **136**, 309, 314, 406, 412, 420, 425, 427, 460
Brown, Pyare Lal 104, **140**, 279, 301, 304, 305, 311-315, 458, 460
Brown, Sahodra Bai 104, 427
Bruenimier, Beth 297
Bryner, Joyce 259, 424
Buddha 375
Buddhist 147, 291, 374, 442
Bundelkhand Christian Education Society 204, 230
Bundelkhand Commissioner 446, 447
Bundelkhand Friends Church ix, 22, 23, 25, 26, 27, 29, 32, 35, 37, 38, 39, 42, 43, 56-58, 65, 66, 71, 76, 78-81, 84, 86, 98-100, 114, 117, 120, 143, 145, 150, 151, 154, 156, 157, 159, 161, 168, 171, 173, 177, 179, 180, 184, 188, 192, 201, 215, 226, 227, 230, 232, 236, 243, 248, 254, 255, 257, 259, 262, 263, 266, 267, 271, 279-281, 285, 288, 289, 293, 295-316, 329, 330, 357, 376, 380, 384, 388-390, 394-400, 403-410, 412, 413, 415-420, 425, 426, 429, 433, 437, 460
Bundelkhand Masihi Mitra Samaj (BMMS) *See Bundelkhand Friends Church*
BMMS Boys' Dormitory (Hostel) 307, 311
BMMS Branch 329
BMMS Church Discipline 225, 311, 314
BMMS Executive Committee 312, 314
BMMS Provisional Yearly Meeting 225, 226, 296, 300
BMMS Yearly Meeting 313, 315, 426
Bundelkhandi 55, 214, 216, 242, 248, 274, 287, 297, 330, 345, 441
Bundelkhandi Gospel of Mark 216, 447
Burch, Rev. Herbert 394, 423

Burki Mela 153
Burns, Norman 266
Bush, Lova 348
Butler, Esther 10

C

(Cain) Johnson, Nirmala 349, 351, 352
Alena **50**, 86-89, 91, 92, 95, 99-101, 108, 110, 117, 118, **123**, **128**, 142, 145, 148, 149, 155, 156, 161, 164, 165, 173, 188-190, 198, 202-205, 207, 208, 211, 216, 222-225, 232, 233, 236, 276, **319**, 424, 427, 439, 442, 447, 461
Calvin, John 264
Calvinistic Theology 264
Cameron, Alexis "Lexie" 360, 365
Camp Caesar, W.Va. 193
Campbell, Edith 433
Campus Crusade 333
Canadian Anglican Church 360
Canadian Army 63
Canadian Presbyterian Girls' School 61, 256, 281
Canadian Presbyterian Mission (CP Mission) 117, 197, 291-293, 339-341, 345, 350, 351, 444
Canadian Presbyterian Women's Board 230
Cardis, Captain 155
CARE, Inc. 275
Carey Baptist Church 340
Carey, William 263
Cartmel, Bea 360
Cartmel, Daryl 360
Caste System, The 74-76, 87, 101, 154, 155, 233, 248
Catholic Church 375
Catholic Medical Mission Sisters 368
(Cattell) Brantingham, Barbara Anne 120, **123**, **128**, 147, 156, 206, 221, 263, 280, **325**, 351
Cattell, Catherine DeVol xi, 119, 120, **123**, **128**, **132**, **135**, 141, 142, 145-147, 156, 158, 160, 161, 164, 167, 170, 172, 173, 175, 177-180, 182-187, 190, 192-194, 202, 204-208, 210, 211, 216-221, 224-226, 229, 233, 236, 240, 241, 251, 253, 258, 260, 263, 267, 276, 277, 279, 280, 284, 285, 289, 294, 298, 300-302, 306, **325**, 339, 344-351, 386, 424, 425, 427, 428, 429, 444, 449
Cattell, David 120, **123**, **128**, **131**, 147, 156, 157, 177, 182, 206, 220, 241, 242, 289, 301, 302, 452
(Cattell) Lupton, Emelyn J. *See Emelyn J. Lupton*
Cattell, Dr. Everett Lewis xiv, 119, 120, **123**, **128**, **131**, **135**, 141-148, 150, 151, 153, 155-160, 163-165, 167, 168, 170, 172, 173, 175-185, 187, 190-194, 201, 202, 204-208, 210-212, 215-221, 224-228, 230-232, 234-236, 238-241, 243, 244, 247, 254, 257-269, 261-266, 269-271, 274, 276, 277, 280, 284, 285,